**Keep this book. You will
need it and use it throughout
your career.**

About the American Hotel & Lodging Association (AH&LA)

Founded in 1910, AH&LA is the trade association representing the lodging industry in the United States. AH&LA is a federation of state lodging associations throughout the United States with 11,000 lodging properties worldwide as members. The association offers its members assistance with governmental affairs representation, communications, marketing, hospitality operations, training and education, technology issues, and more. For information, call 202-289-3100.

LODGING, the management magazine of AH&LA, is a "living textbook" for hospitality students that provides timely features, industry news, and vital lodging information.

About the American Hotel & Lodging Educational Institute (EI)

An affiliate of AH&LA, the Educational Institute is the world's largest source of quality training and educational materials for the lodging industry. EI develops textbooks and courses that are used in more than 1,200 colleges and universities worldwide, and also offers courses to individuals through its Distance Learning program. Hotels worldwide rely on EI for training resources that focus on every aspect of lodging operations. Industry-tested videos, CD-ROMs, seminars, and skills guides prepare employees at every skill level. EI also offers professional certification for the industry's top performers. For information about EI's products and services, call 800-349-0299 or 407-999-8100.

About the American Hotel & Lodging Educational Foundation (AH&LEF)

An affiliate of AH&LA, the American Hotel & Lodging Educational Foundation provides financial support that enhances the stability, prosperity, and growth of the lodging industry through educational and research programs. AH&LEF has awarded millions of dollars in scholarship funds for students pursuing higher education in hospitality management. AH&LEF has also funded research projects on topics important to the industry, including occupational safety and health, turnover and diversity, and best practices in the U.S. lodging industry. For more information, go to www.ahlef.org.

Convention Management and Service

Educational Institute Books

Convention Management and Service

Eighth Edition

Milton T. Astroff
James R. Abbey, Ph.D.

American
Hotel & Lodging
Educational Institute

Disclaimer

This publication is designed to provide accurate and authoritative information in regard to the subject matter covered. It is sold with the understanding that the publisher is not engaged in rendering legal, accounting, or other professional service. If legal advice or other expert assistance is required, the services of a competent professional person should be sought.
—*From the Declaration of Principles jointly adopted by the American Bar Association and a Committee of Publishers and Associations*

The authors, Milton T. Astroff and James R. Abbey, are solely responsible for the contents of this publication. All views expressed herein are solely those of the authors and do not necessarily reflect the views of the American Hotel & Lodging Educational Institute (the Institute) or the American Hotel & Lodging Association (AH&LA).

Nothing contained in this publication shall constitute a standard, an endorsement, or a recommendation of the Institute or AH&LA. The Institute and AH&LA disclaim any liability with respect to the use of any information, procedure, or product, or reliance thereon by any member of the hospitality industry.

Cover photo: The Orange County Convention Center, Orlando, Florida.

Contents

Introduction

Sweeping changes have taken place in the meetings and conventions industry since the first edition of *Convention Management and Service* was printed—many of them since the seventh edition was published in 2006! A number of trends have greatly impacted the meetings and conventions field, and it is imperative that hotel executives keep abreast of these changes in order to stay competitive.

Technology has played a pivotal role in the changing face of meetings and conventions sales and services. Today's hospitality professionals have more efficient ways to reach meeting planners and promote their properties, and new advances in technology have streamlined organizing for group sales and following up with optimum service. And technology is not only important to hotel executives—meeting planners and attendees now expect the latest advances, from sophisticated audiovisual equipment to high-tech room amenities.

Today's meeting planners are not the inexperienced, perhaps occasional, planners of yesterday—they are more likely to be knowledgeable and professional. A growing number are taking advantage of certification programs. They have become adept in all aspects of the meetings and conventions sales and service process and they expect the best when it comes to their functions.

In order to provide the high quality of service expected by today's meeting planners, successful hotel executives must have a complete grasp of convention sales and service. Having this knowledge not only enables you to successfully sell to and service the meetings and conventions segment, which has become increasingly important for hotel profitability, it also offers the opportunity for you to enjoy an exciting and rewarding career with practically limitless potential.

Convention Management and Service was written to serve as both a primer for those interested in meetings and conventions as a career path, and as an updated resource for those who are already involved in this exciting segment of the hospitality field. The first seven editions of this book have been tested on the firing line in university classrooms and in hotel sales offices throughout the world, and seasoned industry professionals worldwide have given glowing reviews to this comprehensive text. Neil Ostergren, CHSE, past president of the Hospitality Sales and Marketing Association International (HSMAI), says:

> *Convention Management and Service* is the most complete and up-to-date textbook that I have come across in my 35 years in the hotel industry. The 18 chapters are full of pertinent information, not just for students being introduced to the industry, but for seasoned professionals as well. Anyone seriously interested in advancing his or her career in today's hotel industry who does not read this book will, in my opinion, be less successful in reaching his or her full potential.

To maintain this level of credibility, the contents of this eighth edition have been substantially updated with information from current trade journal articles, seminar notes, book reviews, and input from industry leaders. Topics have been added or expanded, and the text now includes additional examples of standardized forms developed for industry-wide use by the Convention Industry Council (CIC).

The first half of the book offers practical insight into the various types of meetings and conventions, the types of organizations that stage these events, and how to reach and sell to this important group segment. This portion of the book includes in-depth discussions on developing a marketing plan (the cornerstone to successful sales and marketing), analyzing a hotel property to determine which segments of the group market can be sold to and serviced successfully, practical advice on reaching each of the group market segments, implementing successful sales strategies, and finalizing a group's events through negotiations and letters of agreement:

Chapter 1   provides an overview of today's meetings and conventions market and the trends that are impacting this segment today.

Chapter 2   discusses the marketing plan and its components and details how to put a marketing plan into action.

Chapter 3   takes a look at various sales structures and positions, and demonstrates how sales functions are managed.

Chapter 4   focuses on the characteristics of the association meetings market and how to identify and reach key decision-makers.

Chapter 5   covers the requirements of the corporate meetings market and how to sell to various types of corporate clients.

Chapter 6   offers practical tips for reaching nonprofit and SMERF groups, govern-ment agencies, labor unions, and the incentive travel market.

Chapter 7   covers sales strategies, including personal sales calls, telephone sales, sales blitz selling, trade show selling, and selling with convention bureaus.

Chapter 8   discusses how to develop an advertising strategy to maximize print advertising, electronic advertising, and collateral materials.

Chapter 9   provides an in-depth look at contract negotiations, detailing the points that should be covered in a letter of agreement/contract.

The second half of the book details the various aspects of convention service. To ensure that an event flows smoothly, effective service procedures must be implemented and followed by a staff that is skilled and knowledgeable in the various aspects of each function. This section details specific requirements for group events, including guestrooms, meeting and function rooms, audiovisual requirements, food and beverage service, and other aspects of convention service, such as event registration, convention security, and other services:

Chapter 10   provides an overview of the service function, detailing several management options for large and small properties.

Chapter 11   covers managing guestrooms through the effective use of reservation systems, check-in and check-out procedures, and room block management.

Chapter 12   discusses the pre-convention meeting and the importance of resumes, banquet event orders, communication, and follow-up.

Chapter 13   provides a detailed look at function rooms and meeting setups and how to manage function rooms, and offers a preview of meeting rooms of the future.

Chapter 14   offers an in-depth discussion of food and beverage service, including the types of food and beverage functions, pricing, and post-function actions.

Chapter 15   covers today's audiovisual requirements, including the types of audiovisual equipment typically used, as well as audiovisual pricing policies.

Chapter 16 discusses some of the other requirements for successful group events, including registration, convention security, and guest/companion and children's programs.

Chapter 17 explores the world of exhibits and trade shows, focusing on such topics as types of exhibits, key personnel, and exhibit billing procedures.

Chapter 18 is an in-depth analysis of convention billing procedures and details how to conduct a successful post-convention review.

Comprehensive appendices at the end of several chapters include a sample marketing action plan, a convention service questionnaire, a behind-the-scenes look at a trade show, and a resume questionnaire for servicing meeting groups. Case studies at the end of the text focus on practical topics, offering students the opportunity to apply their critical thinking skills.

Text Features

Each chapter contains numerous cross-referenced illustrations, actual industry examples, and quotes from successful hotel sales and services managers to enhance comprehension and encourage retention of the text material. In addition:

- "Best Practices" industry examples are included in several chapters, and periodic "Putting It All Together" exercises enable students to create sales and marketing strategies to execute successful functions based on concepts discussed in the text.
- "Internet Exercises" provide the opportunity for students to critique actual industry examples and gain additional knowledge of topics discussed in the text.

End-of-Chapter Material

In addition to a chapter summary, which also provides a brief introduction to the next chapter, end-of-chapter material includes:

- Additional References—other material that provides in-depth information on topics covered in the chapter.
- Internet Sites—a listing of websites for the firms and organizations mentioned in the chapter.
- Review Questions—questions designed to pull together and integrate the basic concepts of the chapter and provide an opportunity for the reader to see how his or her own values will affect the way management principles will be applied.
- Key Terms—a glossary of the terms (which are bolded in the text) that have been introduced in each chapter.

New to This Edition

This eighth edition has been updated substantially to reflect the latest developments in the meetings and conventions industry. New additions and updates include:

- Expanded coverage of key industry trends, including the "greening" of meetings, social responsibility, the latest developments in technology, social media, and the rise in the popularity of second-tier cities.
- New special-interest boxes on such topics as boutique hotels, positioning conference centers, meeting rooms of the future, and a day in the life of a convention service manager.

- New and updated charts and graphs.
- Updated advertising examples, photographs, and illustrations.
- An increased global perspective, featuring examples from Canada, Mexico, Europe, and Asia.
- Numerous new interviews with and profiles of prominent industry profession-als, including David Brudney (advice for new salespeople), Don Freeman (trade shows), Cindy Estis Green (database marketing), Anne Hamilton (Disney Meet-ings), and Roger Helms (third-party meeting planners).
- Over 35 new Internet exercises on topics including meeting contracts, property press kits, convention press releases, banquet menus, and customizing group events.

Instructional Support Package

A comprehensive instructor's guide to assist teachers in the classroom use of the text is available. The instructor's guide provides a sample lesson plan and class activities, includ-ing suggested guest speakers, an optional test, individual/group activities (including case studies in some chapters), and PowerPoints.

This new, expanded edition of *Convention Management and Service* is an invaluable resource that will enable students and hospitality professionals alike to stay up-to-date in the ever-changing meetings and conventions industry. It is the author's hope that, using the tools provided in this text, YOU will find success and career satisfaction in this challenging and rewarding field.

James R. Abbey, Ph.D., CHA
Las Vegas, Nevada

Acknowledgments

Over the years, students and instructors have provided reviews and suggestions for improving the text and Instructor's Manual, and seasoned industry professionals have contributed their knowledge, expertise, and advice to ensure that *Convention Management and Service* remains one of the most comprehensive, practical, and up-to-date textbooks available for the meetings and conventions field. It would be impossible to list everyone who has contributed, of course, but each is gratefully appreciated (several of these industry professionals have been profiled at the beginning of chapters and within numerous chapters in the text). The author would, however, like to extend a special "thank you" to two professors who have contributed to this eighth edition and its accompanying Instructor's Manual:

- Katie Davin, associate professor and director of hospitality education, Johnson & Wales University, for her suggestions on improving the Instructor's Manual.
- Dr. Dan Spencer, associate professor of tourism and hospitality, Black Hills State University, who supplied several new and expanded PowerPoint presentations for the Instructor's Manual and provided content suggestions for the text.

The author also wishes to express his gratitude to his Las Vegas–based assistants who contributed to the production of this book:

- Donna Merrill, a professional advertising writer and editor who has worked on a number of editions of this book as well as on the author's *Hospitality Sales and Marketing*, assisted in the editing of this text, typed additions and corrections, and proofread the book in its various stages.
- Robert Wais, a talented graphics artist who has worked for prestigious companies in the United States and abroad, scanned the new illustrations, designed graphics, and is responsible for the layout of this text.

Last, but certainly not least, the author wishes to express his appreciation to the hospitality firms (large and small), trade publications, and hospitality professionals who not only contributed their expertise, but also granted permission for the use of their forms, exhibits, and advertisements to enhance the text of this book.

Chapter 1 Outline

Competencies

1. Describe the convention and meetings industry today, and identify organizations involved in the advancement of professionalism within the industry. (pp. 3–6)

2. Describe the scope of today's meetings market, including the various types of meetings hosted by the convention and meetings industry. (pp. 6–10)

3. Identify the different types of organizations that hold meetings, and describe types of group customers. (pp. 10–16)

4. Describe the various types of meeting facilities. (pp. 16–20)

5. Describe trends in the meetings industry. (pp. 20–32)

The Meetings Market: Types of Meeting Customers

Keith Patrick
Director of Convention Services
Pinehurst, Inc., North Carolina

"Meeting terminology is important. Those in the hotel business who aspire to be true professionals seek to understand the differences in order to help the meeting planner produce a successful event. As a convention sales or service professional, you'll be working with an ever-increasing professional group of people referred to as meeting planners or convention managers. Only by knowing the groups and the purpose of their meetings can you help them toward the accomplishment of their goals."

1 Introduction to the Convention, Meetings, and Trade Show Industry

MEETINGS AND CONVENTIONS play a significant role in the workings of associations, corporations, nonprofits, government agencies, technical societies, and even social groups. People need to come together for a number of reasons — to share information, to receive training and product knowledge, or just to connect with their peers. As a result, meetings and convention business may account for as much as 70 percent of the sales volume at major U.S. hotels, while smaller properties generally realize 15 to 20 percent of their revenue from the group segment.

Meetings are also big business in Canada, where meetings were attended by 70.2 million participants, resulting in $32.2 billion in direct spending and the creation of 235,500 full-year jobs (see sidebar titled "Meetings Activity in Canada"). More than 75 percent of these meetings were held in hotels and resorts. Similar results can also be seen in Europe and Asia, where the acronym MICE (meetings, incentives, conventions, and exhibitions) is used to describe the meetings sector.

Meetings and conventions business doesn't just fall into the laps of hospitality properties, of course. In order to effectively sell to and service the group market, you have to know the types of meetings that are held, determine who holds these meetings, and recognize the types of facilities that each segment of this market requires. You also need to keep abreast of trends in the meetings industry to stay a step ahead of your competition. In this chapter, we will provide an overview of today's meetings market, and we will discuss the trends that are shaping the needs of this market segment and their impact on the hotel industry.

MEETINGS ACTIVITY IN CANADA	
Total meetings	671,000
Total participants	70.2 million
Full-year jobs (equivalent)	235,500
Direct Spending	$32.2 billion

Source: Meetings impact research study conducted by Toronto-based Meeting Professionals International Foundation Canada. To download MPIFC's complete research results, visit www.mpiweb.org.

The Convention and Meetings Industry Today

Projections based on the most recent study commissioned by the Convention Industry Council (CIC) found that the average association delegate spends $283 per day and that approximately $122.31 billion annually is generated directly from meeting, conventions, expositions, and incentive travel (see Exhibit 1).[1] And this figure, which reflects the economic impact in the United States alone, is only a fraction of the $315 billion—supporting nearly four million jobs—generated indirectly from the convention business; local transportation companies, hotel suppliers, retail stores, and other businesses all benefit (see Exhibit 2).

While leisure travelers may represent larger numbers for the hospitality industry, meeting attendees—who frequently travel on an expense account—bring in the lion's share of revenue in addition to benefiting properties by filling "soft spots" and generating word-of-mouth business. Therefore, the lucrative convention and meetings market is becoming an increasingly important—and competitive—target market.

Exhibit 1   Where Association Delegates Spend Money

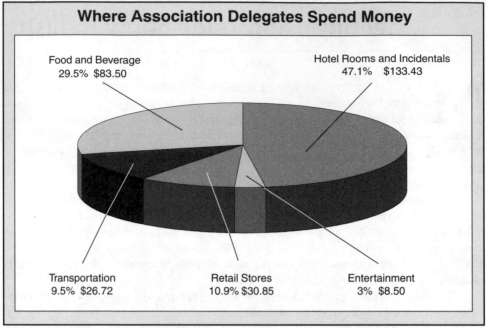

Where Association Delegates Spend Money

Food and Beverage
29.5% $83.50

Hotel Rooms and Incidentals
47.1% $133.43

Transportation
9.5% $26.72

Retail Stores
10.9% $30.85

Entertainment
3% $8.50

The International Association of Convention and Visitors Bureaus determined that the average association meeting delegate spent approximately 283 dollars per day at national and international conventions. It is important to note that this survey includes only association delegates; corporate delegates can be expected to spend an additional twenty to thirty dollars per day, as many are on expense accounts and usually entertain potential clients while attending meetings and conventions.
Source: Adapted from the Destination Marketing Association International's Expenditure and Impact Survey (EXPACT).

No longer are conventions attended primarily by males. According to recent figures, as many as 44 percent of association meeting attendees and 39 percent of corporate meeting attendees are women. Therefore today's accompanying spouses are often husbands instead of wives!

Meeting and convention attendees are also just as likely to be single as married, and are typically younger (25 to 40 years of age) and more affluent than convention delegates of two decades ago. But despite increased spending power, meetings are no longer attended primarily for fun; in most cases, meeting attendance must be considered worthwhile enough to justify the expense and time away from the office.

The economy has also played an important part in changing the meetings and convention market. For example, the previous 80 percent deduction for business meals and entertainment has been reduced to 50 percent, forcing meeting planners and convention delegates to "cut corners" and look for the best deals. This trend, in addition to deregulated airlines and increased competition for meetings and convention business in the hospitality industry, has resulted in increased negotiation for group transportation, discounted room rates, low- or no-cost meeting space, and inclusive packages. Contracts for hotel services are now the norm, and many corporations and associations are signing multiple-meeting contracts. This trend not only provides a savings to the organization (contracts usually guarantee a percentage off the rack rate in exchange for multiple business), but also gives the advantage of having only one contract for multiple events.

Exhibit 2   The Economic Impact of the Meetings Industry

Summary of Economic Impacts

Convention & Exhibitions $ 67.9 (55.5%)	Meetings $48.2 (39.4%)	Incentive Travel $6.2 (5.1%)

$122.31 Billion in Direct Spending   **2.0 Million FTE Jobs**

$16.7 Million in Total Direct Tax Impact

Multiplier Effect

$315.4 Billion in Total Economic Impact   **3.84 Million FTE Jobs**

While direct spending from meetings totaled approximately $122.31 billion, supporting 2 million full-time equivalent (FTE) jobs, the total impact of the meetings market business has an even larger, more far-reaching effect on the nation's economy. As a result of meetings and conventions, the demand for auxiliary goods and services also rose, generating a total of $315.4 billion, supporting 3.84 million FTE jobs.
Sources: Forecasted in *The Economic Impact of Conventions, Expositions, Meetings & Incentive Travel Study,* conducted by Deloitte & Touche for the Convention Industry Council (CIC) and *Groups and Meetings: Marketing Opportunity Redefined,* published by PhoCusWright, Inc.

Many hotel contracts are negotiated by meeting planners who, unlike the meeting planning clients of the past (who typically had little knowledge of the requirements for a successful meeting), are highly trained professionals. Twenty-five years ago, the Convention Industry Council (CIC) administered its first certification exam to just a handful of meeting planners who had taken its educational courses. Today, over 14,000 meeting professionals hold the CIC's Certified Meeting Professional (CMP) designation, and additional courses and certifications are offered by a number of other organizations as well (see box titled "The ABCs of Certification"). Professional groups such as Meeting Professionals International (MPI), the Professional Convention Management Association (PCMA), and the Society of Incentive Travel Executives (SITE) have been formed—and joined in force by meeting planners—for additional training and networking. A Certification in Meeting Management (CMM) program, for example, is offered by Meeting Professionals International (MPI). This program, begun in Europe at the request of meeting planners who wanted a more comprehensive educational program, was recently approved for the United States. Viewed as a graduate curriculum for meeting planners, the CMM program provides senior-level certification on a global scale.

The Convention Industry Council (CIC), recognizing the need for hospitality professionals to have guidelines and examples of common industry practices, has developed a number of standardized forms and tools under its APEX (Accepted Practices Exchange) umbrella. One of the most useful, whether you are a student or a seasoned professional, is a comprehensive listing of the terms commonly used in the hotel industry (see box titled "APEX Industry Glossary"). We urge you to refer to this glossary — and to the additional tools developed by the CIC — to better learn how to sell to and service the meetings market.

APEX Industry Glossary

The Accepted Practices Exchange (APEX), an initiative of the Convention Industry Council (CIC), developed a comprehensive glossary of terms that are typically encountered when dealing with meetings business — from setting up programs and meeting the specific needs of meeting planners to negotiating the final contract.

These standardized terms guarantee that everyone is "on the same page" when requests are made — there is no doubt as to what a planner needs when he or she requests a lavaliere microphone or a podium. Of equal or even greater importance are standardized definitions of common meetings contract terms, such as arbitration, audit, and slippage.

With approximately 4,000 terms defined, a student or an inexperienced meeting planner can become well-versed in meetings terminology by simply typing in a search term. The glossary is also an invaluable tool for seasoned professionals, as it is updated periodically with new terminology. To view this useful tool, which can be used to supplement the terms you learn in your text, log on to www.conventionindustry.org/glossary.

Source: Courtesy of the Convention Industry Council (CIC).

The Scope of Today's Meetings Market

Despite rising costs for transportation and hospitality services, more and more meetings are being held. They are held for a variety of purposes: to keep abreast of today's ever-changing technology; to keep sales goals on track; to meet for group motivation and rewards; and many more. No longer are meetings limited to a few annual conventions that simply require a large ballroom for a general session and a few food functions or small business meetings where attendees are informed by a speaker armed only with a flip chart and a few marking pens. Today's attendees—and planners—expect a lot more. Hotel **business centers** that are complete with computers, fax machines, and sophisticated communications equipment have become commonplace; state-of-the-art audiovisual equipment is expected; and many conventions have taken on the appearance of lavish productions—complete with exotic foods and decor—to attract attendees.

As with other industries, however, the hospitality industry is greatly affected by economic conditions and other outside factors. After the tragic events of September 11, 2001, for example, the meetings market suffered a dramatic slump as many people were hesitant to travel long distances — especially by air. Another slowdown took place as a global recession impacted both businesses and the traveling public. Many meeting planners had to justify the time and expense of meetings held off company premises, while other corporate planners were forced to scale back their formerly lavish affairs and forego the use of upscale properties in the face of public outcry over the appearance of excess in a down economy. Association meeting planners and planners for social groups were also forced

The ABCs of Certification

CMP — Certified Meeting Professional
Convention Industry Council
www.conventionindustry.org
CHSP — Certified Hospitality Sales Professional
American Hotel & Lodging Association
www.ei-ahla.org
CHME — Certified Hospitality Marketing Executive
Hospitality Sales and Marketing Association International
www.hsmai.org
CEM — Certified in Exhibition Management
International Association of Exhibitions and Events
www.iaee.com
CITE — Certified Incentive Travel Executive
Society of Incentive & Travel Executives
www.site-intl.org

CDME — Certified Destination Management Executive
Destination Marketing Association International
www.destinationmarketing.org
CSEP — Certified Special Events Planner
International Special Events Society
www.ises.com
CMM — Certification in Meetings Management
Meeting Professionals International
www.mpiweb.org
CPCE — Certified Professional Catering Executive
National Association of Catering Executives
www.nace.net
CGMP — Certified Government Meetings Professional
Society of Government Meetings Professionals
www.sgmp.org

Increasingly, people within an industry seek to become "certified" or "licensed" in the skills of their profession. While certification is not essential, many meeting planners and suppliers recognize the importance of education, and take advantage of opportunities to improve their skills and update their knowledge through programs offered by their professional associations. The meetings industry is filled with an "alphabet soup" of certifications, many of which are earned at the association's regional conventions, at regional seminars, or through courses offered over the Internet. Many of the industry leaders who have contributed to this text have completed one or more of the certification programs listed above.

to rethink meeting locations and programs in light of shrinking travel budgets for both the groups and attendees.

Today, however, demand is slowly increasing — although many of today's meetings are smaller and planners may scale back certain options, such as food and beverage, for meeting attendees. Beverly Kinkade, vice president and director of association sales for the Sheraton Corporation, says:

> Small meetings are up, and so is training activity. Convention attendance is up in all industries. There is greater demand across the board.[2]

Now planners are seeing how economic cycles play a vital role in how hotels respond to group business. The greater demand, which is due in part to there having been virtually no growth in the upscale and luxury property category, has resulted in:

- Tighter availability of rooms, especially at peak times
- Fewer concessions on food and beverage functions
- Less flexibility in "comp" allotments
- Tougher negotiations of other amenities

Bruce Harris, past president of Experient, the nation's largest independent meeting planning company, says:

> Hotels put an end to some of the "ridiculous" concessions, certain things they felt they had to do to book business despite the fact that they hurt their ability to be profitable.[3]

Although the meetings industry is facing an uncertain economic climate worldwide, meeting planners will still face higher rates and stiffer penalties if they fail to fill space as hotels struggle to keep pace with rising costs. But, since the hospitality industry is highly cyclical, a wise hotelier knows that business lost today may be business lost tomorrow, when it is needed. Hotels are looking to hold on to future group business by working with planners, often suggesting flexibility with dates; groups looking for value as well as availability, for example, are urged to consider off seasons rather than peak periods for their meetings.

You still face a great deal of competition in selling your site and facility for today's meeting. If you land a piece of business, you remain very much involved. You have a strong vested interest in the success of the convention. If it goes well and you gain the approval of the event sponsors and attendees, you stand a better chance of getting the repeat business and recommended business that is so very important in the career of anyone in the hospitality business. To successfully compete in the marketplace, it is important to know:

- The types of meetings held
- Who plans and holds meetings
- The types of group planners with whom you'll deal
- The types of properties that can successfully accommodate
  different meeting groups

Types of Meetings

In the interest of simplicity, we will use the term *convention business*. But we are actually dealing with an entire spectrum of meetings of all types. It would be simpler if all events were just called *meetings*; after all, that's what they basically are. But that's not the way it is. There are a number of not-quite synonyms for the term, with nuances of difference.

Convention. The most commonly used term in the field is **convention**. The dictionary tells us that a convention is a meeting of delegates for action on particular matters. These may be matters of politics, trade, science, or technology, among others.

Today's convention usually involves a general session and supplementary smaller meetings. Conventions are produced both with and without exhibits. Most conventions have a repetitive cycle, the most common of which is annual. Giving market reports, introducing new products, and mapping company strategy are some common objectives of a convention. The general session usually requires a ballroom or large auditorium for the whole group. Specific problems are discussed in smaller groups, using a number of small breakout rooms.

Conference. A *conference* is a near-synonym for a convention, usually implying much discussion and participation. The word "convention" is used in trade circles for regular meetings of a general nature; the term "conference" is used frequently in technical and scientific areas, although it is used in the trade as well. The differences are those of semantics rather than execution. A conference program commonly deals with specific problems or developments and may or may not have smaller breakout meetings. Conferences may be small or large in attendance.

Congress. The term *congress* is most commonly used in Europe and in international events. It usually refers to an event similar to a conference in nature. Oddly enough, only in the

United States is the term used to designate a legislative body. Attendance at a congress varies a great deal.

Forum. A meeting featuring much back-and-forth discussion, generally led by panelists or presenters, is often called a *forum*. Much audience participation is to be expected, with all sides of a question aired by both panelists and the audience. Two or more speakers might take opposing sides and address the audience rather than each other.

A moderator will summarize points of view and lead the discussion. The audience is usually allowed to ask questions, so a number of microphones must be supplied by the hotel.

Symposium. A *symposium* is similar to a forum, except that conduct seems to be more formal in a symposium. Whether by individuals or panels, presentations are made. Some audience participation is anticipated, but there is generally less of the give-and-take that characterizes a forum.

Lecture. The *lecture* is even more formal or structured, using individual presentation, often by just one expert. It may or may not be followed by questions from the audience. Lectures vary widely in size.

Seminar. The *seminar* format tries to get away from the idea of a presenter or presenters addressing an audience from a platform. A seminar usually involves much participation, much give-and-take, a sharing of knowledge and experience by all. It usually is under the supervision of a discussion leader. This format obviously lends itself to relatively small groups; when such a meeting grows, it generally changes to a forum or symposium.

Workshop. The *workshop* format calls for general sessions involving only small groups that deal with specific problems or assignments. Whether or not the term is used, the workshop format is commonly used by training directors for skill training and drills. The participants actually train each other as they share new knowledge, skills, and insights into problems. Obviously, it is characterized by face-to-face dealing, with a great deal of participation by all.

Clinic. Used a great deal in training activity, the *clinic* offers drills and instruction in specific subjects. It is almost always limited to small groups interacting with each other on an individual basis.

Retreat. A *retreat* is usually a small meeting, typically in a remote location, for the purpose of bonding, intensive planning sessions, or simply to "get away from it all."

Institute. Conferences, seminars, and workshops are often offered by an *institute*, which is frequently established within a trade or profession to offer extended educational and training opportunities. The term is often used to suggest further meetings on the same topic. For example, an institute might offer continuing training programs every quarter of the year.

Panel. The *panel* calls for two or more speakers offering viewpoints or areas of expertise. It is open for discussion among the panelists, as well as with the audience. A panel is always guided by a moderator and may be part of a larger meeting format.

Exhibitions and Trade Shows. An *exhibition* usually describes an event held in conjunction with another meeting, such as a convention. The exhibition format is used for display, usually by vendors of goods and services, and has a built-in audience since it is held as part of a convention (see Exhibit 3).

The term **trade show** is used to describe a show that is held for its own sake. In Europe such exhibits, generally held without any type of program, are called *trade fairs.*

Another term used interchangeably is *exposition.* Most industrial, professional, and scientific trade shows are not open to the public. When large-scale exhibitions are open to the public, they are referred to as **consumer shows** (examples are home shows, flower and garden shows, auto shows, and boat shows) and a modest admission fee is typically charged. Because consumer shows are designed to attract a local clientele, they do not generate a large amount of room revenue for community hotels.

But the trade show concept is often attractive to meeting planners, whose meeting costs can be defrayed by the revenues generated from exhibitors, who are charged for their booth or table space. The concept of a "marketplace" showcasing a vast array of new equipment, technology, and ideas often boosts delegate attendance. An interesting convention program coupled with the showcase of the trade show combines to form a strong magnet, drawing increased delegate attendance benefiting show organizer, exhibitor, and attendee.

In the past few years, trade shows have increased in scope, with some—such as the Consumer Electronics Show (CES) or annual or bi-annual home builders shows—attracting thousands of attendees. This growth has resulted in a new industry substructure which includes trade show planning specialists, convention planning services, and auxiliary firms supplying trade show equipment and labor.

Persons and companies who sponsor and manage trade shows often hold membership in the International Association of Exhibitions and Events (IAEE). IAEE has over 3,000 members who plan nearly 5,000 shows and exhibitions annually.

Meetings. All the terms we've defined represent meetings of a sort. When none of the terms seems to apply, the event can always be called simply a *meeting.* This is particularly true when all the attendees are members of a single organization, meeting to discuss organizational affairs, such as stockholder meetings, board of directors meetings, etc. These can attract both a local and an out-of-town clientele, and range from a few attendees to large groups. It is important to understand these various differences in terminology in order to grasp the kind of event the client is trying to produce and to help the meeting planner to effectively carry it out. Much of it has to do with the projection of a desired image. While meeting descriptions are not scientific terms but rather are loose, often interchangeable ones, proper terminology can help people work together to achieve a tone or image for an event, and in that sense terms are important. For example, a *seminar* connotes something more cerebral than a *convention.* A *conference* in Chicago may be termed a *congress* in Geneva. A *conference* conjures up a picture of a small group in shirt-sleeves, while a *lecture* promises a more formal presentation to a passive audience. Accurate communication is needed in the convention business, and the ability to use proper terminology is important. Those in the field should understand the various terms used to describe meetings and use them correctly to achieve the professionalism expected by today's more sophisticated meeting planners.

Who Holds Meetings

Once you have determined that convention business, whatever the terminology, is worth going after, the next question deals with determining who holds meetings. Corporations and associations represent the two major types of meeting sponsors. But nonprofit organizations such as governmental agencies, labor unions, and fraternal and religious organiza-

Exhibit 3   Trade Show Exhibition

This photograph depicts the Canadian International Auto Show, a large trade show held at the Metro Toronto Convention Centre. The facility's convention service manager and the meeting planner created a master layout that the exhibition company used to divide the event space into displays for the individual exhibitors.
Source: Courtesy of the Metro Toronto Convention Centre.

tions also hold conventions, meetings, and trade shows. For convenience, we have broken today's convention business into three major categories:

- Corporations
- Associations
- Nonprofit organizations

Corporations. The corporate meeting is of extreme importance. Such meetings can be likened to an iceberg. A small tip protrudes above the surface while a huge mass floats beneath it. Companies have no need or desire to publicize their meetings, but meet they do. And often. They hold small meetings, large meetings, and middle-sized meetings. Business executives stress communication, and one of the most fundamental methods of intracompany communication is the meeting. Company meetings are a prime part of the market and growing rapidly.

Attending conventions and conferences is very definitely a part of professional and business activity. Such expenses as transportation, lodging, food, entertainment of clients, and registration fees are tax-deductible as business or professional expenses. Companies that stage meetings for dealers or their own staffs may deduct the cost of such events as business expenses. This has been a strong stimulant to meetings and conventions. It is also a strong factor in site selection, as those who attend look to such business trips as quasi-vacations.

Pharmaceutical, financial, and insurance companies are important to the hotel sales manager because they are such prolific meeting sponsors. There are continuing training programs for personnel. The prize, however, is the *incentive trip* for their top salespeople. These deluxe events are produced in various sizes and durations. Such trips are free to the attendee but are not planned exclusively for recognition and recreation. Most insurance companies schedule training and sales technique workshops in conjunction with such trips. Incentive trips are promoted a year in advance and therefore require more advanced planning. However, so many insurance company meetings are produced in such a variety of sizes and types that the insurance company meeting planner is a prime contact for all hotels, from the large property to the small inn.

Associations. The most visible convention organizers are the many associations throughout the country—indeed throughout the world, because many of them are truly international. Associations vary in size and nature. Their scope ranges from small regional organizations through statewide associations to national and international ones. Associations can be divided into several general categories:

- Trade associations
- Professional and scientific associations
- Technical societies

Trade associations. Trade associations are usually considered the most lucrative form of meeting business because their members are composed mostly of executives who have made it in business. Such conventions are often held in conjunction with exhibits.

A good example of such a group in the hospitality industry is the National Restaurant Association, which meets annually in Chicago with more than 110,000 in attendance. Big industrial suppliers of kitchen equipment and restaurant supplies do a great amount of selling during the convention.

It is a rare trade that doesn't have at least one association. Many have several national ones, involving different levels of the trade. It is common for the manufacturers in a trade to have their own association; the wholesalers and distributors to have theirs; and the retailers, still a third.

The photographic industry shows this pattern. There is the Photographic Marketing Association, whose members are retailers and photofinishers. They hold an annual convention of national status followed by a regional one six months later. The National Association of Photographic Manufacturers is a smaller group made up exclusively of domestic manufacturers. Its members meet once a year, while its boards and committees meet more frequently. The Photographic Manufacturers and Distributors Association has a broader membership base made up of foreign and domestic companies. In addition, there are a number of regional associations of independent camera dealers that hold regional exhibits and meetings. All of these organizations are trade associations.

Professional and scientific associations. The numerous associations in the professional and scientific fields are also inveterate meeting holders. Their subject matter ranges far and wide, but they all share a love for meetings. Each profession has its national association as well as state chapters.

The American Medical Association and the American Bar Association are well known to almost everyone. The Hospitality Sales and Marketing Association International (HSMAI) is a good example of a professional association in the hospitality industry, meeting annually for a major get-together and holding a number of regional and state workshops throughout the year.

Technical societies. Associations also are found among technical professions. The Society of Motion Picture and Television Engineers holds two national conventions a year. The Professional Photographers of America holds a national event annually, and most states have chapters that hold annual conventions of their own. In addition, there are specialty groups such as wedding photographers and newspaper photographers that have their own

---

A Successful Career Servicing the Meetings and Conventions Market

Anne Hamilton
Vice President, Resort Sales & Services
Walt Disney World Resort
Orlando, Florida

I grew up in the hotel business. My father owned several small properties on Miami Beach, so I learned the ins and outs of hotel operations from an early age. After graduating from Florida State University's hospitality school, I joined Hyatt in its corporate training program. I had rooms experience at that point, so I worked in food and beverage to balance myself.

In 1996, I joined Disney, and today I'm responsible for all sales and services related to meetings, conventions, and incentive programs at Walt Disney World Resort. We are fortunate to have an incredible team here at Disney — individuals who really want our meeting attendees to have a tremendous experience. My challenge is to keep this powerful team motivated and excited about coming to work every day.

I love the fact that my job is different every day. The meetings business is ever-changing. Meeting planners have become increasingly professional. They are more focused on attendee experience, achieving results, and realizing a return on their meeting investment.

Being a mentor is very important to me at this point in my career. I get great joy out of helping people become successful and realize their potential. I love articulating the benefits of a convention sales and service career, and I work closely with students at Rosen College. My advice to those just starting out in the hospitality/meetings industry is to seek a variety of work experience, understand that you are always on the journey of learning, and to embrace change. There are times when things go great and times when they don't, but you pick yourself up and learn from it (I've applied that to my personal life as well). I love this industry. Life couldn't be better.

---

associations and conventions. Think of any profession or career and you'll find at least one association. Librarians, teachers, hospital administrators, engineers—all have associations.

Nonprofit Organizations. There are many nonprofit organizations that just don't fit into the above slots, but they take no back seat when it comes to meetings. We have all seen political conventions on television. The camera shows the main floor, but think of the demand for smaller meeting rooms, suites, food functions, and so on. The story is repeated on a more modest scale on the state and regional level. All add to the market.

Hotels house weekend seminars on sex and marital problems, women's roles in the world, and social problems, to mention a few. The meetings of nonprofit organizations are just like those of other associations, and should be sold and serviced just like them.

Nonprofits fall into three categories:

- Government agencies
- Labor unions
- SMERF groups

Government agencies. Many branches of the government have a need to hold meetings off government premises for government employees or with the public. The Department of Agriculture, the Department of Commerce, the World Health Organization, and the United Nations affiliates are prolific meeting planners.

These agencies are funded in a variety of ways. Chambers of commerce are usually membership organizations that are privately funded. The Department of Agriculture, of course, spends public money. The labels are not important so long as you understand how they operate, what their meeting needs are, and how you can sell and serve them efficiently.

(A word of warning may be in order here. There is a love for acronyms among associations and governmental agencies that can drive the outsider up the wall. Each association seems to feel that the world is focused on it and that everyone knows what XYZ stands for. It also leads to crossed lines. Take "AMA": it can refer to the American Medical Association or the American Management Association, both prolific meeting holders. It takes a bit of caution. Listen carefully and take good notes. Take nothing out of context. Soon, you'll talk in acronyms, too.)

Labor unions. Labor unions have become one of the most important economic forces in the world. The largest unions are in the construction, manufacturing, mining, and transportation fields.

Labor unions are organized on four levels: local, state and regional, national, and international. Each level represents countless meetings and conventions, providing a fertile market for hotels. Most union members spend slightly less than the average convention delegate, but they still provide hotels with a sizable piece of business.

Large labor union conventions are similar to political conventions. They are held annually or biannually and include committee meetings, debates, speeches, and guest speakers.

SMERF groups. The industry has coined an acronym for certain nonprofits—the term SMERF (which stands for social, military, educational, religious, and fraternal) has come to represent a major market segment for many properties because of the large number of room nights these groups occupy each year—largely during property slack times.

SMERF groups have three common characteristics: they are very price sensitive; they are more likely to book meetings during the hotel's off-season; and they very often have nonprofessional planners who change from year to year.

Religious groups, for example, are not traditionally big spenders, but they are a viable market. Denominations hold regional and national meetings as well as seminars and ministerial workshops. Their events frequently begin on Monday and close on Thursday, providing weekend resort properties with midweek business.

Educational associations, too, are typically price sensitive, but they can be prime sources of business. Educational groups not only hold a number of national meetings, but every state has at least one teachers' association as well. In addition, educational business is particularly attractive to hotels, as these groups frequently meet during the slow summer months.

Veterans' groups and military associations can also be good business, especially for resorts. Many of these groups have large annual conventions as well as both large and small reunions, and attendees may be bigger spenders than those in other SMERF groups.

Although "big spenders" are not the norm (attendees tend to double and triple up in rooms, eat most meals off-property, and spend little money in lounges), SMERF groups are proving to be increasingly important for properties.

Barbara McDonald, national account manager for Sheraton Corporation's Chicago sales office, says:

> SMERF business used to be the lowest-rated business. The perception
> has been that these meetings are groups like fraternity chapters coming
> to have a beer brawl in your hotel, and that's just not so. The SMERF
> market is just as important as the corporate and other markets because the
> SMERF groups fill our down time. It's that simple. Also, small SMERF
> business can lead to much larger business. If a CEO comes in with his

fraternity and likes the hotel, you could have just landed another piece of business.[4]

According to Warren Breaux, assistant vice president of national sales for Hyatt Hotels Corporation:

> Hotels must have at least 70 percent occupancy to get a return on the investment of building the property. The four-and-a-half months worth of weekends, holidays, and seasonally distressed times are very difficult to fill, but this is a market that can help fill it. We would certainly rather fill our rooms at a reasonable, yet lower, rate than let these rooms go vacant. But we can't use that philosophy 365 days a year.[5]

SMERF groups do not follow a normal business schedule, and shop for the best rates, but they provide an excellent source of revenue during slack times. A property that can offer discount rates—and is willing to assist the largely nonprofessional meeting planners—can find that SMERF groups may make a considerable impact on the property's revenues.

Types of Group Customers

Since group meetings customers represent so many different types of organizations, from trade and professional associations to corporations and businesses to SMERF groups, you will likely work with different types of meeting planners with varying degrees of expertise. Meeting planners fall into four basic groups:

Full-Time Meeting Planners. Large national associations and corporations that look to convention revenues to financially support their organizations are most likely to staff full-time, professional meeting planners. These planners know exactly what is required to stage a successful event and will be thorough and timely in presenting information and instructions to the hotel.

Single-Event or Part-Time Planners. These meeting planners typically work for smaller companies or associations that do not have enough meeting activity to warrant a full-time meeting planner. The experience of these planners will vary; some will have little or no knowledge of the mechanics of running a meeting and will look to your hotel for assistance. It will be necessary to provide these planners with a timetable of the hotel's needs and deadlines and to assure them of your commitment to helping them stage a successful event. Other part-time planners have extensive knowledge of the meetings process. It is important, therefore, to ascertain the planner's knowledge and experience and to respond accordingly.

Committees. Many associations and nonprofit groups have committees that are involved in initial suggestions for meetings, screening of meeting sites, and the actual planning of meetings. As with single-event or part-time planners, the experience of committee members may vary and the hotel may be faced with multiple or conflicting decisions. You can minimize potential problems by suggesting that one person be put in charge and by offering your hotel's expertise in helping to make decisions.

Third Party Planners. An increasing number of meetings are being booked by third parties, such as meeting management firms, association management companies, and travel

---

Meeting Planner Profile

Today's meeting planners spend thousands of hours a year planning events from simple training meetings to huge conventions involving thousands of participants and hundreds of exhibitors. It is an exciting and varied career, and one which is constantly evolving. So who is the "typical" meeting planner of today?

According to a survey conducted by *Meetings & Conventions* magazine, today's professional meeting planner fits the following profile:

- Female (62% versus 38% male)
- Works in a department with a dozen other people
- Has been at the same job for nine years
- Earns $55,000 a year (salaries range from $25,000 to $100,000 or more; 50% of all meeting planners make $30,000 to $59,999)

Duties typically include: budgeting; site selection; negotiating with hotels, airlines, and vendors; program planning; trade show and exhibit planning; food and beverage selection; hotel and ground transportation arrangements; and post-meeting evaluation, including surveys of participants and an evaluation of the facility and service provided at each function.

In order to stay on top of market conditions, most belong to one or more professional associations, and find the following skills most useful for their profession: excellent oral and written communication and organizational skills; leadership qualities; flexibility; and the ability to handle pressure.

Joan Eisenstodt, a meeting manager with over 30 years of experience, suggests that you ask yourself the following questions to determine if you have what it takes to become a successful meetings professional:

- Do you like to plan parties, work schedules, your day, and so forth?
- Do you have a date book or personal digital assistant (PDA) that you update regularly and that includes everything you need to do for weeks or months in the future?
- Do you like to organize your bedroom, car, workplace, and so on? Is your idea of fun organizing a closet for someone?
- Are you very organized, almost to the point of obsession?

Joan Eisenstodt

---

agents. If this is the case, you will be dealing with an intermediary, not directly with the company, association, or nonprofit organization holding the meeting. Most of these third parties are experienced planners, but there may be cases in which you will need to assist the intermediary in making decisions about the event. If problems arise, you should first deal directly with the intermediary; you must use discretion regarding contacting the group that the intermediary represents, only going to the group after exhausting all other avenues (and thoroughly documenting your attempts to resolve problems).

While the above profiles will help you determine how much assistance might be needed from the hotel, each group and each planner is different. All meeting planners, regardless of their level of expertise, expect you to get to know them, their group, and the purpose of their meetings so that you can best meet their needs.

Types of Meeting Facilities

When the term "meeting site" is mentioned, hotels and resorts typically come to mind (downtown, suburban, and resort hotels host about 70 percent of all meetings). But hotels encompass a wide variety of choices. There are resort hotels, downtown hotels, suburban hotels, airport hotels, and large motels and motor hotels, and some are better suited for holding varying types of meetings. Airport hotels, for example, are excellent choices when the planner needs to get attendees to a central, convenient location, and these hotels may be an excellent choice for one-day or overnight meetings. Resorts, which are often the choice for annual conventions and incentive trips, offer a respite from the work world and appeal to attendees with families. But there are now a number of alternatives to "traditional" hotel and resort venues.

Planners who wish to book into a hotel can now opt for all-suite or boutique hotels or book their meetings into other, "nontraditional" venues, such as conference centers, cruise ships, and college campuses. In this section, we will take a look at some of these alternatives and see how they are impacting the hotel industry.

All-Suite Hotels. All-suite hotels were originally positioned to attract two market segments: business travelers who wanted "more than a room," and the relocation market. All-suite hotels, with their separate living rooms, complimentary "perks" such as breakfasts and cocktail hours, and homey atmospheres, serve as "temporary residences" and are especially attractive because their features are available at rates competitive with standard hotel rooms. Many meeting planners as well are attracted by the features offered by all-suite hotels.

First, all-suite hotels are ideal for board meetings and small training sessions, as each suite can serve as a small breakout room, and the atmosphere is conducive to conducting both business and personal conversations. Second, all-suite hotels solicit the small markets that are virtually ignored by larger properties; large properties are often perceived to be more interested in serving groups of 200 or more, while groups of 50 or less seem to get far less of the hotel staff's attention. Third, the worries about room assignments are eliminated—every attendee is offered a suite and therefore receives VIP treatment. In addition, meeting planners of small, regional meetings find that attendees are willing to pay for the perceived value of a suite over a conventional hotel room.

Many chains are targeting the small meetings market by developing all-suite properties. Embassy Suites, a member of the Hilton family of hotels and a forerunner in the development of all-suite properties, has formed a national group and meeting planning service department and offers a specific website to planners arranging meetings for groups of 300 or less. To attract small corporate meetings, Marriott also offers all-suite properties (with approximately 3,000 square feet of meeting space) to accommodate groups of 300 or less.

Boutique (Lifestyle) Hotels. Relatively new as a meetings venue, **boutique (lifestyle) hotels** were introduced by Ian Schrager, the successful operator of Studio 54. Schrager's concept for his venture into the hotel business, Morgans Hotel, incorporated concepts and features that were new to the industry at the time, including "lobby socializing" and the "urban spa."

Designed with unique architecture and decor, boutiques were originally targeted toward Gen X and Y travelers, who looked for high-tech amenities, all the comforts of home, and a unique experience (see Exhibit 4). Their small size (typically 150 rooms or less, although some boutiques may be larger) quickly caught the eye of corporate meetings planners, whose meetings are typically attended by 50 people or less.

The advantage to the small size of boutiques was that corporate buyers could buy out the property for complete privacy, and the hotel's staff was totally dedicated to their group. The size was also conducive to innovative programs, as decor could be quickly changed and various areas of the hotel — the rooftop, lobby, and grounds as well as restaurants and bars — could be modified to meet the group's needs.

Exhibit 4   Boutique (Lifestyle) Hotels

Boutique (lifestyle) hotels are characterized by their unique architecture and decor, as well as their small size (usually 150 rooms or less). These hotels are attractive to meeting planners who wish to avoid being lost in the crush at a large hotel, and planners often buy these properties out — ensuring that their groups will have privacy, the undivided attention of the staff, and a unique experience.

This photograph pictures corporate attendees around a fire pit at the Ventana Inn and Spa, a Joie de Vivre boutique hotel in Big Sur, California.

Source: Courtesy of Joie de Vivre Hospitality. Fire pit photograph by Kodiak Greenwood.

The growing popularity of boutique hotels led to a boom in the genre; Bill Kimpton was another leader in the boutique industry, and Schrager later teamed up with Marriott to create Edition Hotels. Other major chains that have entered the boutique market include Choice Hotels (Cambria suites), Hyatt (Hyatt Place), InterContinental Hotels Group (Indigo), and Starwood (the aloft and element brands); Hilton also operates several boutique-style hotels.

Conference Centers. **Conference centers**, which are typically designed to accommodate meetings of between 20–300 people and generally host groups averaging 70 attendees, differ from hotels in several ways. First, the *design* of conference centers typically differs from meeting facilities offered by hotels and resorts. Meeting rooms are situated away from high traffic areas to minimize distractions, and offer conveniently located breakout areas that are constantly refreshed. Since many conference sessions run for several hours, meeting rooms are designed for endurance and comfort and are equipped with commonly used audiovisual equipment (see Exhibit 5).

Most conference centers, since they are geared toward meetings and study, offer guestrooms that provide extra work and study space, and their on-site facilities may include small offices, libraries, and computer centers. Even the dining rooms are designed to facilitate small group interaction. Most feature half walls, large plants, and other decor that offer privacy. And, to provide for greater flexibility, many offer buffet meals rather than set menus.

Conference centers also differ from hotels in terms of *pricing policy*. Most conference centers offer their own version of the *Full American Plan*—a package price, available

Exhibit 5   Conference Centers for Business and Pleasure

Boardroom meeting setup at Dolce Hotels and Resorts' Lakeway Resort and Spa in Austin, Texas. The property, a conference center that is a member of IACC, is not the traditional, institutional-like conference center of yesterday. Although it offers the dedicated meeting space long associated with conference centers, the Lakeway offers a fine-dining restaurant, bar, and lounge, as well as numerous resort amenities, including a spa, a marina for water activities, tennis, and easy access to four nearby golf courses.
Source: Courtesy of Dolce Media Center.

either per day or per person, that includes rooms, meals, **continuous breaks**, meetings rooms, audiovisual equipment, and other needs. This "one-stop shopping" for a **complete meeting package** eliminates unexpected charges and is considered a real value by many meeting planners.

Planners also appreciate that conference center *meeting room bookings* can be made on a 24-hour basis. Therefore, if a meeting runs longer than expected, the group doesn't have to be concerned about incurring additional, often exorbitant, rental costs or having to vacate to accommodate another group.

Dolce Hotels and Resorts, which has broadened the appeal of conference centers with the addition of fine dining and resort-style amenities, is one of the largest operators of conference centers, with over two dozen facilities in the United States, Canada, and Europe. Benchmark Hospitality International is another major operator of conference centers, and several hotel chains, such as Hilton, Marriott, and Wyndham, are also active in the conference center market.

The International Association of Conference Centers (IACC) was founded to assist properties in targeting the conference center market. IACC members include conference centers and related firms and suppliers. To qualify for membership in the IACC, a property must derive a minimum of 60 percent of its business from meeting-related activities and must offer a "total and balanced meeting environment."

Other Nontraditional Facilities. Other types of nontraditional facilities chosen by meeting planners may include condominium resorts, convention centers, cruise ships, and college and university facilities. Cruise ships, for example, can be a popular choice for incentive meetings, and, as with conference centers, the cost of meals is included in the fee. The Radisson chain launched the *Radisson Diamond*, a ship designed solely to handle the group market. While it merged with Seven Seas Cruises and is no longer devoted strictly to the meetings market, meetings still account for about a third of the ship's business.

🖳 *INTERNET EXERCISE*

IACC Conference Centers

Visit the website for the International Association of Conference Centers at www.iacconline.com. View the area titled "Understand the IACC Conference Center Difference" and then navigate the site to answer the following questions:

1. What are the differences between conference centers and conventional hotels and resorts in each of the following areas:

    *   Focus and market segments
    *   Facility design
    *   Furnishings and equipment
    *   Food and beverage service
    *   Personnel

2. What are some of the industry *standards* and *guidelines* for conference centers?

3. What environmental initiatives are recommended to member conference centers?

4. What scholarships and awards does this trade association offer to students?

Meeting planners with limited budgets can opt for holding meetings at college and university campuses. While facilities, equipment, and such features as dining options and recreational amenities may vary, these settings can provide a casual, focused atmosphere.

Today's meeting sites offer a wide variety of choices, advantages, and disadvantages. No matter what type of facility is selected by the meeting planner, however, the principles outlined in this chapter can be applied to all venues.

Trends in the Meetings Industry

The expanding convention business has been—and will continue to be—impacted by a number of recent trends. Properties and managers who wish to continue to successfully compete for the meetings dollar should be aware of the impact of the following trends.

Continued Globalization

The unprecedented events of the past two decades—the opening of trade in European bloc countries; new hotel development in China, India, and the Middle East; the passage of the North American Free Trade Agreement; and the establishment of the European Economic Community, to name just a few—opened up a vast new market for the convention industry. Potential business was no longer limited to 300 million Americans, but a global village of seven billion people with growing economies. **Globalization** has impacted the convention industry in two significant ways.

First, despite a generally sluggish economy, the lifting of trade restrictions ushered in a boom in world tourism and business travel, increasing attendance at more meetings and conventions at domestic properties.

Peter Nathan, President of PWN Exhibicon International in Westport, Connecticut, says:

Globalization has impacted the exhibition industry in a way that nobody could have foreseen. Today, with the World Wide Web, there's a tremendous ability to create business opportunities overseas. Nearly all major trade show companies have offices overseas that can do the work you used to have to handle yourself.[6]

Second, the economy was ripe for foreign hospitality interests to buy domestic properties. This means there is additional competition for both foreign and domestic convention business, resulting in the need for more creative marketing on the part of domestic properties to attract international business—and keep domestic meetings and conventions.

Popularity of Second-Tier Cities

As costs for hotel rooms and transportation continue to rise in many major cities, budget- conscious meeting planners search for more economical sites. Milwaukee, Wisconsin; Hamilton, Ontario; and Charlotte, North Carolina, are just a few examples of what has become known in the industry as **second-tier cities** (see Exhibit 6).

Meeting planners who face the challenge of "selling" attendees on these seemingly less exotic locations usually find attractive incentives. In Charleston, West Virginia, for

Exhibit 6   Promoting Second-Tier Cities

Second-tier cities, such as Charlotte, North Carolina, are a popular choice with meeting planners who want to save money, receive attentive service, and introduce attendees to locales with a different "flavor" and unique attractions. To convey what Charlotte has to offer, the Charlotte Regional Visitors Authority had to look no further than the city's name. Its creative advertising campaign highlights the phrase "a lot" in Charlotte, and the campaign's theme line, "Charlotte's Got a Lot," effectively communicates that the idea is much like the city itself: the closer you look, the more pleasantly surprised you are.
Source: Courtesy of Charlotte Regional Visitors Authority.

example, delegates can go white water-rafting or take a cruise on the *West Virginia Belle* during their free time—activities that cannot be enjoyed in Chicago or New York. Attendees for the most part have responded favorably to these diverse activities, and have also noted the friendliness of the people living in second-tier cities. And all of this is usually enjoyed at a much lower cost than attendees would pay to meet in a larger city.

In addition to lower room rates—and often lower transportation expenses—second-tier cities often offer better service. Besides being enthusiastic about new business and "rolling out the red carpet," hotels in many second-tier cities often focus on one meeting at a time.

The growth in the choice of second-tier cities has led to the building of convention centers in many of these cities to better serve smaller association and corporate business meetings with larger facilities and up-to-date communications and audiovisual equipment.

Growth of Third-Party Meeting Planners

Today, it is not always easy to identify the meeting decision-maker. While hotel salespeople formerly dealt almost exclusively with corporate, association, and nonprofit meeting planners, third-party planners (either independents or meeting management firms) are becoming more prevalent in the industry.

Corporate downsizing, the increased complexity of negotiations, and increased use of Internet technology has many organizations looking *outside* their staffs for meeting planning services. Since these intermediaries are hired "out-of-house," a new industry buzzword— **outsourcing** —has been coined. Corporations typically outsource to such intermediaries as travel agents, destination management companies, and incentive travel houses. Associations and nonprofits generally look to meeting management companies or association management companies to assist them with their meeting needs. Therefore, as a hospitality salesperson, your customers will not only be association or corporate executives, but also the meeting management firms that represent them.

These third-party planners act as liaisons, bringing their clients' needs for sleeping rooms, food and beverage, and meeting facilities to hotels. Jeff Heckard, with the Westin Innsbrook Resort in Palm Harbor, Florida, says:

> Our hotel books a lot of business from third-party planners located all over the U.S.: corporate, association, SMERF and non-profits.[7]

Third-party planners can be broken down into several categories:

- Meeting management firms
- Association management companies
- Destination management companies
- Incentive travel houses
- Travel agents

Meeting Management Firms. *Meeting management firms* are private contractors (companies or individuals) who provide planning services directly to a client. Increasingly, planners are leaving their associations and corporations to set up shop as independents. Such planners are generally easy to work with because they are experienced. They function as intermediaries, and are paid a fee, which can vary. Some independent meeting planners simply assist corporate in-house meeting planners; others are responsible for the entire execution of the meeting. Interestingly, these companies often employ former hotel salespeople who know how to negotiate with hotels.

The largest of the **meeting management companies** are Experient, Conference Direct, and HelmsBriscoe. To demonstrate the importance of meeting management firms, Experient (and the clients it represents) was the largest single group customer of Starwood, Hyatt, Marriott, and Radisson hotels last year.

Meeting management companies search out hotel sites and aid their clients

Delegating Tasks	
WHAT SERVICES DO THIRD-PARTY PLANNERS PROVIDE FOR YOUR ORGANIZATION?	
Facility research and selection	51%
Planning entertainment, social and sports functions	51%
Negotiating with facilities	50%
On-site staffing	49%
Destination research and selection	48%
Transportation arrangements	40%
Vendor research and subcontracting	28%
Trade-show planning	19%
Planning incentive travel programs	13%
Negotiating with airlines	8%

in conducting meeting programs (the sidebar titled "Delegating Tasks" illustrates the services most often offered to meeting groups by third-party planners). These third-party planners make their money by charging a flat fee to the meeting organization or by seeking a commission from the hotel.

Association Management Companies. *Association management companies* work for smaller associations that do not employ a full-time professional staff. In most cases, employees of these firms work through the board of directors of associations to manage meetings and plan conventions and other activities. Often these firms provide management services for two or more associations.

SmithBucklin and Associates, the largest of the association management firms, manages the affairs, including annual meetings, for several meeting and event organizations. The Center for Exhibition Industry Research (CEIR), a source for trade show statistics and education, and the Society of Incentive and Travel Executives (SITE) have turned over their management to SmithBucklin.

Destination Management Companies. These firms offer convention and meeting services at the host city. **Destination management companies** may arrange for room accommodations, restaurant reservations, airport shuttle service, entertainment, technical services (teleconferences, audiovisual presentations, etc.), and special programs for attendees and spouses. The impact of these *local experts* is detailed in the box titled "The Growth of the Destination Management Industry."

Most destination management companies remain "behind the scenes," assisting the meeting planner with the details of the meeting. This type of firm knows the host city, and can provide in-depth information on the destination, both in terms of suppliers and extra convention activities (special sightseeing tours, etc.). In Europe, a destination management company is generally called a **professional congress organizer.**

Incentive Travel Houses. Incentive travel houses deal directly with arranging incentive travel packages for corporations wishing to reward or motivate their staffs or their customers. These packages are usually "first class" and involve an exotic or popular resort location. They typically include a number of "perks" and special amenities not commonly associated with regular hotel and travel packages.

The Growth of the Destination Management Industry

Karen Gorden
President, Activity Planners

After air travel allowed greater numbers of participants to attend conventions at a national level, ground operators began offering transportation and later "Ladies Programs" for the wives of attendees. Ground operators later added special events and themed parties to their list of services. As the role of these "local experts" grew, the industry began referring to them as destination management companies, and these DMCs continued to expand their role in the meeting, convention, and travel industry. As corporate meetings and retreats became more common, many DMCs added additional services, such as motivational speakers, educational seminars, and personalized merchandise and gift items, making them a "one-stop shop" for meeting planning. Since the role of DMCs is to keep their city "fresh" in the eyes of repeat visitors, DMCs continually updated their services and style and, recognizing a need for regulation and standardization, created the Association of Destination Management Executives (ADME). The non-profit, non-partisan, international trade association defines DMCs as "professional services companies possessing extensive local knowledge, expertise, and resources, specializing in the design and implementation of events, activities, tours, transportation, and group logistics." The growth from ground operator to destination management company in just over 30 years is only the beginning. With developments in technology, such as the World Wide Web, the average traveler is more educated than ever before, making the job of the DMC a continuous challenge to keep abreast of the ever-changing demands of the marketplace.

Travel Agents. Some travel agents have expanded their traditional role of selling package tours, transportation, and guestrooms to offer meeting planning services to corporate accounts. Mega travel agencies such as BTI America (with 100 meeting planners) and American Express (48 planners) plan everything from board meetings to trade shows.

This transition came naturally, as travel agents were able to keep abreast of changing airline price structures and routes, and many corporate meeting planners are now turning to travel agents to arrange everything from transportation to rooms to meeting space. Since not all travel agents are experienced in meeting planning, corporate clients must carefully select those who have this expertise, and properties may have to work more closely with those who are just learning the meetings field. This association can prove extremely profitable, however, both in terms of meetings business and other individual and group bookings at the property.

Increased Use of Technology

New advances in computer, telephone, and video technology have radically changed the ways hotels do business and communicate with clients. This new technology includes:

- The Internet
- Fax and e-mail capabilities
- Video conferencing
- In-room technology
- Social media

The Internet. When asked about the most significant change in the meetings industry over the past ten years, Peter Yesawich, CEO of Ypartnership (a marketing, advertising, and public relations agency), responded: "…it is the evolution of the Internet and the way technology is now used to plan meetings."[8]

Maureen Callahan, vice president of marketing for Destination Hotels and resorts, agrees:

> The meetings industry has been revolutionized by technology. Web sites are now the ubiquitous solution for meeting research, planning, and booking. Current Web technology allows access to detailed property data, interactive 3-D site tours, rate planning, site comparisons, and an experiential orientation to hotels and resorts. Web cams provide real-time views of properties, and, with the advent of Travel 2.0, planners can "chat" with other planners on key issues, gather information on meeting experiences at properties, and obtain referrals and recommendations. The business of planning and booking meetings is very transparent with these ever-evolving tools.[9]

Meeting planners now use the Internet to search for properties that meet their requirements, "tour" properties, and even auction their event for the best price. At conventionplanit.com, for example, meeting planners can search a database of more than 14,000 meeting venues and then forward an RFP (request for proposal) to the desired property. Other sites offering searchable databases can be found at the end of this chapter. Some sites offer meeting facilities only, while others offer direct access to other service providers, such as transportation companies and other key suppliers.

While many meeting planners still rely on site visits to make a final decision, an increasing number are viewing properties through the "virtual tours" offered on hotel websites. These tours, which vary in their degree of sophistication, are replacing brochures (including video brochures) and even DVDs as an effective way to present a property. If the planner likes what he or she sees, it only takes the click of a mouse to contact the hotel for additional information or an RFP.

A growing number of planners are using the Internet to promote their events, especially conventions. A link to event information may be set up on the group's website, a separate event site may be set up by the planner, or the hotel may include a dedicated page for the group on its own website. These sites provide a number of advantages to both membership and planners. Members have ready access to housing and program information as well as a convenient payment option. Planners benefit by getting early cash flow (as opposed to waiting until members register at the event), being able to obtain a detailed tally of the number of delegates who will be attending, and being able to prepare convention materials ahead of time, such as badges and packets that include tickets to specific functions.

Another trend is the use of interactive event sites as part of meetings. These sites, set up by meeting personnel, allow attendees to reference materials both before the event begins and at the meeting, and they usually provide a means of continued group interaction through the use of meeting blogs. Providing materials in this way eliminates the need for copious amounts of paper and note-taking at the meeting.

Hotels are also using the Internet to create a presence for their properties, link to other sources of meeting planning business, and conduct market research. Hotel chains use corporate websites to link their properties; a meeting planner can log on to the corporate site and call up a number of locations. But even small properties, realizing that they are now advertising to a global market, are developing websites.

In addition to the value of having an individual presence on the web, many hospitality properties are benefiting from alliances with other entities that service the meetings market.

Hotels can be featured on or linked to websites hosted by their destination cities, their local convention and visitors bureau, or other firms and organizations that offer services to the meetings industry, such as Expedia (expedia.com).

Last, but certainly not least, the Internet can be used as a powerful research tool. Hotels can use the Internet to research their competition, their target markets, and current economic trends that impact business. Logging on to a competitor's website provides a wealth of information on its facilities and ability to service meetings. Accessing a particular corporation or association can yield contact information and pertinent facts about meeting history. As an added benefit, the Internet can provide the names of businesses and associations that were not even previously considered by the property.

To keep pace with the changes brought about by technology, today's hotel salespeople are expected to be computer literate. Not only will they be using the Internet for research and bookings, they will most likely use computerized applications for most aspects of the sales and service process.

Fax and E-Mail Capabilities. Although the Internet is increasingly being used to transmit information, *fax transmissions* are still a powerful tool for communicating with meeting planners. *Broadcast fax* is used to send updates on the property and other announcements to meeting planners at regular intervals. *Fax-on-demand* provides a source for meeting planners for meeting room specs, open dates, banquet menus, and other meeting-related information by simply dialing a property's fax number. Fax is still an easy and fast way to transmit an existing document.

E-mail (electronic mail) is popular for communicating both inter-office and inter-property and with meeting planners and other possible sources of business. The advantage of e-mail over fax (which is simply a copy of a document) is that e-mail can be edited; a copy of a contract, for example, can be mailed to a meeting planner, who can edit it and return it to the hotel with a minimum of effort.

Yet another application of e-mail is the ability to stay in touch with contacts, even when the hotel salesperson or meeting planner is unavailable. An automatic response to incoming e-mails can alert the sender that the person is currently unavailable and provide information on when he or she will return — and provide alternate contact information, such as a cell phone number, in case of emergencies.

Video Conferencing. *Video conferencing*, also called *teleconferencing*, has been in use for some time, using satellites to link groups and speakers. New technology has greatly enhanced transmission quality and sound, and has led to other improvements, including multimedia presentations, video-enhanced speakers, instant replay, and "live projection" (projecting a close-up image of the speaker onto a large video screen to bring him or her "closer" to the audience). One of the most exciting innovations in video conferencing is **telepresence**, which uses special studios and advanced audio and video equipment to give the impression that participants are in the same room as participants in remote locations. Telepresence suites feature a half conference table that faces large video screens on the opposite wall (see Exhibit 7). To enhance the illusion of a face-to-face meeting, participants at remote locations are projected life-size at eye level at a "matching" half conference table, and even the walls of the remote suite are painted the same color as the walls in the other participating suite.

Since telepresence equipment is expensive, it was previously used only by major multinational companies. Although many hotels do not have enough requests for this service to justify the expense, Marriott International and Starwood Hotels & Resorts have

Exhibit 7   Telepresence—Video Conferencing Goes High-Tech

Participants in a telepresence suite at a "hub" location interact with participants at a remote telepresence suite using high-tech video and audio. The immersion experience includes the projection of life-size images (at eye level) on the screens, and studios that "mirror" each other with half conference tables and matching decor, giving the impression that the attendees are in the same room.
Source: Courtesy of TANDBERG.

become leaders in equipping properties with telepresence studios, which typically rent for $500 per hour. While this fee may sound high, telepresence can be a cost-effective alternative to getting participants together by conventional means, such as time-consuming and expensive air travel; travel and rooms are only needed for participants who will participate from the "hub" location.

In-Room Technology. *In-room technology* already includes the availability of fax machines, voice mail services, and computer hookups in guestrooms. Many meeting planners now demand wireless and high-speed Internet access in guestrooms. Other applications include in-room video checkout, voice or electronic control of thermostats and lighting levels, in-room television channels that offer "tours" of the property and display convention programs and other pertinent information to guests, and other innovations.

Brian Beamish, a supplier of voice-processing systems, states:

> Soon the widespread telephone technology will be linked to computer networks on the information superhighway. I can see an e-mail message from the Internet triggering the light on the telephone to indicate there's a message waiting. Similarly this could also work voice-to-text. Someone could send out a message over the Internet by simply speaking into the phone.[10]

At theWit Hotel, a Doubletree boutique property in Chicago, in-room innovations include touch-screen access to a number of services, including ordering wake-up calls (choices include messages from celebrities), contacting valet personnel, accessing needed services from housekeeping, making restaurant reservations, and looking up flight and weather information. High-tech innovations can also be found at the MGM Grand Mirage's City Center project in Las Vegas. Scot Campbell, chief information officer for the project, offers this description of the guestroom experience:

> Upon entry, lights slowly brighten, music plays, and curtains automatically part to reveal sweeping city or mountain views. From the keyless entry to the monitored minibar to the one-touch Good Night button, the guestroom technology at City Center properties rivals that of many "smart" luxury homes.[11]

Social Media. Today, both hotels and meeting planners are making extensive use of **social media** — including business and social networking sites, blogs, and podcasts — to share information and build relationships using the Internet. Joining online networking communities such as Facebook, LinkedIn, and Twitter, where people can share information, photographs, videos, and music, has become increasingly common — and can be an effective way to keep in touch and build relationships with "friends" and "followers." In fact, many hotels now include links to their social media pages on their websites.

It is important to note that social media is unlike traditional advertising — hotels should use social media to create *dialogs* with their customers; social media strategies should be designed to talk *with* customers, not *at* them.

David Nour, CEO of the Atlanta-based consulting firm BeOne Now, says:

> The number-one enemy of doing social networking well is corporate culture. It takes a very different mindset, a very different approach. Most companies are afraid of putting a blog out there because they don't know what customers are going to say. They should be thinking in terms of what they could learn from this vast audience that can give them candid input.[12]

While technology, including social media, e-mail, and web presences, enable hotel salespeople, convention service managers, and meeting planners to share information and communicate quickly and efficiently, it is important to take heed to the words of Jerry Wayne, vice president of sales and marketing for the Greenbrier, who says:

> In my 30 years of sales and marketing experience, there has never been a substitute for personal relationships. In today's world of electronic communications, those relationships are declining. We are a people business, and those of us that have developed personal relationships with our customers will continue to have their loyalty.[13]

Extended Use of Revenue Management

Over the past few years, hotels have joined the ranks of airlines and cruise ships in using yield management—setting prices based on demand. With today's technology, prices can be revised instantaneously as availability and demand warrant.

While this strategy has proven effective in filling rooms, hotels generally realize revenue from a number of sources. Hotels today are interested in more than rates, dates, and space. They are basing pricing on demand, but applying the approach to all the property's profit centers, not just guestrooms. Hotels are now evaluating a group's spending patterns and potential for utilizing meeting space, food and beverage services, and other property facilities and services (such as spas) before booking them.

Kostas Trivizas, director of revenue management for the Savoy Group, London, explains:

> Hotels receive combined requests for meeting rooms, food and beverage, guestrooms, and all of these requests come with a different profit margin, so you want to find the right mix that optimizes the one profit margin at the end for all the departments together. This requires specific forecasting—demand for guestrooms with meeting rooms, meeting rooms with banqueting rooms, or banqueting rooms alone, or meeting rooms alone. Often what happens is that yield managers end up trying to do tactical optimizing—last-minute close up of rates. Revenue management gets to the root, such as correctly formulating pricing issues.[14]

Mr. Trivizas feels that revenue management is one of the most challenging aspects in the industry, and predicts that revenue management director positions, which are marketing-driven, will become more commonplace.

Already, hotel chains are evaluating convention and meeting groups with revenue management software. Salespeople input estimates of room revenue and catering revenue in dollars per night, suite and hospitality revenues, arrival and departure patterns, room to function space in square feet per night, and date requirements of prospective meetings. The software then evaluates the business according to what is already on the books, historical trends, and forecasts of potential bookings. Meeting groups are assessed on their ability to meet revenue expectations in food and beverage purchases, audiovisual rental, recreational usage, and even retail spending.

Complex Contract Negotiations

According to Roger Dow, a longtime executive with Marriott International who became president and CEO of the Travel Industry Association of America, planners of 25 years ago had three basic questions, "How does your space look, will I fit, and will you give me good service?" Today, however, hoteliers are focusing more on the bottom line, and protecting themselves with contracts that include attrition clauses, due diligence, and other measures to minimize losses from cancellations and other issues arising from group business.

Dow says that both sides are putting far more time and energy into contracts rather than the old concerns of space and service, creating a tension that did not exist in the days before contracts became a matter of prime importance. Dow says, "The handshake and the relationship are still there, but then comes the 30-page contract."[15]

Jonathan Howe, president and founding partner of Howe & Hutton Ltd. (and the General Counsel for MPI), adds:

> Negotiations have taken on a new complexion. Contracts have gotten much more complex and extensive, and we have the whole request for proposal process now. There is a lot more counseling and active

involvement by lawyers through the whole process — from the outset
to final bill reconciliation.[16]

Some meeting planners today feel that they spend an inordinate amount of time on
legal issues. Deidre Ross, CMP, director of conference services for the American Library
Association, says:

> I feel like an attorney. I'm looking at contracts all the time. It didn't
> seem to be that legal when I started. It was friendlier, and even though
> people have good relationships now, when it's a contract it's a contract.
> We didn't even use to use that term—we called it a letter of agreement.[17]

Most organizations now have attorneys who look over hotel contracts, and more
meeting planners are being taught the nuances of contract negotiation, especially when it
comes to cancellation clauses and attrition.

"Green" Meetings and Social Responsibility

Many hotels — especially those in drought-prone areas — have practiced water conservation for many years by reducing the number of times that sheets and towels are replaced
for guests staying over several nights; switching to water-saving shower heads, faucets,
and toilets; and offering water at meals only upon request. Today, as a greater emphasis
has been placed on the environment, customers are actively seeking out businesses that are
doing their part to conserve, and "going green" has become a hot trend in the hospitality
industry — which includes **"green meetings."**
Laurence S. Geller, chairman and CEO of Strategic Hotels & Resorts, says:

> The customer is dictating that the hospitality industry go green. If you
> don't see it today, you will tomorrow. Get ready. Every group meeting
> planner is going to check your carbon emissions. You better build it green
> or convert it. Because if you don't, customers won't come.[18]

Hotels are responding to the demand by instituting green practices in a number of
areas:

- *Energy efficiency and conservation.* The use of efficient technologies
  for heating and air conditioning units, food service appliances, lighting, and transportation. The use of alternate forms of power, including
  wind power, solar power, and geothermal sources.
- *Water efficiency and conservation.* Conservation practices for linens.
  The installation of water-efficient toilets and shower heads. The use
  of recycled water for landscaping.
- *Sustainable food.* Increased use of organic and locally grown food
  items, reducing both the amount of pesticides and fertilizers that harm
  the environment and the amount of fuel used to transport food.
- *Recycling and composting.* The recycling of such items as glass, plastic, metal, paper, ink and toner cartridges, and grease. Composting
  of food waste, either on property or through an outside composting
  service.
- *Green building and construction.* The use of environmentally friendly
  products, such as stone and recycled materials, in construction. Archi-

tecture that makes use of natural sources of energy (skylights, solar panels, and so on).

- *Education.* Making both property staff and guests aware of conservation efforts to enable them to actively participate in recycling and other programs. For example, meeting planners should be made aware of options to reduce paper, such as using electronic signs, online registration forms, and electronic note-taking, document downloads, and surveys.

In order to help keep up-to-date on conservation technology and products — and to get the word out about their green efforts — a number of hotels are joining associations that provide comprehensive guidelines and offer opportunities to promote green efforts. The Green Hotels Association (www.greenhotels.com), for example, offers a 135-page guide on going green and a catalog of environmental products. The association's website also provides links to member hotels and approved vendors, and offers travel tips.

In Canada, hotels can join the Hotel Association of Canada (HAC), which offers one to five green keys to hotels that meet guidelines for environmental management, indoor air quality, solid and hazardous waste, land use, and community outreach. The Green Key Eco-Rating Program can be viewed at www.hacgreenhotels.com.

Once a hotel has its green programs in place, it is important to get the word out. Don't forget to advertise your programs and certifications (see Exhibit 8), and make the community aware of your efforts through press releases, articles, and green events — such as a recycling event or the cleanup of a nearby park. This type of activity is growing in popularity as people take a more active role in environmental issues.

Social Responsibility. As people get more involved with the environment and wish to commit to being a "good neighbor," more meetings focusing on **social responsibility** are

Exhibit 8   Promoting Green Meetings

This ad for The Banff Centre, an IACC conference center in Alberta, Canada, promotes the property's commitment to green meetings — at no extra cost to the meeting planner. The ad also focuses on the property's unique location in an UNESCO World Heritage site teeming with natural wonders.
Source: Courtesy of The Banff Centre, Banff, Alberta, Canada.

🖥 INTERNET EXERCISE

Green Meetings

Hotels have recognized the need to stage environmentally friendly meetings. Each of the following hotel chains has an environmental policy and/or initiative. Log on to the websites of these hotels to answer the questions below:

- www.fairmonthotels.com
- www.kimptonhotels.com
- www.rosenhotels.com

1. Review Fairmont's "Eco-Meet: Green Meeting and Conference Planning Guide." What does Fairmont recommend in each of the following areas: external accreditation; waste management; water conservation; air quality; and energy efficiency?

2. What Earthcare products and practices are standard at all Kimpton boutique hotels? How does Kimpton integrate its Earthcare program into events and meetings?

3. In what specific ways is Rosen Hotels helping to reduce environmental concerns and promote green meetings?

---

being held. Social responsibility refers to incorporating volunteer activities into the meeting program.

Instead of spending their spare time lounging around the pool or taking in local attractions, more meeting attendees are expressing an interest in doing something for the local community. Hotel chains are responding to these requests by offering such programs as Fairmont's Meetings that Matter and the Ritz-Carlton's VolunTeaming, a program that incorporates volunteer and *team-building* activities.

While team-building frequently involves outdoor, physical efforts such as rock climbing, ropes courses, and white-water rafting, volunteering is also an excellent way to bring groups together to accomplish a common goal. A team may build bicycles for a local children's organization, for example, or accomplish another task to benefit a local or national charitable organization.

Summary

As you can see from this overview of the convention and meetings industry, there are a number of factors that must be taken into consideration after the decision has been made to solicit this lucrative market segment. To successfully compete for meetings business, you must have a working knowledge of the various types of meetings and the groups that typically hold them, be aware of the types of facilities that can best sell and service the various segments within the meetings market, and stay abreast of trends impacting the industry to enable you to develop effective strategies for attracting meetings business.

 ## Endnotes

1. EXPACT 2008 Convention Expenditure and Impact Study.

2. Amy Tiebel, "What Buyers Need to Know in a Seller's Market," *Convene*.

3. Ibid.

4. Dara Wilson, "SMERF GROUPS: Second-Class No Longer," *Association Management*.

5. Ibid.

6. "Expert Voices on 30 Years," *Meeting News*, January 29, 2007.

7. Barbara Ann Cox, "The Third-Party Meeting Planner Is an Asset to the Hotelier," *Florida Hotel and Motel Journal*, June 2002, p. 32.

8. "Winds of Change: Four Trends that Will Change the Meetings Industry," posted on www.meetingsnet.com, January 31, 2007.

9. Maureen Callahan, "Confidence, Integrity, and a Competitive Spirit," *Meeting Planners Guide*, Spring 2007.

10. Deborah McKay-Stokey, *Future Hotelier*.

11. Jay McDonald, "Hotel Tech 2.0," *Elite Meetings* (www.elitemeetings.com).

12. John Buchanan, "How Social Networking Is Changing the Hospitality Marketplace," *HSMAI Review*, February 2009, pp. 28, 29.

13. "Leadership: A View From the Top," *HSMAI Foundation*, July 2009, p. 15.

14. "Profit Performance: A Primer for Mastering Revenue Management," *World Hospitality*, February 2000, p. 4.

15. Dave Kovaleski, "The Meeting Industry Grows Up," *Corporate Meetings & Incentives*, March 2005, p. 28.

16. "Expert Voices on 30 Years," *Meeting News*, January 29, 2007.

17. Ginny Phillips, "Legal-Sized Planners," *PCMA Convene*, June 2004, p. 55.

18. Jim Butler, "Green Gems from the Los Angeles Hotel Investment Conference," *ehotelier.com*, February 13, 2008.

🔑 Key Terms

all-suite hotel—A hotel that features rooms larger than typical guestrooms, with a living or working space separate from the bedroom(s).

boutique (lifestyle) hotel—A small, trendy hotel typically known for its unique architecture and decor. Frequently bought out by meeting planners to ensure privacy, attentive service, and a unique experience for meeting attendees.

business center—A facility that offers key equipment and services typically found in a business traveler's home office, including computer access, fax machines, and copy machines. Many offer secretarial and other services, such as shipping.

complete meeting package—An all-inclusive pricing plan (including lodging, all meals, and support services) offered at conference centers.

conference center—A property specifically designed to handle group meetings. Conference centers are often located outside metropolitan areas and may provide extensive leisure facilities. May be certified by the International Association of Conference Centers (IACC).

consumer shows—Exhibitions that are open to the public; they usually require an entrance fee. Also termed a public show.

continuous breaks—Refreshment areas that are continually replenished while the meeting is in session. This allows attendees to break at will, in groups or individually, with the assurance that refreshments are always available to them.

convention—A meeting of delegates for action on a particular matter. Usually involves a general session and supplementary smaller meetings. Conventions are produced with and without exhibits.

destination management companies—Professional management companies specializing in the design and delivery of convention events, activities, tours, staffing, and transportation, utilizing local knowledge, expertise, and resources.

globalization—The international consolidation of big business and the growing trend for countries to allow free transfer of goods and services across national boundaries.

"green" meetings—Meetings that include practices, products, and services that are less harmful to the environment. Elements may include using less paper by employing electronic means to convey information, choosing recyclable products, and using meeting rooms that are built using natural materials and environmentally friendly lighting.

incentive travel houses—Full-time professional travel companies that make arrangements for companies that wish to offer incentive trips.

meeting management companies—Companies, representing another organization, that handle site selection, negotiations, and turn-key support for an event.

outsourcing—Subcontracting a task or responsibility to a supplier to handle some aspect of an event.

professional congress organizer (PCO)—European term for a DMC (destination management company). Local supplier who can arrange, manage, and/or plan any function or service an event.

second-tier cities—Smaller cities and suburbs of major cities that offer the meeting planner an attractive location and at the same time provide less costly accommodations and transportation.

social media—The tools and platforms that people employ to converse with each other and publish/share content online. These tools include blogs and podcasts as well as sites designed to share photos, videos, graphics, bookmarks, and other content.

social responsibility—Meetings that include a combination of volunteer and team-building activities.

telepresence—A high-end form of video conferencing that uses studio-quality audio and video and life-size images of participants at other locations to make the video conference as much like a face-to-face meeting as possible.

trade show—An exhibition with displays, generally held within a trade industry or discipline. May be independent or in conjunction with a convention. Not open to the general public.

 # Review Questions

1. Why is it important for hotel people to understand the differences between various types of meetings? After all, aren't all the definitions synonymous?

2. Distinguish between a congress and a conference, a symposium and a workshop, a trade show and a consumer show.

3. What are the types of meeting planners a convention sales or service manager might be working with? How are these planners different?

4. How do conference centers differ from hotels?

5. Why are many meeting planners choosing second-tier cities for their conventions?

6. What are the characteristics of SMERF groups?

7. Describe the competitive advantages of all-suite hotels in the meetings industry.

8. Briefly describe the important and changing role of third-party meeting planners in the meetings market.

9. Explain how technology is reshaping the relationship between meeting planners and hotel salespeople.

10. What is revenue management and how is it affecting the way hotels sell and service the meetings industry?

 ## Additional References

Fundamentals of Destination Management and Marketing, Richard Harrill, Editor, Educational Institute, American Hotel & Lodging Association, 2005. www.ei-ahla.org

Meetings, Expositions, Events, and Conventions, G. G. Fenich, Pearson Prentice-Hall, 2008.

Professional Meeting Management, Fifth Edition, Professional Convention Management Association. www.pcma.org

 ## Internet Sites

For more information, visit the following Internet sites. Internet addresses can change without notice. If a site is no longer available at the address listed below, a search engine can be used to find the new address or additional, related sites.

Benchmark Hospitality
www.benchmark-hospitality.com

British Exhibition Contractors Association
www.beca.org.uk

European Federation of Conference Towns
www.efct.com

The Green Meetings Industry Council
www.greenmeetings.info

Independent Meeting Planners Association
  of Canada
www.impaccanada.com

International Association of Professional
  Congress Organizers
www.iapco.org

International Congress and Convention
  Association
www.icca.nl

SmithBucklin
www.smithbucklin.com

Chapter 2 Outline

Competencies

1. Distinguish sales from marketing and describe the "four Ps" of marketing. (pp. 37–39)

2. Explain the importance of a marketing plan, list the four steps of a marketing plan, and describe how marketers conduct market research. (pp. 40–55)

3. Describe how marketers select target markets, position their properties, establish objectives and action plans, review and monitor their marketing plans, and put their marketing plans into action. (pp. 55–65)

Charles Walhaven
Director of Convention Services, Meetings.com
Nashville, Tennessee

"Knowing what aspects of your meeting facility are most important to meeting groups is essential. The foundation of any marketing plan is the property analysis. A property analysis is a written, unbiased self-appraisal used to assess the strengths and weaknesses of your hotel. Know everything about your property—and experience it from a meeting planner's point of view. Your interaction with a planner will be more successful if you understand his or her objectives, format, and requirements, and if you are able to demonstrate exactly how your property can meet those needs. Your creativity and knowledge of your property's capabilities will help you meet the needs of your target markets."

2 Developing Your Marketing Plan

T HE CONVENTION BUSINESS is a potentially lucrative market segment that can be serviced by almost any type of property. But this does not mean that a hotel should just plunge headlong into attempting to capture all the convention business it can handle. Going after convention business without a sense of what the property can deliver may lead to costly mistakes, including misdirected advertising, fruitless sales calls, or, worst of all, poor service.

Tom McCarthy, past president of the Hospitality Sales and Marketing Association International and a leading trainer and consultant, advises:

> You definitely need a written marketing plan. When plans are verbal, they change frequently and confusion among the troops always results. Laying out your plan in writing for the entire year helps you to budget more accurately than making decisions as you go, but 75 percent of what I see in typical hotel sales/marketing plans is worthless—just filler to make the plan more important than it is.[1]

In this chapter, we present a practical step-by-step approach to developing a marketing program. The case study of the Rolling Green Resort will be used to explain key marketing concepts. Many of the figures and examples in this chapter are related to this case study, so it is important that you not only read the text but also review these examples (and the captions to each) for a better understanding of each application. The numerous illustrations are from actual forms used in the hospitality industry today. Therefore, you are not just learning theory—you will see exactly how marketing concepts are put into practice.

The marketing plan will be our base. We will refer to it often, so it is necessary to grasp the concept thoroughly.

The Difference Between Sales and Marketing

Before we explore the foundation for convention sales and marketing, there is an important question that needs to be addressed: What exactly is **marketing?** Some people think that marketing and **sales** are synonymous. Others think that marketing is no different than the age-old sales and promotion concept; they consider the combination of sales, advertising, promotion, and merchandising to be marketing. Neither is correct.

There is a clear distinction between marketing and sales. The terms are not synonymous—sales and marketing are *not* equal; marketing is more than sales. Marketing is the combining, blending, integrating, and controlling of all the factors that have an influence on sales. Being market-minded is much broader than being simply sales-minded. Marketing is strategic and directive. It is goal-oriented, and the goals are concise and measurable. It is the groundwork, the research, the *plan* on which sales promotion is based (see box titled "The Difference Between Sales and Marketing").

In the recent past, the demand for hotel rooms was far greater than the supply; there simply were not enough rooms to go around. It didn't matter what type of rooms were built; the customer had no alternative choices. A marketing plan that was customer-oriented was not needed to sell the product.

But the hospitality industry of today is far different. The city that once had a single inn now has four or five new hotels, each of them unique. Where formerly the demand exceeded the supply, the reverse is now true in many markets.

Now, the lodging industry is realizing that its problems are not unlike those of companies specializing in tangible products. Thus, many hotels are attempting to come to grips with what marketing means in an effort to apply marketing management principles. Hotels that wish to effectively compete must become marketing-oriented. The future belongs to those who are customer-oriented, those who are in the business of meeting the changing needs of the public—not just in the business of maintaining hotel rooms.

THE DIFFERENCE BETWEEN SALES AND MARKETING

MARKETING	SALES
Focuses on market analysis, planning and control of changing market variables.	Focuses on field work and desk work to sell to the consumer.
Focuses on long-term trends and creating new products, markets, and strategies for future growth.	Focuses on short-term considerations—today's products, markets, consumers, and strategies.
Focuses on profit planning, including determining the optimum market segment mix.	Focuses on volumes and quotas, current sales, bonuses, and commissions.

The Importance of Marketing

Like other industries, the hospitality industry is subject to both controllable and uncontrollable variables that will affect sales efforts. External variables, such as weather conditions, fuel shortages, and airline strikes, are largely uncontrollable. Other market variables, however, are inherent to all properties and can be controlled through marketing strategies to attract and retain new and repeat business.

These controllable variables, called the **marketing mix**, consist of "four Ps"—product, place, promotion, and price. *Product*, in the hospitality industry, consists both of physical facilities—guestrooms, banquet space, meeting facilities, and recreational amenities—and of more intangible factors—such as service and the vacation or meeting experience itself. Since a large part of the hospitality product is intangible (you are often selling a property's atmosphere), most marketing strategies will emphasize *benefits* rather than the more tangible physical *features* offered by a property. *Place* refers to the accessibility of the products to its consumers. Hospitality products, of course, do not have to be distributed to the consumer; instead, the consumer must travel to them. This accessibility may be facilitated by marketing strategies which involve intermediaries, such as meeting planners, tour operators, and travel agents.

Promotion includes both persuasion (getting the consumer to buy) and communication (developing a relationship with the client). In the hospitality industry, communication plays an especially important part in determining exactly what a meeting planner wishes to purchase and is just as important as the actual promotion of the property. *Price,* the fourth factor, is one of the crucial concerns of the marketing mix. Since price is often an important consideration when dealing with the meetings market, this variable should be taken into consideration when establishing room rates for the varying market segments (see Exhibit 1).

Many large properties (250 rooms or more) employ a *director of marketing* to plan, direct, and control all of these factors. It is his or her job to establish programs, policies, and objectives to adapt to changing customer needs. The marketing manager must know and understand such concepts as capital markets, break-even analysis, and cost control, as his or her function includes establishing long- and short-range sales goals.

The marketing manager's job begins with planning. He or she must constantly plan new ways and activities to adapt to the changing needs of the customer while providing continuity to the hotel and improving its image and salability.

Exhibit 1   The Importance of Price in Promoting the Hospitality Product

Within Your Budget. Beyond Your Expectations.

At Marriott, we have a history of providing successful, risk-free meetings, at surprisingly affordable prices. You can rely on us to help plan your event, every step of the way. No matter what your particular needs. And you can be sure of working with professionals, who'll do whatever it takes to make your meeting special. So give us a call. And spend less than you bargained for, to get more than you bargained for.

Marriott.
HOTELS·RESORTS·SUITES

1-800-831-2878

Many sources of group business, including associations, government groups, the SMERF market, and small corporations, are especially price-sensitive. This ad addresses the consumer's concern over price—while still promoting the services offered by the property at an affordable cost.

The Marketing Plan

While the fast-paced and ever-changing nature of the hospitality industry seems to be better suited to short-term sales efforts rather than long-term marketing strategies, there are many advantages to long-range marketing planning. Having a detailed, written plan creates an awareness of the problems and obstacles faced by the property and helps managers to think ahead to make better use of the property's resources. In addition, a written **marketing plan** sets responsibilities, coordinates efforts, and helps evaluate the results of marketing and sales efforts. As an added bonus, the research done in the early stages of developing the marketing plan can identify opportunities to increase revenues in some market segments and point out previously ignored segments.

To be most effective, a marketing plan should cover a *three-year period*. While many properties feel that a yearly marketing plan is enough, a twelve-month plan may restrict sales efforts to already established guest bases. Many corporations and associations make meeting commitments well beyond one year, and short-term sales goals may eliminate the opportunity to capture a larger share of the lucrative conventions and meetings business.

A three-year plan, of course, may be broken down into yearly segments with specific goals for each time period. Many convention-oriented hotels set a targetable plan with well-defined objectives and detailed action plans for the first year of the three-year cycle, and identify broad goals for years two and three. Periodic review of the plan is essential, especially if there are drastic changes in the economy or personnel, enabling advertising and direct sales efforts to be adjusted to adapt to these changes.

The marketing plan will serve as the property's "road map," and should include programs to attract business to each of the property's **revenue centers**—rooms, banquet facilities, meeting rooms, restaurants, and so on. Because these programs should complement rather than compete with one other, it is important to define specific objectives for each revenue center, and to be sure that these objectives—and strategies for attaining them—are understood by each staff member.

While the director of marketing is ultimately responsible for the property's marketing plan, many properties have recognized the benefit of a team effort in the development of effective sales strategies. In a marketing team or *sales committee* approach, representatives from each revenue center provide detailed information on the workings of their departments and offer specific strategies for review. As one consultant emphasizes, "None of us is as smart as all of us." This type of team effort not only gives the director of marketing better insights on how to best promote or improve day-to-day operations, but also provides an excellent way to sell the entire property.

For example, Tammis Anderson, general manager of the Hassa Yampah Inn, actively involves all her department heads in the development of the marketing plan. Every year, the department heads "retreat" for a few days off property to ponder the current year's results and the opportunities that may present themselves in the coming year. The department heads are then held accountable for goals that are agreed upon and they monitor the marketing plan to ensure that it is being executed, adjusting it periodically based upon changing market conditions. This marketing committee approach has resulted in revenue increases in all of the property's profit centers for every period over the past two years.

The Four Steps of the Marketing Plan

No matter what approach is taken, a marketing plan consists of four basic steps (see Exhibit 2):

- Conducting market research
- Selecting target markets and positioning the property
- Establishing objectives and action plans
- Reviewing and monitoring the marketing plan

To ensure a better understanding of these steps, we will be using the fictitious Rolling Green Resort as a case study (see box titled "The Rolling Green Resort Case Study").

Step #1—Conducting Market Research

Before you sell any product, you must know its strengths and weaknesses in order to determine how to best promote it. This is where the first step of the marketing plan, conducting market research, is invaluable. In selling the hospitality product, it is not enough to know what your property has to offer; you must also determine what competition you face and what trends in the marketplace may affect future sales and marketing efforts. In order to determine how to best position your property in the marketplace, it will be necessary for you to gather research information so you may conduct a:

- Property analysis
- Competition analysis
- Marketplace analysis

The findings from these three types of research will be used as the foundation to plan the most effective marketing strategies for your property, and will set the stage for the

Exhibit 2   The Four Steps of the Marketing Plan

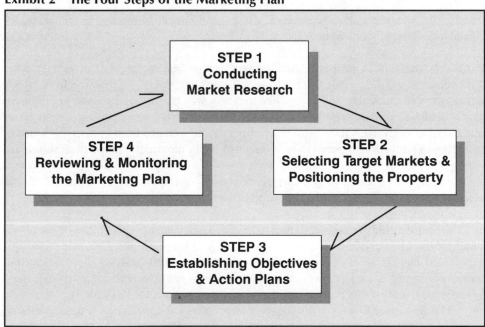

In today's highly competitive hospitality industry, it is essential to have a systematic approach for increasing sales. A well-developed marketing plan serves as a blueprint for the sales effort, and provides an effective sequence that minimizes wasteful effort. Marketing plan development, therefore, is a never-ending process. After one marketing plan cycle has been completed, results are evaluated and the process returns to the research portion of the marketing cycle to ensure that up-to-date sales guidelines and strategies are employed.

The Rolling Green Resort Case Study

The 320-room property is located forty miles north of St. Louis, a metropolis of over three million people. Situated on the banks of the Pritchard River, it is in a renowned vacation area featuring high wooded hills, picturesque fruit and dairy farms, country estates, historic battlefields, and a national cemetery. A small community nearby, Forest Glen, serves as a shopping center for the approximately 1,200 rural residents of the valley.

The resort is about two miles off U.S.16, a main four-lane north-south highway that is fairly heavily traveled by tourists going south in the winter and north in the summer. This transient trade constitutes the bulk of the resort's business, which is good in the peak summer months and for a few weeks in the winter. But business is generally poor in the spring, fall, and late-winter months.

The Rolling Green Resort's revenues currently consist primarily of room sales to individuals and a minimal amount of banquet business—despite the fact that the property has an excellent dining room and boasts a ballroom that can accommodate 600 people on the second floor. Both the first-floor dining room and the ballroom overlook the river, and both feature charming outside patio/balcony areas. On the lower level, there are several rooms of varying sizes which are now being used only for storage.

Property recreational amenities include a large swimming pool, three lighted tennis courts, and riding stables. The resort is in close proximity to a number of riding, hiking, and biking trails, and bicycle rentals are available in Forest Glen. In addition, there is a small dock that is adequate for three or four small boats and can be used for fishing, although the resort does not offer any organized river activities.

The general manager of the resort is an elderly gentleman who knows the hotel business, but he is unable to come up with any ideas to increase occupancy. The property's board of directors has appointed you as their marketing manager, and it is your job to create a marketing plan that will meet the property's goals of attracting additional business—perhaps including the meetings market, which has not previously been targeted—and increasing occupancy during the slow periods.

---

targeting of specific market segments and the development of marketing strategies designed to sell the property to each.

Property Analysis. A **property analysis** involves an honest appraisal of exactly what a property has to offer. Since this analysis will form the base of information from which virtually every marketing and advertising decision will be made, any error in judgment here will almost certainly result in mistakes in your marketing and advertising strategy. In order to most objectively judge a property, input can be solicited from a variety of sources, including employees and guests. You might also try to picture the property as if you are seeing it for the first time—become a guest yourself and experience the property from a guest's perspective. Later, as you analyze other parts of the property, put yourself in the place of a meeting planner seeing the property for the first time.

Strengths and weaknesses analysis. While it may seem superfluous, this analysis should always be done in writing (even if you feel you know the property inside and out), and should include all of the property's revenue centers. This analysis should *detail the property's strengths and weaknesses, provide columns for comments on areas that need improvement, and specify cost estimates and completion dates* (see Exhibit 3).

The first place to start is with the property's physical appearance. Since customers, including meeting planners, form a negative or positive first impression from the appearance of the property, and appearance often plays a large part in sales promotion, a hotel with a neat eye-catching appearance (see Exhibit 4) is a step ahead of a more lackluster competitor.

First, the entrances, grounds, and exterior construction should be assessed with a critical eye for improvement. What is the overall general appearance? Is there ample parking?

Exhibit 3   Sample Property Analysis Form

PROPERTY ANALYSIS - ROLLING GREEN RESORT			
AREA	**STRENGTHS**	**WEAKNESSES**	**RECOMMENDATIONS**
Exterior	Attractive and appealing, newly designed entrance	Lack of seating/relaxing area near entrance	Veranda entrance could be more inviting with addition of comfortable chairs
	Clean, good repair, freshly painted	Dumpster area visible from west wing	Construct fence to conceal trash area
Meeting rooms	Ballroom can accommodate 600 persons Ballroom overlooks river	Rooms on main level are not utilized	Convert storage rooms to meeting and function space
Parking	Convenient to rooms	Driveway is in need of repair	Repair asphalt cracks in drive
	Lot has perimeter fence and landscaping	Perimeter fence is too low for security purposes	
		Very narrow driveways at hotel entrance	Research feasibility of widening entrance
		Difficult to enter driveway because of traffic	
Rooms	Comfortable, modern decor	Not entirely secure	Install stronger window locks
	Easy to keep clean	Little consistency in door locking systems	Install high-quality door latch mechanisms
	Cable television	Small bathrooms	Rent out less desirable rooms last
	Easily accessible		
	Refrigerator in each room		
	Effective air-conditioning		
Reputation	Friendly, clean hotel, modern, charming	Positioning is as an average facility	Use slogan or marketing strategy
	Courteous staff	More individual than group business	Involve hotel in more community support
	Moderate-priced rooms	Not a well-known property	
Location	Riverfront	Far from downtown and airport	Develop shuttle system for groups
	Accessible to expressway		Billboard advertising on highway
	Popular vacation/resort area	Two miles off main road	

To provide the best source of information possible about a property, a property analysis should be written out, and include an objective look at the property's strengths and weaknesses. This is only one of several pages in the Property Analysis. Similar comparisons should be done for every area that can affect the property's profitability, including restaurants, lounges, room service, catering, convention services, shops, recreational amenities, housekeeping, bell staff, reservations, and accounting and billing, as well as other influences, such as local attractions, pricing, and brand awareness. This type of analysis provides a means of taking stock of what the property has to offer, what areas need to be upgraded, and what steps can be considered to improve weaknesses. An estimate of the cost and completion date for each recommendation should be specified; some property analysis forms include columns for this information.

Exhibit 4   Convention Hotel Construction

The Mandarin Oriental, Las Vegas, the smallest of the three hotels at MGM-Mirage's CityCenter project and the only free-standing, non-gaming property on the Las Vegas Strip, was built exclusively to serve small, high-end groups. Promising to "set a new benchmark for service" in Las Vegas, the property will handle only one group (about 150 rooms and 400–600 participants) at a time, and the entire hotel staff, including a meeting concierge and butler, will focus on the group's needs.

The Mandarin Oriental, Las Vegas offers 12,000 square feet of meeting facilities, including a 7,650-square-foot ballroom, a divisible 810-square-foot event space, and a 20-person boardroom. All meeting spaces have outdoor balconies and floor-to-ceiling windows overlooking the Strip, offering planners the option of natural sunlight.

Other hotels in the CityCenter complex that offer convention space are the ARIA, which has 30,000 square feet of high-tech meeting space on three-levels, and the Vdara, which caters to smaller groups (under 150 people) with 10,000 square feet of meeting space as well as the Sky Pool and Lounge that can accommodate groups of up to 1,500.
Source: Courtesy of Mandarin Oriental, Las Vegas.

FACILITIES THAT MEET THE NEEDS OF THE MEETINGS MARKET

William Cox, the architect for the Boca Raton Hotel in Boca Raton, Florida, conducted a study to determine an ideal design and layout for function rooms at convention-oriented properties. His research showed that a different type of facility was needed for servicing groups than for catering to individual guests, and he recommended the following design guidelines to the Boca Raton management:

1. A large hall capable of seating and feeding at one time the total number of guests the house is designed to accommodate.

2. Meeting rooms for groups ranging in size from 20 to 100. The total area of these rooms should equal or exceed that of the banquet hall.

3. Large and small meeting rooms that can be partitioned easily and quickly to adapt to individual group requirements.

4. Built-in audio and visual aids in each meeting room, with individual control stations in each possible subdivision of the space. The speaker should be able to control lights, sound, and projection from a single station.

5. Stage facilities in the main banquet room for a single performer or production of musical shows.

6. Exhibit space with adequate electrical service, water, and gas. Another special requirement: doorways must be high enough and wide enough to accommodate a tractor-trailer.

Cox's recommendations can be applied by any property seriously considering the convention business.

Source: William Cox, "Design Guidelines for Convention Resorts" (highlights from a speech at a meeting of the American Hotel & Lodging Association's Resort Committee).

Are outside areas well-lighted and secure? The exterior of the property should be evaluated in terms of traffic flow, accessibility, eye appeal, and compatibility with local surroundings.

Next, make a detailed, room-by-room and facility-by-facility inspection. Are rooms clean and in good repair? What type of dining facilities are offered by the property? Are kitchen facilities modern and up to code? Do you have an on-premises lounge or nightclub? Does it offer entertainment—and what type? What is the condition of the common areas—are they clean, inviting, and well-lighted?

Put yourself in the place of the meeting planner. In terms of facilities, what do you offer? Location? Adequate transportation? Ample meeting space and up-to-date audiovisual equipment? Meeting rooms that are free from distraction? A highly trained staff? A well-lighted and secured environment that will make women attendees feel more comfortable?

Hotels vying for convention business should assess their function space and what equipment they have available or can obtain from local suppliers. It is wise for a hotel to prepare a printed list of its group-function business equipment, including the kind and quantity available and the locations of the specific pieces of equipment. This itemization can serve both as a selling tool when presented to a meeting planner and as an inventory list for the property.

In some cases, properties wishing to target a specific market segment, such as the meetings market, have designed special facilities to appeal to their target markets (see box titled "Facilities That Meet the Needs of the Meetings Market"). While this type of renovation may not be practical for all properties, the property analysis can give valuable clues as to what property modifications are needed to attract specific business.

And what about recreational amenities? Do you have indoor/outdoor swimming pools? Do you offer easy access to golf and tennis? Do you have an exercise facility? How good are your recreational amenities in relation to those of your competitors?

Your inspection of the Rolling Green Resort has shown the exterior to be charming and in good repair, although the wide veranda could be made even more inviting with the addition of comfortable chairs. The guestrooms, ballroom, and kitchen facilities are modern and adequate, but you are determined to make better use of the wasted space on the lower level.

Your tour of the grounds has shown that the driveway to the property is in need of minor repair—and perhaps widening—and that parking facilities are minimal. The pool area is large and clean, but is probably underused; its size and convenient proximity to the kitchen facilities offer excellent possibilities for food and beverage functions.

In addition to taking stock of the physical aspects, the property analysis also takes into consideration such intangible factors as the property's reputation and quality of service. Reputation includes how the property is perceived—is it classified as an inn, hotel, or resort? Is it considered upscale, budget, or family-oriented? How would guests describe the atmosphere—relaxing, bustling, or business-like?

As far as the Rolling Green Resort's reputation, it is perceived as modern yet charming, but—unfortunately—the property seems to be a well-kept secret. Aside from a directional sign on the highway, nothing has been done to promote the property. There is a definite need for you to get the word out.

A property's location can also be a selling point. Is it within easy access to major highways or airports? Are there other historic or scenic attractions or major amusement centers close by? Are there annual events that draw people to the area?

The Rolling Green Resort has the advantage of being located in a particularly popular vacation area—and can capitalize on a number of scenic attractions. Its location on the river can also be a selling point. Two drawbacks come immediately to mind—it is a considerable distance from the nearest airport, and, because of its location off the highway, may not be accessible year-round in inclement weather.

Business status and trends summaries. The last part of your property analysis helps you assess your property's current position in the marketplace by examining the property's sales history and current guest base. This part of your research, known as the **business status and trends summaries**, traces the property's past, present, and potential operating statistics, including sales patterns over a three- to five-year period (see Exhibit 5). Such analysis helps to track the "soft spots"—low business periods—inherent to hospitality sales, and can disclose sales areas that need improvement.

These charts show the history of occupancy and activity by month for all profit centers. Without this, it is difficult to determine objectives and action strategies for the coming year.

In addition to looking at room statistics, it is also necessary to determine the makeup of your property's **business mix**. How old are your guests? Are they singles, married couples, families? Middle-income, high-income? Sports-minded? Drinkers? This information, which is extremely useful in planning marketing strategies, can be obtained by designing a

Exhibit 5   The Business Status and Trends Summaries

MONTHLY OCCUPANCY AND AVERAGE RATE

Month	2008		2009		2010	
	Average Rate	Occupancy Percent	Average Rate	Occupancy Percent	Average Rate	Occupancy Percent
January	69.00	50.5	74.50	46.7	86.70	59.6
February	61.50	52.4	71.00	52.6	85.45	62.0
to Dec.						

BANQUET FOOD AND BEVERAGE REVENUE (in thousands)

Month	2008		2009		2010	
	Food	Beverage	Food	Beverage	Food	Beverage
January	7691	761	6541	531	14126	1646
February	10250	1614	4694	1911	17120	3361
to Dec.						

RESTAURANT FOOD AND BEVERAGE REVENUE (in thousands)

Month	2008		2009		2010	
	Food	Beverage	Food	Beverage	Food	Beverage
January	15461	8761	18640	7640	21013	9641
February	20911	11411	22611	11311	23415	11421
to Dec.						

FUNCTION ROOM REVENUE (in thousands)

Month	2008		2009		2010	
	Food	Beverage	Food	Beverage	Food	Beverage
January	1290	330	1700	410	2690	491
February	810	240	1423	467	2870	502
to Dec.						

Exhibit 5 continues on the following page

guest questionnaire and perhaps offering an incentive (a free dinner for two, a week-end at the property, etc.) to ensure guest participation. The box titled "A Guest History Analysis" illustrates a sample guest registration card that is typically used to obtain guest information, but more extensive surveys can also be developed.

This type of analysis of guest history and future prospect information is referred to as **consumer research**, and it can take many different forms. At the Conrad International

Exhibit 5 *(continued)*

GEOGRAPHIC ORIGIN OF GROUP BOOKINGS

Missouri	Number by City	Total by State	State Percent
Kansas City Springfield Joplin Jefferson City	51 36 32 24		
TOTAL		143	34 percent
etc.			

GROUP ROOM NIGHTS BY MARKET SEGMENT

Segment	Jan	Feb	Mar	Apr	May	Jun	to Dec.
Corporate Group							
Insurance	621	541					
Computer	29	59					
Incentive	43	122					
Other							
Association							
National	330	461					
State and Regional	461	296					
Other	69						
SMERF							
etc.							

This market research, which is also called an occupancy and activity analysis, traces the property's past and present operating statistics and aids in forecasting future activity. While most properties keep guestroom statistics, it is also important to monitor the activities of other revenue centers, such as restaurants and banquet operations, and to determine where the property's customer base is coming from—and when. Additional data that should be included in charts such as this one includes average rate by market segment, fair share and actual market share, restaurant and banquet covers, and check averages, all broken down by month, week, and day of the week. These statistics make it easier to develop effective marketing strategies to both existing and new markets.

Centennial in Singapore, Theresa Choo, director of sales and marketing, says part of her research includes talking with current guests, an often overlooked source of ready information. She says:

> In the elevator, I introduce myself and try to find out what the guest needs. I invite ten guests a week to have tea with me and ask them if what we are giving as value-added perks is actually what they want.[2]

Another key area for research is the **geographic origin study**. Not only is it important to know who your guests are, but also where they come from. Identifying **"feeder cities"**

A Guest History Analysis:
A Valuable Key for Building Business

PLEASE PAY LAST AMOUNT

)|(Hilton Inn St. George, Utah

1450 HILTON INN DRIVE
ST. GEORGE, UTAH 84770
(801) 628-0463

GUEST REGISTRATION   34725

Names _____

Address _____

City or Town _____ State _____ Zip _____

Firm _____

MAKE OF CAR	LICENSE No.	MODEL	STATE

MY ACCOUNT WILL BE PAID BY
☐ CASH   ☐ CHECK   ☐ CREDIT CARD _____
TYPE AND NUMBER
I AGREE TO THE CORRECTNESS OF THIS STATEMENT AND PERSONALLY ASSUME LIABILITY

SIGNATURE

X _____

REMARKS

NOTICE TO GUESTS   SAFETY DEPOSIT BOXES ARE PROVIDED FOR DEPOSIT OF VALUABLES. THE HOTEL IS NOT RESPONSIBLE FOR VALUABLES NOT DEPOSITED

ARRIVED	DEPARTED	ROOM	RATE	CLERK	NO. GUESTS

Consumer research is an invaluable tool for both protecting a property's current customer base and for developing strategies to increase new and repeat business. While other guest market research, such as geographic origin, may be obtained from responses to advertising or direct mail campaigns or from post-departure guest surveys, one of your most valuable resources can be found in-house: *guest registration cards*. Guest registration cards are an effective way to determine the geographic origin of a property's guests, and offer a wealth of other information, including:

- The number and type of guests (individual business travelers, family leisure travelers, group commercial business, etc.)
- The source of the reservation (travel agent, meeting planner, guest direct, etc.)
- Reservation date (which will help to determine the lead time required)
- Length of stay
- Room rate and revenue generated (room, food and beverage, gift shop, valet, etc.)
- Personal information, including name, address, city, state, and zip code (a ready-made mailing list)

This knowledge helps a property to determine which market segments (and guests) are sources for the most business, and, by learning what zip codes are producing the most business, the property can direct advertising (or rely on repeat business and target other geographic areas).

By determining guest origins, patterns, and needs, a property can develop strategies and programs to increase potential business. If, for example, guest market research reveals that 80 percent of the property's business comes from within the state and that these in-state guests travel an average of three weekends a year, the property could consider quarterly mailings offering special packages to these guests to entice repeat business. A fishing tournament, a "Get-Away" weekend, etc., are just two examples of possible strategies. And, besides offering a great potential for repeat business, former satisfied guests are an invaluable source for building additional business through word-of-mouth referrals. Such referrals make it even more important to keep in touch with customers. It is costly to get a guest the first time; it is vital to get business again.

or "catchment areas" can result in a more effective use of time and money. The smaller the geographic areas used as categories, the better. It is more useful to know, for example, that a guest came from Chicago than to know that a guest came from Illinois. This breakdown by cities and even zip codes can help the property to direct advertising to those areas which are most likely to produce guests.

Geographic and zip code information can come from a number of sources, beginning with the guest registration card. Other sources of information include responses from advertising or direct mail campaigns. This information should be updated regularly to avoid having to deal with thousands of guest registration cards at one time and to ensure that the correct areas are being targeted.

Competition Analysis. In addition to analyzing your own property, it is of prime importance to know your competitors and evaluate their strengths and weaknesses in comparison with your own so you can emphasize your strengths in areas where you know competitors are weak. It is not enough to be *customer-oriented;* you must also be *competition-oriented.*

Generally, your competitors are comparable properties in the immediate area that offer similar facilities and room rates and service similar markets. In the case of large convention hotels, however, the nearest competition may be hundreds of miles away (for example, the Rosen Centre Hotel in Orlando might be competing with the Cloister Sea Island in Georgia for an East Coast meeting). Your own **competitive set** will usually include four to six properties that are the most important competition for your hotel. Two key forms that are used to assess the competition are the competitive rate analysis form and the competitive analysis—need fulfillment by market segment form (see Exhibits 6 and 7).

To completely and effectively assess your competition, fact sheets should be prepared to compare: guestroom and function room rental rates; banquet menu pricing; function room square footage and quality of meeting space; typical number of guestrooms allocated to groups (called the group room allotment); and services offered to meeting groups, i.e., audiovisual, airport shuttle, express check-in, and so on.

A **competition analysis** should be done at least quarterly, and information gathered from a variety of sources. The most useful source is a firsthand look at the competitor. Walk

Exhibit 6   Competitive Rate Analysis

COMPETITIVE RATE ANALYSIS									
Hotel **Rates**	Rolling Green			Arrowhead Conference Center			Hilton Inn		
	Single	Double	Suite	Single	Double	Suite	Single	Double	Suite
Rack	84-92	94-102	130+	100-105	105-110	160	102-116	102-118	140+
Corporate	80	80	120	98	104	140	88	88	130
Tour	62	72					85	92	
Convention	78-90	88-100	120+	85-100	90-105	140	88-98	94-104	130+
Club Floor	90	100					115	125	
Government	68	78		85	90		85	90	

This form compares the rates of your property against those of the competition. Note that ALL types of rates are included—rack, corporate, convention, tour, club floor, and government. In today's technological market, rates comparisons should also be made for website rates and rates from Internet global distribution sites. In addition to benchmarking rates, hotels also gauge competitor activities in areas such as occupancies, group bookings, guest relations, promotional programs, use of advertising, selling methods, market penetration, and market segmentation mix. To monitor these areas, fact sheets are often prepared on each competitor. This comprehensive type of analysis can point out specific areas in which your property differs from the competition and can help you determine how to set your rates in order to better compete for specific market groups.

Exhibit 7   Competitive Analysis—Need Fulfillment by Market Segment

Needs and Wants of Target Markets	COMPETITORS			
	Rolling Green Resort	Hilton Inn	Arrowhead Conference Center	Comments
COMPETITIVE ANALYSIS **NEED FULFILLMENT BY MARKET SEGMENT**				
Corporate Meetings Market				
AV equipment	1	3	3	Our access to outside AV firms is limited
Security	3	2	2	
Training atmosphere	2	2	2	Our secluded location is a benefit to corp planners
Space on short lead time	3	2	3	
Soundproof meeting rooms	2	2	1	
Master account billing	3	2	3	
Efficient check-in, check-out	2	2	2	
Wake-up, message service	2	2	2	
Quality food service	2	2	3	
Association Meetings Market				
Comp. room policy	3	2	2	We offer 1 comp for 40, rather than 1 comp for 50 rooms booked
Exhibit space	1	3	1	
Accessible location	1	3	2	
Overflow arrangements	1	3	2	
Assistance with housing	2	2	2	
Spouse programs	2	3	2	
Reasonable room rates	3	2	2	Key: 3 = superior
Recreational amenities	3	1	1	2 = average 1 = poor
Convention coordinator	3	2	2	

A competitive analysis can take many forms, including just a simple feature-by-feature comparison of the competitors' facilities with one's own. The most pertinent information can be gained by evaluating how one's property "stacks up" in specific market areas. This is one type of form used to compare the services offered to each market segment. Market segmentation is the practice of targeting segments of customers within the overall marketplace. Isolating target markets and determining how well your property fills the needs and wants of each segment is extremely helpful in finding your competitive advantages. Once determined, these advantages can be used to differentiate your property in the form of positioning. This form illustrates just two market segments. You should assess the needs and wants of all market segments you are targeting—the corporate individual traveler, the travel agent market, the incentive group market, the family market, and so on. The key is to find a "difference that makes a difference" to each targeted customer.

💻 *INTERNET EXERCISE*

Marketing Intelligence

The purpose of this exercise is to show the depth of research information available. There are a number of firms that provide information that can assist hotels in developing marketing plans. Smith Travel Research, for example, compiles and maintains a comprehensive database of global hotel performance information. Log on to their website at www.strglobal.com and click on "Products" and then "Revenue, Sales and Marketing." Scroll to the following reports: Star Program, Profitability/Host Reports, and Lodging Market Data Bank. Click on "North American Sample" for each to answer the following questions:

1. In the Competitive Set Report, what three statistics are used to measure your hotel against the competition?

2. At full-service hotels, what percentage of hotel revenue is derived from guestrooms?

3. What percentage of total revenue is spent on marketing?

4. Explain how information from the "Lodging Market Databook" assists in the preparation of sales and marketing plans.

It is important to note that statistical information alone is useless—hospitality marketers must make decisions and take action based on what they learned from these intelligence reports.

---

the properties of competitors. For an even clearer picture, actually staying at competitors' properties is essential. Converse with their guests, talk with competitor's employees, pick up their literature, and study their advertising. Also, check your competitors' reader boards every day (some hotels display "welcome" messages on their outside signage; others have listings of the day's meetings on boards near the lobby or meeting areas of the hotel). Tracking your competition's meetings business provides an opportunity to prepare a game plan to land these groups in the future. If it is not possible to check the competition's reader boards on a regular basis, a reader board service is offered by the Knowland Group (www.knowlandgroup.com).

You can also get literature from convention and visitors bureaus and your local chamber of commerce. Check the telephone directories, hotel chain directories, and travel guides to try to determine just what features are being promoted and to whom. Internet searches can also yield extensive information. Most convention hotels host Internet sites that you can access for a fast, comprehensive analysis of competitive properties. Smith Travel Research is another site that can be used to provide competitive intelligence and historical trends. For a fee, the firm will provide industry data customized to your local market and competitive set.

This analysis of the competition can help to point out market segments that are not being serviced at your property and can provide valuable clues as to how you can change your own marketing strategies to generate additional business.

As far as the Rolling Green Resort is concerned, there is obviously no local competition for rooms, but this is a rare case in the hospitality business. In most locations—even small towns—there is at least one other competitor (and oftentimes many more) that may offer a different type of product or may target a market segment that your own property is overlooking. The Rolling Green Resort has identified the Arrowhead Conference Center and the Hilton Inn as competitors. Both are located in the outskirts of St. Louis.

Marketplace Analysis. The **marketplace analysis**, also known as a *situation analysis,* evaluates the environment in which the property operates (see Exhibit 8) and the property's

Exhibit 8   The Marketplace Analysis

MARKETPLACE ANALYSIS

Part I

OPPORTUNITIES	EFFECTS ON BUSINESS
The St. Louis Airport is expanding and bringing in two new regional carriers.	Easier accessibility to the city. These airlines service several of our feeder cities.
The local college has made arrangements with several companies to hold seminars and workshops on electronics this spring and fall.	Possible room nights from students and instructors, and meeting space for meetings, classes, and seminars.
Archaeological dig in Majestic Canyon has uncovered an ancient Indian burial ground. An influx of scientists and historians have begun a major investigation of the area. etc.	Possibility of room nights from those not wishing to sleep on site, and day rooms from those who wish to shower and clean up after the dig. Also increased business in food and beverage areas.

Part II

PROBLEMS	EFFECTS ON BUSINESS
The highway from St. Louis is scheduled to be repaired in May.	Guests will experience some delays during May. However, when construction is finished, the repairs and additional lane will make access to our resort easier and faster. Also a possibility of increased restaurant business from the workers.
A new Starwood W hotel has been proposed. Construction is to commence late next year. etc.	This property is to be located midway between our property and St. Louis. If developed, this will be increased competition; and Sheraton is strong in the corporate market and has a good, established reputation.

This marketplace analysis looks at the environment in which your hotel operates and assesses the effects of political, economic, sociological, and technological factors (these are often termed the "uncontrollable variables"). The marketplace analysis generally consists of two parts, one titled "Opportunities and Effects on Business"; the other titled "Problems and Effects on Business." These studies detail influences (both positive and negative) that may have an effect on your business and provide a way to determine how these opportunities and challenges can impact your property. You should use this environmental scanning to monitor your environment in order to design strategies that will help you to avoid potential problems while taking advantage of the opportunities provided in your marketplace environment. This exhibit is abbreviated—you undoubtedly will identify several additional marketplace opportunities and problems that could impact your hotel in the immediate and long-term future.

---

operating status in that environment. The marketplace analysis identifies factors that can affect business, such as the cost of travel and government regulation, and also includes research on the environment around the property. This latter research can include the population and projected growth of the local community, the economic trends being experienced by local industry, the traffic counts for nearby highways and airports, recreational amenities and attractions in the area, and unique area activities—such as fairs, festivals, rodeos, etc.—that attract crowds. Not all of these factors will affect your property—the key is to recognize those that do impact you, and, where possible, capitalize or counteract them.

Data for the marketplace analysis can be found in census information, industry reports, periodic updates from the chamber of commerce, and even the local newspaper. Becoming involved in community affairs is another way to learn what is going on in the area and how trends may affect business.

In the case of the Rolling Green Resort, the marketplace analysis may reveal that there is little going on in terms of population growth and projected changes in the economy. If you were to find out that a light industrial park was proposed nearby, however, that information would greatly impact your property.

While the research phase of the marketing plan is very important, the crucial exercise is not to merely collect data but to *interpret* property, competition, and marketplace information. Bill Watson, former senior vice president of marketing for Best Western, advises that "researchers must put less emphasis on data and more on the interpretation of the data. They must work toward turning data into useful information. Collecting data for its own value is like collecting stamps. It's a nice hobby but it does not deliver the mail." The key is to "boil down" the statistical information gathered in order to select appropriate market segments and to help form strategies for reaching them.

In the case of the Rolling Green Resort, for example, your research has shown that you could indeed service at least some portion of the meetings market if you were to formulate a plan to better utilize the "wasted" space on the main level. It may be viable to turn one or two rooms into attractive conference rooms, or to add a business center or other facilities—such as an exercise room or child-care center—to attract this additional business.

As you can see, the research step of the marketing plan can be an involved and time-consuming process. Therefore, some hotels hire outside experts to assist with the research step of the marketing plan. Outside consultants provide an opportunity for you to get a fresh look at what the property is doing to maximize sales. When the Ritz-Carlton Kapalua on Maui wanted to validate its sales strategy, for example, it brought in David Brudney, a hotel industry consultant.

He reports:

> I spent an hour each with every member of the sales and marketing team and half a day with the GM; I spent a full day visiting the competition.... Then I came back and did a report on why group business had dropped. I interviewed incentive houses and validated why incentive business had dropped.[3]

Brudney says his evaluation included questions dealing with account coverage, handling the SMERF market, and group sales strategy (whether proactive calls were made, how many sales calls, how many site inspections). He also evaluated where leads were coming from, what hired parties the hotel was using to generate leads, and whether or not salespeople were receiving proper direction.

Step #2—Selecting Target Markets and Positioning the Property

How do you choose your **target markets**? The obvious first step is to target groups you are already serving. The information obtained from room reservation cards may show that a majority of your guests come from metropolitan St. Louis. If so, direct advertising there.

Next, chart the number of room nights you are currently selling to each market segment by month (see Exhibit 9). If you are realizing a high occupancy from associations or sports teams, for example, expand your efforts to those market segments.

You will also want to target markets that would be the most profitable to your hotel, not only in terms of rooms revenue but additional revenue from such sources as meeting space, food and beverage, and other property profit centers. **Segment profitability** is determined by analyzing the purchasing patterns of past customers. For example, your hotel may already be targeting sports teams, but what is the profit potential of targeting executives (both international and domestic) with unlimited expense accounts? When selecting target markets, you should keep in mind that a balanced guest mix is ideal. A full-service hotel, for example, will want to target several markets: meeting rooms may be used primarily by out-of-town convention groups during the week and by local groups on weekends, while the property's restaurant may serve local business clientele at lunch and hotel guests for dinner.

Marketing goals should be set and hotel salespeople should be trained to target business from potentially more profitable groups. If, for example, your hotel doesn't generate acceptable revenues in its profit centers from association meeting attendees, who tend to be more price-conscious, perhaps you should target other segments that tend to spend more freely on restaurant meals, recreational amenities, and gift shop items, such as business travelers on expense accounts.

Then, determine what other markets you may adequately service (see box titled "Selecting Target Markets"). A property such as the Rolling Green Resort would be an attractive destination for market segments such as honeymooners, business travelers, and families. Its location and atmosphere would be ideal for "murder mystery weekends" or special educational seminars or retreats.

Exhibit 9   State and Regional Associations Occupancy Chart

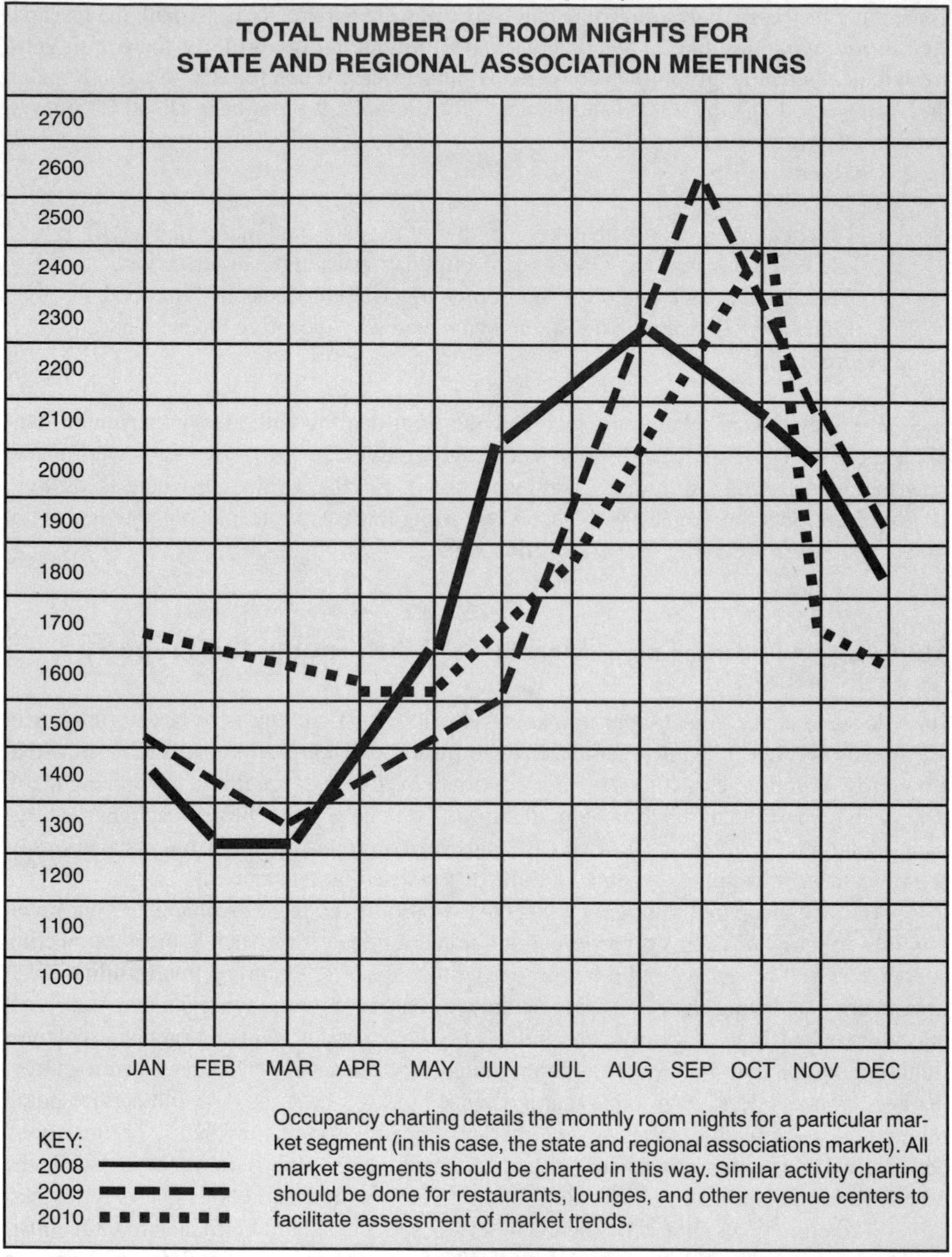

TOTAL NUMBER OF ROOM NIGHTS FOR
STATE AND REGIONAL ASSOCIATION MEETINGS

KEY:
2008
2009
2010

Occupancy charting details the monthly room nights for a particular market segment (in this case, the state and regional associations market). All market segments should be charted in this way. Similar activity charting should be done for restaurants, lounges, and other revenue centers to facilitate assessment of market trends.

In order to determine the most effective marketing strategies, properties should chart the number of room nights they realize from each market segment they serve. This occupancy chart for the state and regional associations market sub-segment provides such information as the number of guests and peak months of occupancy, and is useful to forecast trends and direct advertising.

The property's guest mix should be reviewed periodically. Since the objective in selecting target markets is to create a mix of business that will generate the greatest revenue and produce the most profit, changes in strategy may be necessary during the course of the year. Defining and redefining markets is a continual process, and adjustments to the marketing plan are frequently required as conditions change.

The conventions and meetings industry has been shown to be a lucrative market segment that should be targeted. While the Rolling Green Resort is probably inadequate to handle large conventions, what other segments within the convention and meetings industry can it service? What specific needs of meeting planners does it meet? Your location away from the bustle of the city may be an inducement to St. Louis businesses wishing to hold training sessions in a quiet, yet convenient, location. And, many small meetings and seminars do not require large facilities—or even have a food function. Are there state or regional associations that can be targeted? SMERF groups? Other groups that you can adequately serve?

Due to its historic setting, the Rolling Green Resort might also appeal to historical societies, educational groups, and veterans' groups. And the nearby city of Forest Glen should not be overlooked as a potential source of business from wedding receptions, awards banquets, and other community functions. Perhaps the resort could promote regional activities, such as a dairy festival, or sponsor a sports team to attract visitors to the area.

Once you have selected your target markets, you must then determine how to best *position* the property to each of them. **Positioning** refers to the perception of a property by the guest. It is a composite of the property's reputation, what it stands for, and how it differs from the competition. In short, it is the property's image or uniqueness—which gives you the wherewithal to sell it to your guests. Kathleen A. Girard, vice president of marketing at the Hotel Millennium in New York City, says:

> Knowing your product and how to position it is a fundamental key to success in the hotel business. You have to have a very strong identity from the moment you open your door, and you must not compromise it. Otherwise people get confused. You have to know who your audience is, who buys. Many hotels don't know who they are. They try to be all things to all people, and certain market segments clash. Conventions clash with the individual business traveler, for example. It's better to do a few things very well rather than do a lot of things in a mediocre manner.[4]

To effectively sell a property, your perception of it and your customers' perception of it must match (see box titled "Positioning Your Property"). An example of success in positioning is the Mercedes-Benz automobile. The name immediately conjures up the image of a luxury car.

The property's positioning plays an important role in advertising. It enables you to create the advertising which will project the image you want for the property.

You may, for example, wish to position the Rolling Green Resort as an attractive small meetings destination. Or, you may wish to "play up" the historical significance or the tranquility of the area to attract associations or retreat business.

Step #3—Establishing Objectives and Action Plans

One of the attractions of the convention business is that it fills many rooms at a time—and business can often be controlled to fill those rooms at the most advantageous times, such as during the off-season or slow periods. To best take advantage of marketing opportunities, however, it is necessary to set specific objectives and develop plans to help bring about the desired results. And, since marketing goals cannot be met without sales, it is wise to look at each revenue-producing center and set goals for each.

Selecting Target Markets

The primary purpose of the research phase of marketing planning is to identify three to five priority needs for the property and ways to meet those needs. The study of the property, competition, and marketplace (the business status and trends summaries, in particular) assist the marketing team to identify areas needing sales activity and when specific business is needed.

Once a property's priorities are identified, market segments can be selected that can meet these priorities. Hotels are always looking for ways to improve their customer mix; they must periodically evaluate their customer mix in order to drop or replace low-rated segments and boost business from segments that are more profitable.

Noted industry marketing consultant Tom McCarthy suggests that properties ask the following five questions to best determine which market segments to target:

- Does the property meet the needs of this segment?
- How does the competition meet the needs of this segment? The number and quality of competitors in the area weighs heavily in determining whether or not to solicit a specific segment.
- Does this segment meet the property's needs? Look at the list of the property's needs and determine whether the segment will provide the kinds of business that will satisfy those needs.
- How much business is the property getting from this segment at present? If it is getting some business from this segment, there is likely to be more out there.
- How much time and money will it take to solicit this segment vis-a-vis its long-term potential?

In today's market, properties are being more selective, not only in regard to the market segments they are targeting, but even as to the particular customers they are booking. Transients pay higher rates than groups, so in periods of high demand, some meetings business is given "back burner" treatment. The type of group is also being closely scrutinized; those with substantial banquet business, for example, are of more value to hotels.

Barbara Best, National Accounts Director for Hyatt Hotels, says, "Smart hoteliers want to have a mix of business, but we are trying to learn how to best manage that mix." In periods of high demand, hotels can indeed be more selective—but their selectivity is often at the expense of the meetings industry. Lynn Tiras, president of International Meetings Managers in Houston, Texas, says, "Hotels are looking at the whole picture to see if a particular piece of business is of value to them, and they are turning away business that doesn't have enough food and beverage or whatever.

"In some cases I can understand it, like when they don't want to tie up all their meeting space for a group that may not need any sleeping rooms or F&B, but they are going way beyond what's reasonable in some cases too."

Obviously, a property must make sound business decisions, but it must be careful, too, not to jeopardize future business. Weighing out a property's priorities, current business relationships with the meetings industry, and market trends is essential to help a property to effectively manage its customer mix without jeopardizing future business.

To illustrate how these strategies are put into practice, let's go back to our case study of the Rolling Green Resort. The property's marketing team, for example, has decided not to solicit individual government business because the segment is too rate-conscious, and also determined that there is no substantial room night volume from the leisure sport fishing traveler. The marketing team instead decided on the following priorities and selected the marketing segments listed in the accompanying chart to meet the property's needs.

(continued)

| Market Segments Targeted to Fill Priorities ||
Priorities	Market Segments to Be Given Emphasis to Solve Priorities
Priority #1 **Midweek Business** **Year-Round** This is our area of greatest opportunity for significant increases. We have some corporate individual travelers, but if this can be expanded and coupled with the corporate meetings market targeted, we will be able to create a strong corporate base to fill this need.	• Corporate Individual • Corporate Meetings • Intensive Training Meetings
Priority #2 **Shoulder and Value Season Group** Early fall and late spring are our shoulder periods, with winter being the off season. The association market (particularly state and regional groups) have been our strongest in the past. We will concentrate our efforts in this market and also with the SMERF market to target groups into the shoulder and value seasons.	• State and Regional Associations • Educational Groups • Government Groups • Religious Groups in Preparation for Christmas and Easter Pageants • Medical Associations • Veterans Groups
Priority #3 **Banquet Business** Has not been pursued actively in the past. Efforts will be directed to maintain current customer base with increases in average check, banquet beverage revenue, and to target into the weekends.	• Local Corporate Groups • Weddings and Bridal Fairs • Reunion Business • Civic Groups

Marketing Objectives. At the beginning of each year, research data should be used to set specific goals for each market segment. To arrive at these goals, certain questions need to be answered:

- When are the property's peak periods? In what months does business need to be increased?
- What revenue centers need more sales effort? Does the restaurant do more business during some months? Would offering family rates help to boost room occupancies?
- What market segments can be reached to increase business? What priority should each be given?
- What steps can be taken to generate additional revenues in each segment?

Marketing objectives should be set for each market segment, revenue center, and revenue-producing service (the property's laundry, valet parking, gift shop, and so on). These goals must be clearly defined *in writing* so that everyone involved gets the same information. In addition, the goals must be realistic yet challenging; if a property is currently experiencing an average occupancy of 65 percent, it is unrealistic to expect to set a goal of 100 percent—but the sales staff can shoot for a more reachable, yet challenging, goal of 80 percent during certain months.

Setting specific goals helps in the monitoring process. Room nights can be tracked and restaurant covers counted periodically to ensure that marketing goals are being met.

Developing Action Plans. Once objectives have been outlined, **action plans** must be developed to meet those objectives. Action plans spell out how you will use the marketing mix (price, promotion, product, place) to reach each target market. This is the real meat of the marketing plan. There should be detailed action plans for each market segment and revenue center, and, since action plans can be compared to "mini" marketing plans, they should incorporate the following six areas:

1. *A description of the market segments or types of business to be solicited.* Will the plan target business travelers? Local associations?
2. *A specific description of the target customer.* If the target segment is local associations, this portion of the action plan will include the names, addresses, and telephone numbers of local contact persons.
3. *Rates, special plans, or promotions that will be offered.* This should include any discounted rates for association groups, a possible free room for a tour operator, and special package rates (rooms, food service, entertainment) for groups.
4. *Specific Objectives.* Here, the objectives are clearly spelled out. The plan should not just call for "increasing room occupancies," but rather should specify the room night and revenue goals by month for the entire year. These types of objectives enable the sales department to plan strategies to meet its goals.
5. *Action Steps.* This portion of the action plan involves the actual steps that should be taken to carry out the marketing objective. Perhaps some promotional literature will be developed. An "open house" may be held to introduce the local meeting planners to your facilities. In the case of the Rolling Green Resort, you may plan an advertising campaign directed to those leisure travelers within a two-day drive of the property (see Exhibit 10).
6. *Budgeting.* It is not enough to simply set goals. Enough money has to be allocated to help achieve them. You should go through each strategy and action step to determine what each will cost.

As you can see, action plans are specific and therefore require personalized attention. It is highly recommended that the action plans be assigned to specific individuals who can oversee their part of the total marketing effort, and dates should be specified for accomplishment. The chapter appendix provides a detailed description of how each of these six areas are applied in the Rolling Green's market segment plan for increasing corporate meetings.

Budgeting. Some properties base their marketing budget on what was spent the previous year. We feel that the marketing budget should be based on your strategies/action steps. Set goals for each market segment, identify what action steps are needed to meet these goals,

Positioning Your Property

Branding is essentially the name recognition of your property by the public, and is critical to a property's success. Just as the "golden arches" are immediately linked to McDonald's, it is imperative for a property to establish a readily recognizable image in today's competitive hospitality industry.

One example is the Sensational Meetings program offered by Omni Hotel. The chain has uniquely positioned itself by not only offering meeting space, but also creating an environment for three types of meetings—energetic, challenging, and recognition. This is accomplished by offering innovative banquet menus as well as custom-tailored environments to meet the planner's goals for each type of meeting.

The chain, which first won the top award for "Guest Satisfaction Among Upscale Hotel Chains" from J.D. Power and Associates in 2005, describes its positioning and advertising as appealing to both sides of the brain (emotional and logical). Christine Connolly, Omni's director of corporate communications, says: "We try to fill a very unique niche between the luxury level and the simply upper scale. You get all or most of the services that you would see in a luxury hotel like the Ritz-Carlton or the Four Seasons, but at a price and at a rate that is sensible."

But positioning is more than just catchy symbols or logos. In today's competitive marketplace, proper positioning enables you to:

1. Identify possible competitive advantages.
2. Select the *right* competitive advantages.
3. Deliver your property's chosen position to carefully selected target markets.

To effectively position your property, the following factors should be taken into consideration:

- *Physical Attributes*—Is your property a "classic" hotel with a colorful history? Does it feature unique construction or features—formal gardens, waterfalls, etc.? How is it different from other properties in your area?
- *Service*—How efficient is your check-in and check-out service? How long is the wait at your restaurant? Do you offer specialized service needed by guests (computers, FAX service, children's programs, etc.)?
- *Personnel*—How are your customer-contact people perceived? Are they courteous and friendly? Can they communicate well and respond to guest needs?
- *Location*—Where is your property located—beachfront, mountain, mid-city, airport, etc.? Is it conveniently located (or, conversely, remote)? What aspect of your location gives you an advantage over the competition?
- *Image*—How is your property perceived by the public—luxury, family, business-traveler friendly? Do you have a distinctive image that differentiates you from your competition? Does your property live up to its perceived image?

Your property's projected image must effectively meet the needs and wants of each of your targeted market segments. You must find opportunities to determine and promote what each segment needs. What benefits do they seek? What needs are currently unmet—and what needs can be met or improved? What innovations are needed to attract unreached market segments? And, most important, are those additional segments worth going after?

Exhibit 10   Targeting Prospective Customers

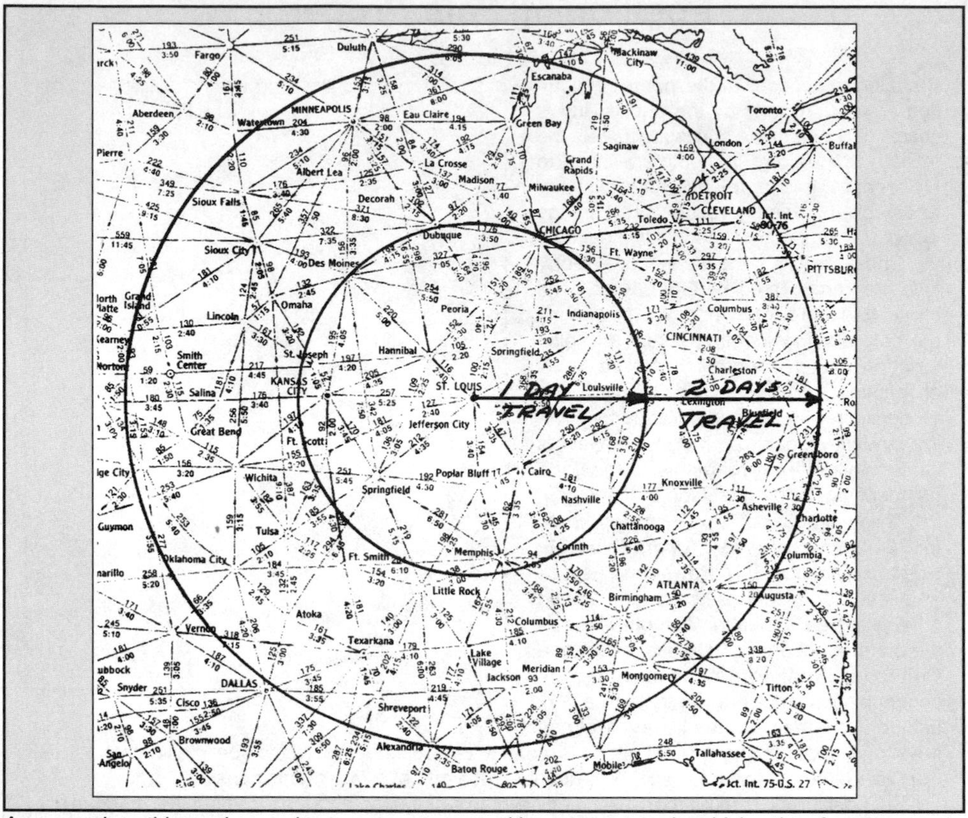

A map such as this can be used to target customers with a one- or two-day driving time from a property. This part of an action plan can be incorporated into either a direct mail or print advertising campaign to target the business or leisure travelers most likely to visit the resort. (Map by permission of Rand-McNally.)

and then determine how much money should be allocated. As we mentioned in the discussion on developing action plans, there needs to be a specific budget set for each revenue center and for each market segment (see Part VI of the chapter appendix). This type of fiscal planning ensures that there are enough dollars spent in the most effective areas.

While there are several types of budgeting, one of those most commonly used is **zero-based budgeting**. This method of allocating money is based on a "task method"; money is budgeted at levels to get the job done, but each expenditure must be justified. This approach assumes that the marketing department starts with zero dollars and that every expense is analyzed on the basis that it will yield more favorable results than spending the amount in another way.

Since this budget is based on the tasks that need to be done, *it can only be completed after an action plan has been developed.* In this way, the property can be sure that there has been enough money allocated to meet the objective. If, for example, you have determined that an extra six sales calls a month are needed in the St. Louis area, you can easily determine the amount of money needed to take care of that portion of the action plan.

Another advantage of this system is that once money has been committed to a certain department or market segment, there is some room for adjustment. If advertising costs less than estimated, for example, you may opt to increase advertising or divert the excess money into additional sales calls. In order to readily see what is available, however, a budget form must be developed that provides instant access to information (see Exhibit 11). The budget form, when completed, is your most important budgeting tool. It not only specifies your original budget, but also breaks your budget down into spending for each market segment.

The use of computers in hotel sales offices has greatly facilitated the budgeting process. Computers can forecast based on previous and current expenditures, and provide instant printouts to let you know where you stand on dollars allocated for your marketing strategies.

Step #4—Reviewing and Monitoring the Marketing Plan

Despite the best planning, outside influences (an energy crisis, a natural disaster, etc.) or inherent weakness in the marketing plan (unrealistic goals, lack of provision for personnel turnover, etc.) make it imperative to periodically review the marketing plan. This evaluation should be done at regular intervals—each month, each quarter, or at the end of an advertising program—to ensure that marketing goals are on track and that money is not being wasted on strategies that are not producing the desired results.

John Hogan, director of education and cultural diversity for Best Western International, says:

> Once the actions steps are reviewed and approved by the manager or owner, a follow-up system needs to be implemented. Each month, the action steps need to be individually reviewed. Marketing and sales plans are only effective if managers, owners, and sales staff view the process as living and important. Regular reviews of tactics that do and do not work are essential to long-term success.[5]

Goals that have been clearly spelled out are easier to monitor and revise. For example, if specific goals have been set to increase room occupancies in the winter months by 15 percent or to cater an additional ten wedding receptions during the month of June, it is a simple matter to count room nights and banquet activity. Other types of monitoring can include the recording of room nights by market segment, charting and comparing room nights or restaurant covers before and after an advertising campaign, and determining what zip codes are producing the most business.

In the case of the Rolling Green Resort, for example, you may have coded newspaper advertising to determine which cities are responsible for generating additional business. If you see that there is little response from the Chicago area, you may opt to channel advertising dollars being spent there into more lucrative areas, such as the St. Louis market, or try for a better response by advertising in travel guides or specialty magazines instead.

Before scrapping a part of the marketing plan, however, you must ascertain if the strategy was given enough time to work (as we have learned, some corporations and associations make booking commitments years in advance and a one-time direct mailing may not bring immediate results) and determine if there could be other reasons for a lack of response (inclement weather in the Chicago area, for example, may have prohibited people from traveling). Sometimes, all it takes is a little corrective action—such as targeting a market segment during a month in which it is more likely to book—for a strategy to bring about increased business. In other cases, an evaluation may show that a more effective marketing strategy is needed to reach a particular segment. Perhaps rooms are priced too high to attract a price-sensitive group, or a specific benefit offered does not have enough appeal. A periodic evaluation will point out these weaknesses and give the property an

Exhibit 11　Sample Marketing Budget Form

NAME OF PROPERTY													
Marketing/Sales Methods		**Last Year**			**Next Year**								
Merchandising/ In-House Promotions	Actual Expenditures	Budgeted Expenditure	Variance	Budget	Allocation by Target Markets							Comments	
a. Display Material	$	$	$	$	$	$	$	$	$	$			
b. Special Events	$	$	$	$	$	$	$	$	$	$			
c. Free Samples	$	$	$	$	$	$	$	$	$	$			
d. Prizes	$	$	$	$	$	$	$	$	$	$			
e. _____	$	$	$	$	$	$	$	$	$	$			
Subtotal	$	$	$	$									
Travel Trade Marketing													
a. Print Materials	$	$	$	$	$	$	$	$	$	$			
b. Travel/Trade Shows	$	$	$	$	$	$	$	$	$	$			
c. Familiarization Trips	$	$	$	$	$	$	$	$	$	$			
d. _____	$	$	$	$	$	$	$	$	$	$			
e. _____	$	$	$	$	$	$	$	$	$	$			
Subtotal	$	$	$	$									
Other Marketing Programs													
a. Marketing seminar	$	$	$	$	$	$	$	$	$	$			
b. _____	$	$	$	$	$	$	$	$	$	$			
c. _____	$	$	$	$	$	$	$	$	$	$			
Subtotal	$	$	$	$									
TOTAL	$	$	$	$									

A summary budget should be prepared combining the budgets developed for each of the market segment plans. This format is especially helpful when developing a marketing budget because it lists anticipated and actual amounts expended the previous year, provides a variance column, and allocates the current budget into targeted market segments.

opportunity to either revise strategies or goals or to focus its marketing efforts in other directions.

This process of monitoring, evaluating, and correcting is the final phase of a marketing cycle that returns once again to the research stage in order to keep abreast of market trends and new ways to reach and retain business.

Putting a Marketing Plan into Action

The marketing plan is not developed to sit on a shelf collecting dust; it should be an integral part of sales and promotional efforts and referred to often. Once the marketing plan has been prepared, it should be distributed to each department, and its objectives and how to meet them explained to all of those who are involved in particular parts of the marketing effort. Juergen Bartels, past president of Westin Hotels, says of his chain's marketing plan, "It's not a dead plan, it's a lively plan; we work from the plan every day."

Since the marketing plan is the foundation for sales efforts, it is important that the entire sales team become especially familiar with the goals and objectives outlined. From these goals and objectives, sales goals and quotas are set and specific market segments are targeted. It is important that everyone on the sales team thoroughly understand their role(s) in the marketing effort, and utilize the research collected to position the property to appeal to potential sources of business.

The implementation of the marketing plan will impact everyone at the property, not just those in the sales department. Each department should be appraised of the sales department's goals—and the strategies for achieving these goals—and all departments should be made aware of the integral part they play in the overall success of the property's sales efforts. If a marketing team approach was used to develop the marketing plan, each department's representative can serve as a "team leader" to ensure that his or her department remains on track.

For long-term success, effective and complete communication between sales and operations is essential. The sales team has to "sell" internally to the rest of the hotel staff as well as to potential guests, so regular meetings should be held with such staff as front desk personnel, housekeepers, accounting staff, engineering personnel, cooks, wait staff, and so on. Topics for discussion can include how groups and individuals book at the hotel, how much time and effort it takes to get groups, how future and repeat business depends on service, how the hotel staff's responsiveness is essential to total guest satisfaction, how the market is competitive, and how each staff member makes a difference in sales and service.[6] With this approach, line staff will understand how satisfied guests are the key to the property's profitability, which, in turn, results in additional compensation and benefits to them, and they will become willing participants in the property's overall marketing efforts. Another marketing textbook sums up the importance of having—and following—a good marketing plan as follows:

> A good marketing plan provides direction for an operation. It states where you are going and what you are going to have to do to get there. It builds employee and management confidence through shared effort and teamwork toward common goals. It recognizes weaknesses, emphasizes strengths, and deals with reality. It seeks and exploits opportunities. And, last but certainly not least, a good marketing plan gets everyone into the act.[7]

Summary

Today's meeting planner has a myriad of choices, so competition for the meetings market has become fierce. Attracting and keeping customers requires a planned, carefully researched and thought-out effort, and a written marketing plan is a must for every hospitality establishment. In this chapter, we have discussed the four steps inherent to each marketing plan and how to implement the marketing plan. Although the marketing effort will involve the entire staff of the property, the main thrust begins in the sales department.

 ## Endnotes

1. Tom McCarthy, "Better Late Than No Plan At All," *Lodging Hospitality,* January 2007, p. 3.

2. "Marketing Research Includes Talking to In-House Guests," *World Hospitality*.

3. Harvey Chipkin, "The Sales and Marketing Audit: A Proven Way to Build Business," *HSMAI Marketing Review,* Summer 2003, p. 33.

4. *World Hospitality,* May 2000, p. 10.

5. John Hogan, MBA, CHA, MHS, "Marketing Plans Must Be a 'Living Being': They Cannot Sit on Shelves!" hotel-online.com, June 2004.

6. John Hogan, MBA, CHA, MHS, "Everyone Should Know What the Sales Department Does," hotel-online.com, September 2004.

7. Stowe Shoemaker, Robert C. Lewis, and Peter C. Yesawich, *Marketing Leadership in Hospitality and Tourism,* Fourth Edition (Prentice-Hall, 2007), p. 569.

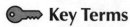 **Key Terms**

action plans—The specific steps taken to achieve marketing objectives.

business mix—The variety or mixture of guests who stay at a property. For instance, business may consist of 20 percent association meetings, 15 percent corporate meetings, 15 percent SMERF groups, 40 percent leisure travelers, and 10 percent transient guests. Also called customer mix.

business status and trends summaries—Reports that assess the property's current position in the marketplace by examining the property's sales history and current guest base. Part of the property analysis.

competition analysis—An evaluation of competitors in order to identify their strengths and weaknesses in comparison to your own. Part of the market research step.

competitive set—A group of properties that are the most important competition for a hotel in a given market.

consumer research—Marketing research aimed at providing a profile of present and future guests.

feeder cities—Geographic areas from which business is derived, but where a company may or not have a property of its own. For example, Calgary, in Alberta, may be a feeder city for Vancouver, in British Columbia, Canada.

geographic origin study—Research identifying key feeder cities and the zip codes from which guests are generated. Part of the business status and trends summaries.

marketing—The practice of combining, blending, integrating, and controlling the factors that influence sales.

marketing mix—The combination of the four "Ps" of marketing—product, price, place, and promotion—used to achieve marketing objectives for a target market.

marketing plan—A written guide detailing sales, advertising, and promotion programs used to attract business to the property's revenue centers.

marketplace analysis—An evaluation of the environment in which the property operates. Assesses both opportunities and problems in the marketplace, and determines how they impact the property. Part of the market research step.

positioning—A strategy to develop the product and service as distinct in the minds of consumers. Positioning attempts to distinguish a firm from any of its competitors.

property analysis—An evaluation of a business's facilities, services, and programs to determine strengths and weaknesses. Part of the market research step.

revenue center—A hotel division or department that sells products or services to guests, thereby directly generating revenue for the hotel. Also called profit centers, these may include food and beverage outléts, room service, retail stores, recreational facilities, and other services, such as laundry services and valet parking.

sales—Direct selling efforts through face-to-face calls, telephone calls, and mailings.

segment profitability—The profitability of a particular type of consumer or market segment, determined by analyzing the revenues generated through the sale of products and services to that type of consumer or segment.

target markets—Market segments that a property singles out as having the greatest potential, and toward which marketing activities are directed.

zero-based budget—A budget that starts at zero and requires planners to justify expenditures for each activity. The process of building a budget without the benefit of a previous year's budget.

Review Questions

1. What is the difference between sales and marketing?

2. The marketing plan should cover what time frame?

3. List the four steps in developing a marketing plan.

4. Research should be conducted in what areas before developing action plans?

5. What factors should be considered when selecting target markets?

6. What is meant by zero-based budgeting?

7. Choose two lodging properties and assess how each has positioned itself in the marketplace. Include a discussion of the following factors: physical attributes, service, personnel, location, and image.

Additional References

Heads in Beds: Hospitality and Tourism Marketing, Ivo Raza, Prentice-Hall, 2004. www.prenticehall.com

Hospitality Marketing Management, Fifth Edition, Robert Reid and David Bojanic, John Wiley & Sons, 2010. www.hospitality@wiley.com

Hospitality Sales and Marketing, Fifth Edition, James R. Abbey, AH&LA Educational Institute, 2008.

Internet Sites

For more information, visit the following Internet sites. Internet addresses can change without notice. If a site is no longer available at the address listed below, a search engine can be used to find the new address or additional, related sites.

Association for Convention Marketing
Executives (ACME)
www.acmenet.org

Best Western International
www.bestwestern.com

Boca Raton Resort and Club
www.bocaresort.com

D.K. Shifflet & Associates
www.dksa.com

Hospitality Sales and Marketing
Association International (HSMAI)
www.hsmai.org

J.D. Power and Associates
www.jdpower.com

Ypartnership
www.ypartnership.com

Smith Travel Research
www.smithtravelresearch.com

Chapter Appendix

Sample Marketing Plan

This excerpt from a hotel marketing plan illustrates a detailed market segment plan for the corporate meetings market. The Rolling Green Resort would prepare detailed action plans for each market segment and revenue center. This third step is the core of the marketing plan. The statistics gathered on the property, the competition, the marketplace, and the target customers in the first two steps might encompass more pages in the plan, but success is based on how well the action plans are developed and implemented.

As you read this action plan, note how complete and specific it is, providing a "road map" for the coming year. The strongest marketing plans result from the input of people from all areas of the property. Therefore, brainstorming sessions with key personnel are essential to developing effective action plans.

Market Segment Plan

Corporate Meetings

I. Description

The Rolling Green Resort will aim at expanding its share of the corporate meetings market. Types of meetings sought will include: corporate sales, training and development, distributor and dealer, executive conferences, product presentations, stockholder, board and management meetings. Our property should target local, statewide and national corporations who have yearly meetings in our area.

II. Target Customers   Number

   A. Present Local Files   98

   B. Priority Accounts—present high-volume accounts and   5
      those in the area not using us at present, but are known
      to produce high volume business

      • Pritchard Data Services
      • Harper and Associates
      • Stewart Group
      • Stubs Real Estate Investment
      • Adam and Bre Corporation

   C. St. Louis Prospects

      • Companies of over 50 employees within selected SIC   120
      numbers in following zip codes:
      63111, 63137, 63128, 63104, 63121

- Companies of over 100 employees within selected SIC numbers in all other zip codes within metropolitan area ... 70

D. Tri-County–St. Louis Area (other than above zip codes)

All companies with 100+ employees plus the following companies if they have less than 100 employees:

- Top 10 law firms, stockbroker-investment firms, leasing firms, relocation firms, insurance companies, advertising agencies, real estate main offices ... 200

- All branch and regional offices of Fortune 500 companies ... 24

- All companies of 50+ employees moving in from outside Montcalm County ... 73

E. Kansas City, Springfield, Chicago (within one-day drive)

- All manufacturing and insurance companies with 100+ employees ... 55

- All branch and regional offices of Fortune 500 companies ... 62

- MPI (Meeting Professionals International) and SCMP (Society of Corporate Meeting Professionals) members in these cities ... 325

F. Four-State Region

- Top 30 seminar companies ... 30

- Fortune 500 company home offices ... 150

- ASTD (American Society for Training and Development) members in the four-state region ... 917

Total Target Customers ... 2026

III. Rates, Special Plans, Packages, and Promotions

A. Seminar/Training/Corporate Group Package:
Available on selection of specific dates.
Minimum of 25 sleeping rooms include:

(continued)

	Single	Double, Per Person
Room (per person)	$80.00	$40.00
Tax (7%)	5.60	2.80
Meeting Room	4.00	4.00
Continental Breakfast	3.50	3.50
Lunch	7.50	7.50
AM/PM Refreshment Breaks	3.00	3.00
All Food Tax (7%)	.98	.98
All Food Service (15%)	2.10	2.10
	$106.68	$63.88
Above package including dinner		
Dinner	15.00	15.00
Tax	1.05	1.05
Food Service	2.25	2.25
	$125.00	$82.18

B. Extended-Stay/Early Arrival

If stay is extended to include Saturdays, free unlimited use of the championship golf course and tennis facilities, along with free champagne brunch will be provided. For new bookings arriving on Sundays rather than Mondays, free welcome cocktail parties will be organized and tickets given to a local show or performance.

IV. Objectives and Goals

Based on a review of our property, the competition, and the marketplace, we have identified fall and spring as our most important priorities for the coming year. The corporate market is targeted as one segment to fill this need. Our objective is to increase our corporate group rooms business from 6% to 10% of our total rooms business, increase our annual room sales revenue from $622,542 to $669,400 (7% increase), and increase average daily rate from $72 to $79 for this segment. Monthly targets are identified below:

Room Nights and Revenue Goals From Corporate Meetings												
	J	F	M	A	M	J	J	A	S	O	N	D	Totals
Room Nights	700	850	900	800	700	600	550	550	600	750	900	600	8500 room nights
ADR	78	78	80	80	80	75	75	75	78	82	82	78	$78.75
Room Rev (000)	54.6	66.3	72.0	64.0	56.0	45.0	41.3	41.3	46.8	61.5	73.8	46.8	$669.40

V. Action Steps

A. Sales/Direct Mail

Step No.	Method	Target Customers	No.	Details	Qtr.	Sales Days	Resp.
1	Telephone	Present local files	98	Survey their satisfaction over the telephone. Give comp one-night stays to any who were dissatisfied.	1	5	AH JM
2	Telephone	Priority accounts	5	Have contact with these accounts a minimum of once a month. Include entertainment at hotel, sporting events, or other local activities to build relationship.	1,2,3,4	20	AH JM
3	Personal Blitz	St. Louis prospects and those in Tri-County St. Louis area	287	Personal visits by sales staff to outline our services and deliver small gifts such as a business pen.	2,4	15	TS AH JM
4	Phone Blitz	Planners in key feeder cities of Chicago, Kansas City, Springfield, and Four-State Region	1539	Promote our package and familiarize the company with our product.	1,3	25	AH TS JM
5	Direct Mail	Previous corporate meeting customers	250	Send personal thank you letters for their past business and ask them to rate satisfaction by returning post-paid questionnaire.	1	4	AH JS
6	Telephone	Previous corporate meeting customers (not returning questionnaire)	70 (est)	Survey satisfaction over the phone. Provide comp room night to any who were dissatisfied.	1	3	AH JS
7	Telephone	Tri-County St. Louis, Kansas City, Springfield, and Chicago areas of of over 100 employees	340	Call for initial qualification to determine if file should be set up (at least 30 room nights per year). Set up appointments.	2	6	JM TS
8	Direct Mail	ASTD members in Four-State region	1000	Promote our package and familiarize with our product special rates, etc. Mail-in response card enclosed.	2	25	TS JM AH
9	Telephone	ASTD members in Four-State region	100	Respondents to mailing.	3	25	JM AH

B. Advertising

Media
The Trade Journal Magazine (2 col x 5") 12 times
Corporate Market Review (5 col x 8") 6 times
The St. Louis Directory—Annual

(continued)

C. Merchandising
   Development of the following brochures and flyers:

	Total
Meeting Planners Informational Brochure, 4p4c	1,500
Hotel Fact Sheet (group) 8"x11" 2c	1,000
Meeting Package 4p4c	5,000

D. Public Relations and Publicity
   Contact local TV stations, major newspapers, and the
   Convention Authority announcing prominent corporate meetings.

E. Internet
   Add Facebook and Twitter links to property's website.   2,000
   Develop a blog offering advice to corporate clients.   2,000

VI.   Budget

A.   Sales
     Dues and Subscriptions
           The Trade Journal Magazine $500
           Corporate Market Review   350 $850
B.   Advertising
     Media
           The Trade Journal Magazine
                 2 Col x 5" @ $800 x 12x   9,600
           Corporate Market Review
                 5 col x 8" @ $750 x 6x   4,500
           The St. Louis Directory
                 Annual   1,000 $15,100
     Direct Mail
           American Society for Training and
                 Development (ASTD) $3,000

           Brochures and Flyers
                 Informational Brochures   1,650
                 Hotel Fact Sheets   1,200
                 Meeting Packages   2,400 $5,250
     Production costs (ads and brochures) $5,000

     Other Selling Aids—Gifts for Blitzes $6,000
                              Total Corporate $35,200

Summary

Corporate meetings business is one of our priorities for the coming
    year. The estimated 8,500 room nights is 10% of total rooms busi-
    ness, and the $35,200 is 9.2% of the total marketing budget.

Chapter 3 Outline

Competencies

1. Identify factors to consider when organizing for convention sales. (pp. 75–80)

2. Describe typical sales and marketing staff positions, and outline the roles of regional and national sales offices and independent hotel representatives. (pp. 80–90)

3. Explain how to manage the efforts of the sales team in terms of establishing standard operating procedures, conducting sales meetings, assigning account responsibility, and evaluating the sales effort. (pp. 90–95)

4. Explain the various records and filing systems maintained by a sales office. (pp. 95–107)

5. Describe technological applications for a sales office. (pp. 107–114)

Organizing the Sales Office

Beverly W. Kindade, CHME, CMP
Vice President Industry Relations
Starwood Hotels & Resorts

"The role of the sales department in pursuing the convention business is vitally important. With today's competitive hotel environment, it is imperative to have sales policies and procedures in place to smooth the communication both within the sales office and other areas of the property. In order to reach occupancy and revenue goals, the sales office must not only be organized and staffed with enthusiastic, knowledgeable people but also have an efficient filing system, written operating procedures, and an effective system for monitoring both function room and guestroom bookings."

3   Organizing for Convention Sales

APPROXIMATELY 50 PERCENT of the lodging industry's total receipts are derived from the meetings market, making it a prime target for many properties. But in today's highly competitive marketplace, it is simply not good enough to send salespeople out into the field to solicit meetings business. Tapping this lucrative market requires an efficient, organized sales endeavor.

This chapter deals with how to organize the sales effort by creating a sales office—both the physical plant and the personnel in it—that maximizes a property's potential to sell to and service the convention and meetings market. We will also discuss some of the positions within sales, and see how sales efforts can be structured and managed for optimum results.

Sales Structures

Two trends have greatly impacted the way hotel sales departments do business. First, acquisitions, mergers, and consolidations have occurred in the lodging industry at a record pace as companies realize the value of acquiring multiple brands and the cost savings from combining departments. In recent years, numerous acquisitions have taken place: Marriott's purchase of Renaissance and Ritz-Carlton; Starwood's takeover of Sheraton, Le Meridien, and Westin; Fairmont's purchase of Delta Hotels; and Hilton's acquisition of Doubletree, Red Lion, Embassy Suites, and Hampton Inns.

Today, a handful of firms own nearly 100 brands. To increase efficiency, these hotel companies are consolidating their operations and relying more on regional and national sales offices. Rather than having a dozen individual properties call on a potential client for meetings business, chains are assigning a single salesperson to represent every brand in the hotel company's portfolio to the client. This concept will be discussed in greater detail later in the chapter.

Second, marketing functions have increasingly been incorporated into sales. More hotels today are focusing on the overall bottom line, not just rooms revenue from meetings business. While rates, dates, and space are still important, more properties are evaluating a group's spending patterns and potential for revenue property-wide before booking them. This trend, called revenue management, has led to revenue management positions and departments within many sales offices, and revenue management is expected to expand throughout the industry. A detailed look at revenue management will be provided later in the chapter.

Small Properties. All hotels, whether they are large or small, should have some kind of sales department from which sales efforts are directed. At small properties, a salesperson usually handles all types of business. He or she may call on meeting planners, travel agents, tour operators, and other sources of potential business. Still smaller hotels may have to combine sales operations under another department—or even have the general manager direct the sales effort, with the GM often designating one day a week for personally making sales calls.

Regardless of size, every hotel has "non-sales" employees who could be recruited to assist in the sales effort. If a food service employee and two front desk people, for example, would each make five calls per week to qualify new prospects, fifteen calls per week—750 calls a year—could be made!

Large Properties. Larger properties generally have a specialized sales staff and operate out of a separate sales office. It is best, if at all possible, to have full-time sales specialists for convention sales. In the largest organizations, the degree of specialization is carried still further, with salespeople assigned to market segments. One sales staffer may go after association business, another goes after corporate meetings business, still another focuses on incentive programs. Obviously, such concentration is practical only for chain operations. It is not essential to successful selling to break down the task so finely, but this should tell you that each segment of the market has its own appeal.

The Sales Office

The sales office is often the first contact a client has with the property, and first impressions can make the difference between sales success or failure. To be effective, the sales office (and effort) must be properly organized. This organization should include both a sales philosophy as well as a physical office layout conducive to generating sales.

The Function of the Sales Office. As we have said, the sales office must be established and organized to enable it to meet the overall goals and objectives of the property's marketing plan. The sales department should be structured so that group business is not only solicited but also properly serviced by being given authority over other departments that will be involved in servicing group business (see Exhibit 1).

However the sales office is organized, it is crucial that all employees understand their roles in meeting the goals set forth in the marketing plan. Property salespeople should be professional, knowledgeable, and service-oriented. All property employees, whether they be field salespeople or the receptionist at the sales office, should be aware of their importance in the marketing effort. Walk-in clients, for example, should be greeted promptly and made to feel at home, and the receptionist or secretary should be able to answer any immediate questions a visitor may have.

The Physical Layout of the Sales Office. Both the location and the appearance of the sales office are important. Sales offices should never be hidden away in the basement or an unused guestroom; nor should they be located in "goldfish bowl" areas off the main lobby. Ideally, a property selling meeting and banquet facilities should locate the sales office adjacent to these areas.

The sales office should appear tasteful and professional, with a minimum of clutter, be well-lit and ventilated, and have comfortable seating and reading material available. Property information sheets and brochures, sample menus, complimentary letters from satisfied meeting planners, and perhaps albums of past events or news clippings about the property are informative—and good pre-sale tools. Sales-office decor can also include photographs of guestrooms, banquet rooms, and the sales and managerial staff, as well as feature awards received by the property. This type of decor helps to familiarize the client with the property's facilities, and can also help to develop confidence in the property.

Exhibit 1   Typical Convention Hotel Organization Chart

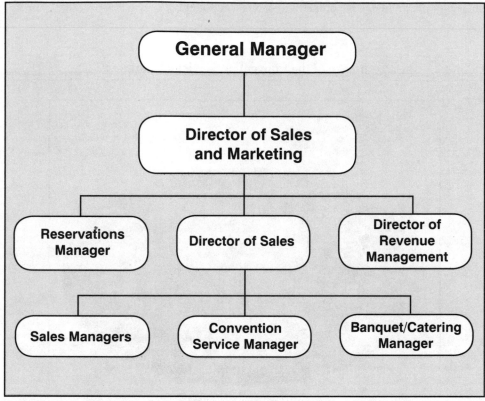

Organizational structures within properties vary, but this chart shows the typical management structure of a large convention hotel. In this example, the reservations manager, director of sales, and director of revenue management report directly to the director of sales and marketing. All three are sales-focused positions that are considered equal in terms of position level, and they will interact with each other on a regular basis. It is important to note that the director of sales is increasingly being given authority over other departments, such as banquets and catering, to enable the sales staff to deliver what it promised to clients.

How the Sales Office Interfaces with Other Departments

Before the hospitality industry became more marketing-oriented, the sales department was usually a separate entity responsible only for filling guestrooms and function space. Today, however, it has become imperative for not only the director of sales but also his or her staff to move into the mainstream of the day-to-day marketing operations of the property.

This is especially true in dealing with convention and group meetings business. In addition to ensuring that guestrooms are available, it is imperative that the director of sales and his or her sales staff work closely with a number of other departments, especially:

- Convention services
- Banquets/catering
- Revenue management

Convention Services. A good convention services department is essential for repeat bookings. Meeting planners must be satisfied with meeting space, the handling of functions, the availability of equipment, and the service attitude of the staff in order to book repeat business or recommend the property to others (see Exhibit 2).

Exhibit 2   The Importance of the Convention Service Department

Crowne Plaza Hotels & Resorts, which positions itself as "The Place to Meet," developed a series of ads to promote the chain's commitment to successful meetings. In addition to ads that promote the chain's two-hour response to meeting inquiries as well as daily meeting debriefings, the series includes ads such as this one, which introduces the Crowne Meetings Director. These members of the convention service staff are experts in the field of meeting planning, which enables them to assist meeting planners with all of their meeting needs.
Source: Courtesy of Crowne Plaza Lexington, The Lexington House.

The convention service manager serves as the on-the-scene contact between the convention organizer and the hotel. He or she is the one who sees that all provisions of the contract are carried out, and is the one who must be prepared to cope with the requests—and emergencies—that come up as the convention nears and during the event itself. This position is a very crucial one and should never be downgraded. The convention service manager must have sufficient stature and authority to cope with the unexpected (see Exhibit 3).

Sheraton, in recognition of the importance of convention services personnel, defines its convention and conference service professionals as follows:

> A Convention and Conference Service Professional is a diplomat, accountant, psychologist, juggler, mind reader and goodwill ambassador with an impelling attention to detail. It's one of the most challenging and rewarding jobs in the hospitality industry.
>
> It's challenging because you get to wear so many hats. You deal with a lot of different personalities and a lot of demands are made on you. Details and deadlines define your workday.
>
> It's rewarding because you get to see a project through from start to finish, knowing that you helped make it all happen. You make meetings for two thousand or two dozen run like clockwork. And you make customers come back again and again, just because you did a good job.[1]

Banquets/Catering. Although some people feel that the banquet/catering department does not belong under the authority of the sales department, we feel that control of all function space should be overseen by one person—the director of sales. This eliminates confusion and communication problems, since choices must sometimes be made regarding who will get a function room on a certain night. This decision must be made with an eye toward the overall scheme of things, and this falls within the responsibility of the sales executive.

For the sake of argument, let's look at what would happen if this were not the case. This partial organization chart has the banquet manager reporting indirectly to the assistant manager. When a client requests banquet space, the banquet manager will book one of the hotel's banquet rooms. While this action seems efficient enough on the surface, the sales department often needs the function rooms should any convention group be booked.

This could happen in the event of a communication breakdown. If the banquet department booked a function room and the sales department unknowingly booked the same room for a training seminar, the hotel would be placed in an embarrassing position and would most likely lose business.

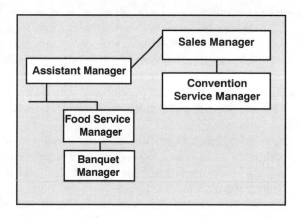

Revenue Management. With today's trend toward combining sales and marketing efforts, revenue management has become increasingly important to hotels. Properties that previously relied on the director of marketing and the director of sales to realize maximum profit potential are now creating a specific position dedicated to forecasting supply and demand and researching the potential profitability of groups.

Swissotel, for example, employs a revenue manager to decide price structure based on the date, season, day of the week, competitive situation, and the potential of the group. A state-of-the-art computer system is at the heart of the revenue manager's decision-making process, and predictions can be made for weeks—even months—ahead. While the position is fairly new and can be expected to change, the HSMAI expects that the revenue manager position will be firmly integrated into hotel sales offices in the next few years.[2]

The Sales and Marketing Staff

The sales staff is the first contact that many people have with a hotel. Corporate and non-profit/association meeting planners first establish contact with the hotel through the sales office. Their first impressions are formed by the warmth, personality, and public contact of the sales staff.

Positions within Sales

While the sales effort itself should be coordinated by one person—the director of sales—there are a wide variety of positions within the sales department. While each individual on the sales staff is given certain responsibilities, it is important to remember that sales is a *team effort.* The efforts of each member must be coordinated with those of the others on the sales team for maximum results.

The Director of Sales and Marketing. The director of sales and marketing spearheads the sales effort by setting objectives and monitoring action plans. He or she works closely with the director of sales to ensure that sales goals are being met and that the sales effort is kept within budgeted limits.

The Director of Sales. The director of sales, who may be called the sales director or vice president of sales at some properties, is responsible for executing the marketing plan formulated and accepted by top management. It is his or her job to coordinate and direct the efforts of the sales staff. All sales promotional programs must be channeled through him or her for approval. He or she works closely with the general manager or director of sales and marketing to determine target markets and to set the budget appropriations for each market segment.

While the scope of this position is often argued, it is our belief that the director of sales should be given all the authority necessary to ensure that sales goals are met. This may include becoming involved in a number of areas, including advertising and public relations, budgeting, and any other function of the hotel that directly or indirectly affects the sales effort. The salary for this position will vary depending on the type of hotel (see box titled "Typical Salaries and Bonuses for Directors of Sales").

Sales Managers. Depending on the size and type of property, there may be a number of additional sales managerial positions. The *convention sales manager* is responsible for soliciting convention trade for the hotel (see Exhibit 4). It is his or her job to identify and contact the associations, corporations, and fraternal organizations that could use the hotel for their conventions. Convention sales are generally made through personal visits, so the convention sales manager must build a relationship of confidence with the prospective client. Due to long lead times, a convention sales manager may need three to five years to get specific convention business.

TYPICAL SALARIES AND BONUSES FOR DIRECTORS OF SALES		
Type of Property	Median Base Salary	Median Bonus
All-Suite/Extended-Stay	$ 70,355	$ 4,200
Commercial-Transient Hotel with Limited Meeting Space	$ 94,551	$11,165
Conference Center/Meeting and Convention–Oriented Properties	$105,270	$ 881
Resort Properties Targeting Leisure and Convention Guests	$111,650	$12,982

The above figures show the median annual salary and bonuses earned by the director of sales at various types of properties. Compensation for this position varies based on a number of factors, including property revenues and geographic location as well as type of property.

The *convention service manager,* while not always considered an actual member of the sales team, works hand in hand with the convention sales manager. His or her job is to coordinate and service the conventions booked by the property. The convention service manager takes over after the sale has been made and begins to work out the fine details with the convention group. In addition, any problems that arise during the convention will be directed through convention services. The convention service manager must work closely with all departments, coordinating the efforts of the food and beverage department, the front office, and the banquet setup crew to see that things run smoothly in the exhibit area.

Since this is such an important position, as the convention service manager is ultimately responsible for the success or failure of a meeting, it has become increasingly common for CSMs to become certified. There are a number of certification programs available to ensure that CSMs provide the best in service to meetings groups. The "Best Practices" box in this section details just one of these programs—the Meeting Maestros Program developed by Delta Hotels in conjunction with PCMA.

A *tour and travel sales manager* is responsible for developing group and charter business for the hotel. He or she works closely with travel agents, tour wholesalers, tour operators, and transportation companies. This person is generally instrumental in putting together tour packages and must have expertise in the pricing and promotion of group packages. The tour and travel sales manager may also put together group incentive packages.

Some properties may also employ a *director of advertising and public relations* whose job it is to coordinate all promotional materials and public relations and to make the final decision on advertising media (radio, television, Internet, social media, magazines, newspapers, billboards, direct mail).

The Sales Staff. The property's salespeople are the key to sales success. These are the people who prospect, set appointments, and make personal calls on prospective clients. They must be professional; knowledgeable about the property, the competition, and their markets; and must possess excellent organizational and oral and written communication

Exhibit 3   The Communication Role of the Convention Service Manager

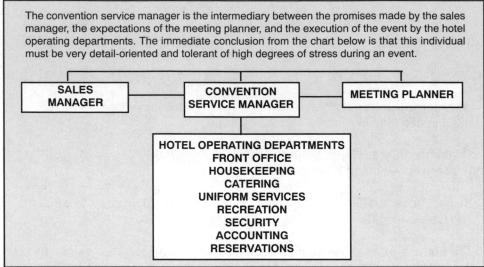

The convention service manager is the intermediary between the promises made by the sales manager, the expectations of the meeting planner, and the execution of the event by the hotel operating departments. The immediate conclusion from the chart below is that this individual must be very detail-oriented and tolerant of high degrees of stress during an event.

SALES MANAGER — CONVENTION SERVICE MANAGER — MEETING PLANNER

HOTEL OPERATING DEPARTMENTS
FRONT OFFICE
HOUSEKEEPING
CATERING
UNIFORM SERVICES
RECREATION
SECURITY
ACCOUNTING
RESERVATIONS

The convention service manager acts as the on-site connection between a meeting group and the host property.

skills. Today's sales professionals must also be computer-literate, as most hotels utilize computerized sales systems.

Ironically, the increased use of technology sometimes impacts relationships between salespeople and clients. The use of the Internet by meeting planners to research possible sites, "virtual tours" of properties, and other technology (such as electronic transmittal of contracts) have sometimes minimized face-to-face contact between meeting planners and hotel salespeople.

This makes it all the more important for salespeople to commit to building long-term relationships with customers. **Relationship marketing**—the building and maintaining of lasting relationships with customers—is important in today's competitive environment. Meeting planners are more likely to feel comfortable with a salesperson who has performed well in the past, and may even take familiarity and trust into consideration over other factors, including price.

Unfortunately, meeting planners are sometimes unable to work with the salesperson who assisted with a past function. The turnover of sales personnel in the hotel industry is considerably higher than turnover in other industries. According to a recent Dartnell's Sales Force Compensation Study, the annual turnover in sales personnel in all industries is 14.1 percent; in the hospitality industry, turnover more than doubled at 30.5 percent. And the percentage may actually be considerably higher, as hotels do not consider transfers within the company as employee turnover. Greg Marshall, executive director and meeting planner for the Gift and Home Trade Association, has experienced problems with staff turnover firsthand. His take on the situation:

> From the time I signed the contract to the time the program was held, I had two different salespeople and four different convention service managers. It was like I was always starting from square one, educating the new person I was assigned about my group and the goals of our conference. Today, one of the first things I ask during site inspections is, "What's your staff turnover like?"[3]

Best Practices

Delta Hotels and PCMA Team Up to Offer the Delta Convention Services Manager (CSM) Meeting Maestros Program

Delta Hotels, which has hotels throughout Canada, launched the Delta Convention Services Manager (CSM) Meeting Maestros Program, developed and sponsored by Delta Hotels and PCMA. The intensive three-day course focuses on the complex and changing role of the convention service manager, and features such topics as building client relations, adult learning, food and beverage, and technology.

All Delta CSMs are required to take the course, which centers on deliverables such as guaranteeing that all Delta CSMs will be PCMA-trained professionals, that meeting planners will be recognized on a personal level, and that Delta will deliver the fastest response in the industry. Sharon Bolan, director of learning and development for Delta Hotels, says:

> We wanted it to be known that if you're planning a meeting with Delta, you will work with someone who's trained specifically for that. We wanted everyone to be trained to the same standards. So it made sense that we would look for a [standardized] training program, and PCMA was able to customize it.

Darrin Stern, who helped develop the content of the course and facilitated it, says that the course was designed *by* meeting managers *for* meeting managers. According to Stern, one of the areas of the program that generated the most discussion among participants was the section on adult learning, specifically how a room setup affects learning.

Danny Champagne, manager of convention services for the Delta Centre-Ville, says:

> This three-day class made us realize what our clients are experiencing while they're at our property. I think that it brings new meaning to customer service for our clients. They already know that they are important to us, but the difference now is that they have the assurance that the convention services managers across Delta Hotels are devoted to their meetings and that we give guarantees to them in order to provide them with the level of service they deserve.

Turnover is especially frustrating for meeting planners who have developed a good working relationship with salespeople and other property staff. Jackie Brave, a partner with Accenting Chicago Events and Tours, says:

> There has been so much turnover of personnel at hotels that it's hard to keep up with who is where. It's very difficult to create relationships with people who disappear at a moment's notice.[4]

The compensation structures employed by some hotels may be contributing to the problem. Some hotels opt to reward salespeople for performance, paying a commission rather than a salary, so there is a tendency for salespeople, especially younger salespeople, to opt for compensation from the generation of new business rather than commit to building relationships with current customers.

Clerical Support. To enable salespeople to handle the most important aspect of their jobs—selling —it is essential that a property employ a good clerical staff that can maintain careful and detailed records, make intelligent use of this data, and assist in follow-up. While responsibilities may vary from property to property, the main function of the clerical staff

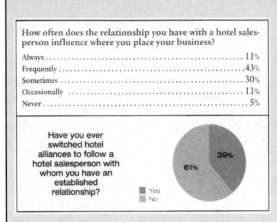

The Importance of Relationships

How often does the relationship you have with a hotel salesperson influence where you place your business?

Always 11%
Frequently 43%
Sometimes 30%
Occasionally 11%
Never 5%

A key element in securing—and retaining—meetings business is building solid relationships with clients. *Meetings & Conventions* magazine recently polled hotel salespeople and meeting planners regarding how each felt about developing relationships. This chart shows that 84 percent of planners said that their relationships with hotel sales people "Always," "Frequently," or "Sometimes" influence where they book their meetings. Approximately 40 percent of planners surveyed have followed salespeople from one hotel company to another because of the importance of established relationships. Further, 65 percent said their relationship with a hotel's convention service manager is very important when selecting a site. This study clearly demonstrates the need for salespeople to focus on consultative and relationship-based selling and concentrate on building personal relationships with meeting planners. It is very likely that some of your prospects and your hotel's best customers are at the top of your competitors' hot prospect list, so it is extremely important to begin building a relationship at the very beginning—and giving a high priority to seeing that the relationship flourishes.

Building relationships in a high-tech age is critical. Jack Schmidt, regional director of sales and marketing for Destination Hotels and Resorts, observed: "What has happened is that the Internet and electronic distribution channels have driven people apart—we're doing business with machines and information, versus people today. And what that has done is depersonalize the sales process.

"It's more difficult to build relationships now because it's more difficult to get past e-mail and voice mail and even meet with planners. What used to be a relationship is becoming a transaction. New technologies have made us more efficient, but much less effective."

Since building relationships gives salespeople an edge in capturing business as well as fostering future business, salespeople would do well to follow the example of the late Bob Keilt, who built and kept lifelong relationships by being attentive and thoughtful, beginning with going to the airport to pick up important meeting planners who were in town for site visits. That personal touch and thoughtfulness, of course, left a lasting impression—meeting planners remembered Bob when making choices about properties and booking future events. His efforts paid off in a big way, enabling him to meet his primary goal: "I strive to develop such strong relationships with my accounts that I own their business."

Source: Jack Buchanan, "A Meaningful Relationship: How Technology Affects the Connection Between Hospitality Marketers and Meeting Planners, *HSMAI Marketing Review,* **Spring 2008, p. 58.**

is to provide support at the home base and to handle walk-in clients in the absence of sales personnel.

It would be penny-wise and pound-foolish to foot the considerable expense of fielding a sales staff only to skimp on the support at home. The period of sales effort before signing a convention can be very long, and salespeople must be continually in touch with the meeting planner. With today's high cost of sales calls, a follow-up system of letters and phone calls generated by a well-trained clerical staff is essential. The clerical staff will also maintain careful, detailed records of your prospects' convention activities, personnel changes, and other data that may help win the sale.

Supplemental Sales Staff

It is often impractical and uneconomical for hotels to cover all the market bases with their in-house staff. To gain representation nationwide, chain properties supplement their staffs'

Exhibit 4   Sheraton's Job Description for the Convention Sales Manager Position

Job Title:	Convention Sales Manager
Department:	Marketing
Reports to:	Director of Sales

Basic Functions: Reviews with Director of Sales the marketing strategy that will obtain maximum occupancy levels and average rate. Responsible for all convention group business related to the market segments as they relate to annual revenue projection.

Scope: Sales manager will be the primary person for booking of long-term convention group business, with "long-term" being more than six months out.

Work Performed: Initiate prospecting and solicitation of new accounts; manage current accounts to maximize room nights from the account in relation to the hotel marketing plan; responsible for administrative efforts necessary to perform the aforementioned.

1. Quotas for this position are:

Room nights per month	1200
Soft spot percentage	20
Phone calls per week:	
Trace:	20
Prospecting:	25
Personal calls per week	10
New accounts per week	10

Individual to supply weekly, monthly, and annual reports supporting productivity standards.

2. Probe for customer needs: rooms, suites, desired dates, day of week pattern, program agenda, food & beverage requirements, and degree of flexibility in each of the aforementioned areas.
3. When available, obtain information on the group's past history, i.e., previous rooms picked-up, arrival/departure pattern, and double occupancy percentage.
4. Review availability of client's REQUIRED DATES AND ANY ALTERNATE DATES which should be offered. The dates presented to the customer should satisfy the customer's needs while allowing the hotel to maximize occupancy and average rate.
5. Negotiate with the customer: day/day of the week pattern, day-by-day room block, group rates (within guidelines as set by DOS, comps, and function space.
6. Tentatively block rooms and function space in accordance with office policy.
7. Confirm in writing all aspects of the meeting. Check to ensure they received the signed contract.
8. Upon receiving the signed contract, process definite booking ticket, definite function room outline, and credit application.
9. Oversee, manage, and track the way in which reservations are to be made.
10. Periodically contact the customer while in-house to be certain all is in order and going well.
11. Conduct exit interviews with customers to determine their level of satisfaction and ask for additional business.
12. Send letter of appreciation to customer.

Supervision Exercised: Supervise and share one secretary with another individual.

Supervision Received: Primary supervision from the Director of Sales. Initial training, and retraining as needed, also received from the Director of Sales, as well as direction as to room merchandising.

(continued)

Exhibit 4 *(continued)*

Responsibility & Authority:	Upon satisfactorily completing rooms merchandising and operational training, the individual will have the authority to make decisions and confirm dates, room blocks, and rates to the clients.
Minimum Requirements:	Bachelor of Arts or Science degree—preferably business, hotel, or restaurant administration. Individual must also be professional in appearance and approach.
Experience:	Minimum of two years' experience in hotel sales.
Sales Competencies:	1. Ability to negotiate. 2. Accounts strategizing. 3. Ability to prospect. 4. Ability to judge profitablility of new business. 5. Knowledge of product. 6. Knowledge of competition. 7. Ability to make presentations. 8. Ability to organize and plan. 9. Ability to utilize selling skills. 10. Ability to overcome objections. 11. Ability to problem-solve and make decisions. 12. Ability to write effectively.

A job description is a detailed listing of the function and organizational relationship of each employee. This job description for the convention sales manager shows the many facets of this important job and details the qualifications required for the position. Note that under "Work Performed" both room night and activity goals are stated. Top salespeople like to have their efforts measured against predetermined goals. Quality of calls is more important than quantity; therefore, room night/revenue goals are most important. However, maintaining activity goals such as number of phone calls, personal sales calls, and new accounts per week leads to more room nights booked and more revenue.

sales efforts with *regional and national sales offices,* while independent properties turn to *independent hotel representatives* to help them with regional and national sales efforts.

Regional and National Sales Offices. Many national chains are reorganizing their sales function from a property basis to a regional basis. Marriott, Hilton, and Starwood, for example, are merging sales departments from several properties into one central location. As this happens and the number of "unassisted" sales continues to grow as planners take advantage of Internet virtual tours and electronic transactions, individual salespeople in the future will only sell to their property's larger accounts, and sales staffs at the property level will be reduced in favor of regional sales reps (see box titled "Marriott's New Sales Structure—Sales Force One").

One of the reasons for the success of regional and national offices is their use of *corporate sales staffs* in regional sales offices. The **regional sales office** serves as an intermediary between meeting planners and individual properties by providing a central information point that directs meeting planners to the property that best fits their needs.

The corporate staff solicits business for any hotel in the chain, and there are a number of advantages in this approach (see sidebar). First, customers

---

What Meeting Planners Say About Regional and National Sales Offices

- "They've invaluable. They open doors."
- "They offer one point of contact for all hotels and brands within the chain."
- "They know our company, our history, our culture, our attendees, and whether or not a particular property is the right fit for our group."
- "They tell our story to individual hotels, so we don't have to repeat basic information about ourselves."

Marriott's New Sales Structure: Sales Force One

J.W. "Bill" Marriott, the chairman and CEO of Marriott International, shared details about the chain's renovated sales structure in one of his recent blogs, which are designed to not only provide information and insights about the chain, but, most importantly, to develop relationships with the public. Below are excerpts regarding the purpose and workings of the chain's new sales strategy:

"The hotel business is a people business. It's about the one-on-one experience. And it's about building a relationship, anticipating needs, and selling our group customers the way they want to be sold.

"A few years after we opened a hotel in Lincolnshire, Illinois, I visited the property and asked them how the sales process was going. Well, the manager of the hotel said, 'My sales manager went in to see a major client last week. When he walked into the office, there was the sales manager from the Residence Inn and the sales manager from the Courtyard. It seemed like all three of our brands were there to compete for the same piece of business. Of course, when I talked with our customer, he said, "I don't like to be sold this way. Have one person represent Marriott for all your brands."'

"So that's why we're rolling out what we call Sales Force One. That allows our salespeople to create a one-on-one customer relationship and represent all our brands with an individual customer. This means our sales teams—no matter where they are—will have access also to the information about that particular customer, and our meeting planners will not have to continue to inform the latest salesperson about who they are and how much business they give us.

"The new framework moves the majority of our salespeople out of individual properties and into centralized sales offices in metropolitan areas. Meeting planners have one contact person at the nearest regional office who helps place meetings among Marriott brands, including Marriott, J.W. Marriott, Ritz-Carlton, Renaissance, Courtyard, and Residence Inns."

Source: Bill Marriott blog (www.blogsmarriott.com) and Robert Carey, "'Sales Force One' Alters Marriott's Reps Structure," *Meeting News,* **January 2008, p. 1.**

who have experienced good service and a successful meeting in one hotel of the chain might be induced to stay within the chain for their next meeting. Even when convention organizers have to move around the country to increase attendance, they may be sold on staying within the chain. Secondly, it is easier for a meeting planner who is scheduling ten similar meetings in many parts of the country to book all of them at once with a single salesperson. Once a salesperson has broken through to close a sale, the way to booking additional locations is easier. Still another advantage comes into play when a meeting planner cannot get a free date at one hotel. The chain may be able to offer another hotel on that date, whereas an independent property loses out when firm dates cannot be met.

Several hotel chains, including Mandarin Oriental, Taj Hotels, Orient-Express, and Hyatt, have developed computer systems that link their convention hotels with their regional and national sales offices. These systems give instant electronic access to group booking data, including availability, rates, and dates, and, in addition, track client histories and account activity chain-wide. With such information at their fingertips, many regional sales representatives are now empowered to block space, print out proposals for any hotel on the system, and book business on the spot. The hotel's director of sales is then notified by electronic mail for approval of the agreement. Regional sales offices also serve the properties within a chain's region by providing promotional materials and public relations.

Independent Hotel Representatives. Many hotels do not feel they can adequately cover all of their market bases with an in-house sales staff; they often supplement the staff with an **independent hotel representative**. These outside individuals or firms represent the property as a "long arm" of the sales department.

Because hotels have different needs, the services provided by independent hotel representatives vary widely. In some cases, the representative may be hired simply as a field salesperson, soliciting clients who are impractical for the hotel's in-house staff to reach. Other hotels may use larger representation companies, whose services include consulting, market analysis, advertising, and public relations in addition to sales.

Because of economics, independent hotel representatives usually represent more than one property. This causes many hotels to balk at the notion of being represented by such firms. Quite logically, they question having a competitor represented by the same firm. Hotel representatives answer this criticism by saying they represent properties of different sizes and market emphasis, not similar clients seeking the same clients.

Should a hotel use an independent hotel representative? If you can afford to field your own staff and it performs satisfactorily, that's fine. If you can afford only limited sales efforts, a representative may offer another dimension. What counts is the amount of sales generated.

A hotel should investigate the benefits offered by an independent hotel representative firm. Such firms usually specialize in a particular market, while overlapping to other sources of business. If your target market is the convention trade, be selective, and choose firms that actually specialize in this area. Since the majority of association and trade convention groups are headquartered in Washington, D.C., Chicago, or New York, your chances of reaching the convention market are greatly increased if your representative has an office in one of these locations. Just two examples of such firms include the Krisam Group, headquartered in Washington, D.C., and Hinton and Grusich, based in Chicago.

There are a number of factors that you will want to consider in making your decision (see box titled "How to Choose an Independent Hotel Representative"). In addition, you may wish to consult similar-sized properties who are using a representative you are considering. Ask them about the effectiveness of the representative, especially in regard to areas in which you feel you may have difficulties.

HOW TO CHOOSE AN INDEPENDENT HOTEL REPRESENTATIVE

Choosing an independent hotel representative is not to be taken lightly. Take the same care in hiring a hotel representative as you would in hiring an in-house executive. Here are questions to help you to determine whether an individual or firm would be an asset to your sales operation:

1. How many hotels does the firm represent? Has it extended itself so much that it may not be able to meet your needs?
2. Does the firm represent competing properties? If so, how will this affect its handling of your account?
3. Does the representative specialize in the targeted markets you are seeking? Does he or she have knowledge of the group and convention business? Is the firm doing business with organizations you have targeted?
4. Does the firm have offices in the cities that are your major market areas?
5. Is the representative's staff knowledgeable about your type of operation? Does his or her staff have a hotel background?
6. How does the representative regard service? Do you want him or her to be an extension of your sales staff? Is he or she willing to be part of your team?
7. Can he or she deliver needed supporting services and advise you on brochures and other printed materials?

🖳 INTERNET EXERCISE

Independent Hotel Representatives

Independent hotels frequently look to independent hotel sales representatives or firms to assist in their sales efforts. These firms, which usually have offices in major cities such as Washington, D.C., Ottawa, Canada, and Chicago, have their own portfolio of clients and act as an extension of the independent hotel's sales office, much like the national and regional sales offices of the major chains.

Not only do representation firms field a staff of salespeople in key geographic areas, they also reach meeting planners at trade shows. Instead of buying a booth as a single entity, hotels can split the cost with other properties in the rep firm's portfolio. This is especially beneficial, as it can cost up to $20,000 to exhibit at some meeting planner trade shows.

The Ambrose Hotel's director of marketing, speaking of the hotel's representative firm, states:

> They are an adjunct to our sales effort. It's like having an additional arm that reaches farther than we could on our own and multiplies our efforts. They have enough representation to cover what we can't.

To answer the following questions, log on to the websites of these hotel sales representative firms:

- Krisam Group—www.krisam.com
- David Green Organization—www.dgoinc.com
- The Hyland Group—www.hylandgroup.com
- Hinton and Grusich—www.hintonandgrusich.com

1. What types of hotels does each firm represent?

2. How many regional offices does each have and in what locations?

3. What industry events and trade shows do they attend on behalf of the hotels they represent?

4. How is each paid?

5. Compare and contrast the companies. What are the strengths and weaknesses of each? Which firm do you think is best for a hotel targeting the meetings market?

6. Explain how hiring an outside sales rep firm provides independent hotels some of the same benefits of being a "brand," but without having to give up anything that made them independent in the first place.

If you opt to go with an independent hotel representative, it is important to remember that these firms are generally hired on a contract basis, usually paid a fee, and receive a set percentage of the volume of business they directly book for the hotel. They must be given clear guidelines on what type of business the property is soliciting and what rates the property will accept.

In other words, the hotel representative should work within the framework of the property's marketing plan, and, as an extended member of your sales force, should be thoroughly familiar with the property's facilities, rates, and operating procedures. Personal visits and tours by the management should be encouraged. The representative should be given organization charts, operating manuals, and materials detailing charges for meeting rooms, guestrooms, and other facilities. Most importantly, the representative should be given a copy of the property's marketing plan—with specific objectives spelled out for him or her to meet.

In addition to hiring outside independent sales representatives, many independent hotels join global referral associations, such as Preferred Hotels, World Hotels, Leading Hotels of the World, Relais & Châteaux, and Small Luxury Hotels of the World. These firms provide similar services as representation firms (personal selling, advertising, sales promotion, and public relations) as well as central reservations systems and loyalty rewards networks.

The selling point for many independent hotels is the reach realized from these firms' global reservation systems. Many independent hotels are family-owned and simply do not have the resources to open offices in Washington, D.C., Toronto, London, or Milan. Referral associations make a global presence possible—and provide association with other prestigious hotels within the group. Additionally, member hotels get access to discounts on goods and services due to the association's volume purchasing. These associations also provide valuable training and networking opportunities.

Managing the Sales Effort

While hiring good salespeople, whether they be in-house staff or independent hotel representatives, is an important step toward achieving sales goals, the sales effort itself must be structured and managed properly for maximum effectiveness. Managing the sales effort involves a number of areas: the development of standard operating procedures (SOPs) for salespeople and convention staff; periodic sales meetings to discuss goals and problems; the prioritizing of accounts; keeping accurate records; and, most important, the monitoring and evaluating of progress.

Standard Operating Procedures

An effective sales effort begins with standardized guidelines for each step of the sales and servicing process. Each salesperson should be made aware of the sales office's **standard operating procedures (SOPs)**. These are instructions explaining how recurring business activities should be handled.

Each hotel salesperson should have a three-ring binder containing the property's standard operating procedures on his or her desk in order to keep everyone "on the same page" for consistent selling. Written SOPs presented together in a manual provide a constant reference for sales and banquet personnel, and are an essential training tool for new employees. Areas that might be included in a SOP manual include:

- Function book control and procedures
- Guestroom control book procedures
- Booking policies
- Rate guidelines for high and low demand periods
- Credit/deposit/cancellation policies
- Policies regarding VIP and complimentary rooms
- Meeting room rental fees and procedures
- Banquet and room reservation cut-off dates
- Convention service standards and procedures
- The organization chart and specific job descriptions for the sales department

The sales department's SOPs can be added to or amended as situations warrant, but it is important that each person involved in the sales effort be made aware of any changes. These written SOPs help to eliminate costly errors by ensuring that each member of the sales team follows the same procedures when booking and servicing groups.

Sales Meetings

Just as written procedures are important, good communication is also essential to an effective sales effort. Sales meetings are an excellent way to ensure that all people involved in the sales effort have the same information and can help to eliminate potential problems by identifying and dealing with them early.

While the number and type of sales meetings may vary, the most commonly used meetings are *weekly and monthly staff meetings, weekly function meetings, weekly revenue management committee meetings, marketing team meetings, and periodic (usually annual or semi-annual) sales meetings for all employees.*

- Weekly and monthly sales or staff meetings are usually headed by the coordinator of the sales effort; this may be the director of sales and marketing, the director of sales, or the sales manager at larger properties, or the general manager at small properties. Held to discuss any changes in the sales or promotional effort, the progress on certain accounts, new and tentative bookings, sales goals, and potential problems, these meetings are usually attended by all sales personnel and the heads of any departments affected by the sales effort (convention services, banquet/catering, front desk, etc.). Since the mutual exchange of ideas and information is vitally important to any sales effort, these regularly scheduled sales meetings should also include a period of open discussion or a brainstorming session.

- Weekly function meetings generally include only the department heads involved in selling to and servicing the convention market. These meetings ensure that every area of the property is adequately covered when making commitments to groups, and help to ensure that specific business is understood and properly handled.

- Weekly revenue management committee meetings, which typically include the general manager, director of revenue, director of sales and marketing, director of sales, catering/food and beverage director, controller, reservations manager, and front office manager, have grown in importance because the new reality is that not all revenue is created equal, necessitating that everyone work together to maximize revenues. It is no longer enough to simply book group business; managers must determine their clients' present and future value.

  Today, pricing strategies are based on a calendar that forecasts high-, medium-, and low-demand periods. The objectives of revenue meetings, then, are to review the forecast calendar, and update it with new demand information, competitive influences, and reservations activity in order to reset or confirm pricing. Management can then inform the sales team of how much it can negotiate with meeting groups based on anticipated demand for the dates requested.

- Many properties hold an annual or semi-annual sales meeting for all the property's staff. The marketing plan—and each employee's role in it—is presented, and specific information, such as advertising and promotional efforts

Exhibit 5   Key Account Management Spreadsheet

KEY ACCOUNT MANAGEMENT SPREADSHEET

Name of account and key contact	# of times account was called on last year	# of times we expect to call on account this year	Estimate of room night potential from account	
Stubbs Insurance Mark Steward	4 Personal calls 4 Telephone calls	5 Personal 5 Telephone	25 r.n. x 12 mo. @ $75 = $22,500 20 r.n. x 12 mo. @ $80 = $19,200 30 r.n. x 2 days x 4 @ $72 = $17,280 125 r.n. x3 days @ $75 = $28,125 Total $87,105	

Prioritizing accounts can be accomplished easily if a salesperson takes a look at all of his or her accounts and judges them by the same criteria. A spreadsheet such as this one provides a place for necessary data and enables the salesperson to see the profit potential of each account at a glance. Since each of a salesperson's 300–400 accounts are assessed, the director of sales can review the spreadsheets with salespeople on a periodic basis (usually the end or beginning of a year) to reassess priorities.

and their affect on individual departments and employees, is discussed. This benefits both employee and management, providing an opportunity to obtain ideas and suggestions from employees working in day-to-day operations.

Assigning Account Responsibility

Keeping the sales staff abreast of current information and goals is only part of the management of the sales effort. It is the responsibility of the director of sales or other leader of the sales effort to ensure that accounts are being distributed and handled in the most productive and cost-effective manner for optimum results.

There are many variables in assigning responsibility. Some directors of sales feel that accounts should be assigned by market segment; if he or she has three salespeople, for example, one might be assigned to corporate meetings, one to association business, and one to the SMERF market. While this may seem practical on the surface, there may be a drastic imbalance within the market segments. The salesperson assigned to corporate meetings, for example, may end up with more accounts than he or she can handle.

The director of sales may see this imbalance, and assign two people to cover the property's most lucrative segment. This approach, too, may present problems, since most corporations find it more comfortable to deal with only one contact person at a property.

Home Run Accounts

In most situations, there are a few accounts on which you should concentrate, because these key accounts can have an immediate impact on your business. *Home run accounts* are those accounts that are likely to generate the greatest revenue.

To manage accounts properly, you must *fully qualify* the contact. Full qualification involves gathering all information necessary to place a dollar value on the account's potential business. For example, a corporation contact might state they average 25 room nights per month for their own executives, another 20 room nights for visiting clients, quarterly two-day workshops for 30 persons, and a large new product showcase annually, requiring 125 guestrooms for the three-day event. From this information, it is now possible to estimate the potential dollar volume the account represents for your hotel (see Exhibit 5).

		KEY ACCOUNT MANAGEMENT SPREADSHEET		
	Estimate of food and beverage potential	Estimate of meeting room revenue potential	Total potential dollar value of account	Level of account priority (Level 1 through Level 5)
	40% of Room Revenue = $34,842	4 Workshops — Complimentary function space Product Showcase — 1.00 per square foot for exhibit hall = $10,000	Rooms $86,105 Food & Beverage $34,842 Meeting Space $10,000	Level 1 — High Potential Account

One solution is to *assign specific accounts, rather than market segments*, to each of the salespeople; one salesperson would be responsible for all the business generated by a particular organization. This type of account assignment is beneficial to both the salesperson and the client; it provides one contact person and helps to build rapport that may generate future business. If this approach is taken, it is important to distribute accounts with particular attention to the number of accounts, their geographic area, and the market segments into which they fall. In terms of numbers, it is usually considered best to assign accounts equally. If, for example, a property expects to target 900 accounts over the coming year, each of the hotel's three salespeople should be given 300 of them.

This number can vary based upon the location of the accounts. If, for example, a property can target a nearby industrial park, it is easier for a salesperson to handle these accounts than it would be for a salesperson to adequately cover accounts spread over a two- state area. In this case, the salesperson covering the local area can be assigned a larger number of accounts.

The market segment factor comes into play when determining just how much business will be generated by each account. A salesperson assigned to a large corporate account, for example, can expect to cover a great deal more business—meetings, award ceremonies, the annual convention, etc.—than a salesperson assigned to an association that stages just one annual convention. In this case, or in the case of the salesperson who shows particular expertise in servicing a specific market segment, accounts can be redistributed for the best results.

Key Account Management. Once accounts have been assigned, the typical salesperson may find that he or she is looking at 300 to 400 sources of potential business. Selling to and servicing these accounts will involve making sales calls, setting appointments, and following up—all activities that will generate a mountain of paperwork. So how does a salesperson decide how to handle the monumental task of effectively selling to his or her accounts? The solution is **key account management**.

Key account management involves prioritizing accounts based on their profit potential. This is important because, generally, 20 percent of a salesperson's accounts generates 80 percent of the business. Look at accounts individually to determine which ones have the highest potential for generating business and organize your time to sell and service these accounts. Key account management, then, involves ranking accounts. This is usually done on five levels:

- *Level 1* consists of all new and established accounts with a high potential for business. These are the accounts that will warrant your highest attention. As a general rule, a minimum of five personal calls and five telephone calls should be allocated to these accounts annually.

- *Level 2* consists of high potential accounts that are already providing a good share of business. Of course you want to continue to follow up on these lucrative accounts, but they don't require the same amount of personal attention and they can usually be serviced by four personal and four telephone calls annually.
- *Level 3* consists of new accounts with medium potential and established accounts that are not generating the medium potential expected of them. These accounts generally require three personal and three telephone calls each year.
- *Level 4* consists of accounts with medium potential providing an acceptable level of business. These accounts are normally followed up with two personal and two telephone calls annually.
- *Level 5* consists of low potential new and established accounts that do not warrant a great deal of time. These accounts require little more than token attention, such as a personal visit while on a sales trip to a more lucrative account or a telephone call after all the other business has been handled.

The level of each account can be determined by preparing an account "spreadsheet" (see Exhibit 5) and by discussing questionable accounts with the director of sales. When setting account levels, however, remember that your priorities may change as your accounts and prospects change. Perhaps a company that had a low potential level because of its distance from the property may expand into your area or an association that had previously met at another hotel chain may have become dissatisfied and is now looking for another meeting place. These scenarios, which are not that uncommon, show the necessity for qualifying each account (see box titled "Home Run Accounts") and for personally reviewing your accounts to determine how much time and effort should be spent to realize maximum sales potential.

It is also important to note that the goals set for a salesperson will affect how he or she manages accounts. Most hotels measure sales productivity and provide salespeople with bonuses and incentives based on both the amount of revenue generated and the number of room nights booked. If salespeople were measured strictly by the number of room nights booked, there would be a tendency to book business at almost any rate rather than the highest possible rate. Some properties set goals for high and low periods, for example. In this case, a fairly low priority account may provide the business needed during a slow period—and help achieve an individual sales goal. It is also important to maintain a balance between maintaining good customer relations and prospecting for new customers. In some cases, salespeople will have sales goals based on business from current customers and business to book from new accounts. All of these variables will Exhibit into managing accounts for maximum benefit.

Evaluating the Sales Effort

To ensure that the sales office is operating at top capacity, it is necessary to periodically review both the salespeople and the organizational structure itself. Salespeople should be monitored to determine if they are meeting their personal quotas. They should also be evaluated as to how they are using their general sales abilities—are they prospecting, developing concrete leads, and following up? Do they have a good service attitude? Are they managing their time properly? These evaluations should be made at least quarterly to enable sales management to control small problems that could develop into major difficulties. One seasoned sales professional says:

> Review the activity of a salesperson to check what's being done and to make sure the person's performance is in line with corporate or property sales procedures. Review each salesperson's weekly sales activity report with the salesperson. You also want to look at the follow-up accounts to see if the trace system is working accordingly. Pull some files to see how accounts are being handled.[5]

New salespeople should be reviewed more frequently to ensure that they are on track. To assist in evaluations, each salesperson should maintain a **reader file**. This file contains copies of all correspondence and call reports generated by a salesperson. Each salesperson's reader file should be evaluated weekly by the director of sales.

The organizational structure of the sales office should also be reviewed to determine if current efforts make the most of the strengths of its staff and contribute to the property's bottom line. This involves taking a look at a number of factors. Are lines of communication open with both the sales staff and other departments on the property? Has authority been clearly delegated—and is the scope of that authority understood? Are duties and responsibilities being carried out? Is sales follow-up—correspondence, telephone calls, etc.—being handled properly? Is there an adequate support staff?

Sales Records and Filing Systems

A hotel sales department should have an efficient system of sales records and files. Effective sales promotion requires it. Vast amounts of client information must be documented and filed, accurately and up-to-date, if they are to be meaningful. Similarly, forms and records are valuable only if the information they contain is accessible. If you cannot locate the needed information quickly, the system isn't much good.

While most hotels today use computerized systems for recordkeeping and managing sales efforts, some smaller properties still use manual systems. And, if a computer system is used, it is still customary to maintain "hard copy" files and maintain a paper trail of customer business. Even when correspondence, contracts, and other paperwork inherent to sales efforts are sent electronically (e-mail or fax), they are printed out and placed in a customer file.

In this section, we will discuss the basic forms that are used for the sales function. While computerized systems are widespread, we will first show the manual version of each form to aid in understanding before illustrating the computer counterpart of each. Later in the chapter, we will show how the computer is used to manage the service function and how technology can enhance sales efforts and profitability.

Hotel Filing Systems

The late C. Dewitt Coffman stated that "the maintenance of accurate and up-to-date file systems is the single most important mechanical operation of any sales department. Without minutely accurate file records, the sales department is without ammunition." When selling, especially to groups, sales personnel need easily available, up-to-date information.

Methods of Filing. Most hotel filing systems, whether they are manual, computerized, or a combination of both, fall into three general categories. *Alphabetical filing* is done by the title of the organization, firm, or association (or by the name of the contact person), and is often used by hotels. Many properties find this to be the easiest method of filing.

The second method of filing is by *key word of the title.* This type of filing is advantageous when the exact name of the organization is not known. For example, the Association of Petroleum and Oil Products would be filed under the word "petroleum." Or, several key words could be used (in this case, the account could also be filed under "oil").

The third method of filing is *numerical.* Each file carries an assigned account number and a corresponding set of file cards is kept by the number and name. This method is often effective for larger file systems, and while it has not always been widely used, it is becoming more popular as hotels turn increasingly to computer technology to assist in keeping account records. Most computerized systems enable the salesperson to access accounts by a number of criteria, including account number, name, key word, and other specialized searches.

Elements of Filing Systems. Most hotel filing systems share three common elements:

- The master card
- The account file, and
- The tickler (trace) file

As each of these elements is explained and illustrated, keep in mind that systems will vary slightly from hotel to hotel.

The **master card** serves as a summary for the sales effort. It details such information as contact names and titles, addresses, telephone numbers, month or months in which the group meets, the size of the group, where it has met in the past, who makes the initial and final site decision, and other pertinent information (see Exhibit 6). The master card serves as a data bank of prospects and is often color-coded to draw attention to specific areas. If you are going after groups in a specific area, for example, you may color-code the cards by geographic location. Or you may color-code cards based on the month of meetings, to attempt to fill holes in your property's calendar. Groups can also be color-coded by size or other key factors.

Large companies having a number of divisions usually require a master card and several "trailer cards." The master card would detail information on the corporate level, while the trailer cards would contain contact names, meeting dates, and similar information for divisions in the company. A company such as General Electric, for example, would have a number of trailer cards.

The computerized version of the master file enables the salesperson to instantly access the account and add an unlimited amount of material to each account file. The file can be broken down into several screens (or windows) that provide a variety of additional information: account history, name of contact person, etc. (see Exhibit 7). Using a computerized master file eliminates the need to make copious notes on an index card, and necessary information is immediately available on a computer terminal.

The **account file** serves as the basic group business record, and its file folder should include all correspondence and related materials (contracts, past convention programs, tear sheets from trade papers, etc.). The account file is usually a standard-size file folder (see Exhibit 8), and, like the master card, it may be color-coded to draw attention to specific data.

If a file needs to be removed from the file cabinet, a guide card detailing the name of the group, its file number, the date of removal, and the initials of the person requesting

Exhibit 6   Sample Account Master Card—Manual System

Jan.	Feb.	Mar.	April	May	June	July	Aug.	Sept.	Oct.	Nov.	Dec.	1 to 100	100 to 250	250 to 350	350 to 500	Over 500

Convention Group *NATIONAL LIVESTOCK DEALERS ASSO.*   *N-02197*

Main Contact   *DAVID PRITCHARD*   Title *ASSO. MANAGER*

Address   Phone
City
Other Contacts

How is Decision Made   When

Date	City	Hotel	Attend	No. of Hotel Rms.
				Exhibits
				Functions

The master card provides a summary of convention information on a 5x8-inch card. Master cards can be color-coded by geographic location, month of meeting, or other category to assist salespeople in soliciting business or following up on the account.

the file should be placed in the file drawer in place of the file. This enables the sales staff to keep track of the file's whereabouts.

The **tickler file**, also known as a *trace file, bring-up file,* or *follow-up file,* is an effective follow-up tool. Tickler files may come in various forms; some are card files with monthly dividers and card separators marked 1 through 30 or 31 (see Exhibit 9), others are accordion-style files with multi-pockets. And, there are systems designed to fit within a letter-sized file cabinet. In all of these systems, cards are filed by month and day.

The tickler file, used properly, works very well, costs little, and takes little time to implement. It works this way: you make contact with a prospect who indicates that no meeting plans will be finalized until October. Obviously, you want to contact the person before then—perhaps by the middle of September—so you place a card, a note, or a copy of some correspondence in the pocket marked September 15. This type of system eliminates reliance on memory, and ensures good follow-up—*if* you remember to remove everything in the pocket on each day of the month!

Several computerized versions of the tickler file are available. Specialized hotel software, such as Delphi, not only reminds salespeople of important dates, but also offers additional sales tools. The computerized trace report shown in Exhibit 10, for example, breaks down the day's business into several categories. The salesperson can take advantage of this to prioritize his or her work and schedule each day to make the most of sales opportunities. But even salespeople who do not have access to hotel-specific software can utilize other programs, such as Microsoft Outlook, to help organize their work. The Outlook program features a daily calendar and task list.

Exhibit 7   Computerized Master Card Files

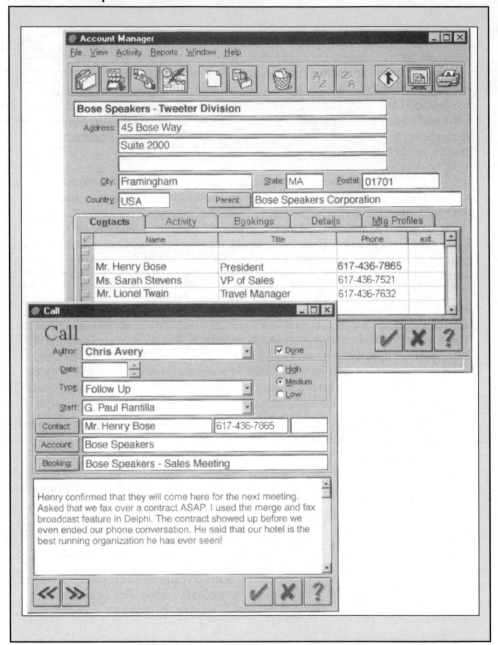

This computerized version of the account master card enables the salesperson to instantly access the account—and add an unlimited amount of material to each account's file. The file can be broken into several screens (or windows) which provide a variety of additional information—account history, name of contact person, etc. Using a computerized master file eliminates the need to make copious notes on an index card—and the need to spend a great deal of time in locating the necessary information (it can all be done at the salesperson's desk).
Source: Delphi 7/Newmarket Software Systems, Inc., Durham, New Hampshire. For more information, browse the company's website at www.newmarketinc.com.

Exhibit 8   Sample Account File

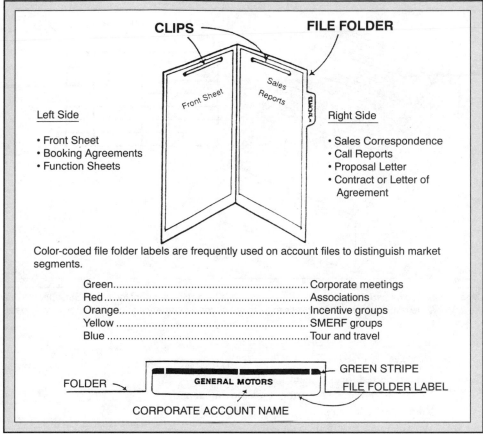

Color-coded file folder labels are frequently used on account files to distinguish market segments.

Green...Corporate meetings
Red..Associations
Orange..Incentive groups
Yellow ....SMERF groups
Blue ....Tour and travel

The account file is usually kept in a standard file folder and contains all of the group's information, including sales call reports, tentative and definite booking information, function sheets from past business, and correspondence generated relating to the booking. Information is placed in the file in chronological order (with the newest on top) and secured with clips to prevent loss. Like the master file, account file folders may be color-coded to call attention to specific characteristics of the group.

Control Books and Sales Forms

In addition to files, the sales office utilizes a number of control books and sales forms in selling to and servicing the group sales business.

Control Books. In selling public and banquet space to convention groups, for example, the salesperson must be sure that the assigned space will be available. Overbooking is eliminated by the use of a hotel **function book** (see Exhibit 11).

The function book serves as the hotel's "bible" when it comes to booking meeting and banquet space, so there should only be one book to prevent mismatched entries or **double bookings**.

The most common type of manual function book is a large book with a page for every day of the year. The function book has a number of vertical columns, providing space for such information as:

- The name of the organization or person requesting space
- The contact person (name, title, address, telephone)

Exhibit 9   Sample Tickler (Trace) File—Manual System

NATIONAL LIVESTOCK DEALERS ASSN.   N-02197
                                               PA
Trace:

DATE	INL.	DATE	INL.
Jan. 12	M.A.		
June 15	M.A.		

Divided into months and days of the month, the tickler file helps with account follow up. Salespeople use the tickler file to remind themselves of calls to be made or correspondence to be sent on a specific date.

- Type of function
- Time required for the event
- Total time required (for setup, breakdown, cleanup)
- Number of attendees
- Type of setup required
- Rates charged
- Contract status
- Other remarks

There should be at least one section for each meeting or function room, with space to cover specific time periods in each day. If a manual system is used, all bookings should be made in pencil, the name of the group should be recorded exactly as it appears on the file to facilitate future referencing, and the starting and ending times should be recorded to enable the property to book another event if possible.

To eliminate possible errors, only one person should be given control of the function book. This may be the convention sales manager, or, at properties with a large staff, the senior sales executive. Single-person control of the function book is essential; convention space cannot be sold efficiently without this control.

There may be instances in which the same space is desired by two groups. In this case, sales managers will try to determine the best "fit" for both the hotel and the group. Factors to be considered are the likelihood that the space will actually be filled, the estimated profitability of each group, the status of the group (regular client or new business), the likelihood of repeat business, the long-term profitability of each group, the possibility that one group would consider an alternate date, and the group's convention history.

In addition to controlling meeting space, it is also necessary to control guestrooms. Properties use a **guestrooms control book** for this; at some properties this book is referred to as the *rooms control bible.* This ensures that rooms are available for groups. This book is used by the sales department to stay aware of the number of rooms it can sell, as hotels

Exhibit 10   Sample Ticker (Trace) Report—Computerized System

The Durham Resort
Morning Report for Ralph Johnson
September 21, 1999

Rooming List Due

Group Name	Date	Day	Room Type	Agree	Block	Pickup	New Block
Mt. Hope Radiology Dept.	2/ 2/ 00	Wed	Run of House	25	25	_____	_____
	2/ 3/ 00	Thu	Run of House	25	25	_____	_____
	2/ 4/ 00	Fri	Run of House	300	300	_____	_____
	2/18/00	Fri	Run of House	25	25	_____	_____

Deposits Due

Group Name	Arrival Date	Trace Date	New Status/ New Trace Date
Acorn Dry Cleaning	3/20/00	1/10/00	_____ ___/___/___

Verbal Definites - Contract Due

Group Name	Arrival Date	Trace Date	New Status/ New Trace Date
Jacobs Wedding	9/1/00	1/15/00	_____ ___/___/___

Tentatives - Decision Due

Group Name	Arrival Date	Trace Date	New Status/ New Trace Date
Automobile Travelers Assn	3/24/00	11/20/99	_____/ ___/___/___
Arizona Building Company	4/30/00	12/20/99	_____/ ___/___/___

Leads - Decision Due

Group Name	Arrival Date	Trace Date	New Status/ New Trace Date
Balloon Industries	2/1/00	11/1/99	_____/ ___/___/___

Source: Delphi Newmarket Software Systems, Inc., Durham, New Hampshire

This report not only replaces the cumbersome manual tickler file, but also offers additional sales tools to the salesperson. The trace report, for example, breaks down the day's business into several categories. The salesperson can take advantage of this feature to prioritize work and schedule each day to make the most of sales opportunities.

Exhibit 11   Function Book Reservation Sheet

WmGrant
HOTEL

FUNCTION BOOK RESERVATION SHEET

Group Name _____   Comments _____

Contact _____   _____

Address _____   _____

Phone _____   _____

Dates In House _____   _____

A G E N D A

DAY/DATE	TIME	FUNCTION	SET-UP	# OF PEOPLE	ROOM NAME

Meeting Space Charges:

Sales Rep _____

Date _____

Option Date _____

Date Entered _____

Entered By _____

The sales or catering manager must fill out this form and submit it to the person responsible for monitoring the hotel's function space. In addition, one copy of this form will go into the account file and another copy to the salesperson's reader file.

often stipulate a maximum *group allotment*—the number of rooms available for sale to groups— to ensure that a proper market mix of group, tour and travel, and individual guest business is maintained. Demand fluctuates by time of year and by day of week, so the group room allotment varies considerably. For example, the summer months are generally soft convention months, so a 400-room hotel might only do 25 percent of its business with meeting groups and 75 percent with individual travelers.

Although these percentages may be reversed in the typically busy convention periods of spring or fall, hotels rarely, if ever, will sell the entire hotel to convention groups. Individual corporate and leisure travelers are consistent year-round producers, and selling out to a convention will alienate travelers displaced by convention groups.

The guestrooms control book's format usually consists of monthly report sheets with space for the group's name and guestroom commitment by day. These "forecast sheets" are dated and bound in book form, providing projections several years ahead.

As with the function book, all entries should be made in pencil. Often, definite bookings are listed on the upper half of the page, while tentative bookings are entered on the lower half.

It is extremely important for the hotel sales office and the front desk/reservations department to have good communication and contact with one another. Because both are booking business, it is imperative that room sales are not overlapped. Traditionally, reservations has reported to the front office manager, but reservations are increasingly being placed under the sales department in many convention-oriented hotels.

Most hotels also computerized their function and guestrooms control books (see Exhibit 12). This method still provides control, since only authorized personnel can add or change information (while information is being changed, the system goes into a "read only" mode until the information is updated). However, the information is readily available to salespeople, either in-house or from a remote location.

Before Hyatt Hotels updated their function books, Gordon Kerr, Hyatt's senior vice president of Management Information Systems, said:

> Each hotel kept this giant diary with function room bookings written in it. If a customer called Hyatt headquarters in Chicago to book a function room in San Francisco, for example, the manager of the San Francisco hotel had to be called to check availability. Customers eager to book space would wait hours, or even days, to receive a reply. By that time, many would-be customers had found space elsewhere. With the computerized system, Hyatt users can check availability and book function rooms at any connected hotel from any hotel in the network.[6]

Wendy Bonvechio, director of sales and marketing, Sheraton Seattle Hotel & Towers, says:

> Automation is very important to our business. A problem that has been completely eliminated is the inevitable double booking that occurred with the manual systems. With automation, the computer won't allow you to double book. Our customers demand automation because it is quicker, makes us more efficient, and virtually eliminates mistakes. It's no longer an option, but a necessity in order to compete in today's market.[7]

Sales Forms. Once a sales commitment has been made, there are a number of forms used to follow the sale to the final execution of the function. The *tentative booking sheet* (or report)

Exhibit 12   Computerized Function and Guestrooms Control Book

THE RIVERVIEW HOTEL

Date printed: October 1, 20__   Time printed: 11:59 AM

DELPHI — Function Space Profile   Page: 1

Report for Oct 1 20__ to Oct 31 20__

Room Name	Time Period	We 1	Th 2	Fr 3	Sa 4	Su 5	Mo 6	Tu 7	We 8	Th 9	Fr 10	Sa 11	Su 12	Mo 13	Tu 14	We 15	Th 16	Fr 17	Sa 18	Su 19	Mo 20	Tu 21	We 22	Th 23	Fr 24	Sa 25	Su 26	Mo 27	Tu 28	We 29	Th 30	Fr 31
WASHINTN	M				D	D	D	D				D	D						T	T	T											
	L				D	D													T	T	T											
	A				D														T	T	T											
	E																		T	T	T											
ADAMS	M																		D	D												
	L																															
	A													T	T								D	D								
	E				T	T	T		T	T																						
JEFFERSON	M				D	D	D					VD	VD	VD	VD	VD	VD															
	L											VD	VD	VD	VD	VD	VD															
	A																															
	E																															
MADISON	M											VD	VD	T	T	T					D	D	D					T	T	T		
	L											VD	VD			T	T	T										T	T	T		
	A																															
	E																															
MONROE	M																		T	T	T											
	L																		T	T	T											
	A																		T	T	T											
	E																		T	T	T											
JACKSON	M						VD	VD	VD					D	D	D																
	L						VD	VD	VD					D	D	D																
	A																															
	E																															

Many hotels are using computerized function and guestrooms control books to provide instant access to information by sales personnel, who must often provide an immediate answer regarding the availability of function space or rooms. These reports are very similar to the manual reports kept by some hotels. The main difference is that the computer generates these reports automatically by using booking information already entered into the system. These sample reports were generated by Delphi System, software specifically designed to meet the needs of the hotel industry. (continued on next page)

is used if a date has not been confirmed or if details have not been worked out (see Exhibit 13).

In the normal sequence of events, a convention organizer may inquire about the availability of the property on certain dates. Requirements are discussed, but perhaps there are circumstances that must be resolved before setting a definite date. Perhaps board approval is needed or, in the case of a corporate meeting, a supervisor must be consulted. The meeting planner then asks for an **option** on the space, and a *hold* is placed on the room(s).

This means that the hotel has agreed to hold the space pending final confirmation by the client. Some properties are cautious about tentative bookings; they do not want to lose out on other business while protecting a tentative account that may not "go definite." That is why it is important to limit the length of the hold by designating an *option date*. An option

Exhibit 12   *(continued)*

THE RIVERVIEW HOTEL

Date printed: August 27, 20__   Time printed: 11:41 AM

DELPHI — Group rooms Control Report for 20__ June

	1 Sun	2 Mon	3 Tue	4 Wed	5 Thur	6 Fri	27 Fri	28 Sat	29 Sun	30 Mon	Total Rooms	Total Guests	Ave. Rate	Room Revenue	Decision Date	RT	SRC	Stat	Date Entered
DEFINITES for CORP.																			
D.E.C.											500	500	124.00	62,000.00	8/27/96		TRB	D	8/27/96
Mass Bay Co											200	200	118.00	23,600.00	8/27/96		TRB	D	8/27/96
I.B.M.											90	90	125.00	11,250.00	8/27/96		TRB	D	8/27/96
Coastal Inc.											15	15	128.00	1,920.00			TRB	D	2/13/96
CORP.	0	0	0	0	0	0	0	0	0	0	805	820	122.69	98,770.00				D	
TENTATIVES for CORP.																			
Lotus Dev. Co.			5	5	5	5					20	40	145.00	2,900.00	8/27/96		SB	T	8/27/96
Crimson Trvl						6					24	48	118.00	2,832.00	8/27/96		RWH	T	8/27/96
Eastern Inc.											35	70	130.00	4,550.00	8/27/96		RWH	T	8/27/96
Lotus Dev. Co.											15	30	121.00	1,815.00	8/27/96		RWH	T	8/27/96
Intel Corp.											9	27	121.00	1,089.00	8/27/96				
Eastern Inc.											4	4	145.00	580.00	8/27/96				
CORP.	0	0	5	5	5	11	0	0	0	0	107	223	128.65	13,766.00				T	
DEFINITES for Assoc.																			
Travel Assoc.	25.	25	25								75	75	108.00	8,100.00	9/30/96		KL	D	3/10/96
N.A.F.E.											30	60	127.00	3,810.00	8/12/96		CRW	DD	8/12/96
U.S.ASSOC.											120	240	120.00	14,400.00	8/1/96		TS	D	8/10/96
U.S.ASSOC.							7	7	7	7	63	126	112.00	7,056.00			TS	D	8/10/96
U.S.ASSOC.							5				20	20	120.00	2,400.00					
ASSOC.	25	25	25	0	0	0	17	7	7	7	308	521	116.12	35,766.00	.			D	
TENTATIVES for ASSOC.																			
Vets Assoc.	2	2	2								6	12	121.00	726.00	8/25/96		TRB	T	8/25/96
N.A.R.R.P.	10	10									20	40	120.00	2,200.00	8/25/96		TRB	T	8/25/96
Data Systems			6	6	6	6					48	96	131.00	6,288.00	8/25/96		TRB	T	8/25/96
D.P.A.			10	10	10						30	60	145.00	4,350.00	8/25/96		TRB	T	8/25/96
Mutual Assoc.					3	3					24	48	131.00	3,144.00	8/25/96		TRB	T	8/25/96
Mont Ward Co.											40	80	100.00	4,000.00	6/24/96		EP	T	6/24/96
Newsweek											16	32	131.00	2,096.00	8/25/96		RWH	T	8/25/96
N.A.F.E.											36	72	127.00	4,572.00	8/12/96		TRB	T	8/25/96
Int'l Assoc.											8	16	118.00	944.00	8/25/96		TRB	T	8/25/96
Womens Assoc.											4	8	110.00	440.00	8/25/96		TRB	T	8/25/96
Manufact. Assn											48	96	127.00	6,096.00	8/25/96		TRB	T	8/25/96
N.A.T.C.O.							45				270	540	234.00	63,180.00	8/25/96		TRB	T	8/25/96
Dental Assoc.								2	2		4	8	110.00	440.00	8/25/96		TRB	T	8/25/96
Central Assoc.									30	30	60	120	120.00	7,200.00	8/25/96		TRB	T	8/25/96
US Yacht Club									4	4	8	16	131.00	1,048.00	8/25/96		TRB	T	8/25/96
ASSOC.	12	12	18	16	19	9	45	2	36	34	622	1244	171.58	106,724.00				T	

(Continued from preceding page) Tentative and definite bookings in the function book and guestroom control book are monitored on a regular basis. At the weekly sales meeting, discussion will center on booking activity and how to best manage the guestroom and function space inventory. The computerized function and guestrooms control books will help the sales team to look at business on the books and manage it for the benefit of both the hotel and meeting planners.

date is the date by which the client must confirm the order or release the space. If this period is too long, the hotel has severely limited its freedom to seek another customer, but the date should be long enough to enable the client to secure the necessary approval. A typical first option agreement might read:

> This tentative room block is being held on a first option basis until [date]. Following this period, all space outlined above will become subject to availability unless prior arrangements for an extension have been made.

Exhibit 13   Tentative Booking Form

| OPRYLAND HOTEL | TENTATIVE SALES BOOKING SHEET | FILE NO _____ TODAY'S DATE _____ SM _____ DOS _____ |

NAME OF GROUP _____   FILE NO   TODAYS DATE   S.P.I

YEAR	DAY											
	DATE											
	ROOMS											

ROOMS	NO	RATE	ARR	DEP		CONTACT/ADDRESS _____
I/C						
DBL/DBL						
KING						
SUITE						TEL. NO. DECISION DATE

RESERVATION COPY

DATE	DAY	TIME	FUNCTION	SETUP	# OF PEOPLE	ROOM

HISTORY: 19 ____ HOTEL _____ CITY _____ / 19 ____ HOTEL _____ CITY _____
HISTORY: 19 ____ HOTEL _____ CITY _____ / 19 ____ HOTEL _____ CITY _____

FUNCTION BOOK

MARKET RESEARCH COORDINATOR

SALES MANAGER'S FILE

DIRECTOR OF SALES

This form is used pending final confirmation of an event or function. Tentative bookings are often made when a client is interested in the space but needs to work out additional details or get approval. Using this form, tentative details are entered into the function book in the event that the function is confirmed (note the space for the option date, *the date by which a final decision must be made).*

A *definite booking form* is used after business has been confirmed. It is processed when a contract or letter of agreement has been signed and when the business is scheduled for a specific date. The form includes a number of details needed to properly service the function, such as the number of attendees, setup requirements, etc. The date and details will be entered into the function book (and guestrooms control book, if required).

Once a group "goes definite," establish a **working file** for the event. This file differs from the account file. The working file contains only the information relevant to the event. It is the file from which the convention service department works. Once the event concludes, the working file is broken down and appropriate materials are returned to the account file. Some hotels file the folders chronologically, but because the function book already lists all events in such order, you may be more comfortable filing alphabetically. It doesn't matter so long as there is some chronological system to remind the hotel of pending events.

After the convention is booked, other forms may also be necessary. In some cases, details such as a date, room requirement, or guestroom figure may change. It is then necessary to complete a *change form* to ensure that these changes are made. There may be many times when a piece of business which was considered definite is cancelled. In such a case, a *cancellation form* must be filed. Since there may be a number of reasons for the cancellation, some properties follow up the cancellation form with a *lost business report* that details the reason for the cancellation.

Some properties use a general form that eliminates the use of several of these forms. And, in addition to these general sales office forms, salespeople also utilize a number of forms for their individual use to track their progress in selling to accounts.

Sales Office Automation

Over the past several years, there have been dramatic changes in the way hotels do business. Today's advanced technology has eliminated much of the "drudge work" that was an inherent part of the sales effort. Paperwork that used to be done by hand (notes about sales calls and account requirements, for example), taking hours to prepare, update, and analyze, is now readily available by calling up a screen on a computer terminal. In this section, we will take a look at how the computer is drastically changing the face of the sales office—how it is not only helping to eliminate time-consuming paperwork, but how it is being used to personalize presentations, create lists of potential contacts, and forecast future demand for guestrooms and meeting rooms.

Advantages of Automation

Hospitality industry professionals agree that up to 70 percent of a salesperson's time can be spent on non-sales activities, such as call tracing, checking the availability of rooms, blocking rooms and space—and simply running back and forth to filing cabinets to retrieve information. The computer has changed all that. No longer is it necessary to search for lost files or prepare reports by hand; this data is readily available on individual computer terminals.

In addition, the computer frees salespeople from the office. If a salesperson is out making calls, information can be accessed by other salespeople or the clerical staff if immediate action is required. And, pertinent information (often in the form of reports) is instantly available to other departments requiring it (the banquet/catering department, reservations, etc.).

Computers make it easy to "personalize" important documents such as contracts and correspondence. They also simplify mass mailings, generating mailing labels (often by zip code or group type) in a fraction of the time it would take a secretary to sort through records and type labels to specified target groups. Sales management uses computers to evaluate both individual and departmental performance—the computer can provide detailed reports of sales calls made, the amount of business booked, and the potential area for future efforts.

New Advances in Hotel Computer Systems

While hotels have used computer systems for booking reservations for many years, only relatively recently have sales offices been automated to provide up-to-date information to salespeople and sales management. Tim Grover, regional director of sales and marketing for Starwood Hotels & Resorts Worldwide, states:

> For any hotel sales force, automation is critical. Delphi (software for hotel sales and catering) controls more than 80 percent of the market; it is considered the "Microsoft" of hotel sales and catering systems. They have a Windows-based version for managing sales contracts, group room blocks, and catering space. It is also user-friendly and can generate a variety of reports. Delphi software also functions as an excellent contact manager. Every conversation with a client about an event is documented and accessible to our entire sales team. And, finally, it helps us manage our revenue more efficiently. Knowing what's on the books at any given time for both room sales and catering is a valuable asset that benefits both the customer and the hotel.[8]

In addition to the access to this information, we have also seen how computers are being used to eliminate the large amount of paperwork generated by the sales department. One of the most important ways in which a computer is being used, however, is to assist the sales department in organizing and analyzing information about meeting groups. Database management programs provide a way to keep a service history of all client bookings, including the expected and actual number of attendees, the number of guestrooms booked, the types of functions booked, average room rate and average check, etc. **Database marketing** becomes a simple process. If a salesperson wishes to target groups that meet in the western regions of the country, for example, the computer will produce a list of accounts that meet that criteria for the salesperson to contact (see box titled "The Hidden Opportunities with Database Marketing").

The "Virtual" Office

Besides eliminating much of the drudgery of keeping records and accessing the information necessary to sell to and service meetings business, computers are playing an increasing role in improving the efficiency of property salespeople. No longer does it take days to answer inquiries or check date availability. Nor do salespeople have to sell from their own property. Many of today's salespeople are using technological advances to create "virtual offices"—armed with a laptop computer, an e-mail address, and a Blackberry, they are free to go where the business is—while still maintaining close contact with their home property. The Blackberry, which provides features including a calendar, address book, task list, and memo pad, also offers a Corporate Data Access feature that provides access to a property's customer relationship management (CRM) database and other pertinent corporate information. Not only does this mean that salespeople can keep up-to-date while away on business, but technology has also resulted in a growing number of hotel salespeople being home-based. Starwood, for example, estimates that about half of its 100 salespeople selling its Sheraton brand are home-based, and this trend is expected to continue.[9]

Laptop computers are the main component of a virtual office. While they are portable enough to be carried in a briefcase, they provide the capability of tapping into the property or chain's computer system to check for room availability, rates, and other information needed by potential clients. Most are equipped with fax modems, enabling the salesperson to check availability, generate a reply or proposal for the meeting planner, and immediately fax the document to the customer.

Swissotel, a hotel chain with properties in the United States, Europe, Asia, and the Middle East, was one of the first hospitality firms to "go virtual." Their United States national account team is equipped with laptop computers and accompanying personal digital assistants (PDAs) which enable salespeople to get immediate availability and rate information. The laptops are also used to send and receive faxes and, since they store property photos and detailed information about guestrooms and meeting space, they can be used to create customized presentations for meeting planners.

Swissotel president and CEO Andreas Meinhold says of the system:

> In a sense, Swissotel has packed its bag and taken itself on the road using specially adapted laptops and connectivity links. Because our salespeople are tapped into the property-management system, they're able to operate out of their virtual office as if they were behind the front desk of any Swissotel.
>
> Our account managers will be able to spend their time just selling, not focusing on administrative tasks. They can work when they want and where they want, and really spend their time focusing on our customers' needs.[10]

Electronic mail (e-mail) offers a number of advantages to salespeople. First is its speed. No longer does it take days to send correspondence to a client and wait for a reply. With e-mail, the salesperson can send off a message or proposal, get a reply, and respond to the reply within a short period of time (unlike telephone messages, e-mail can be directly responded to as soon as it is received; there is no need to talk to the home office, hang up the phone, and look for and dial the client's number). Second, although it is private, a number of the same messages may be sent to different contacts at one time (if a salesperson wants to get the word out about a new promotion, for example, the message can be generated once and e-mailed to several potential customers). Third, e-mail allows for flexibility. A number of messages—either the same or different—can be generated at one sitting and one or all can be sent at the same time. Conversely, an e-mail recipient can pick up all of his or her e-mail messages at once and respond as time and priorities allow. Last, but certainly not least, is the versatility of e-mail. E-mail communications can range from a short note requesting specific information to a large file of text and graphics; even software applications can be transferred via e-mail.

THE HIDDEN OPPORTUNITIES WITH DATABASE MARKETING

Database marketing allows hotels to develop personal long-term bonds with customers. Sometimes called relationship marketing or loyalty marketing, this approach departs from the mass marketing that has long been used to reach meeting planners. Few industries maintain the information about their customers that hotels keep—files that not only indicate guest requirements but make it easy to identify customers for future communications. Every hotel has account files, including information on past groups and registration cards from individual guests. The most frequently asked question is, "How long do we keep these records?" A more important question is, "What can the information in these files do for us?" The history in these files is the foundation for database marketing.

As competition has heated up in the past five or ten years, hotel operators have scrutinized marketing expenditures more carefully than ever. What they have learned is that *it's five to seven times more expensive to acquire new guests than it is to retain existing ones*. Your best customers are those who have purchased recently, purchase frequently, and deliver the greatest contribution to revenue.

Guest folios, registration cards, and group history on meeting planners form the core of your database; they allow you to personalize service to meet guest needs, thereby improving the guest experience and reinforcing loyalty.

Hotels typically use database marketing to analyze travel and spending patterns of market segments. Database programs allow you to easily trace and maintain customer controls, call up any customer record quickly, generate call-back schedules, follow-up letters and mailings, as well as mail merge to individual or a large number of customers.

Establishing relationships and a dialogue with customers is fast becoming a requirement for survival in the hotel industry. Whether a hotel continues to rely solely on its guest history system or decides to invest the time and money in a more sophisticated database system, one thing is certain: Hotel managers who know the most about customers and are able to harness resources for quick response to threats and opportunities will enjoy a tremendous advantage in the competitive decade ahead. If you cannot move quickly enough, your competitor across the street surely will.

Contributed by Cindy Estis Green, managing partner of The Estis Group and founder of Driving Revenue.

Other technological advances that have made it easier for today's hotel salespeople to concentrate their time on selling include computerized Rolodexes; "memo" machines; personal organizers; and electronic dictionaries, spell checkers, and translation devices. These advances can enhance efficiency and professionalism and give the salesperson more time do what he or she was hired to do—sell rooms and meeting space by going where the business is and focusing on the needs of potential clients.

Mike Mulcahy, a sales manager for the Sheraton City Centre in Washington, D.C., armed with his laptop and Blackberry, spends four days a week in New York City soliciting meetings business. He feels the arrangement is beneficial to both the hotel and the meeting planner. Mulcahy says:

> The bottom line is, I'm giving the planner more personal service by being here and meeting with them—there's nothing like being there and reviewing room availability on screen with the client. And, not only that, but taking it a step further and generating the contract and having them sign before you leave. The level of immediacy is far greater.

Additional Uses of Automation

In addition to automating sales records and enhancing the effectiveness of the property's salespeople, the computer and other facets of today's technology are being used to boost productivity and increase efficiency by:

- Generating daily, weekly, and monthly reports
- Providing rooms and equipment inventory
- Generating mailing lists
- Using word processing functions to generate contracts, proposals, routine correspondence, and so on

Personalization. In terms of word processing, the computer age has also ushered in an age of personalization. Today's meeting planners want to be more than an account number. Computer data banks make it easy to personalize correspondence and even routine contracts to meet this need.

Some of the advantages of using word processing, with a special emphasis on personalization, include:

- Letters need to be written only once and can be stored on file for future use.
- Spelling can be verified with the system's dictionary, and most systems offer a grammar check as well.
- Mailing lists for meeting planning organizations can be merged with inhouse lists (duplicate entries are purged, resulting in a single, clean file).
- Standard paragraphs can be recalled for insertion into proposal letters and contracts.
- Information from a previous function can be used in a follow-up letter; for example, "Do you wish to use the Monte Carlo room for your awards banquet again this year?"
- Filing is correctly done accurately, automatically, and quickly, eliminating the most hated clerical job in the office.

Simple mass mailings can be effectively personalized with the name of the contact person and his or her group. This information can be merged into a routine sales letter to give the impression of a personal touch. And, as with computerized sales records, this type of automation frees the sales department's clerical people to pursue other, more productive duties, such as setting appointments or following up on accounts for salespeople.

Yield and Revenue Management. Another vital use of the computer has been in the area of market analysis. **Yield management**, which is based on the forecasted demand for function space and guestrooms, is becoming an increasingly important tool in filling both meeting rooms and guestrooms while increasing profitability for the hotel.

Although yield management has been used by airlines and cruise ships for a number of years (rates have long been based on the customer's willingness to pay), the hospitality industry was relatively slow to capitalize on this concept. With software programs designed specifically for hotels now on the market, however, yield management is becoming an increasingly important tool in determining how to fill rooms for the most profitability.

Today, most hotels constantly monitor their business mix (business travelers, leisure travelers, and the meetings segment) to maximize revenues. They can forecast what rates they want over certain days and determine how much group business they want to see over specific dates.

Fred Shea, Hyatt's Chicago-based vice president of sales, says:

> A ceiling is put in place based on what we think the transient demand will be. But it is constantly being re-evaluated. As we get closer to the group block ceiling, we begin to re-evaluate whether the rate should go up or down, based on the overall demand we are getting.[11]

Savvy meeting planners who know a hotel's target business mix for the days of their meeting can leverage that information in deciding whether to place the business early and be guaranteed their desired meeting space or wait to see if demand falls off and they can get a better rate. They are also aware that past data is the hotel's internal tool for determining how much group business a property wants to sell over particular dates. If their group traditionally has a high profitability, it is looked on as a more favorable piece of business and the planner may be able to negotiate a better rate.

🖥 *INTERNET EXERCISE*

Hospitality Revenue Management Software

IDeaS Revenue Optimization is one of the leading providers of hospitality revenue management software. Its system aids in forecasting and pricing group and meetings business.

Log on to the company's website (www.ideas.com) and click "On-Demand Webinars." Register as a student and use your school as the company name. Click on "Resources" and then "On-Demand Webinars." Watch one of the webinars and report what new insights you have learned about the application of revenue management.

Feel free to chose any webinar topic that interests you, but the following two webinars are excellent, and they specifically relate to the material in this chapter:

- How to Conduct an Effective Revenue Management Meeting for Your Hotel
- Group/Corporate Business—Taking Advantage of This Market Segment

---

Revenue management takes yield management a step further by not only assessing a group's potential for rooms revenue but also looking at the group's projected impact on the property's overall bottom line. Kevin Kowalski, vice president of brand marketing for Atlanta-based Crowne Plaza Hotels & Resorts, says that, with increased demand, hotels need to take a second look at their business mix to increase their profitability. He explains:

> We can concentrate more on getting group business that is better value-related, and less on SMERF [social, military, educational, religious, fraternal] groups, which generate less ancillary revenue.[12]

Revenue management takes into consideration the size of the group, its spending history (not just in terms of rooms, but overall spending at the property's other revenue-producing outlets, such as restaurants and recreational facilities), and future revenues for the hotel (additional bookings by the group and individuals, referrals, and so on).

Case Study:

The Breakers Adopts Automated Sales and Catering System

Founded in 1896 and listed on the National Register of Historic Places, The Breakers Palm Beach is one of America's legendary resort destinations. The 560-room, Italian Renaissance–style hotel is located on 140 acres of oceanfront property in the heart of Palm Beach, Florida. With the commitment of its original owners, The Breakers has invested $250 million over the past two decades in its ongoing revitalization and enhancement of its multi-faceted amenities—most recently, the dramatic transformation of the shoreline into a luxurious beachfront experience.

A Reason for Change

For years, The Breakers Palm Beach relied on its own homegrown management system to manage its sales and catering processes. Jim Mostad, director of sales for the property, acknowledged that the program simply wasn't doing the job anymore. Because a significant percentage of The Breakers' revenue comes from groups and events, the hotel was in need of a solution designed to meet its intensive volume of meeting business. Additionally, the resort's sales, catering, and conference divisions comprised many moving parts that needed to be more organized and efficient while also continuing to provide the superior service the hotel's clients had come to expect.

In short, Mostad and his team needed to bring the resort into the next generation of technology and implement an entirely new sales and catering system. The Breakers chose the Delphi system for automating their sales, marketing, and catering processes, along with the company's Diagrams, a powerful design application that empowers the staff of The Breakers to quickly, easily, and accurately generate customized floor plans for meetings and events.

Mostad says of the change:

> As with any major software transition, the sales and catering team had some trepidation, but only months into the implementation, The Breakers Palm Beach reaped the benefits of the comprehensive system and its helpful reporting capabilities.

Jim Mostad
Director of Sales
The Breakers Palm Beach

Source: Adapted from Newmarket International's website (www.newmarketinc.com). Photographs courtesy of The Breakers.

Real-Time Information Leads to New Revenue Opportunities

The Breakers Palm Beach has seen tremendous productivity increases since the implementation. Response time between catering and sales is much improved, along with returning and customizing RFPs (Request for Proposals). Additionally, a salesperson can send a draft contract to a customer instantaneously, allowing the resort and the customer to review it together. This feature pleases the customer and makes for a speedier process all around.

In addition to managing the day-to-day sales and catering operations, Mostad is excited about the ease in managing revenues using the automated system:

> Knowledge is truly power. Our automated system gives the sales team the information they need to work independently and take action right away. We can now better evaluate the resort's availability, giving us an overall convenience and ease of use we didn't have before. The Breakers can now access how they are doing by market segment at any given time. We now know what was booked and why; moreover, we can accurately assess the implications of taking business or booking an event. Predicting, forecasting, and knowing where the opportunities exist are extremely beneficial to The Breakers' bottom line.
>
> The system allows us to see where we stand, the actual business on the books, and truly have an understanding of where we are right now. This results in better forecasting, better selling strategies, and, ultimately, recognizing new opportunities for our property.

Source: Adapted from Newmarket International's website (www.newmarketinc.com). Photographs courtesy of The Breakers.

Summary

Organizing for sales is essential if a property is to capture its share of the lucrative meetings and convention market. In this chapter, we have discussed how sales are structured on a number of levels. We have detailed the importance of the physical layout of the sales office as well the relationship of the sales department with other property departments that will be involved in servicing a group's business, discussed the various positions within sales, and introduced types of supplementary sales staff, including regional sales offices and independent hotel representatives.

Managing the sales effort at any level involves utilizing a number of forms to successfully follow up on business booked and to ensure successful execution of a group's events. We have looked at a number of these forms, including the function and guestrooms control books, as well as forms that enable salespeople to manage their time and enable them to focus on key accounts. We have also seen how the computer has changed the way in which salespeople do business, making it far easier and more efficient to reach and service their customers.

In many ways, technology has created an impersonal way of doing business. Salespeople benefit from the convenience and option of doing business 24/7, and the Internet is an important tool for prospecting and finding business. However, it is *personal service* that generally distinguishes one salesperson from another. The hospitality business is still a "relationship" business—the personal touch of interacting with meeting planners face-to-face or over the telephone is still the most effective means to book business.

Endnotes

1. Sheraton's Convention and Conference Service Standards Manual.

2. Lalia Rach, Ed.D., "The Current and Future Marketing Professional," *HSMAI Marketing Review.*

3. Peggy Swisher, Andrea Dole, and Michelle Russell, "Driven by the Bottom Line," *PCMA Convene,* June 2007, p. 32.

4. Megan Rowe, "15 Things That Drive You Crazy and What to Do About Them," *Corporate Meetings & Incentives,* October 2003, p. 17.

5. Howard Feiertag, "Educated Sales Effort," *Hotel & Motel Management,* April 7, 2003, p. 16.

6. Courtesy of Hyatt Hotels Corporation Sales Automation System, Datamation.

7. William Duncan, "Booking Streamlined by Next Generation of Hospitality Software," *Convene.*

8. "How Technology Is Refining Hotel Operations," *Convene,* December 1999, p. 124.

9. Beth Rogers, "Working at Home," *HSMAI Marketing Review,* Spring 2000, p. 34.

10. Laura Ross-Fedder, "Computers Empower Swissotel Sales Staff," *Hotel & Motel Management.*

11. Cheryl-Anne Sturken, "As They See It: How Hotels Evaluate Group Business," *Meetings & Conventions,* May 2005, p. 49.

12. Ibid.

 ## Key Terms

account file—A standardized folder holding the information needed to serve a client.

database marketing—The process of using guest folios, registration cards, and group histories of meeting planners to develop relationships and dialogue with customers.

double booking—Reserving space for two groups to use the same space at the same time; neither can be fully accommodated as contracted.

function book—Master control of all banquet space, broken down on each page or screen by banquet rooms, with a page or screen for each day of the year.

guestrooms control book—A book or computer program used to monitor sleeping room allocations to groups.

independent hotel representative—An individual or firm that acts as an addition to the hotel's internal sales staff.

key account management—Prioritizing of accounts based upon their individual profit potential.

master card—An index card that contains a summary of everything needed for a sales effort, including the organization's name, the decision-maker(s), key contacts, addresses, telephone numbers, and so on. Cards may be color-coded to accent key factors. Many properties today use computerized versions of the master card.

option—Meeting space or guestrooms that are reserved by the meeting group but not yet under contract. A hotel extends a right of first refusal to either confirm or release the space if there is demand from another group.

reader file—A file containing copies of internal and external correspondence generated by a salesperson. Useful for reviewing the performance of the sales staff.

regional sales office—Sales offices for chain properties that are located in places other than the property. Help promote and sell individual properties.

relationship marketing—Marketing that views customers as assets and emphasizes retaining customers by nurturing and sustaining relationships with them.

revenue management—The practice of assessing a group's overall profitability on the property's bottom line. Not only is the group's impact on guestrooms and meeting space revenues assessed, but also its spending in other areas (from restaurants to retail) as well as its potential for future business.

standard operating procedures (SOPs)—Written instructions explaining how business activities should be handled.

tickler file—A follow-up file used to remind salespeople of correspondence, telephone calls, sales calls, or other business activities that must be handled on a particular day. A computerized version is commonly used by today's hotel salespeople.

working file—A file set up as soon as a booking is definite, containing information relevant to the event.

yield management—A technique used to maximize the revenue/profit of the hotel by basing prices for guestrooms and banquet space on supply and demand.

Review Questions

1. How is the sales department perceived within the organizational structure of the hotel? Why is it necessary for the sales department to assume authority over other departments?

2. Identify the three departments that the director of sales and his or her staff must work most closely with. Why is it crucial that sales interfaces with these departments?

3. Sketch job descriptions for the various positions within the sales department. How will these vary between large and small properties?

4. What is an independent hotel representative? What considerations are important in choosing an individual or firm to effectively represent your property?

5. What are the key elements of a sales office filing system? Why is each important?

6. Discuss the importance of the function book and guestrooms control book. Why is it important that only one person control these books when a manual system is used?

7. How has computer technology changed the sales office? How is automation being used to enhance the sales effort?

Additional References

Convention Tourism, Karin Weber and Kaye Sung Chon, The Haworth Press, Inc., 2002.

Hospitality Sales: A Marketing Approach, Margaret Shaw and Susan Morris, John Wiley & Sons, 2000.

Journal of Convention and Exposition Management, K. S. Chon, The Haworth Press, Inc. www.haworthpressinc.com

Internet Sites

For more information, visit the following Internet sites. Internet addresses can change without notice. If a site is no longer available at the address listed below, a search engine can be used to find the new address or additional, related sites.

Delphi/Newmarket Software
www.newsoft.com

Delta Hotels
www.4deltahotels.com

Hilton Hotels
www.hilton.com

Hospitality Sales and Marketing Association
   International (HSMAI)
www.hsmai.org, www.revmanagement.org

Hospitality Industry Technology
   Exposition and Conference
www.hitechshow.org

International Association of Hospitality
   Accountants (IAHA)
www.iaha.org

Starwood Hotels
www.starwood.com

Chapter 4 Outline

Competencies

1. Explain the importance of conventions to associations, and identify factors that association meeting planners consider when making a site selection. (pp. 119–122)

2. Describe the different types of association meetings. (pp. 123–129)

3. Identify characteristics of association meetings that are important for selling to the association market. (pp. 130–136)

4. Identify who typically decides where to hold an association meeting and those who may influence that decision. (pp. 136–140)

5. Describe the tools salespeople use to locate associations and to find information about the meetings associations hold. (pp. 140–145)

The Importance of the Association Market

Kathy Dixon Leone
Vice President of Sales
Boca Raton Resort and Club

"The association market provides a tremendous base of business, both in the meetings the market holds, and the meetings it can generate through the exposure a property gains by hosting its corporate membership. If serviced properly, it can provide a base of business that can be the foundation of a property's success for years to come."

4   Selling the Association Market

I N THE FIRST THREE CHAPTERS, we've studied the importance of the convention business and the trends impacting it, the marketing plan—the cornerstone of sales—and the organization and operation of the sales office. In the next three chapters, we will take a look at the major meetings market segments in detail. The two most prominent target markets, the association and corporate meetings segments, will follow a similar outline:

- What planners look for in selecting sites,
- The kinds of meetings held and the characteristics of each type,
- Key decision-makers, and
- How to locate sources for business.

According to a Convention Industry Council study, associations spend more than $81.94 billion a year on meetings (see Exhibit 1). It comes as no surprise, then, that hotel chains such as Fairmont, Four Seasons, Hilton, Hyatt, Marriott, and Starwood have convention properties in major cities and look to association meetings to fill 30–40 percent of their rooms annually. The historic Boca Raton Resort and Club attributes approximately 65 percent of its annual sales volume to groups and meetings; 40 percent of its sales from meetings are realized from the association market. That's a lot of business, and it warrants careful study of the kinds of meetings that associations hold and how you can capture your share of this lucrative market.

Revenue Producers

Its convention is of extreme importance to an **association**. It is the single largest source of associations' non-dues revenue (see box titled "The Principal Sources of an Association's Income"). According to *Convene* magazine's Meetings Market Survey, associations derive

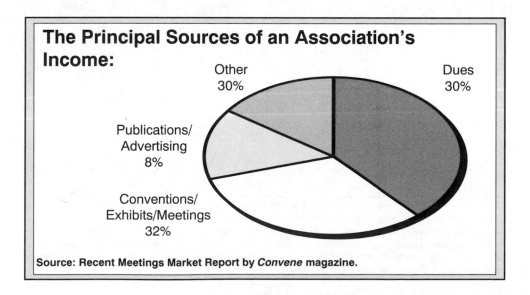

The Principal Sources of an Association's Income:

Other 30%

Dues 30%

Publications/ Advertising 8%

Conventions/ Exhibits/Meetings 32%

Source: Recent Meetings Market Report by *Convene* magazine.

Exhibit 1   Associations Are the Most Visible Convention Organizers

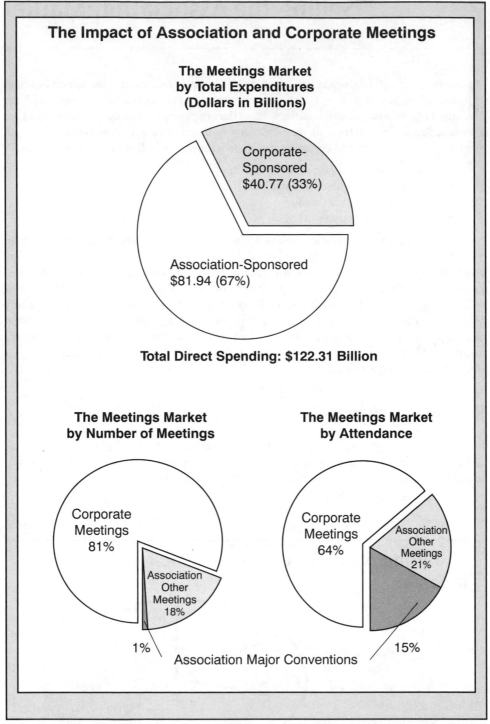

The Impact of Association and Corporate Meetings

The Meetings Market
by Total Expenditures
(Dollars in Billions)

Corporate-
Sponsored
$40.77 (33%)

Association-Sponsored
$81.94 (67%)

Total Direct Spending: $122.31 Billion

The Meetings Market
by Number of Meetings

Corporate
Meetings
81%

Association
Other
Meetings
18%

1%

The Meetings Market
by Attendance

Corporate
Meetings
64%

Association
Other
Meetings
21%

15%

Association Major Conventions

While corporations provide a larger market in total number of attendees and meetings, the spending of associations is approximately twice that of corporations. The principal reason for this difference in spending is that associations generally include a trade show as part of their conventions.
Source: Updated from *The Economic Impact of Conventions, Expositions, Meetings and Incentive Travel Study* conducted by the Conventions Industry Council and a recent Meeting Market Report by *Meetings & Conventions* magazine.

about 32 percent of their annual income from conventions and exhibitions. Membership dues range from twenty-five dollars or so to several thousand dollars annually in more affluent associations, but almost every association views its convention, meetings, and exhibits as prime sources of revenue.

Associations earn money from conventions in several ways. One is with exhibits. The group may rent the exhibit hall of a hotel or convention center for one to three dollars per square foot, depending on demand and season. The association then subleases the space to exhibitors for considerably more—up to fifty dollars per square foot in some cases.

Registration fees at such events also add to the association's coffers. When a convention "package" includes a number of meal functions, it is not uncommon for the package to cost the delegate several hundred dollars. The hotel is paid only for the actual number of meal tickets collected or the number of meals the meeting planner guarantees, which adds more to the profits of the convention, since not every person attends every event.

Associations earn additional money from the advertising in their publications and programs. And when a participating company sponsors a segment of the program and picks up the tab, the association's costs are further reduced.

Thus, when you consider how important conventions are to membership retention and to revenue production, it becomes apparent that these events are absolutely essential for the well-being of an association. They constitute a major effort on an association's part, and they are planned and conducted as such.

Requirements for Association Meetings

Site selection is crucial to the success of a convention. Mike Welch, executive director of the Credit Union Executives Society of Madison, Wisconsin, has said:

> We look for good facilities, pleasant weather, an attractive location, and a city that's near the largest concentration of members. We also consider who else is going to be there and when. For instance, when our annual convention is taking place in a city, we don't want to go there for a seminar for a year or two.

Exhibit 2 details some of the other factors that meeting planners take into consideration when making a site selection. These considerations include:

- *Adequate meeting space.* The organizer is always concerned about your ability to house the general assembly and smaller sessions. He or she is interested in space for workshops and committee meetings, as well as your ability to handle food functions expertly without encroaching on the meetings.

- *Enough guestrooms.* We don't know a single convention organizer who doesn't prefer to house the entire group in one hotel. Suites are needed in addition to singles, twins, and doubles. When a single hotel can't house the entire group, two or more hotels in close proximity are the most desirable.

- *Adequate exhibit space.* Exhibits mean money for the association and are an attraction for the members. Planners look for adequate exhibit space, located conveniently to housing. Hotels with exhibit facilities have an advantage. When larger exhibits require exhibition halls, the preference is for setups near

Exhibit 2   Factors Considered Important to Association Meeting Planners in the Selection of a Facility/Hotel

Association Planners

Factors Considered Very Important	Major Conventions	Association Meetings
Number, size, quality of meeting rooms	90%	67%
Negotiable food, beverage, and room rates	84	70
Cost of hotel or meeting facility	83	76
Number, size, and quality of sleeping rooms	78	59
Quality of food service	70	61
Availability of meeting support services and equipment, such as AV equipment	54	43
Availability of exhibit space	53	28
Efficiency of billing procedures	50	52
Previous experience in dealing with facility and its staff	49	40
High-speed Internet access	47	46
Assignment of one staff person to handle all aspects of meeting	46	45
Efficiency of check-in and check-out procedures	42	39
Meeting rooms with multiple high-speed phone lines and computer outlets	38	38
Proximity to shopping, restaurants, and off-site entertainment	28	19

Source: Recent Meetings Market Report by *Meetings & Conventions* magazine.

Although the purpose of a meeting ultimately determines the facility selection criteria, this exhibit gives insight into general factors of importance to the association meeting planner. Negotiable rates and costs continue to be an important aspect of hotel selection for conventions and meetings.

the hotel. Delegates prefer not to travel between hotel rooms and convention areas.

• *An attractive location.* A location need not be a resort to attract different groups. Chicago gets lots of business because of its central location. That's very important to many busy groups.

   Other groups may like to combine the show with other business. Your city may be in the heart of their business world. Attendance is also easier to stimulate if people don't have to travel too far. Easy driving distance may mean an extra ten percent registration. Many associations do like resort locations. You may be able to offer that, or perhaps you are located in great tourist country. Put simply, you have to offer something attractive to each group. It might be the draw of your city or destination, or your proximity to a major airport, or your reputation for superior customer service.

• *Service.* Last, but probably most important, the meeting planners look for service. They want some assurance that you have an experienced staff that is interested in doing a good job. Each convention event is a custom job and many things can go wrong. Convention planners live with such hazards and justly feel that your staff should have the expertise and the desire to keep the show moving. Service is what brings repeat and recommended business.

Guest satisfaction is a major concern of meeting planners. This photograph from Shangri-La Hotels and Resorts emphasizes the chain's "Service with a Smile" promise.
Source: Photograph courtesy of Shangri-La Hotels and Resorts.

Kinds of Association Meetings

The first kind of association meeting to come to mind is the *annual convention.* Certainly this is the most visible, and the largest, but there are many other occasions for associations to meet. For example, lots of planning is required in staging a convention, and *board and committee meetings* are often scheduled for this very purpose, as well as at other times for many other purposes; these meetings may require a meeting room at a hotel property. In addition, *state and regional conventions, conferences, seminars, and workshops* are conducted throughout the year by most associations (see Exhibit 3). These are all sources of good business for hotels. It is a rare property that cannot handle some kind of association business. You may not necessarily be able to handle the major events but there are many others that you can service.

Annual Conventions

Almost every association has an annual convention. The annual convention is a ritual in associations of all types—international, national, regional, and state.

Attendance varies, of course (see box detailing "Delegate Attendance at Annual Convention"). Some conventions are truly huge affairs. The Chemical Society draws between 20,000 and 30,000; others have fewer than 100. The mean attendance is about 1,500 people. Conventions vary only in scale, maintaining similar philosophies and motivations.

Since 60 percent of all national meetings and trade shows have an average attendance of 300 or less, even small properties can take advantage of this lucrative market. And, small

Exhibit 3   Summary of Types of Association Meetings Other Than Major Conventions

Type of Meeting	Total Meetings	Average # Planned	Average Attendance	Average # Days Duration	Average # of Months Lead Time
Board Meetings	68,100	3.4	28	1.8	5.6
Training/Educational Seminars	56,800	9.5	119	21	7.0
Professional/Technical	40,900	4.6	163	23	7.1
Regional/Local Chapters	27,200	6.5	153	1.9	6.1
Other Meetings	34,000	5.6	507	3.3	9.9
Total/Average	527,000	15.5	146	2.0	7.1

The average association meeting planner works on over 15 meetings per year.
Source: Recent Meetings Market Report by *Meetings & Conventions* magazine.

properties can benefit from the large conventions by making arrangements with neighboring properties to handle overflow business generated by large groups.

Exhibits are a major part of association meetings, especially trade and technical societies. Two-thirds of the annual association conventions are held in conjunction with a trade show or exhibit. These conventions attract an average of 265 exhibitors using an average of 56,000 square feet of exhibit space. Exhibits are a source of essential income to associations, and very important to exhibitors, too.

There are conventions without exhibits, of course, and it is also not unheard of for a convention to stage a major program with exhibits in one hotel and another program without exhibits in another. Sometimes an event may be held in a city because of the presence of another convention with an exhibit.

Most conventions include a **general session** (also called a plenary session) attended by everyone, along with a number of smaller meetings. These smaller meetings are often termed **breakout sessions**, where the group divides into smaller meetings, and **concurrent sessions**, where meeting sessions on different topics are scheduled at the same time.

Delegate Attendance at Annual Convention	% of Associations
Fewer than 100	32%
100–149	6
150–299	22
300–900	17
1000+	23
	100%

Average delegate attendance: Male   830
                                                    Female   610
                                                                   1440

Source: Recent Meetings Market Report by *Meetings & Conventions* magazine.

Re-Branding Conference Centers

Dolce Seaview Resort

In 1981, Andy Dolce founded Dolce International, which would grow into a chain of 26 unique properties in the United States, Canada, and Europe. Committed to an environment that reflected his clients' need for environments that inspire creativity and learning, Dolce elevated the meeting and conference model, offering luxury services not found in typical conference centers and pioneering the Complete Meeting Package (CMP), which offers assistance to meeting planners with all the details of their meetings at an all-inclusive package price.

Each of the unique properties in the chain is geared toward business travelers, with wireless high-speed Internet access in meeting rooms, public spaces, and guestrooms; a 24/7 technology help desk; fully equipped business centers; and in-room business amenities; but each also provides upscale guestroom amenities, such as luxury bed linens and pillows, fine dining restaurants, and fitness facilities that range from spas to championship golf courses. Teambuilding/group activities can also be included in a group's agenda.

Despite the special services and amenities offered at the chain's properties, meeting planners felt the term "conference center" was too confusing — they thought of conference centers in terms of meeting space only. In response to focus groups held with planners, Dolce International became Dolce Hotels and Resorts in 2008. This change enabled the chain to more accurately reflect the services and amenities offered to hotel guests — and it was also adopted to appeal to leisure and transient business as well as the meetings market.

Dolce Hayes Mansion Banquet Setup

Conference centers typically capture a mere 10–11 percent share of the meetings market business, while approximately 90 percent of this segment opts for hotels and resorts when booking meetings. Dolce says:

> We've been fighting for that 90 percent the last 20 years. We figured it is best to join them, to change our image and call ourselves hotels and resorts. Our tagline is, "Meet with Inspiration."

Meetings are still the chain's core business (eighty percent of its $350 million revenue is meetings-related). The company's goal, however, is a 70/30 percent business/leisure mix with a higher level of occupancy, and the chain also has plans to double in size over the next five years. The first addition will be a $70 million conference hotel and resort in Munich, Germany.

Sources: Roger Carey, "Seizing the Moment," *Successful Meetings*, **May 2009, p. 34; photographs courtesy of Dolce Hotels and Resorts.**

Sometimes, the general session runs concurrently with the exhibit hours; sometimes they run in tandem so as not to compete for members' attention.

It is a rare convention without food functions. Many groups sell a complete convention package for their event. The package includes registration fees and prepaid tickets to all food functions and special events.

You can see at this point that a convention, especially a large one, calls for a number of rooms of different kinds. Large rooms are needed for the general assembly, the exhibit, and the food functions; smaller rooms for committee and board meetings, workshops, and smaller food functions; and suites and similar rooms for hospitality centers.

Often a hotel cannot handle an entire convention because of its size, so several hotels may band together to sell an association as a team. The hotel business is odd in that strong competitors often become partners in a project, and both can enjoy additional business as a result. Even a piece of a convention event may be profitable, as well as giving the hotel a foot in the door for future business.

There is another variation of the national convention—the exhibit without convention program. These events, often called *exhibitions*, *expositions*, or *trade shows*, sometimes are not even sponsored by an association but by individual entrepreneurs or companies. These events can bring you business even if you cannot house the exhibit itself. Many an exhibition becomes the focal point of the industry or trade it serves and gives exhibitors the opportunity to hold sales meetings and dealer meetings in conjunction with the event.

Things You Can Count on When Meeting at a Dolce Hotel or Resort
• **Package pricing.** Each property offers a package plan that includes conference rooms, guestrooms, three meals, continuous refreshment service, conference services, and basic conference technology.
• **Skilled conference planners.** A designated conference planner is assigned to each group.
• **Ergonomic seating.** Dolce has precise standards for chair seat width and depth, height adjustment, upholstery, casters, and other factors.
• **Comfortable writing surfaces.** Table specs include non-reflective, hard writing surfaces —and they must be long enough to allow at least 30 inches of space per occupant. Draped, skirted banquet tables are not acceptable.
• **Continuous refreshment service.** Refreshment stations are located outside meeting rooms.
• **Technology support.** Skilled technicians are available on site for immediate response.
• **Secure storage.** Groups that have multi-day meetings can safely store their materials and equipment in the conference room overnight.

State and Regional Conventions

While the national or international association convention is the prize for large hotels, the state and regional convention can be targeted by hotel properties of all sizes (see Exhibit 4).

The major difference between a regional convention of a national organization and one staged by a state or regional association is sponsorship. A state association usually holds an annual meeting for its members within the state, although in recent years state organizations have ventured beyond state borders on occasion. Many national associations, even those with affiliated state chapters, hold regional conventions to supplement their national ones. Of interest is the recent growth in regional association meetings. When finances are short, many association members skip the big annual conventions, and attend smaller, shorter meetings that are closer to home. As a rule, the regional event is smaller than the national one both in attendance and size of the exhibit. Again, some regional conventions have exhibits and others don't. There is no rule of thumb.

Exhibit 4   State and Regional Association Market at a Glance

State and Regional Association Market at a Glance

Location

This segment of the association market is usually an offshoot of the national or international association. Groups usually rotate their convention among the major cities within the state or region and rely heavily upon local support for invitation. They meet four to six months before or after their affiliated national convention.

Facilities

Preferred facilities include free and ample parking, as a high percentage of attendees drive. Access to public transportation is not critical; therefore, suburban hotels are often used. Most conventions require ballrooms for plenary sessions or banquets as well as several breakout rooms for seminars.

Price

Double occupancy is common, so hotels should consider a flat rate, perhaps a compromise between the single and double rates. Attendance is voluntary, so the decision-maker is price-sensitive. They often will schedule their meetings during a hotel's off-periods and will schedule a Thursday arrival/ Sunday departure or Friday arrival/ Sunday departure.

Services

Preferred services include business services such as fax machines, office copiers, typing, and word processing. Other services include audiovisual equipment necessary for presentations and occasionally exhibit halls for table-top exhibits.

Decision-Makers

These groups usually do not have a paid staff or a permanent office, but rather are administered by volunteers and committees on a part-time basis. The local chapters frequently submit bids or invitations to host a regional or state meeting. Because volunteer staff changes annually, it is important to actively solicit and update files frequently to determine decision-makers.

Best Ways to Reach Market

Check the yellow pages under "Associations" in all major cities (most are headquartered in a capital city due to lobbying efforts). Most states have an affiliate of the American Society of Association Executives (ASAE) and publish a list of their members. Local convention and visitors bureaus and chambers of commerce will normally supply a listing of professional associations in their area. Personal contacts and direct mail are the most effective means to reach the decision-makers.

The major difference, as far as hotel people are concerned, has to do with who makes the decisions about when and where the event will be held. The sidebar titled "State and Regional Association Planners Cite the Top Ten Attributes for Convention Site Selection" details some of the factors important in site selection. State and regional conventions are an important source of business for both large and small hotel properties (see Exhibit 5).

According to the *Association Meeting Trends* report, only ten percent of all state and regional conventions had an attendance of more than 1,000; 75 percent had less than 500 attendees, making this an ideal market for smaller properties.

Since chapters of national associations meet within the state or regional boundaries, it is a market that can be reached relatively easily. Sources for locating state and regional business include:

- Chambers of commerce and convention and visitors bureaus.
- The Yellow Pages of telephone directories for capital cities.
- Newspapers from capital cities or feeder cities.
- The American Society of Association Executives (ASAE). Hotel salespeople can join such groups as the Washington Society of Association Executives (WSAE) or the California Society of Association Executives (CSAE) as allied members.

State and Regional Association Planners Cite the Top Ten Attributes for Convention Site Selection		
Attribute	**Percent**	**Rank**
Proximity of hotel to meeting facility	71.4	1
Capacity of meeting rooms	65.6	2
Hotel cleanliness	62.8	3
Number of meeting rooms	61.6	4
Quality of food and beverage	59.8	5
Banquet space	59.0	6
Complimentary meeting space	57.3	7
Meeting room rates	56.7	8
Friendliness of hotel personnel	56.7	9
Problem-solving skills of hotel personnel	56.4	10

Source: Jeong-Ja Choi, Ph.D., and Carl A. Boger, Jr., Ph.D., "State Association Market: Relationships Between Association Characteristics and Site Selection Criteria," *Journal of Convention & Exhibition Management*, The Hawthorne Press, Inc.

Once a group has been located, it is important to remember that in many cases the meeting planners may be committees or inexperienced planners and that lead time is usually fairly short. A property that shows a willingness to assist with meeting planning will gain an edge over the competition.

Another way to solicit this market's business, which is an important source of revenue for off-peak periods, is to offer inexpensive room rates. Many attendees pay their own expenses, making room rates especially important to them. And, because spouses usually attend, a property that offers a single/double occupancy flat rate for these groups is especially attractive to this lucrative market.

Conferences

Associations have become frequent stagers of conferences, primarily to supplement the annual convention program with a specific program made timely by new developments. The recent debates over stem cell research and national health care, for example, precipitated a number of conferences.

The number of conferences held within an industry varies, of course. They have become commonplace in the technical, scientific, and professional worlds. A breakthrough in an electronic process or medical treatment, or a change in corporate law or tax structure brings on a rash of conferences.

Seminars and Workshops

Closely allied to the conference, but on a more modest basis, is the seminar. Association seminars are usually tied in with training and continuing education, such as the training of apprentice craftsmen, the updating of scientific and engineering personnel, or the presentation of marketing developments within an industry. Such seminars are presented around the country to small groups. Such business is within the scope of almost any hotel property.

Exhibit 5   Marketing to State and Regional Associations

The Bavarian Inn Lodge & Conference Center in Frankenmuth, Michigan, America's largest Bavarian-themed resort, is located in the heart of Michigan's "Little Bavaria." The property targets the statewide and regional conference market by promoting its meeting amenities, on-site facilities, and proximity to local attractions.

Board and Committee Meetings

Association business regularly calls for smaller meetings. The board of directors may meet on a regular basis, not necessarily in the city of the association office. These meetings are often set in attractive locales as a way of encouraging outstanding people to serve, since they are not paid. Attendance at board meetings may range from ten to twelve to up to two hundred. The hotel chosen for such meetings is in a prime position to sell the property for the national convention, and for business emanating from the board members' own organizations.

Committee meetings may range in size from ten to fifty people and are held at varying rates of frequency. These events, too, can be serviced by hotels of any size as long as they are geared for meetings.

Characteristics of Association Meetings

Association meetings of all types follow similar patterns; understanding these patterns will help you sell them intelligently.

Cycle and Pattern

Conventions are held on a regular time cycle. The most common is annual, although about ten percent of associations hold two conventions a year and there are some that convene only every two years. The one-year cycle is often supplemented in a national organization with one, two, or even three regional conventions on a smaller scale.

Conventions most frequently begin on Sunday and run through Wednesday or begin on Thursday and check out on Sunday (see Exhibit 6). The reason for this pattern is the airfare savings realized with a Saturday night stayover. These Saturday night stayovers, required by most airlines to qualify for reduced airfares, have boosted the occupancies of many downtown hotels that previously saw weekends as their slowest periods. Meetings and conventions that previously began on Mondays have moved registration to Sundays whenever possible so attendees can take advantage of the lower airfares. Exhibit 7 shows Marriott's attempt to secure Sunday registrations.

Exhibit 6   Monthly and Daily Meeting Pattern of Associations

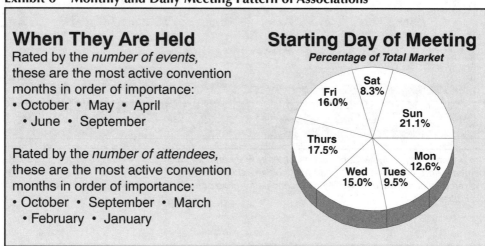

Source: By permission of *Successful Meetings* magazine.

A strong geographic pattern is also indicated. Jeff Sacks, CMP, an executive with Experient, the world's largest meeting management company, states:

> A smart organization will rotate its annual convention across the map. This strategy not only allows you to meet in all regions where your membership is based, but it also benefits membership growth and recruitment in addition to keeping the meeting fresh in terms of climate, attractions, time zones, and cost of attending.[1]

Most associations alternate between the East and West in site selection. The most popular variation calls for a Midwestern city every two years, with eastern and western cities alternating during the other two years. Typical examples follow:

	2010	2011	2012	2013	2014
National Conventions					
ABC Assn.	New York	Los Angeles	Washington	Denver	Boston
XYZ Assn.	Chicago	New York	St. Louis	Las Vegas	Milwaukee
Regional Conventions					
ABC Assn.	San Diego	Atlanta	Phoenix	Miami	San Francisco
	Cleveland	Kansas City	Cincinnati	St. Louis	New Orleans
XYZ Assn.	Los Angeles	Dallas	Philadelphia	Boston	Miami
	Atlanta	Seattle	San Diego	Detroit	Los Angeles

The important factor is the area of the country, not the specific city. The pattern may call for a Midwest location, which could be St. Louis, Chicago, Cincinnati, or other cities in the Midwest. The Southeast could be served with Atlanta, Miami, Tampa, or Memphis. In Canada, Toronto, Quebec, and Halifax might be considered if the group is considering an eastern location. Much depends on the geographic interests of the association members. If

Exhibit 7 Capturing Sunday Meetings Business

Convention start and end dates are an important factor for hotel profitability. A Tuesday–Thursday convention, for example, is problematic for many hotels. To maximize revenues, hotels seek to book groups arriving on Sunday and checking out on Wednesday, and groups checking in on Wednesday and departing on Sunday. Sunday arrivals are especially important to city hotels, which traditionally see Sunday as the lowest occupancy day of the week. David Horowitz, of the Hyatt Regency Century Plaza in Los Angeles, states: "A Sunday arrival is much more valuable to us than a Tuesday arrival."
Sources: Tom Isher, "The Ugly Meeting," *Meetings & Conventions*, **October 2006, p. 8. Photo courtesy of Marriott Portland Downtown Waterfront.**

there is no special interest factor, the site selectors attempt to provide an interesting place to serve as an additional attraction. Exhibit 8 shows how hotels in three different geographic areas have teamed up to attract meeting planners who must rotate their locations.

Exhibit 8   Hotels Team Up to Offer Diverse Locations for Association Meetings

Because associations generally rotate convention sites throughout the country, a joint marketing effort can be an excellent way to capture association business. A geographically diverse collaboration has paid off for three cities' convention and visitors bureaus — Visit Pittsburgh (www.visitpittsburgh.com), Travel Portland [Oregon] (www.travelportland.com), and Visit Milwaukee (www.visitmilwaukee.org) — who offer the advantage of a cost savings for a multi-year contract as well as favorable geographic locations. The partner cities offer a discount to planners booking in Pittsburgh, Portland, and Milwaukee in a multi-year deal.

Craig Davis, vice president of sales and marketing for Visit Pittsburgh, says, "The customer base is associations who tend to rotate meetings around the country. The whole basis for this working is that the cities have to be similar in size, share a customer base, and rarely compete with each other."
Source: Maxine Golding, "Groups Reap Benefits of Bureau Collaborations," *Experient Meeting Mentor***, Fall 2008, p. 1.**

The scheduling of regional events calls for a frank recognition that some members will not travel too far for the event. One association executive told us that his records show a hard core of regulars come to the convention every year no matter where it is held. This group is supplemented by members who come from within three hundred miles. Obviously, he holds regional conventions to keep his members involved. Perusal of the meeting pattern should show you when the group would next consider your part of the country.

Geographic Restrictions

Many state organizations, as part of their constitutions, have limited site selections to within their own states. This is also true of regional associations. There may be further restrictions because of the narrow interests of the program or the nature of the association's business.

There has been some deviation from such rigid limitations in recent years. One device that association executives have used to break out of the pattern is a reciprocal agreement with another state organization. Thus a Colorado chapter might meet in Massachusetts one year and the Massachusetts chapter would meet in Colorado. This satisfies the political aspects of catering to local businesses while providing a novel site to stimulate attendance.

Lead Time

Association conventions are planned well in advance, with a **lead time** of two to five years the norm for conventions, a lead time of one and a half to two years for state and regional events, and somewhat less than a year for other types of association meetings. Even decisions finalized two years in advance are the result of research and discussion that took up to five years. The larger the convention, the greater the lead time. Meeting planners are well aware that every hotel is not suitable for their convention. They want time to visit the site, check with past clients, and check other alternatives before making the decision.

This long lead time can be frustrating for the new hotel or the new hotel sales manager, but it is the pattern for association conventions. And the clear pattern enables you to decide when you can best propose your property to have the best chance of success.

Kinds of Sites

Association business does not all go to the same kind of property. This is hardly surprising, considering the many kinds of associations and societies and the many types of meeting events they hold. Requirements and preferences could scarcely be expected to be uniform, but it is a rare hotel property that cannot serve some sort of association event.

Meetings are held in various types of facilities, depending on the size, nature, and duration of meetings. Types of meeting facilities commonly used by associations include downtown hotels, airport hotels, suburban hotels, resorts, convention centers, conference centers, college/university campuses, and the association's headquarters (see box titled "Types of Facilities Used").

The kind of site selected generally reflects the group size, degree of sophistication, and members' affluence. Obviously, a 200-room hotel would not be considered for a 500-person convention, unless it is in cooperation with other hotels. The basic requirements must be met—an auditorium for the main assembly, exhibit space if needed, support rooms for committees' and exhibitors' meetings.

Types of Facilities Used		
	For Conventions	For Other Association Meetings
Downtown hotels	62%	68%
Resort hotels (not including golf resorts)	24%	36%
Suburban hotels	15%	36%
Suite hotels	12%	13%
Airport hotels	8%	22%
Golf resorts	7%	14%
Gaming facilities	5%	5%
Residential conference centers	3%	9%
Nonresidential conference centers	1%	6%
Cruise ships	1%	3%

Association planners prefer downtown hotels. Average room rate paid by association attendees is $172. Two-thirds of major association conventions involve exhibits, utilizing an average of 56,000 square feet. Note: Totals exceed 100% due to multiple responses.
Source: Recent Meetings Market Report by *Meetings & Conventions* magazine.

We have discussed geographic considerations. Add to that ease of transportation and how important the association executive thinks that is. It is hard, for example, to find a more accessible place than the hotels near O'Hare Airport at Chicago. If the executive believes that such a site would draw more attendance, he or she may choose it.

There are other geographic factors involved. Many convention organizers want the vacation element working for them. How many extra registrations can a site such as Toronto or Las Vegas or Colorado Springs draw? That's the name of the game. There are many ways to enliven a regularly scheduled convention. Good, stimulating programming is the ideal way, but it's very hard to execute. It is often easier to stage the event at a lovely resort and keep your people happy by exposing them to "the good life."

Downtown properties are commonly used for association meetings.
Source: Photograph courtesy of Hyatt Regency, Calgary, Canada.

Sports also play a role in site selection. Golf, tennis, swimming, and boating are factors considered by convention planners as they analyze their people. Some fervent golfers on the board may very well swing the decision to a property with a famous course and favorable climate.

Voluntary Attendance

It should be clear by now that the association convention planner has to *attract* members to the annual event. One might think that business and professional interests would suffice as a magnet. Undoubtedly they do draw a certain number, but there are an indeterminate number of fence-sitters. Should they go this year or should they skip it? This is where site attraction plays such an important role, and the meeting planner is aware of it.

The option to attend is the member's own. He or she may demand that both business needs and vacation desires be satisfied. If your property or region has tourist attractions, you should make sure that these are all part of your presentation. Whether it is the opera at the Lincoln Center or shopping at Saks Fifth Avenue in the Big Apple, exploring the winding streets of Quebec City (the only fortified city in North America), or white-water rafting in Vancouver, British Columbia, a hotel's attraction is more than just its decor and facilities. Learn what positive aspects of your property you can project. Sales may depend on it.

As a bonus, records show that spouses come too when the site is attractive. That results in double-occupancy revenues and longer stays. Vacations with tax-deductible expenditures also help turn out the members.

Convention Duration

The average duration of a convention is three to five days (see Exhibit 9). This is generally true for national events, although smaller affairs may last only two or three days. Seminars, committee meetings, and the like can last just a day or two. Most conventions with exhibits meet no fewer than three days. There is quite a lot of additional business to be picked up

Exhibit 9   Average Duration of Association Meetings

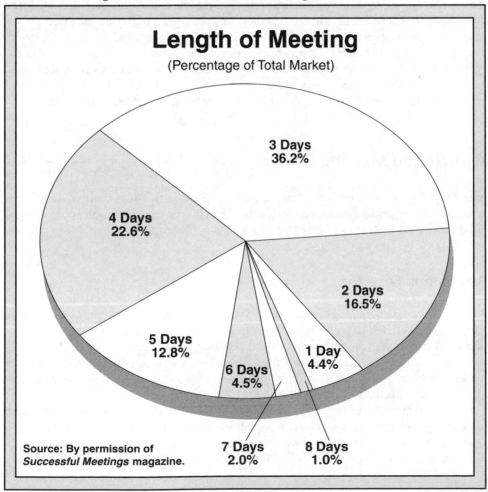

Length of Meeting
(Percentage of Total Market)

3 Days 36.2%
4 Days 22.6%
2 Days 16.5%
5 Days 12.8%
1 Day 4.4%
6 Days 4.5%
7 Days 2.0%
8 Days 1.0%

Source: By permission of *Successful Meetings* magazine.

as a result of such conventions, as many exhibiting firms hold sales meetings just before the event. This is true, too, for the association's board of directors and many committees. Look also for small associations among delegate groups who meet each year at the major convention.

Price

Your rate schedule is an important consideration for the association executive. We refer to your guestroom rates, not so much to your charges for meeting rooms, food functions, etc., although they will be reflected in the overall registration fee and charges for individual events. Guestroom rates must be aligned with the kind of people expected to attend. This is where the full range of hotels comes into play.

Many a convention organizer sticks with the traditional downtown hotels because of price. The older properties, built years ago at lower costs and lower mortgages, often can offer lower rates. That means nothing to some associations. But to others, it can mean the difference between choosing your property and rejecting it. Price can be a factor. Keep in mind that it is not always the most important one, even though it is always brought up.

Here, too, some study of where the group has met will help. If its history discloses successful years at places such as the Fairmont in San Francisco, the Plaza in New York, and the Four Seasons in Ottawa, you can feel pretty sure that the convention organizer wants the best places for his or her people and that they are accustomed to paying the price. On the other hand, one convention organizer told us that her people were middle-level employees who traditionally paid their own way to the convention. When she booked at a more expensive place, she invariably received an increased number of complaints from members.

There is no right price level. It must suit the group you are trying to sell. Or, more accurately, it must suit the picture the association executive has of his or her people.

Association Meeting Decision-Makers

Selection of the convention site—both city and hotel—is a two-step process. The first is screening all suggestions and solicitations; the second is the final approval. We have separated the two because not all people are active in both phases.

Association Director

Almost every association has a permanent executive person. The title may be executive secretary, executive vice president, or executive director. Usually, he or she is the administrator of the association, and a very important person to hotel people.

Your sales effort starts with this decision-maker. A well-run sales staff of a hotel or convention bureau will treasure a file on each association and its key people; the list always starts with the executive director (see Exhibit 10).

The executive director is a key person for the initial screening of suitable convention sites and swings great influence over the final selection as well (see box titled "Executive Directors Speak Out About How Sites Decisions Are Made"). After all, this executive enjoys a continuity in office that the elected officials do not have. The elected officials may

Exhibit 10   Typical Job Titles of Association Decision-Makers

Job Title	Association Planners
Executive Director/Conventions/Conference Planner/ Coordinator/Manager/Director	43%
President/Executive Vice President	20
Meeting Planner/Coordinator/Manager/Director	8
Assistant to Executive	1
Treasurer	3
Director of Education	3
Marketing Director/Coordinator/Officer	1
Board Member/Program Director/Member Services	1
Other	20
Total	100%

Source: Recent Meetings Market Report by *Meetings & Conventions* magazine.

serve for a year or two and then pass on the reins to the next team. But the executive director continues in office, and does so with the backing of the key members of the association.

The executive director doesn't work alone, however, especially in larger organizations. Since most of the administrative work has nothing to do with the convention activities, the executive director often has a staff member specifically assigned to convention planning. In the largest organization, this person may have a staff as well. This convention planner thus is another person you should consider as very important when you make your presentation. He or she reports to and works closely with the executive director. Often the executive appoints a site selection committee to do **site inspections**. This group visits cities and hotels and is responsible for securing convention space arrangements for the association.

Executive Directors Speak Out About How Site Decisions Are Made

Garis Distelhorst, National Association of College Stores:
"Our process is collaborative. The meetings staff screens proposals and prepares a list of four or five cities. At that point, my role is to determine if there are any that wouldn't work and to suggest any destination not on the list that we might want to do additional research on. We try to follow an East/West/Central rotation. We focus on second-tier cities that are going to treat our meeting as a big deal."

Ron Moen, American Association of Orthodontists:
"Preliminary screening is the responsibility of the director of meetings. Actual site reviews of two or three cities on the short list are conducted by the director, myself, and the member of the board who will be president in the year that the meeting will be held. A committee of the board rubber-stamps our recommendation...when it's unanimous."

Dan Weder, Institute of Food Technologists:
"The recommendation comes to me. I visit cities in the running and make the site decision. While it ultimately goes to the executive committee for approval, in 30 years they've never failed to ratify a selection."

Source: Drs. J. Dana Clark, Catherine Price, and Suzanne Murrmann, "Collaborative 'Buying Centers': How Associations Choose Destinations," *Convene*.

Small associations that cannot afford a full-time executive may choose to hire the services of **association management companies**. These organizations function as the executive and office staff for a number of associations that otherwise would have to make do with volunteers. In this way the associations enjoy professional management at costs they can afford.

There are approximately 500 association management companies in business today, managing the affairs of over 800 national associations and more than 1,000 state and regional associations.

If an association employs an association management company, you may find yourself dealing with one man or woman responsible for several convention bookings. The advantage to you is that when selling to these organizations you are not talking about a group coming back in four or five years. One of their clients may be interested in your property later in the same year. Many of these management organizations specialize in one or two industries. If your hotel's history shows a concentration of certain types of associations, such as automotive or computer groups, it would be wise to link with those association management organizations that represent these types of associations.

The trade association representing association management organizations is called the Association Management Companies Institute (www.amcinstitute.org). This group holds an annual meeting and trade show, and is an ideal target market for smaller lodging properties.

There are independent companies that fill this role as well. The Alliance of Meeting Management Companies (www.ammc.org) and the Independent Meeting Planners Association of Canada (www.impca.canada.com) are two examples of independent companies.

🖥 *INTERNET EXERCISE*

Multiple-Association Management Companies

 Many small associations cannot afford a full-time association executive to manage their groups. These smaller associations, therefore, often contract with a multiple-association management company that will serve each association as needed, including selecting convention sites and planning conventions at an affordable cost.

These multiple-association management firms have organized their own trade association, the Association Management Companies Institute. Log on to their website (www.amcinstitute.org) to answer the following questions:

1. What is an association management company and who do these companies serve?

2. What specific services does the AMC Institute offer to its members?

3. Are hotels allowed to join the organization as associate members?

SmithBucklin Chairman & CEO Henry S. Givray speaks to executive Boot Camp participants about leadership.

Next, log on to the websites of Talley Management Group, Inc. (www.talley.com) and SmithBucklin (www.smithbucklin.com), two of the largest multiple-association management companies, to answer the following questions:

1. Approximately how many associations does each represent?

2. What services does each provide?

Convention management companies work either for a negotiated fee or a percentage of the registration fees as an incentive to stimulate attendance. Such management firms obviously are important. They influence site selection and are also the people who work with the hotels to execute the meeting.

Association President and Officers

The power of the president varies greatly among associations. As mentioned, the president usually serves for a year or two. He or she may serve as an honorary figurehead or may flex a great deal of muscle. You really have no choice but to pay a lot of attention to this key person. In almost all cases, keep in mind that he or she shares in the initial screening of a selection site and is certainly in on the final decision.

When you build your files on association personnel, take notes on the vice presidents and secretary/treasurers as well. Many of these officers are future years' presidents. A recent study suggests:

> It is not uncommon in associations to have a new chairperson every year. Often, this chairperson has substantial power over staff and other members....Such power may include the ability to affect the list of sites initially being considered and one that is eventually chosen as the convention location in the future. Because of the lead time necessary to plan major conventions or trade shows, many of these meeting sites are picked years in advance. At the same time, many associations also know in advance who the association president will be in any given year. Either tradition or bylaws regulate much of the decision power on site selection to the person who will be president during the year of a particular convention. Therefore, marketing strategies not only need to be aimed at the current chair or president, they need to identify and court future leaders. A long-term relationship between the hospitality marketer and the association chair(s)-to-be can impact how they use their influence in your favor for the year they are in power.[2]

Committee Chairperson

Certain committee heads get involved in the initial suggestions and screening. This depends on the nature and structure of the organization and the subject of the event. They most definitely are a factor in site selection for seminars dealing with the committee's subject matter.

You can see that a fair number of hands get involved in creating the original list of proposed places and in the preliminary screening to narrow down the choices. If you are eliminated in the final selection, it may mean loss of business that year, but you may well be in line for

---

Profile of Association Meeting Planners

- 75% are female; the average age is 50.
- Spend an average of 60% of their professional time on meeting planning activities.
- Have been arranging meetings for 13 years.
- Decision-making responsibilities include: selecting hotels (87%); selecting locations (78%); setting budgets (78%); planning entertainment (76%); trade show/exhibit planning (66%); and planning meeting agendas (58%).
- Approximately one-quarter have earned profession certifications, and the majority hold membership in a meeting planning association such as MPI, ASAE, or PCMA.

Source: Recent Meetings Market Report by *Meetings & Conventions* magazine.

a booking when the cycle brings the association back to your part of the country. There may also be some consolation prizes in the form of selection for lesser events such as committee meetings or seminars.

Board of Directors

The final list is usually presented to the board of directors for the final selection. It is worth emphasizing that the recommendations of the executive director usually are accepted. Some get their way all the time; some must deal more politically and tactfully. But the executive director remains the single most important person you must sell to get association business. These directors may not rule autocratically, but they manage to get their own way most of the time. You may lose the business at the directors' meeting, but without the support of the executive director, you never even get that far. Generally, *all* the finalists have won the director's approval.

Other Influences

It is common practice in many scientific and technical societies for local chapters to make an **association bid** for the national event. That is not to say they *bid* in the sense of offering money. Rather, they request the honor of playing **local host** to the national group and offer their efforts to make the convention a success. This is especially true with international societies; an invitation from a national chapter is required before a location is considered.

Hotel salespeople are aware of this practice. We know of cases in which a local delegate to an international congress has been approached by a convention bureau or hotel. An appeal is made to his local pride and to any other emotions that can be brought to bear. It is not uncommon in such cases for the bureau or hotel to bear the costs of the delegate's travel, a hospitality suite, and the presentation to the board. It is wise to assure the delegate that the bureau or hotel would supply clerical support to enable the delegate to fulfill his role of host.

It doesn't always require such effort. Appeals to local delegates or chapters often bring results merely because of civic pride and a willingness to help local businesses. Look around your city and make friends with people in local association chapters. At the very least, you may pick up a local banquet or one-night meeting.

It is important when you enlist the aid of local members to impress upon them that you and your establishment are fully capable of handling the business. They may very well feel uncertain about the wisdom of getting involved and perhaps fear the embarrassment of a debacle at the national convention. But then you have to convince any prospect at any level that you and your staff are competent and interested in doing a good job. Those are the two key points you must make over and over — that your staff has the *expertise* and the *desire* to do whatever must be done to execute the meeting properly.

Sources for Finding Association Business

Associations are readily located, fortunately. The national ones seem to be clustered in a relatively few cities. The Washington, D.C., area is home to more associations (3,500) than any other city, with New York City (1,900) and Chicago (1,200) placing second and third. Other major U.S. headquarter cities include Austin, Indianapolis, Los Angeles, Milwaukee,

Oklahoma City, Philadelphia, and Richmond. In Canada, sources for association business can generally be found in Ottawa and in the capitals of the provinces.

Directories and Databases

Several volumes offer detailed listings of associations. One is *Who's Who in Association Management,* published by the American Society of Association Executives, 1575 I Street, NW, Washington, DC 20005. It lists approximately 8,000 associations. The list is available for sale and, under certain circumstances, for direct mail rental. It is a valuable reference.

Other directories include the *National Trade and Professional Associations of the United States* and its companion publication, *State and Regional Associations of the United States.* Each offers over 7,000 listings. The publisher is Columbia Books, Inc., 8120 Woodmont Avenue, Suite 110, Bethseda, MD 20814. The publisher will rent the list for direct mail use and will supply various breakdowns and services at prices quoted on request.

The *Encyclopedia of Associations* (and its companion, *Geographic Index of Associations*) is published by Gale Research Company, 27500 Drake Road, Farmington Hills, NJ 48331 (1-800-877-4253). Contact the publisher for prices.

The Salesman's Guide publishes directories of association, corporate, and incentive meeting planners (see Exhibit 11). Each listing includes the names and titles of the meeting planners, their addresses, number of conventions and meetings held, past and future sites, months held, and the type of facility utilized. These directories can be ordered from Douglas Publishers (1-800-793-4209).

Databases are also available to assist hotels marketing to association planners. The Internet offers several sites that provide information on associations. Associations, publications, and independent organizations are making important facts and figures available to enable interested hotels to better identify true prospects for their particular property.

Concept Marketing Group (www.marketingsource.com), for example, offers two on-line directories of interest to hotels targeting associations. Their directory of associations is a comprehensive source of information on over 45,000 associations and non-profit groups in the United States, while their Canadian associations directory lists 13,500 associations throughout Canada, providing mailing addresses, contact person and title, and telephone and fax numbers.

Recently, the Destination Marketing Association International (DMAI) ended its code of confidentiality regarding information provided by member bureaus. All historical and demographic meeting information in its new Meeting Information Network (MINT) is now accessible through their local bureaus. This database contains some 31,000 meeting profiles going back over the past four years and the future site-selection information for over 15,000 organizations. The report includes the decision-maker's name, history of past meetings, start and end dates, registered attendance, number of guestrooms used, number of meeting rooms used, square footage of exhibit space, and definite and tentative future bookings. Approximately 1,500 new histories are added yearly. This information is invaluable, providing a factual convention operations history of these leading convention organizations.

Most meeting planners are eager to verify information for these databases on their organizations' meetings for two reasons. First, this history provides them with information useful in negotiating with hotels. Second, planners recognize that database information allows hotels to target their prospects, eliminating misdirected efforts and reducing the number of cold calls from suppliers who do not have enough rooms and/or meeting space for their meetings.

Exhibit 11 Sample of Information Provided by Directories

36

CALIFORNIA – HUNTINGTON BEACH

ASSOCIATION	MEETING PLANNERS	CONVENTION BOOKINGS	■ TYPE OF MEETING / NO. MEETINGS PER ANNUAL	† MONTHS HELD	NO. OF DAYS	★ NO. OF ATTENDEES	O TYPE OF FACILITY
UNITED STATES LIFESAVING ASSN (USLA) PO BOX 366 HUNTINGTON BEACH, 92648 714-536-5283/FAX: 714-374-1500	BILL RICHARDSON (Pres) *Speaker* *Exhibit Space*	05/93 Florida Keys 11/93 Chicago 05/94 Seattle *Booked 6 mos in advance*	C		3	B	DAR
WESTERN ECONOMIC ASSN INTL (WEA) 7400 CTR AVE # 109 HUNTINGTON BEACH, 92647 714-898-3222/FAX: 714-891-6715	ELDON J DVORAK (Exec Vp) VERONICA M DVORAK (Dir Of Conf)	06/91 Seattle 06/94 Vancouver 07/92 San Francisco 07/95 San Diego 06/93 Lake Tahoe *Far East* *Booked 1 yr in advance* *South Pacific* OC	C M	 1	3-4	E	DRC
WYCLIFFE BIBLE TRANSLATORS (WBT) P O BOX 2727 HUNTINGTON BEACH, 92647 714-969-4600/FAX: 714-969-4661	RON OLSON (Assoc Dir) GERALD ELDER (Treas) *Speaker*	OC	M 12	V	3	A	
THE ELECTRICAL MANUFACTURING & COIL WINDING ASSN INC PO BOX 278 IMPERIAL BEACH, 91933 619-575-4191/FAX: 619-575-5009	CHARLES E THURMAN (Exec Dir) *Speaker*	10/91 Boston 10/93 Chicago 09/92 Cincinnati 09/94 Chicago 06/93 Hong Kong *Far East* *Booked 2-3 yrs in advance* OC	C M 2-3		3-4 3	E A	AC
AMERICAN COLLEGE OF TRIAL LAWYERS (ACTL) 8001 IRVINE CTR DR STE 960 IRVINE, 92718 714-727-3194/FAX: 714-727-3894	ROBERT A YOUNG (Exec Dir)	*Booked 2-3 yrs in advance*					
INTERIOR DESIGN EDUCATORS COUNCIL (IDEC) 14252 CULVER DR SUITE A331 IRVINE, 92714 714-551-1622	CANDEE ERWIN (Exec Secy) *Exhibit Space*	04/92 Alexandria	M 6	4	4	C	D
MOTORCYCLE INDUSTRY COUNCIL (MIC) 2 JENNER ST SUITE 150 IRVINE, 92718 714-727-4211	PAMELA AMETTE (Vp) CATHY WILSHIRE (Asst Prog Dir) *Speaker*	02/94 Cincinnati 02/95 Cincinnati *Booked 2 yrs in advance*	C M 1	 10	1 3	A U	C C
MULTI LEVEL MARKETING INTL ASSN. (MLMIA) 119 STANFORD CT IRVINE, 92715 714-854-0484/FAX: 714-854-7687	DORIS WOOD (Pres.) *Exhibit Space*	09/91 Toronto 08/92 Orange County *Canada* 02/93 Orange County *Europe* *Far East* *Booked 3-5 mos in advance* OC	C M 4	 1, 4, 7, 10	4-5 2-3	B U	AR
NATIONAL ASSN OF NAMEPLATE MANUFACTURERS (NAME) 17300 RED HILL AVE STE 100 IRVINE, 92714 714-261-9588/FAX: 714-261-2594	JAMES A KINDER (Exec Vp) LINDA BRADY (Dir Of Educ) *Speaker* *Exhibit Space*	03/93 Naples 10/94 St Louis 09/93 New Orleans 03/95 Palm Springs 03/94 Scottsdale *Mexico* *Booked 2 yrs in advance* *Caribbean* OC	C M 1		1-2 4-5	D B	D DR
NATIONAL MIDAS DEALERS ASSN (NMDA) 14795 JEFFREY RD STE 202 IRVINE, 92720 714-551-1289/FAX: 714-551-0621	MYRON P GORDON (Exec Dir) FRANK MAGLIOCCO (Assoc Exec Dir) *Exhibit Space*	10/91 Las Vegas 09/94 Boca Raton 11/92 New Orleans 10/93 Colorado Springs *Canada* *Booked 2-3 yrs in advance* OC	C M 10	 1, 2, 3, 4, 5, 6, 7, 8, 9, 10, 11, 12	4 1-4	C U	DR A

■ TYPE OF MEETING (C) Convention Data (M) Smaller Meetings & Seminar Data
† MONTHS HELD (1) Jan (2) Feb (3) Mar (4) Apr (5) May (6) June (7) July (8) Aug (9) Sept (10) Oct (11) Nov (12) Dec (P) Spring (S) Summer (F) Fall (W) Winter (V) Various
★ NUMBER OF ATTENDEES (U) Under 50 (A) 51-100 (B) 101-200 (C) 201-500 (D) 501-1000 (E) 1001-5000 (F)Over 5000
O TYPE OF FACILITY (D) Downtown (A) Airport (R) Resort (C) Convention Center

The Nationwide Directory of Association Meeting Planners, *available from* The Salesman's Guide, *lists the names and titles of over 10,000 meeting planners from over 6,500 major associations. The directory details the number of meetings held annually, the months in which they are held, the approximate number of attendees, and the geographic location of the meetings. Of special interest to hotel salespeople: the type of facilities used by each group.*
Source: *The Salesman's Guide.*

🖥 *INTERNET EXERCISE*

Links to Meetings-Related Websites

Listing your property with online meeting directories is a cost-effective method of reaching meeting planners. The websites listed below allow meeting planners to search for hotels and send out requests for proposals (RFPs). Hotels listed generally pay the site a commission for each RFP that results in a booking. These sites also offer the opportunity for hotels to purchase banner ads and priority listings. The volume of RFPs from these sites continues to grow as meeting planners see "online shopping" as one of the most desirable ways to research hotels. Log on to the following websites to answer the questions that follow:

- Worktopia (www.worktopia.com)
- CVB Hot Rates (www.cvbhotrates.com)
- Cvent (www.cvent.com)
- Meeting Broker (www.meetingbroker.com)

1. Which online marketplace focuses on smaller groups?

2. Which site is affiliated with the Destination Marketing Association International (DMAI)?

3. Which site advertises that it has over 75,000 supplier profiles and claims that over 250,000 meeting planners visit its site each month?

4. Which is the lead management program for Newmarket International and has partnered with Cvent, Worktopia, and StarCite to send leads directly to hotel users of their Delphi sales and catering software?

Databases provide a valuable service in building your prospect file for sales campaigns. One subscriber to databases says, "We feel it is an innovative way to find pre-qualified profiles and a really efficient way to pursue business. By receiving the profiles, we save hours of time that would otherwise be spent on cold calls."

Specialized Periodicals

There are a number of periodicals that serve the association market. Some go only to association personnel; others are distributed to both association and corporate personnel. Their advertisers are hotels, convention bureaus, airlines, and other suppliers in the convention industry.

Associations Now is published monthly by the American Society of Association Executives. Its circulation consists of the members of this prestigious organization. The list is available for rental for direct mail under specific circumstances. The Association Directory & Buying Guide lists members with their addresses and telephone numbers, which makes it most useful. Vendors may join the society as associate members.

Association Meetings is published six times a year. It is circulated to full-time managers of societies and associations as well as volunteer/member part-time managers, and others. A sales lead service is available to advertisers.

Association News is a monthly magazine directed to state and regional associations. If this is your target market, you might consider advertising in this publication.

Convene is published ten times annually by the Professional Convention Managers Association (PCMA).

Meetings & Conventions is a monthly publication whose circulation also contains association personnel. Its circulation is available for rental for direct mail. Advertisers get a reader service card system plus a sales lead service in the association and corporate fields.

Medical Meetings magazine, published eight times annually, concentrates on a specific segment of the field. The circulation is formed from medical societies and associations, biomedical corporations, hospitals and medical centers, and government and foundation organizations. They, too, offer a reader sales lead system.

These are prominent publications but not the only ones. For a comprehensive list of trade publications directed to the meetings industry, visit www.conventionplanit.com. Click on "For Planners Only," scroll to "Industry Resources," and click on "Trade Magazines." Many of these publications offer free subscriptions to those involved with the convention and meetings industry. Information as to the particular segment each serves should be obtained from the publishers. Begin today to advance your knowledge by submitting your information and subscribing to publications of interest.

Hotel Records

If you are newly assigned to a hotel convention sales staff, one of the first things to do is to closet yourself with the function books and other records from the past few years. Much can be learned from them. Identify your most lucrative association accounts and determine why they are your best producers — and how you can find similar business. How many groups met in your house but never returned? It is amazing how many times business is lost because no one followed up and pressed for more business.

Your hotel records will also offer clues to personnel changes. If a group didn't return, a new executive director could offer another chance. You could call and indicate that his group had met successfully at your hotel and perhaps persuade the group to book again. You also should try to find out where the previous director is now located. After all, he or she selected your hotel previously and may be amenable to doing so again. No sales staffer should rely on a past customer's memory to bring him or her back. Sales life is not that easy. You must go after business.

Keep in mind that the easiest prospect is a satisfied past customer. Referrals and recommendations from satisfied planners are excellent ways to prospect for new business. Don't wait for details of a planner's event to sit dormant in your property's records — planners are happy and motivated upon the completion of a successful event; that is the time to ask for referrals. Potential prospects who have been introduced through a referral will have a much greater close rate — 50 to 90 percent higher. When meetings go well, you have excellent prospects for repeat business. If they do not go well, it is imperative to find out why. It could be something that you must prevent from happening with other clients, or it may be something that you have already corrected and you could then press for business. Some of the best business relationships result from clearing up past grievances, many of which could have been eliminated in the first place had sales executives better understood the needs of association meeting planners. To minimize problems with members of this market segment, some hotel chains are offering specialized training to their sales personnel (see "Best Practices" box).

Hotel records may also lead to other prospects gleaned from local small bookings. A dinner meeting handled solely by the banquet manager may indicate only a local chapter. But this small bit of business of dinner for twenty or so may be just the Trojan horse you need to penetrate the state or national parent organization. Much can be learned from the members themselves. At the least, a follow-up phone call will increase the chances for more local business.

It is important to realize that much association business must be cultivated over the long haul, so don't get discouraged. The road to that major booking may have to go through many minor bits of business before you score the big one, or before scoring at all. Maintain a good follow-up system, keep after target associations, and you'll get your share.

Summary

In this chapter, we have discussed the importance of the associations market to hotels and identified some of the factors that hospitality firms need to consider if they wish to target this market segment. It is essential to know the types of meetings that associations hold, the characteristics of these meetings (cycle and pattern, geographic restrictions, lead time, kinds of sites desired, and price considerations), and to determine the key decision-makers and how to reach them. A hotel that does its homework can attract business that will fill rooms and bring revenue to the property's other facilities in what would normally be slack months, and may generate significant repeat business from association meeting attendees.

Best Practices

Marriott Hotels & Resorts and PCMA Team Up to Help Hotel Sales Executives Think Like Association Meeting Planners

The Certified Association Sales Executive (CASE) Marriott/PCMA Program is an intensive nine-week course designed exclusively for hotel sales executives who sell to the association market. Louis Nicholls, senior account executive for Marriott International and a CASE graduate, says:

> This course specifically targets issues that pertain to our industry and our day-to-day roles in it.

The CASE program, which is open to all Marriott employees involved in association sales, gives the sales executives the opportunity to "get inside the heads" of their association clients through a combination of online learning, instructor-led training, and firsthand experience with association personnel. Jessica van der Gaast, a senior account executive at the San Francisco Marriott, who had never been on the association side of meeting planning, says:

> I had the opportunity to observe the roles and responsibilities for each staff member of the association, sit in on important meetings, and observe first-hand the decision-making process and structure of the organization. I had one-on-one discussion time with each staff person, including the executive director, and learned about current technology and changes in society in terms of how they affect the organization and its strategic planning.

Through this course, hotel salespeople get a real sense of how associations operate in terms of structure and timing issues. This understanding helps them to see associations as valuable business and be able to offer solutions to help this segment meet their objectives.

Source: Ginny Phillips, "Creating a Niche," *Convene*.

Endnotes

1. Jeff Sacks, CMP, "Site Selection," www.pcma.org/templates/Conferon/charts/Ch2_1.htm.

2. J. Dana Clark, Michael R. Evans, and Bonnie J. Knutson, "Selecting a Site for an Association Convention: An Exploratory Look at the Types of Power Used by Committee Members to Influence Decisions," *Journal of Hospitality & Leisure Marketing*.

Key Terms

association—A group of people joined together for a common purpose.

association bid—A regional chapter requests the honor of hosting a national convention.

association management companies—Firms that function as the executive and office staff for a number of associations.

breakout session—Small group sessions within the meeting, formed to discuss specific topics.

concurrent session—Meeting sessions on different topics scheduled at the same time.

general session—The main meeting attended by the majority of the association members. Also called a plenary session.

lead time—The time between the booking and the actual meeting date.

local host—A group of local people that carries out the strategies and policies established for the organization of an event held in their geographic area. Also called an organizing committee.

site inspection—Tour of the property conducted by representatives of the association or corporation in order to determine whether the hotel is suitable to host the meeting/event.

Review Questions

1. Conventions are extremely important to associations for financial reasons. Explain why.

2. What kinds of meetings do associations hold? What type of facilities are best suited to each?

3. How do state and regional association meetings differ from the national association meetings?

4. Identify the monthly and daily meeting pattern of association meetings.

5. Attendance for association conventions is voluntary. How important is price to association executives? What implications does this have on a hotel's sales efforts?

6. What individuals in the association make the site selection decision?

7. List sources for locating associations.

Additional References

Contemporary Hospitality Marketing, William Lazer and Robert A. Layton, American Hotel & Lodging Educational Institute, 1999. www.ahlei.org

Destination Marketing for Convention and Visitors Bureaus, Second Edition, Richard B. Gartrell, Kendall/Hunt Publishing.

Internet Sites

For more information, visit the following Internet sites. Internet addresses can change without notice. If a site is no longer available at the address listed below, a search engine can be used to find the new address or additional, related sites.

American Society of Association
  Executives (ASAE)
www.asaenet.org

Association Directory
www.assoconline.com

Association Meetings
www.meetingsnet.com

Association News
www.schneiderpublishing.com

Canadian Society of Association Executives
www.case.org

Convention Industry Council (CIC)
www.conventionindustry.org

European Society of Association Executives
www.esae.com

Meetings and Conventions
www.meetings-conventions.com

Professional Convention Management
  Association (PCMA)
www.pcma.org

Competencies

1. Identify factors that corporate meeting planners consider when making a site selection. (pp. 149–155)

2. Describe the different types of corporate meetings. (pp. 155–161)

3. Identify characteristics of corporate meetings that are important for selling to the corporate market. (pp. 161–169)

4. Identify who typically decides where to hold a corporate meeting. (pp. 169–176)

5. Describe the tools salespeople use to locate corporations and to find information about the meetings they hold. (pp. 176–181)

Selling to the Corporate Meetings Market

Helmut Knipp
President and Chief Operating Officer
Lexington Management Corporation

*"**Qualify** and **quantify** are two of the most important steps in the solicitation of any account. You have to know the potential an account has before you can make intelligent rate and solicitation decisions. With our salespeople, we stress the importance of doing research on our customers. Two other areas require mentioning. One is to take outstanding care of the customers you have. It is much more costly and time-consuming to find new customers than it is to take care of existing ones. The second area is prospecting. A salesperson must make new contacts all the time. Ask your existing customers for other contacts in their business or trade. Read the newspapers and trade journals for leads and prospects."*

5 Selling the Corporate Meetings Market

TODAY'S CORPORATION is a complex organization. The geographic marketing range has grown to the point that most companies now market nationally or internationally. The structure of larger companies is more detailed and multifaceted than ever before. Modern executives who received their training with such companies in mind are keenly aware of the vital need for *communication*. Meetings remain a most basic form of communication within companies. You are concerned solely with those company meetings that take place off company premises, and there are enough of them to satisfy any enterprising hotel sales staff.

If the association convention business represents the best-known and most visible segment of the meetings field, corporate meetings offer the greatest potential for growth. You must, however, keep up with the latest trends to be ready to meet the needs of this market. Today's corporate meeting planners are shifting their focus in terms of meeting locations as well as the size and "flavor" of their events. A recent survey by StarCite, a leader in meeting management, meetings procurement, and online event registration, showed that 70 percent of meeting planners are meeting closer to home and that 43 percent are changing the ambience to reflect backlash against what appears to be corporate excesses.

The new "normal" environment calls for meetings that are sensible, practical, and responsible—with an emphasis on value, convenience, and service.[1] This means that companies are meeting closer to home (with regional rather than national meetings) or in less expensive second-tier cities. Corporate meetings are also getting smaller due to budget cuts, and may include virtual components, such as teleconferencing and "webinars," to save on travel costs.

Corporate meetings are also more likely to be more strategic and practical. Certain elements, such as elaborate meal functions and big-ticket entertainment, are being scaled down or eliminated as companies seek to be more fiscally responsible. In response to this trend, a new industry buzzword, **strategic meetings management**, has been coined to reflect how corporate meeting planners strive to prove to their bosses that meetings and events can be strategic assets to their companies.

Although the volume of corporate business is greater than that of the association segment, corporate business is not as visible. Since company meetings are varied and are controlled by a wider variety of personnel, they are harder to dig out. But they offer a great deal of group business potential that no hotel should ignore.

Fortunately, hotel marketing people do not have to decide which segment of the market—associations or corporations—to sell. The two are a digestible mix, and a successful property enjoys its share of both kinds. The ratio of each really reflects upon the kind of property you have, what you are equipped to handle, and where you are located. While some hotel features and benefits appeal to both markets, there are significant differences (see Exhibit 1). Examine your hotel with an eye to what corporate meeting planners want and the kinds of meetings they hold.

Exhibit 1   Comparison of Association and Corporate Meeting Groups

FACTOR	ASSOCIATION	CORPORATION
Attendance	Voluntary	Mandatory
Decision-making	Decentralized; often committee	Centralized (usually one person)
Number of meetings	Fewer, but larger attendance	More, but fewer attendees per meeting
Potential for Repeat Business	Some, but must rotate sites	High
Room Block	Must track reservation pickup closely	Stable
Spouse Attendance	Common	Seldom
Exhibits	Frequent; heavy demand for hospitality suites	Less frequent
Site Selection	Need to build attendance with attractive locations; sometimes political	Seek convenience, service, and security
Geographic Pattern	Rotate geographically	No set pattern
Lead Time	Long (usually two to five years)	Short (often less than one year)
Billing Format	Individual Folios	Master Account
Risk of Cancellation	Minimal	Higher; penalty clauses and advance deposits are common
Arrival/Departure	More likely to have early arrivals	Few early arrivals or departures
Price	More price-conscious; generally good negotiators	Less price-sensitive
Convention and Visitors Bureau Involvement	Frequently utilize convention bureaus, especially with citywide conventions	Seldom contact convention bureau
Reservation Procedures	Generally use postal reply cards or Housing Bureau	Frequently provide a rooming list
Attrition Concerns	Over 50% of association meeting planners cite attrition as a major issue in contracts	Only one in four corporate planners mention attrition as a concern

If you pursue a career in convention sales and services, you must have an understanding of the critical differences between association and corporate meetings. This knowledge will be vital when responding to a request for proposal (RFP) or selling to meeting planners face-to-face.

Requirements for Corporate Meetings

The factors that make a hotel attractive for association events hold true for most corporate meetings too. Keep in mind that corporate meetings vary a great deal in size, scope, and purpose. It is important, therefore, to match the planner's needs with the hotel's facilities.

Quality food service. Food and beverage functions are major contributors to the success or failure of corporate meetings. Long after other meeting details are forgotten, corporate attendees remember an elegant banquet, a unique refreshment break, or an unusual theme party.

Hotels can increase the comfort level in this area by having staff that assures the meeting planner of the property's attention to all the details of food and beverage functions. Mark Beaupre, executive chef at the 1,000-room JW Marriott Orlando Grande Lakes in Orlando, Florida, always meets with meeting planners beforehand. He says:

> The idea is to build relationships, especially if the meeting is, say, three years away. I assist the sales managers, and that really adds to the comfort level of the person responsible for the event. By the time the group gets here, I have talked with and e-mailed him or her many times. During the event, every evening I sit with the planner over a glass of wine, and we talk about that day and the one to follow.[2]

Crown Room Banquet Setup.
Photograph courtesy of the Hotel del Coronado, San Diego, California.

Corporate meeting planners consistently rate quality of food service as very important in choosing a hotel or facility (see Exhibit 2). The planner of today is continually encouraging the staff to surpass a previous year's convention program. To gain its share of repeat business, a hotel must continue to upgrade menus, contribute to the uniqueness of each event, and create an occasion that will be long remembered.

Adequate meeting space. It is hard to hold a meeting efficiently if the meeting rooms are too small—or too large (although surplus area may be screened off). When you go after company business, discuss room requirements in detail. The main room may need support from a number of small rooms. If your layout shows these nearby, you have a strong selling point. The traffic flow pattern of the meeting is very important.

In addition to adequate meeting space, many of today's corporate meeting planners require "high tech" equipment and Internet access in both meeting rooms and guestrooms. Since most corporate meetings are about productivity and businesspeople most generally come to these meetings armed with their laptops, hotels that wish to capture this market segment must offer such services as High-Speed Internet Access (HSIA) and/or Wi-Fi—wireless technology that allows attendees to log on to the Internet using radio frequencies (wireless technology is commonly offered in lobbies and other public areas as well as in meeting rooms and some guestrooms).

The Internet is frequently used for demonstrations and business applications at corporate meetings, and attendees tap into the Internet to maintain productivity while on the road, including keeping in contact with customers via e-mail. In many cases, hotels are charging a daily fee (which can be a separate charge or included in the room rate) for both wired and wireless Internet access, or are "bundling" these services with other amenities, such as a continental breakfast and newspaper for Concierge Level service.

Still other hotels offer **business centers** for guests requiring Internet service or other office-related needs, such as faxing, copying, and shipping. Some business centers offer secretarial services and tech support, while others are self-service (see box titled "Hotel Business Centers").

Service. Companies meet for good reason, and they don't want problems. They want service—good service. They want what was promised, and on time. The reward is repeat business. Except for incentive programs, corporate meetings promise the most repeat business. Many planners mention good service first when asked what they look for in a meeting site.

HOTEL BUSINESS CENTERS

Technology has revolutionized today's hotel guestrooms, which increasingly feature high-speed wireless Internet service, fax machines, media hubs, and other amenities, such as large desks (often stocked with office supplies) and ergonomic chairs. Wi-Fi is typically offered in hotel common areas.

Despite these innovations, many business travelers still have a need for additional services, such as copying, printing, and shipping. Hotels have responded to this need by offering business centers equipped with computers, scanners, printers, copy machines, and other office equipment. Equipment offered varies greatly, as does other services offered and costs for the use of the center's amenities.

At some hotels, business centers offer secretarial services and tech support. At the L'Enfant Plaza in Washington, D.C., the business center is staffed from 7:30 a.m.–6:00 p.m. daily, and offers such services as mailing and shipping and the production of name tags, badges, and tent cards. Limited, automated service is offered 24 hours a day. Other hotels simply provide equipment, which can be accessed with cash, credit card, or a pre-paid card that can be purchased through the hotel. The Hillcrest Hotel, located in Revelstoke, British Columbia, has had great success with its pre-paid cards, which cover the price-per-minute set by the hotel for the use of business center equipment.

The costs of investing in a business center can be quite high, of course, so some hotels turn to companies such as Hotel Internet Services (HIS), which offers the Bizcenter™ System. Hotels can purchase, rent, or enter into a revenue-sharing agreement with the company, which provides self-service office equipment and tech support to such chains as Best Western, Comfort Inn, Crowne Plaza, DoubleTree, JW Marriott, LaQuinta, Radisson, and Wyndham Hotels & Resorts.

Although there have been some declines in the use of business centers as more businesspeople travel with laptops and other electronic devices, other travelers appreciate the convenience that these centers offer (especially the self-service centers that are available 24-hours a day). In response to the need for such services as copying and the printing of boarding passes, some properties are now offering Internet kiosks in lobbies or secluded areas in the hotel instead of investing in a full-service business center. Other properties are making their business centers more attractive by creating spaces that combine work with relaxation and socializing—the ME Cancún in Mexico, for example, offers eSpace, a bar that features 10 flat-screen computer screens so guests can check e-mail messages and order coffee or Coronas any time of the day; the JW Marriott Grand Rapids also offers bar service in its business center.

Source: Photograph courtesy of Crowne Plaza Hotels.

Exhibit 2   Factors Considered Important to Corporate Meeting Planners in the Selection of a Facility/Hotel

Factors Considered "Very Important"	Corporate Planners
Number, size, and quality of meeting rooms	82%
Negotiable food, beverage, and room rates	82
Cost of hotel or meeting facility	81
Quality of food service	75
Number, size, and quality of sleeping rooms	74
High-speed Internet access	55
Availability of meeting support services and equipment, such as AV equipment	54
Efficiency of billing procedures	51
"Green" practices at the facility	51
Meeting rooms with multiple high-speed phone lines and computer outlets	49
Assignment of one staff person to handle all aspects of the meeting	48
Previous experience in dealing with the facility and its staff	45
Efficiency of check-in and check-out procedures	43
Availability of exhibit space	39
Provisions of special meeting services, such as pre-registration, special equipment, etc.	37
On-site recreational facilities (swimming pool, tennis, spa, etc.)	37

Corporate austerity programs, coupled with a greater awareness of the size of meeting expenditures, have caused corporate planners to rank the cost of a hotel or meeting facility and negotiable food, beverage, and room rates high on their list of factors for site selection. The quality of food service, which was formerly their first priority, moved to fourth place on their list.
Source: Recent Meetings Market Report conducted by *Meetings & Conventions* magazine.

Enough guestrooms. No company likes to split up at a meeting, chancing the "loss" of attendees during the walk or cab ride to the meeting site. They prefer to house everyone under one roof. This is a difficult problem to overcome if you can't offer it but your competitor can. Hotels combine presentations to large groups but the first choice is invariably a single hotel housing all attendees.

Convenient location. Location is very important to the corporate meeting planner. Travel means company money. Time spent traveling and at the meeting itself means time off the job. That's a prime factor. A convenient location is a strong sales asset. Company planners use downtown hotels, airport hotels, and suburban locations, especially for regional meetings and training sessions.

Attractive location. Business officials have a clear image of their company, and they want to meet in a hotel consistent with that image. This does not necessarily mean a posh place, but an attractive place. Boutique (lifestyle) hotels are often a popular choice (see box titled "Boutiques (Lifestyles) Attract Corporate Groups").

For incentive trips, it goes without saying that the hotel and the area must have tourist attractions. The basic concept is to reward those who meet targeted goals. The prize selected must stimulate extra effort. The approach for incentive meetings is quite different from that of sales meetings, but the two are often intertwined. A working sales meeting requires solely a *suitable* hotel site; an incentive meeting requires a most *desirable* one.

Security. Corporate meetings are private affairs to a far greater extent than most conventions. The discussions are not meant for the ears of people outside the company, and, because of the increasing competition in the marketplace—especially in the computer and

Boutiques (Lifestyles) Attract Corporate Groups

In the mid-1980s, nightclub entrepreneur Ian Schrager introduced the first boutique hotel, a trendy, small property that featured chic décor, plenty of natural light, and lobbies and bar areas designed for socializing. Typically small (150 rooms or less), boutique hotels were originally built to appeal to a young, hip crowd by offering the "comforts of home" in an upscale, yet relaxed atmosphere that was enhanced by attentive service and the "gadgets" and facilities that were an essential part of their everyday lives.

It wasn't long before the meetings market discovered boutique hotels. Attracted by their small size, which offered both personalized service and attention to their group as well as security for meetings, meeting planners increasingly began buying out boutique hotels for their meetings.

Sarah Clark, vice president of corporate communications for the Preferred Boutique arm of the Chicago-based Preferred Hotel Group, says:

Source: Photograph courtesy of Inter-Continental Hotel Group.

> A buyout gives a group tremendous focus throughout every aspect of the meeting. The entire staff is dedicated to the group, and the property is always available for their enjoyment.

Lindsey Ueberroth, managing director for the Preferred Boutique chain, adds:

> One of the advantages that boutiques have is that they can offer much more flexibility and personalized service than a big hotel can. The management at a boutique tends to be hands-on, so you're working with the general manager of the hotel, not just the sales and catering managers.

In addition to the increased flexibility and the unique guest experience offered by boutiques, Jacques-Olivier Chauvin, CEO of Relais & Châteaux, a Paris-based company that represents upscale boutique properties worldwide, says of the security issue:

> We've seen a significant growth in executive retreats, board meetings, and events for luxury goods and car launches. If a group is staying in a large hotel, there's a risk that confidential information will be disclosed. With a buyout, the property is secure because it's just you.

The growing popularity of boutique hotels did not go unnoticed by the large hotel chains. Starwood, which was first to jump on the boutique bandwagon with its W Hotels, now also offers the Aloft and Element brands. The InterContinental Hotel Group launched Indigo, Choice Hotels offers Cambria Suites, and Hyatt serves boutique customers with its Hyatt Place brand.

Sources: Jennifer Nicole Dienst, "All Yours: Buying Out a Small Luxury Hotel," *Meetings & Conventions*, December 2007, p. 39; Tony Bartlett, "Lofty Lifestyle: New Boutique Brands are Transforming the Hotel Scene, *Meetings West*, May 2008, p. 24; and Steve Bjerklie, "Big Fish, Little Pond," *Smart Meetings*, July 2006.

other high-tech fields, security has become an even more important issue for corporate meeting planners. If your property understands this need for additional security and can offer viable solutions, you will have a far greater chance of securing corporate meetings business. Mary Kay Hokanson, a meeting planner for Allianz Life Insurance Co. of North America in Minneapolis, has one particular clause that she's very careful about including in her meetings contracts:

> We always request that no other financial services institution is holding a meeting at the hotel the same time we are. Our independent producers sell a variety of products and we want their meeting to be a total Allianz experience.[3]

Folding vinyl partitions and meeting rooms right off busy lobbies leave corporate planners cold, as does unrestricted access to meeting rooms and areas in which equipment and displays will be stored. In some cases, the planner may even worry about communications sent to the property's fax machine or the security of the property's phone system.

If you hope to handle this type of high-level meeting, you must be prepared to answer these concerns. First, offering a layout of the traffic pattern of the property can be an asset if the group's meeting and storage facilities will be isolated from the main flow of traffic. Second, you may offer additional security measures, such as assigning one or two trusted employees to freshen meeting rooms and watch over unoccupied facilities. Third, the business may be so attractive that you will want to go to the extra expense of hiring outside security guards or setting up a dedicated fax line for the group. If the company will be the only group meeting in the hotel at that time, you have an additional selling advantage. This is an asset for small properties, turning what may be considered a liability (small size) into a positive attraction. This is also a strong selling point for resort properties; the remoteness of a location may be an additional sales point for the security-conscious client.

Kinds of Corporate Meetings

Corporate meetings business has been increasing more rapidly than any other market. Hundreds of thousands of meetings are held all over the country throughout the year, and the spectrum of meetings attended is broad. Among the prevalent types of company meetings are:

- National and regional sales meetings
- New product introduction/dealer meetings
- Professional/technical meetings
- Management meetings
- Training meetings
- Stockholder/public meetings
- Incentive meetings

Each will be considered in detail, but Exhibit 3 summarizes several key characteristics. The most widely attended meetings are for sales and marketing purposes and training, each type totaling over 12 million attendees. On average, the highest attendance is at new product introduction meetings (163 attendees) and the lowest at training meetings (73 attendees) and management meetings (42 attendees). The average number of off-premises meetings planned yearly by corporate planners is 19.4.

The kinds of companies holding meetings are diverse. Insurance, banking and investment groups, and automotive and other industrial and manufacturing concerns are just a few of the sources of corporate meetings business. It would be more difficult to find any sizable organizations that do not hold meetings—and lots of them.

Exhibit 3   Summary of Types of Corporate Meetings

Type of Meeting	Off-premise Meetings	Average # Planned	Average Attendance	Average # Days	Average # of Months Lead Time
Management Meetings	205,276	6.2	42	2.2	3.5
Group Incentive Trips	75,628	3.8	130	5.0	8.2
Training Seminars	302,512	10.0	73	2.5	3.7
National/ Regional Sales Meetings	226,884	6.7	94	2.7	3.8
Professional/ Technical Meetings	118,844	6.2	89	2.3	5.3
New Product Introductions	32,412	3.3	163	2.1	3.7
Stockholder Meetings	10,804	1.8	79	1.7	5.2
Other Meetings	108,040	12.3	183	2.3	9.1
Total/Average	1,080,400	19.4	78	2.7	5.5

Note that the average lead time for corporate meetings is less than one year, the attendance is generally less than 100 persons, and the duration of most corporate meetings is two to three days.
Source: Recent Meetings Market Report by *Meetings & Conventions* magazine.

National and Regional Sales Meetings

The best-known company meeting, and one of the largest sectors of the corporate meetings market, is the **sales meeting**. The nature of a national sales organization makes it a natural for meetings. These events are scattered throughout the country. With new products and new sales developments appearing all the time, there is constant need to meet face to face with the sales team, at every level. There are national sales meetings with everyone present, meetings of regional sales managers, and regional sales meetings run by regional sales managers.

In order to save money and maximize company productivity, many firms today are combining meetings or holding different meetings back-to-back at the same property. When companies use the same hotel for back-to-back meetings, they not only save on hotel rooms, food and beverage expenses, and on-site staff costs, but they can also save money by using the same off-site venues, entertainment, speakers, production equipment, and ground transportation.

In some cases, companies will combine a large sales meeting with smaller meetings either the day before or the day after the "main event." In other cases, companies use the same facility for both training meetings and incentive trips. David Lutz, past president of the Twinsburg, Ohio–based meeting planning firm, Experient, says:

> We're seeing it [combining meetings] happen to a much greater degree than ever before, and we're seeing it across industry segments.[4]

Attendance at national sales meetings averages about 150 for three to four days. Regional sales meetings are smaller, averaging 65 in size over two to three days.

The reasons for the sales meetings are many, often dealing with several objectives. The annual sales meeting may involve new product introductions, new company policies and suggested sales techniques to overcome problems, or it may simply be a morale builder and stimulator to cap a successful year and to start work on the next one. Sales meetings come in all sizes, at any time of the year, and all mean good, regular, repeat business for hotels.

Sales meetings are generally staged and controlled within the sales and marketing departments of each division of a company.

New Product Introduction/Dealer Meetings

Sales executives often hold national and regional events to meet with dealers or distributors. New product introductions are very important in these meetings, too. The introduction of new sales and advertising campaigns calls for carrying the message out to the hinterlands. The very heart of the sales and marketing philosophy is to sell your own staff first and then your distributors and dealers and their staffs, and to work them up to new levels of enthusiasm. This approach results in many meetings around the country.

As in the case of sales meetings, **dealer meetings** can be very small, such as a cocktail reception for a dozen or so for one evening, or great affairs involving thousands and running three to five days. The Ford Motor Company spent several million dollars for a live Broadway-type stage show, combined with a multimedia presentation, at the large Las Vegas Convention Center. The affair called for several days of rehearsals and two weeks of back-to-back charter flights from all parts of the country. The production was worthy of any on Broadway, yet had a run of only two weeks. If the objective of the meeting is achieved, the meeting is a success and the cost accepted as necessary and worthwhile.

Dealer meetings, in addition to being attended by sales personnel, also attract top company management, stockholders, and the press. Since these meetings are often "gala affairs," they provide an excellent opportunity to "show off" the property and book additional business from both company personnel and "outside" attendees. There is no better sales presentation than a successful execution of a meeting on premises. This is the opportunity to display your hotel at its best.

Professional/Technical Meetings

The need to update technical personnel increases every year. The volume of technical development and innovation is hard to envision. In only the last 100 years—just four generations—man has created the automobile, the airplane, the computer, the spaceship, and the laser. An engineer or scientist cannot afford to stop learning, or he or she will soon be obsolete. To give you some idea of the scope, General Electric has some 30,000 engineers, representing an enormous investment in technical talent that requires constant updating. It is a resource that needs to be safeguarded against personnel obsolescence.

Company **professional/technical meetings** often take the seminar and workshop formats. Independent consultants, educators, and even vendors are invited to demonstrate and lecture.

Management Meetings

Just as sales and technical personnel meet, so do all levels of executives. Far-flung organizations mean that there is a need even at the top for executives to get together for discussion.

Such meetings may be regular events, such as board meetings, or may be called in response to a special situation. These are usually small meetings, but they call for the finest in accommodations and service. An important characteristic of such meetings for hotel salespeople is that each attendee is a potential customer for meetings within his or her own division or company.

Management meetings most commonly last for two days and follow no special locations rule, ranging from convenient downtown or airport locations to remote resorts and lodges.

Training Meetings

Training of personnel on all levels is an important activity of the larger corporations. Companies may conduct training in technical skills such as welding, machinery repair, and maintenance. Computer systems result in more training sessions. Sales personnel receive training, as do executives.

About half of training directors conduct programs off company premises. These **training meetings** are held on a regular basis and usually run about three days. Attendance is usually small. Most training groups number fewer than 100, and most are nearer 60. Groups of ten to 15 are not at all rare, so even small hotels can handle these meetings.

That is not to say that training directors are satisfied by just any facility; they have firm criteria. They do, however, deal with small groups that are easily accommodated. They want meeting rooms with

Source: Courtesy of the Emirates Academy of Hospitality Management and Jumeriah Hotels.

permanent walls instead of screen dividers, rooms good for audiovisual use, easy access to meeting rooms without distraction from other hotel activities, and prompt service for food functions such as refreshment breaks and lunches. Well-lighted and well-ventilated rooms with adequate space for either classroom or U-shaped seating (there is often a preference for extra-wide 24- or 30-inch tables), and guestrooms with well-lighted work space (desks or large tables) are especially attractive to training meeting planners.

Training directors do not need prestigious locations and impressive surroundings. They are more likely to choose hotels that are convenient to airports, highways, and parking. Training directors have no need to change locations to stimulate attendance or interest.

They make excellent customers because they tend to come back to hotels that have worked out well. Dependability, reasonable prices, and good service all count a great deal toward repeat business.

Many hotels and motels have done well with this kind of business, to the point of having almost permanent commitment of certain meeting rooms and a constant use of a minimum number of guestrooms by a single company. Chains find this to be good business, too, as many national companies rotate similar training sessions to several cities around the country.

Regular business bookings can also be picked up when personnel become acquainted with a property while attending a training session.

An odd characteristic of training meetings is the frequent reluctance to use the term *training*. At lower levels, employees look for training and will regard it as an added benefit and frequently stick with an employer that offers it. But sales and middle-level people at times resent the thought that they *need* further development. The situation is dispelled by tact, so don't be surprised to see *workshops, seminars, management development,* or simply *meetings* being booked by training directors.

Another type of training meeting that is promoted under a different name is the *corporate retreat*. Corporate retreats are typically held for small groups to foster relationships and team-building, and they may include challenges and strategic games to enhance communication and problem-solving skills. In most cases, a remote location is chosen, but that does not mean that participants are deprived of creature comforts. Many corporate retreat packages offer deluxe accommodations, meal functions, and a number of recreational options (see Exhibit 4).

The position of training director has broadened in many companies over the years. Today, you may find your key decision-maker under a title reflecting involvement with *human resources*.

Stockholder/Public Meetings

Companies find it necessary at times to hold meetings for non-employees. These typically fall into the category of **stockholder/public meetings**. The annual stockholders meeting can range from a mere formality attended by a handful to a fairly active one-day event involving a goodly number, with lunch and refreshment breaks. These seem to vary with the economic climate.

Public relations and industrial relations departments also hold meetings and exhibits to tell their stories. They, too, add their bit to the growing number of corporate meetings.

Incentive Meetings

Each year, as millions of people exceed their business goals or quotas, many are rewarded by a trip—trips that collectively mean close to $6 billion to the travel industry. Up to 45 percent of that figure is spent on hotels alone. Meetings are included in 85 percent of all incentive trips, and those meetings are called **incentive meetings**.

Incentive travelers may be suppliers, dealers, customers, salespeople, or other employees. They must qualify in some way to participate.

What do incentive customers want? Above all, they look for first-class service. Companies offer these trips as rewards to top performers, so they want them treated in a special way.

Exhibit 4   Attracting the Corporate Retreat Market

Cowboy Ethics Bootcamp at the Alisal

A unique corporate retreat designed to boost morale, raise standards and rejuvenate the spirit of integrity. Join us as we team up with renowned author and speaker Jim Owen to create the first-ever "Cowboy Ethics® Bootcamp".

PACKAGE INCLUDES:

• Studio accommodations for four days and three nights
• Welcome basket (includes book "Cowboy Ethics")
• Welcome reception- meet James Owen "Cowboy Ethics" author
• Breakfast, lunch and dinner, including wine with dinner
• Private winemaker's dinner
• Three workshop sessions with James Owen
• Free time for golf, tennis, lake activities, spa activities, horseback riding & more
• Taxes and service charges

THE ALISAL
Guest Ranch and Resort

Package Price:

$2,250 single occupancy all inclusive.
$3,000 double occupancy all inclusive.

10 room minimum.

1054 Alisal Road
Solvang, CA 93463
1-800-425-4725
sales@alisal.com

Corporate retreats are usually held for small groups at remote locations, such as the Alisal Guest Ranch and Resort in the Santa Ynez Valley in Solvang, California. The property's accommodations include 73 studios or two-room suites, none of which include a television or telephone in order to enhance the retreat atmosphere (participants' messages are delivered by staff members). Also included in this particular retreat's package are a welcome basket and reception, three meals daily, workshops, and free time for recreational activities, including golf, tennis, lake activities, and horseback riding. Team-building activities, such as a ropes course, mini Olympics, and other strategic games, can also be added to the program.
Source: Courtesy of the Alisal Guest Ranch and Resort.

For hotels that can deliver what these customers want, the benefits are substantial. First, bookings are guaranteed. This means easy forecasting and a break-even factor that's minimal compared to other markets. Second, incentive participants typically make use of all hotel facilities, such as restaurants, bars, and room service. Third, incentive meetings mean high-dollar revenues. Average room rates

Group Reward Travel	
Percentage of corporate planners who arrange incentive trips	33%
Average number planned	3.8
Average number of attendees	130
Average duration	5 days

Source: Recent Meetings Market Report by *Meetings & Conventions* **magazine.**

are usually higher, with double occupancy most common, and they spend more on banquets than do many other meeting segments.

Characteristics of Corporate Meetings

Any meeting should have a clear objective, a logical attendance group, and a site and structure to suit the event. When we discuss characteristics of company meetings, keep in mind that we are talking about many different *kinds* of meetings—all sizes and shapes, instigated by many causes, planned and executed with rare exceptions by a variety of people.

But this very difficulty in describing a "typical" meeting should be most encouraging to hotel staffs. It is a most unimaginative hotel salesperson, or a particularly primitive hotel property, that cannot come up with some part of this market that can be sold and serviced well. This is the time to ignore what facilities you may lack and concentrate on what you *have*. Select that portion of the market that you can target and call your own. Think in terms of your own sales campaigns and the kinds of hotel properties that can handle the situations discussed in this chapter.

Small Meetings

As we mentioned in the introduction to this chapter, a number of factors, including a fluctuating economy and public scrutiny of events deemed as corporate excesses, has resulted in companies scaling back large events and booking smaller meetings. According to a recent Meeting Planners Intention Survey conducted by PCMA, American Express, and Ypartnership, 52 percent of meetings booked had an attendance of 100 or less, while 67 percent of meetings planned were for fewer than 50 attendees.[5]

This trend is good news for small and mid-size lodging facilities, boutique hotels, and conference centers, which can easily serve this excellent market. And larger hotels, such as Gaylord, are attempting to capture a share of small meetings business with a hotel-within-a-hotel concept. Major chains such as Hilton and Marriott are also reaching out to the small meetings market, offering convenient, online tools that make it easier for corporate meeting planners to book their small meetings on a 24/7 basis—without having to deal with a hotel salesperson.

The Hilton chain, which introduced Hilton Meetings to offer personalized services for meetings of under 50 attendees, also launched e-Events, which offers online planning and booking tools (for events requiring 25 rooms or less) at a number of its brands (see Exhibit 5). Bob Brooks, vice president—eSales Strategy and Performance for Hilton Hotels Corporation, says:

> We developed e-Events to address the growing needs of people to plan, book, and manage their events online at their convenience. Our research continues to reflect the ongoing trend of many first-time planners—primarily GenX and GenY users—who drive the online booking process. With the majority of today's consumers Internet savvy, our goal is to make online bookings of events and meetings as commonplace as online airline bookings.
>
> Once an event is booked online with e-Events, customers have immediate access to additional online booking tools and resources that

allow them to manage their rooming list and create a customized page for their event. In our effort to continue enhancing e-Events, Hilton has also introduced customized menus.

Marriott offers a QuickGroup booking site on its website (www.marriott.com). The site was designed for convenient booking of group blocks of between ten and 25 rooms for up to seven nights at participating Marriott, Renaissance, JW Marriott, Courtyard, Residence Inn, SpringHill Suites, Fairfield Inn, and TownePlace Suites.

Meeting planners have instant access to meeting space floor plans and dimensions, and several electronic tools are available—including space and budget calculators, online rooming and group lists, web pages for groups, and step-by-step meeting guides—to assist meeting planners on a 24-hour basis.

Exhibit 5   Booking Small Meetings Online with Hilton's e-Events

The e-Events online booking and planning tool, which is offered by hotels in The Hilton Family, including Embassy Suites Hotels, makes it easier for planners to book their events and manage their small meetings at a time that is convenient for them. Online booking is growing in popularity, and allows planners ready access to information—without the need of calling a hotel directly and dealing with a hotel salesperson.
Source: Courtesy of Embassy Suites Hotels, a member of The Hilton Family.

Time Cycle

Corporations tend to meet midweek and throughout the year (see Exhibit 6). Company meetings seem to follow a demand schedule instead of the fixed-time cycle that is common with associations. A meeting is planned and executed as the need arises. After all, a company meeting doesn't require the time needed by associations to build attendance. A simple directive from the top brass is all that is needed to ensure that everyone will attend the meeting.

Exhibit 6   When Corporate Meetings Are Held

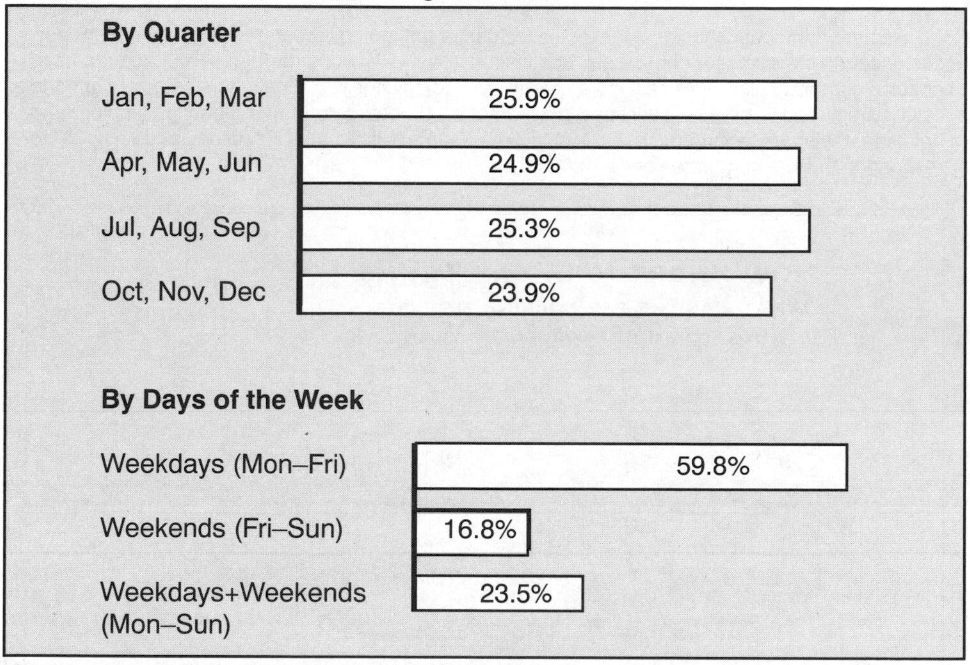

By Quarter

Jan, Feb, Mar	25.9%
Apr, May, Jun	24.9%
Jul, Aug, Sep	25.3%
Oct, Nov, Dec	23.9%

By Days of the Week

Weekdays (Mon–Fri)	59.8%
Weekends (Fri–Sun)	16.8%
Weekdays+Weekends (Mon–Sun)	23.5%

The beauty of corporate meetings is their consistency. Corporations meet regularly throughout the year and generally follow a mid-week pattern.
Source: State of the Industry Report by *Successful Meetings* magazine.

Lead Time

The planning period for company meetings is relatively short, rarely longer than a year. In the case of incentive trips, some consideration about the general area may be made some eight months to a year in advance, and, in the case of great numbers, the time may stretch to two years. But that is still much shorter than the lead time of many associations.

The annual sales meeting is usually planned eight to twelve months prior to convening. Corporate structure in this decision-making is simple. Some middle-level person, or perhaps two, will suggest, investigate, and screen properties and pass along the recommendation to one executive who generally makes the final decision. In some companies, one person does it all, which certainly can shorten lead time. There are many variations, of course.

Most other company meetings have a very short lead time—less than three months is becoming typical. Due to changes in the economy, the introduction of new products and companies, mergers and acquisitions, and breakups or expansions, businesspeople meet more often on short notice (see box titled "Shrinking Lead Times"). Short lead times are

---

SHRINKING LEAD TIMES

According to a study by *Meetings Today*, 74 percent of all corporate meetings can be classified as short term, having a turnaround time of 90 days or less. Rich Del Colle, the Boston-based meeting planner for Hewlett-Packard Co., explains:

> Today's pace has picked up from 10 years ago. Before, business used to be five days a week, but now it's 24 hours a day, seven days a week. That's what people expect, and you need to keep customers happy and get your products out there.

Another contributing factor is the increased use of technology. Internet virtual tours of properties, electronic requests for proposals, and instant communications through e-mail and fax have enabled corporate planners to act more quickly. Technology has replaced the numerous telephone calls, letters, and in-person site inspections formerly inherent to corporate meeting planning, and hotels that wish to capture their share of this market must have the technology and flexibility to respond to today's corporate needs.

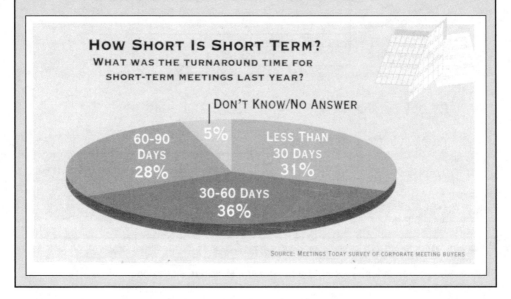

HOW SHORT IS SHORT TERM?
WHAT WAS THE TURNAROUND TIME FOR SHORT-TERM MEETINGS LAST YEAR?

DON'T KNOW/NO ANSWER

60-90 DAYS 28%

5%

LESS THAN 30 DAYS 31%

30-60 DAYS 36%

SOURCE: MEETINGS TODAY SURVEY OF CORPORATE MEETING BUYERS

---

especially prevalent in the technology and pharmaceutical industries due to product break-throughs. Nearly every company meeting planner can recall instances when it seemed like the meeting was needed for the next day. There is one kind of company meeting that we refer to as a *crisis* meeting. That follows when someone says, "Let's get everyone together as soon as possible and talk this thing out!"

It is too late to start selling your property at that point. If you had been in there selling, or had enjoyed some business from that company before, you might get a chance at this business. Certainly, there is no time for anyone to shop around. The situation calls for fast action and the meeting generally goes to a place the company has used before or to some wide-awake salesperson who had been in there pitching at the time.

It is such types of corporate business that must fill the gap when the convention function book is less than filled. The unexpected sales meeting, the crisis that calls for facing dealers or distributors, the new modification for which service personnel must be trained—all these bring opportunities for business meetings. These are meetings executives don't discuss when you talk to them. You must sell them on the idea of using your facility when the need next arises, and hope you made enough of an impression that they'll remember.

Geographic Patterns

There is no general geographic pattern for company business. To begin with, there is often no reason to vary sites to attract attendance, as in the case of associations. When the vice-president of sales calls a meeting in Chicago or Montreal at the first of the month, it is not surprising to find the sales staff in Chicago or Montreal at that time.

There is also no reason not to go back to the same hotel if it performed satisfactorily. The main reason for another selection may very well be mere boredom on the part of the meeting planner or his or her boss. It really depends on the kind of meeting. The annual meeting, with much hoopla and singing of the company song, may call for a variety of sites from year to year, but the hastily organized meeting doesn't. In fact, a strong case can be built for repeating at a hotel proven dependable by the last meeting, or at least for some hotel that had been pushing for the business.

Training directors, in particular, prefer to deal with the same hotel on a consistent basis. Some feel that with only small meetings to offer, they reach the status of *important customer* only through the promise of repeat business. Most training directors feel the need for distraction-free, classroom-type isolation, with a good supply of audiovisual equipment and service. Once having worked out such an arrangement with a suitable facility, they are understandably loathe to change.

There is some geographic factor involved, but it is the most obvious one. An Atlanta hotel obviously will have a better chance at getting a regional sales meeting for a staff covering the southeastern states than will a hotel in Boston or St. Louis. Time, the cost of transportation, and convenience are all factors affecting the geographic location.

Imagine the assignment given to the company meeting planner to arrange for a series of regional meetings for an international sales staff. He or she might plan to use hotels in New York, Chicago, Seattle, Los Angeles, Atlanta, and Toronto. If you have a hotel in any of these general areas, geography will work for you and give you a chance at the business in your sector. But the planner is also free to meet in Ottawa instead of Toronto, in St. Louis or Milwaukee instead of Chicago, in Boston or Philadelphia instead of New York.

This is where selling comes in. The hotel sales staffer must present the hotel positively and turn what might be a liability into an asset. If Kansas City is less glamorous than New York, it is more centrally located. If your property is not downtown, it offers fewer distractions, easier access by automobile, and free parking. If it is downtown, it offers more opportunities for entertainment. A salesperson should concentrate on the property's positive factors instead of being haunted by its shortcomings.

Company meetings, unlike many association meetings, rarely have regulations against meeting anywhere. The company president or board may favor some types of sites and frown on others in keeping with the image they want to project, but that's not the same as restrictions written into a constitution or bylaws.

Kinds of Sites

What kind of hotel does a company prefer? The answer has as many variations as there are companies and kinds of meetings (see Exhibit 7). A meeting planner should select a site to benefit from its locale and the hotel's attractions. The hotel that would be good for an incentive trip or annual dealer meeting may not be the wisest choice for that crisis meeting or training session.

Exhibit 7   Types of Facilities Used by Corporate Meeting Planners

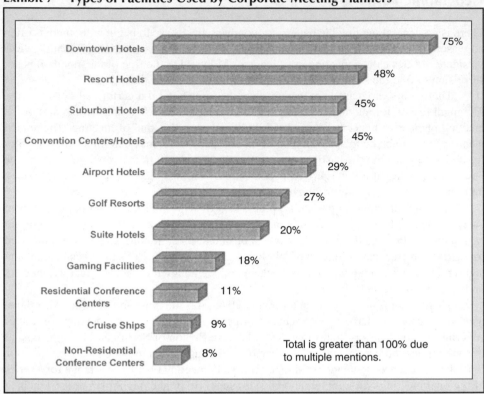

Meeting planners, who typically pay an average daily room rate of $184.00, prefer downtown hotels, followed by resort hotels and suburban hotels. The key selection criteria is generally the purpose of the meeting.
Source: Recent Meetings Market Report by *Meetings & Conventions* magazine.

For a successful sales and marketing career, help your customer achieve the kind of meeting he or she wants. Try to get those meetings that go well in your establishment. Let the ones that get away be those that really should be held in some other type of hotel.

Give careful thought to the kind of meetings most suitable for your hotel. Is yours a downtown hotel? Then stress its convenient location, especially when some people participate in only part of the program. Comfortable and familiar, the downtown hotel is a frequent choice.

Is yours a suburban hotel/motel? It offers easy access by auto and free parking. Stress its informal atmosphere. Will the meeting be the only one in the house? That is considered by many corporate planners to be so important that it may be the very factor that swings the business to you.

Airport location? The obvious advantage is convenience when air transportation is used, plus all the features of the suburban hotel. Once small properties, airport hotels come in all sizes today.

Resort? This is the obvious choice for incentive meetings, but is also often chosen to get away from the distractions of the city. Resorts in the off-season offer excellent rates, charm, exclusivity, industrial security, physical beauty and a good image.

Conference center? Conference centers are growing in popularity with corporate meeting planners, and many major hotel companies, including Marriott, Hilton, and Sheraton have noticed this shift and are becoming key players in the conference center segment.

While the few conference centers of past decades had a "going back to school" stigma, today's state-of-the-art facilities are often the choice of corporate planners looking for high-tech presentation equipment and locations that minimize distractions.

Boutique (lifestyle) hotel? Many corporate groups prefer full buyouts of these hotels for the privacy offered.

These are but a few benefits and characteristics of each type of property. You should be able to add others and to present your property positively as the one that best fits the meeting planner's event.

Attendance

One characteristic of corporate meetings that makes them popular with hotel people is the predictable attendance. Whether attendees come alone or with their spouses, attendance is nearly always mandatory. A rooming list submitted before the event is usually accurate. Barring mishap or illness, no-shows are minimal. Nancy Holder, RJR/Nabisco's conference planner, says:

> In corporate planning, if you book 200 rooms, you're going to use 200 rooms, unless there's an emergency. In other areas of planning (associations), you have to convince people to come. In the corporate world, if the CEO tells you to show up, you're going to show up.[6]

While attendance at corporate meetings is mandatory, one problem associated with corporate meetings is the risk of cancellation of the entire event. Poor financial returns or unexpected delays may result in a corporate official changing or cancelling the meeting. For this reason, most hotels now require nonrefundable deposits and have included stringent cancellation clauses in their contracts with corporate groups.

Care should be taken to get a VIP list. It can be embarrassing to everyone to have the fledgling sales trainee assigned to the fine corner room and the vice president of sales in a minimum single. If no VIP list is submitted, bring up the subject yourself and help your customer create one. If no need exists for him or her, fine. But check it out and at least flag a few names for preferred treatment. Those executives' comments may determine whether you get the group again.

Duration

Most corporate meetings are short. Some are limited to a single day and others may run as long as five days, but three days are about the most common. Arrival on the previous evening is popular so that the meeting can start early the next morning. Cocktail receptions and/or brisk action at the hotel bars add to the profits to be derived from corporate business.

Take care to coordinate the final day meeting program with your policy on check-out time. Plan ahead. If you can't gracefully extend the normal check-out time, perhaps you can arrange to check all the luggage with the bell captain or arrange for all luggage to be placed in just a few rooms before the check-out deadline. If you don't look ahead and decide how you will cope with the many requests at the last minute (or even with the entire group checking out late without even discussing it with you), your staff will be forced to improvise. And they may not always handle it as you would like.

Bring the matter up with the meeting organizer even if he or she doesn't. State your policy and suggest how to arrange matters. You can arrive at an agreed-upon arrangement. At the very least, you have alerted the planner to a potential problem.

Exhibits

The exhibit is a trademark of the association meeting for the most part. Corporate meetings, however, frequently have exhibits too. It is not uncommon, for example, for such meetings to display new products or to use live presentations on a grand scale. Thus you can expect requests for stage facilities and exhibit space when servicing corporate events.

The most recent *Meetings & Conventions* Meetings Market Report found that roughly 50 percent of corporate meeting planners plan trade shows for their companies. While the average number of attendees (1,210) is less than the number of attendees at association trade shows, the average duration of the show is similar (about three days). Therefore, meeting groups that hold trade shows in conjunction with their meetings are potentially very profitable for your hotel.

Corporate Trade Shows	
Percentage of planners involved in trade shows	53%
Average number planned	9.1 events
Average number of attendees	1,210
Average duration	3.3 days

Source: Recent Meetings Market Report by *Meetings & Conventions* magazine.

Meeting Room Requirements

There is a need for large and small meeting rooms, varying from event to event. Some meetings call for small committee-type rooms. In many training setups, the main group breaks into units of as few as ten people who meet separately for awhile, then reconvene in the main meeting room. Most meeting organizers prefer such *breakout* rooms to be right at hand.

If your hotel has such rooms in the same wing of the building, you have an edge when you solicit such business. It leaves something to be desired if the group has to huddle around a few tables in different parts of the main meeting room. It certainly is difficult to attract such a group under those circumstances if the competition can offer more suitable arrangements.

With corporate meetings, there is little likelihood that meeting rooms will have to be changed at the last minute. Association meetings, on the other hand, have higher attendance and the program often features concurrent meetings (several topics covered at the same time in various meeting rooms). The more popular topics may draw a larger audience than anticipated, requiring the meeting room set up staff to bring in extra chairs or make other arrangements (which may include moving the meeting to a larger room).

One Meeting, One Check

It is nice for a hotel to have most group business paid for with one check. That's one appeal of corporate business. Many companies pay all the expenses for their employees; others have different guidelines. Discuss with the meeting planner what he or she will approve for payment on the master account and what the individual must pay for upon checkout. Your front desk must be informed. Your credit manager may want to do some homework on the customer-corporation and may propose a schedule of payments, beginning with a deposit. As a general rule, corporate business is paid for en masse.

Multiple-Booking Potential

Hosting company meetings offers the opportunity to promote other business. Each person attending the meeting has sampled your hotel. If the impression is favorable, you may become the first choice whenever that person stops in your city on business trips. Or you may benefit from recommendations to others both in and out of the organization. Remember that most association boards include businesspeople who hold their own organizational meetings.

Help to execute a smoothly functioning meeting and you can pick up future business from the company as well. What appears to be a single meeting may be repeated in several parts of the country. This is a great situation for hotel chains. One person may order meetings in a number of locations, and that person may handle the logistics of all those meetings. There is often enough flexibility in the designation of the cities to be used that a chain may sell dates in a number of different properties.

The appeal to the meeting planner is achieving the status of a more important customer, and he or she has only to explain his or her needs once and have them duplicated in different hotels.

Surprisingly, however, chain loyalty is not a trademark of corporate meetings. A survey of corporate meeting planners conducted by *Meeting & Conventions* magazine determined that only 25 percent of corporate meeting planners used the same hotel chain for the majority of their meetings.

What does this mean to a single-location hotel? In order to compete with a chain effort, the individual hotel must present a good case for being the best choice in the city. Ideally, that image would be so strong that a meeting planner normally using a chain for the entire group of meetings would break that pattern when it comes to your city.

Many wise hotel salespeople cooperate with their counterparts in independent hotels in other cities. They try to get the meeting planner to buy from independents as often as possible, and make it easy for that to happen by recommendations and the passing of the sales lead to each other. Independent hotels in different cities recognize that they function as true allies in the sales competition with chains. This concept has helped in the development of the hotel representative who, with a stable of independent hotels, can offer the same kind of "one-stop shopping" as the chains.

Corporate Meeting Decision-Makers

No sales effort succeeds unless it is directed at the person or persons with the authority to make the decision. The convention sales picture is no different. Your story may be a good one, but it will be to no avail unless it is told to the right person.

Who is the *right* person? Not only does it vary from company to company, but it may vary from year to year within the same company. But some titles do keep coming up and they certainly represent a starting point for sales penetration (see Exhibit 8).

Exhibit 8   Meeting Planners' Corporate Positions

Job Title or Position	Corporate Planners
Corporate Executive Management	24 %
Meeting Planning/Convention Management	30
Sales/Marketing	11
General/Other Management/Administration	17
Other	18

Many corporations do not have professional meeting planners. Therefore, in prospecting for business, it is wise to know the common job titles for corporate decision-makers. These are summarized above.
Source: Recent Meetings Market Report by *Meetings & Conventions* **magazine.**

To find the decision-maker, you have to ask the right questions. "Who coordinates your meetings?" is not a good question; the person who coordinates the details of a meeting may not be the actual decision-maker. It is far better to ask, "Who is responsible for deciding which hotels your company uses for meetings?" With this approach, you will be able to make immediate contact with the decision-maker or recommender rather than having to deal with one or more "go-betweens," saving valuable time and effort.

Another approach, which may require slightly more time and effort, but which may also prove profitable, is to start at the top of the company and work downward. While speaking with the president of a company may not result in an immediate booking, this contact can prove valuable in two ways: you won't be referred to someone below the decision-making or recommending level, and a referral "from above" is a great door-opener.

Once the key contact is determined, you should pay attention to tomorrow's decision-makers. As the account is worked and information is secured on the organizational structure, "star performers" should be identified and relationships with them cultivated. Knowing the people who are likely to succeed present decision-makers can pay dividends in the future.

Full-Time Meeting Planner

When companies have centralized meeting planning activity, you deal with a full-time meeting planner. Hopefully, this should make your job easier because you deal with an experienced, knowledgeable pro who knows what he or she wants and how to go about getting it.

It is easier to deal with someone who knows what he or she wants. It can protect you from overlooking something in the arrangements. Both parties want the same thing—a smoothly run meeting—and it helps if both parties are expert. Build a reputation for

---

Profile of Corporate Meeting Planners

- 72% are female; average age is 48.

- Spend an average of 53% of their professional time on meeting planning activities.

- Have been arranging meetings for 13 years.

- Plan most of their meetings (58%) for 50 or fewer people.

- Duties include: selecting hotels (88%), selecting locations (81%), planning entertainment (72%), setting budgets (70%), planning meeting agendas (51%), arranging for transportation (air, 54%; rental cars, 42%), and trade show/exhibit planning (51%).

- Only 19% are Certified Meeting Professionals (and only 4% are Certified Meeting Managers), but 28% are members of Meeting Professionals International (MPI).

Source: Recent Meetings Market Report by *Meetings & Conventions* **magazine.**

competence and fair dealing and you are on your way to a successful sales career in the convention field.

The organization that represents corporate meeting planners is Meeting Professionals International (www.mpi.org). Membership is comprised of 24,000 members that belong to 71 chapters worldwide.

Company President

Smaller companies seldom have enough meeting activity to warrant a full-time meeting planning employee. In many such companies, the decision-maker is the president or some counterpart, such as a partner or chairman. It is understandable that the president of a large corporation such as General Motors will not be involved in such decisions, but the president of a company employing several hundred people might get involved in the national sales or dealer meeting. Never worry about making contacts too high up the corporate ladder. If he or she isn't involved personally, a president is seldom hesitant about naming the right person. And the recommendation of the president does you no harm when you deal with subordinates.

Administrative assistants to company presidents are also influential in meeting site decisions. Hyatt and the International Association of Administrative Professionals (IAAP) determined that meeting and event planning is an administrative professional's second most time-consuming office activity; 81 percent of administrative assistants plan four off-site meetings annually.

Marketing and Sales Executives

Marketing and sales executives are key people. The exact title may be *vice president, sales* or *marketing director, or manager* or *product manager.* They may operate on a regional, national, or even international basis. The bulk of corporate meetings involves the important areas of sales and marketing, so it makes sense to zero in on these people.

Such executives don't join meeting planning societies. They don't think of themselves as meeting or convention planners. But they do plan many of them, or, more accurately, are involved with planning them. They call the meetings, control the kind of meetings they want, and most often have the most important voice as to where and when they will take place. That makes them very important people for you to contact.

Advertising and Sales Promotion Managers

One step down the corporate ladder is the *advertising* or *sales promotion manager.* One person may carry both titles because the work is interrelated. In addition to usual duties, such middle executives frequently handle meeting planning functions. There is no relationship in such assignment to the size or type of company. If the company does not have a full-time meeting planner, the task is assigned to some departmental or divisional manager, and since it involves marketing activity, the advertising or sales promotion manager is often selected.

At the very least, such middle managers get involved in the initial screening of a site and the planning and execution of a meeting. They could be your first hurdle. You need them to recommend your property. In some cases, that is sufficient; in others, the final selection is made by their boss—the vice president, director, or manager of sales and marketing. Some people freely admit when their authority is limited, but some find it too painful to do so.

It helps you to know who the final decision-maker is, but you have to pay attention to the level that screens, too, or you may never get to the final selection stage. Make sure that your presentation summarizes your strong points very clearly so that they may be passed along in discussion with others.

Other Corporate Executives

Not all meetings stem from marketing divisions. Other executives get involved with staging meetings and therefore influence site selections. They carry titles such as *manager of corporate relations, public relations, industrial relations,* or *communications.* Such personnel may very well be active in sales and marketing, too. Corporate organization charts seldom indicate anyone as meeting specialists, yet many executives are. The executive in charge of meetings may have that assignment for a period of time and then it may pass on to another. The role of meeting planner is often a part of the career path for upward-bound middle management.

Passenger Traffic/Corporate Travel Managers

Many companies maintain a travel desk, which handles arrangements for employee business travel. When plane or hotel reservations are needed, they are requisitioned through the passenger traffic personnel. Traditionally, these corporate travel planners were responsible for booking hotel rooms and travel for individual corporate executives, and commonly negotiated with hotels and travel providers for a *commercial rate*, a lower rate guaranteed to their personnel.

Increasingly, however, because of consolidation of the meetings and travel departments at a number of corporations, the responsibilities of corporate travel planners have expanded to include planning meetings. These personnel, therefore, not only negotiate for rates for guestrooms but also for meetings space and food and beverage functions.

Membership in the National Business Travel Association (NBTA), an organization of corporate travel managers, once consisted of corporate travel planners who dealt primarily with individual travel for their personnel. Today, 94 percent of NBTA members are involved in planning meetings for their corporations. In order to better assist corporate travel planners, especially those new to the meeting planning area, the NBTA offers training classes and joined the Convention Industry Council (CIC) to provide additional opportunities for the education of their membership.

The NBTA, which has branches in Canada (called the National Business Travel Association—Canada) and in Asia (called the National Business Travel Association—Asia Pacific), sponsors an annual trade show in August. A similar organization for corporate travel planners, the Association of Corporate Travel Executives (ACTE), is a global association of over 60,000 travel executives in 82 countries. ACTE also hosts a trade show as well as educational conferences. The shows of both of these organizations are well-attended by hotels seeking to build corporate group travel business, especially since the position of corporate travel manager is expected to grow in scope.

Procurement (Purchasing) Managers

Another answer for companies that wish to cut costs by consolidating their meeting and travel departments is to structure meeting planning within the procurement (purchasing) department. The involvement of the procurement department in meeting planning is changing the nature of planner/hotel relationships. While hotels traditionally have dealt directly with the meeting planner (who answered to his or her company or organization regarding the meeting budget), the procurement department is increasingly involved in the decision-making process—from selecting hotel sites to approving menus and costs for food functions.

While meeting planners generally have some knowledge of the nuances of meeting costs, such as paying more for guestrooms or food functions to enable them to receive free meeting space, for example, procurement managers often look at buying hotel rooms and services in much the same way that they look at purchasing other commodities; in other words, they want to get the best price possible. And this doesn't mean strictly in terms of rooms or meeting space; procurement managers also look for the best values in such products and services as audiovisual equipment, decorators, and so on, which can result in decreased revenues for the hotel.

This trend has not only resulted in increased competitiveness among hotels, but has also affected the way in which salespeople do business. The decision-maker for a corporate meeting may now be the procurement manager, and the salesperson dealing with this decision-maker has to be able to prove the value of what his or her hotel has to offer. This can include explaining everything from the quality of the hotel's food to its reputation for high service standards to something as intangible (but important) as the experience of the attendees.

Fred Shea, vice president of sales for Hyatt Hotels Corp., says:

> Our sales managers have to show price value, but not just price, because dates and rates are all online, right there for the customer to see. We are training our people how to do a better job of making that procurement customer understand the value that goes back to them, both in service and actual attendee experience.[7]

Training Director

Training directors use a wide variety of hotel types. Airport and other suburban locations are popular because of ease of access and parking. Small resorts and boutique hotels are used in the off-season, especially when executive development programs call for more prestigious sites. With lower budgets, training directors make good use of secondary hotels, off-season rate breaks, and all-cost packages.

Training departments usually handle their own meetings, even in cases where the company already has a setup for sales meetings. You may sell the sales department for their meetings but still have to sell another group for training sessions.

Training directors' requirements do not differ from the requirements of others who plan small meetings, but they are less likely to be permissive about such things as audiovisual equipment, permanent dividing walls, low-hanging chandeliers, and nearby distractions in the hotel. Actually, these specifications are similar to those that any good meeting planner would want (see Exhibit 9).

Exhibit 9   Advertising to Planners of Small Meetings

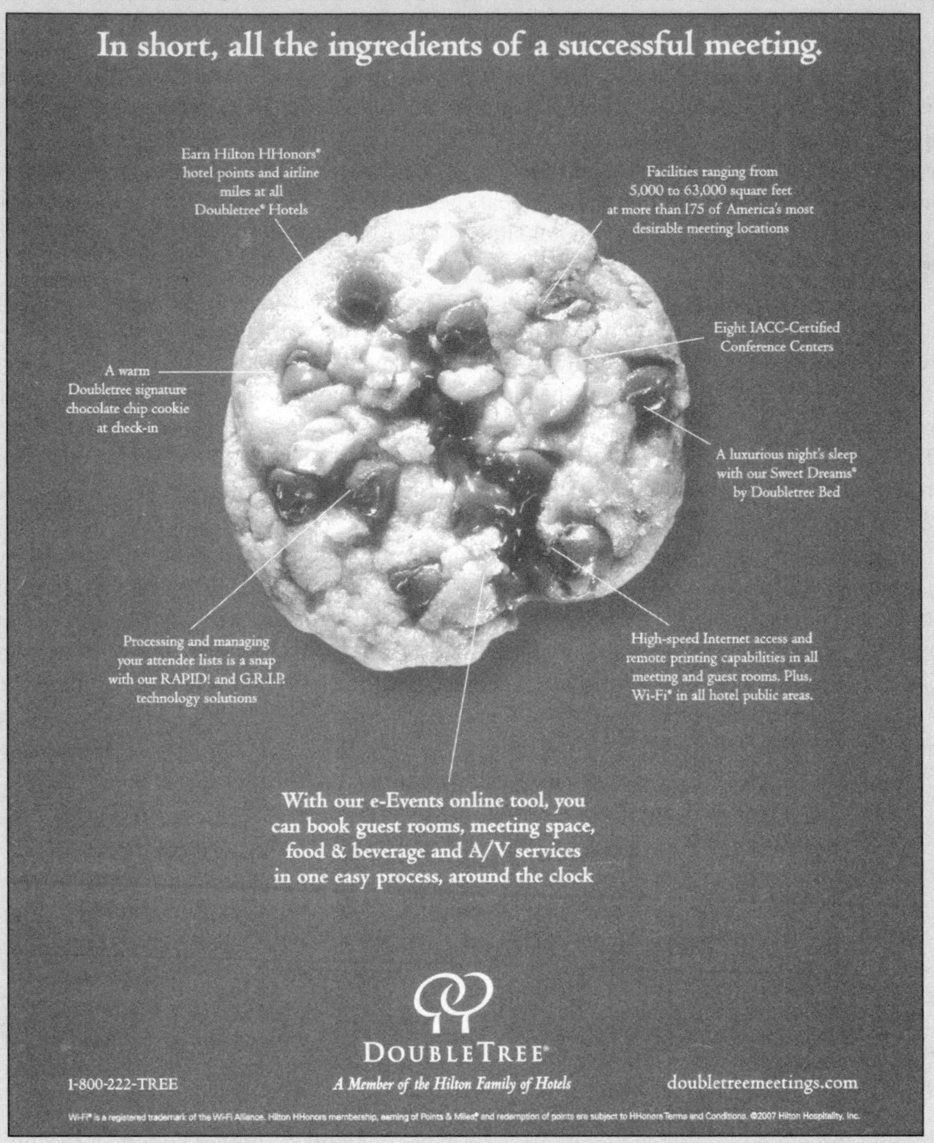

This ad for the DoubleTree chain promotes the services and amenities that are offered to meeting planners at the chain's hotels and conference centers, including the e-Events online tool, which allows meeting planners to book everything needed on a 24/7 basis.
Source: Courtesy of DoubleTree.

Meeting Specialists/Third-Party Planners

Just a few years ago, nearly all corporate meetings were planned by in-house departments. Due to downsizing, many companies, like associations, are looking outside their own organizations for meeting planning services. Some of these **third-party meeting planners** only get involved in larger meetings. Others select hotels, airlines, destination management companies, and other meeting services. They conduct site searches, negotiate rates on behalf of

Generating Sales from Third-Party Planners

Roger Helms, Founder & CEO

HelmsBriscoe

Scottsdale, Arizona

We are an international travel and meeting planning company that plays "matchmaker" between companies looking for hotel rooms and meeting space and the venues that can meet these needs. We're a wonderful resource for meeting managers because we free up their time to focus on content and the delivery of the meeting's message. We also offer them the advantage of our volume purchasing, which means better pricing and more lenient contracts (hoteliers favor us because we provide business they weren't reaching and we save them the cost of setting up sales offices in markets we've penetrated).

In 1992, while working as a sales and marketing executive with the Registry Hotel Corporation, I spotted a void—and the opportunity to act as "resource firm to the conference industry." That same year, I teamed with Bill Briscoe, a 14-year Registry veteran, and HelmsBriscoe was born.

Since that time, we have grown to become the largest purchaser of group hotel rooms in the world. We have a network of nearly 1,000 associates, most former seasoned hotel salespeople, in over 30 countries. We work with hotels throughout the world on a daily basis and are compensated by the hotels that pay us a placement fee based on room revenue. Our company represents clients ranging from fraternal organizations holding reunions to large corporations launching new products—anybody who plans meetings. We started as a very small boutique company and have been fortunate to maintain this great culture and sense of communication and community as we grew the organization. The dedication and passion of our associates, as well as the technology to communicate globally, has made this possible.

As is always the case with the future, the only constant is change. Staying ahead of industry trends and client needs is a key component of our company's success. The difference between a good company and a great one is that some will learn nothing and some will learn a great deal and become better and stronger. I'm proud to say that I believe HelmsBriscoe fits into this latter category.

the companies and associations they represent, and assist in conducting meetings and conventions. Travel organizations are called in at times, especially for incentive programs. These organizations are important sources of business.

Third-party companies have become prominent sources of meetings business. According to a Future Watch survey by Meeting Professionals International, about 20 percent of events are outsourced to these kinds of planning firms. Hotel chains now focus their efforts on deriving their business from the biggest clients and have justified this approach based on the rationale that 80 percent of group business comes from 20 percent of their clients. Therefore, third-party leads will grow in importance.

Steve Armitage, vice president of sales and managing director of Hilton Hotels, says:

> We want to increase our market share with key accounts, and the more business we get from an organization, the better positioned we can be to partner with them on the rates they need for an event to be successful.[8]

Third-party companies make their money by charging a management fee to the meeting groups they represent or by charging the hotel a commission on the room rate. Obviously, hotels would prefer that these third-party planners secure their fee from the groups

---

💻 *INTERNET EXERCISE*

Third-Party Meeting Planners

Corporations often outsource their meeting planning to third-party meeting planning firms. These firms will take site inspection trips and negotiate meeting contracts for their clients. Because they represent several companies and bring a large volume of business to hotels, they claim to be able to negotiate a better meeting package than a company could get when acting alone. The salespeople who work for these third-party firms are independent contractors, and many have worked in hotel sales positions and have their own corporate meeting contacts.

Log on to the websites of the companies below and answer the questions in this exercise:

- Experient—www.experient-inc.com
- Conference Direct—www.conferencedirect.com
- HelmsBriscoe—www.helmsbriscoe.com

1. What services do each of these companies offer?

2. What are the benefits for hotels that partner with these firms?

3. How are each of these companies paid—by the meeting planner or are they paid a commission by hotels for booking business?

---

they represent, but, recognizing the volume of business provided by third-party planners, many hotels are willing to pay commissions.

Many smaller associations and corporations have limited bargaining power when negotiating with hotels. But when they outsource their meetings to a large third-party planner they often realize the advantage of volume savings. To get more personal attention—and perhaps greater concessions from hotels—it is likely that more planners will turn to third-party meeting management companies to locate and negotiate facilities for their meetings.

Sources for Finding Corporate Business and Decision-Makers

It's a great big business world out there, and while you may be eager to just get out there and knock on doors, that isn't the recommended use of time. Tom McCarthy, a veteran of hotel sales, believes prospecting should be more calculated:

> A salesperson might have a territory that includes 35,000 companies. If a salesperson can qualify 20 new prospects a week, it doesn't take much figuring to determine that the salesperson can qualify about 1,000 accounts a year.
>
> Wouldn't it make more sense to work with a list broker and pick 1,000 companies in advance that would be assigned the salesperson (based on proximity, size, and type of business), rather than just telling the person to "hit the bricks"? Do we think the person will call on the best 1,000 out of the 35,000 by chance?
>
> Here we are working with computers and sophisticated software and still living in the 19th century when it comes to the most basic principles of prospecting.[9]

In today's competitive environment, prospecting for new business is essential, but going up and down the street knocking on doors is not the way. Once you know the kind of corporate executives you want, there are a number of ways for you to reach them effectively.

Special Meetings and Business Publications

The corporate meetings business is served by several publications that have literally done your job of sorting out those executives interested in meetings. It is hardly a surprise, therefore, to find that advertising appearing in these publications seems to be an industry rundown of the leading convention hotels. These magazines also offer advertisers sales lead services, providing the names of and data about likely prospects.

Leading publications include *Corporate & Incentive Travel, Corporate Meetings & Incentives, Meetings & Conventions, Meeting News,* MPI's *One+, Smart Meetings, Successful Meetings,* and *Financial & Insurance Meetings.* Most of their circulation is to readers in the corporate area, and all have Internet sites for instant access.

There are other publications of interest to hotel marketing people, although they do not specialize in conventions; they either deal with related editorial subjects or reach the executives likely to make meeting decisions. Most relevant is *Sales and Marketing Management.* As its name implies, the publication is directed to sales and marketing executives who are frequently involved with meetings.

General business publications can be considered as well. Although these publications are not directed specifically to executives who are involved with meeting decisions, their circulations reflect profiles similar to those of meeting planners. Hotels with adequate advertising budgets can promote their meeting facilities in such publications as the *Wall Street Journal, Business Week,* and *Fortune.*

Trade Directories and Publications

It is possible to develop sales leads by working your way through a specific industry. If your records indicate meetings of similar companies, it may be that industry is a fertile field for more business. The insurance industry, for example, is a prolific meeting group. There is even an association of meeting planners solely within that field. Other individual trades and industries may offer names of companies similar to those that have met in your hotel.

The *Dun & Bradstreet Million Dollar Database* (www.dnbmdd.com), which was formerly available in directory form but is now posted online only, lists the largest businesses in the United States and Canada and their officers. Hotel salespeople can search by specific companies or by specific industries.

Standard & Poor's Net Advantage (www.netadvantage.standardandpoors.com) is a similar database that lists over 60,000 companies and provides addresses and basic information on key personnel, number of employees, and revenues.

Meeting Professionals International Membership Directory is available to members and allied members of Meeting Professionals International (MPI), 1950 Stemmons Freeway, Dallas, TX 75207. To obtain a copy of this guide—the best-known source of corporate meeting planners—hotel people must join the organization along with a meeting planner.

Best Insurance Reports, published by A.M. Best Company, Ambest Road, Oldwick, NJ 08858, lists some ten thousand executives of insurance firms. A.M. Best Company also offers extensive online information that can help hotel salespeople identify principal officers and get company names and addresses at www.ambest.com.

The *Corporate Meeting and Event Planners Directory* lists more than 14,000 meeting planners in the United States and Canada. Listings include key information such as addresses, telephone numbers, websites, when and where meetings are held, number of meetings, average meeting length, and the type of facility used. The directory is available from Douglas Publications, 2807 No. Parham Road, Suite 200, Richmond, VA 23294 (1-800-762-9600). The company also offers several hospitality databases (broken down into such categories as Association Meeting & Event Planners, Corporate Meeting & Event Planners, Medical Meeting & Event Planners, and Premium, Incentive & Travel Buyers) at its web- site, www.douglaspublications.com.

Trade Associations

If you feel that specific industries might be worth following, call on the executive directors of their trade associations. *You should be calling on them anyway for their own association business,* but they can also be a prime source of leads. They can pinpoint the larger companies in the trade and those in your part of the country. Their trade directories could be a good source of leads and a good addition to your mailing list.

Many meetings are held in the principal locale of the sponsoring company. It makes sense, therefore, to study directories of businesses within your city, state, or area of the country. Chambers of commerce could also supply such lists.

The local library, chamber of commerce, and state industrial commission are also excellent sources for local leads. Most offer publications that list businesses according to North American Industry Classification System (NAICS), developed by the federal government. In many cases, your property may already have a breakdown of businesses booked by NAICS code; this makes it particularly easy to target other businesses from the same category.

Don't neglect to solicit the local branches of national organizations. You may be told that meeting decisions are made at the national headquarters, but don't ignore the local firms. It is common for a corporate meeting planner to ask a local district manager about a suitable hotel in the area. The order may come from corporate headquarters, but the important input could come from your own area.

In addition, local branches often hold meetings of their own, albeit smaller ones. Local dealer meetings, training sessions, and regional sales meetings are often within the responsibility of the regional sales manager. Going after the regular commercial business of a branch sales office may give you a chance at some group business as well.

Internet Sites

Another effective way to find meeting planners is to visit Internet sites that provide membership information and search services. One of the largest is MPIWeb, the website of Dallas-based Meeting Professionals International. MPI has more than 71 chapters in 51 countries, including 30 in North America, and you can click on "MPI Chapters" to find chapters in specific geographical areas. The site offers a free search service (a hotel salesperson does not have to be a member or associate member of MPI to use the search feature) that allows you to select such items as "Meeting Consultant/Independent Planner." By entering a specific city and state, you will be provided with a list of updated names and contact information.

💻 *INTERNET EXERCISE*

Garnering Sales Leads from Cyberspace

There are a number of websites that allow meeting planners to conduct detailed property searches on the Internet. Three popular sites are:

- Convention Planet—www.conventionplanet.com
- Elite Meetings International—www.elitemeetings.com
- Groople—www.groople.com

Log on to each of these sites to answer the following questions:

1. Which site offers the "RVP Valet" tool? How does this site's request for proposal (RFP) differ from the other two sites'?

2. Which site offers the greatest number of facility listings for meeting planners to consider?

3. Which site requires members to pay a listing fee to be included on the site?

4. Which site targets SMERF meeting planners?

5. In your opinion, which of these three sites would meeting planners find to be the most user-friendly?

This is just one of the many sites available on the Internet. LinkedIn (www.linkedin.com), a business-oriented, professional networking social media site, allows salespeople to reconnect with past and present business contacts. Hoover's (www.hoovers.com) offers an online directory that provides information on 32 million companies. This directory lists the names of key decision-makers in various industries, allowing a hotel salesperson to build customized lists of prospects. Tools such as this directory and other directories available online are great tools for reaching the corporate market, allowing you to expand contacts at companies you are presently doing business with and identify other potential customers in the same industry. Online directories offer varied services, such as access to financial data and the ability to download reports or lists; some charge subscription fees.

Steve Tremewan, director of marketing at the Radisson Resort and Spa Scottsdale (Arizona), says:

> We used to do research at the library and subscribe to all the local newspapers in our target markets. But now we are able to do most of our research on the Internet.[10]

He still reads local newspapers in his property's major target areas, but their online versions rather than printed publications, to determine if new businesses may be coming to town as well as what conferences and meetings are scheduled to be held. He also uses these and other online sources to find contacts in market segments that his property wishes to target.

Convention and Visitors Bureaus

Many hotel salespeople are also finding that working with their city's convention and visitors bureau can be an excellent way to build corporate business. While CVBs formerly dealt exclusively with associations business, many are now targeting smaller corporate markets and can provide leads for your property.

Just a few years ago, the Destination Management Association International (DMAI) held its first Destinations Showcase event in New York City to promote CVB services to corporate planners. While many corporate decision-makers had not previously used CVBs, interest in using them as "one-stop shopping" venues has increased. If a corporate meeting planner is interested in booking space in Orlando, for example, he or she need make only one call to the CVB; the CVB will respond with information on only those hotels that meet the planner's needs.

Properties can also find additional leads by participating in the destination marketing efforts of CVBs. Many of them participate in trade shows promoting their destination city, and participating properties may either send salespeople to meet with show visitors or make promotional materials available at the CVB's booth.

💻 *INTERNET EXERCISE*

Prospecting Tools for Hotel Salespeople

The Knowland Group offers a number of prospecting tools for hotel salespeople. Log on to their website, www.knowlandgroup.com, browse the site, and view the "Insight" video to answer the following questions:

1. How can the site's satellite imagery and Internet mapping tool be used to prospect for new meetings business?

2. What service is available for targeting sales leads that have used your direct competitors?

3. Using the site's database of group events, type in a city of your choice and determine the number of hotels and events that were surveyed there in the most recent month.

4. Why is the site's reader board service a valuable resource for lead generation?

Lateral Referral and Account Penetration

Many hotel people are content when they get meetings business from a large corporation. But hosting company meetings offers the opportunity to promote even more business. Just help to execute a smoothly functioning meeting and your hotel will have an edge on the competition when it comes to additional business from the firm.

Some companies are so large that employees in one division have little or nothing to do with those in other sectors. If your meetings business comes from a product manager in one division, give serious thought to following up with everyone who has the title of product manager in that and other divisions of the company.

The operating structure of the company may be uniform throughout, and if the product manager in one instance has the meetings responsibility, it is likely that others would too. If not, the manager will likely be able to point you to a decision-maker. Your case is stronger if you can get a recommendation from your original product manager customer. Even if he or she doesn't know the others personally, an endorsement from someone within the firm should open some doors.

Such lateral referrals and complete **account penetration** of all sectors of a large firm is the sign of a successful hotel sales manager. Think of the large companies in your area as a multi-divisional entity simply loaded with business potential. To ensure that you have reached all potential decision-makers and other influential staff members, you can employ a technique called **account mapping**. Neil Salerno, founder of the Hotel Marketing Coach, explains:

> An excellent technique to penetrate larger corporate accounts and get more of their business is account mapping. Place the name of a decision-maker on a chart. Now, add who your contact reports to and who reports to them. If you don't know, find out and contact the additional staff members. Once they have been contacted, add them to your chart and continue the process. The end result should be a virtual organizational chart of the company. This chart or map will ensure that you are doing business with every mover and shaker in that company.[11]

This will also help your prospects for business in other companies. You will gain an insight into corporate structure that will help you analyze other companies in the same industry. The structures are generally similar. It certainly provides you with a good starting point by knowing the titles you are seeking. Understanding the corporate setup and who most likely has the meetings chore gives you a big leg up to penetrating and selling corporate business.

Other opportunities await at the property level. Local suppliers, such as your produce wholesaler, dairy operator, insurance agent, and other suppliers of products and/or services, are potential sources of meetings business. Even if a property's suppliers do not require meeting space for themselves, many belong to trade, professional, or civic organizations or social or religious groups. The property's suppliers, then, could very well be in a position to recommend the property as a meeting site for future meetings of their respective organizations.

One industry consultant advises:

> Look through the newspaper for announcements of meetings being held at competitors' properties—and try to get them for their next meeting. Look through the business section of the newspaper and trade journals for companies moving to town and for promotions or honors given to officers of companies. All of these are good lead opportunities.[12]

The hotel's employees are also good sources of meetings business. Many employees belong to organizations (bowling teams, garden clubs, the P.T.A., religious groups, etc.) that meet regularly or have need of function space for special occasions such as installation dinners, awards nights, and other events. Hotel employees could very well influence the choice of "their" property for those events.

Summary

In this chapter, we have taken an in-depth look at the corporate meetings segment, which is typically viewed as the most profitable group market segment. Not only does this segment often pay higher rates for rooms (despite meetings held during slow seasons), but it also can add to the hotel's bottom line with food and beverage, audiovisual, and recreation revenues. We have discussed the kinds of meetings held by corporations and the characteristics of the various company meetings. We have determined who the key corporate decision-makers are likely to be and how to find them. This lucrative market segment is becoming increasingly important to hotels, and hotel salespeople who understand the requirements of corporations and can match these requirements to their properties can successfully target the corporate market.

Endnotes

1. John Anderson, "In Front of the Curve, *Smart Meetings,* November 2009, pp. 39, 41.

2. Terence Baker, "Coffee With…Mark Beaupre," *Meetings & Conventions,* May 2004, p. 12.

3. www.meetingsnet.com/financialinsurancemeetings/maginsurance_leveraging_smallmeetings_spend_0509/index.html.

4. Marshall Krantz, "Combo Meetings: Seeking Efficiencies," *Meeting News,* October 11, 2004, p. 1.

5. Macie Schreibman, "Small Meeting Myths," *Smart Meetings,* November 2009, p. 43.

6. Michael Adams, "Career Jumping," *Successful Meetings.*

7. Cheryl-Ann Sturken, "Making Inroads," *Meetings & Conventions,* April 2005, p. 44.

8. "Hilton Makes Fast Progress Absorbing Promus," *Meetings News,* March 20, 2000, p. 53.

9. Tom McCarthy, "Get Your Sales Management Ready for the 21st Century," *Hotel and Resort Industry.*

10. Cheryl-Ann Sturken, "Making Inroads," *Meetings & Conventions,* April 2005, p. 44.

11. Neil Salerno, "Are You Being Out-Hustled by Your Competition? How to Dominate Your Hotel's Market Set," www.hotelmarketingcoach.com/are_you_being_outhustled_by_you.htm, November 1, 2009.

12. Howard Feiertag, "New Sales Teams Often Miss Opportunities," *Hotel & Motel Management,* July 21, 2008, p. 10.

 ## Key Terms

account mapping—Determining the arrangement of and relationships between various company personnel to ensure that a salesperson has made contact with every potential decision-maker or influential staff member.

account penetration—The process of determining new sources of business within an organization.

business center—A facility that offers key equipment and services typically found in a business traveler's home office, including computer access, fax machines, and copy machines. Many offer secretarial and other services, such as shipping.

dealer meetings—Meetings held on a regional and national basis for dealers and distributors. Usually held to introduce new sales and advertising campaigns and new products.

incentive meetings—Meetings held during incentive trips given to employees, distributors, and dealers as a reward for top performance.

management meetings—Relatively small meetings consisting of top management, often requiring upgraded accommodations and services.

professional/technical meetings—Meetings held in order to update the company's technical personnel, usually taking the form of seminars/workshops.

sales meeting—Often a meeting dealing with such company objectives as product introduction, sales policies, company goals, and a discussion of sales techniques; or held to boost morale.

stockholder/public meetings—Meetings for non-employees.

strategic meetings management—A return on investment program implemented by corporations to bring accountability, consolidation, collaboration, and cost-consciousness to the meetings management process.

third-party meeting planners—Outside individuals or firms that handle meeting planning for companies. Services may include site selection, negotiations, and assisting in all phases of staging the meeting

training meetings—Meetings held to update personnel in new company policies, methods, or procedures. Usually fairly small in size.

 Review Questions

1. There are many similarities between association meetings and corporate meetings, but there are also clear distinctions. Contrast the two considering lead time, attendance, and kind of site required.

2. Company meetings come in many sizes and shapes. If you were the sales manager of a small property with limited meeting facilities, what types of company meetings would you target?

3. Discuss the multi-booking potential of corporate meetings.

4. As with associations, finding the key decision-maker within a corporation is of utmost importance. Why is this problem so acute in the corporate meetings market? List probable decision-makers within the corporate structure.

5. What role do local chapters or business offices of regional, national, or international corporations play in the determination of meeting sites?

6. Discuss how hotels are upgrading guestrooms with extra services and "perks" to meet specific business traveler needs.

7. List the major sources for finding corporate meetings and tell how each is used to develop a client base.

 Additional References

Meetings, Expositions, Events, and Conventions: An Introduction to the Industry, George G. Fenich, Prentice-Hall, 2008.

Cindy Estis Green, "The Information Revolution in Hospitality: A Guide to Intelligent Marketing 2000-2020," *The HSMAI Foundation Research Review.* hsmai.org

Internet Sites

For more information, visit the following Internet sites. Internet addresses can change without notice. If a site is no longer available at the address listed below, a search engine can be used to find the new address or additional, related sites.

Alliance of Meeting Management
  Companies
www.ammc.org

Association for Corporate Travel Executives
  (ACTE)
www.acte.org

Corporate & Incentive Travel
www.corporate-inc-travel.com

Corporate Meetings & Incentives
www.cmi.meetingsnet.com

Independent Meeting Planners Association
  of Canada (IMPAC)
www.impaccanada.com

Meeting Broker
www.MeetingBroker.com

Meetings & Conventions magazine
www.meetings-conventions.com

Meeting News magazine
www.meetingnews.com

Meeting Professionals International (MPI)
www.mpiweb.org

National Business Travel Association
  (NBTA)
www.nbta.org

Small Market Meetings
www.smallmarketmeetings.com

Smart Meetings
www.smartmtgs.com

Successful Meetings magazine
www.successmtgs.com

Chapter 6 Outline

Competencies

1. Describe the nonprofit organizations market and explain how to sell meeting services and products to it. (pp. 187–189)

2. Identify SMERF organizations and explain how to sell meeting services and products to them. (pp. 189–200)

3. Summarize sales considerations for selling meeting services and products to the following markets: goverment agencies, labor unions, incentive meetings, insurance/financial service meetings, and medical meetings. (pp. 200–213)

Successfully Targeting SMERF Groups

Lyn Matthew, CHSE
Director of Sales and Marketing
Embassy Suites Resort, Scottsdale, Arizona

"The remaining group market segments, commonly referred to as SMERF (Social, Military, Educational, Religious, and Fraternal) as well as government, union, medical, insurance, and incentive markets are by far the most diverse and challenging. Research is critical in determining which groups can best be served by the property. Since a property can be perceived in many different ways by targeted prospects, it is important to communicate the benefits that highlight the planner's needs and wants. Meeting needs vary widely. The astute sales executive must carefully match property capabilities with the needs of the conference planner. By selling the benefits of the property relative to the conference needs and wants, the sales executive has the opportunity to become a top producer while at the same time satisfying the needs of the meeting planner and paving the way for future bookings."

6   Selling Other Markets

T HIS CHAPTER INTRODUCES the third major source for meetings business: nonprofit organizations, including SMERF groups, government agencies, and labor unions. Also included is a discussion of three other major meeting segments: incentive meetings and insurance/financial service meetings, both of which are prominent corporate types; and medical meetings, which are a type of association meeting.

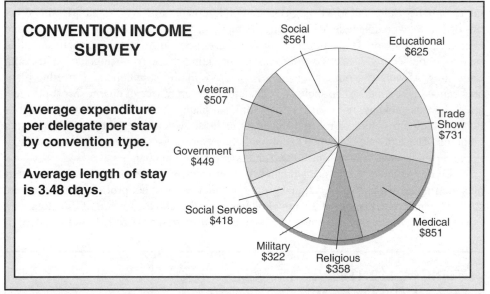

CONVENTION INCOME SURVEY

Average expenditure per delegate per stay by convention type.

Average length of stay is 3.48 days.

- Social $561
- Educational $625
- Veteran $507
- Trade Show $731
- Government $449
- Social Services $418
- Military $322
- Religious $358
- Medical $851

This chart illustrates the average expenditure per delegate per stay for the SMERF groups that we will discuss in this chapter. Medical groups and trade shows have the highest average expenditures, while military and religious groups are the most price-conscious and spend the least money. While most of the SMERF groups fall below corporations and associations in terms of convention expenditures, these groups typically meet during months in which corporations and associations are not holding group meetings and conventions, making them a very attractive source of business for hotels.

The "Market at a Glance" boxes in this chapter give a snapshot of these groups. They identify each segment's key characteristics, including location requirements, facilities commonly used, price range, services needed, typical decision-makers, and the best ways to reach each market. This will enable you to identify the group(s) best suited to your property and develop strategies to capture their business (a list of the major associations to which planners in these categories may belong is also listed at the end of the chapter).

Nonprofit Organizations

Although many organizations cannot be termed associations, they are structured in similar fashion. They have members, are nonprofit, and were created to accomplish some common purpose. Some, such as the Red Cross and the Boy Scouts and the Girl Scouts, promote charitable causes. In addition to meetings business, these types of organizations, which exist through fund-raising, may be excellent sources of business for your banquet department. Others of this category include political clubs and parties, which need hotel meeting accommodations for their regular conventions and frequent meetings. Still others include social, military, educational, religious, and fraternal (SMERF) groups; government agencies; labor unions; and medical groups, which will be discussed in greater detail in this chapter.

Selling to these organizations is much the same as selling to trade associations, although it is difficult to find a central source that identifies these organizations, since they are so varied. The records of a convention or tourist bureau may be of some help, and there are also directories from which a list of nonprofit meeting groups can be compiled. The *National Directory of Nonprofit Organizations* lists 265,000 organizations indexed by activity and zip code.

Another particularly good avenue for reaching nonprofit, cost-conscious groups is the Hospitality Sales and Marketing Association International's Affordable Meetings® series of shows, which include Mid-America (Chicago), West (Long Beach, California), and National (Washington, D.C.) shows. Named the most popular meetings events in an online survey conducted by *Meetings & Conventions* magazine, these events include a 650-booth trade show as well as seminars for planners and hospitality suppliers, and meeting planners can attend both the trade show and educational program free of charge. Most planners attending this show are not members of traditional planners' associations such as MPI or PCMA; they are volunteer meeting planners or those whose titles don't imply meeting planning. These people plan such events as hobby conventions; military reunions; educational, religious, and fraternal meetings; and government meetings.

Once you have determined which of these groups you can best service, you can start by soliciting local chapters of national groups. Generally, most nonprofit organizations are staffed by permanent employees and volunteers and overseen by a board of directors. Site selection processes will vary, but recommendations are usually passed along to a board of

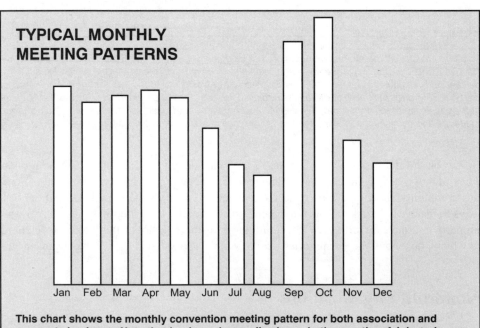

TYPICAL MONTHLY MEETING PATTERNS

Jan Feb Mar Apr May Jun Jul Aug Sep Oct Nov Dec

This chart shows the monthly convention meeting pattern for both association and corporate business. Note that business is usually slower in the months of July and August. Targeting SMERF groups, which normally meet in these months, can help increase business over these "soft spots."

The SMERF Market at a Glance

- Many SMERF meeting planners work part-time or are volunteers.
- SMERF attendees tend to stay together in the hotel for food and beverage. Many groups have up to three meals in the hotel.
- Attendees bring their families. While one member is in meetings, other family members are visiting attractions.
- 32% plan one to three off-site meetings a year; 27% hold up to 10 off-site meetings annually.
- Attendance projections are reliable and less likely to be affected by economic downturns.
- 70% of SMERF meeting planners report attendance of less than 500 persons; 50% reported that attendance at their largest event was less than 500.
- 43% have meeting budgets of less than $100,000.
- A little over half of SMERF annual events include a trade show or exhibition.

Types of Facilities Used by the SMERF Market:

Urban/Midtown Hotels	65%	Convention Centers	29%
Suburban Hotels	44%	University Facilities	20%
Conference Centers	36%	Arenas/Stadiums	7%
Resorts	32%		

Source: Patricia Sherman, "SMERF Events," *Expo*, **February 2008, and Howard Feiertag, "SMERF Business Ideal to Help Fill Weekend Room Nights,"** *Hotel & Motel Management.*

---

directors for a final selection. Lead time tends to be shorter than that of most trade associations; a lead time of one to two years is most common.

Since most local committees are made up of volunteers, it is a good policy to assure them of your aid should they succeed in getting the national organization to schedule its event at your property. If you offer to extend help for the chores associated with being the host chapter, this may encourage them to push for consideration of your locale as a meeting site.

As a further selling point, don't be reluctant to point out the many economic benefits to the community when a convention is held there. Research has indicated that delegates to regional and state conventions account for expenditures of about $165 a day for three or four days.

Once you are past the local chapters and have penetrated the national organization, you will usually find that there are experienced meeting planners on the staff. Some of these national organizations do a great deal of convention work. They will work with you in the manner of association staffs, especially if you have been successful in getting the local chapter to request the position of host chapter.

The SMERF Groups

One of the most important subsegments in the nonprofit organizations market are the **SMERF groups** (see box titled "The SMERF Market at a Glance"). This acronym represents the collective group of **S**ocial, **M**ilitary, **E**ducational, **R**eligious, and **F**raternal groups. These groups, though typically price-conscious, are economically viable to properties (large and small) both because of their sheer numbers and their ability to fill "soft spots," as most meet during the typically slow summer months (see box titled "Typical Monthly Meeting Patterns").

Social Groups

People are avid "joiners," and there are groups for almost every interest. Just looking through the "Groups and Organizations" listing in a local telephone directory may yield such prospects as chess clubs, ethnic groups (Italian-American clubs, etc.), garden clubs, and bowling leagues. These organizations may be local, or they may be part of a regional or national organization. No matter what their size, these social groups should not be overlooked as potential sources of business. Since most SMERF meetings are not driven by business needs, but rather by social and personal ties, they are generally more recession-proof than other types of meetings. Even a small local group may require meeting space or can generate meals business, while large groups can be an excellent source of banquet and convention business. Many social clubs hold awards banquets or fund-raising functions, or can be a source of business for annual events such as Christmas parties and installation ceremonies. Groups such as garden and craft clubs often host local shows or fairs,

Social groups meet to share common interests, and, depending on the type of group, can prove to be an excellent source for meeting rooms business as well as food functions.
Source: Photograph courtesy of Loews Hotels.

which not only result in meeting space sales, but may bring in out-of-town business and generate publicity for your property. Most social group decision-makers are inexperienced in meeting planning. Louise Hurlbut, vice president of marketing for Groople, an agency that specializes in group online travel arrangements, says:

> These groups are often run by volunteers or by people who may not handle an event from year to year. So when you're dealing with a less experienced audience, you may need to help them through the process by providing them the tools that make it easier for them to find the appropriate facilities and travel arrangements for their group.

Military and Other Reunions

The reunions market, which consists of family, class, and military reunions, is a rapidly growing market segment. This segment is an excellent source of flexible weekend business.

Military Reunions. In recent years, military reunions in particular have paved the way for an entire new industry that assists in planning these nostalgic events. Bob Brooks, president of THE Reunion Network, Inc., estimates the military reunion market to be worth $15 billion a year in air travel, hotels, food, drink, and entertainment.

In the past, military reunions, which typically draw 100 to 300 people or more, were planned by nonprofessionals. Because of the rising demand, however, several resources were developed to assist inexperienced meeting planners.

THE Reunion Network, established to provide assistance and training, publishes a newsletter, *TRN News,* that offers tips for planning a successful reunion and provides additional services to planners, such as offering lists of "reunion friendly" hotels. Military reunion planners can also look to other publications, such as *Reunions Magazine, Military Reunion News,* and *The Reunion Handbook: A Guide for Reunion Planners,* for assistance in planning their meeting. In addition to these resources, Service Reunions, a registry listing over 9,000 military units, helps planners in the most difficult part of their jobs: locating members. This service, which lists planners by state, military service, size of meeting, and month of meeting, also provides telemarketing lists, making it an invaluable resource for properties that wish to target this lucrative market. There are also a number of other resources for hotels wishing to target military reunions (see Exhibit 1).

Military reunion business has several notable characteristics (see box titled "The Military Reunion Market at a Glance"). For the most part, reunions are held from April to October, and occupancies run from Thursday or Friday through Sunday (the average length of stay is 2.5–4 days). There are an estimated 15,000 military reunions held annually. Most groups meet annually or biennially, and many will seek your professional expertise in setting up their meeting.

Most military reunion programs include a Saturday night banquet, a memorial service, and a short business meeting. Also critical to military reunion groups is an adequate hospitality room in which attendees can share stories and consume food and drinks. Ted Dey, president of Armed Forces Reunions, Inc., which books more than 30,000 room nights a year for military reunions nationwide, says:

Exhibit 1   Sources for Finding Reunions Business

Properties wishing to target the lucrative reunions market can utilize a number of sources to find leads:

Publications

Reunions Magazine P.O. Box 11727 Milwaukee, WI 53211-0727 800-373-7933 www.reunionsmag.com	Reunion Research 40609 Auberry Road Auberry, GA 93602 www.reunited.com/tomstips	Reunion Research Publisher of: *Family Reunion Handbook* *Reunion Handbook:* *A Guide for School &* *Military Reunions*

Books on Reunions   ### Reunion Planning

Reunions: Step By Step TRN 5688 Washington St. Hollywood, FL 33020 800-225-5044	*Reunions for Fun-* *Loving Families* by Nancy Funke Bagley Brighton Publications P.O. Box 120706 St. Paul, MN 55112 800-536-2665	THE Reunion Network 5688 Washington St. Hollywood, FL 33020 800-225-5044

In addition, hotels can join such organizations as THE Reunion Network. This group publishes *TRN News,* a free newsletter for reunion planners, and offers help—including lists of "reunion friendly" properties—to inexperienced meeting planners. In addition to being included on THE Reunion Network's list of contact properties, your hotel can advertise to meeting planners in the newsletter.

The Military Reunion Market at a Glance

Location: Family and/or military-oriented destinations that can offer a combined vacation/reunion. Past destinations have included San Diego, California, Daytona Beach, Florida, Branson, Missouri, San Antonio, Texas, and Norfolk, Virginia. Almost any city with popular local attractions or a good climate, however, can compete for this market.

Facilities: Programs usually consist of a short business meeting, a memorial service, and a Saturday night banquet. Requirements include limited audiovisual equipment, but there must be enough banquet space to seat the entire group and their spouses at one time. A hospitality room is usually required.

Price: Since many attendees are on fixed incomes, this group is very cost-conscious. Properties that offer low rates, free or low-cost meeting space, or discounts to local attractions are especially inviting.

Services: Properties targeting this group can expect to assist with the planning of functions, as many military reunions are planned by nonprofessionals. Some groups will also require special meal menus.

Decision-Makers: Contact must be made with individual military unit or group to determine the decision-maker.

Best Ways To Reach Market: Join THE Reunion Network, and advertise in *TRN News*. Other advertising opportunities include *Reunions, the Magazine* and *Military Reunion News*. Find contacts through the *Military Reunion Handbook*, and purchase lists or labels from Service Reunions National Registry. Attend military reunion training conferences and organize fam trips for military reunion planners.

The hospitality room is the reunion. That's where it happens. The ideal hospitality room would be one that's large enough to accommodate tables of memorabilia and where attendees are allowed to bring their own liquor.[2]

Room occupancy is usually 75 to 150 per night, although this can go higher for larger reunions. Since many attendees are on fixed incomes, paying their own way, they are extremely price-conscious. Attendees often share rooms with spouses or friends.

🖳 *INTERNET EXERCISE*

Hotels Offer Tools for SMERF Meeting Planners

Hilton Hotels offers a number of tools and checklists for SMERF meeting planners, who are typically less experienced than planners for associations and corporations.

Log on to their website, www.hiltondirect.com, which is billed as Hilton Hotels' meeting site search service, and scroll down to "Tools." First, click on "Checklists" to review the various Hilton Direct checklists available to the SMERF market. Then, click on "RAPID!" and "G.R.I.P" to view Hilton's numerous web-based aids for meeting planners.

1. What is Hilton's G.R.I.P. program?

2. What is their RAPID! program?

3. List the advantages meeting organizations receive by using Hilton's Personalized Group web page.

Hotels with planned spouse programs have a competitive edge in attracting this market. Attendees are typically male, but spouses have a strong voice in the decision to attend. One meeting reunion planner states:

> All of the men have something in common, but almost none of the women do. If you do the job right, the wives will send the check in the day the registration notice arrives.[3]

Military towns also have an edge, as veterans like to visit their old haunts and tour bases, ships, and museums. The Pensacola, Florida, Convention and Visitors Center, for example, touts its history as "The Cradle of Naval Aviation." The Montgomery, Alabama, Chamber of Commerce estimates that military reunions have a $10 million annual impact on the local area economy because the Air Force keeps its historical records at a base there. Or, a site may be chosen for its uniqueness. The Hangar Hotel in Fredericksburg, Texas, for example, is reminiscent of a World War II hangar and offers a number of nostalgic touches, including a 1940s-style diner with a menu that generates déjà vu for military reunion attendees.[4]

In order to assist planners in selecting venues for military reunions, THE Reunion Network, the organization of military reunion planners, is now planning and organizing familiarization trips for their members. These fam trips are sponsored by the THE Reunion Network and the convention and visitors bureaus of military reunion-friendly destinations.

Class and Family Reunions. Class and family reunions differ from military reunions in terms of size, meeting frequency, and types of programs. Recreational amenities are considered very important, and there may be several food and social functions but little in the way of meeting space needed. Like military groups, however, these groups pay their own way, and usually provide a good number of double occupancy rooms.

Class reunions are the largest in terms of numbers of events and number of attendees. However, attendees stay an average of just one night in a hotel. Family and military reunions, on the other hand, draw fewer people but the attendees stay for a longer period of time—an average of two nights in the case of family reunions and about three nights at military reunions.

Although most family reunions are hosted by nonprofessionals, there is a growing number of trained class reunion meeting planners. The National Association of Reunion Managers (NARM) is an organization that offers meeting planning training and networking. In addition, exhibiting at the African-American Family Reunion Conference, held annually at Temple University in Philadelphia, is an excellent way to reach potential customers. According to the National Coalition of Black Meeting Planners (NCBMP), African-Americans are an excellent source of reunions business, especially if your city can offer points of interest relative to the black heritage (museums, entertainment, etc.) and your property is sensitive to African-American issues.

Source: Photograph courtesy of Pifemaster Productions.

Exhibit 2   Reunion-Friendly Hotels

Host your special reunion at the
Holiday Inn Bayside overlooking beautiful
San Diego Bay. Our experienced staff will
assist you in planning the perfect event.

- Beautiful and spacious guest rooms
- Tropical courtyard with heated pool, spa, shuffleboard, billiards
- Family style restaurant and cocktail lounge
- Non-smoking and disabled rooms
- 9-hole putting course, exercise room
- Free parking and airport transfers

Special Reunion Features

- Complimentary one-night stay for reunion planner with site inspection
- Complimentary hospitality suite
- Welcome letter and box of chocolates in each room
- Senior discounts in our restaurant
- Special reunion rates

SAN DIEGO BAYSIDE

4875 North Harbor Drive • San Diego, CA 92106
(619) 224-3621 • Fax: (619) 224-3629
(800) 650-6660
www.holinnbayside.com • email: dos@holinnbayside.com

This ad for the Holiday Inn, San Diego Bayside, promotes an experienced staff who can assist the planner in organizing a "perfect event" as well as special reunion amenities, such as special reunion rates, a complimentary hospitality suite, and a welcome letter and gift of chocolates in each room.

Other ways to target the class and family reunions market are to advertise in *Reunions Magazine*, a Milwaukee-based monthly publication, and to work closely with your local convention and visitors bureau or chamber of commerce. These organizations are often contacted by individuals or groups wanting information about "reunion-friendly" hotels (see Exhibit 2).

Leads can also be obtained on the Internet. Over 5,000 *family reunion* planners visit Family Reunion Hotels (www.familyreunionhotels.com) every month. Great Reunions (www.greatreunions.com) is the largest *class reunion* planning organization.

Educational Meetings

The educational meetings market is an excellent market segment for filling rooms during slow summer occupancy periods. Elementary, high school, and college teachers and others affiliated with academic programs are prime sources of convention business. They hold a number of meetings, and every state has a teachers' association of some sort as well. In addition, most states have continuing-education requirements that necessitate periodic seminars and classes for teachers.

Most educational meetings are relatively short (sometimes lasting only a day), and meeting planners look for accessibility and value. Since most attendees come at their own expense, they are extremely price-sensitive. Properties that are located close to major transportation arteries or an educational center (college, university, etc.) and can offer reduced room rates are especially attractive.

Since this market is so diverse, there are many potential contact persons. Cooperative extension services often sponsor seminars, and the state director is the decision-maker (a county agent's directory is an excellent source of contact names). Alumni offices and divisions of continuing education at local colleges and universities are sources of leads for meetings business, and admissions offices can provide transient business from visiting parents and prospective students. Other leads can be obtained through the administrative offices at a local educational institution or board of education. Personal contacts and referrals are often available from college professors and teachers who belong to professional associations.

A pamphlet specifically keyed to the educational meetings market is *Educational Associations and Directories.* Providing the names and addresses of educational offices, it can be obtained from the Superintendent of Documents, U.S. Printing Office, Washington, DC 20401. The *National Directory of College Athletics* identifies personnel in the athletic departments of universities and colleges throughout the United States. This directory can be secured by writing to Collegiate Directories Inc., P.O. Box 450640, Cleveland, OH 44145. Or, you may wish to utilize the *Blue Book of College Athletics,* published by Athletic Publishing Company, P.O. Box 931, Montgomery, AL 36101.

Many hotel chains exhibit at the annual Travel, Events and Management in Sports (TEAMS) conference and expo. This convention provides networking opportunities and one-on-one appointment sessions. Information on upcoming events can be found at www.teamsconference.com.

Religious Meetings

Religious groups are an excellent source of business for gatherings both small (board meetings, committee meetings, seminars, and workshops) and large (area and regional meetings and conventions). Large conventions of 10,000 to 45,000 attendees are a common annual occurrence. The last survey by the Religious Conference Management Association (RCMA) shows that religious meetings have grown by 195 percent over the last decade. A property that understands the unique needs of religious groups can take advantage of this opportunity to fill "soft spots"—most groups meet over a three-day to one-week period during the summer months (see box titled "Religious Meetings at a Glance").

Most large religious meetings are "family affairs," and meeting planners tend to choose locations that are family oriented (Orlando, Anaheim, Indianapolis, Toronto). Mike Blackwell, festival coordinator for the United Church of God, speaking of his Branson, Missouri, meeting, says:

> Many of our members make this their family vacation. All ages attend, so
> we have to have a destination with something for everybody.[5]

Religious meeting attendees often make up for their lack of alcohol consumption in food consumption. D'Wayne Leatherland, meeting planner for the Church of the Nazarene, states:

> Our meetings history supports the claim that our group likes the "f" in
> food and beverage.[6]

He suggests that hotels convert bars into ice cream parlors or coffee shops during his group's meetings, turning lost alcohol revenue into food revenue.

Most religious meeting attendees pay their own way, so they are price-sensitive and usually opt for double-occupancy rooms, but religious meetings can be profitable to a hotel because they do not displace corporate or association business. Because these groups are value-conscious, religious meeting planners negotiate lower rates by booking on holidays and weekends and seeking shoulder or valley periods. Vaughn Hall, director of convention sales and marketing for the Santa Clara, California, Chamber of Commerce/Convention and Visitors Bureau, says, "We've targeted the religious market because our weekends are slow and it's a good filler market for us."

There is another very good reason to target this market. Many religious groups do community service projects when they visit a city. In Indianapolis, for example, 2,000 meeting attendees helped local neighborhood associations rehabilitate ten houses and clean up city parks. Other groups work at soup kitchens or run blood drives.

Religious Meetings at a Glance

Attendance: Consists of hundreds of organizations from dozens of denominations throughout the United States and the world; may range in size from small board meetings to mega-conventions of up to 75,000 (see photo). May consist of clergy, lay people, or both; are often family affairs.

Location: Favor family-oriented cities such as Orlando, Anaheim, and Atlanta. Also prefer second- and third-tier cities, generally in the South or Midwest, such as Birmingham, Branson, Indianapolis, and St. Louis. Mark McCulley, CMP, festival administration manager for the Worldwide Church of God, evaluates each city for facility size and quality; affordability of hotel and convention facilities; area attractions and amusements; friendliness of the city; and overall entertainment value of the region.

Facilities: Need a wide selection of meeting and convention space—small meeting rooms for seminars, workshops, and meetings; large convention halls to hold large crowds. Often require numerous breakout rooms and have many, often simultaneous, meal functions.

Services: Restaurant availability is a high priority. According to April McWilliams, V.P. of Sales for the Greater Birmingham CVB, "Whenever people finish up with a meeting, they're always hungry. They want a place to eat, so it's important that hotels or centers have restaurants open for them, even if it's just for pie or coffee." Some religious groups will require special menus as well (i.e., Jewish Kosher foods).

Price: Middle- to low-budget hotels are preferred, since most attendees pay their own way. Double occupancy is the norm. Property-offered discounts and complimentary transportation are valued. However, the once-pervasive image of penny-pinching religious meeting attendees is no longer valid. Anne Hamilton, vice president of resort and sales services for Disney, states, "Disney World has 25 resorts at four price points and religious meeting attendees stay at all of them."

Decision-Makers: Most national events are planned by professional meeting planners. Local and regional events are planned by a committee or the leader of the organization.

Best Ways To Reach Market: The RCMA (Religious Conference Management Association) is a national organization representing over 250 denominations and religious organizations. They publish a monthly magazine, *Religious Conference Manager*, and a membership directory.

Religious groups, such as the Promise Keepers, a men-only ministry based in Boulder, Colorado, generate over 7,200 conventions and meetings internationally and represent 30 million nights of hotel accommodations annually.

Summary of Types of Religious Meetings		
Type of Meeting	**Total Attendance**	**Average No. of Days**
Convention/Conference	10,871,566	4.0
Board	121,449	2.3
Committee/Seminar	626,571	2.2
Retreat	465,729	3.4
Other	1,804,442	2.8
Total	14,889,757	
Types of Meeting Facilities Used		
Downtown Hotel		17.2%
Conference Center		16.6%
Suburban Hotel		12.8%
Camps/Retreats		11.2%
Resort Hotel		11.1%
Convention/Civic Center		11.1%
Airport Hotel		10.5%
College/University		7.6%
Cruise Ship		1.9%

Source: "RCMA Survey," *Religious Conference Manager*, **June 2008, p. 24.**

Many of the large religious meetings are planned by professional meeting planners, many of whom belong to the Religious Conference Management Association (RCMA). This group was founded in 1972 and has approximately 800 meeting planner members and 2,100 associate members that represent hotels, convention bureaus, and other suppliers. RCMA members are responsible for over 2,000 meetings a year, and represent more than 250 denominations and religious organizations.

RCMA's Annual Conference and Exposition is an ideal arena for direct sales to this market. The group also publishes a monthly magazine, *Religious Conference Manager*, and a membership directory. Properties seeking the religious market would find associate membership in the organization to be an excellent investment.

Another group of interest is the Christian Meetings & Conventions Association (www.christianmeeting.org). Hotels can join the association as supplier members, and the organization's website features a "Supplier Search" tab. The group holds an annual convention and exposition each spring.

Fraternal Meetings

Fraternal organizations can be broken down into two categories: "The Greeks," which are the familiar college campus societies; and fraternal service groups, such as the Benevolent Protective Order of Elks, the Fraternal Order of Eagles, the Lions Club, and the American Legion, to name a few.

College Fraternal Groups. National fraternities and sororities, which number 55 and 26 respectively on college campuses across the country, typically meet during the summer months at events planned by a paid executive. The activities of this vast market are coordinated by three major groups: the National Interfraternity Conference (NIC), which represents 48 fraternities; the Panhellenic Conference, the female counterpart of the NIC; and the Fraternity Executives Association (FEA), whose membership is made up of paid executive

---

Sources for Reaching the Fraternal Market

Fraternal Executives Association

Attendee Profile: College fraternity executives (executive directors and national presidents) from the top college fraternal organizations in America.
Program: Fraternity-related suppliers from the hospitality industry can socialize with executives and participate in a trade show.
Contact: Fraternity Executives Association, www.fea-inc.org.

National Panhellenic Conference

Attendee Profile: College sorority executives (executive directors and national presidents) from the top women's fraternal organizations in America.
Program: Geared mainly toward hospitality industry suppliers, the best opportunity for business development occurs during the trade portion of the event.
Contact: National Panhellenic Conference, P.O. Box 90264, Indianapolis, IN 46268 (313) 872-3185.

National Interfraternity Conference

Attendee Profile: National fraternity executives and college fraternity advisors from throughout the country.
Program: Mainly fraternity related; the trade show portion of the event offers the best opportunity for business development.
Contact: National Interfraternity Conference, Inc. 3901 West 86th Street, Suite 390, Indianapolis, IN 40268-1791 (317) 872-1112.

---

officers from a number of fraternities (see box titled "Sources for Reaching the Fraternal Market").

The size of most general membership meetings, held during the months of June through August, ranges from approximately 150 to 800 or more. Multiple-occupancy rates are high, since spouses or fellow students often share rooms. Meeting agendas typically include a banquet lunch, so properties wishing to service this market must have ample facilities to seat the entire delegation at one time. Lead time is typically two to three years.

In addition to general meetings, sororities and fraternities hold educational retreats and leadership training institutes, which are usually held during the school year to train newly elected officers. While some of these meetings are held on college campuses for cost-effectiveness, properties that can offer discounted rates may be able to capture some of this business.

Other possibilities for business include national board or council meetings, which usually consist of the governing boards of sororities and fraternities. Since group size is small, ranging from six to 125 people, and meetings are shorter, these meetings are often held on weekends (usually during the months of October and February). Airport facilities and properties close to the campus can often draw this type of business.

A subsegment for special consideration is African-American fraternal organizations. Consisting of eight major fraternities, these groups have annual or biennial conventions of 2,000 to 20,000 people. Besides generating high attendance, the advantage of servicing this market is that the membership is generally older and more affluent than the typical collegiate fraternity member. Alumni chapters play active roles in these organizations, and

attendees tend to have more disposable income than their college counterparts—which translates to higher entertainment, catering, and alcoholic beverage revenue for hotels.

In addition to the traditional Greek societies, there is another group of professional or honorary societies that should also be included in this category. Some examples include Alpha Omega, a professional dental fraternity, Sigma Delta Chi, a professional journalism society, and Delta Epsilon Sigma, a scholarship honorary society. Some of these host large conventions, meeting on an 18-month rotational basis in the months of August and December. The December conventions, held between Christmas and New Years Day, are an excellent way to fill this traditionally slack time. These groups can be reached through related professional associations or through contact with the American Society of Association Executives (ASAE), since many of these meeting planners belong to that association.

Service Fraternal Groups. Service groups also hold a number of meetings and special events throughout the year. While many of these (such as the Elks, Shriners, and the American Legion, for example) have their own meeting facilities, they can be excellent sources of business for special occasions, including fund-raising events and annual functions such as Christmas parties. This group may also play host to regional and national conventions or generate rooms business from out-of-town guests attending local functions.

Both fraternal and service groups' regional and national meetings are usually family affairs and are often presented to delegates—who pay their own way—as a vacation-convention combination. Planners, therefore, look for recreational amenities as well as value.

Some service organizations have special needs. Lions Clubs International, for example, strives to serve people with sight challenges, and more than five percent of the attendees at the group's annual meeting are blind. That means that meeting planner Renee Aubin must look for a destination that doesn't require a lot of walking yet has enticing activities close by for the group's multinational attendees. She found that "Montreal excels as an easy multilingual destination with a compact downtown and tantalizing pre- and post-convention tourist opportunities." She adds:

> It was one of the best cities, with its housing package and diversity.[7]

There are a number of ways to reach this lucrative market segment. Sororities and fraternities can be reached by contacting college campuses and their alumni associations or by contacting the national governing groups mentioned in this section. Service groups may be found in local telephone directories or through chamber of commerce listings.

To solicit this market on a larger scale, you may wish to consider participating in three events held by major fraternities and sororities. The Fraternal Executives Association (FEA) holds a meeting and vendor trade show during the first two weeks of July, while the National Interfraternity Conference (NIC) holds a larger event during the first week of December. While this event also includes a trade show, it is less hotel-specific than FEA's. The National Panhellenic Conference (NPC), which is held in October, also features a trade show and gives vendors the opportunity to meet with the executives and staff members of 26 attending sororities.

Government Agencies

Another frequently overlooked—but potentially lucrative—nonprofit market segment is government meetings business (see box titled "The Government Meetings Market at a Glance"). This market segment can be an excellent source of conventions business, especially when agencies deal with business groups. The Department of Commerce, the National League of Cities, and the Department of Public Health are three examples of government agencies.

It is difficult to generalize about the kind of business that comes from government agencies. It varies a great deal, as does interest in different parts of the country. We are strong believers in "fishing expeditions." Go into any local government office and ask the supervisor about meetings held by his or her department or any emanating from the national or state office. This takes patience and hard work, but you may be able to add a number of prospects to your lists. And don't overlook chambers of commerce. Some are funded by local governments, while others are independent membership organizations; in either case, local chambers can be excellent sources of meetings business.

The Government Meetings Market at a Glance

Location: Preferred locations are those that are easily accessible. Cities to which airlines offer direct flights and discounted fares are given priority. Government planners must be sensitive to the public appearance of booking a resort or elegant location.

Facilities: Preferred facilities offer double-double guestrooms and reasonably priced restaurants. Most meetings involve training, so quality meeting rooms and audiovisual support are prime concerns.

Price: Generally are cost-conscious. Planners must deal with a strict bid process and sparse per diems. Hotels bidding must know how to fit within government per diem guidelines; rates quoted must include taxes.

Services: All "low-cost" or "no-cost" services that the property can provide are solicited by planners, i.e., free shuttle van from airport, complimentary coffee breaks, and waived meeting room rental. Require flexible payment schedules, as the government is often slow in paying.

Decision-Makers: Meetings are planned at the local, state, and federal levels. Key contacts include the agency director, training officer, contract specialist, and procurement officer.

Best Ways to Reach Market: Join the Society of Government Meeting Professionals. SGMP's monthly chapter meetings, national newsletter, directory, and annual conference are excellent for identifying and contacting prospects. List your property in the *Official Airline Guide Government Edition* and subscribe to the *Commerce Business Daily,* a publication listing requests for meeting proposals.

If the people expected to attend meetings are government employees, it would help if you learned what the current **per diem** allowance—the fixed amount of money allowed for government employees for each day of travel away from the office—is for your city. It is seldom a generous sum, and employees often add to it out of their own pockets. If you can offer a meeting package of lodging and meals that is covered by the per diem allowance, you will be more likely to attract this market segment.

When going after government business, you will find that it is not too different from dealing with corporations. You deal with a strata of executives, and when you get to the person of authority, you can close the deal. You can expect many small meetings, on short notice, just as you do in corporate business. Government meetings are generally held during the normal work week, so lodging is typically required Mondays through Thursdays.

The majority of government meetings are held for training purposes, and there are several key needs that must be met in order to attract this business. First, accessibility is important; direct flights at discounted rates are a major factor in the choice of locations. Second, most agencies look for free meeting space; a property that hopes to secure government business must make this concession in exchange for guestroom business. Third, government meetings are on a tightly controlled per diem basis; a property that can offer a rate within government guidelines has a distinct advantage in attracting this market. Government agencies are also often slow in paying (it can take as long as 45 days to receive payment); a property must be able to work within government payment schedules. Since lead time is short (less than one year), government agencies often keep files on properties that meet their requirements and can book meetings on short notice.

Since most meetings are training meetings, the meeting planner is often a training officer, contract specialist, or procurement officer. Although properties will usually work with one of these people in regard to meeting details, site selection is often based on two

Five Steps to Capturing Government Meetings Business

1. Become FEMA certified.

Hotels that wish to do business with the U.S. government must be certified by FEMA (Federal Emergency Management Agency). You can become certified by logging on to www.usfa.fema.gov/applications/hotel and clicking the "Register" link. The form can be filled out online or you may download a PDF version.

If you are unsure if your property is already FEMA approved, you can use the website's search tool to determine your current status.

2. Register your property with the Central Contractor Registration.

Hotels that wish to be considered for government business must be listed with the Central Contractor Registration. The registration form can be accessed at www.ccr.gov.

3. Determine and be able to comply with government per diem rates.

Per diem is the allowance that the government pays for daily lodging (including taxes), meals, and incidental expenses in any given city. These rates are tied to local markets, and they change periodically. To determine current per diem rates for your area, log on to www.gsa.gov/perdiem.

4. List your property on government-related websites.

Business Partner Network, accessible at www.ccr.gov, is an official vendor service for the U.S. government; registration with the Central Contractor Registration will make your hotel's information available to government meeting planners. You can also list your property on www.fedtravel.com. This website provides information on FEMA-certified hotels that offer government contract rates.

5. Join organizations for government meeting planners.

Joining one or both of the following organizations can provide opportunities to network with government decision-makers. Each also offers education on ways to capture the government meetings market.

The Society of Government Meeting Professionals (SGMP)	**The Society of Government Travel Professionals (SGTP)**
900 King Street, Lower Level Alexandria, VA 22314 (703) 549-0892 www.sgmp.org	4938 Hampden Lane #332 Bethesda, MD 20814 Washington, DC 20815 (202) 363-7487 www.sgtp.org

distinct types of price submission: Invitation for Bids (IFB) and Request for Proposals (RFP).

The IFB procedure uses sealed bids that are mailed or hand-delivered to the requesting government office in sealed envelopes until a preset bid-opening date. All prices are announced during the bid opening. The RFP is a confidential method of selection. The government is free to negotiate with a supplier who meets government standards. Once a final selection is made, the property must prove that it can provide the contracted services (physically and financially).

There are several sources for locating government business. Local legislators can be invaluable contacts; often, the suggestions of a legislative committee will result in a booking. Direct mail contact may also be made with various government agencies and officials. A direct mail package might include a government rate sheet, third-party endorsements from government groups that have met at your property, and an offer for a member of the agency to visit your hotel. Advertising is another option frequently used to reach the government market. The box titled "Five Steps to Capturing Government Meetings Business" provides a five-step action plan for soliciting the multi-billion-dollar government meetings market.

Labor Unions

The labor union meetings market has become so important that many properties employ sales personnel to specifically target this category. There are over 150 unions in the United States and a similar number in Canada, and most hold meetings fairly regularly. In addition, most unions stay with a property with which they have been satisfied, providing an excellent opportunity for repeat business.

Union meetings, which are usually held only at hotels that are unionized, fall into three general categories: national conventions, regional conferences, and executive and committee meetings.

National conventions are usually held every two years, with site locations shifting between eastern and western regions. National conventions typically generate:

- High spouse attendance
- High per-person expenditures
- A number of social programs
- Several sponsored functions, providing good food and beverage revenue

Because of their size, national conventions are held at large properties that can provide the rooms and meeting space needed to accommodate the delegates and their spouses. The general session, which typically takes on a political atmosphere, is the focal point of the convention and is usually attended by all of the delegates. Sophisticated audiovisual equipment is often required, as is media accessibility, since prominent political speakers are often part of the program.

In addition to the large amount of space needed for the general session, sufficient space is needed for the various social functions in the program. These may range from banquets for the entire contingent, to breakfast meetings for key leaders, to a number of hospitality suites.

Regional conferences are usually held in central locations. Meetings typically last two to three days and draw attendances of 200 to 500 delegates. As in the case of national conventions, meeting planners seek out properties that can accommodate all of their delegates and offer sophisticated audiovisual equipment.

Executive and committee meetings, which number as many as four a year, are usually held in the union's headquarters city. Since participants are key union people, attendance is smaller (15 to 20 people). These meetings are important to a property, however, as the success of a small meeting may lead to the booking of larger meetings and conventions.

Contact persons for union business include the general secretary of a union for national conventions and the secretary-treasurer for executive and committee meetings. Meeting planners are professional and well-disciplined, and the selling process must include a sense of trust based on personal relationships and the ability to meet the meeting planner's needs. Directories that can be helpful in locating labor union business include the *Directory of Unions and Labor Organizations* and the *Directory of Labour Organizations in Canada.* Information on labor unions can also be found with an online search.

Incentive Meetings

While incentive travel is a part of the corporate meetings market, this important market segment is sufficiently different to deserve special mention, especially due to its growing impact and importance to resort properties.

What is **incentive travel**? It is a travel award—often a deluxe tour package—offered as motivation to employees and customers to put forth extra effort and meet criteria established by the program sponsors. Since the trip is a reward for selling (or buying), incentive meeting planners seek first-class accommodations and service, and look for locations that offer good weather, sightseeing, recreational facilities, entertainment, and a choice of restaurants (see Exhibit 3).

The economic environment has a great impact on the degree of incentive travel. When times are tough, it becomes critical to motivate employees and customers. Incentives have been proven to increase employee and distributor participation in moving products and services. Travel incentives, which are recognized as effective motivators, have been used to improve morale, reduce turnover, and achieve special sales targets. They have also been used to get dealers to concentrate on specific brands and to increase purchases.

Travel award programs are frequently established for automobile dealers, appliance distributors, insurance salespersons, and other employee and customer groups. The

Exhibit 3   Factors Important to Incentive Travel Planners When Selecting Group Destinations

Factors Considered "Very Important"	Group Incentive Trips
Climate	92 %
Sightseeing, cultural, or other extracurricular attractions	82
Safety and security of destination	81
Availability of hotels or other facilities suitable for meetings	78
Affordability of destination	75
Glamorous or popular image of location	71
Ease of transporting attendees to and from location	64
Transportation costs	62
Availability of recreational facilities, such as golf, tennis, swimming, etc.	56
Distance traveled by individual attendees	50
	Total is greater than 100% due to multiple mentions

Since incentive travel is largely motivational—a reward for a job well done—incentive travel planners have different requirements than general corporate meeting planners. Interestingly, while climate is ranked number one on the list, the safety and security of a destination is now also a top concern.
Source: Recent Meetings Market Report by *Meetings & Conventions* magazine.

insurance, auto parts, and electronics industries are the heaviest users of incentive travel (see Exhibit 4).

Most incentive trips last five days to a week (occasionally longer), and have an average attendance of approximately 105 people to ensure that everyone involved gets special attention. While most incentive trips have typically been group affairs, *individual incentive travel* is a trend that has been gaining momentum (see Exhibit 5). Many qualifiers prefer to take an individual trip with a significant other. Approximately 35 percent of all incentive trips are individual rather than group trips.

Why is incentive travel so important to hotels? Typical per-person costs for a group incentive trip average about $3,600. Also of importance is that many incentive travel trips include spouses. The presence of spouses not only contributes to increases in the double-occupancy figures of a property (which, in itself, has a favorable effect on operating results), but is also a factor in increased spending. The award winners will often spend their own money on "extras," such as gift items, recreation, and entertainment options not included in the award package.

Obviously, incentive trips call for a desirable vacation setting. All the tourist attractions come into play here—be it a natural attraction, an ideal climate, excitement, or even some tie-in with the industry or company. The experienced incentive planner will analyze his or her people carefully to decide what type of site and program will draw the greatest number of people. It may be a big-city trip, a trip abroad, a cruise, or an exciting visit to a playground such as Las Vegas or Hawaii. At the Hilton Waikoloa, for example, the lobby of the hotel features a lagoon populated by dolphins, and guests are transported to their rooms by boat. This type of "fantasy resort" is extremely popular among incentive meeting planners. A Pocono resort, a ski lodge in Colorado, or a country club with a famous golf course may be just the thing for a smaller group. In addition, 32 percent of American corporate planners sponsored incentive programs outside the United States. The

Incentive meeting participants are increasingly looking to be pampered at resort spas. Studies by the International Spa Association suggest that spas are viewed as a means of escaping pressures and getting re-energized.
Source: Photo courtesy of Banyan Tree Phuket (Thailand), one of the luxury properties in the Banyan Tree Hotels & Resorts chain.

Exhibit 4   The Top Ten Users of Incentive Travel

TOP 10 USERS OF INCENTIVE TRAVEL
(BY INDUSTRY, IN MILLIONS)

Insurance	$342.9
Auto parts, Accessories	$203.2
Electronics, Radios, TV	$189.5
Automobiles and Trucks	$149.8
Heating and Air Cond.	$123.3
Farm Equipment	$108.6
Office Equipment	$101.6
Appliances	$78.0
Building	$75.7
Toiletries	$66.7

Percentage of Field Represented by Top 10 **56%**

This graph shows the industries that rely most on incentive travel to motivate their staffs and promote sales, and gives an idea of the scope of this lucrative market segment. Properties wishing to target these groups may wish to invest in the Directory of Premium, Incentive and Travel Buyers. *This directory, available from the Salesman's Guide, Inc., is organized by industry and contains a list of corporate buyers along with buyer profiles to help qualify them.*
Source: Society of Incentive Travel Executives.

sidebar titled "Top Factors When Selecting Hotels for Incentive Trips" details what incentive planners look for when selecting a particular hotel for their events.

Much less is called for in the way of meeting facilities for incentive groups than for a convention or conference, as the meeting business that is conducted is much less complex. Usually a general assembly hall and banquet facilities will suffice. The accent is on the vacation activities, and the business connection is definitely of the soft-sell variety. Almost any resort property should be able to handle this type of business.

If your property could be considered a candidate for incentive travel, you would greatly benefit by developing a marketing strategy to reach incentive travel planners.

Top Factors When Selecting Hotels for Incentive Trips	
Quality of food service	64%
Number, size, and quality of sleeping rooms	63
Negotiable food, beverage, and room rates	61
Efficiency of billing procedures	59
Number, size, and quality of suites	45
Cost of hotel or meeting facility	44

Source: Recent Meetings Market Report by *Meetings & Conventions* magazine.

Exhibit 5   Sample Incentive Travel Ad

Marriott Individual Incentives gives companies an alternative to group incentive trips. Sharon Walters, director of sales and marketing for Marriott, states, "It's important to us that our customers can build their own products because one size doesn't fit all. We give companies a lot of ways to tailor a program because they know who they're trying to motivate and what the budget is" Marriott promotes its program in print ads such as this one, which appeared in Corporate Meetings & Incentives *magazine.*
Source: Courtesy of Marriott International Hotels.

There are a number of ways to reach this market segment. Contacts and leads can be developed through the Society of Incentive Travel Executives (SITE). SITE has dozens of chapters throughout the world, and the association's website (www.siteglobal.com) includes a search engine that enables planners to search hotel partners by type and location. SITE also publishes an annual directory of incentive travel executives and sponsors an annual trade show called the Incentive Travel and Meeting Executives Show, where incentive travel suppliers such as hotels, attractions, and airlines can exhibit their products.

The international marketplace (primarily Europe, Asia, and Canada) has also become an attractive area. Convention bureaus and hotels can attend key international shows such as the Canadian Travel Expo (held in Toronto), the Asian Business and Incentive Show (in Singapore), the European Incentive Business Travel Meetings Expo (staged in Barcelona, Spain), and the Incentive Travel Exchange in Las Vegas.

Still another option is dealing with **incentive travel houses** (see box titled "Incentive Travel Houses"). While repeat business from groups is rare because destinations are varied each year, incentive travel houses, which represent several different companies, can provide repeat potential; they often will return different groups to a property that they have successfully dealt with in the past.

Advertising is yet another way to reach this market. Unlike ads to corporate meeting planners, which stress a property's professionalism in handling meetings, incentive travel ads must stress the desirability of your location and the recreational and entertainment amenities available (see Exhibit 5). The two principal trade publications for reaching incentive planners are *Corporate Meetings & Incentives* and *Corporate & Incentive Travel*.

INCENTIVE TRAVEL HOUSES

E. F. MacDonald is generally regarded as the innovator in incentive travel. Working as a stock boy in a luggage factory, he observed an NCR representative picking up merchandise. He learned the luggage was intended as incentive prizes for dealers. He conjectured that if luggage could be used as an incentive, so could travel. From this was born the specialized incentive travel agent. E. F. MacDonald (now Carlson) was soon joined by other firms. Creative Group, Inc., Maritz Travel, Peak Performance, and others have moved in to capture a share of this growing market. At one time, incentive travel was planned exclusively by the company, but the tremendous growth in incentive travel created a demand for full-time professional incentive travel companies (houses). These organizations fall into three basic categories:

1. *Full-service incentive houses*—These organizations offer clients a wide range of services, from program planning and development to implementation. This type of firm handles both travel and merchandise fulfillment, and offers specific measurement criteria, promotional materials, and sales campaigns based on each company's goals.

2. *Travel fulfillment companies*—These organizations handle the travel planning while the corporate clients design and operate their own incentive programs.

3. *The travel agency with an incentive division*—This type of firm does not offer marketing services, but has personnel that specialize in incentive trips.

These companies see to the details of the incentive program. They negotiate with airlines and hotels and then package the transportation, lodging and meeting accommodations, meals, tours, and entertainment. They often prepare the promotional literature and may even get involved in setting the goals of the program. Before the group arrives, the agent visits the site and reviews with the hotel the arrangements for servicing the group. The agent sees the group through its stay, serving as the liaison between the group and the hotel. In essence, then, the agent serves as a bona fide meeting planner, seeing to the needs of the group he or she represents. Minneapolis, Chicago, and St. Louis are the locales of the top incentive travel companies in the country. Large hotel chains and convention bureaus often schedule an "incentive house blitz" to these cities to solicit these companies.

Insurance/Financial Service Meetings

While insurance companies fall into the corporate market category, they deserve special attention because they spend more money on meetings than any other industry. In addition, insurance and financial services meeting planners anticipate an increase in incentive, sales, and training meetings in the future as insurance companies are consolidating and merging at a significant pace. A recent study reports that one in three have acquired another company within the last two years. These mergers mean more meetings as field forces and home offices must learn each others' culture and practices.

There are over 6,000 insurance companies in the United States and Canada, and each holds about 20 meetings a year, ranging in size from 20 attendees at small workshops, to conferences of 200, and major conventions of 3,000 or more. These national conventions are the largest, held annually for three to five days and planned a minimum of a year in advance.

Regional meetings are smaller and held more frequently than national meetings, and tend to be sales-oriented. While expenditures per person are typically less, resorts are considered for this type of meeting. Convenience and accessibility are the important factors in site selection; lead times average six to nine months.

Local meetings are usually held in hotels, and are primarily training seminars and board meetings. Local meetings may have a lead time of as short as two weeks, and proximity to the home office is a prime consideration in site selection, as is quality of service and facilities.

Although the insurance industry sells two basic types of insurance, life insurance and casualty insurance, most business comes from the life insurance segment. Life insurance companies employ large sales forces with regular training meetings and conferences. This segment also holds a large number of incentive meetings to keep its sales staff motivated.

Whether large or small meetings are planned, this group is not overly price-conscious, and the availability of recreational amenities often plays a role in site selection. The agenda of a small meeting usually calls for business meetings in the morning and afternoon and scheduled recreational or social activities in the evening. At larger meetings, business sessions are held in the morning, recreational activities are offered in the afternoon, and social functions figure prominently in the evening. Since spouses are usually invited to large regional and national meetings, the availability of spouses' and guests' programs is a plus when attempting to solicit insurance company business.

To solicit this lucrative market, you should start at the company's home office. There may be a number of decision-makers within the company (see box titled "Insurance/Financial Services Company Decision-Makers"). Many large insurance companies have their own travel departments, often staffed by five to seven meeting planners. When selling to this market segment, it is important to remember that even the persons responsible for the meeting planning in smaller companies are highly skilled professionals who are good negotiators who demand the same quality in their suppliers.

Because insurance companies plan numerous similar training and sales meetings over a large geographic area, they often look to hotel chains for one-stop shopping for meeting sites. Sharon Chapman, CMP, CMM, of Berkshire Life Insurance Co., says:

> Hotel-chain national sales offices are a real time-saver. I can go through one contact rather than call each individual property, and the national sales offices understand my business. They can tell me if a property I'm thinking about will fit my needs, make other recommendations, and find the best value.[8]

Insurance/Financial Services Company Decision-Makers

A recent survey by the *Financial and Insurance Meetings* magazine determined that the principal job titles for insurance company decision-makers were:

Job Title	Insurance Planners
Vice President	28%
Director of Meetings	26%
Marketing/Administrative Executive	25%
Meeting Planner	16%
President	5%
	100%

Statistics from the survey also revealed that:
- 80% were female;
- their average age was 44;
- planners had an average of ten years of experience;
- there were approximately five persons in their department;
- 79% host golfing events (typically three annually);
- 69% rate a spa facility at their meetings as important or very important.

The meeting planning department typically resides in the marketing/communication division of the company.

As in other meeting market segments, third-party planners are increasingly being used by the insurance industry. Approximately one-third use incentive travel houses and/or meeting management companies to assist in site selection and program planning.

When targeting insurance meeting planners, a professional, well-prepared, and sincere approach is the best, whether you are reaching them through advertising or direct sales. They typically conduct their own site inspections, and detailed letters of agreement are important to them. The better you understand their needs for each meeting and demonstrate how your property can meet the high standards of the meeting planner, the better chance you will have in securing their business.

Most insurance/financial services executives and meeting planners belong to trade associations, the two most well-known being Meeting Professionals International (MPI) and the Financial & Insurance Conference Planners Association (www.ficpnet.com). The Life Insurance Marketing Research Association (LIMRA) is also a key life insurance trade organization (its members write more than 90 percent of all life insurance). Allied membership is available in most associations serving this market, and this would be a worthwhile investment in gaining insurance groups meetings business.

According to a recent survey, insurance meeting planners are also turning to technology to search potential sites. Some 88 percent said that they researched hotel chains' websites. Establishing a web presence, then, can greatly enhance your chances of tapping into this lucrative market.

Medical Meetings

Last, but certainly not least, is the medical meetings market. While this market segment may be part of the associations market, this dynamic and rapidly growing segment merits additional attention (see box titled "Medical Meetings at a Glance").

Today's ever-changing technology and healthcare reforms make it mandatory for medical professionals to keep abreast of how the latest trends impact their profession. It is estimated that medical and healthcare groups currently hold over 35,000 meetings annually, and this number is expected to grow dramatically for a number of reasons:

- Medical professionals must stay current on new treatments, potential cures, and the latest surgical procedures and medical techniques.
- Modern advances such as lasers, ultrasound, and electrodiagnostic machines are changing the way medicine is practiced. Trade show exhibitors and product demonstrations provide opportunities to introduce medical professionals to the latest technology.
- Doctors and other healthcare professionals must earn Continuing Medical Education (CME) credits to maintain certifications. The most popular places to earn CME credits are forums sponsored by medical societies, associations, universities, and private providers.
- The constant emergence of new medical specialties (and subspecialities) has spawned a number of new medical organizations. This trend will create additional continuing-education needs.
- Globalization has also impacted the medical profession. Record numbers of international attendees have been reported at the medical meetings held in the United States, and more American medical professionals are attending meetings abroad.

Most medical meetings are small (the majority have 200 or less in attendance) and are usually held in sites close to major medical facilities. While most meet during peak periods (fall and spring), some groups also meet during traditional "soft spots" (summer and winter

---

Medical Meetings at a Glance

Location: Meetings are normally attended by an average of 200 people. They require a large meeting room and a number of smaller breakout rooms. The nature of the meetings is best suited by a quiet location in close proximity to a medical facility. Most meetings travel from city to city, other meetings are sponsored by associations. National association meetings are usually held in a vacation location to draw the most delegates.

Facilities: Medical meetings usually involve the use of audiovisual equipment during demonstrations. Most association meetings require exhibit space as well as meeting rooms and banquet facilities.

Price: This group is not overly price-conscious, but as they join managed care organizations they are given a budget. Professionals in the medical field need these meetings in order to gain certifications and stay current in their practices.

Services: Many require faxes, voice mail, photocopiers, and computers. A health club is an excellent selling point.

Decision-Makers: The decision-makers are experienced professionals in associations. The newer meetings are coordinated by hospitals and managed health care organizations. The managed health care facilities are also requiring doctors to attend certain seminars in order to stay abreast of the latest medical developments.

Best Ways to Reach: Many medical meeting planners are members of PCMA and receive *Convene* magazine. The *Medical Meeting and Event Directory* lists over 10,000 executives who plan off-site meetings. Healthcare Convention and Exhibitors Association and the National Pharmaceutical Council sponsor many conventions, as do hospitals.

months). And, since many medical groups plan several meetings a month, there is a great potential for repeat business.

Medical meetings require a high level of presentation. Technical presentations, in which demonstrators can interact with the audience and take questions from all over the world, are sometimes done via satellite. One medical meeting planner explains:

> We show live surgeries on a big screen. Our camera work allows for close-ups and instant replays. Busy physicians are drawn to medical meetings with new techniques and new knowledge.[9]

Requirements for medical meetings also include several breakout rooms for small group discussion and good message service. For larger medical meetings, exhibit space with adequate electrical outlets will be needed. The Center for Exhibition Industry Research reports that nearly 25 percent of all exhibitions are medical or healthcare shows. Since most meetings are technical meetings, medical groups prefer to meet in a quiet location; a meeting booked near rooms used for a college reunion or a bowling league will lose future business.

One difficulty with medical meetings is that the amount of function space they require is incredibly high relative to the number of guestrooms typically used. Therefore, they are sometimes not a good piece of business for a hotel, particularly during high-demand periods. Meeting planners have responded to this dilemma with a space-saving technique that is becoming increasingly used for medical and scientific group meetings: **poster sessions** rather than formal verbal presentations. Using horizontal corkboards, presenters can post a visual summary of their findings, experiences, or opinions instead of giving an oral presentation from a platform.

A sub-segment of the medical meetings market that warrants additional attention is the multibillion-dollar pharmaceutical industry. Pharmaceutical companies primarily hold meetings to introduce new products to their sales staffs and to doctors who are likely to prescribe the latest medications. While pharmaceutical meeting are similar to other medical meetings in that they often have short lead times due to the latest breakthroughs, there are also two other major concerns that must be taken into consideration when targeting this sub-segment.

The first is *security*. Since the pharmaceutical industry is an extremely competitive industry, with companies striving to be the first to introduce new products, a hotel that can offer complimentary paper shredders and secure storage in meeting venue offices has an advantage over another property that cannot do so. Some pharmaceutical companies also insist on a non-compete clause—requiring that the hotel not book simultaneous meetings for two or more pharmaceutical companies.

The second consideration is *image-oriented*. Pharmaceutical companies must operate under spending guidelines issued by the Pharmaceutical Research and Manufacturers of America (the PhRMA Code) as well as the FDA and the Office of the Inspector General. A meeting for doctors, therefore, cannot be booked at a five-star hotel, which gives the impression that doctors are being bribed to prescribe the company's products. This does not mean, however, that pharmaceutical meetings cannot be booked at desirable locations offered by such chains as Hilton, Loews, and Sonesta. The key is to be able to offer an upscale meeting at a moderate price.

KSL Resorts, a collection of distinctive resorts that includes the Homestead, Vail Mountain Lodge and Spa, and La Costa Resort, trains its entire staff—from sales, catering, and convention services to hotel operations—in the nuances of pharmaceutical meetings. One topic covered by the company's Pharmaceutical Expertise Program, for example, details an option for getting around the luxury-image issue—individuals are charged for spa services rather than having them charged to the master account. The program also provides information on which companies are competitors, which eliminates the problem of booking two competing groups at the same time, while still being able to service the meetings of two or more non-competitive groups.

It is fairly simple to reach this lucrative and growing market segment. The typical medical meeting planner is an experienced professional; most belong to the Professional Convention Management Association (PCMA), a trade association originally formed for medical meeting planners and now open to all association planners. This association holds an annual meeting in January, and is an opportunity for hotel salespeople to interact with planners. You can also place print ads in the numerous medical periodicals and journals published for doctors, dentists, and the scientific community (see Exhibit 6).

Exhibit 6   Advertising to Medical Meeting Planners

This print ad, which appeared in Medical Meetings *magazine, attracts medical meeting planners with a catchy headline (the medically related "Intensive Care"), and promises a "clinically tuned" solution to meeting needs.*
Source: Courtesy of Ojai Valley Inn & Spa.

Summary

In this chapter, we have detailed the types of meetings held by nonprofit organizations and specialized segments of the corporate meetings market. We have seen how nonprofits, though largely price-sensitive, can add to a property's bottom line by filling typically slow periods and providing potential repeat business (a chart listing these organizations, number and composition of members, membership restrictions, major meetings, and publications to reach them is included at the end of this chapter). And we have seen how other segments, such as labor unions and incentive travel, can be lucrative for specific types of hotels. In this chapter we have determined:

- Each segment's characteristics and needs.
- The kind of meetings they hold.
- What they look for when selecting a property.
- The decision-maker for each market segment.
- How to locate key sources of potential business

These crucial factors are essential in determining what type(s) of group business your property can handle.

Endnotes

1. Beth Rogers, "SMERF: A Multi-Billion Dollar Market Worth Pursuing, *HSMAI Marketing Review*, Spring 2007, p. 22.

2. Larry Keltto, "Tailor-Made Meetings," *Association Meetings*, April 2005, p. 32.

3. Fred Gebhart, "Reunion Meetings," *Meeting News*.

4. "Front Words," *Reunions*, February/March 2005, p. 4.

5. Patricia Sherman, "SMERF Events," *Expo*, February 2008, p. 3.

6. June Norman, "Moving Toward the Mainstream," *The Meeting Manager*.

7. Larry Keltto, "Tailor-Made Meetings," *Association Meetings*, April 2005, p. 29.

8. Regina Barban, "Insight 2005," *Insurance Conference Planner*, January 2005, pp. 22–24.

9. Joseph Dabrian, "The Changing Pulse of Medical Meetings," *The Meeting Professional*.

 Key Terms

fraternal organizations—Groups in which membership is based on common personal interests rather than on common work or career responsibilities.

incentive travel—Travel financed by businesses as an employee or dealer reward for outstanding performance.

incentive travel houses—Full-time professional travel companies that make arrangements for companies that wish to offer incentive trips. Usually represent several different firms.

per diem—The fixed amount of money given to government representatives for each day of travel away from home. Government employees have a fixed amount of money that they can spend per day on food, beverage, and lodging.

poster session—Display of reports and papers, usually scientific, accompanied by their authors or researchers. Can also refer to a session dedicated to the discussion of posters shown inside the meeting area. When this discussion is not held in a special session, it can take place directly between the person presenting the poster and interested delegates.

SMERF groups—An acronym for the nonprofit organization market segment made up of social, military, educational, religious, and fraternal groups.

 Review Questions

1. What are SMERF groups? Why are they an important market segment? What SMERF market segments show the most potential for future growth?

2. How does dealing with government agencies differ from dealing with other meetings groups? What types of hotels are best-suited for the various types of government meetings?

3. What types of meetings do labor unions typically hold? What factors are important to planners booking labor union meetings?

4. What makes the incentive market different from the corporate market in general? What types of properties are best-suited to handle this market segment? What types of amenities would you stress if you were trying to attract the incentive market?

5. What are the characteristics of insurance meetings? What types of hotels might be most attractive to this type of business?

6. Cite several reasons why the medical meetings market segment is likely to grow.

7. Who are the key decision-makers for each of the segments discussed in this chapter? How can each type of meeting planner most effectively be reached?

Internet Sites

For more information, visit the following Internet sites. Internet addresses can change without notice. If a site is no longer available at the address listed below, a search engine can be used to find the new address or additional, related sites.

African-American Fraternities/Sororities: The National Pan-Hellenic Council
www.nphc.org

Collegiate Directories, Inc.
www.collegiatedirectories.com

Fraternity Executives Association
www.fea-inc.org

Insurance Conference Planners Association
www.icpa.org

National Association of Reunion Managers
www.reunions.com

National Interfraternity Conference
www.greeklife.org/nic

National Panhellenic Conference
www.greeklife.org/npc

Professional Convention Management Association
www.pcma.org

Religious Conference Management Association
www.rcmaweb.com

Reunion Planners
www.classmates.com

Summary of Sources for Reaching Meeting Planners

Meeting Planning Associations	Number of Members	Composition of Members
American Society of Association Executives www.asaenet.org	25000	84% association executives 16% suppliers (hotels, convention bureaus)
Financial & Insurance Conference Planners www.ficpnet.com	470	All insurance planners, full or part-time Suppliers cannot become members but can attend meetings
International Association of Exhibitions and Events www.iaee.org	3600	54% trade show managers 46% suppliers; suppliers may join as associates
Meeting Professionals International www.mpiweb.org	24000 in 42 countries	50% meeting planners (45% corporate, 19% assoc., 19% independent, 8% other), 50% suppliers
National Business Travel Association www.nbta.org	2500	Corporate travel managers and travel service providers
National Coalition of Black Meeting Planners www.mcbmp.com	1500	Professional meeting planners, suppliers, and contractors
Professional Convention Management Association www.pcma.org	5000	60% suppliers, 40% meeting planners
Religious Conference Management Association www.rcmaweb.org	2900	Meeting planners, contractors, suppliers of religious organizations or denominations
Society of Government Meeting Professionals www.sgmp.org	3500	51% suppliers/contractors, 49% meeting planners
Society of Incentive Travel Executives www.site-intl.org	2000	Hotels, airlines, cruise lines, tour operators, travel agents, and official tourist organizations as well as supporting organizations

Membership Restrictions	Convention	Publications
Active members must be executives of non-profit associations; suppliers may be associate members	Annual meeting and exposition in August	*Associations Now* magazine
Must be employed by an insurance company or insurance association	Two: Annual meeting in November, summer forum in June	*Insurance Conference Planner* newsletter
Trade show managers; suppliers may join as associates	Two: Mid-year in June, annual meeting and expo in December	Weekly newsletter
Open to all meeting executives; the number of supplier members must be matched by the number of planners	Two: Trade shows in July, education conference in January	*One + Magazine,* newsletter to chapter leaders, newsletters from special interest groups
Suppliers may join as allied members	Annual meeting in August	Daily news brief
Only professional meeting planners with at least one year experience	Two annual meetings: one in spring, the other In fall	*The NCBMP Newsletter*
Members responsible for meetings of nonprofit associations; affiliate members may be vendors or independent planners	Annual convention held in January	*Convene* magazine and *PCMA Perspectives*
Restricted to religious organizations	Annual meeting held in January or February	*Religious Conference Manager* magazine
Restricted to government meeting planners, suppliers, and contractors	Annual meeting in May	*The Society Page* newsletter plus the *Membership Directory*
Application needs approval, letter of recommendation	Annual meeting held in November	Monthly newsletter as well as *Insite* magazine

Chapter 7 Outline

Competencies

1. Explain the steps in making a personal sales call. (pp. 219–230)

2. Explain how to conduct telephone selling effectively in meeting and convention sales. (pp. 230–235)

3. Describe the convention and meeting sales techniques of sales blitz selling, trade show selling, selling with convention bureaus, site-inspection selling, and familiarization tours. (pp. 236–248)

Common Sense Strategies for Convention Sales

Charlotte St. Martin
Executive Vice President Operations and Marketing
Loews Hotels

"Salespeople close sales. They do their research; they follow-up; they are consistent and persistent; they do what they say they will do and they deliver what they say they will deliver. I firmly believe that establishing that relationship [with a customer] is the single most important thing a salesperson can do to make a sale. Research and planning are critical to any discipline in the sales process, whether it be personal sales calls, sales blitzes, booth selling at industry trade shows, site inspections, or telephone sales."

7 Selling to the Meetings Market

THE SIZE AND DIVERSITY of the meetings market makes it a viable target market for all types and sizes of hospitality properties.

There are two basic ways to reach this lucrative market: *selling* and *advertising*. In this chapter, we will take a look at some of the most effective direct sales tools used by properties today:

- Personal sales calls
- Telephone selling
- Sales blitz selling
- Trade show selling
- Selling with convention bureaus
- Site inspection selling and familiarization tours

Selling to the meetings market has changed dramatically in recent years. The Internet has changed how event planners search for hotel information and how they book their meetings, leading to changes in how salespeople do their jobs.

Personal Sales Calls: Mastering Consultative Sales

The most effective tool in convention sales, or any other kind of sales, is the personal sales call. This type of face-to-face selling works well with both professional and occasional meeting planners. The personal sales call offers the opportunity to present your case in a detailed manner, to answer questions immediately, and to read the reaction of the prospect so you can gain a better understanding—and take remedial action if necessary.

Roy Stone, senior vice president, sales and marketing for Accor Hotels, believes that even with so much media attention given to social communities, text messaging, and digital channels, the personal sales call is still the most effective method to reach meeting planners:

> You can make telephone calls, send e-mails, and Skype, but nothing beats sitting down across from a person and demonstrating that you are interested enough to be there and that you want to listen to them. Body language is so important, and you don't get that any other way except meeting someone face-to-face.
>
> Obviously, in today's fast-changing world, it's critical that you efficiently drive your share in the online environment, but the sales function must be there taking its place in your toolbox.[1]

In today's competitive environment, salespeople have to do more than simply sell meeting space and guestrooms; they must become *consultants* who identify customers' needs and provide solutions by adopting selling methods tailored to potential meeting customers. Although **consultative selling** is a low-pressure form of personal selling, it is a highly effective sales strategy and well-suited to hospitality sales. The focus here is to build relationships—not just get an immediate sale, but to create and keep long-term clients.

The personal sales call consists of six essential steps (see Exhibit 1). Each of these steps is vitally important in presenting your property effectively to the meeting planner, and we will cover each of them in the following sections.

Exhibit 1   The Six Steps of a Sales Call

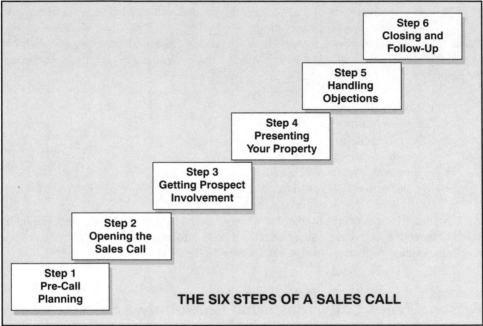

The sales process is a systematic series of actions that directs the meeting decision-maker toward a buying commitment.

Step #1: Pre-Call Planning

While getting out there and selling is the best way to ensure that you will generate meetings business for your property, there is another—quite logical—step that should always precede the selling process: *pre-call planning*. While this planning (and the research inherent to it) may seem time-consuming and tedious, the keys to effective selling are:

- Knowing your property.
- Knowing your competition.
- Knowing your prospect.

Knowing your property can help your sales effort in two ways. First, you will know exactly what you have to sell. You will know your property's strengths and weaknesses—and how to showcase or downplay them as needed. Second, and just as important, knowing basic facts about your property will give you the confidence you need for making a sales call. You won't have to worry about what questions a prospect will ask—you will already have the answers to most of his or her concerns (how many rooms are available, the size and capabilities of meeting rooms, audiovisual equipment available, etc.).

William Tiefel, vice chairman, Marriott International, and chairman emeritus, the Ritz-Carlton Hotel Company, advises salespeople to:

Learn as much as you can about the business through a variety of jobs. It's a mistake to go right into sales and then try to learn by osmosis, or by working a week here and there and think you really know the hotel. The best-prepared salespeople are those who have product knowledge. I don't think you get as much from a training program as you do when you experience something long-term. We (Marriott) have a myriad of sales schools and activities for people at different levels in the organization, which is great. But I still think the basic concept of knowing the product is important.[2]

Since it is virtually impossible to memorize every detail about your property, many hotels prepare a **property fact book** to assist their salespeople (old and new) to know enough about the property to properly present it. Exhibit 2 provides a beginning outline of the key elements in a property fact book. Every salesperson should know these important facts. This information can be updated as necessary and serves as an excellent tool for the selling process.

Knowing your competition can also help you to better sell your property. If you know a competitor's rates are slightly lower than yours, for example, you may expect a prospect to raise an objection—and you can be prepared to justify your additional cost by pointing out your property's special amenities, free parking space, or some other feature that the meeting planner may perceive as well worth the rate difference.

Fred Shea, vice president of sales at Hyatt, says:

Our hotels always want you to know what they're up against because, hopefully, they know the strengths and weaknesses of hotels in their competitive set and can sell against that. If, as a hotelier, I'm bidding in a vacuum, I'll give what I think is our best bid, but if I knew that a competitor had more services to offer, it may compel me to do different things.[3]

The third phase of pre-call planning, *knowing your prospect,* is essential for tailoring presentations to meet the needs of meeting planners. David Scypinski, senior vice president of Conference Direct, believes that hotel salespeople must know the customer as never before:

It's not enough to know your customers' products, services, and objectives. You have to know everything about their business and industry. Hotel salespeople should understand how the organization they are trying to book makes money and how large their budget is. There's no substitute for knowing your customers' organization, business needs, and objectives.[4]

Many properties—even those that utilize mailing lists to develop new sales leads—send out surveys or make telephone calls to gather information about potential prospects (see Exhibit 3). And, don't forget the benefit of obtaining information right under your own roof; talk to meeting planners currently using your property and ask them about potential leads (and their requirements).

Once you decide that a prospect is indeed a valid one, you must make contact to try to sell. Sales calls in which you initiate the contact without any degree of interest indicated by the prospects are called **cold calls**. The anticipated percentage of success in these cases is

Exhibit 2   Outline for Property Fact Book

GUESTROOM INFORMATION	RESTAURANTS & LOUNGES	MEETING AND BANQUET FACILITIES

Priority I
 	
Number of rooms
Number of singles/doubles/
   suites
Size of rooms—square
   footage
Number of floors
Phones in rooms
Fire alarms/detectors in rooms
Handicapped rooms
No-smoking rooms
Amenities in rooms
 	
Priority II
 	
Room rates
Check-in/check-out times
	Priority I
	
	Seating capacity
	Number of tables and types
	Atmosphere/interior design
	No-smoking sections
	Dress requirements
	Pricing by restaurant
	Restaurant positioning
	
	Priority II
	
	Menu style/theme
	Types of food by restaurant
		Priority I
		
		Location of meeting rooms
		Square footage/seating
		   capacity
		Utilities available
		Exhibit space
		Meeting room rental rates
		
		Priority II
		
		Function room furniture
		Audiovisual capabilities

Priority III
 	
Customer mix
Average occupancy
   by day of week
Average length of stay by
   segment
Sales budget
Profitability by segment
Group check-in/check-out
   procedures
Front desk staffing
	Priority III
	
	Entertainment
	Reservation policy
	Cocktails available
	Wine cellar/list
	Food served in lounge
	Special promotions
	Opening/closing times
		Priority III
		
		Banquet seating capacities
		Banquet menu
		Theme parties
		Outside services
		Types of banquet specialties
		Beverage service
		Banquet staffing levels

New salespeople cannot learn everything about a property in their first week. To help them gain knowledge in a logical order, questions about each area (guestrooms, restaurants and lounges, meeting and banquet facilities, etc.) should be arranged by priorities. At the end of week one, a salesperson should master all Priority I questions; and each week, master another priority level. The director of sales should assign the responsibility of updating and maintaining the property fact book to one specific person in the sales department.

understandably lower than when you are dealing with past customers or recommendations. It is often a problem just getting in to see the right person.

While the primary purpose of cold calls is to find the name of the decision-maker and to determine prospect needs, these types of calls are often not well-received by meeting planners. Harlan Didrickson, operations and events manager at Skidmore, Owings & Merrill, a Chicago-based architectural firm, says:

> I work in an almost constant state of chaos, so cold calls are very irritating. They're a waste of my time, and I find them rude.[5]

Didrickson's opinion is shared by 51 percent of 235 meeting planners surveyed by *Meeting News*. Receiving cold calls was the top complaint among respondents, who say that salespeople should do their homework before making cold calls. It is a waste of both the planner's and the salesperson's time, for example, if a small hotel calls a planner who books only with large hotel chains.

You can increase the efficiency of such efforts if you precede your visit with some sort of preliminary campaign. You might send your convention facilities brochure to the contact person, along with a personal letter. Follow up with another letter if you hear nothing within a few weeks. Then call for an appointment. If you fail to get an appointment, try again.

Your most effective calls will likely be **appointment calls**, where you have prearranged a visit with the prospect, but don't completely rule out calling without an appointment. When you are already in the area for another appointment, a cold call is worth a try. Cross-index your prospect list geographically. Mixing cold calls with your appointments will increase your number of sales calls. Cold calls sometimes work, but even if you cannot get in to see the right person at that time, you stand to lose little except a few minutes' time.

Exhibit 3   Sample Sales Prospect Card

Date of Contact _____ Trace Date _____
Name of Contact _____New Prospect ☐ Yes ☐ No
Company Name _____ Type of Business _____
Address _____ Telephone _____
_____ Fax _____
Prospect's estimated sales potential:
Room nights _____
Meetings/banquets _____
Dollars _____
Facilities/services needed:
_____
_____
_____
Background information on prospect and company:
_____
_____
_____
Salesperson's Name _____

To make the most of a sales call, it is helpful to have some basic information about the needs of a prospect. A sales prospect card can help the salesperson to determine how to best structure his or her presentation to appeal to the needs of the client.
Source: Used with permission of the Grand Traverse Resort, Traverse City, Michigan.

Advice for New Hotel Sales Professionals

David Brudney, ISHC

David Brudney & Associates

Carlsbad, California

Today's hospitality sales professionals must deal with a much more sophisticated, knowledgeable and demanding meeting planner. Never has it been more critical for sales directors and managers to know their "stuff" and share their knowledge; to master the art of people-connecting; and to respond quickly and accurately at all times.

If you are new to hospitality sales, you most likely are a member of a new generation of salespeople. Therefore, you need to understand that in order to be successful—and, more importantly, to sustain that success over the years—you need to balance time spent on the computer against time spent on the telephone and out on personal sales calls.

Your generation of sales professionals is the most tech-savvy of any generation in the history of the hospitality industry. You are masters of the Internet. You fully expect information to come customized and instant. History? That's all about yesterday. What's important today is today.

You may expect instant success from your efforts in selling room nights and F&B events, and become impatient when you find that you can't close a piece of business quickly via e-mail and text messaging.

From day one you will need to begin mastering the "high-touch" aspects of direct selling: selling on the telephone and selling when making outside sales calls, selling at trade shows, on fam trips, and anywhere you find yourself face-to-face with potential clients. Remember always that you live by *relationships* with support from technology.

You new generation of sales pros must not fail to learn that one-on-one sales, on the telephone and at clients' places of business, will always be the cornerstone to professional selling.

What is the best advice I can give to the new generation of hospitality sales professionals? It is all about relationships. Build and maintain solid relationships that will support you for the life of your sales career.

Sales success, to use an analogy from baseball, is accomplished not so much from achieving a high "batting average" as from your total number of hits. More "turns at bat" (sales calls) mean the chance for more "hits" (sales).

Once you have completed the research phase of your pre-call planning, assemble the materials needed to make an effective presentation. A well-organized and professional **presentation book** should include only that information pertinent to each prospect's needs. Fumbling through too many materials in a sales kit may result in a loss of presentation momentum. Most sales kits contain basic information such as a general property information sheet, a meeting and banquet room information sheet, a convention brochure, and other visual aids, including color photographs, a map of the property, etc. Many properties also include third-party endorsement letters, also called *testimonials*, which are letters of recommendation from meeting planners who have used the properties' facilities. If these are used, however, they should be relevant to your prospects. A letter from an association meeting planner praising your theme party, for example, would have little significance for a corporate meeting planner wishing to hold a training session.

If your property targets a number of market segments, you should consider preparing a presentation book tailored to each of those segments. While incentive and tour groups can be adequately served with glossy brochures and information on local attractions, meeting planners require "working documents." Your presentation book for meeting planners should include meeting space layouts on white, uncoated paper to allow the planner to easily make notes during a site inspection. These diagrams (ideally one per page) should include all specifics for meeting rooms, including anything that impacts the usable square footage of the room, and you may also want to include specifications for alternative room setups.

Additional "must haves" in a presentation book for meeting planners include large, detailed area maps with clear driving directions (these should be designed to enable the planner to fax or otherwise duplicate them), audiovisual price lists, parking information, transportation information (such as airport shuttles, hotel shuttles to nearby destinations, and so on), dining outlets (including types of cuisine, hours of operation), detailed summaries of guestroom types and amenities, and business center information.[6]

Step #2: Opening the Sales Call

Selling is essentially helping someone to buy. Open your sales call in such a way that it puts the customer at ease so that he or she can build rapport with you. Your opening should consist of an introduction, a statement of the purpose of your call (and its benefit to the prospect), and a bridge statement that leads into the actual presentation. You can start by introducing yourself and your property ("Good afternoon, Mr. Jones. I'm Dan Merrill from the Golden Gate Resort in San Diego, California."), while offering a brief but firm handshake. You may also wish to add a few words at this time to show your interest in the prospect. For example, "I've heard so much about what your firm has been doing in the area of microcomputers, and I'm looking forward to hearing more about your innovative uses of microchips." But take care not to get so immersed in discussion about the company that you neglect your objective.

As soon as possible after the introduction, state the purpose of your call. Can you offer the prospect additional meeting space or are you there to try to win back former business? After stating your purpose, you should present a benefit or two that will give the prospect a reason to listen to you. Once you have stated your property's benefits, lead into the body of the sales presentation with a bridge statement. This statement asks the prospect for permission to continue, and is usually in the form of a question: "Would you be interested in learning how other associations used one of our theme parties to increase attendance?" or "May I show you just a few examples of our state-of-the-art audiovisual system?" If the prospect gives a positive response, you have the green light to continue. If the prospect is not interested, thank him or her for meeting with you and ask for an appointment in the future.

Step #3: Getting Prospect Involvement

Involve the prospect in the sales process to determine his or her needs. Do it by asking questions, and always ask *before* making your presentation. Two types of questions are generally used: close-ended questions and open-ended questions.

Close-ended questions require a specific reply. These include such queries as, "How many training meetings do you stage each month?" or "What is your average attendance at your annual convention?" **Open-ended questions**, on the other hand, give the prospect an opportunity to express his or her feelings. Open-ended questions such as, "Why do you think last year's meeting was so successful?" or "What factors are most important to you in selecting a resort?" will provide clues into what is important to the prospect and can help you to adjust your sales presentation to meet those concerns.

Effective questioning is among the more critical aspects of selling. Decide what information you need from the prospect in advance, and use it as a checklist for asking questions during your sales call.

Take notes when questioning. Prospects appreciate the fact that you are taking time to write down their concerns, encouraging them to give additional information. Additionally, your notes become the basis for your presentation as well as a part of your sales file when trying to book the client's next meeting.

Don't forget that the most important skill in gaining client involvement is *listening* to the client's responses. Sal Dickinson, president of Dickinson Associates, a consulting firm to hotel sales executives, stresses that successful salespeople are active listeners who relate to the prospect's needs and desires. He says:

> Get to know your prospects' needs better than the competition by being a better listener. Do your due diligence and research well. Knowledge is power, and the more you know, the more effective you'll be. Come armed with solutions, not features, and spell out how what you have will be valuable and make life easier.[7]

Step #4: Presenting Your Property

While every salesperson should have a prepared and rehearsed sales presentation that addresses the needs of each market segment, you increase your chances of a sale if you custom-tailor this general presentation for specific clients. Most clients are really interested only if what you offer will benefit them. Rather than being a product-seller, become a problem-solver; always present your property's features as benefits to the client (see Exhibit 4).

Your presentation should directly address the client's needs—and should include visual aids such as pictures, charts, and graphs to enable the planner to envision how your property will work for his or her meeting. Many salespeople today use more sophisticated

Exhibit 4   Turning Features into Benefits

Feature		Benefit
All of our breakout rooms are adjacent to the room where your general session will be held	SO THAT	no time will be wasted between sessions and you will be able to keep your meeting on schedule.
We offer 24-hour room service	SO THAT	those attendees who must check-in late may still enjoy a late meal in the comfort of their room.
Every room has a desk	SO THAT	your meeting attendees will have plenty of room to review and work on handouts they receive during the daily meeting sessions.
We have a health club and spa	SO THAT	your trainees can relax and unwind after a day of intensive educational meetings.
Benefit		**Feature**
Those attendees who check-in late may still enjoy a late meal in the comfort of their room	BECAUSE	we offer 24-hour room service.

Salespeople who present only features rely on their prospects to interpret how those features can benefit them. Instead, salespeople should try to influence the interpretation by always linking features with benefits and explaining to prospects how the features will benefit them and enhance their meetings. To assist you in thinking "benefits," the words "so that" can be used to tie the two. The selling sentence can also be reversed, using the word "because" to link the benefit to the feature.

visual aids—PowerPoint slide presentations or DVD brochures—but the important factor is how these presentations relate to the client.

Tom McCarthy, CHME, CHA, past president of Hospitality Sales and Marketing Association International, suggests that each hotel create several five- to six-minute introductory presentations (with pictures) to be used at a prospect's office, a one-minute presentation to introduce your hotel over the telephone, a presentation to use on a tour of the hotel, and presentations to overcome the most frequently raised objections. Salespeople should then rehearse these presentations before actually giving them to prospects.[8]

When presenting, use testimonial letters and publicity reprints to increase your credibility. Prospects are more likely to believe the good things their peers and unbiased reviewers have to say about your property than what a salesperson might say. Third-party endorsements from meeting decision-makers in the same segment as your prospect are best; use association-related letters when selling to association meeting planners, corporate letters when presenting to corporate decision-makers, and so on.

Once your presentation is completed, make a transition statement (which can be as simple as asking, "Do you have any questions?") that may lead to a close—or to what is often the next phase of the sales call, overcoming objections.

A major advantage of personal sales calls is immediate feedback and two-way communication. Research conducted by Meetings News *found that 85 percent of meeting planners affirmed their preference for face-to-face contact when asked, "What is your preferred method of professional networking?" And, a recent survey by the Hospitality Sales and Marketing Association International (HSMAI) found that hotel salespeople believe that person-to-person sales provides the best return on investment of all selling and advertising methods.* **Source: Photograph by Alan Cresto. Courtesy of Loews Hotels.**

Step #5: Handling Objections

It is a rare meeting planner who will not have some questions or objections. It is important, therefore, to anticipate the most likely areas of concern and to be able to respond immediately.

The most common objections involve concerns over price or product, or simply a lack of interest. *Price* objections ("Your competitor has cheaper rates") can often be overcome by pointing out a compensatory benefit ("Perhaps. But our meeting package includes free meeting and function space as well as free golf and tennis facilities."). Whenever possible, try to get the focus off price ("Putting price aside for the moment, do you have any other concerns?"). This tactic may work if you can demonstrate how your property meets the client's needs so well; then, price diminishes in importance.

Product objections ("Your property may not be as attractive to our attendees as the new resort in your area") may be handled in a number of ways. Try restating the objection and offer a positive response: "I gather that you don't feel our property is modern enough. Although we are an older property, our rooms and meeting space have been completely renovated and we offer all amenities found at new properties in our area. Clients tell us our property has a great deal of character and charm."

Lack of interest objections ("We are happy with our present hotel") can be overcome by finding out why the client is satisfied and offering comparable—and additional—benefits. Or, you may point out that a change of site may prove to be stimulating to the attendees. A change in site could then be considered acceptable to the planner, and you offered an alternative without the implication that the selection of the previous property was wanting in any way. If nothing changes the client's mind at that time, it is still a good practice to ask to be considered for a meeting or function in the future. There are many factors that may come into play at some future date that may open the door for you.

When handling objections, it is vital that you *never* knock your competition. At best, this is unprofessional; at worst, the meeting planner may feel that your words reflect on his or her judgment—and you may lose any possibility of booking a sale at that time or in the future.

Step #6: Closing and Follow-Up

While many salespeople enjoy presenting their product, some hesitate when it comes to asking for the sale! The skill of closing, however, can be learned, and can be more comfortable when salespeople realize that clients *expect* to be asked to book at the property.

There are two types of closes: trial closes and major closes. **Trial closes** are used to elicit responses from the client, and are generally used to build an "agreement staircase." In other words, the salesperson periodically asks for a positive client response ("Don't you agree that our audiovisual equipment will greatly enhance your training sessions?" or "Don't you think our ballroom would make an elegant setting for your awards banquet?" or "Don't you find our golf course to be one of the finest in the state?"). Positive responses, repetition of benefits by a client, and positive nonverbal signs (frequent smiles, the client leaning forward, etc.) are excellent indicators that the salesperson can proceed with his or her major close.

Many hotel salespeople have a specific room they use when making their sales presentations. One salesperson told us, "I always use our boardroom when closing. It overlooks our fountains, waterfalls, and the golf course. If prospects are hesitant, I point out the view and ask if their board wouldn't appreciate the scene."
Source: Photograph courtesy of Fairmont Chateau Lake Louise, Banff, Alberta, Canada.

The **major close** is the question or statement that asks for the sale. It should be attempted as soon as the client has reached a peak of excitement, and should elicit a commitment. This close should be as direct as possible ("May I reserve space on a definite basis?"), and after making it, you should stop talking and give the client a chance to respond. Avoid the temptation to keep talking—you may inadvertently say something that brings up concerns the client had not previously considered!

Once your call is completed, leave as soon as is politely possible. And, whether you have made a sale or not, always follow up your sales call promptly with a thank you letter. This gesture shows your commitment to customer service and may result in future sales.

If a commitment has been made, follow-up is even more important. You will want to service your client with frequent post-sale contacts, including keeping him or her informed on the progress of preparations for the function. Find out the client's preference for communicating—by phone, fax, or e-mail—through their assistants. It is also important to check with the planner during the function. Arlene Sheff, CMP, a planner for Boeing Company, recently held a meeting and said she:

> never saw the salesperson once on site. I spoke to him on the phone several times before the meeting, but while the meeting was going on, he never came by even once to see how things were going. If a hotel salesperson wants my repeat business, they need to track me down and check on my meeting. It's all about building a relationship with me.[9]

Contacting the client after the function to ensure that all went according to plan is also essential. Never assume that a lack of complaints means that the client was satisfied. Follow-up is the key to building long-term relationships. Remember: customers don't care how much you know until they know how much you care.

This type of commitment leads to customer rebookings and word-of-mouth referrals for additional business.

Telephone Selling

One of the problems with personal calls is that they are getting increasingly expensive. Many properties are cutting down on the expense of personal calls by stepping up their use of the telephone, especially as a tool to screen prospects and to set appointments with clients.

Although telephone calls should not be a substitute for as many personal visits as you can manage, you should become proficient in using the telephone as a means to increase customer contact, screen prospects to make personal calls more effective, and offer immediate assistance to clients in the event of urgent situations.

Telephone Techniques

Since using the telephone is much more impersonal than talking face-to-face with a prospect, it is important that you and your salespeople develop techniques to make the most efficient use of this sales tool. As with a personal sales call, *preparation* is the key. Before making a call, you should have an outline of what you are going to cover. A clearly typed topical outline will help you maintain control of your thoughts and maintain a logical flow in your conversation. You can even use a prepared presentation—as long as it doesn't sound "canned." Along with your outline or presentation, you also want to keep pertinent backup information—room rates, function room sizes and capacities, availability, and so on—at hand so that you never have to fumble while searching for it. Also, keep paper and pencil handy to jot down notes or to remind yourself of information requested by the client.

Using the telephone involves the mastery of several simple techniques. Always hold the receiver slightly away from your mouth and speak slowly and distinctly. Immediately identify yourself and your property. Put your personality into the call—be cheerful yet professional—and always be willing to listen to the prospect's views. Don't be reluctant to ask the prospect to spell his or her name if it isn't clear. Few people mind repeating or spelling their name.

Screening Prospects

The telephone makes it easy to prequalify prospects before making appointments for personal calls. The Kingsmill Resort in Williamsburg, Virginia, employs a sales assistant to use the Internet and the telephone to determine prospects' meeting plan profiles. The sales assistant obtains the decision-makers' names, contact information, meeting frequency, length of meetings, arrival and departure dates, number of attendees, type of property preferred, and any other information needed to qualify a group. Profiles are then turned over in a written report to the appropriate salespeople. Letting a sales assistant do the screening allows salespeople to spend 100 percent of their time selling. Many properties use sales lead services, often referred to as *tip sheets,* to analyze information about frequent convention and meeting planners. All of these names will not be high-priority prospects; they must be scanned to determine those who best fit into your marketing plan. But, since other hotels are receiving the same tip sheet, you must take quick action after an initial screening. Since you already have basic information about each lead, you can tailor your telephone calls to these prospects.

Other prospects can be interviewed directly by salespeople, who will enter information that could be helpful in a sales presentation on a **call report** (see Exhibit 5). This form can help the salesperson to determine the needs of the prospect—if the prospect represents viable business. In some cases, marketing surveys are conducted by members of the property's clerical staff, while large properties and chains may have an entire department that surveys potential prospects (see the telemarketing section in this chapter). Training clerical staff specifically in telephone techniques pays dividends.

Setting Appointments by Phone

Since cold-calling is less effective than calling on prospects who are already interested in what the property has to offer, the telephone is a useful tool for setting appointments for sales presentations.

One of the most challenging tasks in using the telephone to set appointments is getting by the intermediaries—the receptionist, secretary, administrative assistant, etc.—to reach the decision-maker. The intermediary is often your contact person in determining who makes the decision for holding meetings and can be your best friend—or worst enemy; his or her response and level of assistance can make the difference between whether you get an appointment or not! These people can be an added source of information, too. It is important, then, to build rapport with these support people. They should always be treated with respect, and, for best results, should be told the objective of your call—and how it will benefit their boss.

Meeting planners are usually busy, and their time is scarce, so you should remember that the objective of your call is usually to simply set an appointment—not to make a sale. Once you have reached the decision-maker, the telephone appointment call involves three steps: opening the call, the presentation, and setting the appointment (see Exhibit 6).

Telephone Sales Call Follow-Up

It is just as important to follow up on your telephone calls as it is on your personal calls, especially since a telephone call does not leave as lasting an impression as a personal visit. Since you are either looking for information or an appointment when you make telephone contact, you should take the time to write a friendly note thanking the prospect for his or her time or confirming an appointment date.

Use this further contact as an additional pre-sale tool. Along with a professionally typed letter, include requested information (room rate sheet, menus, etc.) or some hotel brochures to familiarize the prospect with your property before you arrive. Then, a few days later, you can call the prospect to verify that he or she received your materials.

This type of follow-up not only keeps you in the prospect's mind, but also demonstrates your property's commitment to customer service. Meeting planners, especially those who are nonprofessionals or those with limited experience, are more likely to choose a property that has demonstrated its willingness to work closely with its clients.

Exhibit 5   Sample Call Report

RED LION HOTELS®

CALL REPORT

FIRST CALL

REPEAT CALL

FILE NO.

COMPANY / ORGANIZATION:

STREET ADDRESS

CITY   STATE   ZIP

CONTACT: PHONE:

DOES YOUR COMPANY HAVE MEETINGS?   ☐ NO   ☐ YES   HOW OFTEN?

SIZE   CONTACT

WHEN IS YOUR NEXT MEETING?   WHERE

DO YOU NEED GUEST ROOMS?   ☐ NO   ☐ YES   HOW MANY

WHO MAKES THE RESERVATIONS?

DO YOU NEED OUT OF TOWN RESERVATIONS?   ☐ NO   ☐ YES   WHERE?

DO YOU HAVE SUCH THINGS AS:

- CHRISTMAS PARTIES

- AWARDS BANQUETS

- OTHER

ARE YOU OR ANYONE ELSE IN YOUR
COMPANY AFFILIATED WITH AN ASSOCIATION?

COMMENTS:

SALESPERSON   DATE

FORM NO. 001-547 (4/88)

Call reports are used by salespeople to survey the needs of a potential contact and to trace the follow-up on each account. At some properties, surveys are taken by support staff and the names of qualified prospects are passed on to the salespeople for follow-up.

Exhibit 6   Sample Script for a Telephone Appointment Call

There are three steps in making a telephone appointment call once you have reached the decision-maker: opening the call, the presentation and setting the appointment. Sample statements include:

Opening the Call

"Hello, Mr. Stubbs. My name is Diane Street, sales manager of the Oakbrook Hotel, the new hotel just down the street from your offices. Since we are neighbors and so convenient, I thought you would be interested in hearing about our hotel and the affordable meeting package we have just designed for local businesses."

The Presentation

"Mr. Stubbs, from my research, I've learned that you schedule intensive training meetings lasting two or three days with several evening working sessions. We have developed a 24-hour meeting program for companies with needs such as yours. The program reserves your meeting rooms on a 24-hour basis so that you will not be inconvenienced with removing training materials each evening and resetting equipment the next morning. In addition, our copying equipment is available to you 24 hours a day for any timely additions or changes in your handout materials."

Setting the Appointment

"I know you'll be impressed with our state-of-the-art meeting rooms and our convention service staff who will assist you in staging successful training meetings. When could we meet for lunch to discuss your upcoming employee development seminars?

"Would you prefer the beginning or later part of the week? Is 11:30 or 12:00 most convenient for you?

"Great. I'll see you Thursday at 12 noon at our concierge desk. I'll have my name tag on so you can recognize me.

"Thank you for your time, Mr. Stubbs. I'm looking forward to meeting with you personally. Have a good day."

Source: Photograph courtesy of Swissotel.

Note that the salesperson clearly identified herself and her hotel, stated the purpose of her call, and explained how the prospect would benefit from an appointment, appealing to his need for convenient meeting facilities. Note that in setting the appointment, she asked forced-choice questions, giving the planner a choice between two positive alternatives.

Handling Inquiries

In today's high-tech world, many meeting planners prefer doing business via e-mail. Today, Hilton (as well as other hotel chains) equips its salespeople with BlackBerry hand-held wireless units to enable them to read and respond to e-mail communications quickly, as timing is critical for clients with short-term meetings, and the hotel that responds first often gets the business. Larry Luteran, vice president of industry relations for Hilton, says:

> Speed to market is critical now. A good response time used to be two days, then it was 24 hours, and now it's a few hours.[10]

Inquiries about your property also come via requests for proposals on the Internet or your hotel's website; by fax, telephone calls, or mail; and from walk-ins. Walk-ins should always be immediately referred to a hotel salesperson; other inquiries require an immediate follow-up by telephone (see Exhibit 7).

Exhibit 7   Crowne Plaza's Guaranteed Response to Meeting Inquiries

In today's competitive marketplace, it is essential that hotels make immediate responses to inquiries. This ad for the Crowne Plaza Hotels & Resorts promotes the chain's 2-Hour Response Guarantee, which promises to respond to a Request for Proposal within two hours or the chain will take 5% off the group's master account.

A large number of properties use voice mail systems. While these systems are convenient, many planners are put off by them. They want a timely response, so sales department phones should be answered by a live person. Not only does this show that a property is interested in the planner's business, it provides the opportunity for the salesperson to determine the prospect's needs.

A recent survey by *Meeting News* found that meeting planners' chief complaint about hotel salespeople is their failure to respond to inquiry calls, requests for proposals (RFPs), and e-mails in a timely manner. Quality Track International, a leading provider of group sales mystery shopping services to the hospitality industry, conducted an independent test on 750 hotels and found that 28 percent of new group sales are lost, ignored, or abandoned. Meeting group sales are a significant source of revenue for most hotels, yet over one-fourth of initial customer contact inquiries go unanswered!

Inquiry calls should be handled like sales calls, and all inquiries—no matter what their source—should be followed up by a phone call. Salespeople are not simply order takers. During the call, the salesperson should ask enough questions to be able to present the property effectively. By getting to know the prospect and his or her needs, even if the property cannot handle the business at that time, a relationship has been built and there is a greater potential for future business.

Telemarketing

Besides individual telephone calls, the hospitality industry is making extensive use of **telemarketing**—large-scale telephone qualifying and research—to identify potential prospects. While the larger chains have used telemarketing for some time, the practice has become more widespread. Smaller properties have found that telemarketing can be an invaluable tool to reach prospects before sending salespeople out on expensive sales calls.

Telemarketing falls primarily into two basic categories: qualifying and market research. When a property simply wishes to obtain information, smaller properties can utilize additional staff—secretaries, front desk personnel, etc.—to assist in a telephone effort. It should be noted, however, that this type of "telephone blitz" is not true telemarketing—which is a specialized program backed by technology that offers instant access to information.

For large-scale efforts, a professional telemarketing staff is trained to work from prepared scripts. Using such a script, an experienced telemarketer may reach 50 or more prospects a day, either to obtain information or to present the property and close a sale. Reduced sales budgets have caused many properties to increase telemarketing efforts, especially to reach prospects in distant areas that you cannot get to economically.

A good telemarketing script must be short enough to keep the prospect on the line, but long enough to get the desired information or sale. It should also be specific, with benefits to the client spelled out early. It should be structured to draw the prospect into the conversation and offer the opportunity for him or her to become involved by expressing views and needs. When pressing for an actual sale, follow the same steps as you would in a personal sales call.

Telemarketing is also used for market research, to determine exactly what meeting planners are looking for. Such information is used to upgrade facilities and services, making it easier for salespeople to present the property as meeting the needs of meeting planners.

No matter what type of telemarketing program is implemented, is it essential that it be as disciplined as any other form of selling. The staff should be thoroughly trained, and there should be clear-cut goals and follow-up to ensure that goals are being met.

Sales Blitz Selling

A **sales blitz** focuses on contacting potential clients in a concentrated area over a brief period of time (usually three days), and is an effective tool for both reaching and qualifying new business (see Best Practices box titled "Hyatt's CRUNCH Time Maximizes Sales Blitz Success"). A sales blitz may consist of simply "cold calling" on businesses and associations in an area, but unannounced, random sales calls on meeting planners are usually not a good idea. Planners often feel such calls are intrusive and discourteous. Instead, hotels should carefully plan and identify prospects prior to a sales blitz—and, ideally, send prospective clients a letter advising them of the coming visit.

Other sales blitzes may be more elaborate. A new property, for example, may wish to use the sales blitz technique to introduce itself to the community; the blitz would serve as a way to invite potential clients to attend a special property presentation. If a sales blitz is used to introduce a new property or to promote a special property presentation, however, extensive planning is needed. The program may include audiovisual presentations, property tours, and food and beverage functions. In many cases, notables such as local or national celebrities or political figures are invited to stimulate interest and lend credibility to the property. No matter what type of program is planned, however, its ultimate purpose should be to demonstrate a property's ability to handle meetings business. It is of obvious importance, therefore, to get as many of the prospects to attend the event and receive the special presentation.

Still other properties join up with their local convention and visitors bureau to conduct a sales blitz. In this case, several entities are involved (the CVB, area hotels, destination

---

Best Practices

Hyatt's CRUNCH Time Maximizes Sales Blitz Success

When the Hyatt chain sought to jump-start its sales efforts, it organized a program called CRUNCH TIME, which stands for: Close tentative business; Refer new business; Unite our forces; Network our clients; Clean up data base; and Have fun. The program translated into a massive 12-day sales blitz that involved more than 600 corporate and property salespeople targeting 40,000 potential customers.

The program, which included incentive prizes for top performers in a number of categories (number of calls made, revenue, referrals, and so on), was kicked off when corporate headquarters sent lists of clients to be called on to individual hotels and regional offices. The lists were generated to minimize possible overlaps, and were followed up by electronic CRUNCH Grams to stimulate interest in the program and keep salespeople up to date on the campaign's progress (salespeople sent in their results every three days).

CRUNCH Time resulted in a total of 36,219 contacts made by 566 employees. Nearly 2,200 of these calls led to business closings, generating $30 million in bookings, including a single $600,000 piece of business and several bookings of approximately $500,000 each. In addition, some 1,250 referrals were sent property to property, which would likely result in additional business.

Not only did the program generate sales and sales leads, it also led to camaraderie in the sales force, and CRUNCH Time was deemed so successful that the chain planned to repeat it at least annually and expand the program to targeted segments with Catering CRUNCH and Corporate Traveler CRUNCH.

management companies, and area attractions) in a coordinated sales effort to attract a specific market. In Orlando, the CVB has entered into a partnership with the Rosen College of Hospitality Management, and students make prospecting calls for the bureau.

Whether a sales blitz will lead to a property presentation or will be used simply to survey potential clients, most properties begin planning several weeks in advance. Sales letters are often sent out to prospective clients to advise them of the coming visit. This strategy leads to "warm calls"—contacts with planners who have some idea of what the property can offer. Proper preparation is important, as it will result in the sales blitz participant getting in to see more prospects and create an atmosphere conducive to selling.

When planning a sales blitz, a city directory is used to map out specific target areas. Providing each participant with a list of prospects in a concentrated area greatly reduces the traveling time involved, enabling a sales blitz participant to make 75 to 90 calls over a three-day period.

In most cases, the sales blitz is used simply to collect information, qualify prospects, or invite prospects to that special property presentation, so it is not always necessary to tie up the property's sales staff in a sales blitz effort. Some properties hire a temporary sales blitz staff or utilize sales-oriented college students for blitzes over break periods.

Each person involved should clearly understand the purpose of the blitz, including how many calls he or she is expected to make and what questions he or she can answer (if using an outside blitz team, participants are usually instructed to refer contacts to a member of the property's sales staff). Sales blitz participants should be given an adequate supply of survey sheets (see Exhibit 8) and collateral materials, such as property business cards, convention brochures, and low-cost specialty items imprinted with the property's name and telephone number to keep the property's name in front of the prospect.

A great deal of effort is put into a sales blitz, so proper follow-up is important to maximize results. It is wisest to evaluate the results of a sales blitz on a daily basis. This enables the sales manager to determine if there are any leads that should be followed up immediately, to make any changes in strategy (if, for example, there seems to be considerable interest in one geographical area, some participants can be redirected to that location), and, in cases where incentives are offered, reward the day's most successful participant (thereby motivating the other participants).

Trade Show Selling

Trade shows provide an opportunity for a property to reach meeting planners (see Exhibit 9). One of the advantages of trade show participation is that you will meet people who are buying. Anne Marie Spatharakis, senior account executive for the Renaissance Hotel in Washington, D.C., extols the advantages of trade shows:

> Trade shows are great places for big sales to happen. Calling on customers individually takes a lot of time and effort, but at shows you have everyone either buying or selling, so there is a collaborative spirit where quality matches are made.[11]

Another advantage is the relatively low cost. While trade show participation requires effort and expense, it can be cost-effective. According to the Center for Exhibition Industry Research, the average dollar amount to close a sale from a trade show lead is $625, while it costs $1,117 to close a personal sales call. And, if your convention bureau is exhibiting in a trade show, it may be possible for your property to share booth space and expenses with

Exhibit 8   Sample Sales Blitz Survey Sheet

Sales Blitz Survey Sheet

Organization_____

Address_____

_____Zip_____Phone_____

Contact_____Title_____

Contact_____Title_____

1. How many meetings do you have a year?_____When?_____
   Size_____ Who plans them?_____

Contact_____Title_____

When is your next meeting? _____

Where are meetings usually held? _____

2. Do you have incoming visitors that require sleeping accommodations?

   Yes_____ No_____ How many per month?_____

   If yes, where are they housed?_____

   Do you reserve the room? Yes_____ No_____ (If not, who does?)

   Contact_____Title_____

3. Does your organization plan such things as:

   ___Christmas Parties?   ___Retirement Dinners?
   ___Award Dinners?   ___Other Social Events?

   Are you the organizer, or is there a social chairman?
       Yes_____ No_____ Contact_____

4. Are you, or any of your associates, affiliated with any other organizations or associations that might have need for meeting or banquet space? Yes_____ No_____

Name_____Contact_____

Comments:

Taken by: _____Date Taken_____

Source: Howard Feiertag, "Blitzes and Sales Calls: Indispenable Selling Tools," *HSMAI Marketing Review.*

During a sales blitz, survey sheets are used to record prospect information. Once qualified, the prospects with the highest potential for business will merit additional contact. Besides this vital information, additional questions might include: "Who else is involved in decision-making?" and "How are meeting sites selected?"

the bureau. In addition to these benefits, trade shows also provide excellent opportunities to see what your competition is doing!

There are also some disadvantages to selling through trade shows. First, there is the initial cost and transportation of a property's display; these expenses are especially prohibitive for small properties that must compete with the elaborate displays of larger competitors. Secondly, your competition is likely to be participating in the same show and wooing

Exhibit 9   Trade Shows for Reaching the Meetings Market

Exhibit Shows	Number of Exhibitors	Usual Attendance
1. American Society of Association Executives Annual Meeting & Expo	800	5,000
2. ASAE Springtime	800	5,000
3. Incentive Travel & Meetings Exec Show (The Motivation Show)	963	14,319
4. Religious Conference Management Association Annual Conference	688	1,250
5. Meeting Professionals International Annual Meeting	350	1,700
6. Health Care Convention & Exhibitors Association Annual Meeting	130	600
7. IAEE Expo! Expo!	125	1,000
8. HSMAI's Affordable Meetings	550	1,800
9. DMAI's Destination Showcase	300	1,150
10. IMEX Incentive Meetings Show	3,000	7,000
11. EIBTM Barcelona	3,300	7,500

Thirty years ago, the only major industry trade show was the American Society of Association Executives Expo. Today, there are a number of shows aimed at different segments of the meetings industry. Above is a brief listing of national and regional exhibit shows, and recent attendance figures. When selecting a show at which to exhibit, keep in mind your primary target markets and plan your trade show strategy specifically for these markets.

the same target markets you are trying to attract. And, lastly, your booth time may be taken up by a number of meeting planners who will not generate business for your property.

To make the most of trade show selling, planning is again the key (see Exhibit 10). A pre-show action plan identifying potential clients and a strategy for contact and follow-up is an excellent way to ensure that the maximum benefit is derived from trade show participation. Strong potential business should be targeted, and your representatives should find out where these planners are staying; this enables your reps to see planners that don't make it to the property's booth. It is best, therefore, to allow at least two days to make calls before the show opens and to allow at least one day after the show to follow up on new local contacts made through the show.

Both your booth and personnel should adequately reflect your property's image and professionalism. Personnel should always be friendly, courteous, and informative, and the booth should be arranged in a manner that involves the prospects. Rather than setting tables across the booth, it is more effective to place tables along the sides and back to draw people into the display. Giveaway materials should be kept to a minimum; it is a mistake to offer too many giveaways. Most meeting planners prefer to travel light and do not wish to be overwhelmed by too many materials. It is far better to show a video brochure and/or give live presentations at scheduled times. These can be enhanced by one or two pieces of concise, informative material accompanied by your business card.

No matter how simple or elaborate your display, it is important to always remember your purpose: selling. It is important to qualify prospects. If your property is a resort, for example, it would have little appeal for a meeting planner seeking airport hotels at which to hold training meetings. While you shouldn't discount these prospects entirely—they may have contacts who can use your property or may have use for your property at a later date—it is important to deal primarily with meeting planners who offer a high potential for business for your property. In other words, you must quickly qualify prospects to determine how much time you should spend with them. A survey sheet or questionnaire is an excellent way to determine if a booth's visitor is a good prospect. If he or she is unlikely to have a need for your property, be polite but brief and move on to a better-qualified prospect as soon as possible.

Trade show selling is not complicated if you have set clear-cut goals for before and during the show and have established guidelines for follow-up. The contacts made at a trade show should be followed up as quickly as possible after the show to keep your property fresh in the contact's mind. This interest and demonstration of your property's commitment can result in both business from your trade show contacts and referral business in the future.

Exhibit 10   Exhibiting at Trade Shows

Exhibiting at Trade Shows

Before

- When choosing trade shows, ask show management for a rating ratio of meeting planners to salespeople.
- Contact previous exhibitors; ask about attendance and quality of prospective buyers. Set measurable sales and qualified-lead goals.
- Use pre-show promotions. Target important prospects by mail or phone. Arrive early to make sales calls in the area prior to the show.
- Be prepared with meeting planner kits for distribution at the booth.
- Meet with the sales team to clarify team objectives, set individual goals. Train salespeople with written sales scripts. Role-play different sales situations—using a sales brochure, qualifying prospects, and securing information from prospects.
- Design a custom lead form to qualify your prospects.

During

- Set up the booth in advance and assign salespeople to no more than three-hour shifts before a break.
- Ask quick, qualifying questions to help determine interest. Be courteous and friendly but discontinue discussion when the visitor is not a prospect.
- Smile; act and look knowledgeable; stand, don't sit; don't smoke, eat, or drink in the booth.
- Use prospect's business card to take notes of specific needs for follow-up.
- Schedule sales team meetings before and after each day of the show to discuss problems and solutions and to coach the sales team.

And After the Show

- The sixty days after the show are most critical. Assign responsibility for following up on leads and appointments; establish deadlines for follow-ups.
- Review exhibit objectives to see if goals were attained. Each dollar invested should return ten dollars in sales.
- Use the telephone, mail, and e-mail to follow up. Make sure all your leads are followed up within 48 hours after the show and your results will soar.

Used with permission of Howard Feiertag, CHSE, CMP.

To make the most of trade show exhibiting, the above list details what to do before, during, and after a trade show.

DESTINATION MARKETING

Over a century ago, in 1895, Detroit hotelier Milton J. Carmichael presented an idea of promoting the city as a whole to help build individual hotel business. The concept proved to be so successful that the Detroit hoteliers created the nation's first convention bureau. Before long, the idea spread to other cities, and today hundreds of such bureaus exist around the world.

The convention bureaus' primary objective is *destination marketing*—promoting their respective areas as a whole to attract meetings and convention business. To do so, convention bureaus engage in advertising campaigns, participate in trade shows, and offer a number of services to meeting planners, including general destination information, centralized housing of convention delegates, and registration services.

Once given a meeting's requirements—dates, rates, and space—bureaus go to work for planners. The bureau usually arranges site inspection visits. After a group is booked, the bureau's focus shifts from marketing to service.

While the scope of services offered by bureaus depends largely on staff size and budget, some bureaus have become very innovative. The Chicago Convention and Tourism Bureau utilizes its in-house telemarketing department to help planners build attendance at conventions. Using a prepared script and a database of the convening group's members, the bureau's staff makes up to 2,500 calls free of charge. This service is credited with increasing convention attendance in the Windy City by as much as 16 percent. With each additional attendee representing an average of $800 in spending, such effort benefits both planners and local businesses.

GOOD SPORTS

Play is serious business. That's why we renovated our 13,000 seat arena, cultivate lush, green fields and keep plenty of rinks on ice.

Whether you seek the swish of the net, the crack of the bat, or room to run, you'll find the perfect facility in Providence/Warwick, Rhode Island. We know good sports.

Look for us at TEAMS to learn more about Rhode Island.

PROVIDENCE · THE CREATIVE CAPITAL

Providence Warwick Convention & Visitors Bureau · 401-456-0200 · www.GoProvidence.com · sports@GoProvidence.com

 Hilton Providence *Providence Biltmore* — A Rhode Island Tradition Since 1922 — **THE WESTIN** PROVIDENCE

Selling with Convention Bureaus

Even if you represent a large property with extensive convention facilities, a local convention bureau can be an invaluable partner in selling to the meetings market, even serving as an extension of your property's sales staff. Bill Snyder, past president of the Anaheim Convention and Visitors Bureau, states:

INTERNET EXERCISE

Destination Marketing

Log on to the website of the Destination Marketing Association International (DMAI), the membership association for convention and visitors bureaus, at www.destinationmarketing.org. Navigate the site to answer the following questions:

1. How do convention bureaus help meeting planners?

2. If convention bureaus don't charge for their services, how do they make money?

3. What resources and benefits are available for student members of this organization?

4. DMAI maintains the Meeting Information Network (MINT), an online database that contains profiles of more than 40,000 events conducted by more than 20,000 organizations. How can this extensive database help hotels to garner leads and qualify prospects?

A Bureau's function is to bring conventions, trade shows and tourists to its respective area. A secondary objective is, of course, to offer those services which necessarily follow the attraction of conventions, trade shows and tourists.

A Bureau should be the nucleus for the sales effort in the visitor industry for that community and should also represent the point of "one stop shopping" for any prospect or client contemplating holding a convention or trade show in that city. A Bureau must be impartial in its representation of its facilities if it is to be successful.[12]

Convention bureaus are structured in different ways. Some are membership organizations to which hotels, transportation companies, restaurants, and local merchants turn to organize efforts to bring in convention business. Others are funded through **room taxes** and work to promote general tourism (see Exhibit 11). In some cases, they operate exhibition halls that were built with public funds.

The convention bureau's sales office is set up similarly to a hotel sales office, but on a larger scale. Its job, sometimes called **destination marketing**, is to sell the city, bring conventions to the area, and to make the group's stay productive and enjoyable (see box titled "Destination Marketing"). When a bureau receives a letter or phone call from a meeting group saying the city has been selected for its convention, the bureau sends out a **convention lead form** to local hotels (see Exhibit 12). Many bureaus now distribute this information electronically, sending leads to selected hotels via the Internet. The hotel may then contact the group.

In addition to providing leads to area hotels and convention support firms, the bureau also assists in executing conventions, often supplying registration clerks, guides, spouses' program personnel, and so on. Most important for hotels, most convention bureaus also provide a housing bureau for placing delegates in the city's hotels when large conventions are booked.

If your area has a convention bureau, it most likely is a member of the Destination Marketing Association International (DMAI). If so, you are fortunate, because DMAI offers a wealth of detailed, confidential information to assist you in your selling efforts. Each

Exhibit 11   Funding of Convention and Visitors Bureaus

Bed Taxes in Selected Trade Show Cities

City	Bed Tax
Houston	17%
Chicago	15.4%
Anaheim	15%
Atlanta	15%
Los Angeles	14%
Boston	12.5%
New York City	13.25% + $2.00 per night
Las Vegas	12%

Las Vegas boasts far and away the largest bureau budget, double that of Hawaii, which in turn is nearly double that of Reno.

Annual Bureau Budgets (in millions)

City	Budget
Las Vegas	$124,000,000
Hawaii	$62,600,000
Reno	$32,200,000
Orlando	$25,700,000
Los Angeles	$22,000,000
Kissimmee	$20,000,000
Atlanta	$16,700,000
Miami	$15,600,000
San Diego	$15,200,000
San Francisco	$14,300,000

Hotel room taxes are often the largest source of revenue for convention and visitors bureaus. These taxes, also known as bed or pillow taxes, are levied on a percentage basis of room rate, and nationally account for over 60 percent of the typical convention and visitors bureaus' budgets. These taxes sometimes generate controversy, however, as they are not always used to promote the city as a convention, group meeting, and vacation destination. In some cities, these taxes are instead diverted to fund community programs.

DMAI member receives and files reports dealing with convention performances and characteristics of all associations that convened within the member's city. This data includes promised attendance and actual attendance figures, prices paid, concessions granted, and almost everything else you would want to know about a prospect. When you track a convention over a period of five years, a pattern emerges that enables you to decide whether or not you have a good chance to get such business—and how to go after it.

In addition to maintaining records on major associations and corporations, bureaus also subscribe to key association and corporate publications, such as the *Encyclopedia of Associations* and *The Directory of Corporate Meeting Planners,* and make them available to local hotels for research. These publications, among others, are invaluable in securing the meetings market, but are often too expensive for individual properties to purchase.

Exhibit 12   Sample Convention Lead Form

SAN FRANCISCO
CONVENTION & VISITORS BUREAU
1390 MARKET STREET, SAN FRANCISCO, CALIFORNIA 94102

CONVENTION LEAD FORM

Date ___xxx___

TO _____ All major hotels

FROM _____ Matt Miller

GROUP _____ XYZ CORPORATION

CONTACT _____ Mr. John Jones _____ **TITLE** Convention Manager

ADDRESS _____ 6000 K Street N.W.

CITY _____ Washington, DC 20097 _____ **PHONE** (202) 123-4567

ATTENDANCE 500 _____ **NO OF ROOMS** 350

EXHIBIT SPACE NET SQ FT _____ 4000

REQUESTED DATES _____ February 3-6, February 10-13, **2012**
arrivals 2/2 or 2/9; departures 2/7 or 2/14

MEETING REQUIREMENTS

2/2 or 2/9	6 p.m. reception for 300 people
2/3 or 2/10	8 a.m. breakfast for 150
	12 noon lunch for 500
	9:00-5:00 general session for 500 theatre style
2/4 or 2/11	9:00-12 noon 5 workshops for 100 each theatre style; afternoon free
2/5 or 2/12	9:00-12 noon general session for 500 theatre style
	12 noon reception & lunch for 500
	2:00-5:00 5 workshops for 100 each
2/6 or 2/13	9:00-12 noon general session for 500 theatre style
	7 p.m. reception & dinner dance for 500 people

San Francisco is definite; hotel selection within three months

Please copy the Bureau on all your correspondance

History

2010	New Orleans	476	registered; 327 rooms used
2011	Las Vegas	498	registered; 319 rooms used

This is an example of a form sent by the San Francisco Convention & Visitors Bureau to hotels in the city, advising them of an upcoming convention. Note that the form includes the group's requirements (number of rooms, types of functions that will be held, room space requirements, etc.) to enable hotels to decide if they can realistically service the business.

INTERNET EXERCISE

Virtual Site Inspections

Interactive, 360-degree, and 3-D virtual site inspections are now available on the websites of some hotels. For example, Starwood Hotels has rolled out a virtual event planner that allows meeting planners to view photos of sample event setups (including classroom, theater, cocktail, and banquet setups) that they can customize. Details can be modified—from linen color and the placement of tables and chairs to adding a stage or dance floor. Other hotels offer virtual tours that are less interactive, allowing only a 360-degree pan around empty rooms.

Visit the websites below and assess each from a meeting planner's perspective:

- www.radisonblu.com/hotel_berlin/meetings/virtual-tour
- www.sheraton.com/virtual
- www.mandalaybay.com

1. Do you think virtual site tours can replace physical site inspections?

2. What considerations important to event planners cannot be shown in a virtual site inspection?

3. Search the Internet and find other hotels or convention centers that offer virtual tours on their websites. What features do you find most appealing and why? If you could design a virtual site inspection, what features would you include?

The most important facet of working with convention bureaus, however, is the advantage of pooled resources. The convention bureau serves as a coordinator when the size of an event makes it mandatory to present the sales proposal as a group and to house the delegates in a number of hotels. And, since the convention bureau's function is to promote the area as a whole, its efforts—exhibitions at trade shows, print advertising, and direct mail efforts—will directly benefit your property and serve as an additional marketing resource in helping you to obtain business.

Site Inspection Selling and Familiarization Tours

One of the best ways to show exactly what your property has to offer is to invite the meeting planner to visit it personally. This can be done in two ways: on an individual basis *(site inspection selling)* or in a structured group setting *(familiarization tours)*, which offer a number of planners the chance to experience what the hotel has to offer.

Many meeting planners will not book a site unless they have had the opportunity to see it personally. In a recent survey conducted by *Meetings & Conventions* magazine and NTM Research, 90 percent of all planners reported that they personally visit potential meeting sites before making a final decision (see sidebar titled "Shopping Around").[13]

Therefore, a **site inspection tour**, at which prospective clients are invited to personally tour your hotel, is an ideal sales situation. Site inspection selling is most effective if the following guidelines are followed:

- Always schedule a visit when the property is busy. This will give the planner an opportunity to see your efficient service in action—and will give credibility to your claims of excellence.

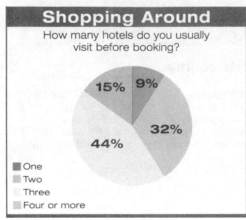

Shopping Around

How many hotels do you usually visit before booking?

9%

32%

44%

15%

- One
- Two
- Three
- Four or more

Source: Art Pfenning, "Site Visits Still Key,"
Meetings & Conventions.

- Don't be too busy, however, to devote time to the planner. He or she should be greeted like a guest, and should have the opportunity to meet those people with whom he or she will be dealing (the catering manager, convention services manager, and so on).
- Alert the staff of the impending site inspection. If possible, post a photograph of the meeting planner and provide pertinent information to enable employees to greet the planner by name.
- A welcoming note from the general manager upon the planner's arrival and a brief visit with the general manager sometime during the visit are good gestures. Many planners indicate they can tell a lot about how a hotel is run by meeting the general manager.
- Feature only those items of interest to the planner. Don't waste everyone's time showing your state-of-the-art audiovisual equipment to a planner whose focus will be social functions or recreational activities.
- Train a number of staff personnel to serve as "tour guides" in the event a salesperson is away. These staff members should be able to answer questions—and sell features as benefits. It is also helpful if they can offer supplemental material, such as photographs of past successful events, third-party endorsements, and so on, to capture the planner's interest.
- Remember the purpose of suggesting a site inspection: selling. Knowing your property, competition, and prospect are keys. Follow the six steps of personal selling discussed in the opening of this chapter. Laura Anevedo, meeting planner for Alder Droz, Inc., says:

> My favorite part about site inspections is being able to visualize my next meeting taking place at the prospective property. Usually the salesperson is putting his/her best foot forward in order to capture the business and is really excited about showing off the property. If the salesperson has done homework on my past programs, he/she can really be influential in my ultimate decision to book a program at that property.[14]

Many of today's meeting planners, especially those who plan a number of small meetings, do not have time to personally tour every hotel that can potentially stage their meetings. Hotels are responding by offering *virtual site tours*. While some hotels already offer photographs and moving images of their guestrooms and their meeting facilities on their websites, it is much more effective for a hotel to combine this sales tool with an actual telephone call with a salesperson. In this way, the salesperson can determine the planner's needs and steer him or her to specific features of interest as well as answer any questions that might arise.

If a hotel targets several market segments, it should consider tailoring virtual tours to individual segment needs. Some hotels create a "bank" of digital photographs to enable them to present features most important to a potential client. Whether these photographs are presented online or e-mailed to the client, you will capture far more business if a "live" representative from the property walks the prospect through the presentation.

Familiarization (fam) tours require more planning than individual site inspection visits, and, since they can be expensive for the property, involve qualifying prospective visitors. Michael Smith, Director of Convention Sales for the Portland, Oregon, Visitors' Association, states:

> We do not invite people just because they happen to plan meetings. Unless they are seriously thinking of meeting in Portland, they are not invited. Our members need to know that the people we are bringing in are legitimate and the trip is an investment.[15]

Qualified meeting planners may be contacted either by mail or telephone, and should be given a reasonable lead time to make plans (four to six weeks is the norm). The planners invited should have similar professional needs. One planner stated:

Best Practices

Sheraton San Marcos Qualifies Prospects for Fam Tours

George Mittler, Director of Sales at the Sheraton San Marcos in Chandler, Arizona, also believes in qualifying prospects, and achieved remarkable results from his semiannual fam tours. He explains:

> At the Sheraton San Marcos Resort, we have found the formula to successful fam trips. After spending $40,000 on our two semiannual fam trips, we booked $900,000 in business as a direct result of the trips. Resorts generally strive for ten times the return on the money invested in a fam tour, but we consistently come back with more than 20 times the investment. In fact, on every fam tour we've organized in the past two years, we've booked business while meeting planners were still on-site.
>
> Competition in our area is stiff, so you have to develop a niche. Ours has been to go above and beyond what the competitors offer. We sell service and successful meetings. We train our people, and everybody from the general manager to the busboys sells the resort. Our philosophy of involving the entire staff as salespeople is the reason we convert so many fam trippers into clients.
>
> To fascinate the fam trippers, we stage three major events while they're here: a Meeting Planners Invitational Golf Tournament, Dinner in the Desert, and a 50s Night or a Casino Theme Night dinner-dance. The whole point of these extravaganzas is to demonstrate to planners how the San Marcos can plan and carry out theme events.
>
> Since it costs about $400 to $500 per person, not counting airfare, to host fam-trip guests, we pre-qualify fam trippers. The days of "'Come eat my shrimp and drink my booze" are long over, so we make sure these people are qualified. To cut costs, we also co-sponsor with a local airline.

Source: From correspondence with George Mittler, director of sales, Sheraton San Marcos.

> I hate to go on fams where everyone is an association planner and I'm the only corporate planner. They show you everything from an association standpoint, and there's a big difference.

The property should let attendees know exactly what the fam tour involves: its duration, what is included (meals, transportation, etc.), and whom the invitation includes (spouse, other members of the selection committee, etc.). When the meeting planners arrive for the tour, they should be greeted individually and given a schedule of events. Events should be planned to show prospects exactly what the property can offer (see "Best Practices" box titled "Sheraton San Marcos Qualifies Prospects for Fam Tours"). Staff members usually handle property tours, although an outside person (a member of the local convention and visitors bureau, for example) may conduct off-property tours of the area's leisure and cultural activities.

As with individual site-inspection selling, property salespeople should try to get a meeting commitment before the guests leave the property. If this is not possible (in some cases, for example, the planner must report back to the site selection committee), the fam tour should be followed up as soon as possible. Many properties include a questionnaire in their follow-up letter, asking what the participants liked and disliked. This type of questionnaire not only can assist the property to plan better fam tours, but can also be used to provide insights into the needs, likes, and dislikes of the individual participants.

Fam tours not only bring business from the participants, but can influence their peers as well. Today, a number of properties are using technology to make their fam tours available to a wide audience of meeting planners. A fam tour, marketed to a specific segment of planners, is videotaped and is made available on tape and on the property's website. This not only enhances the experience for the participants but also provides a "virtual tour" of the property—and feedback from the attendees—to other meeting planners.

Summary

As you can see, personal selling—whether it be an individual effort, such as a face-to-face sales call or telephone call, or a strategy to sell to groups at a trade show—plays a key role in booking meetings. In this chapter, we have looked at the six steps of a personal sales call, examined how the telephone is used in selling to the meetings market, and discussed other direct sales tools, including the sales blitz, trade show selling, selling with convention bureaus, site inspection selling, and "fam" tours.

Endnotes

1. Yeoh Siew Hoon, "Don't Forget the Power of the Sales Call," *Hoteliers: Hospitality, Hotel & Travel News,* December 9, 2009.

2. "Interviews With Marketing Leaders," *HSMAI Marketing Review,* Spring 2002, p. 35.

3. Rayna Katz, "Planners as Honest as Relationships Dictate," *Meeting News,* May 3, 2004, p. 1.

4. "A New Approach to Selling," *The Meeting Professional,* February and April 2000, pp. 43, 46.

5. Rayna Katz, "Planners, Sales Reps Often Out of Sync," *Meeting News,* March 15, 2004, p. 10.

6. Joan Barker, "Stand Out in the Crowd," *HSMAI Marketing Review,* Fall 2002, p. 17.

7. Robert Gilbert, "Mastering the Basics," *Lodging,* October 2003, p. 33.

8. Tom McCarthy, "Don't Forget to Rehearse," *Lodging Hospitality,* January 2005, p. 22.

9. Becky Cumming and Melina Legos, "Squaring Off," *Successful Meetings,* June 1999, p. 37.

10. Rayna Katz, "Hilton Eases Buying Process Via Package of Web Enhancements," *Meeting News,* January 31, 2005.

11. Ruth Hill, "Lost and Found," *HSMAI Marketing Review,* Spring 2003, p. 47.

12. From correspondence with Bill Snyder, past president, Anaheim Convention and Visitors Bureau.

13. Art Pfenning, "Site Visits Still Key," *Meetings & Conventions,* April 2004, p. 24.

14. "In the Trenches," *Meetings in the West,* July 2000, p. 6.

15. Suzanne Miller and Ross Weiland, "Planners Want Better Fam Trips," *Meeting News.*

 # Key Terms

appointment call—A prearranged appointment with a prospect to introduce the features and benefits offered by a property. During this visit, the salesperson may or may not attempt to close the sale.

call report—A document, usually resulting from some personal contact, that provides general information about an account (address, contact person, etc.) as well as remarks on the needs of the group and any action steps that can be taken to sell the hotel's products and services to the group.

close-ended question—A question requiring a specific answer that often can be given in just a few words.

cold call—A fact-finding call on a prospect with whom there has been little or no previous contact; often made without a definite appointment. Sometimes referred to as canvassing.

consultative selling—A customized sales presentation approach in which the salesperson is viewed as an expert and serves as a consultant to the prospect. This involves identifying the prospect's needs and recommending the best solution for them—even if that solution does not include the salesperson's products or services.

convention lead form—Information sheet used by convention and visitors bureaus to circulate announcements about meetings to hotels, destination management companies, and other potential suppliers.

destination marketing—Promotion of a particular location as a meeting site and/or tourist attraction.

familiarization (fam) tour—Free or reduced-rate trip given to meeting planners, travel agents, travel writers, and other sources of potential business to acquaint them with a property or destination, and to stimulate the booking of an event.

major close—A question or statement at the end of a sales presentation that asks for a definite commitment on the prospect's part.

open-ended question—A question that gives a prospect the opportunity to express his or her feelings and knowledge.

room tax—Tax placed on hotel/motel room rentals. Generally all or part of the revenues generated from these taxes are used to finance the operation of convention facilities. Also called a bed tax or occupancy tax.

presentation book—Sometimes called a sales kit, this sales tool provides detailed information on a property's facilities and services. Materials should include floor plans, photographs of rooms and creative banquets, sample menus, complimentary letters from satisfied guests, and favorable press comments. In some cases, special presentation books are prepared as handouts for meeting planners visiting the property on fam tours.

property fact book—A summary of what a lodging property has to offer, including: number and types of guestrooms; room rates; booking policies; food service available, including menus, seating capacities, and hours of operation; descriptions, layouts, and capacities of meeting and banquet facilities; recreational facilities; and area amenities. The property fact book is used as a tool for salespeople, enabling them to translate the property's features into benefits.

sales blitz—Concentrated canvassing by several sales representatives of a selected geographic area over a specific time period in order to gather information on potential leads.

site inspection tour—Prospective customers visit the property and are given a tour that showcases such features as guestrooms, meeting facilities, food and beverage facilities, recreational amenities, and other property services, such as valet parking, shuttle service, and other services that may give the property an edge in the site selection process.

telemarketing—The systematic use of the telephone for marketing or sales purposes.

trial close—A statement or question posed by the salesperson during a sales presentation that seeks to evoke a positive response from the client.

 # Review Questions

1. Identify the steps in making a personal sales call. Why is each important?

2. List the steps in making a telephone appointment call. Why is follow-up especially important after making telephone contact? What kind of follow-up can be done?

3. In what other ways is the telephone used to sell to and service customers?

4. What is a sales blitz? Why can a sales blitz be a cost-effective sales tool?

5. What is a trade show? How can a property make the most of its trade show exhibit?

6. What are the advantages of working with a convention and visitors bureau to secure business?

7. What is a "fam" tour? What steps should a property take to ensure that a "fam" tour is successful?

 # Additional References

Fundamentals of Destination Management and Marketing, Rich Harrill, AH&LA Educational Institute, 2005.

Hospitality Sales: A Marketing Approach, Margaret Shaw and Susan Morris, John Wiley & Sons, 2000. www.hospitality@wiley.com

Hospitality Sales and Marketing, Fifth Edition, James R. Abbey, AH&LA Educational Institute, 2008. www.ahlei.org

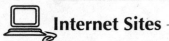

Internet Sites

For more information, visit the following Internet sites. Internet addresses can change without notice. If a site is no longer available at the address listed below, a search engine can be used to find the new address or additional, related sites.

Chicago Convention and Tourism Bureau
www.chicagoil.org

Destination Management Association
  International (DMAI)
www.dmai.org

Hospitality Sales & Marketing
  Association International (HSMAI)
www.hsmai.org

Sales & Marketing Executives (SME)
  International
www.smei.org

Chapter 8 Outline

Competencies

1. Describe how hospitality companies use print media and technology to advertise. (pp. 253–266)

2. Identify the purpose and types of collateral materials hospitality companies use in advertising. (pp. 266–272)

3. Explain how to conduct a direct mail campaign. (pp. 272–274)

4. Summarize the process of planning an advertising strategy. (pp. 274–284)

5. Describe how public relations and publicity can help a property reach meeting planners. (pp. 284–286)

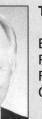

The Planners' Perspective on Advertising

Ed Griffin, Jr., CAE
President/CEO
Florida Hotel and Motel Association
Orlando, Florida

"Advertising wins when the meeting planner understands both the benefits and the unique qualities of a product or service. The hotel must explain how the product will satisfy the planner's needs. In order to do that, the advertiser must know what's important to the planner. Planners want to know about such things as room capacities, pricing, guarantees, restrictions, and value seasons. Advertisers increasingly compete for the planner's time vs. the planner's wastepaper basket, so it is essential for messages to be direct, simple, and concise. The ad copy must be directed specifically at the planner, with a view to planner benefits rather than product features."

8   Advertising to the Meeting Planner

ADVERTISING CAN PLAY a key role in your sales effort, since its primary function is to generate interest in your property. Advertising supplements your sales effort. It is an invaluable tool for targeting meeting planners who have not previously been reached and offers additional information to those who are aware of your facilities.

When a property advertises, its message is seen by a vast audience, generating potential leads that can be followed up by the sales staff. Marketing efforts, then, should be supported by an advertising and promotional strategy that is carefully planned and executed.

One of the benefits of advertising is that it, like sales presentations, can be "tailored" to meet the needs of potential customers. For example, properties can target the corporate segment, whose meetings are often staged by inexperienced planners, with one type of ad, and target the association segment, which looks for a desirable location as well as meeting planning assistance to increase attendance, with an ad promoting those benefits (see Exhibit 1).

While there are a number of media available, including newspapers, trade magazines, travel guides, direct mail, collateral material, outdoor advertising, radio, television, and the Internet, not all are used to reach meeting planners. You will have to make very specific choices based on your target customers, marketing goals, and budget.

Print Advertising

One of the most effective ways to reach meeting planners is through **print advertising**. Most meeting planners look for information. Advertising in printed media most likely to be seen by meeting planners can increase your property's chances of generating meetings business.

While some properties advertise in such newspapers as the *Wall Street Journal* and magazines such as *Fortune* and *Time*, which are often read by meeting planners, the most promising print media in which to advertise is **trade magazines**, especially specialized meetings publications.

Trade Magazines

Magazine advertising offers several advantages. First, ads can be printed in color and photographs reproduced with good quality. Second, many magazines have a long reading life. Back issues of some magazines are kept and reread, often passed on to others, giving ads a longer life. Third, and most important, magazine advertising gives the hotel an opportunity to key its convention promotion efforts to a select group of readers.

Once you have opted to use print advertising, you will need to develop effective print ads. Good print ads don't just happen. They are carefully thought out and targeted toward a specific audience (see Exhibit 2).

The most effective ads follow the AIDA principle, which focuses on *attention, interest, desire,* and *action.* To attract *attention*, your ad must stand out from the rest. In most

Exhibit 1   Sample Print Ad

This print ad for the Wyndham Phoenix appeals to the personal needs of association meeting planners, who answer to a board, attendees, and exhibitors. Promising the services of a skilled professional to ensure that the meeting planner stages a successful event, the ad also promotes special rewards for booking a meeting at the hotel. This ad includes all the successful elements of a print ad: a headline (promoting a benefit), a photograph, copy to support the benefit in the headline, and a logo and contact information at the lower portion of the ad.

cases, this is done through the use of a **headline** or eye-catching illustration. If an illustration is used, it must tie in with the copy of the ad. Whenever possible, use *color* to attract attention. If your budget prohibits using full-color ads, even a property with limited funds can use black plus one other color to draw attention to key points.

To keep the reader *interested*, your **body copy** should be specific and to the point. Don't be reluctant to use plenty of white space and large or bold type for easy readability. Use bulleted lists for key points. Keep the copy simple, using short sentences and words that are easy to understand. Make your ad quick to read and easy to comprehend.

To build *desire*, the text should present your features as benefits and tell the reader why your property is different. If you offer special services to meeting planners, tell them so — and offer this as a benefit to them. The print ad in Exhibit 3, for example, promotes

Exhibit 2   Effective Print Ads Boost the Bottom Line

This ad is from Hilton Hotels' award-winning "Travel Should Take You Places" campaign. This ad, directed to meeting planners, was one of several ads that stressed that traveling should be more than going from point A to point B; each of the ads in the series promoted the belief that travel was transformative, and that travel should be an enriching experience — a "voyage of self-discovery and enrichment." As a result of this series of ads, online bookings, average daily rate, and RevPar all rose for the chain.

the unique guarantee offered to meeting planners who booked meetings in 2009 and 2010 at The Broadmoor in Colorado Springs. In an unprecedented move, the hotel promised to waive all master account fees if a meeting or incentive program didn't meet the planner's expectations for value, service, facilities, and quality. The ad appeared in several major

Exhibit 3   Promoting a Unique Benefit in Print Ads

While it is important for every hotel to offer a benefit that differentiates them from the competition, this is especially important in the luxury segment. In February 2009, The Broadmoor, an upscale meetings property in Colorado Springs, Colorado, offered a benefit never before offered to meeting planners: "The Broadmoor Guarantee." The offer was clear and simple: "Your meeting is exceptional. Or it's free. Period."

No other U.S. hotel has matched the Broadmoor's offer, as many hoteliers are fearful that clients will take advantage of guarantees and revenues will be lost. But when a hotel guarantees its product, it sends a message that the property is confident in its products and services.

Source: The Broadmoor, Colorado Springs, Colorado.

magazines, including *Corporate & Incentive Travel, Successful Meetings*, the *Meetings & Conventions Official Meetings Facilities* guide, *Insurance & Financial Meetings Management*, and *MPI One+*, as well as online on several websites (Mimegasite.com, MCMag. com, and TradeshowWeek.com) and on The Broadmoor website (database messaging and video messaging).

You may also want to include photographs of your expertise in action. But don't make the mistake of including a photograph of an empty room — nothing looks more sterile; portray action by including people in your meeting or function room photographs.

Last, but certainly not least, you will want to create an ad that stimulates *action* on the part of the reader. Since the primary purpose of your ad is to generate a response, offer a way to do so. In many cases, ads are accompanied by a reply card or include a coupon (or, at the very least, an address) to enable the respondent to request additional information. Today, most properties offer toll-free numbers, fax numbers, web addresses, and e-mail addresses to encourage prompt responses. Peter Warren, past president of the Hotel Sales & Marketing Association International and owner of one of the leading hospitality advertising firms, says:

> The purpose of your ad should be to begin the process of "awareness, interest, desire, then action." A mistake made by some clients is to expect the ad to do everything, so they try to make their ads into brochures. Because a one-page ad cannot tell the whole story, entice them to visit your website where they can find a more compelling story, or call an 800 number for more information.[1]

Always be sure your ad includes your property's name, address, and your **logo**. It is highly effective to have ads that are readily identifiable, and, since your logo is distinctly yours, it should be used in all media efforts (it generally appears toward the bottom of the ad).

Once you have developed the components of your ad, you will have to decide on how you want it positioned in the magazine. Magazine space is sold in a variety of sizes (see Exhibit 4). You will have to determine which size and placement will work best for your ad.

The positioning of your ad is important. Studies have shown that the reader's eye is drawn initially to the upper part of the right hand page. For an ad smaller than a full page, the position on the upper right hand page might mean more readership. It is even more preferable to have your ad positioned in the editorial section of the magazine; when possible, ask that your ad be the only hotel ad on the page. The magazine's placement of your small ad next to competing ads may reduce its efficiency. Sometimes you can negotiate to avoid such circumstances; sometimes an additional fee will guarantee it. Good position, facing editorial copy, will help your ad do the job.

The size and frequency of your ad is largely dependent on your budget (see box titled "Magazine Advertising Rates"). While some properties can afford full-page color ads, other properties have to opt for smaller ads if they are to place them frequently. Ads are like sales calls; frequency is important. Your prospects may require several exposures to your advertising before they respond. Advertising gurus advise you to run ads at least every other month throughout the year. If, in your eyes, a publication doesn't warrant six ads a year, perhaps you ought to rethink your decision to advertise in it at all. Frequency is important for effective advertising.

Exhibit 4   Magazine Space Options

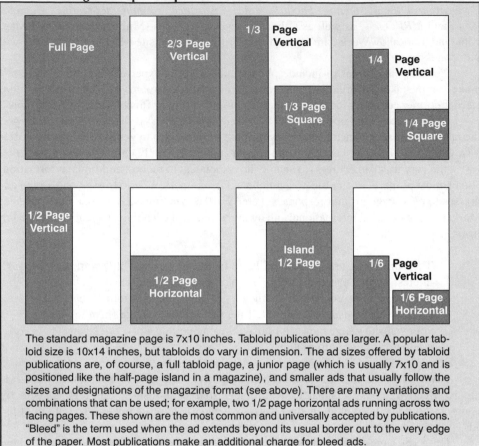

The standard magazine page is 7x10 inches. Tabloid publications are larger. A popular tabloid size is 10x14 inches, but tabloids do vary in dimension. The ad sizes offered by tabloid publications are, of course, a full tabloid page, a junior page (which is usually 7x10 and is positioned like the half-page island in a magazine), and smaller ads that usually follow the sizes and designations of the magazine format (see above). There are many variations and combinations that can be used; for example, two 1/2 page horizontal ads running across two facing pages. These shown are the most common and universally accepted by publications. "Bleed" is the term used when the ad extends beyond its usual border out to the very edge of the paper. Most publications make an additional charge for bleed ads.

Magazine ad space is sold by the page or fraction of a page, and ads can be positioned in standard layouts in a variety of ways. These are some of the sizes and placements most commonly used.

Hotel Directories

In addition to trade magazines, printed and electronic hotel directories (especially those directed to meeting planners) and other business directories are excellent media for reaching meeting planners. These directories list property information in a standard format. The meeting planner has the opportunity to "comparison shop" various factors such as location, facilities, transportation, and price. And while your property is presented exactly as all others in these editorial listings, most directories offer advertising space for your property's print ad.

It is important to note, however, that advertising in these types of directories will differ from your standard advertising. You do not have the continuity that comes with a series of ads in a periodical. You have just the one-time ad in which to make your sales pitch. Readers of directories turn to them for *facts*. Take a leaf from their book and load your ad with details. Your ad should supply all the information necessary to generate an inquiry — and a means for the meeting planner to respond.

Many hotel directories are available online as well as in print. *Meetings & Conventions* magazine, for example, offers a number of guides on its website, www.meetings

Magazine Advertising Rates

Listed below is a sampling of *Meetings & Conventions* magazine's advertising rates. Costs for print advertising vary depending on a number of factors. For example, the use of color is more expensive, but color ads have a greater "stopping power" than black and white advertising. The position of an ad is also a factor; the inside and back covers are the most expensive placements because of their higher exposure. Hotels also have the option of using special inserts for a higher rate. While rates will vary from publication to publication, most magazines offer discounts to frequent advertisers.

A. Black & White

	1x	4x	7x	13x	26x
One Page	$17,015	$16,955	$16,310	$14,955	$14,390
2/3 Page	12,290	12,205	11,780	10,790	10,465
1/2 Page*	9,655	9,570	9,220	8,435	8,195
1/3 Page	6,745	6,725	6,445	5,920	5,790

*Island 1/2 Page plus: $655

B. Color

2-Color: B/W earned rate plus	$1,935
Match Color: B&W earned rate plus	2,545
Match Color Spread: B&W earned rate plus	4,425
4-Color: B&W earned rate plus	5,095
4-Color Spread: B&W earned rate plus	8,895
5-Color: B&W earned rate plus	7,385

C. Covers

	1x	7x	13x
Inside: 2-Color	$24,870	$23,200	$21,095
4-Color	27,955	26,330	24,300
Back: 4-Color	29,340	27,655	25,540

D. Inserts

	1x	7x	13x
2 pages	$16,940	$16,280	$14,960
4 pages	30,495	29,305	26,930
6 pages	41,170	39,565	36,355
8 pages	49,405	47,480	43,630

E. Commission and Credit Policy

15% to recognized agencies. Net 30 days. It is understood that all orders are accepted for space subject to our credit requirements. There are no additional discounts for cash payments.

conventions.com (click on the "Destinations" tab). *The Hotel & Travel Index* can be accessed at hotelandtravelindex.travelweekly.com, and a number of other hotel directories can be viewed at www.issuu.com (type "meeting planner guide" in the search box).

Most directories accept hotel advertising that includes such options as site sponsorships, expanded or premium listings, and various sizes and types of ads. Links to advertising rates and guidelines are usually provided on the home pages of directory sites.

Using Technology for Advertising

Over the past few years, a number of new technologies have made a difference in how hotels market themselves to the meetings market. While print advertising is still an important way to get a property's message out, these new technologies make it even easier for a property to reach new and existing customers and to interact with them in exciting new ways.

The Internet

The Internet is a powerful tool in marketing to meeting planners and other sources of group and transient business. Today, meeting planners and other decision-makers can directly access a variety of travel services over the Internet, and they are finding it indispensible for comparing properties and services. According to the most recent Meetings Market Report, some 99 percent of association planners used the computer to help plan meetings.

Meeting planners cite a number of benefits to using the Internet, including 24-hour availability, a wealth of up-to-date information on potential meeting sites not only locally but around the world, and the ability to "interact" on most sites (see box titled "Rating of Website Elements Used to Help Plan Meetings"). Using the Internet can save time and money and make the planner's job easier. Cathy Shurety, meetings and events coordinator at Aluma Systems in Concord, Ontario, Canada, says:

> The Internet definitely makes it easier for me to do my job. Now when a department comes to me with a meeting request, I can come up with a list of potential venues based on their criteria within half a day. Before the Internet, we mostly looked at local venues. Now I can easily inspect properties anywhere in the world.[2]

Rating of Website Elements Used to Help Plan Meetings

Website elements considered "extremely useful"	Association Planners	Corporate Planners
Floor plans	59	46
Meeting space specifications	50	44
Maps/directions	19	32
Destination information	33	32
Photographs	26	30
Virtual tours	26	35
Meeting management tools	31	21
Facility search	26	15
Special dates/rates	25	27
Video	15	12

This chart ranks what is important to both association and corporate meeting planners who access a convention hotel's website.
Source: Recent Meetings Market Report by *Meetings & Conventions* magazine.

Meetings-related magazines have made the planner's job easier by featuring popular hospitality and planning sites and giving tips on how to use the web. Loews Hotels jumped on the "information bandwagon" by developing a 44-page "Meeting Planners' Guide to Using the Web." The guide featured tips on using search engines and listed top industry sites in addition to promoting the chain's own site and properties.

Property Website. There are other ways in which properties can use the Internet to reach prospects. The first is for a property to set up its own website, allowing meeting planners and other clients to directly access a chain's site for information on specific properties. According to the most recent Meetings Market Report conducted by *Meetings & Conventions* magazine, two-thirds of the meeting planners surveyed access individual hotel sites to make meeting-site decisions. The Internet enables hotels to create high-quality presences via computer. No longer does a property have to rely on constantly updating its color brochure or getting the word out about a new product or service — using the Internet, it can create a graphic presentation featuring full-color images with sound and video and even offer a "virtual" tour of the property.

Hotels using the Internet to market their properties to meeting planners can instanteously provide them with the following:

- A listing of meeting facilities and floor plan diagrams (some hotel websites have floor plans and photos of function rooms with full 360-degree panoramas)
- The name, telephone number, and e-mail address of a contact person
- A form to fill out about their upcoming meetings that can be faxed or e-mailed to the property with the click of a button
- A reservations system that lets the planner guarantee rooms by using a credit card
- Meeting management tools

Features also include interactive electronic brochures, enabling planners to "tour" the facilities or talk to the chef and then tap into the hotel's computer to book function space for banquets and meetings as well as book their guestrooms. Most hotels now have an interactive request for proposal, and it is now possible for meeting planners to do virtually all their meeting business with a property online.

To promote a property, a hotel must first set up its website, which includes its own "address." These sites will vary significantly, depending on the property and the services it promotes, but all start with a "home page" or directory to subsequent pages or "web pages." The home page typically includes the property's name, logo, and a "menu" of information from which to select. If a chain services a number of market segments, it is best to provide links to information of specific interest. Sheraton, for example, offers a "Meeting Facilities" section, Hilton has a "Meetings & Groups" link, and Marriott features a "Meeting Planning" section. The InterContinental Hotels Group offers information for both professional and occasional meeting planners on its website (see illustration on page 263), and the Hyatt chain promotes its online meetings management tools in print advertising (see Exhibit 5).

The best, most effective home pages are visually attractive and should project the company's image or positioning. As with other advertising, the first step is to attract attention, and the home page should also feature navigational links (text, an icon, an image, or some combination) to direct planners to site content that showcases your meeting facilities and other items of interest. Links should include other features and tools that will assist planners, including meeting guides, special offers and promotions, and, most importantly, a way to communicate with your hotel, including Request for Proposal (RFP) forms and links to direct e-mail contacts with key hotel personnel, such as the convention service manager,

Exhibit 5   Online Meetings Management Tools

MEETINGS
AND INCENTIVES
AT YOUR FINGERTIPS.

resorts.hyatt.com

Your complete online planning tool, featuring:

- Searches based on activities, space, rooms, locations and other options
- Robust high-resolution photo galleries for use in presentations and program brochures
- Planning resources and incentive checklists
- Fact sheets, detailed floor plans and capacity charts
- Links to additional destination information

For more information, visit resorts.hyatt.com.

H YATT
RESORTS

Hyatt Resorts promotes its online meeting tools in print ads such as this one. Features include photo galleries for use in event brochures, checklists, fact sheets, and detailed floor plans.
Source: Courtesy of Hyatt Resorts.

💻 *INTERNET EXERCISE*

Property Websites

A growing number of today's meeting planners turn to the websites of convention hotels to compare venues before making meeting site decisions. The four websites listed below have won awards from the hospitality industry for their effective online messages to meeting planners.

Log on to the following sites and go to the meetings and/or convention areas of each to answer the following questions:

- Hyatt Regency Chicago (www.chicagoregency.hyatt.com)
- InterContinental Toronto Centre (www.torontocentre.intercontinental.com)
- Saddleback Resort (www.saddlebrook.com)
- Sheraton Vancouver Wall Centre (www.sheratonvancouver.com)

1. Using the chart in your text titled "Rating of Website Elements Used to Help Plan Meetings," critique each website for content relative to the factors that meeting planners ranked as "extremely useful" in the recent Meetings Market Report by *Meetings & Conventions* magazine.

2. Which sites offer the option of e-mailing a request for proposal (RFP)?

3. Which hotels offer "e-mmediate response" to meeting inquiries, promising instant group date and rate availability?

4. Which sites provide a virtual tour of the property's meeting rooms?

5. Which sites offer a link to the bios and achievements of key meeting staff members?

6. Which websites explain their program for sustaining a natural environment and their "green" policies?

7. Identify the sites that provide testimonials from past clients and guests.

8. Which sites offer links to social networks such as Facebook or Twitter?

---

food and beverage manager, and so on. Subsequent web pages should be designed to be as interactive, informative, and convenient to the user as possible. The web pages should include all pertinent information required by a user (room rates, square footage of meeting space, a biography of your chef, etc.), interesting graphics (photos, charts and graphs, etc.), and up-to-date information.

Marriott, for example, uses its website (www.marriott.com) to offer greater value to meeting planners. The site's meetings section contains a comprehensive suite of tools, including event space calculators, a budget calculator, a planning timeline, publicity and promotion tools, and a food and beverage planner. It also provides a link from which planners can order a free printed meeting planner's brochure. The Hilton chain (www.hilton.com) also offers support to planners with its free meeting planning software (developed with software maker Newmarket) that can be downloaded via the Groups & Meetings section of the website. Planners can use this software to create a custom layout (including seating arrangements, tables, exhibit displays, and other elements) of a meeting room at a specific Hilton hotel or resort.

Most sites now offer the opportunity for planners to search for specific meeting criteria. The planner enters specifics and the computer will search for a "match" for his or her requirements within the chain. And, as we have said earlier, RFPs are usually available. But

This website for InterContinental Hotels Group provides information of interest to both professional and occasional meeting planners. Note the links to customer service, featured offers, and a meeting and event guide in addition to a search feature that enables planners to find potential meeting sites in the chain by city, state, and country.
Source: Courtesy of InterContinental Hotels Group.

sites should also include a direct link to the property sales office or reservation system as well as pertinent e-mail addresses and your property's toll-free and fax telephone numbers.

Links to Meeting-Related Websites. The second way to reach meeting planners is to *link* your property to other meetings-related sites, such as a CVB site, city site, the site of a meeting planner service provider, or the sites of other firms to which planners turn for information. If you are targeting the association market, linking to a CVB site is extremely important; a recent survey indicated that three out of four association meeting planners use CVB sites to plan their meetings. *Convene* magazine publishes an annual website directory that provides the addresses of national and international convention and visitors bureaus, conference and convention centers, hotel chains, hotels and resorts, convention services, and airlines and car rental agencies. By linking with one of these entities, you are likely to reach prospects looking specifically for meeting services.

You can also link to meeting site services, including cvent.com, conventionplanit.com, mpoint.com, sitevisit. com, and a host of others, which compile lists of databases of properties interested in hosting meetings and group business. These services help planners to narrow down choices by filtering such aspects as location, size, and facilities, and then provide electronic RFP forms to send to hotels identified as meeting their requirements. Robert Bennett, vice president of marketing solutions for StarCite, whose technology is used by HelmsBriscoe, says:

> The number of inquiries and leads distributed from our sites has increased 428 percent in the last two years.[3]

A property may also choose to *advertise* on other sites likely to be visited by its targeted segments. One of the most popular choices is a **banner ad** that appears when a site is accessed. Linking and advertising costs vary widely, so it is a good idea to determine the overall benefit. One disadvantage is that many of your competitors may also be linked to the same site, so you will want to promote a unique benefit if you choose to link with other sites or buy space on sites that feature other hotel advertising.

Social Media. A trend that is changing the face of Internet advertising is the explosive growth of **social media**. It has become increasingly common for people to join online networking communities where they share information, photographs, videos, and music, and hotel sales and advertising staff can take advantage of social media to build relationships with meeting planners, network with other hospitality professionals, and advertise.

Hotel salespeople and meeting planners are using such sites as LinkedIn, Facebook, and Twitter as their primary sources for professional networking. And, as social media sites are being increasingly used by hotels as communications tools, many hotel websites have links to their social networking sites on their hotel websites.

Twitter is one such customer relationship management tool that allows hotels to interact with customers, reinforce brand loyalty, and respond to customer service issues in a timely manner — in "tweets" of 140 characters or less. Hyatt, for example, communicates on Twitter under the user name Hyatt Concierge, while Fairmont Hotels & Resorts uses the profile name of Sweet Tweets, and Starwood Hotels & Resorts' Twitter page can be viewed at Starwood Buzz.

While face-to-face communication is most preferred, social networking sites allow salespeople to build and maintain relationships with meeting planners. Salespeople often use social media sites to stay in touch with contacts. If a salesperson is attending a trade show, for example, he or she might alert contacts about being there and try to arrange for a meeting at the event. Hotels can use social media to send out bulletins and audio or video messages regarding an upcoming event or promotion. Carol Verret, a trainer and consultant to the hospitality industry, says:

> Gone are the days when the salesperson booked the business, handed it over to conference services, and pretty much disappeared. The salesperson needs to have a system of communicating with their clients going forward — that can be a periodic newsletter to client groups, blogs that are uploaded to the salesperson's profile on social networks, and/or pushing out an occasional light communication on Twitter!
>
> Use a flip camera to take videos of an event at the hotel or hotel team members doing something unique, like towel sculptures on the bed. Post it on YouTube and your social network pages, and send the link to clients.

Touching accounts and contacts in non-intrusive ways helps keep that person in your tribe.[4]

Travel-related social sites such as TripAdvisor offer travel tips from consumers, and these sites can be excellent advertising vehicles for hospitality firms. TripAdvisor is one of the most popular social media sites for the *leisure market,* with over 30 million visits monthly. Two newly launched social media sites for *meeting planners* are i-Meet (www.i-meet.com) and Meeting Universe (www.meetinguniverse.com). While these sites invite meeting planners to share their opinions on properties from their unique points of view, the sites are in their infancy — and face the challenge of getting busy meeting planners to actually rate hotels and write reviews.

Visitors to online discussion boards — especially those for travel-related topics—can prove to be invaluable by spreading the word about your products and services. In order to help hospitality firms reach out to the tech-savvy consumers who frequent social media and social networking sites, the Hospitality Sales and Marketing Association International (HS-MAI) and the Travel Industry Association (TIA) have partnered to produce an educational report, *The Travel Marketer's Guide to Social Media and Social Networking.*

One of the tools that hospitality firms can use to establish a presence in the world of social media is the **blog** — an online journal of frequently updated articles or comments ("posts") that is easy to create and can be imbedded with images, hyperlinks, and video and audio features. Starwood Hotels' public blog (www.thelobby.com), which features a number of travel-related posts that contain links to relevant hotel information, can be accessed through the Preferred Guest Program pages on the company's hotel brand website. J.W. "Bill" Marriott, Jr., the Chairman and CEO of Marriott International, also launched a personal blog. One of the few industry leaders to have a personal blog, Marriott's focus is on keeping in touch with his guests — and potential customers — through his monthly commentary and photographs.

Of course, using social media is most effective when it is integrated into your hotel's overall marketing plan. If meeting planners are your primary target market, for example, you will want to make contacts and deliver messages that build awareness and share information, including insights into the hospitality industry and techniques for staging a successful meeting.

E-Mail Advertising

According to the most recent Meetings Market Report conducted by *Meetings & Conventions* magazine, 89 percent of meeting planners use **e-mail** for planning purposes. Hoteliers who want to get the word out about their products and services have found e-mail an inexpensive and effective way to advertise. Compared to traditional direct mail advertising, e-mail is highly economical and almost instantaneous. Buggsi Patel, President and CEO of Buggsi Hospitality Group, says:

> We still do direct mail, but we're finding e-mail to be an extremely effective use of our time and money. The Internet is changing the way properties go to market. It's the medium that everyone who is looking ahead is looking to leverage.[5]

As with other advertising, however, planning is needed before sending out e-mail messages. First, using e-mail requires building a database of qualified prospects. Second, content must be developed that will appeal to your various targeted segments. And, last but certainly not least, e-mail must be welcomed by your prospects.

Time and privacy are important to planners, and sending "spam"—the electronic equivalent of unsolicited junk mail—may drive potential customers away. Today's successful e-mail marketers are using **permission marketing** to ensure that their messages make a favorable impression. This strategy involves asking a planner's permission before sending an e-mail about your property. You can create an *opt-in form* on your website to enable meeting planners to enter their e-mail addresses if they wish for you to send updates on your property. Most planners welcome information to help make their jobs easier, and your property should structure its e-mail campaign to alert the planner of seasonal rate changes, special offers, or other items of interest that may make a meeting decision easier (the expansion of your meeting rooms, the addition of a gourmet chef, etc.). When meeting planners share their e-mail addresses with you, they are giving you permission to contact them in the future. Since 80 percent of your meetings business generally comes from 20 percent of the meeting planners with whom you communicate, it is critical to send regular (but pertinent) e-mails to planners who have expressed a willingness to hear from you.

E-mail advertising typically yields responses up to 15 times greater than those generated from direct mail and also has the advantage of doubling as a lead qualifying tool. Hoteliers are also seeing the value of e-mail as a new way to communicate with customers on a regular basis. E-mail is seen as an effective way to nurture customer relations by demonstrating the hotelier's commitment to staying in touch and serving the planner's future needs.

Fax Transmissions

Fax (facsimile) transmissions are useful to provide meeting planners with up-to-date information on new products and services. Faxes provide a copy of the original document — a letter, proposal, advertisement, special announcement, etc. — and are advantageous in that they are instantaneous and many meeting planners make them a priority to read. There are two ways in which fax transmissions are commonly used: fax-on-demand and broadcast fax.

Fax-on-demand offers the latest in property information directly to a meeting planner via a special fax number. This information can be accessed at any time, even when the sales office is closed, and can be updated as required to supply the latest information.

Broadcast fax provides simultaneous transmission of information to a database of interested or qualified prospects. Special announcements, changes in services offered, or other information can be sent to a number of planners at once.

Will technological developments, such as the Internet, e-mail, and fax transmissions, replace personal site visits or diminish the role of the hotel salesperson? A recent study by Meeting Professionals International (MPI) and PlanSoft Corporation found that while technology is a useful tool for initial screening, it cannot replace in-person visits to investigate space for meetings. The large majority of respondents to the survey say that personal contact and building relationships are still essential to the meetings process.[6]

Collateral Materials

Collateral material is supplementary advertising pieces used along with direct mail, magazine advertising, and other promotional efforts. This includes a vast array of promotional materials such as convention and rack brochures, newsletters, postcards, menus, tent cards, matchbooks, and many other items.

The greatest distinction between collateral material and other advertising devices is the directness of collateral pieces. Newspaper advertising takes a shotgun approach; collateral material is more specific and is often directed right to the decision-maker.

Brochures

Perhaps one of the most familiar collateral materials is the brochure. Most convention hotels use two brochures: a standard *rack brochure,* which is directed to the leisure market, and a *convention brochure.* As with other advertising, the focus of these brochures will differ widely. The rack brochure usually promotes rooms, restaurants, and recreational amenities and is targeted to leisure travelers and travel agents. The convention brochure, on the other hand, provides detailed information regarding function space, food and beverage service, and convention services and is targeted to meeting planners.

Printed Convention Brochures. The convention brochure may be prepared in a number of ways. It can be a standard three or four-fold type, loose-leaf pages bound in an attractive cover, or presented in booklet style. Whatever style you choose, remember that it should fit in with your property's overall advertising and project your property's image. In addition, no matter what type is used, it should always contain pertinent information.

When planning your brochure, start with the assumption that your prospect has never seen or even heard of your hotel, and certainly has never been informed of its convention capability. Image yourself as a meeting organizer looking for a suitable hotel for your next event. The information you would want should be presented clearly and concisely. A common complaint from planners is the lack of good, accurate descriptive material from hotels.

A brochure will give the planner enough basic data for preliminary planning (see box titled "Basic Convention Brochure Information").

The larger meeting rooms should be diagrammed, if possible, or at least described adequately. "Large" is not a very accurate phrase. How many people will the grand ballroom accommodate? In what sort of setup (auditorium-style offers greater capacity than seating at round tables, for example)? A good brochure will give enough information so it can be used as a tool by meeting planners to narrow down a field of contestants for meeting functions.

One of the primary sources for ideas for preparing a convention brochure is, of course, existing pieces. Begin collecting brochures. There are some excellent ones in the field. Start a reference file of brochures you admire for one reason or another. They'll give you many ideas you may want to incorporate into your own brochure.

The best brochures show scaled outlines (blueprints) of all major rooms. One meeting planner stated:

> I like to receive a meeting planner's kit, not general information about the
> hotel. I need to see a floor plan with specific seating capacities. It takes
> time and it's expensive for a hotelier to send out information; it should
> be useful.

The brochure need not be so utilitarian that it fails to present your property in a good light. A facility is not chosen merely for its ability to house the event. The beauty of the structure and surroundings, the convenience of the location, and the expertise of the staff

---

BASIC CONVENTION BROCHURE INFORMATION

Your property's convention brochure should provide all the information a meeting planner needs to make a decision on a meeting site. Effective convention brochures should include most — if not all — of the following information:

- Your property's name
- Your property's address and, when possible, an area location map detailing proximity to airports, major highways, and area attractions
- Your property's telephone number (a toll-free number encourages responses) and name of contact person, if applicable (convention services manager, convention coordinator, etc.)
- Your fax number and pertinent e-mail addresses
- Photographs, diagrams, or *complete* descriptions of exhibit space (dimensions, scaled drawings, floor load, ceiling height)
- Audiovisual equipment available
- Other meeting services available (teleconferences, fax service, personal computers, clerical and/or registration help, business center)
- Special services and facilities (photographic services, flowers, entertainment)
- Banquet and beverage arrangements
- Theme party arrangements
- Guestroom information (descriptions, floor plans, room block policy, reservations, rates, arrival/departure information)
- Special procedures (billing procedures, shipping and receiving procedures, signs and notices policy, etc.)
- Recreation and amenities (hotel attractions, spouse entertainment, area attractions)
- Transportation (parking facilities, shuttle service, tours, taxis, public transportation)
- Other general information (climate, dress, gratuities, the availability of room service, etc.)
- References from past conventions
- Checklists and planning guides for the meeting planner

This checklist may also be used for an electronic brochure on the Internet. A website is an ever-evolving marketing tool on which electronic brochures can be updated whenever the need arises.

are all important. But such data should not be included at the expense of basic facilities information. Always include your usual hotel brochure along with your convention brochure.

Design your material to enable your contact to present your case completely and favorably. Good brochures will work for you in sales presentations, mailings, and trade shows, and through intermediaries such as convention bureaus, airlines, and convention specialists.

Electronic Convention Brochures. In addition to printed brochures, many properties produce DVD (digital video disc) brochures. DVD's are both inexpensive and versatile, and a DVD can show a property's selling points in a way that no printed piece can (see Exhibit 6).

A DVD brochure can show the property at various times of the year, and is an excellent resource for the meeting planner who is unable to visit the property in person. DVD brochures can show a property at its best, in a variety of setups (both meeting rooms and banquet facilities), and can also show other important selling points, such as seasonal attractions.

Most DVD brochures are fairly short, running four to six minutes in length, and must present the property's best points in that short time. Many properties, therefore, enlist the services of a firm that specializes in hotel electronic brochures before attempting to shoot one on their own. This may cost slightly more, but the benefits of the expertise of the professional firm (and high-quality shooting techniques) are worth the additional time and expense.

Exhibit 6 Convention and Property Brochures on DVD

Many hotels today supplement their printed convention brochures and property information sheets with DVDs. These virtual presentations enable hotels to provide panoramic tours of the properties' facilities and services at various times of the year. When creating a convention brochure on DVD, however, it is not enough to simply show off meeting and function rooms; meeting planners must be provided with pertinent information, such as room dimensions, room capacities, and banquet menus, that are commonly found in printed convention brochures.
Sources: Courtesy of The Broadmoor in Colorado Springs, Colorado; the Fontainebleu Hotel in Miami Beach, Florida; and Gaylord Opryland Hotel & Convention Center in Nashville, Tennessee.

As with other types of advertising, DVD presentations should project the desired image for your property and should meet the needs of meeting planners by offering pertinent information. The detailed floor plans mentioned above are an excellent selling point, as are interviews with key convention services personnel, a "tour" of the property (preferably when there are groups in-house), testimonials by satisfied clients, and so on. Many properties opt for professional assistance when creating their first DVD, especially if it will be used in conjunction with an Internet marketing program.

Many of today's Internet marketing programs include *electronic brochures*, which are offered on the property's website. Online brochures usually feature "virtual tours" of a property and its facilities, but they also offer several other benefits. First, they can be updated whenever needed, such as for special offers, changes to facilities, and so on. Second, they don't have to be mailed by properties or stored by meeting planners. All a meeting planner has to do is access the hotel's website and view or download the online brochure

---

INTERNET EXERCISE

Digital Convention Brochures

Today, many hotels supplement their printed convention brochures with DVDs and online information. However, some hotels fail to include the detailed information that meeting planners require when they develop their electronic presentations. Meeting planners, for the most part, prefer a brochure that is "long on facts and short on pictures."

One meeting planner states:

> I used to have a file cabinet full of convention brochures. Now I depend on the Internet to provide what I found in traditional sales kits — photos, menus, floor plans with room dimensions.

Log on to the following two hotel electronic brochure sites to answer the questions below:

- MGM Grand Hotel — www.mgmgrand.com/images/pdf/meeting_planner_guide.pdf.
- Snowbird Resort Utah — www.snowbird.com/imagelib/meetings/EntireMPK_144dpi.pdf

1. Compare the two brochures. Which is "long on facts and short on pictures"? Which do you think is most useful to meeting planners?

2. Evaluate each brochure based on the checklist, titled "Basic Convention Brochure Information," in your text.

3. Do you feel these two brochures could substitute for a printed convention brochure?

---

on an "as needed" basis. And last, but certainly not least, electronic brochures are far less expensive than printing full-color collateral materials or preparing a DVD.

As with DVDs, however, the information offered should be pertinent for meeting planners. The guidelines in the box titled "Basic Convention Brochure Information" should be applied to convention brochures developed in every format.

Other Collateral Materials

In addition to brochures, collateral materials may include such diverse pieces as postcards, fliers, maps, menus, tent cards, and newsletters (see Exhibit 7). These materials not only serve to keep your property's name and its features in the prospects' minds, but also can be used by salespeople to enhance their sales presentations.

As with brochures, all pieces used should be carefully planned and integrated into the property's overall marketing and advertising strategy. All pieces should be attractively designed and, as in print advertising, list the benefits offered by your property as well as its features. And, most importantly, printed collateral materials should be targeted to the conventions market (separate newsletters should be developed for the meetings market and the leisure travel segment, for example).

Specialty Items

Collateral materials also include **specialty items** (sometimes called premiums) that are marked with the property's name and toll-free number. These may include such inexpensive

Exhibit 7   Sample Hotel Chain Newsletter

The newsletter is an excellent — and relatively inexpensive — way to convey property information to meeting planners. Newsletters may be produced at the property level or as part of a chain's effort to introduce its properties to meeting planners. Newsletters typically contain such features as property statistics, articles and/or photographs of successfully staged events, personnel profiles, special offers, and general meeting information. Newsletters are typically used in convention kits, enclosed with sales letters, or used in direct mail campaigns, and many can also be accessed on individual property or chain websites.

items as matchbooks or keychains, or "signature" items, such as glassware, plush toys, or sportswear featuring the property's logo.

Chain properties have the advantage of ordering specialty items from the chain's catalog at greatly discounted rates. But even small properties can take advantage of this advertising tool — which, according to the Specialty Advertising Association (SAA), boasts a recall factor of up to 40 percent even after six months. It is fairly easy to find suppliers of specialty items, and costs can be kept down by ordering in quantity and staying with the same imprint.

Select items that reflect the image of your property, not necessarily the cheapest. It is far more cost-effective to choose items that a meeting planner will probably use (keeping your property's name constantly in his or her mind), such as a desk calendar or a coffee mug.

Direct Mail Advertising

Another popular tool in the promotion person's kit is **direct mail advertising**. Direct mail can be used to screen prospects, follow up on advertising leads, and make a printed sales presentation in great detail to many prospects at once — at far less cost than for print or broadcast advertising. Direct mail pre-selects the client and reaches him or her personally and privately. No other media can do this as effectively.

Unfortunately, there are also disadvantages to direct mail. The cost of direct mail efforts has increased over the years, especially due to increasing postal rates. Another disadvantage of direct mail is that pieces frequently end up in the wastebasket. An efficient program that will overcome these difficulties, however, can be produced at almost any budget level.

One factor in the success or failure of direct mail is ensuring that you are advertising directly to your target market. A direct mail campaign is only as good as the **mailing list** used. If your hotel does not have a mailing list, start one immediately. Begin by compiling a list of planners who have met in your hotel in the past. Keep in mind that we are a mobile business society and lists must be updated frequently. Expect many returns and changes of names and addresses after each mailing, and remember to budget for postage due on returned pieces. It is vital to delete the undeliverables and note the changes of addresses on your list so that expensive printing and postage are not wasted in subsequent mailings.

As we have discussed, there are also several directories and a number of publications that supply the names, addresses, and phone numbers of most association, corporation, incentive, fraternal, and other meeting planners. It is also possible to rent names from the circulation lists of suitable magazines.

Convention bureau notices from past years can also be a source of prospects for your mailing list, since major citywide conventions are channeled through the bureau. Groups that have met in years past may hold smaller meetings that you may be able to attract. The convention bureau list might also show some groups have a repeat pattern for the city. These groups should be given a high priority in your sales campaign.

It is a good policy to develop two lists: a *general* one of all prospects you feel reasonably sure are relevant, and a *preferred* list of screened prospects and past customers. You will probably mail more frequently to the second list than to the first.

Before sending any mailings, you should also decide on a follow-up method. Ideally, your direct mail efforts will give you a list of "hot" leads to follow up. The list of new leads generated through direct mail will be wasted if these prospects are not attended to promptly. You may wish to have follow up literature readily available, or forward responses directly to your salespeople for an immediate personal contact.

Direct mail, only one part of a hotel's total advertising effort, should be carefully planned for maximum results. The direct mail campaign must be integrated into the hotel's overall sales objectives, and mail pieces should blend with the property's other media advertising.

Some of the most commonly used direct mail pieces include sales letters, surveys, and postcards, but more creative and elaborate visual aids may also be used (see Exhibit 8). When deciding what types of materials would be most effective to use, several factors must be considered, such as the purpose of the mailing, its scope, and the costs involved.

Writing Better Sales Letters. *Sales letters* are the meat of any direct mailing. Their function is to convince and to sell. Time does not permit a salesperson to make personal calls on every prospect, so the message must be communicated through the written word.

It is effective to use well-written personal letters, with convention brochures as enclosures. Seemingly personal, individually typed letters can be produced using your in-house

Exhibit 8   Direct Mail "Novelties"

The Skamania Lodge promoted its world-class meeting facility, which is located in the Columbia River Gorge Scenic Area, an area teeming with outdoor wonders, with a mailing of hand-carved and painted Chinook salmon (along with campaign literature) to approximately 2,500 meeting planners. The creative, award-winning campaign generated 23 group bookings, resulting in 1,237 room nights, rooms revenue of $212,774, and food and beverage and other revenue of $108,129.
Source: Courtesy of the Skamania Lodge, Stevenson, Washington.

word processing system or local letter shop services. If you want to create more ambitious direct mail programs, use your advertising agency or local creative services to produce the mailing pieces. But don't underestimate the power of personal letters addressed to a person by name. The high cost of brochures and postage make it advisable to polish your techniques (see box titled "Writing Effective Sales Letters").

Many properties find that a number of mailings must be used to achieve best results. A one-time mailing is not too effective unless it is a birthday or holiday greeting or an answer to an inquiry. Direct mail *campaigns*, then, should be a part of your direct mail efforts.

WRITING EFFECTIVE SALES LETTERS

Effective letter writing is a skill than can be developed. Here are a few fundamental techniques that should be used:

- Use the correct titles of hotel personnel and the person with whom you are dealing.
- Be informative but brief. Stick to the facts.
- Be yourself; write like you speak. Write as if the client were with you in the office.
- Emphasize key points by underlining them or using bold-faced lettering.
- Avoid using computer-generated form letters that do not address specific needs.
- *Always ask for the sale* — and provide a means for the client to respond (a reply card, toll-free number, etc.)

Keep in mind that you should always write in the client's language; avoid the use of hotel terms that may confuse or mislead. Don't give the sales copy second billing in direct mail pieces. Be specific, and make your correspondence meaningful and convincing.

When using more than one mailing, the frequency, as well as the content, is important. There is no hard and fast rule, but the maximum interval between mailings is considered to be about two months. Obviously, multiple mailings must never be the same. The first letter must be an attention-getter. Its content must be appealing and retain the reader's interest. Future mailings should be built around the theme presented in the first one, but the information and point of the letters should be different. In some cases, you may want to build on each letter sent. The point of your message may be the same, but the content should be stated differently and creatively or the reader's interest is sure to wane (see Exhibit 9).

Planning an Advertising Strategy

As you can see, there are a number of ways to reach meeting planners, and you must develop a strategy that will work best for your property (see box titled "Selling Sheraton to the Meetings Market"). Developing such a strategy, of course, means working within the marketing plan — and budget — established for your property, and structuring your efforts accordingly.

Some of the factors you will want to consider in devising your strategy include whom you wish to target, what media you will use, and how much money you can spend. Many properties prepare a media chart (see Exhibit 10) to plan advertising placement and expenditures over the course of a year. Annual planning is much more effective than last-minute, haphazard efforts. When you plan on an annual basis, keep in mind that you can schedule

Exhibit 9   Sample Direct Mail Series

The Bloomington Convention & Visitors Bureau in Bloomington, Minnesota, developed a series of four mailings to introduce its Executive Director, Bonnie Carlson, and her staff to meeting planners. Each mailing in the series featured people who would actually help planners in staging their functions, creating an atmosphere of familiarity and trust long before the function was held. Each three-fold mailing had an illustration, a copy panel, and a tear-off reply card. This type of series mailing reinforces your property's message in the minds of meeting planners. If done correctly, planners will actually look forward to additional mailings.

SELLING SHERATON TO THE MEETINGS MARKET

When the Sheraton Corporation sought to position itself to attract meeting planners, it went directly to the source, conducting extensive research with clients to learn what was important to them and what was needed to help make their job easier. The result was the Sheraton Master Plan for Meeting Planners, which responded to the meeting planners' requests for more information to ensure professionalism in the industry.

The Sheraton/PCMA Showcase I is a program for new meeting planners (and serves as a refresher course for full-time professionals). These workshops cover the basics of meeting planning, including site selection, working with properties, room setup, food and beverage planning, etc.

Sheraton developed a comprehensive free meeting planning manual. The manual plays an important part in the chain's advertising, showing its willingness to assist meeting planners and its commitment to successful meetings.

To further enhance its professionalism, Sheraton also launched the industry's most comprehensive training program for its own convention and conference services managers — a strategy that has generated tremendous interest within the industry and adds credibility to the chain's advertising, which positions Sheraton as both dedicated to maintaining high standards of professionalism and being "meeting planner friendly."

Our New Workbook is Used.

Our new Sheraton workbook is already being used by over 100,000 meeting planners and travel planners all over the world.

Created by experienced meeting planners and Sheraton's Convention Service Professionals, this is more than just a workbook; it's a real working tool for planning meetings. It covers everything from budgets to food and beverage, from meeting room set-ups to site selection. It even includes detailed worksheets.

Let Sheraton help you plan your client's next meeting. Order your free *Sheraton Meeting and Conference Workbook* today. It will be new when it arrives, but it will be used right away.

For your FREE Workbook, call 1-800-323-1847 in the U.S. For information or to book a meeting call G.R.A.B. 1-800-343-6320.

Sheraton
ITT

---

your advertising expenditures to match your property's fiscal or budget year. Publications compute frequency discounts on a consecutive twelve-month period. You can, if it suits your purpose, schedule your advertising from March 2011 through February 2012, for example. Also, it is helpful, if you can manage it, to set aside a sum for special situations that crop up during the year.

Reach, Frequency, Timing, and Consistency

When planning your advertising strategy, whether it is print, Internet, or direct mail (or any combination of these), four key factors should be taken into consideration: reach, frequency, timing, and consistency.

Reach refers to the number of different individuals who are exposed to your message during a specific period. This, of course, is determined by the media you select. When targeting the conventions market, for example, you are focusing on a smaller number of specific prospects than if you were targeting the transient market. You should select the media that will be most effective in reaching them (a specialized trade journal, for example) rather than opting for indiscriminate media (a television spot). You are interested in how many potential customers you can reach for each dollar spent.

Frequency refers to the number of times your target audience sees or hears your message. As with sales calls, advertising is rarely effective on a "one-shot" basis; it is usually

Exhibit 10   Sample Hotel Media Chart

Client number: BM100-3
Media: MEETINGS

MEDIA SCHEDULE 01/01/__ THRU 12/31/__

Publications	January	February	March	April	May
Association Management Pub Number Issued Circulation AS700-6A Monthly 21,120 96 Rates 15th of 2nd Month Publication Total $8,372.50				Page 4/C $4,186.00 Or Pg 4C	
Business Travel News Pub Number Issued Circulation BTN15-8A Bi-Weekly 51,046 Jr Pg or 1/2SPD 3 Weeks Prior Publication Total $34,000.00			Jr Pg 4/C $6,800.00 Mtgs Today 22 +BRC	Jr Pg 4/C $6,800.00 Mtgs Tday 19	Jr P4\C $6,800.00 Mtgs Tday 10 +BRC
Corporate & Incentive Travel Pub Number Issued Circulation C0605-6A Monthly 49,698 One Month Prior Publication Total $4,764.00		Page 4/C $4,764.00 DSTNTN Colorado			
Executive Memo **Colorado Soc. Of Assn Executives** Pub Number Issued Circulation COSAE-6A Monthly 250 One Month Publication Total $12,605.50				Page BW $500.00	
Executive Update - GWSAE Pub Number Issued Circulation EU478-6A Monthly 9,000 33% DSCNT Publication Total $12,605.50					Page 4/C $3,740.00 SPGNTME PK
Forum (CSAE) Pub Number Issued Circulation For 10-9 11X/Yr ½ SPD or Pg 6 weeks Prior Publication Total $6,262.37				Page 4/C $1,789.25	
Incentive Pub Number Issued Circulation IN150-6A Monthly 40,281 15th, 2 Months Prior Publication Total $39,467.80				Page 4/C $4,911.30 +BRC	Page 4/C $4,911.30
Insurance Conference Planner Pub Number Issued Circulation IN500-6A Bi-Monthly 7,451 1st of Month Preceding					Page 4/C $2,622.25 Incentive

All listed rates are based on applicable rate card as of the date of preparation and are subject to change.

In order to plan an effective advertising strategy, many properties prepare an annual media chart that lists such data as name and type of publication to be used, size of ad (or length of spot), and advertising expenditures, both for production and space costs. This approach provides an at-a-glance overview of the property's advertising, controls budget commitment, and can also be used to measure the effectiveness of advertising. This sample shows data from January–May; a complete chart would extend through December.

necessary to expose your prospects to your message on a frequent basis — and often in a number of ways, such as the combination of trade journal advertisements and direct mail efforts. It is beneficial to expose your prospect to your message a number of times.

Direct Mail Marketing

Carolyn Hamilton-Proctor
President
Graphic Communications, Las Vegas, Nevada

"Direct mail is a powerful weapon in your sales arsenal. Studies show repeatedly that the direct mail package outpulls any other printed format. Properly used, direct marketing will make your marketing plan more targeted — and more profitable.

"Direct mail makes advertising accountable. Direct mail to meeting planners does not replace journal or directory advertising, rather it complements them. Proper integration of general advertising and direct mail will have a synergistic effect on your profits.

"A solid list of names and current addresses of your guests is worth its weight in gold. Direct mail requires the maintenance of a guest database which includes both demographic and psychographic profiles of your guests. The more specific the guest profile in your database, the more successful your direct mail campaigns can be. Compiled lists that match your guest profile, rented from outside sources, will yield respondents who also can be added to your existing database. Increasing and updating your in-house guest database is an ongoing process."

Timing, then, is an important factor. Some properties prefer to advertise or send out mailings on a *continuing* basis, timing their advertising to appear once a month, for example. There are times, however, when you can take advantage of a *pulsing* approach. Pulsing is used to promote business over slow periods. A property, for example, may wish to offer special rates during its valley periods of early fall and mid-winter, and would advertise over a predetermined time prior to these periods. Similarly, *flighting* (advertising only when managers feel it necessary, with no regular pattern) can be used when it is necessary to promote special packages or events. Perhaps the area will be host to a local festival or special event; advertising can promote the property's participation or proximity to the action.

Most convention publications run special editorial sections throughout the year dealing with meetings in certain geographic areas, such as a city or state, or specific types of properties, including golf resorts, airport hotels, conference centers, etc. Editors and publishers will usually supply the schedule of such features for the full year. When you plan your advertising, you might be able to take advantage of such targeted sections by placing your ad in them while still maintaining your objectives in timing and frequency. There are additional advantages to appearing in editorial sections describing your specific area.

No matter what approach is used for timing, **consistency** in advertising is vital. Your advertising must develop distinguishing characteristics — a logo, special colors or design, etc. — to stand out from the rest. Your prospects should be able to identify your property's ad at first glance.

Not only should your advertising have distinguishing characteristics, but it should also be consistent with and supportive of other elements in your marketing plan. This approach, called **integrated marketing**, ensures that your advertising and marketing activities have a common focus for both your marketplace in general and specific market segments in particular.

Since the purpose of your advertising is to become known and patronized, your advertising strategy should also include a program of follow-up that also involves monitoring and evaluation. *Follow-up* is extremely important, especially in the conventions and meetings market. Most planners are "comparison shopping" and if they have responded to your ad or mailing it is likely they have responded to others. Your prompt handling of an inquiry will demonstrate your commitment to provide efficient service.

At the very least, inquiries should be followed up with a personal letter and information that was requested. Whenever possible, especially if the respondent has included his or her telephone number, make a personal call of thanks and request an appointment. This can lead to an immediate sale.

To develop the most cost-effective program, however, you must carefully *monitor and evaluate* your program periodically. Determine which ads or direct mail pieces seem to attract the most interest; check to see which publications are generating the most leads; and monitor the number of conversions from inquiries. Also, take steps to determine the actual cost per conversion from each type of inquiry. If your ad series is costing $35,000, for example, but you have only generated $15,000 in business, take another look at your ad program.

Exchange Trade Advertising

To cut advertising costs, many properties have looked for alternatives, such as trading out goods and services or sharing advertising expenditures. **Exchange trade advertising** is an arrangement in which the hotel exchanges its services (rooms, food, beverage, use of recreational amenities, etc.) for advertising (newspaper, magazine, outdoor space, radio and television spots). Such arrangements are also referred to as *reciprocal advertising, barter advertising,* and *trade-out advertising,* and can be very worthwhile as long as the hotel fully understands the procedure. It is important to realize that exchange trade advertising is not free; there is a cost to the hotel, and this cost must be budgeted, just as print and Internet advertising costs are. And, whether you are paying cash or exchanging services, your hotel's advertising efforts must be directed to your target markets. If you are trying to build group meetings business, for example, a trade exchange with a billboard specialist would not be the wisest use of your money.

Exchange trade advertising does offer some real advantages to a convention hotel, and its possibilities should be investigated. As with any advertising strategy, there are factors that should be considered and guidelines to follow in order to utilize this type of arrangement for your maximum benefit (see box titled "Making the Most of Exchange Trade Advertising").

The use of exchange trade advertising does require increased recordkeeping, but it also affords yet another benefit — the opportunity to build relationships with media firms. A friend in the media can be a real asset when it comes to editorials and publicity about your hotel (and, the hotel is in a position to extend extra courtesies to the media's important clients). In the final analysis, exchange trade advertising can be mutually beneficial if a fair arrangement is negotiated.

MAKING THE MOST OF EXCHANGE TRADE ADVERTISING

Consider these recommendations for negotiating exchange trade agreements:

1. Consider some variations on the "one-for-one" arrangement, especially when the publication or station approaches you. You could receive $1.50 or $2.00 of advertising for every dollar of hotel facilities, especially if food and/or beverage are included in the arrangement. When such is the case, point out that food and beverage represent an out-of-pocket cost to you, whereas available publication space or radio and TV time ordinarily do not.
2. Consider these limitations, all of which mean money in your pocket: For commercial hotels and motels, (a) rooms only, and then only during periods when you don't expect to be at capacity, or (b) food only, rather than food and beverage. For A.P. (American Plan) or M.A.P. (Modified American Plan) resorts, the room portion only.
3. Bring your advertising agency into the picture and require the publication or station to pay the customary 15 percent commission. Your ad agency will undoubtedly handle the placement of the advertising, and if it receives the commission, you will not be required to pay it.
4. Include as a condition of your reciprocal deal that your facilities are limited to use by certain individuals (publisher, station manager, key executives, employees), and secure in advance a list of those persons.

Cooperative Advertising and Strategic Partnerships

Cooperative advertising also provides an additional way to save on advertising costs. In a cooperative arrangement, several properties — or a property and several related entities, such as a convention and visitors bureau, an airline or car rental company, or local area

🖥 *INTERNET EXERCISE*

Strategic Partnerships Among Cities

Strategic partnerships among destinations that are similar in size, meeting and convention capabilities, and approaches to serving clients' needs are relatively new in the meetings industry, but destination marketing organizations (DMOs) throughout the United States and the world are increasingly combining resources to get more bang for their marketing buck. By partnering, cities gain a stronger marketing presence and maximize collective resources. One city spokesperson states:

> The whole basis for the collaborations to work is that the participating cities are similar in size and hospitality, share and customer base, and rarely compete with each other.

Log on to the following three websites to answer the questions below:

- www.capitalcitiescollection.com
- www.bestcities.net
- www.3cityexpress.com

1. What destinations make up each of these three alliances?

2. Which of the three is a global collaboration?

3. How do the cities in each alliance work together to sell to the meetings market?

4. What incentives does each offer to meeting planners?

attractions — advertise together to both save on costs and maximize results. A cooperative advertisement is illustrated in Exhibit 11.

Exhibit 11   Sample Cooperative Advertising

The perfect mix of business and pleasure.

The Monterey Meeting Connection is a combined meeting facility consisting of the Monterey Conference Center, Hotel Pacific, Monterey Marriott and Portola Hotel & Spa at Monterey Bay.

The only 800+ room waterfront facility between San Francisco and Los Angeles, the Meeting Connection offers an award-winning amphitheater, 61,000 square feet of flexible function space, beautifully appointed accommodations and much, much more…

www.montereyconnection.com

Monterey Meeting Connection Sales (800) 742-8091 • (831) 646-3388 • (831) 641-0699 Fax

Three hotels, the Hotel Pacific, the Marriott Monterey, and the Portola Hotel & Spa at Monterey Bay, teamed up with the Monterey Conference Center to become the Monterey Connection. Promoting the California city as a meeting planner's dream destination, the Monterey Connection collaboration offers over 800 waterfront rooms as well as 61,000 square feet of function space, and an award-winning amphitheatre — all of which can be accessed and booked by contacting the "umbrella" organization.
Source: Courtesy of the Monterey Connection.

Cooperative advertising can be used as either a "one shot" promotion, or, as is done more commonly, in an advertising campaign that promotes the services and attractions available in an area. This type of advertising provides meeting planners with more information and options, and can also prove beneficial to your property. If your property has limited meeting facilities, for example, you can advertise with a full-service meeting hotel, offering your rooms to accommodate meeting overflow.

Strategic partnerships are another form of cooperative agreement. These alliances are relationships between independent parties or chains that agree to cooperate in advertising but still maintain their separate identities. A common example is several hotels combining forces with each other (and often the city's CVB and/or other attractions) to offer a "one-stop shopping" alternative to compete with larger cities (see the "Best Practices" box titled "Hilton Hotels & Sheraton Hotels Form a Strategic Partnership to Capture Meetings Business in New York City").

Susan Henrique is director of sales and marketing for Coastal Fairfield County, Connecticut, which is located near New York City. Her CVB as well as those in Arlington, Virginia (near Washington, DC), Prospect Heights, Illinois (near Chicago), and Irving, Texas (near Dallas), formed an "Edge City Alliance" to promote themselves to meeting planners. She says:

> In an ever-changing economy, meeting planners seek affordable alternatives for their meetings. The program illustrates that there are alternatives, which include accessibility and benefits of the larger destination

---

Best Practices

"Hilton Hotels & Sheraton Hotels Form a Strategic Partnership to Capture Meetings Business in New York City"

The Hilton New York, Sheraton New York, and Sheraton Manhattan, which are about 150 feet from one another in mid-town Manhattan, have 100 meeting rooms, more than 225,000 square feet of meeting space, and a combined total of 5,000 guestrooms. They can also accommodate up to 425 exhibits. Although they are competitors, the three hotels took advantage of an opportunity to market their combined facilities to appeal to meeting planners.

The three hotels created NY 5000, a partnership geared to a joint sales and marketing effort. Christopher Perry, director of sales and marketing for Hilton New York, said:

> We wanted to offer an alternative for conventions that need 1,400 rooms or more on a peak night. We are ideal for events that want to come to New York, would like to stay with two or three hotels, and prefer not to use the convention center. It saves them money on transportation and creates better networking opportunities. We also have a consistency of product and service, including food and beverage.

Although meetings customers negotiate independently with each hotel in order to protect any proprietary information, the hotels have developed a presentation, designed collateral materials, and developed a website, and salespeople regularly meet and make pitches for NY 5000 business when appropriate.

While the three hotels had previously been averaging about eight large meetings jointly, they added four additional large group bookings in the first year of the formation of NY 5000.

Source: Harvey Chipkin, "Success Stories That Inspire," *HSMAI Marketing Review*.

cities without the bigger price tag. We all need help for weekend occupancy and have similar budgets for meetings marketing. The real key is that we are all on the outside looking at a first-tier city.[7]

Members of the alliance see their consolidated efforts as a way to bring their resources to the notice of meeting planners who might not have considered alternatives just across big-city borders. Their strategic partnership also allows individual participants to stretch their advertising dollars; with their participation in the "Edge City Alliance," each property and CVB can get maximum exposure at less cost, enabling them to save money for their own promotional efforts to their other targeted market segments.

Advertising Agencies

A hotel that has its own advertising department should make special efforts to develop material and advertising dealing solely with the convention market. In smaller properties, the sales manager may be his or her own advertising manager. At larger properties, a full creative and production department may be employed.

Such efforts may be supplemented by an outside advertising agency. A properly selected — and properly utilized — agency adds skilled specialists to the work force of any hotel advertising department. Even smaller hotels can afford an arrangement with smaller ad agencies (it is difficult to work without one, in fact). Advertising agencies are not a substitute for your own sales efforts, but they have the skills and the resources to back up the sales department with the required promotional material.

Many convention hotels have found it advantageous to use advertising agencies, but it is extremely important that when a hotel uses an advertising agency that there is agreement as to the direction of the advertising campaign. Naturally, a hotel is more familiar with its strengths than the outside agency. The hotel must communicate its positioning and goals to its agency representative to ensure that the advertising creates the image a property wishes to project and is aimed at its target market(s). To ensure that the property and the agency can work well together, it is important to select an agency carefully (see box titled "Selecting an Advertising Agency"). A properly functioning agency offers you an experienced and objective view of your property's promotional efforts. One advertising executive says:

SELECTING AN ADVERTISING AGENCY

Before you select an advertising agency, you should evaluate your property's needs. Will you need full services or just assistance in placing your own promotional material? How would an advertising agency be utilized — as a supplement to your in-house advertising department, occasionally as needed for research or production, or as an extension of your advertising and sales effort? How much can you afford to spend on outside services?

Once you have established guidelines, informal meetings should be held with representatives of agencies of interest to you. Each representative should provide the answers to the following questions:

1. How long has the agency been in business? Does it have a proven track record in the hospitality industry?
2. Does the agency represent competitors? If so, how will this affect the handling of your account?
3. What services can the agency provide? Does it offer full creative services? market research? media placement?
4. Who will be assigned to your account? How much time can he or she spend learning about your property and its needs? In the event "your" account person is not available, who will be assigned to handle your account?
5. How will costs be handled? Is the agency willing to work within the property's budget?

We're concerned not just about creating and placing [clients'] advertising, but helping them with their in-house promotions in all of their market segments; developing new segments; motivating their salespeople; building their collateral; redesigning Web sites; and managing direct mail promotions....We truly want to become the client's marketing partner, and not just its [ad] studio.[8]

Public Relations and Publicity

While advertising is a powerful method of reaching target markets, you can do more to keep your hotel's name before your potential customers. Advertising and e-marketing coupled with public relations and publicity can form a stronger combination to reach planners.

Public relations is a broad term that encompasses a number of methods of communicating favorable information about a property. Its purpose is to create a positive image about the property. Loews Hotels, for example, began a model program — and won an award — with its Good Neighbor Policy. This community outreach program seeks to address a number of concerns, such as homelessness, illiteracy, and environmental preservation, and mobilizes not only the chain's properties but meeting planners as well. The hotel's contracts include an offer for meeting planners to donate surplus products and materials to a local charity. Donations have ranged from clothing to items from food shows to basic supplies (poster board, masking tape, etc.) that are donated to area preschools.

As with advertising, a good public relations plan must be developed — and people trained to implement it. While every employee — from the general manager to front desk personnel to a valet attendant — plays a role in developing and maintaining a positive image for the property, it is essential that a professional public relations person or staff be employed to oversee the property's efforts in this important area. Small properties may employ one person or work with an outside public relations firm. Large properties may also utilize an outside public relations firm or engage a multi-talented public relations staff. In either case, public relations people or firms will be called upon to perform a variety of duties: acting as the property's spokesperson, contacting the media about the property, maintaining contacts with past guests, and so on.

One of the public relations staff's most important responsibilities is dealing with the media to obtain favorable publicity for the property. **Publicity** is the gratuitous mention of your hotel in newspapers, magazines, and over the airwaves. When you advertise, you pay for space or airtime and control what is said about your hotel and its services. And, with advertising, many readers or listeners may be apprehensive about whether you can or will deliver on your promises. Publicity, however, which comes from an impartial third party, lends credibility to a property.

In the hospitality industry, there are many opportunities to generate good news. Some of it just happens — a celebrity stays at the property, the property wins a prestigious award, a trade magazine does a story on a particular area, and so on. Much of it, however, is created — the hotel sponsors a festival or creates innovative theme parties. Or, the property can get its name in the news through its expansion and renovation programs or the involvement of its staff members in community affairs.

Meetings magazines — one of your best resources for reaching meeting planners — are always interested in stories of interest to meeting planners. Innovative meeting techniques, reports on new methods used to service successful meetings, renovations programs that will impact the meetings industry (the opening of additional facilities, etc.), and personnel changes are all of interest. Some magazines publish "Meeting Calendars" that list major meetings and their venues; these are an excellent vehicle for free listings for your property.

To enhance your chances of being featured in a meetings magazine, consider inviting travel writers from the major magazines (*Convene, Meetings & Conventions, Successful Meetings*) and from magazines directed toward your target markets to stay overnight and experience your property firsthand. This is an excellent way to reap the benefits of editorial coverage — and the resulting publicity.

Make a strong effort to get photographs of meetings in progress at your property. Meetings magazines are always looking for such illustrations. In addition, the organization sponsoring the meeting may use your photographs in their own publicity efforts, giving you additional exposure at the same time. It is not by accident that hotel lecterns carry the hotel's logo prominently across the front panel so that all photos of the speaker show the logo as well.

Trade magazines are spearheaded by an editor who makes the decisions about the subjects of articles and when they will run. They also have a managing editor who coordinates the makeup of the magazine. These people should be on your mailing list to receive publicity materials (press releases, newsletters, personal letters and invitations, etc.), as should editors of major newspapers in your property's target markets. The news generated about your property must meet their requirements of editorial interest, timeliness, and accuracy to be considered for publication.

Almost all properties send out **press releases** about events of importance. Press releases are usually printed on stationery with the property's logo and name, physical address, web and e-mail addresses, and telephone number; and include basic information (time, place, and other pertinent details) and the name of a property contact person. Press releases should always be sent well in advance of a deadline, but it is important to note that there is

---

🖥 *INTERNET EXERCISE*

Providing Media Information Electronically

Today, many media representatives prefer to receive news releases and story ideas via e-mail or from a property's website. Therefore, you should always include a link for the press on your site.

Electronic press kits typically include all the elements found in a printed press kit — fact sheets, biographies and photos of key personnel, the property's brochures, photographs (both interior and exterior shots), mention of awards received by the hotel, and current news releases. Both past and present news coverage can usually be accessed by links to the publication, and the electronic format provides an excellent vehicle for showing video of the property and events staged there. Many hotels and chains offer an image gallery of photographs that can be accessed and used by the media (galleries typically require registration).

Log on to the websites of the following hotels to answer the questions below:

- Hotel Del Coronado — www.hoteldel.com (click on "Press Room")
- Opryland Hotel — www.gaylordhotels.com/opryland (click on "Media Room")
- The Sanctuary at Kiawah Island — www.kiawahresort.com (click on "Press Room")
- Swan-Dolphin Hotel — www.swandolphinmedia.com

1. How thorough are the press kits of each hotel? Do their press kits cover all of the areas mentioned in the introduction to this Internet Exercise?

2. Are both high- and low-resolution photographs available for downloading by the media for use in news stories?

3. Review the current news releases from each of these sites. Identify releases directed to the leisure, family, and meetings market.

no guarantee that your material will be featured — or that it will be presented as written. You are not paying for space and you have no control over editorial content or its presentation.

It is important, then, to plan your press releases to ensure the maximum coverage possible. Since your press releases will be aimed at meeting planners, consider those events and personnel changes most likely to get them thinking about your property. The development of a state-of-the-art audiovisual system, for example, is of interest and is likely to make it to trade magazines. As is news of expansions (again, think how you can best word your release to appeal to the meeting planner — present a benefit in your copy), personnel changes (especially if the staff member is well-known in the meetings field), and special events held by your property — your innovative execution of an elaborate function will appeal to other meeting planners.

In addition to press releases and promotional material to send to respondents, most properties with a planned public relations and publicity strategy prepare a **press kit** to both introduce the property to the news media and to provide back-up information. Press kits generally feature a property information sheet, the property's brochures, biographies of key personnel, and, when available, previous press clippings. Press kits should be updated as necessary and targeted for your property's market segments; a press kit for meetings magazines, for example, would contain different material than a press kit directed to travel writers.

In today's high-tech world, the computer is also being used to get the word out about a property. The Walt Disney World Swan and Dolphin hotels, for example, have a "media only" website to provide journalists with immediate access to press releases, photographs, logos, hotel specifications, dining and entertainment options, and other information online (www.swandolphinmedia.com). Information is continually updated, and the site is "user friendly," enabling writers to cut and paste a press release (or a portion of it) directly into the writer's document.

A good public relations and publicity plan does not just seek to get your property's name in the media. To be effective, *the plan should be integrated into the overall hotel marketing strategy, targeted toward specific market segments, and scheduled to coincide with the property's slow periods.*

Summary

As you can see, a good advertising strategy coupled with a carefully planned public relations and publicity plan can greatly enhance the sales effort and actually "pre-sell" the property by creating awareness and a positive image in the meeting planner's mind. These tools can help the salesperson to close a sale and begin the second phase of his or her job — helping to coordinate the meeting planner's function.

Endnotes

1. "Ad Agencies Are Your Marketing Partners," *HSMAI Marketing Review,* Winter 2003, p. 36.

2. Anne Dimon, "Are You E-Planning Savvy?" *Meetings & Incentives,* June 2000, p. 24.

3. "StarCite, PlanSoft Give Planners Faster Response from Hotels," www.hotel-online.com, April 2004.

4. "Key to New Business Development in 2010 & Beyond," *Hospitality Upgrade,* Fall 2009, p. 123.

5. Marty Whitford, "You've Got Mail," *Hotel & Motel Management,* August 14, 2000, p. 34.

6. Lauren Shababb, "In-Person Inspections, Please," *Successful Meetings,* August 2000, p. 14.

7. Ruth A. Hill, "A United Front," *Lodging,* December 1999, pp. 27–28.

8. "Ad Agencies Are Your Marketing Partners," *HSMAI Marketing Review,* Winter 2003, p. 37.

 ## Key Terms

banner ad—An ad placed on another firm or organization's web page, such as the site of a business- or travel-related entity. Commonly linked to the advertiser's site, banner ads are the dominant form of web advertising.

blog—Personal or corporate online journals that offer reporting and/or opinions about people, things, and events. Blogs are designed to allow readers to post responses or comments, so the most successful blogs generate a high degree of interactive dialogue.

body copy—The main text of an ad.

broadcast fax—A function that transmits fax messages to a large number of pre-selected recipients.

collateral material—Supplementary advertising materials, including brochures, tent cards, key rings, matchbooks, postcards, and video brochures.

cooperative advertising—A pooling of marketing dollars by several tourism businesses for promotional purposes in order to increase market impact and/or reduce costs.

consistency—In advertising, refers to the design of advertising messages for a similar look or sound to enhance audience recognition and greater cumulative impact.

direct mail advertising—Advertising sent via mail to prospects' residences or places of business. Contains copy to motivate the reader to purchase a product or utilize a service and usually includes a means to respond.

e-mail—Electronic mail messages sent via computer.

exchange trade advertising—An arrangement in which the hotel exchanges rooms, meals, recreational amenities, etc. for advertising space or time. Also called reciprocal advertising, barter advertising, and trade-out advertising.

fax-on-demand—A function that provides an immediate response to information requests via fax transmission. In most cases, information is requested through a toll-free number.

frequency—The number of times advertising appears in print or on the air.

headline—The most prominent part of a print advertisement. Used to get attention, it usually promotes a promise or benefit.

integrated marketing—Marketing activities with a common focus on the marketplace or a specific customer segment. The execution of each individual component is consistent with, and supportive of, each of the other elements in the marketing plan.

logo—A unique trademark, name, symbol, signature, or device used to identify a company or other organization. Used in advertising, for promotion, and for image building.

mailing list—A collection of names and addresses of past and potential customers to which mailings are directed. Generally maintained on a computer.

permission marketing—An e-mail marketing campaign in which messages are sent only to those who have requested (opted-in) to receive specific types of information.

press kit—News releases, fact sheets, photographs, news clippings, and other materials, often attractively packaged, designed to give the news media background information about a property.

press release—A prepared statement, usually one or two pages, released to the news media regarding a hotel, one of its products or services, an individual, or a special event. Designed to be newsworthy, can be "for immediate release" or prepared to be released at a specified time or date. Also called a news release.

print advertising—Advertising appearing in print in such media as newspapers, magazines, and directories.

public relations—The systematic effort of a company to create a favorable image in the minds of various segments of the population.

publicity—One facet of public relations, it comprises the gratuitous mention or exposure a company receives from announcements, events, and press releases.

reach—The percentage of different people or locations exposed to a media message at least once during a specified period of time.

social media—The term used to describe the tools and platforms that people employ to converse with each other and publish/share content online. These tools include blogs and podcasts as well as sites designed to share photographs, videos, graphics, bookmarks, and other content.

specialty items—Supplementary advertising items, such as coffee cups, T-shirts, beach towels, and so on, that bear the name of the business and other advertising and contact information. Also called premiums.

strategic partnerships—Relationships between independent parties that agree to advertise cooperatively but still retain their separate identities.

timing—In advertising, refers to the scheduling of ads.

trade magazine—A publication, such as *Financial & Insurance Meetings* magazine, that targets a specific industry or profession.

 # Review Questions

1. What is print advertising? What elements should always be included In print ads? Where can print ads be placed to effectively reach meeting planners?

2. Why is the convention brochure an important sales tool for the meetings market? What information should be included in a convention brochure?

3. Why is direct mail an effective tool for reaching meeting planners? What are the elements involved in an effective direct mail campaign?

4. Why is it necessary to plan an advertising strategy? What factors should be considered?

5. What are exchange trade and cooperative advertising? What are the advantages and disadvantages of each?

6. Why do some properties use advertising agencies? What factors should a property consider when selecting an advertising agency?

7. What is the difference between public relations and publicity? How can each be used to enhance the property's advertising efforts?

 # Additional References

Hospitality Sales and Marketing, Fifth Edition, James R. Abbey, AH&LA Educational Institute, 2008. www.ei-ahla.org

Marketing in the Hospitality Industry, Fourth Edition, Ron A. Nykiel, AH&LA Educational Institute, 2003.

Profits and Pitfalls in Online Marketing: A Legal Desk Reference for Travel Executives. Available in the online store at www.hsmai.org.

The Travel Marketer's Guide to Social Media and Social Networks: Sales and Marketing in a Web 2.0 World, Cindy Estis Green. Available in the online store at www.hsmai.org.

Internet Sites

For more information, visit the following Internet sites. Internet addresses can change without notice. If a site is no longer available at the address listed below, a search engine can be used to find the new address or additional, related sites.

American Hotel & Lodging Association
www.ahla.com

Hotel Marketing
www.hotelmarketing.com

Hotelier
www.ehotelier.com

Public Relations magazine
prweek.com

StarCite
www.starcite.com

Negotiations and Contracts

David C. Scypinski
Senior Vice President of Industry Relations
Starwood Hotels

"The most successful salespeople take a long-term approach to negotiating contracts by looking to develop an agreement that benefits both the hotel and the customer. A one-sided contract may bring in much-needed revenue in the short-term, but may make it impossible to re-book the business. And in this business, as in any other, the key to profitability is repeat business. This is not to say you shouldn't seek to negotiate the most profitable contract possible; but you should be professionally aggressive in your negotiations, looking to balance the financial goals of your hotel and the customer's objectives."

9   Negotiations and Contracts

I N TODAY'S competitive market, hotels largely book business based on its maximum profitability. With the growth of individual business and leisure markets, which tend to pay higher rates than the group meeting segment, properties have become stricter in terms of room rates and contract negotiations for meetings business. But wise hoteliers know that their relationship with planners is equally if not more important. Charging exorbitant rates when demand is high may produce revenue in the short-term, but may adversely affect future business—both from the planner and from potential word-of-mouth referrals.

Today's hoteliers must negotiate contracts that provide optimum benefits to both the property and the planner. In this chapter, we will see how contracts are negotiated, the areas of concern taken into consideration and included in the contract to ensure the successful execution of a function, and detail how hotels use specific clauses to protect themselves financially. This process begins with negotiations.

Negotiations

Negotiations involve two or more parties coming together to reach an agreement for their mutual benefit. This process should be viewed as a friendly, problem-solving partnership, not as a fearful or uncomfortable situation. Negotiating can result in a win-win situation for both your property and the meeting planner when handled properly.

The first step involves preparation by gathering information. Knowledge is power and good negotiation skills begin by researching three key areas: your product, your competition, and the prospect.

Product knowledge begins by studying the *property fact book*. It is nearly impossible to effectively sell features and benefits or to demonstrate how your property is best equipped to meet the prospect's needs without thorough knowledge of your property.

In addition to knowing your property's features, you must also understand *when* your property needs group business, the optimum guest mix, and the average daily rate for each market segment. The bargaining position of meeting planners will vary depending on your hotel's level of business, which can be divided into three categories:

- *Peak* — this is the period when demand for a property and its services is highest and the highest prices can be charged. Also called "high season."
- *Valley* — this period, also known as the "value season" or "low season," characterizes times when demand is lowest. Reduced prices are offered to meeting planners during valley periods to attract business.
- *Shoulder* — this period falls between a peak and a valley. Rooms are available and a mid to high rate can be charged. The shoulder period is the time when many properties concentrate their sales and marketing efforts.

You must know as much about your competitors' products as your own in order to successfully sell against them. When negotiating, emphasize the strengths of your property where you know the competition is weak (this information is available from the property's Competitive Analysis Charts).

Being a good negotiator means learning as much as possible about the buyer. There are several factors to consider when evaluating your prospect's position:

- *Budget.* Knowledge of the meeting planner's past and present budget gives you an indication of how much he or she may be willing to spend on similar events and if price is a major concern.
- *Purpose of the meeting.* Every property has its appeal. If a meeting is for training, a small suburban property can offer the group the option of being the only meeting in the house, which pleases some planners.
- *Dates.* When is the meeting scheduled? How flexible is the group? Do your competitors have the preferred dates open? You are negotiating from a position of strength when you know your competitors don't have the desired dates open.
- *Arrival/departure pattern.* Determine the group's arrival and departure pattern to determine how well the group will fit in with business you have already booked. A Tuesday to Thursday meeting schedule may be problematic, for example, if you have already booked a group that arrives on Sunday and departs on Wednesday. In such a case, you could try a little suggestive selling to the meeting planner: "Yes, we do have some rooms available on Tuesday. However, if you can come in just one night later, we can offer a nice discount. Would you consider that?"
- *Hot buttons.* What are the meeting planner's key concerns and what are the most important buying factors? Is it the availability of special services, such as express check-in/check-out, extra staffing at the front desk, or special meals? Key concerns tell you what to emphasize and also give clues to the importance of price. Obviously, planners who mention VIP service and extra amenities as crucial to their meeting are going to be less price resistant.
- *Past problems.* Did the planner experience problems with another property? If poor food service is mentioned more than once, then price may not be as important a consideration as quality food at next year's event.
- *Group history.* Find out what properties the group has previously used to enable you to compare what you have with what other properties offered. What has been their spending history at previous hotels with regard to various profit centers (food and beverage, shops, spa, recreation, and so on)? What is the guestrooms-to-function-rooms-space ratio? Groups that are function-space intensive may not be a good fit.

  How far back should the group history go? Three years' worth of history should be reviewed. A valuable source for evaluating past history is the Meeting Information Network (MINT) system of the Destination Marketing Association International (DMAI). The MINT system is a shared repository of information, collected by convention and visitors bureaus, about association and corporate meetings. Check the DMAI website, www.destinationmarketing.org, for more information on MINT.
- *Decision deadline.* Your hotel's negotiating position will be affected by how quickly a decision must be made. Your negotiating strategy will be different when dealing with a planner who must make a decision immediately versus a planner who does not have to decide on a site until sometime in the future.

When negotiating, it is essential to look at the **customer's lifetime value**. Would offering concessions for a minor function for the client today result in additional, long-term lucrative business tomorrow? Sometimes, hotels will under-price to gain new customers or be generous to existing customers in order to retain them over the long term. Trade-offs are a part of negotiating, but you should sell value and offer concessions only when absolutely necessary. Successful negotiating is a give-and-take process — the end result is that both parties are satisfied. The planner can look forward to a successful meeting within budget, while your hotel benefits from a profitable piece of business and from the positive relationship that may lead to additional business in the future.

Letter of Agreement/Contract

While contracts are now the norm, the word *contract* frightens many people — people who readily enter into an agreement made formal by a letter. Most businesspeople would not dream of drawing up a contract without legal counsel, but will sign a letter that lists the terms of an agreement. For all practical purposes, a letter of agreement and a contract function the same way, the difference being one of semantics.

A **letter of agreement/contract** should include, in simple language, all arrangements that have been negotiated and agreed to. The contract should be straightforward, free of "legalese," and clear to anyone who reviews it. If necessary, diagrams or examples should be included so that both parties have no questions regarding the terms of the contract. This protects the client and the hotel, but it also does something else of extreme importance. By itemizing all matters to be covered, the letter of agreement is essentially a clearly stated checklist of what is expected of either party. This is vital, because most misunderstandings reflect a lack of communication and a lack of experience by either the hotel executive, the client, or both.

The letter of agreement/contract should cover each point clearly in a separate paragraph or clause, and each topic should have its own header. Each point should be documented. Nothing should be left to verbal agreement. The parties that negotiated the deal may no longer be employed by the hotel or the client when the convention actually takes place. In any case, memory is decidedly fallible. Everything should be included *in writing*. This will eliminate many misunderstandings when the time comes to settle up the accounts, and even prevent malfunctions during the meeting itself.

It is also sound practice to contact a hotel that was previously used as a convention site by the group. This contact can be made by using an **inquiry questionnaire**, which asks a group's former hosts to critique the group for the benefit of a prospective host property (see Exhibit 1). This information is helpful intelligence data to use during negotiations.

Cooperation of this kind is commonplace among hotels. Such inter-hotel conversations will not only make you aware of possible pitfalls with a group, but can also keep you abreast of current practices and trends throughout the hotel industry. Some discretion should be exercised not to make inquiries from a hotel — or a hotel within a chain — that is in a position to make a last-minute bid to book the business. But with some care, past sites of the group could be valuable sources of helpful data.

Before offering a letter of agreement, many hotels send a **proposal letter** to the meeting planner. This proposal letter should spell out exactly what the customer will receive at the hotel. Proposal letters usually follow a standard format, including much of the same information included in the letter of agreement/contract, but they are usually not as detailed. Remember, your written proposal is a selling document and should present your key features and benefits. Include convention brochures, fact sheets, complimentary letters from past groups, and other promotional materials with your proposal letter. The conclusion to your proposal letter should always ask the prospect to take action—to do business with you. Be sure to establish a trace date to follow up every proposal letter.

Exhibit 1   Inquiry Questionnaire

U.S. Grant
H O T E L

AN ATLAS HOTEL

Post Office Box 80098
San Diego, California 92138
(619) 232-3121

Dear Colleague:
The U.S. Grant Hotel is working with:

We understand this group met with you. At your convenience we would sincerely appreciate receiving the following information:

1.

Date							
Original Room Block							
Actually Used							

Meeting Requirements (Program if available):

2.

	Persons	Set-up
General Session	_____	_____
Breakouts	_____	_____

Catered Functions:

3.

	No. of Functions	Persons
Breakfast	_____	_____
Lunch	_____	_____
Dinner	_____	_____
Receptions	_____	_____

4. Comments: _____

Thank you in advance for your cooperation. We will be happy to reciprocate at any time.
Sincerely,

_____
Signature

It is sound practice to track the historical performance of meeting groups. A questionnaire such as this one requests a post-convention critique from hotels used by the meeting group in the past. This information is extremely valuable in negotiations, as it gives the hotel an early sense of whether the group meets its commitments. While it is acceptable practice for competitor hotels to exchange basic information on groups (such as rooms blocked, actual pickup, percentage of double occupancy, number of food functions, and the like), it is a violation of antitrust law and a criminal offense to exchange pricing information (such as room rates or banquet charges).

A proposal letter is normally initiated from a site inspection or a **request for proposal (RFP)** from a meeting planner (see Exhibit 2). A written RFP from a planner includes the group's desired dates, guestroom and meeting space requirements, and the group's meetings history. Since planners often send out a RFP to several hotels at the same time, your response should be timely. Planners expect to receive information on availability and pricing within a day or two of their request.

Should the group accept your proposal, you should send a letter of agreement along with a note of thanks. It is customary for this letter to be sent in triplicate, and to request that it be countersigned by a responsible person from the association (or other sponsoring organization) and returned. As we explained, this constitutes a legal contract whereby both parties have agreed to the terms and arrangements. An alternative to the triplicate-copy method might be a letter from the meeting planner stating that the letter of agreement is correct and accepted.

When sending out contracts or letters of agreement, it is important that the contract be dated. This is extremely important during the negotiation stage, as it ensures that the most current version of the contract will be signed by each party. When it comes to signing, however, the hotel salesperson or another hotel contact should not sign the contract before the meeting planner does. If someone at your property is the first to sign, you do not have the chance to correct anything or change your mind about a point once the buyer has signed (the signatures of both parties constitute a binding legal document). The best policy is to send three originals, asking the buyer to sign two and return them to you and keep the third for his or her files. Then, once the signed originals are received, you can sign both originals and send one back to the meeting planner.[1]

Do not be in a rush to sign the returned contracts. You will want to carefully look them over and initial any changes that may have been made. The customer will also have to initial those changes for them to be binding.

It is worth repeating that a soundly written letter of agreement helps both parties execute a successful meeting and prevents misunderstandings by stating exactly what is to

---

🖳 INTERNET EXERCISE

Electronic Requests for Proposals

Approximately ten years ago, the first online request for proposal (RFP) debuted on the website of the Radisson Miyako Hotel San Francisco. Today, virtually every hotel website has some means for meeting planners to request a RFP online. In fact, hotels are on RFP overload, but RFPs require prompt attention. To ensure that action is taken immediately, Crowne Plaza guarantees a response within two hours or a 5 percent discount will be applied to the final master account.

Visit the websites of the four hotels listed below and download the RFP for each (the RFP is usually found under such menu tabs as "Groups," "Meetings," or other similar tags).

- The Breakers Palm Beach — www.thebreakers.com
- InterContinental Boston — www.intercontinentalboston.com
- Peabody Hotel Memphis — www.peabodymemphis.com
- Renaissance Las Vegas — www.renaissancelasvegas.com

Read through each of the RFPs and answer the following questions:

1. Which of the four RFPs do you think is the most meeting planner friendly? Why?
2. Compare the four hotel RFPs with the Request For Proposal template recommended by the Convention Industry Council (www.conventionindustry.org). To view this template, click on Apex, then Accepted Practices, Requests for Proposals, and the Single Facility RFP.

Exhibit 2   Sample Request for Proposal

Date: 3/1/20__   REQUEST FOR PROPOSAL

20__ Plastic Surgery Senior Residents Conference
Sponsored by the Plastic Surgery Educational Foundation
Galveston, TX

Only possible dates:
April 14-18, 20__
April 21-25, 20__
May 5-9, 20__

EVENT PROFILE:

This meeting provides a forum for third-year residents to present their papers and helps to prepare them for medical practice.

ORGANIZATION PROFILE:

The PSEF is the educational arm of the American Society of Plastic and Reconstructive Surgeons, which is a 6,000 member national medical association representing 97% of all plastic surgeons in the U.S. The ASPRS/PSEF sponsors approximately 40 meetings/year throughout the U.S. and abroad.

ATTENDEE PROFILE: Third-year medical residents; average age early 30's
                           From all over U.S.
                           70% male, 30% female
                           15% traveling with spouse

PROPERTY TYPE NEEDED: City location close to restaurants and nightlife.

GUEST ROOM REQUIREMENTS:

Arrival	Tuesday night	5 rooms
	Wednesday night	120 rooms
	Thursday night	130 rooms
	Friday night	130 rooms; 2 suites
	Saturday night	110 rooms; 2 suites
Depart	Sunday	5 rooms

Notes: Need flat single/double rate. 85% sgl, 15% dbl. 85% non-smoking. Rate-sensitive group.

Concessions: 2 1BR suite upgrades for Assn. Presidents
                1/50 comp
                2 reduced rate staff rooms.

MEETING SPACE REQUIREMENTS:

Day	Time	Function	Attendance	Budget
Wednesday	3:00pm-7:00pm	Registration	2 6' tables	
	6:30pm-7:30pm	Reception	200 people	$30/p
	7:00pm-24 hrs	Exhibit Setup	25 6'tables plus	
			20 double-sided posters	

The RFP provides general information about the requesting organization and event, including specifics about the group's space requirements, a history of the group, and its decision date. The RFP may be mailed, faxed, e-mailed, or, as is becoming increasingly common, sent via the Internet to hotels. In most cases, meeting planners not only request proposals from hotels, but from a number of other suppliers as well, such as service contractors (companies that set up exhibits), security companies, audiovisual suppliers, tour shuttle firms, florists, and housing companies (if the event is outsourced). This particular RFP includes three sheets; only the first is shown. Page two lists daily functions, meeting room requirements, the group's meeting history, and a space hold request; page three provides special requirements, a response date, information on the group's decision date, and the name and contact numbers of the meeting planner. The CIC has created a standardized RFP that can be downloaded at www.conventionindustry.org.

be done, by whom, and at what price. Be sure that there are no "surprises"—each aspect should be reviewed with customers in order to protect your business relationship.

Since nothing is part of the agreement that is not included in the contract or letter of agreement, it is essential that certain information be recorded. Details on essential information and commonly negotiated points are covered in the following paragraphs.

Names of Organization and Hotel

Most letters of agreement or contracts begin with an introduction, known as a **preamble**, that clearly specifies the parties entering into the contract (parties should be identified by name, and the addresses and contact information for both should be listed), a statement of intent by both parties to enter into the contract, and the name or a designation of the event. The preamble also includes the official performance dates of the event (see below).

Official Dates

It sounds basic, but make sure the exact dates of the event are specified (this includes dates for move-in and move-out as well as the dates for event functions). These dates, which are often referred to as the *official dates*, should include not only the date and day, but also the beginning and ending times for each event. This protects the hotel from tying up a room beyond an official cutoff time (you don't want a breakfast ending too late to set up the room for a luncheon or training session later in the day).

Number and Kinds of Rooms

Specify the number of guestrooms to be held, spelling out the number of suites, single, double, and twin rooms. Sometimes a client will want the location of the rooms specified, as in the case of a multi-room structure. If you agree to it, specify the number of rooms in Building A and the number in Building B.

Many hotels present the sleeping room block in a table format, such as the one illustrated on the following page. This table shows the dates and days of the week, the specific breakdown of room-suite types, rates, and the number of rooms contracted for each night.

Also include a reservation **cutoff date.** Attendees who make their reservations after the cutoff date are not guaranteed a room or the negotiated convention rate. If this is the case, attendees must pay the "market rate" for available rooms. A typical clause might read: *"A cutoff date of thirty days prior to the opening of the convention is established. This cutoff date is May 1, 20__. After this date, any of your unused room commitment will be released to the general public. After the cutoff date, we will continue to accept your group's reservations on a space-available basis."*

Meeting planners may ask that the hotel continue taking reservations from attendees at the negotiated group rate (rather than the prevailing rate) after the cutoff date if rooms are still available. Hotels are usually reluctant to continue to offer group rates, especially in high-demand periods. For one meeting planner, this meant that the negotiated $224 per night block rate skyrocketed to $429![2]

Specify the method by which room reservations will be made: by mail, using a pre-printed reservation reply card; by rooming list; through the housing bureau of the convention and visitors bureau; to the hotel directly; or to an "800" number. Also specify who is

ROOM TYPE(S)	ROH	RCST	EXEC	STAFF	Contract
ROOM RATE	**$260**	**1500**	**260**	**165**	
Monday, 10/20				7	7
Tuesday, 10/20				7	7
Wednesday, 10/22	3			7	10
Thursday, 10/23	46	1	5	7	60
Friday, 10/24	46	1	5	7	60
Saturday, 10/25	46	1	5	7	60
Sunday, 10/26				7	7
(2) Executive suites will be at $425					

Key: ROH – Run of House
      RCST – Ritz-Carlton Suite
      Exec – Executive Room

A group's room block should be defined in a table format, with the days and dates down the side. Types of rooms and rates should be noted on the lines for each day, and you may also want to add columns for the number of arrivals and departures on each day of the event.
Source: Courtesy of the Ritz-Carlton, Lake Las Vegas.

to handle the receipt of the reservations—the hotel, the convening group, or a third-party housing company.

Rates/Commisions

Specify clearly the rates for each type of accommodation. If a range is agreed to, list rates from the lowest to the highest. If a flat rate (all guestrooms at the same price) is negotiated, state it clearly. If rooms are to be priced differently in different sections of the hotel, it may be wise to list such rates separately. And when listing rates for suites, be sure to note that the suite includes a parlor and a number of guestrooms, such as a parlor and one bedroom or a parlor and two bedrooms.

Many large conventions are planned well in advance, and most hotels will not quote firm room rates more than a year out. In this case, a formula for establishing future rates will need to be negotiated. Often, a "percentage off rack rate" is used to establish a future rate. For example, if the hotel's current rack rate is $150 per night and the current convention rate is 20 percent less ($120), this percentage would be used to determine room rates at the time of the meeting (attendees would get 20 percent off the rack rate in effect at the time of the meeting). Other formulas used to establish future rates might be to specify a maximum percentage increase from current rates or to tie the future rates to the **Consumer Price Index**.

Applicable taxes should also be spelled out. In most cases, attendees will be required to pay the state sales tax and any applicable room taxes. If service charges and gratuities are also assessed, these, too, should be listed to avoid any unpleasant surprises.

In addition to negotiating with meeting planners, it has become increasingly common for third-party meeting planners to be involved in negotiations. Firms such as Conference Direct, Experient, and HelmsBriscoe are often contracted by groups to negotiate and book hotel rooms, food and beverage, and meeting rooms. Because of the volume of business these firms book, they are paid significant fees, which are sometimes collected as commissions from hotels.

Any contract, therefore, should specify the terms and conditions under which any commissions will be calculated and paid. It is important that all parties involved clearly understand which rates and packages are commissionable and how the commission will be calculated (commissions on some package plans, for example, are paid only on the rooms portion negotiated, while other commission plans pay commissions on the total plan). The contract should also include to whom and when the commission will be paid.

Arrival/Departure Pattern

It is important that you know the group's **arrival/departure pattern**—the dates and times that meeting attendees will arrive and depart. If 400 rooms are being held, it is unlikely that all 400 room occupants will arrive on the same day. You should develop a **flow chart** to reserve rooms in accordance with the agreement. The agreement, for example, might call for 100 rooms for arrival on Monday, January 10, 200 rooms for arrival on Tuesday, January 11, and the remaining 100 rooms on Wednesday, January 12. It is also wise to indicate the breakdown of the rooms into singles, doubles, twins, and suites. You may find arrival dates easier to secure than check-out dates, but these too are of great importance to you.

Since all hotels strive to maximize occupancy, a loss of revenue can result if a group's guests leave early. Many hotels combat this problem by charging an **early departure fee** to any guest who checks out earlier than the original departure date indicated on his or her reservation. Contracts, therefore, should clearly spell out the reasons and amounts of early departure fees — and these, in turn, should be clearly indicated to the group's membership on printed meeting materials (registration forms, housing forms, and so on) and on the group's web page.

Clauses regarding early departures may be negotiated, of course; if a guest leaves as a result of an emergency, for example, the fee is waived. Or, a clause may allow a guest to change his or her departure date at check-in without penalty (the early departure fee would only be charged if the guest checks out before the verified date). Other contracts contain clauses that waive early departure fees for certain attendees, such as the organization's staff members, VIPs, and speakers.

Meeting Space

The experienced convention planner will want you to hold all your meeting rooms and public space until he or she has firmed up the program and the resultant traffic flow pattern. If the event is far in the future and if it will not occupy the entire hotel, this may be difficult. You need public space to sell other meetings. Keep in mind that while eye-catching events are the big ones, most meetings do not fill the hotel; usually there are several in the house at once. The second or third meeting in the hotel, although smaller than the main meeting, represents important income, as well as opportunities to serve repeat customers.

How much of your meeting space to hold is a point to be negotiated, but it is reasonable to hold all rooms that might possibly be used for the event. A date must be set by which the program will be completed to the point that unused public space can be released. If you agree to hold rooms without setting an option or **release date**, you may find yourself unable to use them to solicit other meetings or banquets.

Many meeting planners prefer specific meeting rooms to be named in the contract. This limits your flexibility. If possible, avoid naming the specific function rooms and include a clause to indicate how and when meeting space may be released. For example:

We have reserved function space based on the requirements described to us. The meeting group will provide the final program to the hotel nine months before the meeting. At that time, all space not being used will be released back to the hotel. The specific names of the function rooms will be furnished to you when you are ready to print your program. This allows time for attendance figures to be well established.

Another consideration is the guestroom-to-public-space ratio. Groups and transients are both part of the hotel's overall room demand. Groups book well in advance, so hotels can generally offer them lower rates for a guaranteed block of rooms. The booking cycle for transients is much shorter (a week or two) and they pay higher rates. Depending on demand, a hotel's group room allotment differs daily throughout the year.

Consider a 400-room hotel with a **group ceiling** (targeted number of group rooms) of 300 rooms over a given period and an expected transient demand of 100 rooms. The property is effectively a 300-room group hotel. Revenue is lost if the hotel assigns all its public space to a 200-room group, as that leaves no meeting space for the remaining 100 group rooms.

Meeting groups that are space-intensive but light on guestroom usage, however, should not be immediately dismissed by hotel sales. A group that needs extensive meeting space but not a great deal of sleeping rooms should be encouraged to schedule their meeting to coincide with other events that do not require a lot of meeting space but fill guestrooms, such as a citywide convention or incentive program. In these cases, hotels will tend to have the needed meeting space available without tying up guestrooms needed for other groups, making space-intensive groups a perfect fit.

Complimentary and Reduced-Rate Rooms

It is commonplace in the convention industry for hotels to supply some complimentary rooms, but the number varies a great deal. A hotel may be more generous if the meeting is scheduled during an off-time of the week or season. A more successful hotel may be tougher when it comes to concessions. In most cases, hotels offer complimentary rooms based on the number of guestrooms used. A very common rule of thumb is one complimentary guestroom for every 50 guestrooms utilized and one complimentary suite for every 100 paid room nights. The hotel's policy should clearly be spelled out, as in the sample clause below:

We will be pleased to furnish one complimentary guestroom for every fifty room nights utilized. The complimentary commitment will be provided on a cumulative basis for the length of the meeting. The hotel offers a choice of accounting procedures for complimentary rooms. A bottom-line dollar credit on the Master Account will value each unit at the daily average guestroom rate generated by the group, or guestrooms/suites can be reserved on a complimentary basis to arrival.

Notice that the clause above specifies that comps are calculated on a *cumulative* rather than on a per-night basis. Many meeting planners prefer that rooms be calculated in this way. That is, if a group used 45 guestrooms on the first night and 55 on the second night, a cumulative computation would result in two comp room nights; if the comp rooms had been based on a per-night basis, only one comp room would be earned for the second night. No matter what formula is used to calculate comp rooms, it should be clearly spelled out; hotels should specify if complimentary rooms are based on all nights of a group's stay, including early arrivals and late departures, or only calculated during the official dates of the convention.

A hotel and a client may also agree to a number of reduced-rate rooms. This is usually done for staff members, VIPs, speakers, and performers, and, of course is subject to negotiation. The contract should clearly specify the number of rooms that will be reduced, the rate for each, and, perhaps, the designated occupants.

If charges are to be made for meeting rooms, rates should be specified for each room. As with comp and reduced-rate guestrooms, these charges are usually based on the number of guestrooms used. The contract should specify the guestroom requirement and detail how meeting room rates will be assessed based on room pick-up.

Prior Visits

A hotel often will not charge for guestrooms used by the meeting organizer and his or her staff during visits to the hotel before the event to make preliminary arrangements. This is often done on a *space-available* basis. It is wise to set a specific limit on the number of rooms made available for this purpose.

Working Space

Offices, press rooms, and similar working space should be discussed. If a charge is to be made for them, specify the rates. If no charge is to be made, specify this clearly, but also spell out the maximum number of rooms to be used for this purpose. Many meeting planners insist upon indicating the location of such rooms to make sure the locations are convenient to the meeting sessions.

Registration Control

In the case of association conventions, hotels usually agree to clear all requests for accommodation from people of that particular industry with the convention organizer. You need to do this in order to credit the association with the total number of rooms used in conjunction with the convention. All such rooms should be applied against the guaranteed number of rooms. In addition, a convention organizer often wants to control the use of suites as hospitality centers or even as setups which circumvent the exhibit itself and its booth space and decorating costs.

Exhibit Space

If a charge is to be made for the exhibit hall, say so clearly and state what is to be included in the charge. Items to be considered are hours the exhibit is to be open, electricity, air conditioning or heat, carpeting, and the number of tables and chairs. List what the hotel is to furnish and what must be contracted for with a show decorator.

Secure exact dates for the exhibition from the meeting planner, including beginning and ending times that include an allowance for the move-in and move-out of the exhibits. Many hotels provide forms for the meeting planner to verify dates and times for both the exhibit and exhibitor move-in and move-out.

Some hotels charge on the basis of the number of booths sold by the association. The charge is usually a per-booth rate by day for the duration of the convention, including move-in and move-out days. However, this ties the hotel's rental income to the show manager's ability to attract exhibitors; hotels, therefore, normally levy a flat charge. A fee of two to five dollars per square foot for each exhibit day is quite common.

Food Functions

Meeting planners will not expect you to establish menu prices today for a meeting three years in the future. Most realize that, because of rising costs and daily fluctuations in market prices, catering managers usually won't quote firm menu prices until six months out. But a meeting planner has to make budget projections, so expect experienced planners to negotiate a fixed percentage off the printed menu prices in effect at the time of the meeting or to attach a current banquet menu to the contract and negotiate that prices won't increase by more than a certain percentage each year.

Specify how much notice you require for guarantees on food functions. Most common is 48 hours advance notice, but many hotels have increased their guarantees to 72 hours. If you need more time, and you may over weekends, negotiate it and include it in your letter of agreement. Menus have to be priced and approved. Most hotels will agree to set tables for a percentage above the number guaranteed in order to accommodate additional guests. Many set for an additional five percent, others hold it to three percent, and still others base the percent on the number of persons to be served. For example, a typical contract might include points such as the following:

APEX Contracts Report

On December 16, 2006, *APEX Contracts Accepted Practices*, an educational paper prepared by APEX (Accepted Practices Exchange), an initiative of the Convention Industry Council, was approved by the CIC. Like other APEX guidelines, the report, which focuses on contract issues, was developed by a seven-member panel, but there were some major differences from typical APEX offerings, which typically provide templates to help standardize hospitality industry practices. Tyra Hilliard, a veteran attorney, speaker, and meetings consultant, was the chair of the APEX contracts panel. She says:

> Contracts are meant to be negotiated. This is an educational document, it's not meant to take the place of a negotiation. It's meant to help people understand contracts better so that they can negotiate better.

The panel determined that it was not possible to develop a "standard" contract for a number of reasons, "including the large and multifaceted industry with many different types of vendors, customers, facilities, and requirements, and also because legal considerations and fostering competition would prevent creation of such a document." Rather than suggesting a format for a hotel contract (although the paper includes an outline with a suggested order of clauses), the *APEX Contracts Accepted Packages* paper provides an alphabetical listing of 23 different clauses typically found in hotel contracts, explains the purpose of each clause, and details the factors that should be taken into consideration before including each type of clause in a contract.

To view the complete *APEX Contracts Accepted Practices* paper, log on to the CIC's website, www.conventionindustry.org. Click on APEX tab and then Accepted Practices. Scroll down to APEX Contracts Accepted Practices.

Sources: *APEX Contracts Accepted Practices,* **2006, Convention Industry Council; Corrie Dosh, "CIC Prepares to Issue Educational Paper About Meetings Contracts,"** *Business Travel News,* **September 11, 2006, p. 22.**

A 48-hour guarantee is required on all meal functions. Your catering manager must be notified of the exact number of attendees for whom you will guarantee payment. For functions scheduled on Sunday or Monday, the guarantee must be received by noon on the preceding Friday.

The hotel will set up as follows:

20-100 persons set	*5% over guarantee*
101-1000 persons set	*3% over guarantee*
1001 persons and over	*1% over guarantee*

In the event a guarantee is not received, the original estimated attendance count will be prepared and billed.

When a salesperson quotes food and beverage prices, he or she will note a "price, plus, plus." The price is the price per person and the **plus, plus** represents taxes and service charges added to the per person charge. The actual percentages will vary depending on state sales taxes and property service charges. For example, a Carmel Valley, California, hotel might quote a per person rate for a reception as $20.00 ++. The total price would then be $25.45 — $20.00 plus $1.45 (7.25-percent sales tax) plus $4.00 (a 20-percent service charge).

Refreshment Breaks

It is amazing how many arguments stem from refreshment break arrangements. Many meeting organizers think in terms of coffee shop standards. They do not understand the conditions under which the hotel operates. As a result, much resentment is evidenced, and it is important to explain all that is involved when the hotel supplies refreshment breaks. Spell out the costs and labor required for all refreshment breaks. Include prices for cakes, soft drinks, and juice, too. It is important to the hotel that its clients have faith that the hotel charges are fair.

Liquor

Spell out the hotel's policy on liquor service. Most hotels prohibit meeting planners from bringing in food or liquor from outside the property. State your policy on this matter clearly so that no misunderstandings arise during the meeting. A typical contract clause might state:

No food or beverages of any kind will be permitted to be brought into the hotel from the outside without the written permission of the hotel. The hotel reserves the right to assess a service charge for any food and beverages brought into the facility in violation thereof. If any alcoholic beverages are to be served on the premises (and/or elsewhere under the hotel's alcoholic beverage license) the hotel will require these beverages to be dispensed by hotel servers and bartenders. The hotel's alcoholic beverage license requires the hotel to (1) request proper identification (Photo ID) of any person of questionable age, and refuse alcoholic beverage service if the person is either under age or proper identification cannot

---

> ### 🖳 *INTERNET EXERCISE*
>
> ## Evaluating Contract Templates
>
> On the website of the Institute of Electrical and Electronics Engineers, www.ieee.org/web/conferences/organizers/contracts.html, you can find contract templates developed for negotiations with the following chains and hotels:
>
> • Fairmont   • Starwood   • Hyatt   • Disney (California)   • Hilton   • Disney (Florida)
>
> Download a copy of the group meeting contract for one of the above hospitality entities and identify the following clauses in the contract:
>
> | | |
> |---|---|
> | - Arbitration and Dispute Resolution | - Guestroom Pickup Review |
> | - Attrition | - Indemnification |
> | - Cancellation | - Master Account and Credit |
> | - Complimentary and Reduced-Rate Rooms | Procedures |
> | - Gratuities and Service Charges | - Termination |
>
> Use the information found in these clauses to answer the following questions:
>
> 1. What clauses were developed to ensure the organization is getting the lowest group rate?
>
> 2. How much slippage does the contract allow before attrition charges are assessed?
>
> 3. What information is the hotel required to provide in the post-meeting report?

be produced, and (2) refuse alcoholic beverage service to any person who, in the hotel's judgment, appears intoxicated.

If you charge by the bottle, an arrangement should be made for inventory control and credit given for unopened bottles after the convention. It is important both for the hotel and the client to identify the person authorized to tally the inventory with your staff. The credit could be issued at that time.

Gratuities and Service Charges

Gratuities and service charges should be discussed in advance of the meeting and should be spelled out in the letter of agreement. Most meeting planners view gratuities as part of convention costs, and even though a touchy area, no problems should arise if guidelines are clearly established at the outset. For example, a gratuity clause might read:

Bellperson gratuities of $3.00 per person round trip are mandatory on group arrivals. Maid gratuities of $1.00 per room, per night, are optional, but suggested.

A service charge statement might read:

All catered food, beverage, and related service charges will be subject to the current sales tax. Each catered function will automatically reflect a service charge of 17 percent.

Note that the above clause specifies that the service charge is taxable. Taxes on service charges may vary from city to city, and the amount of tax (if any) on the service charge should be clearly spelled out in the contract.

THE CONVENTION INDUSTRY COUNCIL

The best customers are the ones who really know their business. And they like to do business with vendors who know theirs. It is amazing how rapidly and steadily the convention business grew, with very little done to expand areas of knowledge and expertise. Fortunately, leaders of four associations met in 1949 to come to grips with the situation. This group — including both vendors and buyers — formed a council to establish a set of commonly accepted trade standards.

The Convention Industry Council, as it is now known, adopted four basic objectives:

1. To bring about a sympathetic understanding and acceptance among these organizations of the responsibility of each to the other.
2. To create a sound and consistent basis for handling convention procedures and practices through a program of study and education.
3. To conduct educational and other activities of mutual interest to participating organizations.
4. To acquaint the public with the fact that conventions are essential to industry and to the economy of the community and nation.

The four original organizations were the American Hotel & Lodging Association, the American Society of Association Executives, the Hospitality Sales and Marketing Association International, and the International Association of Convention & Visitor Bureaus.

Today, 34 organizations are on the council, about half representing seller groups and half representing buyer organizations.

Through the years the council has been the educational leader for the industry. It created the Certified Meeting Professional (CMP) program. In 1961 it published the *Convention Industry Council Manual.* This manual presented detailed responsibilities of each of the three groups involved in a convention — the sponsoring organization, the hotel, and the convention bureau — and how they were interrelated. This manual, now in its eighth revised edition, contains useful checklists, forms, and an industry glossary. The CIC published an economic-impact study of the meetings industry and recently completed APEX, the development of accepted practices for the industry.

**34 ORGANIZATIONS COMPOSING
THE CONVENTION INDUSTRY COUNCIL**

Association of Collegiate Conference and Events Directors-International (ACCED-I)
AMC Institute (formerly IAAMC)
Alliance of Meeting Management Consultants (AMMC)
American Hotel & Lodging Association (AH&LA)
American Society of Association Executives and The Center (ASAE & The Center)
Association for Convention Operations Management (ACOM)
Association of Destination Management Executives (ADME)
Council of Engineering and Scientific Society Executives (CESSE)
Center for Exhibition Industry Research (CEIR)
Destination Marketing Association International (DMAI) (formerly IACVB)
Exhibit Designers and Producers Association (EDPA)
Exhibition Services & Contractors Association (ESCA)
Financial and Insurance Conference Planners (FICP) (formerly ICPA)
Green Meetings Industry Council (GMIC)
Healthcare Convention and Exhibitors Association (HCEA)
Hospitality Sales and Marketing Association International (HSMAI)
International Association of Assembly Managers (IAAM)
International Association of Conference Centers (IACC)
International Association of Exhibitions and Events (IAEE) (formerly IAEM)
International Association of Professional Congress Organisers (IAPCO)
International Association of Speakers Bureaus (IASB)
International Congress and Convention Association (ICCA)
International Special Events Society (ISES)
Meeting Professionals International (MPI)
National Association of Catering Executives (NACE)
National Business Travel Association (NBTA)
National Coalition of Black Meeting Planners (NCBMP)
National Speakers Association (NSA)
Professional Convention Management Association (PCMA)
Religious Conference Management Association (RCMA)
Society of Government Meeting Professionals (SGMP)
Society of Incentive & Travel Executives (SITE)
Trade Show Exhibitors Association (TSEA)
U.S. Travel Association (U.S. Travel)

Audiovisual Equipment

Some hotels supply audiovisual equipment from their own inventories; others use local dealers. In either case, it is important to show the rate structure for equipment and services, or to indicate that it is the convention staff's responsibility to make its own arrangements. You may prefer to supply the names of local service companies that deal directly with, and bill to, the client. Some hotels will accept the local dealer's bills and rebill the convention. It is important, then, that there be a clear understanding as to who has the responsibility to provide the necessary equipment so that the client receives the service needed.

Union Regulations

Convention organizers are accustomed to union help and regulations, but you should list the basic workday, rates, and overtime charges. You should also state any out-of-the-ordinary union requirements in your labor contract. Making your client aware of them eliminates much aggravation.

Many astute meeting planners will not sign confirmations or agreements without first checking out union conditions. The hotel has a responsibility to alert the meeting planner to the possibility of local labor contracts terminating before the meeting, any likely labor rate increases, or possible labor disputes.

Master Account and Credit Procedures

The meeting planner will have a master billing account. He or she must furnish the hotel with a list of people authorized to sign for charges that are to be placed on the **master account**. The client must also indicate which charges the convention organizer will pick up for such people as speakers and performers. The client may choose to pay room rate only and let the individuals pay all incidental charges. In the case of a corporate meeting, the arrangement may have to be clarified for each attendee. Make it clear that the master account will have to be verified and initialed before the client leaves after the meeting.

Before extending credit to a corporate group or an association, hotel sales executives frequently request a completed credit application (see Exhibit 3). Calls also may be made to colleagues at properties where the group has met previously. These references, combined with Dun and Bradstreet credit checks, are used to determine the credit limit extended to the meeting group.

Method of Payment

Specify how and when the group's bill is to be paid. If you want a deposit, say so and give the date that it is due. Also negotiate any additional sum to be paid, as well as the final payment.

Most convention organizers prefer to go over the master account before they leave the hotel, but some hotels cannot have it ready that quickly. It is a common practice to leave some portion of the account unpaid, should there be some items that require negotiations or that aren't ready for final accounting. But most hotels do insist that the master account be approved by the client before leaving, while all matters are fresh in the mind and the staff is available for consultation. A statement such as the following might be included:

Exhibit 3   Application for Direct Billing

_____ MARRIOTT'S _____
Camelback Inn
RESORT GOLF CLUB & SPA

P.O. BOX 70 • SCOTTSDALE, AZ 85252 • (602) 948-1700

CREDIT APPLICATION

Direct billing privileges are not automatically extended. To apply for direct billing privileges, please complete and return this application to the hotel. Should you have any questions regarding the status of your application, please call the Credit Manager at (602) 948-1700, ext. 7715 or your Sales Representative.

Name of Group: _____

Address: _____

City: _____ State: _____ Zip: _____

Telephone: _____ Date(s) of Event: _____

References:
Hotel Reference: _____ Contact: _____

Address: _____ Phone: _____

Date(s) of Event: _____ Amount Billed: _____

Hotel Reference: _____ Contact: _____

Address: _____ Phone: _____

Date(s) of Event: _____ Amount Billed: _____

Bank Reference: _____ Officer: _____

Address: _____

Telephone: _____ Account #: _____
(please indicate the acct. # from which payment will be drawn)

Items to be Billed: (Please check)
All Room Charges	( )	
Some Room Charges	( )	please specify
Restaurant Charges	( )	please specify
Banquet Charges	( )	
Recreational Facilities	( )	
Other	( )	please specify
Other	( )	please specify

Estimated Value _____

I have completed this application in behalf of this group and believe all information contained to be correct. I understand that the extension of direct billing privilege is conditional upon our agreement to pay our account in full within thirty days of receipt of the hotel's statement.

Signed: _____ Date: _____

Title: _____

- -

Accounting Department Approval _____

Many hotels do not automatically issue credit to new clients. Meeting groups that do not have a credit history with the hotel must fill out a credit application form. Note that both hotel and bank references are requested on this form.

The hotel will be expending money immediately in labor and services to ensure the most successful meeting for you. Therefore, it is our policy to ask for 75 percent of the master account to be paid prior to your departure from the hotel. The remaining 25 percent will be direct billed.

Termination/Cancellation Clauses

A **termination clause**, sometimes termed a force majeure or Act of God clause, should be included in the agreement for cases when either party might cancel because of circumstances beyond its control. Termination means that both parties are excused from performance without liability. For example, the hotel should not be held responsible for nonperformance in the event of a strike, lockout or fire; or failure of heat, light, or power; or natural disasters. Planners might terminate if there is a change in ownership, hotel chain affiliation, management company, or bankruptcy proceedings by the hotel. Other forces beyond the control of the group or the facility that would apply include weather events, large-scale disasters, or civil unrest.

Exhibit 4   Sample Cancellation Policies of Four Hotels

Anatole Hotel Cancellation Policy

In the event that you have to cancel your meeting within _____ of the actual date, you will be asked to pay a cancellation fee of half the anticipated room revenue. This fee will be used to recuperate loss of revenue which cannot be replaced. In the event we are able to resell all or part of your block, an adjustment will be made.

In the event of a national emergency or an act of God, where you had no control over the circumstances, the above paragraph is null and void. If you are able to rebook the meeting or one with similar requirements within one year of the cancellation date, we will be pleased to apply the cancellation fee to this meeting.

Any controversy or claim arising out of, or relating to the cancellation of the contract or the breach thereof, shall be settled by arbitration in accordance with the rules of the American Arbitration Association, and judgment upon the award rendered by the Arbitrator(s) may be entered in any court having jurisdiction thereof.

South Seas Plantation Cancellation Policy

Cancellation Notice Received	*Cancellation Charge*
0–60 days prior to scheduled arrival date	Full payment on rooms for the duration of the dates agreed upon
60–90 days prior to scheduled arrival date	75% of above
90–120 days prior to scheduled arrival date	50% of above
120–180 days prior to scheduled arrival date	Forfeit deposit

NOTE: Same cancellation policy applies in the event the agreed-upon length of stay of days is reduced.

It is further provided there shall be no right of termination on your part for the sole purpose of holding the same meeting in another city or facility. Neither does South Seas Plantation have the right to cancel your room block if another larger group requests the same space and dates.

Opryland Hotel Cancellation Policy

In the event that it becomes necessary for you to cancel your conference with us, we would be in a difficult position to try to resell your room nights and the cancellation would, no doubt, result in additional lost revenue for our Hotel. We will, however, attempt to resell the room nights that were reserved for you and would only assess a cancellation fee for those room nights not resold over the initially agreed-upon dates. This fee would be based upon the unsold room nights multiplied by your established group rate for that period.

Hotel Del Coronado Cancellation Policy

In the unfortunate event that the Group cancels the meeting due to extraordinary and unforeseeable circumstances, the Group agrees (1) to pay one night's rent for the number of rooms confirmed if the cancellation occurs within one year of the scheduled dates, the night paid for being the night the largest number of rooms had been confirmed, and (2) to pay for the entire number of rooms confirmed if the cancellation occurs less than three months prior to the scheduled dates of the meeting.

Sources: Used with permission of the Anatole Hotel, South Seas Plantation Resort, Opryland Hotel, and Hotel Del Coronado Legal Department, Timothy R. Binder, General Counsel.

The next paragraph after the termination clause should be the **cancellation clause**. *Cancelling* a contract is not the same as *terminating* a contract. Termination means that neither party has any continuing obligation to the other. Cancellation means that one party elects not to perform, which ordinarily requires the payment of damages. Many conventions are planned a number of years in advance, so occasions do arise that call for a cancellation of the event. The cancellation clause should spell out what it will cost the hotel and/or the group if either party should cancel for reasons not identified in the termination clause. Cancellation clauses in hotel contracts often establish cancellation fees on a sliding scale, with the amount increasing the closer the cancellation is to the anticipated date (see Exhibit 4). Planned food and beverage functions might also be factored into the scale. Since cancellation fees are based on lost profits, not lost revenues, the percentage of revenue received by the hotel cannot exceed its profit margin (generally 70–80 percent for sleeping rooms and 30–40 percent for food).

Recently, the Hyatt chain implemented a new standardized contract, which was most notably changed in the area of cancellations. Hyatt now uses a graduated formula for cancellation damages; the closer to the group's scheduled arrival date a meeting is cancelled, the more the group's damages increase. In the event of a cancellation between the time the contract is signed and two years before the meeting date, the charge is 40 percent of rooms revenue and 15 percent of food and beverage and meeting room minimums. Meetings cancelled within six months of the meeting date carry the heaviest charges: 80 percent for rooms; 40 percent for food and beverage and meeting room rentals. If it is the hotel that cancels, it pays the same fee to the group. Because Hyatt either owns or manages under contract all its 120-plus properties, it has little trouble applying the new contract (with its penalties) uniformly.

Damage Clause: Liquidated or Mitigated Damages

To protect themselves in the event of cancellation, most hotel contracts include either a **liquidated damage clause** or a **mitigation of damage clause**. A liquidated damage provision is an agreement by both planner and hotel in advance as to the penalty for cancellation. Damages are collected upon cancellation. With a mitigation of damages clause, the penalty is not predetermined — the hotel must wait until the convention dates actually pass and then prove its actual loss. Tracking and reporting the use of space and then computing actual losses following a cancellation is inconvenient, difficult, and requires waiting much longer to recover damages, so most hotels prefer a liquidated damage clause.

A liquidated damage clause allows the parties to agree in advance as to the amount and method for calculating damages that might be paid in the event of cancellation. Generally, the amount of liquidated damages is less than what a hotel might have received from

LIQUIDATED DAMAGES	MITIGATED DAMAGES
Amount agreeed upon in advance of breach	Actual damages proven after breach
• Predetermined	• Must wait until dates pass
• Risk on hotel	• Risk on group
• No proof problems	• Hard to prove/calculate

Liquidated damages are a compromise that reduces risks to both parties. The hotel is not required to prove its actual loss and no proof of mitigation is required.

mitigating damages, but it is a "sum certain." The liquidated damage clause sets the limits of damages well in advance of the meeting. If the hotel resells some of its rooms, there is no reimbursement to the meeting group.

A liquidated damage clause is generally stated in a sliding scale tied to a percentage of anticipated profits and/or to a specific dollar amount. The amount would be low for cancellations two or three years out and higher for cancellations closer to the meeting date. For example:

Under the terms of this Agreement, the Hotel is reserving for your use the room block and public space requirements described herein. In the event these reserved facilities and related services are not used, the Hotel will experience significant monetary losses.

Notwithstanding any other provision of the Agreement, you shall have the right to cancel this Agreement without cause upon written notice to the Hotel at any time prior to the event and upon payment of an amount based on the following scale:

> *Notice and payment received on or before*   *12/15/10–$183,060*
> *(15 percent of total anticipated profit)*
> *Notice and payment received on or before*   *11/15/12–$366,120*
> *(30 percent of total anticipated profit)*
> *Notice and payment received on or before*   *11/05/13–$854,280*
> *(70 percent of total anticipated profit)*
> *Notice and payment received after*   *11/05/13–$1,220,400*

Computing Damages

The difference between liquidated damages and mitigated damages is that mitigated damages are *actual* charges, and liquidated damages, while predetermined, are less than actual damages. For example, assume a hotel books a group needing 200 room nights at $100 per night; the estimated room revenue for the group would be $20,000.

Group Rooms Blocked:	200 Room nights
Group's Average Rate:	$100
Profit Margin for Guestrooms:	70 percent

What happens if the group cancels? With a *mitigated (actual) damage clause*, the hotel would be entitled to 70 percent ($14,000) of the lost revenues. The hotel collects only 70% of lost revenues because damages are based on *lost profits*, not on lost revenue. Lost profit is defined as gross revenue minus variable expenses.

Hotels track profit separately for each revenue-producing department. The industry average profit margin for guestrooms is 70 percent. Catered food has an average profit margin of 35 percent, while alcohol has an average profit margin of 80 percent.

If the cancellation clause spelled out *liquidated damages*, both the meeting planner and the hotel might agree to a penalty of 20 percent of lost profits if the group were to cancel. In the above case, the damages would total $2,800.

Mitigated (Actual)	Liquidated
$20,000 x 70% = $14,000	$20,000 x 70% = $14,000
	$14,000 x 20% = $ 2,800

With a mitigated damage clause, if the hotel is able to resell 50 of the cancelled rooms, it would credit $3,500 back to the meeting group:

50 rooms resold @ 50 x $100 x 70% = $3,500	$14,000 – 3,500 = $10,500

Carolyn Colton, assistant general counsel for Marriott International, cautions that in calculating a liquidated damage amount the hotel should consider other profit centers beyond sleeping rooms. She says:

> When a group cancels an event, the hotel also experiences substantial damages in lost food and beverage/banquet sales and/or lost fees for use of function space. In addition, the hotel suffers losses in other aspects of its business, such as lost restaurant and gift shop sales, movie purchases, and room service.[3]

Most meeting planners will favor a mitigation of damage clause. Such a clause requires the hotel to try to minimize its damages by working to find business to replace the business lost by cancellation. Hotels that agree to mitigate damages must wait until after the meeting dates have come and gone before determining damages and then are faced with the difficulty of computing damages.

It is common for meeting planners to request that a combination of both clauses be included in the contract. David Scypinski, senior vice president of Conference Direct, warns against this. He says:

> **Include a liquidated damages clause or a mitigation clause, but never both.** Mitigation is the process of reselling your hotel's loss brought about by a cancellation or through attrition. Mitigated damages can only be collected *after* the dates of the cancelled event. Liquidated damages, on the other hand, are damages collected immediately upon cancellation. Obviously, the best cancellation clause includes a liquidated damages proviso, which is what you should negotiate. Sometimes a customer will insist on a mitigation clause. *Reason:* Both the liquidated and the mitigated clauses discount the amount of revenue you'll be able to recover; if you include both clauses, you'll be penalizing your hotel twice.[4]

In summary, when liquidated damages are specified in the contract, there is no room resale provision. The hotel is not required to mitigate damages (do the best it can to resell guestrooms and meeting space). The law is very clear that if the parties to a contract agree to a liquidated damage clause, the injured party does not have to prove its loss — or whether it was able to mitigate its loss. Even if the hotel resells the rooms in question, the meeting group must pay the hotel the negotiated fee, as the hotel is accepting an amount that is less than the actual damages.

Attrition Clause

Attrition is not the same as cancellation. Attrition refers to under-performance — the difference between contract commitments and actual guestroom pickup, food and beverage spending, and meeting room usage by the convening group. If a meeting group or hotel cancels an event, no rooms or services are used. **Attrition clauses** are included in contracts to define the extent of the meeting group's liability to meet its commitments, and these clauses specify damages owed to the hotel for the convening group's failure to meet those commitments.

Guestroom Attrition. Until recently, it was industry practice for hotels to accept the risk of low pickup by agreeing to hold a block of rooms for a group until a specific cutoff date (generally 30 days). After that date, the unusued rooms reverted to the hotel for resale with no additional liability to the group.

Although some hotels still adhere to this practice, most, especially in periods of high demand, have altered their contracts to include attrition clauses. An attrition clause allows the hotel to collect damages if the actual sleeping rooms used are significantly fewer than the group's **block**, the number of rooms originally reserved for the meeting. Guestrooms that are used are referred to as **pick-up**; unused rooms are known as **slippage.**

Attrition clauses protect hotels from excessive losses due to slippage. John Foster, an attorney specializing in meeting law, states:

> Slippage clauses are making planners a little sharper in their forecasting. You're better off in today's climate to underbook your convention than overbook. It's always easier to go back to the hotel and ask for more rooms than to decrease your block.[5]

The number of rooms for which a planner must pay attrition is negotiable. Kristy Sartorious, Director of Sales for Wyndham Hotels in Dallas, says that they allow a group twenty percent attrition off their room block before penalties are assessed. In contrast, Westin Hotels adjusts the percentage from city to city and by type of property (resort versus downtown). For example, the Westin St. Francis in downtown San Francisco allows a ten percent slippage, while the Westin La Paloma Resort in Tucson allows only five percent. The reason for the difference is that downtown properties can more easily resell rooms to business travelers, while resort hotels primarily rely on vacationers.

Attrition fees are generally based on a sliding scale: the fewer the rooms occupied, the greater the penalty (see Exhibit 5). Attrition fees are best negotiated as an exact dollar amount, and should provide several option dates to review the room block with an agreed-upon percentage of reduction. For example:

The Hotel agrees to hold ample inventory to accommodate the rooms reserved in your group rooms contract. In doing so, the Hotel may be put in a position to turn away other groups that may request rooms for the same dates. Therefore, the Hotel limits the amount of attrition or reduction in the contracted room block.

From one year to nine months prior to arrival, the group will be allowed to reduce their room block by twenty percent without penalty. For reduction over twenty percent, a fee of ___ dollars per room will be assessed. From six months to three months prior to arrival, the group will be allowed to reduce their room bock by ten percent without penalty. For reduction over ten percent, a fee of ___ dollars will be assessed.

Food and Beverage Attrition. In addition to attrition fees for sleeping rooms, some hotels are requiring planners to pay fees for meeting space and food and beverage that are not picked up because the group did not meet its guestroom commitment. A food and beverage attrition clause might read:

The number of catered food and beverage functions and the attendance figures for such functions have been taken into consideration in establishing the room rates for this convention. Should any food and beverage functions be cancelled, the Group will be responsible for 50 percent of the estimated food and beverage revenue lost, based on the minimum catering prices in effect at the time of the meeting multipied by the number of scheduled attendees.

In order to avoid attrition fees resulting from low guestroom pickup and under-attendance at food and beverage functions, many hotels and meeting planners negotiate an **audit clause** that provides the means for gathering information and verifying the group's actual performance.

Audits generally consist of reviewing records both prior to and during an event, and they help meeting planners to plan for future events as well as resolve any disputes that may occur during an event. For example, if a hotel determines that a group has picked up less than 80 percent of the contracted room block, an audit may be conducted to determine how many attendees were actually staying in the hotel — but not in the group's contracted block. This would involve comparing the group's list of attendees with the hotel's in-house guest list. If it is determined that the group's actual attendance (including rooms booked outside the block) met the attrition requirement, attrition damages would not be assessed.

If audit clauses are used, they should be specific and detail how audit information will be used to resolve any discrepancies. The contract should specify when audits will take place, who will conduct the audits (hotel staff, meeting staff, outside auditor), what elements will be audited (room block versus room pick-up, food and beverage commitments versus actual covers, ancillary revenue, and so on), and who will pay for the audit if any costs are involved.

Meeting Room Attrition. A meeting room (function space) rental attrition clause might read:

The hotel is currently holding function space based on the attached Schedule of Events. Should it be necessary for you to cancel or reduce the estimated attendance by more than 25% of any of the major functions listed on the Schedule of Events, the hotel will be entitled to liquidated damages based on the following scale:

> *More than 60 days to 120 days prior to the scheduled date: An amount equal to one-half (1/2) of the estimated food & beverage profit based on the minimum estimate of the total cost of the function.*

Exhibit 5   Attrition Liability Calculator

Attrition Liability Calculator
MINIMUM COMMITMENT (I.E. 80%)

	26-Jun	27-Jun	28-Jun	29-Jun	30-Jun	1-Jul	2-Jul	3-Jul	4-Jul	5-Jul	Total
Contracted Block	20	40	80	120	80	40	20	-	-	-	400
80% commitment	16	32	64	96	64	32	16	0	0	0	320
Your group's actual pickup	10	20	40	60	40	20	10	5	0	0	205
A. Per night liability	6	12	24	36	24	12	6	-5	0	0	115
B. Rooms available for sale in hotel*	0	10	25	40	10	6	10	10	0	0	
Liability (lesser of A or B)	0	10	24	36	10	6	6	-5	0	0	87

Room Profit Percentage (100%, unless negotiated to be lower) **75%**

TOTAL LIABILITY
Single Room Rate $200.00 x 87
Room nights X 75% = $13,050

* Total hotel rooms minus comp rooms, unavailable rooms and all rooms sold that day.

This spreadsheet lists a group's daily contracted room book (across the top from left to right). In this example, the hotel allows a 20 percent attrition rate, so the minimum guarantee is found by multiplying each day's room block by 80 percent. The per-night liability is determined by subtracting the actual pickup from the minimum required pickup.

Row B lists the hotel's total number of rooms available for sale for each night of the meeting, and the group is required to pay only for lost profit at 75 percent for each night. For example, on June 26, the hotel's rooms were sold out, so the group did not have any liability on that day. Adding the totals across, however, shows that the group owes the hotel an attrition fee for 87 rooms. At a room rate of $200 per night, the group's total attrition fee amounts to $13,050.

Source: From the *Experient Guide*, published by *Convene* magazine. Used with permission.

> *Less than 60 days prior to arrival date: An amount equal to 75% of the*
> *estimated food & beverage profit based on the minimum estimate of the*
> *total cost of the function.*

These attrition clauses clearly spell out what is required of the group and the specific damages that will be levied should the group fail to live up to its contract. Many meeting planners are vocal against these clauses, claiming that attritition clauses force them to look into a crystal ball. Richard Granger, meeting planner for Allmerica Financial, explains:

> Five years ago you didn't see attrition clauses. Now you're lucky to be
> permitted ten to fifteen percent shrinkage. Attrition clauses are not only
> tougher, but broader. They used to cover only room slippage, but now
> include food and beverage costs too.[6]

Hotels, citing their need to be financially accountable, feel that such clauses are justified and prevent the unethical practice of meeting planners overestimating room counts to obtain additional concessions.

Arbitration/Dispute Resolution

Arbitration is the most commonly used form of **dispute resolution** (other means of resolving contract disputes include mediation and litigation). Arbitration clauses are often used because arbitration provides an efficient, timely, and relatively inexpensive alternative to litigation, which is both time-consuming and expensive due to crowded court calendars and the costs of a trial. An arbitration rather than a court action is usually in the best interests of both the hotel and the meeting planner. A typical arbitration clause might read:

Any controversy or claim arising out of or relating to this agreement, or the breach thereof, shall be settled by arbitration in accordance with the Rules of the American Arbitration Association, and judgment upon the award rendered by the Arbitrator may be entered by any court having jurisdiction thereof.

Warranty of Authority

The principles of agency law specify that if both parties are authorized to sign a contract for a meeting, the contract is still binding on both the hotel and the meeting group if one or both of the signers is no longer with their employer. A warranty of authority clause states that the signers have been granted authority by their respective organizations to enter into an agreement. Such a clause is especially relevant given the turnover of both hotel salespeople and meeting planners and in light of the considerable time frame between the signing of the agreement and the execution of the event.

A warranty of authority clause might read:

The Group Name and the person signing this Agreement on its behalf represent and warrant that the undersigned person is an authorized and appointed agent of the Group Name, fully empowered to bind the Group Name to all provisions contained in the agreement, and that no further action is required on the Group Name's part to enter into this agreement.

This agreement shall be binding upon the Group Name and its successors and assigns.

Insurance/Indemnification

Most hotels stipulate that the meeting group must agree to carry adequate liability insurance that protects the hotel against claims arising from the group's activities conducted in the hotel during the convention. In doing business with associations and trade shows, a hotel incurs specific liability in its relationship with trade show exhibitors. Although exhibitors sublease hotel space from the association or trade show, the hotel should require the exhibitor to sign a "hold harmless" or liability agreement that confirms that the hotel is not responsible for damages or theft of material or equipment. Some hotels extend this to deny accountability for accidents occuring in public areas that are not the result of negligence by the hotel.

Convention hotels also request that a copy of the meeting group's exhibitor contract be submitted to the hotel's convention services department prior to its printing and distribution. The reason for this is to ensure the meeting group and the hotel are protected.

An insurance clause might read:

The group acknowledges that the hotel and its owners do not maintain insurance covering property brought into the hotel by exhibitors and that it is the sole responsibility of the exhibitor to obtain insurance covering such losses. The group shall give written notice of such to any exhibitors. The group is responsible for submitting to the hotel an executed release of liability from each exhibitor.

Indemnification is a word found in many meeting contracts. To indemnify means to protect. An **indemnification clause** (hold harmless clause) provides mutual protection. The hotel and the meeting group indemnify each other. A typical indemnification clause might read:

Each party agrees to indemnify and hold harmless the other from any and all loss, damage, or expense (including attorneys' fees) arising from the negligence or willful misconduct of the indemnifying party, its agents and employees in the performance of its duties and responsibilities under this agreement.

This clause states that each party will be responsible for its own negligence and that each party agrees to hold the other party harmless if the actions of one party cause the other party to be sued or suffer loss.

Other Contract Matters

In addition to the topics covered above, meeting planners may have other concerns, or events may have special requirements. In these cases, additional clauses covering these issues are often added to completed, written contracts as **addendums**, additions that must be signed by both parties for the addendum to be a binding legal document.

Some of these additional clauses may cover such topics as:

- Americans with Disabilities Act requirements
- Overbooking and relocation of "walked" guests
- Construction/renovation

Americans with Disabilities Act (ADA) requirements may be an important aspect of events at which attendees may be visually or hearing impaired or have mobility issues. Under the ADA, both the hotel and the meeting planner are responsible ensuring that guests with disabilities can have equal access to the facilities. Generally, the hotel is responsible for public areas, guestrooms, and restrooms, while the meeting planner must ensure that function room layouts are adequate and special needs are accommodated (a sign language interpreter for the deaf, large-print materials, and so on).

An ADA clause should clearly spell out the special needs that must be addressed, and such clauses may also require that the hotel be in compliance with the ADA and that it is committed to accommodating guests with disabilities and special needs.

Overbooking and relocation of "walked" guests are covered in clauses to establish the requirements for the hotel to make alternative arrangements and/or pay damages when it is unable to honor a booked reservation. In some cases, the hotel will offer several alternatives, such as booking the "walked" guest at a comparable hotel at no charge, providing monetary consideration, or offering special services, such as complimentary shuttle service to the guest for each day he or she is displaced from the hotel. Other considerations may be providing an upgraded room at no extra charge when the guest can return to the hotel and crediting the room toward the group's block.

Construction/renovation clauses may be included if an event is scheduled far in advance of the signing of the contract. These clauses generally stipulate that the hotel and its facilities will be in the same or better condition as they were when the contract was signed, and they detail damages if facilities are under construction or substantially altered when the group convenes. In most cases, the clause will specify that the hotel will notify the group of any changes in the condition of the premises — especially changes that may affect the portion of the facility to be used by the group. As with other clauses, the construction/renovation clause specifies each party's obligations in the event that changes will disrupt the contracted event.

Contract Standardization

To facilitate the formerly time-consuming process of contract negotiation and to meet the requests of meeting planners for more consistency when dealing with properties, the industry has responded with an important trend: the standardization of contracts and other meetings-related paperwork. Following the introduction of the Marriott Meetings Network (see Exhibit 6), a number of chains have developed their own standardized forms and services (see box titled "Contract Standardization").

Standardized contracts, which are most prevalent in the area of small meetings due to their short lead time, essentially provide a heightened degree of communication by standardizing language and covering all relevant issues, and most meeting planners are very receptive to them. Blanca Diaz, manager of corporate event planning at McGraw-Hill in New York, says:

> If I receive a contract that is not that customer friendly, I have to run it by
> the legal department and it delays the signing of the contract. In the past,
> it was nightmarish. Now I'll approve some of the contracts on sight.[7]

There are drawbacks, of course. Some meeting planners, especially independent ones, prefer to use their own forms. Their point of view is that every event is unique and no one form can handle all individual group needs. But their perspective is being overshadowed by the sea of planners who welcome not only standardized contracts, but other standardized forms and services as well — event resumes, banquet event orders (BEOs), and billing procedures and computerized access to such areas as rooming lists. Diana Johnson, conference administrator for 28 events in different cities across the nation, says:

Exhibit 6   Standardized Services for the Meetings Industry

In response to meeting planners' needs for consistency when negotiating with hotels within its chain, Marriott developed the Marriott Meetings Network after two years of intensive customer research. This computerized system enables properties within the chain to standardize contracts and eliminates the need for meeting planners to update contracts. Since a group's paperwork is stored in the chain's computer system, it can be easily retrieved and previous histories can be checked to ensure that the group's requirements are met.

Contract Standardization

Hilton: A leader in standardization, with development of a standardized group resume 20 years ago, the chain now offers standardized contracts and general meeting forms at 52 corporate-owned and managed properties.

Hyatt: Developed Meeting Connection program featuring standardized contract for groups of fewer than 100; now, 104 properties have standardized contracts for larger groups. Hyatt hotels also mail out their standardized resume on computer disks, enabling planners to enter meeting specs into the program and mail or e-mail documents back.

Marriott: Led the industry in meeting paperwork standardization with the Marriott Meetings Network, a computerized network system providing standardized contracts, master billing forms, group resumes, and post-convention reports (see Exhibit 6). Thirty-six of the chain's properties in the United States, Mexico, and Canada offer this service.

Ritz-Carlton: All meeting-related paperwork — contracts, group resumes, banquet event orders, billing formats, and post-convention reports — are standardized at 30 Ritz-Carlton properties.

Renaissance: Offers standardized meeting paperwork (contracts, billing formats, group resumes, and post-convention reports) at 49 Renaissance properties in the United States.

Westin: Provides standardized forms and offers Grouplink, a computerized system that enables planners to enter group rooming lists themselves.

> Once you've read the standard BEO you know the format. You know right where to look to find the same things; meeting setups, guarantee policies, set menus. You don't have to scrutinize it as much.[8]

The standardization of these previously time-consuming preconvention documents and procedures enables both the meeting planner and the convention staff at individual properties to concentrate on servicing the event and offers yet another benefit besides saving time and money — meetings clout. Jack Breisacher, vice president of group sales for Renaissance Hotels and Resorts, explains:

> After all, the customer is often spending a few hundred thousand dollars with us, and all they want to know is how much money was spent in each area. Then they'll take that information to a property next year and say, "Here's what we did, and based on that, here's what we need at this time." It becomes a solid negotiating tool.[9]

Multiple-Meetings Contracts

Negotiating multiple-meetings contracts is becoming commonplace in the hospitality industry. These contracts, which schedule business over a period of one to several years, have grown in popularity — especially with corporate meeting planners, who laud them as time- and cost-saving. A planner from a healthcare organization, for example, says she signs a multiple-meetings contract with a major hotel chain for her group's 200 educational seminars held every year around the country. The contract guarantees a price that is a percentage off the rack rate at each hotel and saves time, eliminating the need to negotiate separate contracts.

Best Practices

Marriott Contracts with MetLife for 15 Incentive Meetings Over a Two-Year Period

MetLife, a large insurance company that previously held its meetings in a number of different hotels, signed a deal with Marriott International to book 15 incentive meetings into the chain's Marriott, JW Marriott, and Ritz-Carlton properties across the country over a two-year period. The deal, which represents 15,000 room nights, came about because MetLife's recognition programs represent some of the company's biggest meetings, and the company's management felt that these meetings were too important for a "cookie cutter" approach.

In addition to the benefits of a meetings consolidation plan that would both save money and create consistency, MetLife gained major clout as a potential client when it put all 15,000 of its room nights on the table to potential hotel companies. Bob Pizzute, AVP, conference planning and event services at MetLife in New York, says:

> When we took an enterprise approach to meeting planning, where all of our distribution channels come to one source for meetings, we became a much larger player in the market.

Negotiations for the actual terms of the contract took months, as there were hundreds of details to be worked out, including space, rates, and concessions. Jeff Calmus, CMP, director of conference planning and event services for MetLife, says:

> Rates were different based on the time of the year and availability, but we had developed concessions that every hotel agreed to.

The successful deal benefited both parties, as MetLife got as good a deal for a 220-room-night program as for a 3,800-room-night program, and Marriott not only benefited from the large piece of business but may see additional income, as Pizzute says he will go to hotel chains with future RFPs. The win/win negotiation between the parties on their first multiple meetings deal (and Marriott's successful execution of the meetings for which it contracted) will likely result in the chain being a strong contender for MetLife's future business.
Source: Alison Hall, "Big Deal," *Insurance Conference Planner.*

Another advantage for the meeting planner is meeting clout; a hotel is usually more open to making concessions for a planner who schedules a great deal of business. Judi McLaughlin, CMP, of Martiz McGettigan, one of the largest meeting management firms in the world, states:

> In many companies, meeting planning is fragmented and decentralized. One of our clients found that it used 29 different properties in Chicago in one year for some 70 meetings. Through consolidated planning, the company has named ten preferred hotels in that city.
>
> The benefits to the company are guaranteed discounts in pricing, overall agreement to standard contracting terms and conditions, increased efficiencies throughout the planning process, and better-quality meetings. And the preferred properties are certain to see a dramatic increase in their market share of the company's business.[10]

There are, of course, some disadvantages for meeting planners, including the difficulty of accurately predicting meeting attendance (unless attendance is mandatory), future developments, such as company downsizing or mergers, and being "locked in" by contracts. In the last instance, the meeting planner is bound by the previously negotiated multi-meetings contract and cannot take advantage of opportunities that arise when other properties can provide the same services at a lower rate.

For hotels, multiple-meetings contracts offer the advantage of guaranteed business, but there is also a major disadvantage: perhaps another group comes along that would generate more rooms or food and beverage revenue for the property. If the space is tied up, the property has no recourse but to let the new business go. It is imperative, therefore, that hotels consider multiple-meetings contracts carefully, weighing the proposed multiple-meetings business while maintaining a degree of flexibility in these contracts, especially those that are a year or more out. Other factors, such as the history and stability of the group or possible business developments on either the part of the group (a possible merger in the group's future, for example) or the property (perhaps the obtaining of new, more lucrative business) should also be considered before entering into multiple-meetings contracts.

Summary

If doing business by letter of agreement/contract seems complex and detailed, think of this format as a checklist or order form. Arranging for a convention requires more than ordering a certain number of guestrooms. Your letter of agreement shows you, the hotelier, what the client expects and also shows the client his or her responsibility. It works out well when thought and time are given to each detail.

The first letter of agreement/contract may be the hardest to write. After you get it polished, save it as a sample. It will save much work if that polished letter and its various clauses are individually stored in a word processor file so that they may be used when you are formulating new contracts or letters of agreement.

As you can see, the hotel industry is working hard to deal with meeting planners on a highly professional basis and to make the process of securing profitable meetings business easier through the development of "win-win" contracts and the standardization of meetings-related services.

Endnotes

1. Howard Feiertag, "We're Into a Seller's Market Again, So Watch Those Contracts," *Hotel & Motel Management*, June 21, 2004, p. 12.

2. James Goldberg, "Seller's Market Means Tougher Terms," *Corporate Meetings & Incentives*, June 2006, p. 28.

3. Carolyn Cotton, "Liquidated Damage Provision Reflects Compromise on Hotel's Part," *Convene*.

4. Correspondence with David C. Scypinski, senior vice president of industry relations, Starwood Hotels.

5. Mary Ann McNulty, "Be Prepared for a Slippage Clause," *Meeting News*.

6. Melinda Legis, "Killer Contracts," *Successful Meetings*.

7. Kenneth Hein, "Standardization Efforts Paying Off," *Meeting News*.

8. Ibid.

9. Ibid.

10. Alison Hall, "Fewer Suppliers, Better Deals," *Corporate Meetings & Incentives*, July 2004, pp. 16–20.

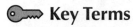 **Key Terms**

addendum—An addition to a completed written document. Must be signed by all parties involved in the contract to become part of a legally binding document. Sometimes called an amendment.

arbitration—The settling of a disagreement by the review and decision of an arbitrator rather than using the courts.

arrival/departure pattern—Anticipated date and times of the arrival and departure of a meeting group's members.

attrition clause—Allows the hotel to impose damages if the actual guestrooms used are significantly less than the rooms blocked. Can also apply to food and beverage and meeting room rental.

audit clause—A clause that allows one or both parties in a contract to perform audits to measure and validate certain aspects in the terms of the contract. Audits ideally should take place through the term of the contract to avoid potential problems from arising.

block—The number of guestrooms reserved for a group.

cancellation clause—Provision in the contract that specifies damages that apply for both parties should either party terminate the agreement. A cancellation is a breach of the contract.

Consumer Price Index—An index that compares the changes of the costs of basic goods and services with the prices previously set in a fixed-base period.

customer lifetime value—The value of profits expected from a customer's future purchases. A corporation or association meeting planner who is satisfied and books several meetings with your property over his or her buying lifetime is more valuable than a one-time purchaser. If the satisfied customer refers other meeting planners, the value would be even greater.

cutoff date—The designated date when the buyer (upon request) must release or add to his or her function room or guestroom commitment.

dispute resolution—The means by which the parties entering into a contract agree to resolve any disputes. These means may include mediation, arbitration, litigation, or other ways to resolve problems.

early departure fee—A set fee charged to a hotel or conference center guest who checks out earlier than the original departure date originally agreed upon.

flow chart—Indicates the arrival and departure pattern of the meeting participants.

group ceiling—The maximum number of guestrooms that can be allocated to groups on a particular day. Sometimes referred to as the hotel's group room allotment.

indemnification clause—Contract clause that specifies compensation for injury, loss, or damage. Also referred to as a hold harmless clause.

inquiry questionnaire—Questionnaire requesting a postconvention critique from hotels used in the past by specific meeting groups.

letter of agreement/contract—Letter from the buyer accepting the hotel's proposal. No legal agreement/contract exists unless both parties have accepted the hotel's proposal.

liquidated damage clause—A contract clause that specifies in advance the exact amount of money parties agree to pay in the event of breach of contract.

master account—One folio for the group on which all charges are accumulated. Also called the master folio.

mitigation of damage clause—A contract clause that requires parties to determine damages after the dates of the canceled event. Mitigated damages are actual damages.

pick-up—Number of guestrooms actually used out of a room block.

plus, plus—Addition of taxes and service charges to the standard prices charged for food and beverage. Designated on a catering contract and a BEO by the notation "++."

preamble—An introductory statement at the beginning of a contract. Identifies the parties involved, a statement of intent to enter into a contract, the name of the meeting or event, and performance dates. Also called a recital or background in some contracts.

proposal letter—A letter sent by the hotel before the letter of agreement or contract that spells out exactly what the customer will receive.

request for proposal (RFP)—Action initiated by the meeting planner for an offer or bid for hotel services.

release date—The date beyond which the hotel is free to rent the unused function space to other groups.

slippage—The number of guestrooms not used from the original reserved block.

termination clause—Contract clause that limits liability should the convention be prevented due to circumstances beyond either party's control. Sometimes referred to as an Act of God clause or a force majeure clause. When a contract is terminated, neither party is considered in breach of the contract.

 # Review Questions

1. Distinguish between a proposal letter and a letter of agreement (contract).

2. What elements should be considered when developing a contract?

3. What is the master account? In what ways is this account billed?

4. What is a damage clause? An attrition clause? What is the difference between a termination clause and a cancellation clause? How extensively are each of these clauses used?

5. What is the Convention Industry Council? What groups make up its membership and what is their role in the convention industry?

6. What are standardized contracts? What types of properties typically use them? What are the pros and cons of using standardized contracts?

7. What are the advantages and disadvantages of negotiating multiple-meetings contracts?

 # Additional References

Hospitality Law, Third Edition, Steven Barth, John Wiley & Sons, 2008.
   www.hospitality@wiley.com

Meeting Manager Standards and Meeting Coordinator Standards, by the Meeting Professionals International Canadian Council and the Government of Canada, Human Resources and Skills Development Canada.
   www.mpiweb.org

Internet Sites

For more information, visit the following Internet sites. Internet addresses can change without notice. If a site is no longer available at the address listed below, a search engine can be used to find the new address or additional, related sites.

American Bar Association Alternative Dispute Resolution Section
www.abanet.org/dispute/drlinks.html

Convention Industry Council
www.conventionindustry.org

Hospitality Sales and Marketing Association International (HSMAI)
www.hsmai.org

Chapter 10 Outline

Competencies

1. Describe the importance of serving convention groups well, and discuss who should coordinate hotel service to groups. (pp. 325–328)

2. Describe the duties and responsibilities of a convention service manager. (pp. 328–334)

3. Describe the duties and responsibilities of various convention service staff positions, and outline the responsibilities of convention service managers at convention and visitors bureaus. (pp. 334–337)

4. Identify issues related to the transfer of responsibility for servicing a group account from a hotel salesperson to the convention service manager. (pp. 338–341)

5. Describe the role of the convention service manager in meeting planning, execution, and evaluation. (pp. 341–343)

The Role of Convention Service Professionals

Devon Walter, CMP
Convention Services Manager
Sheraton El Conquistador
Tucson, Arizona

"Convention service professionals have only one job, and that is to give the meeting professional the best meeting ever. The keys to producing a great meeting are communication and planning. The convention services personnel and meeting professional become a team, and communication between team members is critical. Pre-planning is so important to the success of the meeting. There will always be some little glitch when the meeting is on-site, and that is so much easier to deal with when everything else is running smoothly—because it has been PLANNED. A convention services professional can expect to spend over 40 hours a week at the facility when there is a group in house. Depending on a group's evening activities, the convention service manager may be at the facility quite late, checking on a reception, dinner, or dance. But when the meeting professional and you sit down to conduct the post-convention evaluation and the former says it was the best one ever, that is tremendously rewarding. For those who enjoy working with new people daily, learning about new organizations, working hard, multi-tasking, delegating, administering, coordinating, juggling, creating, and working with details, this is the PERFECT job!"

10   The Service Function

SECURING A CONVENTION is only the beginning; once business has been booked, you must deliver what was promised. How a convention goes out of a hotel is equally—or even more—important as obtaining the group's business. A hotel salesperson does not sell just guestrooms, meeting space, and complicated audiovisual equipment—his or her most important product is reassurance; reassurance that the hotel is capable of handling the group's business. To a great extent, the meeting planner's job depends on how well the hotel does its job.

Hard work and many dollars are invested in advertising and promotional material in an effort to recruit group business. Yet, satisfied meeting planners and delegates are the best and most economical advertising medium. If the hotel performs well, the meeting planner will likely return to the property. Delegates are well-traveled today and expect more from hotels. If your hotel has made a favorable impression, planners may recommend it to their peers, and delegates may stay with you on return visits—and recommend that their business associates and friends do the same.

Since nothing attracts another piece of group business more than a satisfied convention, it is crucial that all promises made in the selling process be fulfilled. An indelible impression will be made when the hotel provides service that is above and beyond the preconvention promises.

Service Is the Key

Sometimes, the service follow-through is regarded as an afterthought to the heavy emphasis placed on selling a convention or meeting. But failure in the essential service phase can be costly. A meeting planner evaluates the success of his or her convention on the extent to which the hotel's commitments were kept. Lack of communication, poorly trained or indifferent employees, failure to heed details, and rude responses to requests are all detriments that may result in lost future business.

How might the hotel better serve the convention group? Most important is a well-trained and courteous staff with a service attitude. The hotel industry is essentially a people business and it is important to communicate the property's willingness to assist the meeting planner during both the selling and servicing process (see box titled "Selling and Servicing Small Meetings"). Hotel staff members should be made aware of the importance of convention delegates and should be trained to understand that nothing short of top performance is expected.

You can build goodwill in other ways—make arrangements with labor if exhibits are used, obtain any official permissions that are required by local government departments such as police or fire, and assist with transportation needs. Help convention delegates schedule their time and keep them informed about the facilities in the hotel. Book special entertainment, arrange tours to points of interest, and provide the highest-quality food and beverage service possible. In short, give convention delegates every reason for staying at your property—and returning in the future.

SELLING AND SERVICING SMALL MEETINGS

The cartoon above humorously depicts the importance of a single hotel contact person, particularly for small meetings, whose planners require easy accessibility to a source of assistance. After the Marriott Corporation conducted an extensive research study of its business, it found that the majority of its properties relied on small meetings to generate group business. The information gathered indicated that the majority of Marriott's group bookings consisted of simple catering events involving room rental, refreshment breaks, continental breakfasts, and a single luncheon. The chain, which recognized that planners staging small meetings look for a single hotel contact, responded with the introduction of a new position, the executive meeting manager. This person, who is responsible for booking and servicing small meetings and catering functions, is viewed as a one-stop shopping source to simplify planning for the small group client.

Other chains followed suit, either designating individuals to work one-on-one with meeting planners or developing programs designed to help planners of small meetings. Hyatt, for example, introduced the "Hyatt Meeting Connection," which offers a toll-free number, a fax number, and a web address to enable a meeting planner to get in touch with the hotel quickly. After the planner provides pertinent details on the date and size of the meeting, the planner is contacted by a Hyatt meeting connection manager who assists with meeting details.

Hilton's program, "Hilton Direct," is targeted to inexperienced meeting planners, as is Sheraton's "One Stop" program. These sources simplify planning to set the stage for suggestive selling and creative presentations, which, in turn, build repeat business and revenues.

With Renaissance Hotels and Resorts' "Meetings Express" service, a sales manager handles meeting details for planners, including guestrooms, function rooms, and audiovisual services. Other programs include Westin's "Westin One Call," Omni's "Omni Express," and Wyndham Hotels' "Wyndham One."

HISTORY OF CONVENTION SERVICES

1960s — *Beginning of the convention service position, but with limited authority.* Salespeople were now confronted with the problem of spending a considerable amount of their time servicing groups. Feeling the need to concentrate more time on the selling of the hotel and its facilities, many sales managers turned servicing over to either the sales secretary or the lowest-level salesperson.

1970s — *Role of convention service manager increased in importance.* As the number and complexity of the meetings held grew annually, so did the importance of the convention service manager. This increased recognition was advanced by the Society of Corporate Meeting Professionals, which opened its membership ranks to convention service managers.

1980s — *Gained industry respect.* Convention service managers formed their own association (seven hundred strong) called the Association for Convention Operations Management (ACOM). Meeting planners came to rely on the dedication, knowledge, and hard work of the convention service department.

1990s — *Elevated to the hotel's executive committee.* Now most of the major hotel chains have a corporate-level position for convention services. Within the hotel, convention service managers generally report to marketing, occasionally to food and beverage or catering, and now increasingly directly to the general manager. In hotels that look to conventions for a major portion of their room nights, the director of convention services is part of the hotel's executive committee.

2000s — *Serve as meeting consultants.* The role of the convention service manager has expanded beyond delivering meetings service. Increasingly, meeting planners look for partners who can consult and present customized solutions to their problems. Most hotel chains have raised the bar, requiring their convention service managers to become certified with the same education and training as the customer.

Regardless of how smoothly a program is planned, snags and slipups inevitably occur. If your hotel helps meeting planners solve these problems, future business is nearly always assured. It may be necessary to shuffle meeting rooms around, help find a last-minute substitute speaker, or prepare a special entree for the wife of the chairman of the board. The attitude with which you accept these common occurrences will, to a great extent, determine the location of next year's convention. The professionalism your staff demonstrates is the hotel's best promotion for future business from the convention organizer and it increases the likelihood of business referrals. If you conquer any crisis that threatens the flow of the meeting, the parting handshake may well be accompanied by the meeting planner's promise, "We'll see you next year."

Who Services?

One of the frequently discussed issues in convention management is the extent to which the salesperson should be involved in the servicing process. The structure of the hotel staff is based on how this issue is resolved.

Some hotels say that a salesperson is just that, and that he or she shouldn't become involved in servicing the client. They claim that the service function is a specialty distinct from selling, and that there is a more efficient use of staff and a higher rebooking percentage when salespeople spend 100 percent of their time selling. Howard Feiertag, a veteran hotel salesperson, says:

> In my opinion, the person who books the business is not the best person to follow through on the details. Large hotels should pass the booking to a convention services manager. Small hotels should pass the food and beverage details to catering and the rooms details to a rooms division manager or front office manager. Although salespeople often do not like to let go of a piece of business, they should turn over the minutiae of the group to the operations staff, remove themselves from the details, and use their skills to book more business.[1]

Others hold that the convention salesperson should handle the sales and servicing completely. They suggest that the sales representative should follow up all hotel visits, write up the actual bookings, and coordinate the servicing of the group during its stay at the hotel. Their position is that the sales manager should sell, arrange, and work with the meeting from beginning to end. They feel that the salesperson who does not get involved in servicing may be concerned only with putting business on the books, thus perhaps making hasty promises that are impossible to keep.

Which approach should you practice? Our experience says "the best approach is the one that works." No one procedure is best for all situations. However, if the size of the hotel justifies an in-house convention service manager, we support separation of sales and service.

The Convention Service Manager

Throughout the text, we have taken the position that the servicing responsibility is handled by the convention service manager. Such a practice assures the association, corporate, or nonprofit executive that whatever his or her requirements—reservations, banquet, meeting room setup—there is one individual with complete authority and responsibility for his or her meeting.

The title *convention service manager* has not been adopted by all hotels. Many use such other titles as conference or convention or service coordinator, convention manager, event coordinator, and, at many smaller properties, banquet or catering manager.

Regardless of the title, the position carries a lot of prestige and a hefty amount of responsibility (Exhibit 1 gives a sample job description that lists the numerous duties of a convention service manager). If any one person can make or break a conference, it is the convention service manager, often referred to as "the person who makes things happen." He or she is the meeting planner's contact person, and so should be readily available to handle all of the convening group's on-the-spot needs. Quite simply, he or she is the single most important communication link between the meeting planner and the hotel.

The convention service manager should not be satisfied with just selling rooms and food. He or she must be a problem solver and an excellent communicator. The convention service manager should request full and detailed information so the hotel can better serve the group. Likewise, the hotel should communicate accurate data to the client.

Horst Schulze, the former president of Ritz-Carlton Hotels, says:

> Hoteliers must understand that a meeting planner has put his job on the line by selecting their hotel. The convention service manager (CSM)

Exhibit 1   Sample Job Description for Convention Service Manager

Job Title:	Convention and Conference Service Manager
Reports to:	Director of Convention and Conference Service
Department:	Convention and Conference Service

Summary of Position

Services all convention and conference groups as assigned by the Director of Convention Service. Plans and coordinates all arrangements (i.e., golf bookings, audiovisual needs, etc.) related to assigned groups to ensure the success of the convention and to promote repeat business.

Scope

This position is responsible for identifying and communicating the needs of the customer to the hotel departments to ensure proper service throughout the hotel operation for assigned groups.

Objectives/ Responsibilities

A.   Plans and executes conventions and conferences as the primary customer contact for assigned groups.   *25% of time*

B.   Coordinates and distributes all interdepartmental paperwork necessary for the successful implementation of assigned groups.
25% of time

C.   Oversees activities of assigned groups, and functions as the onsite contact for the Meeting Planner.   *15% of time*

D.   Assists with training the Convention and Conference Coordinator as assigned by the Director of Convention and Conference Service.
15% of time

E.   Attends daily and/or weekly meetings as assigned by the Director as well as arranges and conducts Pre-Convention and Conference meetings for assigned convention groups.   *15% of time*

F.   Assists in preparation of forecasts and budgets.   *3% of time*

G.   Performs additional tasks as assigned by Director.   *2% of time*

Supervision Exercised

Directly supervises:	Assigned Clerical Staff
Indirectly supervises:	Convention and Conference Coordinator
	Floor Manager
	Support Staff
	Function Book Coordinator

Supervision Received

Responsible to the Director of Convention and Conference Service

Responsibility/ Authority

Employee Relations:
Responsible for communicating and following through with hotel management to ensure that the sales commitment is being fulfilled. Distributes written communications (resumes, event orders) detailing the needs of the customer and the sales commitment. Maintains effective relationship with Sales and Service Staff as well as all department heads.

Materials or Products:
Maintains up-to-date group files to ensure proper coordination of sales commitment as well as customer needs. Maintains trace system for these files.

Equipment:
Assists in properly using and maintaining an adequate inventory of meeting equipment to properly service all functions.

Exhibit 1   *(continued)*

	Financial: Responsible for maximizing revenues associated with meetings for assigned group files as well as maximizing function space usage.
	Business Contacts: Maintains proper communications between groups, outside vendors, and hotel staff. Also responsible for establishing customer relationships that will encourage repeat business.
Preferred Knowledge/ Qualifications	Equivalent Education Level: College degree (or equivalent convention and conference service experience) required.
	Experience: A minimum of two years in convention and conference coordination with exposure to office procedures; experience in function room setups and service; strong interpersonal skills and organizational skills.
	Knowledge Required: Function space configuration, room setups, maximizing space, art of negotiating and selling. General knowledge of hotel management, operations, and facilities.

must build a quality product around that one customer, specifically and individually. The CSM must see himself as a true partner and loyal assistant to that planner. To supply a defect-free meeting, there must be communication between the planner and the hotelier. This communication helps the hotelier understand the planner's desired outcome for the meeting.[2]

The role of convention service manager has grown beyond service to meeting consultant at some hotels (see Exhibit 2). David Kassel, CMP, senior convention service manager, Walt Disney World Dolphin Hotel, states,

> I try to educate the planner on how to do events with a little more creativity. A lot of my expertise is anticipating needs—having the forethought to put myself in the planner's place. It also means that I find alternatives to save them dollars.[3]

Ideally, the convention service manager has the authority to get the job done and to get it done fast. The Loews Hotel chain, for example, has increased the stature of the chain's convention service managers, promoting them to the executive committees of their respective hotels (the executive committee is made up of senior-level hotel managers who report directly to the general manager, and may include the director of food and beverage, the controller, the resident manager, the director of marketing, and the director of convention services). Jonathan M. Tisch, the President and CEO of Loews Hotels, said the change came about because *he listened to meeting planners.* Meeting planners are able to rest much easier when they have the assurance that their liaison has authority within the hotel as well as the responsibility to fulfill their needs.

Leroy Smith, association executive of the National Automobile Association, has suggested that the convention service department should report directly to the hotel's general manager, not to the director of sales.[4] He suggests that hotels should have an organizational structure that gives the convention service manager line control over the functions of the

Exhibit 2   Convention Service Managers as Event Planners

MEETING YOUR NEEDS EVERY TIME

The next time you consider a meeting in the Phoenix area, give us a call and we will help you create an unforgettable event. With our two convenient locations, luxurious amenities, versatile meeting space, and first-class service, the Marriott is the perfect place for any event - business or social. Our professional staff will plan everything for you, down to the last detail and deliver impressive results. We offer up-to-date audiovisual technology and superb catering capabilities to complement our hallmark Marriott service.

IT'S THE MARRIOTT WAY.℠

The Buttes, a Marriott Resort
2000 Westcourt Way
Tempe, Arizona 85282
(602) 225-9000
marriott.com/phxtm

Phoenix Airport Marriott
1101 North 44th Street
Phoenix, Arizona 85008
(602) 273-7373
marriott.com/phxap

Call 1-800-MARRIOTT or visit
marriott.com for more information
or to make a reservation.

© 2007 Marriott International, Inc.

Today's convention service managers do not just sell function space and food and beverage functions. Hotels have recognized the importance of assisting meeting planners with both large and small events, and most CSMs today take an active part in the planning and execution of events. This ad for Marriott Hotels & Resorts promotes the services offered to meeting planners by The Buttes, a Marriott Resort in Tempe, Arizona, including a highly trained hotel staff that will assist in planning every detail to ensure a successful event.
Source: Courtesy of Marriott International, Inc.

front desk, housekeeping, banquet, and food and beverage departments as related to conventions.

The working hours of the person in charge of convention service are often very long (see box titled "A Day in the Life of a Convention Service Manager"). Bill Tobin says of the time he was convention service manager at Caesars Palace in Las Vegas, "I wanted to give the meeting planner the impression that I never went home." One hour before every function, he checked out the facilities with the group's coordinator. This is a commendable policy, but convention managers typically work on three to five meetings simultaneously, each in different stages of completion. This work schedule underscores the need for convention service managers to possess the abilities to organize and multitask, but, no matter how skilled they may be, convention service managers often find they have little time for themselves. Cutting still further into time off are the preconvention and post-convention meetings often scheduled for weekends.

But there are rewards for these long hours. In addition to the salary paid by the hotel, the convention service manager may receive compensation for long hours in the form of gifts and tips from the meeting planner. Association and corporate executives have been known to be extremely generous in saying thanks for a job well done. Further remuneration is sometimes received from the hotel. The Sheraton Waikiki, recognizing the importance of the convention service manager, has given this individual a suite in the hotel. Sheraton Hotels, like a growing number of chains, has also established advisory boards made up of meeting planners to help the chain respond to the needs and concerns of meeting planners. One of these concerns centers on the role of the convention service manager; in many cases, the advisory boards recommend giving convention service managers more authority to ensure that meeting details can be worked out through a single contact person. Brian Stevens, former Vice President, Sales, Hilton Hotels, agrees:

> Today, more than ever, hotels need to make sure their customers work with the most experienced, most highly trained convention service managers possible—or there simply won't be any customers after a while.[5]

How does one become a convention service manager? Most have advanced through either the banquet or front office departments, where they were exposed to the problems frequently encountered in group business. Then some alert sponsor placed him or her over the department. Often the next step up the corporate rung is to convention sales. The salesperson who has had experience in group servicing knows what can be promised and what can be delivered, and thus is a most valued employee. However, many are not sure this move to sales is a promotion, and more and more managers are staying with convention services—or even becoming meeting planners themselves.

Another career move for some is promotion to resident manager. This is not surprising, since the convention service manager interacts with virtually all other hotel departments. In a recent speech, Joyce Inderbitzin of Hilton's Corporate Convention Services estimated that 70 percent of Hilton's general managers were convention service managers at one time in their careers.

Increased Recognition

The convention service manager's position has steadily been elevated in status in hotel organizations. The Society of Corporate Meeting Professionals invited convention service managers to join their ranks and *Successful Meetings* instituted an annual Convention Service Manager of the Year award.

A Day in the Life of a Convention Service Manager

Melissa LaBarbera, the director of convention services at the Fairmont Chicago, becomes involved in each event when the sales department turns over the business to convention services. On a typical day, LaBarbera calls planners to introduce herself; sends out pertinent information on such items as exhibits, production capabilities, and menus; schedules pre-con and post-con meetings; and coordinates event details with other hotel departments. And, during an event, she is personally available to meeting planners and their attendees.

"I make sure I am involved the day [attendees] arrive until the day they leave," LaBarbera says. "Some hotels have 'floor' people who are on site at all times during the meeting. Here, we—the CSMs — are on the floor, right along with the banqueting team." Ultimately, she adds, "It's our job to make the planner look good."

To demonstrate how CSMs do just that, *Meetings & Conventions* magazine followed Patricia Sousa, the conference services manager at the 319-room Omni Berkshire Palace in New York City, on a Thursday in June. Sousa began her day at 9:00 a.m., when she entered her cubicle to catch up on daily reports, telephone calls, and e-mails, and then forwarded pertinent details to back-of-the house departments. Since there were already two financial meetings in-house, and a pharmaceutical client's event was scheduled to kick off that evening, Sousa's presence was required at the daily banquet-order meeting with the kitchen and catering staff, as well as at a weekly staff meeting to review upcoming events for the next two weeks.

By 10:00 a.m., the requirements for the upcoming pharmaceutical event had been changed a dozen times, resulting in numerous calls to various departments to make them aware of the changes. Since the group added a reception, Sousa personally met with the chef before the pre-con meeting at noon. At the close of the pre-con, Sousa gave her business card (on which she had written her personal cell number) to the planner, assuring her, "You may call me at any time, for anything."

Patricia Sousa

Sousa's afternoon was spent reviewing materials for both the banquet order meeting and the staff meeting—and dealing with the unexpected problems that arose when one of the financial meetings ran overtime, requiring the banquet staff to flip the meeting room in a record 17 minutes to accommodate a plated lunch.

At the 4:00 p.m. staff meeting, Sousa again faced—and met—challenges resulting from incoming groups' requests. On this particular day, the staff decided to hire an interpreter to meet the needs of a group from China, and they formulated a plan to provide extra power to high-level VIPs in another group.

At 5:15 p.m., Sousa's day was winding down, although she stayed at her post (catching up on paperwork) through the 6:00 p.m. pharmaceutical dinner. She would continue to monitor events at the hotel until approximately 8:30 p.m. Despite her long hours and the daily challenges, Sousa wouldn't change a thing. "This job is definitely not for everyone," says Sousa. "It's hard, and it is very fast-paced. But I really love what I do."

Sources: Lisa Grimaldi, "Miracle Workers: Profiles of Top CSMs and How They Make Meetings Shine," *Meetings & Conventions*, **December 2005; Cheryl-Anne Sturken, "A (Hectic) Day in the Life,"** *Meetings & Conventions*, **August 2008.**

Convention service managers also have their own organization, the Association for Convention Operations Management (ACOM). Membership includes convention service directors, managers, and coordinators from hotels, and event service managers from convention centers and convention bureaus. Hotel convention service managers can also join the Professional Convention Management Association (PCMA). This organization serves the convention industry with educational resources, networking, and an annual meeting that offers nearly 100 educational sessions to meeting planners.

Marketing gurus tell us that the best future customer is the one you've already got, and hotels are placing a heavy emphasis on the convention service manager's role in rebooking. Increasing the authority and responsibility of this department has been used by hotels to show commitment to the meetings business and convention service personnel.

A profile of ACOM's membership supports this contention. The average tenure is five years in their positions, with less than 10 percent going into sales and marketing. Also, a number report directly to the general manager and are members of their hotel's executive committee, along with the directors of marketing, food and beverage, hotel operations, and the controller. A number of hotel chains have standardized the position of convention service manager and bring these managers together annually for networking and idea exchange. Hilton, Hyatt, Marriott, and Sheraton have established corporate directors of convention services.

Several chains have made major commitments to training their convention service managers and other convention support staff to better assist meeting planners (see box titled "Training Convention Services Personnel"). As part of its recently introduced "Network Plan," the Marriott chain has committed to staffing each of its convention properties with a minimum of two Certified Meeting Professionals (CMPs). Mary Beth Jones, Marriott's vice president of global sales and marketing, says:

> Our basic training for convention service managers comprises a two- to-four week, on-site program combined with courses that can be taken at a company "university" held 11 times a year across the globe. Our success centers around our ability to be consistent at our hotels. The four cornerstones that are key to all Marriott brands are: be the easiest company to do business with; be a consultant and partner in the client's success; deliver flawlessly on the details; and recognize and reward the most loyal customers.[6]

The CMP exam, given by the Convention Industry Council, also figures prominently in the Hyatt chain's "Learning Environment Specialist" (LES) program (passing the CMP exam is a pre-requisite for this advanced training). Developed in association with the Professional Convention Management Association (PCMA), this six-day program offers instruction to help enhance all phases of meeting planning. The Hilton Hotel chain has developed its own program, Customer-Focused Convention Service Skills (CFCSS), to sharpen the skills of its convention service managers.

Convention Service Staff

How the convention service department is staffed depends on the size of the hotel, the percentage of occupancy accounted for by convention groups, the size of the groups using the hotel, and the number and size of the property's meeting rooms. Exhibit 3 illustrates a sample organization chart of a convention service department.

Some properties have expanded their convention service departments, creating new positions to better serve meeting planners (see box titled "Introducing the Conference Concierge"). In addition to the convention services manager, the following list provides the position titles and brief descriptions of the responsibilities of individuals who might work in the convention service department of a large convention-oriented property.

Director of Convention Services—oversees, trains, and assists the convention staff in all phases of managing meeting accounts. Assigns meeting accounts to convention service managers, keeping the workload evenly distributed among staff. Generally reports to the director of sales/marketing, but at large properties may report directly to the general manager.

TRAINING CONVENTION SERVICES PERSONNEL

Many hotel chains have recognized the importance of the service function, and have introduced training programs for their convention service managers and other key convention personnel. This increased knowledge and meeting planning expertise helps build the confidence of meeting planners, and is an important selling point in today's highly competitive meetings market.

Exhibit 3 Organizational Structure of a Convention Service Department in a Large Hotel

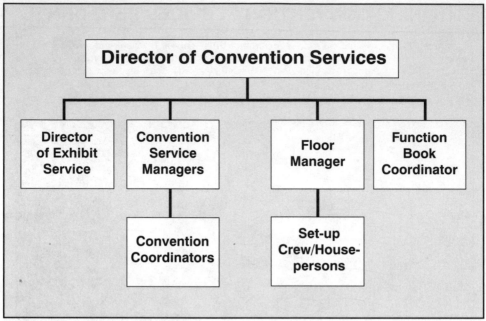

Convention Coordinator(s) — entry-level position in the convention service department. Primary responsibilities are to service small meeting groups and to assist convention service managers.

Floor Manager — responsible for servicing and setup of all meeting room and food and beverage functions. Oversees housepersons to ensure instructions from the specification and function sheets are carried out. At some properties, particularly smaller hotels, this position may be given the title of *Banquet Set-Up Manager*.

Set-Up Crew (sometimes called *Housepersons*) — responsible for the physical setup of all meeting and banquet rooms.

Director of Exhibit Service — works closely with the meeting group's trade show manager when the hotel's exhibition facilities are utilized. This position is only present in hotels with substantial dedicated exhibit space.

Function Book Coordinator — the single person who records entries from the function book reservation forms, responsible for ensuring the accuracy of the function book. This individual works closely with the sales staff, catering, and the convention service manager(s).

Convention Service Secretary(ies) — performs secretarial duties, including typing of correspondence, specification sheets, and function sheets for the convention service department.

Convention Service Managers at Convention and Visitors Bureaus

In addition to the convention personnel employed by hotels, CSMs can also be employed by convention and visitors bureaus. Unlike at hotels, however, CSMs employed by CVBs serve three separate clients—the external client (meeting manager), the internal client (bureau partners), and their employer (the city or CVB organization)—and they generally

INTRODUCING THE CONFERENCE CONCIERGE

As the convention industry has grown, the time commitment of the convention service manager has increased. Hotels that once realized 25 percent of their occupancy from meeting groups now look to capture 40–50 percent of their room nights from meetings, which would stretch even the most capable of convention managers too thin to adequately service business.

In response, Starwood Hotels (owner of the Sheraton and Westin brands, Four Points Hotels, the Luxury Collection, and the new W hotels) is just one of the chains (Hyatt is another) that has introduced a new position: the *conference concierge*. The conference concierge's responsibilities begin when the group arrives. The concierge stays in constant communication with the planner, improving the level of attention and service that meeting planners receive. Typical tasks for the concierge might include getting copies made for the planner at the last minute or assisting with package shipment. With the addition of this position, planners now have two people on site to assist them, and the level of attention is greatly improved.

The new position also frees up the convention service manager to spend more time with advance planning with groups whose meetings may be months in the future. And the position offers an opportunity for those wishing to break into convention services. David Dvorak, convention services vice president for Starwood, says: "The new title creates a great entry-level position because the concierge sees room setups, how to deal with emergencies and meeting planners, and how to multi-task."

provide most of their services prior to the actual event. CVB CSMs are typically an integral part of the sales process, often taking part in the site inspections held before a host city is selected. During site inspections, CVB CSMs assess the group's needs and build a relationship with the planner. Because of their extensive knowledge of the area, CVB CSMs are able to assist meeting planners with finding the products and services needed for their meeting—whether it will be held in a single hotel or citywide, or at an alternative venue, such as a sports arena, college campus, or a fairground—while minimizing costs, as they are familiar with suppliers and discounts available. CVB CSMs also typically assist with such meeting details as housing, registration, tours, and spouse programs, and they also save time for meeting planners by acting as a contact between participating hotels and suppliers. The functions of CVB CSMs may also include such non-traditional services as assisting with special permits in the host city, obtaining sponsorship assistance, and offering creative suggestions for boosting meeting attendance.

🖳 *INTERNET EXERCISE*

Log on to the home page for the Association for Convention Operations Management (ACOM) at www.acomonline.org. Click on "About ACOM" and then "What is ACOM" to learn about the history of this organization for convention service managers (CSMs).

Navigate through the site to answer the following questions:

1. Why should convention service managers in hotels, convention centers, and convention and visitors bureaus join ACOM?

2. What educational opportunities does ACOM offer to its members?

3. How would the organization be beneficial to students?

The Transition

A frequent debate in convention management is, "How and when should meeting planners be turned over to the individual within the hotel who will have charge of coordinating their conference?" Timing depends greatly on the meeting planner, the size and type of the meeting, and how far in advance the meeting has been booked. Four commonly used times for this transition include:

1. *During the site inspection* — The hotel salesperson is the key contact when booking the event, but some planners try to meet the convention service manager during the site inspection visit, saying there is a "reassurance factor" in making early contact with the person who will be handling the details of their meetings.

2. *Right before signing the contract* — Some meeting planners ask for an interview with convention services before signing the contract. This step helps ensure that promises made regarding space, setups, and meeting services can be met. One meeting planner has stated:

> Before signing a contract, I want to meet the convention service manager and let him or her know who I'm bringing in and what my meeting is all about. The salesperson may wine and dine me, but the convention service manager makes it happen. That's the person I'm married to for three days.

3. *Immediately after the point of sale* — If the convention is large and complex, some planners start working with convention services as soon as the contract is signed.

4. *One year before the meeting* — Many planners feel no need to involve convention services before one year in advance to begin the formal planning process. This procedure will not work in the case of short-term bookings that will require immediate contact between the meeting planner and the convention service manager.

🖥️ INTERNET EXERCISE

Log on to the home page of the Association for Convention Operations Management (ACOM) at www.acomonline.org. Click on "Resources," then "CS Tools and Checklists." Next, click on "Convention Services 24-Month Checklist." This checklist is used by the Indianapolis Convention and Visitors Bureau, not by a hotel; hotels generally use checklists similar to those presented in the appendix to this chapter.

These two checklists are tools used by convention and visitors bureaus and convention service managers at hotels to ensure a successful event. After reviewing both checklists:

1. Find and describe three similarities.
2. Find and describe three differences.
3. Explain why it is necessary for convention centers to use 24-month checklists rather than the 12-month checklists typically used by hotels.

Best Practices

Crowne Plaza Hotel and Resorts' "The Place to Meet" Program

In order to better meet the needs of meeting planners, Crowne Plaza Hotels and Resorts, a brand of the InterContinental Hotel Group (which also includes Holiday Inns), offers the "Place to Meet" program, which includes a two-hour response to a request for proposal, the services of a Crowne meetings director (CMD), and daily on-site meeting de-briefings.

Kevin Kowalski, Crowne's vice president of brand management, North America, says the chain's advisory board told hotel management that "meeting planners want an experienced go-to person at the hotel; someone to partner with throughout their event." Therefore, the chain has taken steps to ensure that its convention service managers are a cut above the norm. Tina Lyle, manager of marketing operations, says:

Crowne Plaza's "CMD Boot Camp" whips conference services managers into shape.

"We want them (CMDs) to have the authority and empowerment to make something right, no matter what the service issue might be.... When we started discussing what would enable a partnership between CMDs and buyers, we started looking at certifications, and we saw that the CMP would make our staff focus on the information meeting planners need, instead of just on what the hotel needs. It raises them to a level where they can speak to planners intelligently."

Crowne meetings directors (CMDs) must have at least eight years of meeting experience and must either hold or be working toward holding CMP credentials. To enable their staff to become CMPs, the chain launched a rigorous training program that includes a walk-through of the CMP application and an action plan for those who wish to take the CMP exam.

CMDs are also part of their properties' executive committees, meaning that they are included in weekly management meetings. This enables CMDs to learn about changes at the hotel; report in detail on incoming and departed group business; and work with other hotel departments, from housekeeping to engineering, to address a group's needs. At many properties, CMDs also report to the general manager rather than the director of sales or director of catering.

It is difficult to divorce the salesperson entirely from the service function. The salesperson who simply dismisses a client after the sale, assuming that the convention service manager will shoulder the burden, will probably not get a rebooking. Jim Hill, Director of Sales at the Inverness Hotel and Golf Club in Englewood, Colorado, uses a unique approach to ensure that both the salesperson and the convention service manager are known and trusted by the meeting planner:

> What we've introduced is a buddy system. Each sales associate is working with a conference service manager, and they actually work through the sales process together. From day one, we introduce the conference services manager, who the sales associate knows and has been working with throughout the year.[6]

Repeatedly partnering the convention service manager with a specific salesperson creates strong bonds and efficient teamwork. If the sales staff is deployed by market segments, partnering benefits convention service managers by concentrating their work with similar types of groups. For example, working with a salesperson dedicated to medical groups allows the convention service manager to gain an in-depth understanding of how to service these types of meetings.

The transition from the salesperson to the convention service manager must be handled smoothly. Frequently the client has dealt exclusively with the salesperson for two or three years and has complete trust in the sales staff. The salesperson's exit can be traumatic if the planner has not been reassured of the service manager's competence.

We recommend that once the sale is made the salesperson step aside and turn the meeting over to the service people. We don't believe, however, that the client should be abandoned by the salesperson. We suggest that the salesperson greet the planner, if possible, when the meeting comes to the hotel and reassure him or her that the meeting is in good

THE PERFECT CONVENTION SERVICE MANAGER

The Convention Industry Council advises meeting planners that the "perfect" convention service manager is one who: begins working with the planner as soon as the meeting is booked; knows his or her property and has the respect of people in other departments; has the authority to get things done; anticipates problems and has solutions at hand; offers creative suggestions for set-ups, programs, meals, and entertainment; considers himself or herself an extension of the planner's staff; is flexible and honest enough not to over-promise or to under-commit; balances the needs of the planner with the needs of his or her own property; and treats all meeting planners with equal respect.

Many CSMs think that this description is "too good to be true," especially in regard to working 24 hours a day, although the vast majority of CSMs put in long hours and have little free time. Therefore, it is not uncommon for hotel CSMs to become meeting planners (conversely, it is less likely that a meeting planner will join the hotel industry because of the long, demanding hours).

Hotel CSMs who become meeting planners bring a wealth of knowledge to their new positions. They know how hotels operate and they understand industry jargon. They are also familiar with the issues that are the most important in terms of meeting and event planning, and they know which issues can and cannot be negotiated in contracts.

The convention service manager helps the meeting planner visualize how the meeting room layout will contribute to a successful event.
Source: Courtesy of InterContinental Hotel Group.

Exhibit 4   Sample Letter of Introduction and Timeline Sheet

February 6, 20___

Ray Harper, President
Harper and Pritchard Construction
611 S. Bridge Street
Columbus, OH 48850

Dear Mr. Harper:

I would like to take this opportunity to introduce myself as your Convention Service Manager for your upcoming meeting which will take place at the Las Vegas Hilton during the dates of September 1–4, 20___. I will be responsible for all aspects of your meeting with the exception of food and beverage arrangements, which will be handled by Gus Moser in our Catering Department.

Below I have noted a few of the key items relating to your meeting. Please bring any discrepances to my attention as soon as possible so the appropriate changes may be made internally.

Room Block — 125 king rooms and 4 suites in the North Tower
Room Rate — $110 guest rooms, $150 suites
Method of Reservations — Rooming list
Billing — Master Account

Additionally, please find enclosed a time line for required information which will assist both of us in planning your upcoming convention. This schedule ensures that your program receives the attention and service that it deserves. Please review the schedule and advise me if any dates seem unattainable.

If you will be shipping any packages to the hotel in conjunction with your meeting, please ensure they are addressed to my attention in care of the Las Vegas Hilton Convention Service Department along with your organization's name and date of your function. However, due to storage requirements, we ask that these items be sent as close to the convention as possible.

Sincerely,

Cindy O'Keefe
Executive Director of Convention Se

cc: Sean Steward, Sales Manager
      Gus Moser, Catering Manager

TIME LINE

GROUP: Harper and Pritchard Construction
CONTACT: Ray Harper, President
MEETING DATES: September 1–4, 20___

Listed below are areas of concern with review dates that will assist us both to ensure a successful meeting.

ITEM	DUE DATE
Preliminary meeting program	April 1
Final meeting program	May 1
Credit application finalized	July 1
Cut-off date	August 1
Meeting & audiovisual requirements	July 15
Food & beverage menus finalized	July 15

Please make any changes as necessary, then sign and return the form to me. If these dates seem practical as listed above, I would appreciate your signing and returning this form to me. Thank you.

Ray Harper, President	Cindy O'Keefe
Harper and Pritchard Construction	Executive Director of Convention Services

---

The convention service manager and meeting planner should communicate often—and in writing— from the time the business is turned over to the convention service department. Today, the convention service manager and the meeting planner also exchange e-mail addresses early in the planning stage. Establishing a written timetable with the customer for pre-planning and communicating the group's requirements is essential to effectively service meeting groups. Most convention service managers tell us that their biggest problems in servicing groups stem from not getting enough information from their planners in a timely manner. A timeline such as the one in this exhibit alleviates that problem by setting dates when specific information is needed.

hands. Further, the salesperson should keep in touch and reenter as the meeting closes to suggest a rebooking. It just makes good sense for a salesperson to maintain contact with a client who has bought the property as a meeting site, and could, of course, buy again in the future.

An Overview of the Service Function

Thus far, we've talked about the importance of service, the role of the convention service manager, and his or her position in the hotels' organizational structure. To assist you in understanding the service process, an overview of the convention service manager's role follows. Additional information on each of these steps can be found in the Convention Service Checklist detailed in the chapter appendix.

Step No. 1 — Once a group is booked, the convention service manager reviews all correspondence to find out what information has been documented and what information is still required. Many times he or she will review **account files** from two or three years before the date of the convention. A **sales to service turnover data sheet** is now used by many hotels to quickly bring the CSM up to date on the group. This short form summarizes specifics negotiated by the salesperson, including guestroom block, preliminary meeting program, cut-off dates, and so on. With this information, the CSM begins to assemble the **working file** needed for servicing the group (refer to the chapter appendix, items 1–5).

Step No. 2 — The booking is listed in the function book, and contact is made with the meeting planner through a **letter of introduction** (see Exhibit 4 on the previous page). Note that this letter specifies that the group will be dealing with the convention service manager while in the hotel, and it provides a timeline for crucial components of the event. Meeting planners have stressed the value of a written set of deadlines, saying that timelines give them a "handle" on their events, and help them to ensure that essential information is communicated between the planner and his or her contact at the hotel (whether it be the convention service manager or a designated back-up). At this point, the salesperson goes behind the scenes and the convention service manager begins to get answers to the three basics: *reservations, program, and billing* (refer to the chapter appendix, items 6–10).

Step No. 3 — **Tracing** — using follow-up letters, telephone calls, and personal contact with the meeting executive — is initiated to build a relationship of trust and cooperation be-tween the two parties. Correspondence is made as clear as possible, and includes lots of detail. Technology has made tracing easier, more efficient, and faster. In the past, convention service managers relied on telephones and letters; today, e-mail and faxes are used to speed up the tracing process (refer to the chapter appendix, items 11–27).

Step No. 4 — Details of the program are formulated in a *personal interview* with the meeting planner at least six months before the event. Reservation requests are also mailed to the delegates at about this time in an effort to determine the number of guestrooms (refer to the chapter appendix, items 28–42).

Step No. 5 — A monthly preconvention meeting is held with all department heads to review upcoming groups. All convention *resumes* and *banquet event orders* are discussed in detail (refer to the chapter appendix, items 43–50).

Step No. 6 — Two or three days before the conference opens, a preconvention meeting is held with the front office manager, the supervisor in charge of room setup, the catering manager, and the meeting planner. The entire program is reviewed, the menus are reaffirmed, and the meeting setups are verified.

Step No. 7 — During the event, the convention service manager is on hand as much as possible. He or she will be at each meeting location one hour ahead of time to view the setup, check the audiovisual equipment and exhibit setup, and check security (refer to the chapter appendix, items 51–62).

Step No. 8 — A postconvention meeting is held at the end of the event. All charges to the master account are verified and initialed a second time by the client. The post-convention meeting is a review of the event by those persons in attendance at the preconvention meeting. At this time, the salesperson steps in to sell the group on a repeat convention. When the service department does its job, a rebooking percentage of 70 percent is not uncommon (refer to the chapter appendix, items 63–70).

Summary

Your attitude and professionalism in serving your guests will be what sets you and your property apart from the rest. And the foundation of your professionalism begins with knowledge. You must know what tangible products and services are required by meeting planners and how to deliver the successful meetings and functions that they demand.

In this chapter, we have presented an overview of the convention services structure and the importance of meeting with the planner to ensure that his or her requirements will be met. Armed with this knowledge, you will have the confidence to embark on the most important aspect of your job: building the trust and rapport that results in satisfied customers and repeat business for your property.

Endnotes

1. "Five Tips to Help the Sales Staff Perform at Their Best!" *The Rooms Chronicle*, Volume 8, Number 5, p. 6.

2. "Building Loyalty," *Convene.*

3. Robert Carey, "Leaders of the Pack," *Successful Meetings.*

4. Speech given at a Hospitality Sales and Marketing Association International (HAMAI) meeting in Las Vegas, Nevada.

5. Brian Stevens, "A New Commitment to Convention Service," *Convene.*

6. Terri Hardin, "Convention Services 101," *Meeting News*, December 18, 2008, p. 20.

7. Connie Goldstein, "Productive Meetings," *Corporate Meetings & Incentives.*

 Key Terms

account file—A file prepared by the sales department that includes all correspondence, call reports, and information used in selling a group. Additional information, such as the contract, meeting agenda, room block data, and so on are added to the group's file if business is booked.

letter of introduction—Letter sent by the convention service manager to the meeting planner. Specifies whom the group will be dealing with while in the hotel.

sales to service turnover data sheet—Prepared by the salesperson, this sheet summarizes key information from the account file (room block, meeting program, cut-off dates, and so on) and is given to the convention service manager to assist in preparation of the working file.

tracing—Building a relationship with the client by using follow-up letters, telephone calls, and personal contacts.

working file—A file set up by the convention service manager after a booking is definite. This file initially contains information from the account file. As the service manager works with the meeting planner, additional information, such as the group's resume and banquet event orders, is added. At the conclusion of the event, the working file is broken down and appropriate materials are re-filed in the group's account file for future reference.

Review Questions

1. Should sales department personnel become involved with group servicing?

2. Where does the convention service manager fit into the hotel organizational structure?

3. What types of programs are available to train convention service managers and their staffs to better assist meeting planners?

4. Describe the titles and duties of the members of the convention services staff.

5. What is meant by the transition? At what four times can transitions take place?

6. What is tracing and how is it used to build a relationship with the meeting planner?

7. Briefly define the eight steps inherent to servicing a group's meeting.

Additional References

Hospitality Marketing Management, Fourth Edition, Robert Reid and David Bojanic, John Wiley 2006.

Marketing for Hospitality and Tourism, Fourth Edition, Philip Kottler, John Bowen, James Makens, Prentice-Hall 2006.

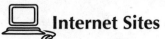

Internet Sites

For more information, visit the following Internet sites. Internet addresses can change without notice. If a site is no longer available at the address listed below, a search engine can be used to find the new address or additional, related sites.

Four Seasons Regent Hotels and Resorts
www.fshr.com

Hilton Hotels
www.hilton.com

Hyatt Hotels and Resorts
www.hyatt.com

Loews Hotels
www.loewshotels.com

Marriott International
www.marriott.com

Professional Convention Management
  Association (PCMA)
www.pcma.org

Successful Meetings magazine
www.successmtgs.com

CHAPTER APPENDIX

CONVENTION SERVICE CHECKLIST

Detailed checklists serve as planning guides and often prevent the overlooking of important items in staging a successful convention. Numerous checklists exist for helping the meeting planner avoid oversights, but few are available specifically for the convention service manager. This is the format used by Penta Hotels and is the best checklist of its type that we have seen in the industry.

Penta Hotels
CONVENTION SERVICE CHECKLIST

NAME OF GROUP   _____

DATES OF MEETING   _____

MEETING PLANNER   _____

MASTER ACCOUNT ADDRESS   _____

_____

TELEPHONE NUMBER   _____

SALES MANAGER   _____

BANQUET MANAGER   _____

TWELVE (12) MONTHS AWAY FROM MEETING DUE DATE	Completion Date
1. Sales manager to turn account file over to Convention Service with a copy of the signed contract, a copy of the approved booking notice, a copy of the approved room block, a copy of the credit form (if credit has not been determined, trace three days and follow-up), and a past history on pick-up for the last two (2) years.	_____
2. Review account file.	_____
3. Verify definite program, confirm diary space, meeting room rental, exhibit rental, set-up charges, and date all space hold to be released (if applicable).	_____
4. Confirm room commitments with Front Office and Group Rooms Control for accuracy, based on past history; block VIP suites. Determine when room rate will be established, and trace if not already established.	_____
5. Determine if all exhibit information is complete in contract and remind account of need for floor plans to be approved, exhibitor's contract to be approved, hold harmless clause signed, insurance certificate for $250,000.00.	_____
6. Initial contact and letter of introduction—obtain names of other key meeting personnel.	_____
a) Request most recent convention history.	_____
b) Review credit procedures and billing address.	_____
c) Review reservation procedures, when mailing will go out, clarify need for approval of reservation form if they act as housing bureau.	_____

6. d)   Check need for hospitality suites, who will use them, their names and addresses, and previous suite number if annual.   _____

    e)   Ask about public relations opportunities, famous people, unusual events, and newsworthy issues.   _____

    f)   Inquire if account is tax exempt; ask for tax exempt form.   _____

7. Discuss their needs and requirements for outside security per corporate policy.   _____

8. Send Penta meeting planner fact book.   _____

9. Send Penta convention kit.   _____

10. Order reservation cards (if the salesperson has already done so, obtain a copy of this form).   _____

SIX (6) MONTHS AWAY FROM THE MEETING DUE DATE

11. Contact public relations for coordination of publicity. Place director of Public Relations in contact with the meeting planner. (If this is applicable.)   _____

12. Accentuate the need for the accounts to provide detailed instructions at an early date so that proper service may be administered.   _____

13. Explain convention resume procedure.   _____

14. Reconfirm staff and VIP housing requirements; double-check suites blocked.   _____

15. Determine audiovisual needs. Discuss how extensive set-ups are. Sell in-house audiovisual company.   _____

16. Discuss registration personnel and procedures. Penta needs to maintain integrity of our property. All signs must be professionally printed; no signs allowed on walls. No signs allowed in the main lobby, except by management approval.   _____

17. Coordinate contact with banquet representative, give name, telephone number, have banquet representative call account.   _____

18. Review account's needs in regard to office equipment, i.e., typewriters, telephones, need for decorations or decorators, florist.   _____

19. Request name of drayage company. Review needs of union labor. This is a union house.   _____

20. Inquire into anticipated companion programs, anticipated bus tours. Coordinate information regarding bus tour loadings and unloadings.

21. Request finalized meeting and exhibit floor plans for approval.   _____

22. Review final meeting schedule and check diary.   _____

THREE (3) MONTHS AWAY FROM MEETING DUE DATE

23. Reconfirm required suites and staff requirements with guest and Front Office.   _____

24. Review billing arrangements, identify all master accounts and authorized signatures.   _____

25. Remind client of cut-off date for rooms. _____

26. If rooms do not materialize, a rental may have to be implemented (if there is not a rental or sliding scale in the contract) by the salesperson. _____

27. Request official printed program. Compare published program to space requirements in regard to time, set-up times, coffee services, etc. _____

SIX (6) WEEKS AWAY FROM MEETING DUE DATE

28. Process letter for VIPs. _____

29. Verify attendance at all functions, establish rental based on contractual agreement, and establish master account and billing instructions along with authorized signatures. _____

30. Secure deposit if required, due 30 days prior to arrival date, unless we have devised a payment schedule. _____

31. Review file on the departmental basis to alert key people of heavy or unusual requirements. _____

32. Review microphone requirements. _____

33. Review lighting requirements and any production set-up needs. _____

34. Review room block against pick-up and cut-off date with the convention service manager. _____

35. Review complimentary rooms. If pick-up is below what the client anticipated, causing a comp room assignment problem, confer with Sales Manager and Convention Service Manager to explore best means of satisfying customer. _____

36. Request complete set-up information. _____

37. Review room registration, check-in arrangements. _____

38. Review special housekeeping requirements, if applicable. _____

39. Obtain a copy of authorized signatures for the master account. _____

40. Review cash advance needs. _____

41. Review safe deposit needs. _____

42. Review shipping arrangements of materials. _____

THREE (3) WEEKS AWAY FROM MEETING DUE DATE

43. Forward resume (specification sheet) and check with Catering on menu progress. _____

44. Distribute resume to hotel departments and include affiliated activities. _____

45. Establish date and time for a pre-convention meeting, process in-house memo. _____

46. Inquire if client wishes to guarantee rooms not picked up. _____

TWO (2) WEEKS AWAY FROM MEETING DUE DATE

47. Order limousine if applicable. _____

48. Re-check program with diary for possible quick meeting room turn-over and enter proper times for all events. _____

49. Review complimentary room arrangements. _____

50. Request posting instructions. _____

FORTY-EIGHT (48) HOURS AWAY FROM MEETING DUE DATE

51. Check hospitality and complimentary orders and VIP reservations. _____

52. Reconfirm pre-con meeting. _____

DURING MEETING

53. Check setting of meeting rooms (a.m., afternoon, p.m.). _____

54. Public Space Mgr. or Asst. to complete checklist for each function room. _____

55. Assist with restaurant reservations for VIPs. _____

56. Review shipping arrangements for postconvention materials. _____

57. Review complimentary room arrangements. _____

58. Compare room pick-up to complimentary list, make necessary adjustments. _____

59. Set up post-convention meeting. _____

60. Verify booth and exhibit hall by walk-through with customer. _____

61. Determine exhibit rental charge if determined by booth. _____

62. Determine repeat booking potential and advise Sales Manager. _____

63. Review master account with account credit department at a predetermined meeting. This should be completed each day. _____

IMMEDIATELY AFTER MEETING

64. Conduct post-convention meeting. _____

65. Call account and send thank you letter. _____

66. Complete report of convention and profit and loss statement and distribute. _____

67. Determine report on abnormal circumstances in the postconvention memo. _____

68. Post-convention report to include under "comments" section an objective evaluation of the hotel's performance. _____

69. Turn file over to Convention Service Manager for review. _____

ONE (1) MONTH AFTER MEETING DUE DATE

70. Break down working file and return appropriate correspondence to account file. _____

Competencies

1. Describe the ways in which meeting attendees make reservations at the hotel that will host their meeting. (pp. 351–361)

2. Identify factors that hotel staff take into account when assigning rooms to meeting attendees and managing room blocks, and describe the importance of good check-in/check-out procedures. (pp. 362–377)

3. Describe how computerization facilitates front office guest service. (pp. 378–382)

A Planner's Perspective on Room Reservations

Sara R. Torrence, CMP
Chief, Special Activities
National Institute of Standards and Technology

"The meetings for which I have been responsible have used a variety of reservations systems—ranging from rooming lists to postal reply cards to call-in reservations, to housing bureaus. We have even used a combination of services, and once created our own housing bureau, through a travel agent, because we were using four hotels for a relatively small international conference (800 attendees—too small to use the CVB housing bureau for the host city). One of the MOST important points about any reservation system is that the Hotel Sales Manager MUST get the details of the convention to the Reservations Department as soon as the contract is signed, and these details must be entered into the computerized reservations system as soon as possible. I cannot tell you how many times I have had attendees call a hotel for a reservation only to find that the Reservations Department has no record of the conference."

11

Guestrooms

T HE LETTER OF AGREEMENT has been signed and countersigned. The dates are firm. The room block is specified in the contract. At this point, many departments and organizations become involved as the service process branches out into different areas.

One of these areas is the assignment of guestrooms, which plays an important part in the success of a convention. Cooperation between your reservations department and front desk and the convening organization's housing staff is essential to ensure that there are no unpleasant surprises for meeting attendees.

Reservation Systems

Guestroom reservation information is typically sent to the group's membership three to six months before the event. The systems that are primarily used today include:

- Postal reply/fax response cards
- Toll-free telephone numbers
- Hotel Internet site reservations
- Rooming lists
- Convention center housing bureaus
- Third-party housing companies

The use of the Internet is making it easier for meeting attendees and other guests to make their reservations. Making reservations using such technology as fax reply cards and hotel websites is especially attractive to meeting attendees because of the convenience and speed of making the reservation and the capability for almost instant confirmation (or notification if there is a problem).

Postal Reply/Fax Response Cards

This housing option calls for the meeting planner to mail reservation forms to his or her membership along with promotional material about the meeting. These **reply cards**, which are printed by the hotel and sent in bulk to the convention group's headquarters, may be self-addressed postal reply cards (see Exhibit 1) or similar information cards that can be faxed back to the hotel.

The convention headquarters sends its promotional material and the reservation cards to its membership from its mailing list. While postal reply cards have long been used by convention attendees, cards that can be faxed are increasing in popularity with both hotels and attendees. Attendees appreciate the ease of faxing, while hotels are more likely to get an immediate response; there is no need to wait for the mail.

To facilitate this reservations process, an effective form is essential. If you have to develop a form or revise one, look at our sample or start from scratch, keeping the following factors in mind:

Clarity:
- Be concise.
- Ask guests to print or type. Allow enough space for hand printing.
- Use standard-sized forms for easy handling and storage.

Pertinent information:
- Include spaces for responses for all the information you will need to process the reservation.
- Arrival and departure date.
- Arrival and departure times.
- Rate requests (unless flat rates are part of the agreements).
- Kind(s) of room(s) requested.
- Number in the party.
- Indicate how long rooms will be held.
- Indicate if and how the room may be held past that time (guarantee or deposit).
- Indicate if deposit is required for all reservations.
- Use self-addressed forms or specify where reservation is to be sent.

Keep the form simple:
- Use terms in common usage. Indicate number of bedrooms in suites.
- Don't ask for unnecessary data.

If the group uses its own housing form, the hotel must approve the reservation card to ensure that all information is communicated to attendees to minimize misunderstandings. The reservation card policy of the Chicago Hilton and Towers reads as follows:

> *The Chicago Hilton and Towers will supply your organization, at no charge, a reasonable amount of self-addressed reservation cards imprinted with the name of your association and the dates of your convention. In the event that your company or association plans to use its own housing form or you intend to use the Chicago Convention and Tourism Bureau for housing, the Chicago Hilton and Towers must approve the copy in writing prior to its being printed in its final form and sent to your members or the Bureau to ensure that all information listed on the form pertaining to the Chicago Hilton and Towers is correct and complete, thus eliminating any discrepancies in room rate when your members receive their confirmations.*

Toll-Free Telephone Numbers

Some convention delegates opt to use the property's toll-free numbers to make their reservations. If this is the case, they should be notified beforehand that they must indicate that they are attending the convention when making their reservations. Another alternative is for the hotel to offer a special toll-free number for the group's use (especially if the group is a large one or if several groups are meeting at the same time).

These measures eliminate several potential problems. Since the hotel and meeting planner agreed to reserve a specific block of rooms, the commitment becomes overestimated if individual reservations are not credited to the group. The hotel may be stuck with unfilled guestrooms and the association will not get credit for the number of complimentary rooms to which it is entitled.

Exhibit 1 Sample Postal Reservation Reply Card

Front of the reply card.

BUSINESS REPLY MAIL
FIRST CLASS   PERMIT NO 5216   ORLANDO, FLA
POSTAGE WILL BE PAID BY ADDRESSEE

NO POSTAGE
NECESSARY
IF MAILED
IN THE
UNITED STATES

ORLANDO **Marriott**
8001 International Drive
Orlando, Florida 32819

ATTENTION:
Reservations Manager

THE ORLANDO MARRIOTT WELCOMES

ARRIVAL DATE _____ DEPARTURE DATE: _____
ARRIVAL TIME: _____ FLIGHT NO.: _____
NUMBER OF ROOMS _____ NUMBER IN PARTY: _____
ADULTS _____ CHILDREN & AGES: _____
SPECIAL REQUEST _____

NAME _____
ADDRESS _____
CITY: _____ STATE: _____ ZIP: _____
TELE # _____
For those who wish to arrive early and/or extend their stay, the
above mentioned special group rates will apply to three nights
before and/or after the dates indicated above - rooms subject to
availability.

DAILY ROOM RATES   SINGLE $ _____ DOUBLE $ _____
SUITE $ _____
CHILDREN STAYING IN THE SAME ROOM WITH THEIR PARENTS
NO EXTRA CHARGE
ALL RATES ARE SUBJECT TO 8% STATE TAX
MAXIMUM NUMBER OF PEOPLE IN ROOM - FIVE (5)
RESERVATIONS ARE TENTATIVELY HELD PENDING RECEIPT OF
DEPOSIT OR AMERICAN EXPRESS OR DINERS CLUB CARD
NUMBER _____ . EXPIRE DATE _____
Special request for location, connecting room, etc., will be noted
but cannot be guaranteed. Suites are space available at rates
above and will be confirmed by RESERVATIONS MANAGER

CHECK IN: _4:00 PM_ CHECK OUT: _11:00 AM_ (AFTER)
Baggage must be checked with the Bell Captain if departure time
is later than 11:00 A.M.

THIS IS A **RESERVATION REQUEST** AND MUST BE ACCOMPANIED BY ONE(1) NIGHTS ROOM DEPOSIT. A WRITTEN CONFIRMATION WILL
BE SENT TO YOU AFTER RECEIPT OF DEPOSIT. ALL REQUESTS MUST BE RECEIVED BY _____. AFTER SUCH DATE, THEY WILL BE
ACCEPTED ON A SPACE AVAILABLE BASIS.

Back of the reply card.

This is a self-addressed postal reply card that is filled out by delegates and returned to the hotel. Other forms of reply cards may include printed return envelopes (usually used when a deposit is required) or a card that may be faxed to the hotel. Whatever form is used, reply cards include such pertinent information as the name and dates of the meeting, and room rates. Many associations include such reply cards with their general mailing detailing the convention program, activities, and costs.
Source: Courtesy of the Orlando Marriott.

Hotel Internet Site Reservations

Today, the Internet has become the predominant way for convention groups to make hotel reservations. A recent study by *Convene* magazine showed that just a few years ago most planners selected reservation cards, forms or faxes over the Internet as their preferred reservation method.[1] Today, however, the Internet wins by a mile as shown in the sidebar titled, "What's Your Preferred Reservation Method?"

Hilton Hotels Corporation is one of many hotel chains that offers group reservations on its HiltonNet website. A planner who has reserved a **room block** at a Hilton property can link his or her organization to a special page on Hilton's site. This site not only provides details about the meeting, but attendees are also given a passcode to access the group reservations module. There, they can book a room at the group's designated rates during a specified time. Hilton's system tracks these reservations and planners can view pickup data via a password protected area of the site. The chain also provides a hard copy of room pickup upon request.

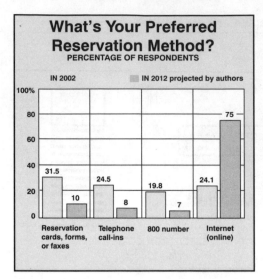

What's Your Preferred Reservation Method?
PERCENTAGE OF RESPONDENTS

IN 2002   IN 2012 projected by authors

Method	IN 2002	IN 2012
Reservation cards, forms, or faxes	31.5	10
Telephone call-ins	24.5	8
800 number	19.8	7
Internet (online)	24.1	75

Rooming Lists

Many hotels prefer to get a consolidated **rooming list** from the planner (see Exhibit 2). When rooming lists are used, reservations are not made with the hotel, but with the housing staff at the planner's headquarters. The meeting planner prepares the rooming list from the reservations received and sends it to the hotel prior to the **cutoff date**. When the hotel receives the list, the front office assigns attendees rooms from the block that is committed to the group and preregisters attendees.

It is extremely important that the front office knows whether a group's reservations are coming individually or through a list. It is standard operating procedure that the trace file on any group for which a rooming list is expected is brought up in sufficient time to remind the customer that the list is expected.

Rooming lists are most commonly used by corporate accounts and incentive travel groups, as their meetings are usually small, attendance is predictable (it is sometimes mandatory), and the organizer is generally picking up the room charges. The convention service manager should encourage the use of rooming lists, when possible, because it reduces the load on the hotel's reservation department.

Convention Center Housing Bureaus

When several hotels are used, the convention is commonly called **citywide** and the reservations may be handled by a convention center **housing bureau** (see box titled "Case Study: City Housing Bureau").

Many meeting planners, however, cite several problems with city housing bureaus. Many are understaffed, especially when it comes to handling large conventions. Meeting planners tell "horror stories" of constantly busy phone lines, long delays when calls finally get through, and delayed **reservation confirmations**. While some CVBs are now offering their housing systems online to eliminate some of these problems, a growing number of meeting planners are turning to other outside sources for their housing needs.

The most recent PCMA Housing Report showed that meeting planners are moving away from using convention bureau housing services and relying more on third-party providers for their housing needs (see sidebar titled "What is Your Preferred Method for Handling Citywide Housing?"). We will take an in-depth look at these third-party housing companies and their impact on the meetings industry in the next section.

Third-Party Housing Companies

Third-party housing providers, private firms that typically use Internet-based technology to make housing arrangements for groups, are often used by large organizations that utilize several hotels for citywide conventions. Associations which need consistency, as they generally rotate their annual conventions geographically, are also turning to third-party providers, citing the inconsistency of housing services offered by CVBs in different cities. And not only are meeting planners using third-party housing companies, many CVBs have recognized the cost savings of using third-party companies and they are now outsourcing housing to third-party vendors.

The growth of third-party providers has been fueled by Internet technology. Internet-based Passkey.com, the largest and best known of the third-party providers, utilizes an accessible centralized database to process housing transactions. Its system also generates confirmations and acknowledgements for attendees and provides reports that enable meeting planners to manage their room blocks. Passkey is now utilized by 85 percent of the major convention cities, including those in Atlanta, Boston, Detroit, and Orlando. The system is also marketed to other third-party housing vendors and to tradeshow organizers and meeting planners who formerly made housing arrangements internally. In addition, the Hyatt and Marriott chains have signed licensing agreements with Passkey, enabling them to pass along the technology

What is your preferred method for handling citywide housing?

For those who outsource, third parties are preferred to convention bureau housing services.

(PERCENTAGE OF RESPONDENTS)

- 8.9 Other
- 34.5 In-house (do it yourself)
- 32.5 Retain Third Party Housing Service
- 24.1 Convention Bureau Housing Service

While a large number of associations handle city-wide housing in-house, planners still rely on outside sources, such as convention bureau housing services and, increasingly, third-party providers.
Source: *Convene's* **Annual Meetings Market Report.**

Exhibit 2   Sample Rooming List

THE
HERSHEY
LODGE & CONVENTION CENTER
ROOMING LIST

Group Name: _____   Send to attention of:

Date: _____

Group Number: _____   _____
(For Lodge use only)   Convention Coordinator

To guarantee your room block, this list must be received 30 days prior to arrival.

ARRIVAL DATE	DEP. DATE	ROOM TYPE	NAME (Last Name First)	SHARING WITH Please also list sharer's data on next line	NUMBER OF PEOPLE OCCUPYING RM	NUMBER OF CHILDREN	COMMENTS

Rooming lists are generally used for small corporate meetings for which the corporation will pay room charges and attendees will be responsible for their incidental charges. Some associations, however, also use them rather than having individual delegates contact the hotel for reservations directly. After the meeting planner obtains room information from delegates, he or she prepares a list to be sent to the hotel by an agreed-upon date. Information typically includes the names of attendees, the type of room desired (and how many will occupy a room), and arrival and departure dates.
Source: Courtesy of the Hershey Lodge & Convention Center.

Case Study: City Housing Bureau

When a convention uses several hotels, the convention is commonly called citywide and the reservations are handled by a city housing bureau. We will illustrate this more complicated reservation system with this case study featuring the hypothetical National Popcorn Association.

National Popcorn Association

The NPA has an active membership of 3,550 delegates. The association executive and the site selection committee have narrowed down their selection for the upcoming annual convention to either Chicago, Miami, or Las Vegas. It will be necessary for such a large group to use a number of hotels, so the planners have been in touch with the convention bureau of each city.

The NPA staff makes personal visits to each site and picks hotels. It then prepares a list of the desired hotels in each city and asks the convention bureau to request room commitments from each property.

The **bid sheet** used by the Las Vegas Convention and Visitors Authority is shown in Exhibit 3. Upon receiving it, the hotel sales department checks room availability for the dates designated. It then specifies the number of singles, doubles, and suites the hotel has available and gives a price range for each. Note that the hotel stipulates a cutoff date by which time the NPA must send a written acceptance of the hotel's offer. The completed form is then mailed back to the convention bureau. The bureau forwards or personally presents the proposal sheets to the association's site selection committee for analysis and a decision.

On the basis of price, location, and service, the NPA chooses Las Vegas as the site for the convention. It also selects a headquarters hotel and designates four others as overflow hotels.

Approximately eight months before the convention, the NPA association executive requests assistance from the Las Vegas Housing Bureau in setting up a reservation system. The association, in conjunction with the housing bureau, prepares a reservation form (Exhibit 4) to be sent to each member, who in turn completes it, writes out a deposit check, and returns it to the housing bureau. The members each indicated their first, second, third, and fourth preferences in hotels, and they have also specified the type of room desired. The housing bureau sorts through the forms and approves reservations on a first-come, first-served basis. As each reservation is approved, the form is returned to the sender, specifying which hotel he or she is to stay in during the convention. If none of the choices are available, the form is returned to the member with a note of explanation and a request for new choices.

As each batch of new reservations is approved, it is sent to the respective hotel and processed there by the reservations department. Each week before the convention, a **reservation housing report** (see Exhibit 5) prepared by the housing bureau is sent to the hotels and to the association to indicate the reservation status of the hotel's room blocks. This report is extremely important to the hotel. If a room block is not filling up as expected, the hotel will probably contact the association and ask for an update on its room commitment. Although the housing bureau specifies a thirty-day cutoff, if only half of the 3,550 rooms commited are reserved, the five hotels might have difficulty in booking the remaining guestrooms.

The handling of the deposit checks by the housing bureau can be avoided if the NPA collects the deposits itself and pays each hotel its respective amount. This procedure is almost the only method some groups use and it is definitely preferred by the hotels.

Once NPA reservations begin to come in, the hotels start convention reservation records and master accounts for the group. Usually a rooming list (see Exhibit 2) is developed and each delegate is assigned a room and sub-account under the master account. If and when checks are received by the hotel, a credit is added to the sub-account.

Exhibit 3   Sample Bid Sheet

LAS VEGAS CONVENTION BUREAU
CONVENTION CENTER · PARADISE ROAD
P.O. BOX 14006
LAS VEGAS, NEVADA 89114

Date: May 15, 20__

FROM: Adam James Stubbs, Convention Sales

SUBJECT: REQUEST FOR ROOM COMMITMENT

THE____National Popcorn Association_____HAS REQUESTED US TO OBTAIN
TENTATIVE / FIRM ROOM COMMITMENTS FOR THEIR CONVENTION IN LAS VEGAS, NEVADA.
FOR MEETING DATES OF___Oct. 18, 20_____THROUGH___Oct. 21, 20_____.
THE_____Abbey Hotel_____AGREES TO RESERVE THE FOLLOWING NUMBER OF
SLEEPING ROOMS AT THE RATES SHOWN BELOW; PROVIDING A WRITTEN ACCEPTANCE
BY THE CONVENING ORGANIZATION IS RECEIVED BY THE HOTEL OR MOTEL PRIOR TO
_____Sept. 15, 20_____.
DATE

NUMBER OF:

SINGLES____*100*_____RATE___*$75-85*_____

DOUBLES____*475*_____RATE___*$85-95*_____

TWINS_____RATE_____

SUITES____*25*_____RATE___*$110--170*___

GRAND TOTAL ROOMS____*600*_____

ROOM DEPOSIT ((IS))(NOT) REQUIRED. (IF REQUIRED, STATE AMOUNT) *$75.00*

SIGNED BY:

Chantal Puepke   *Abbey Hotel*
NAME   HOTEL OR MOTEL

Sales Manager   *May 20*
TITLE   DATE

* * * * *

PUBLIC SPACE AVAILABLE___*yes*_____   *negotiable*____
                                        RATE OR GRATIS

PUBLIC SPACE DESCRIBED ON ATTACHMENT (NOTE TO HOTEL: IF APPLICABLE PLEASE
ENCLOSE BROCHURE)

RESERVATIONS FOR PUBLIC SPACE TO BE REQUESTED AND CONFIRMED BY LETTER.

* * * * *

NOTE: TO BE COMPLETED IN TRIPLICATE. MAIL TWO (2) COPIES TO THE LAS VEGAS
CONVENTION BUREAU. HOTEL OR MOTEL TO RETAIN ONE (1) COPY.

When a number of hotels must be used for large conventions, a bid sheet is filled out by individual properties and returned to the city convention bureau. In this case, the form is filled out in triplicate. The hotel keeps one copy, the bureau keeps another, and the third is incorporated into a summary of local hotel rates that is sent to the organization.
Source: Courtesy of the Las Vegas Convention and Visitors Authority.

Exhibit 4   Typical Reservation Reply Form

APPLICATION FOR HOTEL ACCOMMODATIONS

MAIL COLORED COPY TO:
NPA Housing Bureau
Las Vegas Convention/Tourist Authority
P.O. Box 14006
Las Vegas, Nevada 89114

October 19-21, 20__
Las Vegas Convention Center
Industry Day
October 18th 20__

NPA

COMMITTEE

Send Confirmation to:

Company Name _____

Attention _____

Street Address or P.O. Box _____

City _____ State _____ Zip Code _____

Hotel Preference:

1. _____   3. _____

2. _____   4. _____

Please Reserve The Following Accommodations: (See reverse side for Rates and Map Locations)

. . . . Singles(s) for . . . . .persons(s)   Rate Preferred $ . . . . .per room

. . . . Double(s) for . . . . .person(s)   Rate Preferred $ . . . . .per room

. . . . Parlor Suite(s) with . . . . Bedroom(s) for person(s)   Rate Preferred $ . . . . .per suite

REMARKS: . . . .

. . . .

If Rate Requested Not Available, Next Higher will be Assigned.

List each type of room, its occupants and their arrivals and departures.

Type of Room	**Names of Occupants**	**Arrival & Departure Dates & Hours**
1.		
2.		
3.		
4.		
5.		
6.		

Please Attach List of Additional Names, if necessary.

CONFIRMATION OF THE ABOVE REQUEST WILL BE SENT BY THE HOTEL.
PLEASE MAKE ALL RESERVATION CHANGES DIRECTLY THROUGH THE CONFIRMING HOTEL.

A form such as this one is used when a city housing bureau handles hotel room assignments. The delegate fills out the form and returns it to the housing bureau. Maps (such as the one shown on the next page) and hotel rates are included to assist delegates in determining their choice of hotels. Note that this particular form gives delegates four options when it comes to the choice of a hotel. This practice can be a major factor in hotel overbooking, which is discussed in detail later in this chapter.
Source: Courtesy of the Las Vegas Convention and Visitors Authority.

Exhibit 4 *(continued)*

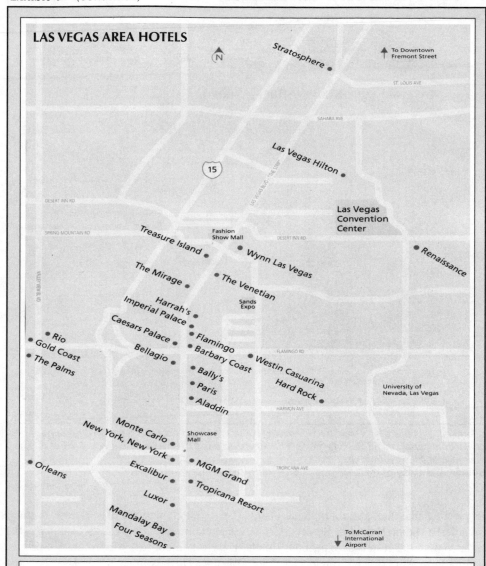

LAS VEGAS AREA HOTELS

Las Vegas Hotel Rates

NPA Industry Day - Oct 18th-Hotel A
NPA Show-Oct 19,20,21 -Convention Center

Room Block	Hotel	King	Double/Double	Parlor Suites *** 1 Bedroom	Parlor Suites*** 2 Bedroom	
1500	A (Hdqtrs)	$110-122 $127-130	$110-122 $127-130	$168-190 $194-225	$201-235 $248-277	*One night room deposit required with reservation
1000	B*	$116-125	$116-125	$170-180	$205-220	** $50 deposit required with reservation
600	C*	$104-108	$108-114	$155-170	$183-198	***Hospitality suites available Rates for special hospitality suites on request.
250	D**	$112-118	$112-118	$170-190	$230-260	
200	E*	$100 S/D Occupancy	$100 S/D Occupancy	$100 S/D Occupancy	$100 S/D Occupancy	All rates subject to12% Clark County Room Tax

Exhibit 5   Reservation Housing Report

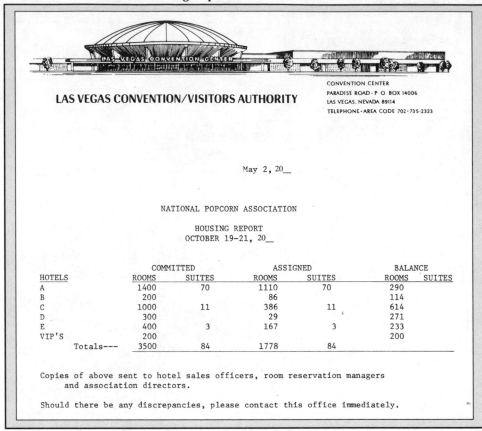

LAS VEGAS CONVENTION/VISITORS AUTHORITY

CONVENTION CENTER
PARADISE ROAD · P O. BOX 14006
LAS VEGAS, NEVADA 89114
TELEPHONE · AREA CODE 702·735·2323

May 2, 20__

NATIONAL POPCORN ASSOCIATION

HOUSING REPORT
OCTOBER 19-21, 20__

HOTELS	COMMITTED		ASSIGNED		BALANCE	
	ROOMS	SUITES	ROOMS	SUITES	ROOMS	SUITES
A	1400	70	1110	70	290	
B	200		86		114	
C	1000	11	386	11	614	
D	300		29		271	
E	400	3	167	3	233	
VIP'S	200				200	
Totals---	3500	84	1778	84		

Copies of above sent to hotel sales officers, room reservation managers
    and association directors.

Should there be any discrepancies, please contact this office immediately.

A form such as this one is used by the housing bureau to inform hotels of the meeting group's pickup on its room commitment. Reports are sent on a periodic basis to enable the individual hotels to adjust their reservations information.
Source: Courtesy of the Las Vegas Convention and Visitors Authority.

to meeting planners at no additional charge. Other hotels and resorts that use Passkey include Fairmont Hotels & Resorts, Hershey Entertainment and Resorts Company, the InterContinental Hotels Group, Omni Hotels, The Broadmoor resort in Colorado Springs, Colorado, and the Hotel Monteleone in New Orleans.[2] The box titled "Hyatt Uses Passkey to Market to Meeting Planners" and Exhibit 6 provide examples of how Passkey is used to attract meeting planners.[2]

Planners now have over two dozen third-party housing firms from which to choose, and the competition has resulted in innovation and better service to the planners that use these services. In many cases, meeting attendees still fax or mail in their housing reservations, but the Internet is expected to account for the majority of reservations received by housing companies in the near future. No matter how reservations are received, these third-party providers prepare a rooming list for the hotel.

Third-party housing firms are the "preferred providers" for large conventions and a growing number of smaller meetings, and it is estimated that about 50 percent of all multi-hotel events are handled by third-party firms. There is a downside, however. Private firms, unlike convention and visitors bureau housing services, charge a fee, often as much as ten percent of the room rate. A CVB will pay this fee when outsourcing its housing, but meeting planners must find a way to pay for housing assistance when it is not provided by the

Hyatt Uses Passkey to Market to Meeting Planners

Hyatt Hotels & Resorts, which has offered the Passkey system to meeting planners for several years at more than 50 of its properties in the United States, Canada, and the Caribbean, has recently added Passkey's GroupLink[SM] enhancement tool to make meeting planners' work even easier—allowing them to track events up to the date of arrival and to manage citywide events. The original Passkey system offered reservation capability, event and hotel information for attendees, and 24/7 access to more than 100 reports, including pick-up and booking reports. The new GroupLink[SM] application provides meeting planners with even more cutting-edge solutions to efficiently manage their events, providing the ability to keep events open through the day of arrival and allowing for complete inventory management from one data source.

Irby Morvant, director of sales and marketing at the Hyatt Regency New Orleans, says:

> Passkey elevates meeting planners to a new level of service and technology by giving them direct access to rooming lists and room pick-ups.

Offering Passkey has resulted in benefits to both the hotel chain and meeting planners. Arnetta Smith, an event manager for the American Petroleum Institute, says:

> I put the link (that Hyatt provides) into the e-mail marketing piece I send out, then attendees can click on it for Passkey, and make their hotel reservations at the same time that they do their conference registration. It's all in one e-mail document. I'm able to go into the Passkey system, quickly retrieve reports on room pick-up, see my numbers, and see who has registered.

In addition to Passkey, Hyatt also offers several other methods for making group reservations, including customized websites for specific meetings (hosted free of charge on hyatt.com), online reservations at hyatt.com, and toll-free numbers.

Source: Hyatt.com.

convention bureau or hotels at no charge. In some cases, the meeting planner will negotiate with the hotel to pay the fee of a third-party provider, passing the cost along to the attendees in the form of higher room rates. Some hotels balk at this arrangement and insist that the service be paid for separately, either by the planner or the attendee, to eliminate artificially raised room rates. Some third-party planners negotiate with the hotel to have their fee paid, much as travel agents are compensated.

No matter how reservations are made, the group's pick-up is important to both the hotel and the meeting group, making it critical to monitor the group's room block. Ideally, the contract will include a schedule of room block review dates. If not, detailed weekly guestroom pickups should be reported to the meeting planner, beginning at either three or four months prior to the meeting date. This is especially important if a housing bureau is handling reservations or if a number of hotels will be used for the meeting. In that case, the housing bureau will send out reservation confirmations, such as the one shown in Exhibit 7, to the hotel or hotels being used as well as to attendees.

As individual reservations arrive at a hotel, the reservations manager monitors the room availability in the group's block. A breakdown of the precise types of rooms booked must be made and kept current. If the reservations department notes that a block does not look like it will fill — or that more rooms are needed in the block due to heavy demand — the sales department should be notified. The sales department can then contact the meeting planner to make whatever room block adjustments are necessary.

🖳 INTERNET EXERCISE

A number of hotel chains, including Hyatt Hotels & Resorts, offer Passkey, the major online group hotel reservations technology supplier, to meeting planners as a complimentary service. Visit Hyatt's web site (www.hyatt.com) and click on "Meetings and Events." Then select "Group Reservation Solutions" to review the Passkey demo and sample reports. Also log on to Passkey's website (www. passkey.com) before answering the following questions:

1. What percentage of the top North American meetings and conventions cities rely on Passkey?

2. Why have many of the major hotel chains, including Hyatt, adopted Passkey technology for handling group reservations?

3. What advantages are offered by group reservation systems to meeting planners? to meeting attendees? to convention and visitors bureaus? to hotels?

4. Explain the value of "RegLink" and "SmartAlerts."

Room Assignment

The front desk carries off most convention and trade show room assignments without incident. Problems do arise, however, and must be handled smoothly.

Prior to the meeting, the convention service manager should review and confirm with the customer:

- The rate structure by category of room
- Complimentary room assignments
- Guestroom priorities for VIPs and speakers
- The room block, including the types of rooms needed by the group
- The group's history in regard to guestroom pickup, no-shows, and cancellations
- The arrival and departure pattern for the group

Rate Structures

Rates are extremely important to the planner. If the rates negotiated are beyond the budget of some attendees, they may book sleeping rooms elsewhere (outside the designated room block). This could significantly impact rental agreements for meeting rooms and could result in attrition fees.

Because most large-scale conventions are planned well in advance, the hotel will not commit itself to any firm rates. This policy is usually made clear during initial negotiations. It is also included in the final contract.

One of the preliminary decisions to be made in booking a convention is what rates to charge for delegates' rooms. Naturally the rates will vary between hotels and even within the hotel itself. Rates are determined according to a number of factors, including season (busy or slow), days of the week, size of the group, length of stay, type of room, number of persons in the room, and the known attendance and difficulty with the group's past conventions. Of course, the interpretation of these factors is up to the individual property. A resort hotel, for example, fills up with social guests on weekends, so it is not likely to offer

Exhibit 6   Attracting Meeting Planners by Offering the Passkey Room Reservations System

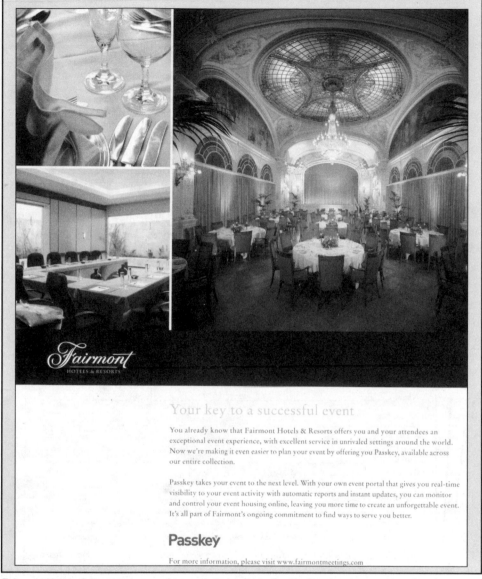

Fairmont Hotels & Resorts is one of several chains that offer the Passkey room reservations system to meeting planners at no cost. This ad promotes the benefit of using the Passkey system to monitor and control event attendance in real-time, which enables the meeting planner to spend more time on other aspects of his or her event.
Source: Courtesy of Fairmont Hotels & Resorts.

discounted rates to a meeting group, while a downtown hotel that realizes the majority of its business during the middle of the week is more likely to offer discounted rates on the weekends.

Many hotels work within the limits of certain rate scales determined by management. The main ones are:

Rack rate. All rates remain as posted, with no discounts or concessions. This is generally preferred by the hotels for easy bookkeeping, but **rack rates** are rarely used for conventions, because convention groups are able to negotiate a group rate lower than rack rates.

INTERNET EXERCISE

Visit the Hilton Hotels website at www.hilton.com and click on the "Meetings" tab. Scroll down to the "Tools for Your Meeting" section.

1. What search criteria is available to meeting planners seeking group value dates?
2. Explain why the Guest List Manager and the Personalized Group Web Pages features are valuable to meeting planners who book with the Hilton chain.
3. Click on the "Learn More" link at the end of the Online Event Planning Tools section. Then click on the Event Planning Checklist and go to the Business Meetings link. Scroll down to see what factors are included for consideration under the Guest Rooms portion of the checklist.

Run-of-the-house-rate. With a **run-of-the-house rate,** all similar rooms except suites are priced at the average between minimum and maximum rates, despite level or location. All guests pay the same rate. This is also called a *flat-rate arrangement.*

Split Rate. Split rates are offered to a group based on the room type. For example, regular guestrooms would be offered at a different rate than tower club rooms.

Exhibit 7 Reservation Confirmation Form

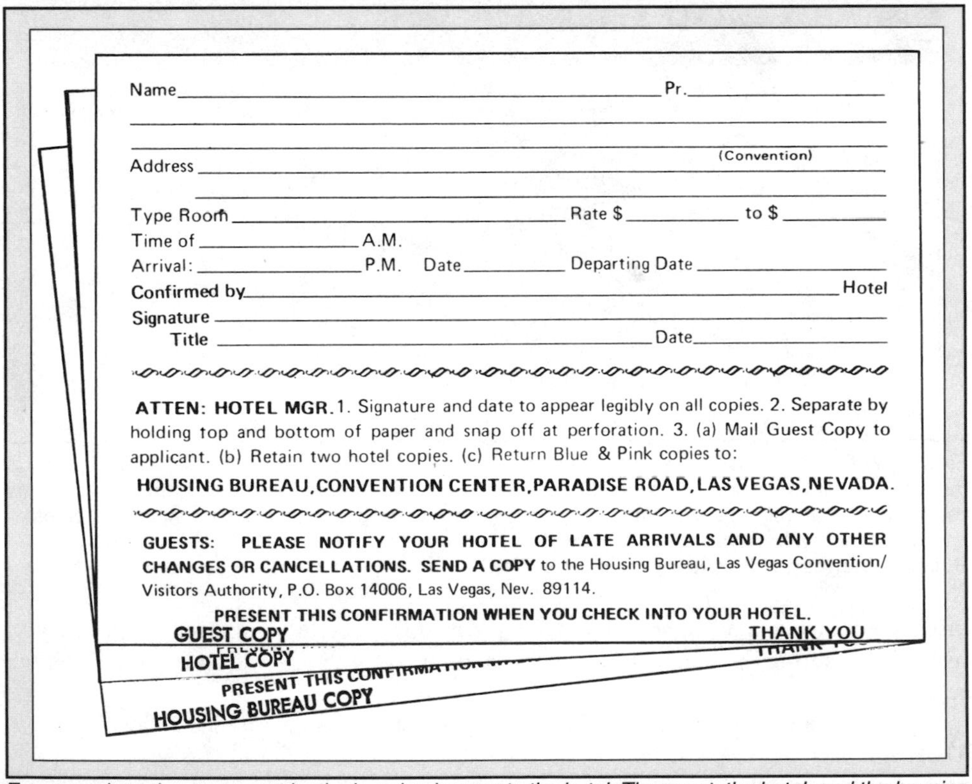
Name ________________ Pr. ________________

Address ________________ (Convention)

Type Room ________________ Rate $ ________ to $ ________
Time of ________ A.M.
Arrival: ________ P.M. Date ________ Departing Date ________
Confirmed by ________________ Hotel
Signature ________________
Title ________________ Date ________

ATTEN: HOTEL MGR. 1. Signature and date to appear legibly on all copies. 2. Separate by holding top and bottom of paper and snap off at perforation. 3. (a) Mail Guest Copy to applicant. (b) Retain two hotel copies. (c) Return Blue & Pink copies to:
HOUSING BUREAU, CONVENTION CENTER, PARADISE ROAD, LAS VEGAS, NEVADA.

GUESTS: PLEASE NOTIFY YOUR HOTEL OF LATE ARRIVALS AND ANY OTHER CHANGES OR CANCELLATIONS. SEND A COPY to the Housing Bureau, Las Vegas Convention/Visitors Authority, P.O. Box 14006, Las Vegas, Nev. 89114.
PRESENT THIS CONFIRMATION WHEN YOU CHECK INTO YOUR HOTEL.
GUEST COPY THANK YOU
HOTEL COPY
PRESENT THIS CONFIRMATION
HOUSING BUREAU COPY

Forms such as these are sent by the housing bureau to the hotel. The guest, the hotel, and the housing bureau retain copies.
Source: Courtesy of the Las Vegas Convention and Visitors Authority.

Effective Guestrooms Management

Kristine K. Gagliardi
Corporate Director of Convention Services
Hilton Hotels Corporation

"During the past several years, I have had the opportunity to develop and implement standardized quality assurance programs for Hilton Hotels convention service departments corporate-wide. During the initial research phase, all existing hotel-wide guestroom block procedures were examined. Aware that Hilton's system-wide computerized reservation/front office system would jointly benefit the group/hotel alliance by means of technical support, it was our intent to offer meeting groups an effective, accurate guestroom system during every stage of the meeting — pre-planning, on site, and beyond to post-meeting information.

"Also important to our research was the initial booking process by sales. Was a group's historical data properly checked? Did this information correlate with the current booking? Was the pattern of arrival and departures in line with the group's meeting program? Did the proposed reservation method work to benefit the group and hotel? Did the group's cut-off date give the group and hotel enough time to react to casualty?

"In order to monitor reservations closely, a convention service file activity checklist was developed to systematically track group pick-up and other pertinent group arrangements. By use of this checklist, the convention service managers could trace group block activity and, if warranted, have subsequent discussion with the meeting planner regarding pick-up information. One week prior to the cut-off, the group was contacted again to re-verify all room-related issues. The checklist once again was to be utilized as a primary tool to initiate action ten days before the group's arrival.

"Equipped with valuable customer information regarding check-in/check-out expectations, the hotel could then prepare a strategy to ensure a smooth arrival. Arrival patterns, transportation methods, and peak check-in times are closely reviewed. The pre-registration of rooms, suites, and VIP accommodations would also be accomplished in preparation for the group's arrival. At the conclusion of the meeting, this information would be compiled into a 'meeting report.' Sent directly to the meeting planner and routed throughout the Hilton system, this report was to cover all aspects of the meeting, including guestroom particulars: reservation method, sequence of hotel reservation pick-up, arrival/departure patterns, final pick-up data, casualty and no-show percentages, suite usage, etc."

Discounted rate. Discounted rates, also called *spread rates,* are used primarily when the result will bring preferred return business, encourage current business, or attract business from the hotel's competition for preferred groups.

It is important to remember that many conventions are planned years in advance, and that rates could vary a great deal over that time. This makes it essential to "peg" a rate of increase to determine the rates that the group will pay in the future.

In most cases, the hotel's rack room rate is used to find the "peg rate." If, for example, the current rack rate is $150 per night and the group rate is $120 per night, the percentage below the peg rate is 20 percent. This percentage would be used to determine room rates at the time of the meeting (attendees would get 20 percent off the rack rate in effect at the time of the function). Other planners insist on more specific room rate guarantees; one planner, for example, specifies the following clause be included in the contract:

> *The Hotel guarantees that room rates extended to the Symposium shall not exceed 85 percent of the rack rate and the present applicable rate shall not increase more than 5 percent per year. The final rate shall be established 12 months in advance of the Symposium.*

Small groups tend toward the use of flat rates, while large conventions find split or discount rates more to their liking. Rack rates are seldom used for conventions unless the group is small or the hotel is running at high occupancy.

Room Types

Single:	A room assigned to one person. May have one or more beds.
Double:	A room assigned to two people. May have one or more beds.
Queen:	A room with a queen-size bed. May be occupied by one or more people.
King:	A room with a king-size bed. May be occupied by one or more people.
Twin:	A room with two twin beds. May be occupied by one or more people.
Double-double:	A room with two double (or sometimes queen) beds. May be occupied by one or more persons.
Mini-suite or junior suite:	A single room with a bed and a sitting area. Sometimes the sleeping area is in a bedroom separate from the parlor or living room.
Suite:	A parlor or living room connected to one or more bedrooms.
Connecting rooms:	Rooms with individual entrance doors from the outside and a connecting door between. Guests can move between rooms without going through the hallway.
Adjoining rooms:	Rooms with a common wall but no connecting door.
Adjacent rooms:	Rooms close to each other, perhaps across the hall.

Discounts typically range up to 30 percent off the rack rate. Naturally, the hotel's objective is to ensure that it gets business, but at the highest possible rate. Questions often asked about the group to determine the amount of discount include:

- How much can they be expected to spend? Will they have cocktail parties? Banquets? Requests for meeting and exhibit space?
- What are the opportunities for future business with the group?
- Is the group willing to put down a firm financial hold on its room block?

Regardless of the rate decided upon, it is important to make the rate arrangements clear. If there is a range of rates, the reservation form should indicate the range and serve notice that rooms in the next higher category will be supplied if those at the requested rate are no longer available. Even if the contract calls for rack rates, it is best to indicate those on the reservation form.

Sometimes the association requests that the hotel charge the delegate more than the agreed-upon room rate and to refund the excess to the association. Hotels generally decline such requests for obvious ethical reasons, particularly if the convention attendee is unaware of the arrangement.

Complimentary Arrangements

Most hotels offer concessions to get group business. It is common practice to extend one complimentary guestroom (**comp room**) for every 50 rooms used, or one suite for every 100 guestrooms.

A rooming list supplied by the meeting planner should specify who will occupy these rooms. To avoid heated arguments at the cashier's window, it is the planner's responsibility to spell out the extent of the complimentary arrangements to the guest and provide a copy to the hotel.

The meeting planner should tell his or her people, especially if complimentary rooms will be used by speakers and program members, what they must pay for themselves and what may be applied to the master account. It is easiest to use complimentary rooms for staff, but that is at the option of the meeting planner. It doesn't matter so long as everyone knows what is expected of him or her.

Some hotels provide a complimentary cocktail party or VIP welcome amenities upon arrival, complimentary travel to and from the airport, and free meeting space. There are no general guidelines for making concessions, but many hotels offer comp rooms and other concessions on the basis of guestroom pick-up. For example, if the group fails to pick up 80 percent of their contracted room block, it may only be allocated one comp room for every 100 rooms used. There is no general guideline. A hotel must use sound judgment and integrity.

Priorities

It is important that the convention planner supply a list of VIPs to the hotel. It is necessary to codify certain types of guests and the accomodations indicated for them. This is certainly important when you have accommodations in different buildings of the hotel. Association officials such as officers, board members, and staff usually get special treatment. Exhibitors, speakers, and entertainers may also require special attention.

It is important to block rooms so that oceanfront rooms and suites in resort hotels and the "best rooms available" in commercial properties are assigned to VIPs without question, regardless of the occupancy of the house. It is often the responsibility of the convention service manager to see that these reservations are in order. He or she should set up a procedure to check the day before arrival on what type of accommodations are blocked for VIPs and also on the day of arrival to make sure that these accommodations are delivered. In addition, the service manager might find out the VIPs' arrival times.

It is the policy of some hotels to have the sales office see that the VIPs get the proper attention. The feeling is that the salesperson's self-preservation is determined by his or her impression on the association's decision-makers, and the decision-makers are usually found on the priority list.

The VIP list should also be coded to include the possible supply of fruit, liquor, and/ or flowers. The allocation of suites is also important, especially if the hotel has a limited number. Discuss this with the convention planner. Some associations have a rule that non-exhibitors cannot maintain hospitality suites.

Take care to hold a small number of rooms in a prime area of the hotel for late priority listings; they inevitably appear late in the game.

Room Types

You must know the number and kinds of rooms to be held. Most agreements with convention planners call for a guarantee of a total *number* of rooms to be used. This may be fine at the negotiating table, but as the event approaches you need to know how many of these are singles, doubles, twins, or suites. Don't forget that there is much confusion about suite designation. Some hotels go so far as to indicate suites as having "one bedroom for two people" or "two bedrooms for four people." In addition, people confuse twins and doubles.

This can be clarified by indicating "one bed for two people" or "two beds for two people." The box titled "Room Types" provides definitions that are common throughout the industry.

The Group History

Since many conventions are booked far in advance, the number of rooms blocked out is an estimate, based on past conventions. Communication between hotel and planner is vital, so regularly scheduled reports should be used to track reservation pick-up patterns.

The letter of agreement should indicate a date by which the organization will either confirm or release the rooms. Reservations received after the cutoff date are accepted on a **space available basis** only, and often the convention rate is not available to reservations received after the cutoff date. In all cases, the reservations should be confirmed individually, with a copy sent to the meeting planner.

The hotel and association should re-examine the room commitment on several intermediate dates and readjust the number if necessary. Most convention center bureaus and hotels provide weekly room pick-up reports, which are also called **booking pace reports**, showing the inventory status of the room blocks to meeting planners. In addition to tracking room pick-up on a weekly basis, the group's historical information (booking patterns and final pick-up information from previous meetings) provides invaluable insights into the likelihood of the group's block being filled. For example, if the hotelier is advised that the majority of the group does not book rooms until four weeks out, he or she will not be alarmed when the block is only half full at six weeks out.

The convention planner must be alert for early signals that might affect meeting attendance. These could be an unusual circumstance, such as the 50th anniversary of the association, an unusually good or bad year, the selection of a prime resort site, or an unusual number of members recruited that year. The smart planners will communicate their apprehensions and revelations to their hotel counterparts so that all attendees may be housed conveniently. Mutual reassurance will reduce the chances of double booking by delegates and overbooking by hotels.

You should not bury your head in the sand and go blithely about your business if you don't receive periodic communiques from your client. D-Day will come and you may face a milling mob around the registration desk or a multitude of unfilled rooms. You cannot afford just to wait hopefully if you don't hear from your client. Keep constant tabs on the reservations being received and interpret how the flow affects the total number of rooms being held.

Constant communication between both parties leads comfortably to the day when the organization executive confirms or releases the number of rooms held. (This is vital to resorts that have little or no business off the street, especially during off-season periods.)

The planner and hotel person who keep in touch constantly and adjust room allotments along the way seem to continue to do business together. They execute meetings together without the shock of housing problems at the outset of the event.

Arrival/Departure Pattern

In assigning rooms, you need an overall pattern that will indicate when people will arrive and depart. The convention planner may have some idea from previous years, but you will have to finalize detailed patterns when you get the reservations from the guests. Even for corporate meetings, where the meeting planner has greater control, attendees frequently arrive a day or two early because of transportation difficulties, personal travel plans, or the attraction of local tourist or recreational facilities.

For example, typical arrivals for a 400-room convention beginning on Monday and concluding on Thursday might look something like this:

Day	Number of Rooms	Flow of Attendance
Friday	20	meeting planner and staff
Saturday	150	early arrivals
Sunday	360	opening of convention
Monday	400	peak convention attendance
Tuesday	400	peak convention attendance
Wednesday	350	early departures
Thursday	30	post-convention meetings and extended days

It is also wise to indicate the breakdown of the group's rooms into singles, doubles, twins, and suites. Arrival dates are easier to secure than check-out dates, but these too are important to you.

Be especially careful if you designate the availability of a *specific* suite. That extra-special VIP suite may be earmarked for the chairman of the board, who may very well decide to test your golf course and arrive a day or two before the meeting or stay in it several days after the event. Impress on your client that you must have advance notice of such plans to make sure the room is available and that there is no conflict with another group.

You will also need to determine the **major arrival/major departure** pattern of incoming convention guests. That is, the dates and times at which large numbers of attendees can be expected to check-in at the hotel and when large numbers of delegates will be checking out. The group's resume should provide this information, which is vital for planning staffing—you will need to have enough desk clerks and bellpersons available for a large influx of guests at particular times. The typical ratio is one bellperson and one front desk receptionist/cashier for every 75 guests arriving or departing. If a group is to arrive or depart en masse, however, one staff person for every 50 guests may be required.

Should the check-in for the group be early afternoon, the hotel may need to set up a hospitality area where attendees can wait until vacated rooms are readied by housekeeping. This is a problem for European hotels because most large planes arrive from the United States in the early morning but check-out time for departing guests is not until noon or so.

Other Hotels

As we mentioned earlier in this chapter, sometimes a number of hotels are to be used for a large convention. In such instances, a competitor becomes a friend. It is nice to have a nearby hotel bail you out with a number of rooms when you may have overbooked. It is just as nice to receive guests from the other hotel when you have a number of rooms available — and to have the favors returned on other occasions. It pays to work together.

Similarly, you may be unable to supply a function room for the convention or for a local customer's banquet. Show the customer that you are interested in his welfare even when you are full by helping him to book the event at another hotel. The other hotel may appreciate the recommendation and reciprocate; your customer appreciates the help and the fact that you didn't turn your back on him when you didn't need the business. Always look to the future. The key to success in the hotel business is a good reputation for expertise and *caring*.

A variation may involve only the use of hotel facilities, such as golf courses or tennis courts. An inter-hotel billing arrangement also must be worked out in the case of multi-hotel involvements, which may bring local bus companies into the act.

Managing Room Blocks

Hotels that cater to group meetings and conventions face potential difficulties when it comes to their rooms inventory. Meeting planners, naturally, want to ensure that there are enough rooms set aside for their attendees—and the number of rooms blocked can play a key role in negotiations for such perks as free meeting space and complimentary rooms. Hoteliers, of course, want to properly house the group, but the hotel's potential profitability can suffer if room blocks are overestimated or rooms otherwise go unfilled (not only do hotels lose money on unsold rooms, but revenue from such areas as food and beverage, recreational amenities, transportation, and other services may be far less than projected).

In this section, we will discuss some of the factors involved in managing room blocks. We will take a look at some of the most common potential problems that may arise when trying to manage room blocks and detail how hotels, meeting planners, and housing providers can work together to ensure that these problems can be avoided or minimized.

🖳 *INTERNET EXERCISE*

Experient, a leading third-party meeting planner, has published an excellent resource titled "Guide to Room Block Management." Go to the Experient website (www.experient-inc.com) and click on "Knowledge Center." Then click on "Experient Publications" to view the 64-page booklet (you will have to register to access resources).

1. What types of historical information are needed to compile a meeting group's history?

2. How does combining housing and registration information in one mailing to meeting attendees aid groups in filling their room blocks?

3. What incentives are recommended for hotels to offer to assist in maximizing room pick-up?

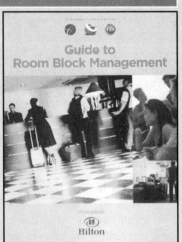

Guide to
Room Block Management

Ⓗ
Hilton

No-Shows/Overbooking

Attendees who fail to check into the hotel despite having a reservation are termed **no-shows**. No-shows may either be guests who fail to attend the convention, whether or not they cancel their reservations, or guests who attend the event but do not use the rooms booked in the group's block. In addition to no-shows, a hotel's profitability can be affected by guests who check out early. An **early departure** is a guest who leaves the hotel earlier than his or her scheduled departure date. Although this is less of a problem for city and airport hotels, which get a certain amount of **walk-in** business, the early departure can be devastating on resort hotels, which usually don't have the advantage of capturing transient business.

Early departures, like no-shows, can result in a significant loss of room revenue, as well as food and beverage, incidental, and recreational income. Scott Boone, vice president of sales for InterContinental Hotels and Resorts, says:

> We've noticed an increase in early departures over the past three to four years, especially with convention attendees. Attendees usually book rooms months ahead for the whole conference, then adjust their schedules and neglect to notify the hotel....We just want guests to focus on their departure date so that we in turn will have inventory to offer.[3]

Underdeparture. Early outs are not the only challenge facing hoteliers in managing group room blocks. At the other end of the spectrum, problems may also arise if the guest decides to stay another day; this is called **underdeparture**. The hotel may have set aside a block of 250 rooms, and if 20 attendees decide to overstay, there may not be enough rooms available for other booked business (this can be especially critical if the group was booked at one rate but the hotel can get a higher rate for the rooms once they are vacated by the group).

Many hotels require a guest to initial the registration card indicating the day of departure; this institutes a contract between the hotel and the guest. The hotel meets its obligation by providing the room through that date. Once the date has passed, the guest may be considered a "trespasser." The hotel has two options: it can enter a new contract at a different rate (the hotel is not obligated to extend the convention rate); or, the hotel may evict the guest (the problem is that in the vast majority of states the hotel has to take the overstaying guest to court, which obviously is costly and time-consuming).

Advance Deposits and Guarantees. The increasing problem of no-shows and early departures has resulted in hotels taking additional measures to minimize losses. The Hospitality Sales and Marketing Association International strongly recommends the use of deposits as a solution to no-shows. With an **advance deposit reservation**, the hotel receives payment for at least the first night's lodging prior to the guest's arrival and is obligated to hold the room regardless of the guest's arrival time. If a guest holding an advance deposit reservation fails to check-in or cancel, the hotel may retain the deposit. A hotel that is going to take deposits must consider the necessary control and recordkeeping involved and the possibility of refunds.

Another solution offered is the use of **guaranteed reservations**. A **credit card guaranteed reservation** is a room being held, using the guest's credit card account number, for which payment is guaranteed; in the case of a no-show, billing takes place in the usual manner. But many hotels cite difficulties collecting such payments. The term is often misinterpreted; guests do not always understand that they are agreeing to guarantee payment regardless of whether or not the room is used.

Because the no-show problem is more significant at high-demand resorts than at city and airport properties, resorts have been the leaders in instituting stricter cancellation policies. In an effort to eliminate no-shows and control rooms inventory, some convention hotels have pushed their cancellation deadline to 72 hours before expected check-in.

Overbooking. In some cases, hotels that have experienced a great number of no-shows (and especially those that cannot rely on transient business to fill unused rooms) try to cover

SOME ASSOCIATION HOUSING POLICIES CONTRIBUTE TO HOTEL OVERBOOKING

In a perfect world, no hotel would ever overbook guestrooms. But hotels can't stop taking reservations when all their rooms "appear" to be sold. Because of "early departures" and "no-shows," hotels that do not confirm more than 100 percent of their rooms run the risk of going 10 percent to 15 percent unsold.

The system is broken, and no one is fixing it. Consider the scenario for citywide conventions. Attendees return a form indicating which hotel(s) they prefer to be in. Registrants are asked to select their top three to six choices, in case the first choice is sold out.

The housing organization attempts to assign the attendees to their desired hotel. If the No. 1 or No. 2 choice is available, there is a high probability the attendee will use the reservation. However, that likelihood decreases the further down the list you go. When all of an attendee's preferred hotels are sold out, most housing authorities will arbitrarily assign a hotel.

This is where the real trouble begins.

Hotels get notification of reservations from the housing organization without knowing if their hotel was a primary request or if it was an "assigned" reservation. (This information would be helpful because there is traditionally a larger "no-show" factor among attendees who are "assigned" rooms.) Many of these "assigned" attendees do not bother to call the hotel to cancel their reservations. Even advanced deposits made by credit card do not deter this practice, because most travelers know that if they challenge a charge, most credit card companies will not pay the deposit to a canceled hotel.

The net result: Hotels that don't overbook during a citywide convention have absolutely no hope of selling out their available rooms.

Another reason for overbooking: when booking many years out, planners tend to be overly optimistic, resulting in hundreds (or even thousands) of excess room nights requested.

If past history doesn't support the block, hotels are caught in a bind. If the group doesn't pick up, many rooms will go unsold. One strategy many hotels employ, whether they admit it or not, is to disregard the contractual block and instead protect a smaller block for the group. This enables the hotel to sell the remaining rooms to any interested buyers, be it other groups or individuals. Ideally, when the cut-off date arrives, the group will be under its contracted block by the same number of rooms that the hotel oversold.

Unfortunately, this is not an ideal world. Walks result when a group picks up beyond its history or when a hotel sells too deeply into its block. This creates the overbooked situation where some attendees have to be "walked" to a different hotel.

The solution here is to establish realistic room blocks based on past performance. After each year's convention, future room blocks should be adjusted to reflect actual growth (or decline) in attendance. This should create a situation in which, at 12 months out, the room block would be within 3 to 4 percent of the previous year's pickup.

This adjustment would give hotels a much tighter comfort level. And, instead of 10 to 15 percent, overbooking could drop to 5 percent or less.

Source: Bruce Harris, founder and past president of Conferon (now Experient), the nation's largest independent meeting planning company.

projected losses by booking more rooms than they actually have available. This practice is known as **overbooking**.

If a hotel overbooks, a convention guest who arrives late may find that there are no rooms available. This constitutes a breach of contract by the hotel, which now owes the latecomer damages. These guests are termed **walked customers**, as the hotel is responsible for finding other accommodations for them. This situation has led many meeting planners to specify that a *relocation, or walk, clause* be included in the group's contract. This clause provides for specific actions by the hotel in the event of overbooking, and may include such points as a complimentary room at a different hotel for each night that the attendee cannot be accommodated at the original hotel, a complimentary telephone call to allow the attendee to inform others of the change, complimentary transportation (or payment of the cost of transportation) to the new hotel, upgraded accommodations if the delegate returns to the original hotel, an in-room amenity upon the guest's return, and a letter of apology to the guest in which the hotel accepts responsibility for the overbooking situation.

Hotels can minimize potential problems from overbooking by contacting properties previously used by the group to determine the group's no-show history. If a group typically fills its room block, the hotel will see less reason to overbook (the property may still oversell to a lesser degree to guard against any slippage). Conversely, it is a smart meeting planner who checks among his or her peers for a hotel's overbooking pattern. Wise planners also inform their members of the practice of hotels to hold reservations only until a certain hour, such as 5:00 p.m. They urge their members to arrive earlier than the hold deadline or to guarantee or pre-pay to make sure they get their rooms.

Attrition

Many hotels protect themselves against no-shows, early outs, and underdepartures by inserting an **attrition clause** into their contracts. Since guestrooms are a perishable commodity, the hotel loses money if it is not able to resell rooms that meeting groups have booked but failed to fill. When hotels book blocks of rooms for groups, however, they normally allow for some **slippage**. While slippage amounts vary, many hotels expect groups to occupy or pay for 80 percent of the rooms blocked. Attrition fees, which are charged to the group, not the individual attendees, apply when the meeting group contracts for a specific number of rooms but the total amount of rooms used is below the original contracted block. Many meeting planners balk at such fees, and some fight the problem by reducing their room block. This practice, however, can cause a different set of problems; booking fewer rooms weakens a planner's negotiating position, perhaps adversely impacting meeting space or reducing the group's number of complimentary rooms.

Attrition has become such a large problem in such a short time that the Convention Industry Council launched Project Attrition, a nine-month study of the problem. The final report can be viewed online at:

www.conventionindustry.org/resources/project_ attrition _report11204.pdf.

While the CIC was developing guidelines that could be used industry-wide, many hotels and convention centers had already taken steps to help meeting planners minimize attrition. Hotels are not in the business of collecting fees; they want to fill rooms. Group guests spend more time in the hotel than other types of guests and therefore spend more money at the property, so it is important for hotels to find solutions to help a group to manage its block. Joel Pyser, vice president of field sales for Marriott, says:

> Attrition is the number-one issue our customers talk about, and we want
> our customers to see us as providing them solutions.[4]

Rather than rely on attrition damages, which rarely make up a hotel's entire loss, many hotels are "partnering" with meeting planners — offering services and suggestions to help planners manage and promote their room blocks to avoid attrition fees. One such service is Hilton Hotels' Group Rooms Identification Program (GRIP) software, which interfaces with the chain's reservation system to provide a cross-reference of the group's reservations list in relationship to the rooms booked within its block. The GRIP system provides immediate, detailed summary reports of rooms booked outside the block, enabling the meeting planner to contact attendees that have made their reservations through other channels and encourage them to rebook their reservations correctly. If attendees do not wish to change their reservations, the GRIP system will ensure that their rooms are credited to the group, resulting in an accurate group history.

Several other properties have created event websites with registration and room reservations capabilities. These sites promote the value of staying at the headquarters hotel, including the proximity to events and opportunities for networking. And, to compete with possible lower Internet rates, some hotels, such as the Starwood chain, fix a price for guestrooms no matter what the source of booking (including the Internet, travel agents, the hotel's own reservations system, and so on).

Booking Outside the Block. When attendees bypass the group's housing service and book rooms at hotels other than those specified by the meeting planner, the hotel doesn't attribute those reservations to the group's block. This practice, called **booking outside the block**, is becoming more common, especially with easy access to hotel information on the Internet and the increasing use of third-party providers.

In some cases, especially when a large convention requires housing the delegates in a number of hotels, delegates may make multiple reservations because they fear they won't get a room at their first-choice hotel. Attendees frequently use the Internet to find travel "deals" (Hotels.com, Expedia, and Travelocity represent 75 percent of online sales).[5] It has become increasingly common to find that 20–30 percent of a group's attendees book their rooms online, whether at the host hotel or at other properties in the convention city.[6]

Attendees who use the Internet may find cheaper rates at the host hotel and book rooms not designated in the group's contract. In other cases, convention guests book into a hotel in which they are members of a loyalty program. Whatever the reason, the group's block is adversely affected, impacting both the meeting planner — who may lose free meeting space and other perks and possibly face attrition fees (discussed later in this section) — and the hotel, which can lose financially when rooms go unused.

Hotels can help meeting planners fill their designated blocks by suggesting that planners "bundle" registration; that is, charge delegates one fee for the entire event (including registration, room, event attendance, and other services, such as transportation). Delegates who book outside the block would be required to pay a higher registration fee or be charged additional fees for specific events, such as an evening banquet. Planners can also discourage booking outside the block by including the reasons for booking within the group's block in promotional materials. Delegates tempted to book outside the block might be persuaded to change their minds when they realize that such benefits as free meeting space, complimentary receptions, audiovisual equipment, and other services are based on filling a guaranteed number of rooms.

Room Audits. As we have seen, attrition can be a problem for both hotels and meeting planners. Not only can failure to fill up its room blocks result in attrition fees for meeting groups, it also affects the group's leverage in future negotiations. If the group's history reflects a lack of room pick-up, it can lose a number of concessions, such as complimentary rooms, free or reduced rate meeting rooms, or perhaps complimentary beverage service between sessions.

Hotels, too, have a vested interest in assisting meeting planners to keep attendees in the contracted hotel and filling their room blocks. Rob Scypinski, vice president of sales for Hilton Hotels Corp, says:

> Keeping people in the block obviously helps the association, because
> they won't run into attrition. It also helps the hotel, because even if we

Industry-Wide Housing Practices

The Convention Industry Council (CIC) has adopted best practices for event housing and registration as part of its APEX initiative. This initiative, which can be reviewed in its entirety at www.conventionindustry.org/APEX/accepted.htm, deals with a number of issues in managing room blocks, including practices for collecting, reporting, and retrieving complete housing and registration data.

Housing and registration accepted practices are organized into two parts — recommended forms for registration and housing, and accepted practices to be followed. The forms, which include templates for housing forms and rooming lists, capture the complete and thorough information required by hotels in order to properly manage room blocks. The forms can be customized to suit the character of the meeting (for example, the housing and registration report can be adapted to any size meeting).

Best practices for blocking rooms, managing blocks, tracking rooms, auditing rooms, and information for post-event reports all make it easier for facilities to control room blocks, reduce rooms outside the blocks, and help clients to minimize attrition. These tools, while primarily a help to reservations departments, can certainly present opportunities for improved customer service by hotel sales and service professionals. These accepted practices were also developed to address housing-related terminology and the role of computerized technology in the industry's housing and registration process as well as room block management.

**Source: *The APEX Housing and Registration Accepted Practices,*
Convention Industry Council.**

get a fraction of the room rate for attrition damages, we don't get them eating in our hotel, watching a movie, or using the high-speed Internet.[7]

One of the most effective ways to fight attrition is by using periodic room audits. We have already mentioned Hilton's GRIP software, which produces reports detailing which attendees are booked under the group's code and such other factors as which attendees are sharing rooms and which channels were used to book rooms. Starwood Hotels & Resorts uses a similar system, Starwood's Reservation Cross Check, in its properties in North America, and Experient offers DQ SureMatch, another automated room block auditing service, to its clients.

No matter which method is used, room audits should be conducted periodically to keep the registration and housing process on track. In order for both the meeting group and the hotel to reap the full benefits of room audits, the contract should include provisions that state how audits will be conducted and how these audits will affect concessions made to the group. This provides an incentive to the meeting planner to stay on top of his or her group's block pick-up and to look for any "red flags" that may affect concessions for the current meeting and leverage for future negotiations. The box titled "Industry-Wide Housing Practices" provides guidelines for maximizing the registration and housing process while minimizing problems with booking and attrition.

Historical Performance

Whenever possible, find out where the group met in previous years. It may be best to do this after the contract is signed in order to maintain business security. Don't hesitate at that point to call the sales manager of the hotels used in the past. They will gladly cooperate

Best Practices

Westin's Creative Approach to Tracking a Group's Historical Performance

The Westin chain uses three interrelated procedures in an effort to assess the accuracy of a convention's commitment by observing its past performance. First, a standard letter of inquiry is sent, along with a questionnaire, to the last two hotels in which the group met. The letter states that the group has booked with a Westin property and asks the hotels to make a post-convention critique of the group. The critiques then are matched with the requirements that have been requested. If there is an indication that the group has exaggerated its needs, the hotel goes back to the customer to clarify the discrepancy.

Westin's second procedure is to question a meeting planner who books a year or more in advance about his or her schedule of upcoming meetings. Through the use of the tickler system, the hotel brings up the file two weeks before the group's next meeting and two weeks after it.

On the first date, the hotel wishes the meeting planner the best with the scheduled meeting and advises the planner of an evaluation questionnaire to be sent in four weeks. The planner usually is impressed with the hotel's meticulous approach to detail, and the hotel can be alerted to any change or trends that might alter the number of guestrooms or function space it is holding for the group.

The third technique used by Westin might be called "pre-participation." When convention groups with complicated programs or unusual requirements are booked, the hotel salesperson and the convention service manager might request to be admitted as observers to the group's next meeting. By observing the meeting process and requirements, the convention service manager is better able to service the group at its forthcoming convention in his or her hotel. And, again, the client is reassured that he or she is in good hands.

When the convention planner and the hotel executive have confidence in each other, they can work things out so that all delegates are housed and no one gets hurt by variations in expectations.

Source: Courtesy of Le Westin Montreal.

because they will want to call you sometime for the same reason.

The historical pattern of a convention tells you a great deal. It can inform you early that this group seldom meets its commitments, or that it always does. You may learn that more attendees show up each year than are expected, or that early departures are common. You may find out that the no-show situation is an ever-present problem, or just an odd one or two that is not of major significance.

If nothing else, these calls will give you insight into the meeting planners and let you know whether you are dealing with well-organized pros who can be relied on to control their conventions, or planners who lack expertise or experience. The more you learn about your customers, the better equipped you are in handling them.

If you do learn that a convention generally fails to fill its quota, don't duck the issue. Call the convention executive and indicate that you know the group had problems in previous years and ask him or her to reconsider the number of rooms to be held. Don't just release rooms without telling him or her, because the planner may have good reason to believe the problems will not reoccur. Corrective steps may have been taken or something may have happened to stimulate attendance. At the very least, you may hasten the room release data and get a more realistic appraisal.

Check-In/Check-Out

A hotel should determine in advance when the heaviest influx of delegates can be expected so it can staff accordingly at the front desk. It would be foolhardy to step off on the wrong foot in the beginning. A delegate who is forced to wait in long lines becomes disgruntled and is a likely complainer throughout the stay.

Check-In Procedures

Arrival lines can be noticeably shortened if a distinction is made between guests with and without reservations. By the process of **pre-registration**, rooms are assigned in advance according to the rooming list provided by the group or developed by the reservation clerk based on reservation requests.

Pre-registration of all guests is being done more frequently. Special receiving desks, and even special lobbies, are being used by some hotels that service extensive group business. Many conventions set up a **housing assistance desk** near the registration area where the meeting planner and members of the housing staff can greet and assist delegates. This desk services attendees who encounter reservation problems. These arrangements minimize lobby confusion, long lines, and slow check-in procedures. Whether individual or group check-in is used, the convention service manager should ask that the meeting planner be present at check-in time.

Check-Out Procedures

A poor check-out procedure can destroy an otherwise perfectly organized convention. The group may have had a smooth meeting for three or four days, with excellent food and beverage service, but this positive experience can be ruined if the delegate arrives at the cashier's window to check-out and is greeted by a long line — or worse, a sharp remark from the cashier. That delegate is very likely to leave with a bad taste, and the goodwill generated by three or four days of good meetings is out the window. Group check-out procedure may be one of the little elements of a convention, but it really counts, particularly if it is not handled expeditiously.

Hotels often establish a **check-out time** of noon or 1:00 p.m. If the wrap-up meeting is a luncheon, late check-out service allows the attendees to attend the conference climax. But if guest arrival patterns prohibit late check-outs, guests should be told to sign out before the luncheon session. Their bills should be ready so that the entire group can be processed quickly and their baggage checked in a convenient storage place until departure time.

The Computer Influence

One of the most important trends for the lodging industry is the increased use of computers. In this section, we will briefly consider how computers have influenced the servicing of groups, from reservations to check-out and billing.

Reservations

Of all front office operations, reservations are most associated with computers. Computerized reservations systems require fewer labor hours and provide higher accuracy than manual systems, allowing reservation clerks to enter, retrieve, modify, and question reservations in seconds. Reservation clerks can check availability from meeting room blocks and print confirmations and registration cards on high-speed printers. In addition, various summary reports, including reservation tally sheets that track room pickup against the block, can be generated to assist managers in scheduling and forecasting.

When the reservation department receives a reply form from a delegate, all the information about the guest is typed into the computer and stored. Once the information is entered, there is no need to duplicate the data. The same information is used for confirmation and deposit receipt notices, pre-registration, check-out, and billing procedures.

Registration and Room Assignment

The Hilton Hotels Corp. is eliminating long lines at the front desk by offering free-standing automated check-in/check-out kiosks at its properties.

The computer saves considerable time in the preparation of rooming lists and room assignments. Pre-registration of convention attendees, particularly corporate groups, begins the night before the guests arrive; the required rooms are blocked off, registration cards are pretyped for each guest, and room keys are sorted. Delegates are listed alphabetically within each convention group and assigned rooms according to the type of accommodation and rate range requested. When delegates arrive, they are given preprinted registration cards, prepared by the computer, which they inspect and sign if all is in order. Some hotels set up separate counters away from the main desk to reduce traffic congestion for pre-registered guests.

To speed check-ins, sophisticated systems are emerging, following the lead of Hyatt Hotels' Touch and Go Instant Check-In Machine. Used much like an ATM machine, these **self check-in, check-out terminals** have been promoted as "line-busting technology," as they eliminate long lines at the front desk by allowing guests with reservations to swipe their credit cards to receive their room keys and printed room number and other information in less than 90 seconds.

Hilton has installed kiosks in over 200 of its hotels, and the chain has high expectations for the technology. Tim Harvey, Hilton senior vice president/chief information officer, says:

Exhibit 8   Computer-Generated Booking Report

The Durham Resort
Bookings Report Short Form
For Bookings Arriving Between February 1 to February 7, 20__

Arrival Date	Days	Account Name / (Total RN) Pattern	Booked By	Stat	Funct Space	Average Rate	Total Contribution
2/ 1- 2/ 3/94	Tue Thu	Adams Point Landing (104) 2 102	LMS	D	Y	100.67	10756.00
		Post As: Adams Point Landing					
2/ 1- 2/ 5/94	Tue Sat	Automobile Travelers Association (119) 20 47 44 5 3	LS	D	N	95.00	8131.27
		Post As: Automobile Travelers Assoc.					
2/ 1- 2/ 4/94	Tue Fri	Grant Retirement Party (70) 1 19 42 8	LS	D	N	79.00	3663.10
		Post As: Grant Retirement Party					
2/ 6- 2/ 7/94	Sun Mon	Wed City Anniversary Celebration (45) 20 25	LS	D	Y	95.00	3174.85
		Post As: Wed City Anniversary Celeb					
2/ 6- 2/11/94	Sun Fri	Society Of Technical Writers (905) 8 103 294 272 218 10	AJ	T	N	68.62	37964.75
		Post As: Society Of Technical Writers					
2/ 7- 2/ 7/94	Sat Sat	New England Conservatory (9) 9	LMS	D	Y	98.00	641.97
		Post As: New England Conservatory					

The Durham Resort
Bookings Report Summary by Market Segment
For Bookings Arriving Between February 1 to February 7, 20__

Market Segment	# of Bookings	# of Rm Nights	Guestroom Revenue	Food Revenue	Beverage Revenue	Rooms Rental	Resource Rental	Other Revenue	Total Revenue
National Association	3	180	21600	5400	1345	600	1200	800	30945
Regional Association	2	1024	112640	28160	4525	500	500	800	147125
State Association	3	0	0	5850	890	1500	250	500	8990
National Corporation	1	0	0	2450	580	250	500	400	4180
Local Corporation	2	70	8750	2580	1200	600	600	400	14130
Tour & Travel	7	347	38864	9716	2500	700	660	1200	53640
TOTAL	18	1621	181854	54156	11040	4150	3710	4100	261010

Data entered into the computer system is often used to generate reports such as booking activity by market segment. Producing such reports manually would require hours of labor.
Source: *Delphi Reports Sampler,* Newmarket Software Systems, Inc., 44 Market Rd., Durham, NH 03824.

Best Practices

GAYLORD PALMS™
RESORT & CONVENTION CENTER

Gaylord Hotels: Using Technology to Better Service Large Groups

Gaylord Hotels, which operates the 2,881-room Gaylord Opryland Resort & Convention Center in Nashville, Tennessee; the 1,406-room Gaylord Palms Resort & Convention Center in Kissimmee, Florida; and the 1,511-room Gaylord Opryland Texas Resort & Convention Center in Grapevine, Texas, is using technology to successfully host large groups and provide convention attendees with comprehensive information about their event online. Computers are used to manage group business, from centrally managing and distributing sales leads to automated check-in and check-out. Craig Ratterman, director of strategic systems, says:

"Gaylord Hotels set up group-specific websites for attendees, and can accept rooming lists from any group that sends them in electronic format. They also use wireless terminals at check-in to give maximum flexibility, and give each attendee an individually customized map with directions to their room and to their conference's registration and location information. With the new Gaylord iConnect technology, convention-goers can also see their group members' phone extensions and check their convention schedule. They can also view a welcome message and other e-mails from their group, check property maps to find their specific events, visit the layout of the exhibit hall, and find out where the booths are—all online."

Source: "Gaylord Gets Groups," *Hospitality Upgrade,* Spring 2003, p. 13.

We've found usage of these kiosks to be exceeding our early expectations, what with some 10% to 12% of our guests [on average] using them, and, in some instances, as high as 35%.[8]

New technology has also ushered in the use of check-out-only kiosks. Smaller and more portable than regular kiosks, they can be placed near meeting rooms or on guestroom floors for more efficient service for groups—guests can check out as they make their way to a meeting or the lobby or during a meeting break. In addition, some hotels offer dedicated kiosks that meeting planners can use to provide customized welcome messages and updated meeting agendas. Agendas can be printed out on attendees' receipts when members of the group check in.

While kiosks can eliminate long waits and may save on labor costs, they do have their drawbacks. First, they are expensive, costing between $10,000–$18,000 each. Second, although customers are becoming more used to self-service terminals, such as ATM machines and airline kiosks, some are hesitant to use the machines for check-in, preferring instead to speak to a front desk clerk. Hotels are responding to this concern by reassigning front desk personnel to assist guests using the kiosks.

For those guests preferring to make accommodation arrangements in the privacy of their home or office, another innovative service that uses today's technology is Radisson Hotel's "Express Yourself[SM]." This program allows guests to check in at their own convenience over the web. First, guests reserve a room via any Radisson booking process (website, call center, hotel direct, or through a travel agent). Seven days prior to the visit, guests receive an e-mail inviting them to "express" themselves by checking in at the Radisson website (www.radisson.com). There, guests enter check-in information and can make requests such as specific room location, preferred amenities (such as high-speed Internet access), and other special service requests. Upon arrival, guests need only identify themselves at the front desk, where they will promptly receive their room key and hotel packet.

Bjorn Gullaksen, Carlson Hotels Worldwide executive vice president and brand leader, says:

> Radisson is taking a bold step to transform what consumer research has consistently shown as the least-desirable experience in the hotel stay— standing in line for a slow check-in or slow check-out. We will never replace the human element of a friendly front desk person, but "Express Yourself" will eliminate the paperwork that has traditionally been the main focus of today's check-in process. By freeing our staff from these procedural restraints, they can now concentrate on welcoming the guest and getting them quickly to their room.[9]

Check-Out and Billing

Throughout the delegate's stay, charges are posted to an electronic folio, either at the front desk or at several *points-of-sale*. Point-of-sale terminals are located in profit centers throughout the hotel and are linked to the hotel's central computer, so guest charges are entered directly to the electronic folio instantaneously. Because vouchers do not have to be physically carried from the points-of-sale to the front desk for posting, time delays and possible revenue loss are significantly reduced. Folios are often preprinted for convention attendees expected to depart on a given day. As delegates arrive at the cashier's window for departure, the clerk quickly scans the folio on the screen for late charges, prints a new folio only for those needing updating, and presents the printed folio. When guests are ready to check out, they are given a running account of their transactions. Computer systems also maintain master accounts for the meeting staff and can separate all charges by specific service location.

Reports and Analysis Applications

The applications of the computer to the front desk operation are not the only benefits that are obtained from such a system. Management information, such as marketing reports and control features, are additional advantages of an in-house computer. An automated sales office can quickly generate lists and reports that would take hours to produce manually. For example, the *Booking Report* shown in Exhibit 8 allows the sales and rooms departments to select and summarize important marketing criteria such as booking status, arrival dates, room night totals, and booking patterns. These statistics are a vital tool to help management plan sales strategies and target promotional efforts.

The computer frees personnel from laborious bookkeeping and paper shuffling, allowing them to provide convention groups with more prompt service.

The front desk is often the first contact for many convention delegates, and a friendly, efficient check-in sets the tone for a successful meeting.
Photo Courtesy of the Madinat Jumeriah Hotel in Dubai.

Summary

A smooth reservations procedure sets the stage for a successful function. Fortunately, today's technology has streamlined the reservations process. Technology has made it easier than ever to process registrations over the Internet—credit card payments can be instantly processed, and confirmations can be immediately sent to both the attendee and the meeting planner. In addition, computer software has greatly facilitated the processing of registration and event information, especially when hotels make use of standardized forms and technology.

The downside of this technology is that attendees are more likely than ever to compare prices and book rooms over the Internet—often bypassing the group's designated block. This makes it necessary for planners to work with hotels to develop strategies to keep their group in their block to avoid lost concessions and possible attrition damages. This process is made easier by educating attendees about the importance of booking within the block—and sometimes offering incentives, such as registration discounts. Hotels can help planners to manage their blocks by providing periodic room audits to "flag" attendees who have bypassed the block and booked elsewhere in the hotel.

Both the hotel and the meeting planner should ensure that reservation information is communicated early and often to ensure that adjustments can be made. Proper room arrangements and efficient check-in and check-out procedures also add to a delegate's favorable impression of the property—and may result in future business from the meeting planner.

Endnotes

1.   Maxine Golding, "Convention Housing," *Convene*.

2.   "The Broadmoor Simplifies Event Management with Passkey," www.hotel-online.com, May 19, 2008.

3.   Linda Humphrey, "Early Check-Out Fees Gaining Momentum," *Business Travel News*.

4.   *Meeting News.*

5.   Mary Ann McNulty, "Pandora's Box," *PCMA Convene*.

6.   Susan Hatch, "Online Booking Blues," *Corporate Meetings & Incentives*.

7.   Jonathan Vatner, "Keeping Them in Line," *Meetings and Conventions*, July 2006, p. 64.

8.   ehotelier.com.

9.   Michael Billig, "Technology Snapshot," *HotelBusiness*.

 # Key Terms

advance deposit reservation—Payment to the hotel (prior to arrival) for the first night's lodging. The hotel is obligated to hold the room regardless of the guest's arrival time.

attrition clause—Contract wording that outlines potential damages or fees that a party may be required to pay in the event that it does not fulfill minimum commitments in the contract.

bid sheet—Form used by local convention bureaus to obtain room commitments and prices from local hotels. The list is later forwarded to the meeting planner or site selection committee.

booking outside the block—Meeting attendees book rooms at hotels other than those specified by the meeting planner or book rooms within the specified hotels but not as part of the conventions group's block of rooms.

booking pace report—A report listing the rate at which reservations are made.

check-out time—The time (set by the hotel) at which guests are expected to vacate their rooms.

citywide—A convention which, because of its size or special requirements, requires accommodations at several hotels for its delegates.

comp rooms—Complimentary rooms; rooms that the hotel offers to a group at no charge in ratio to the number of rooms occupied by the group. The standard is one comp room per fifty rooms occupied.

credit card guaranteed reservation—A reservation made by credit card that assures the guest that a room will be held until check-out time of the following day of arrival. The guest guarantees payment for the room, even if it is not used, unless the reservation is properly cancelled.

cutoff date—The deadline for holding the number of guestrooms booked by a group (the last day a meeting attendee can buy a guestroom from the room block reserved for the meeting). Generally, hotels specify a date (also called a reservation review date) 30 days before the first day of the meeting for the group to either guarantee, add to, or release the guestrooms booked for the convention. Reservation requests made after the cutoff date may be accepted on a space-available basis, but late bookers may not be entitled to the group room rate.

discounted rate—The practice of marking down normal rates by a percentage or dollar amount as a concession to the group. Usually aimed at a specific type of client or offered at a particular time of the year. Also called a spread rate.

early departure—An attendee who checks out of the hotel earlier than scheduled. A fee may be charged by the hotel to make up for lost business. Also called an understay or an early out.

guaranteed reservation—A reservation that assures the guest that a room will be held until check-out time of the following day of arrival. The guest guarantees payment for the room, even if it is not used, unless the reservation is properly cancelled.

housing assistance desk—An area used to provide service to convention attendees who have concerns about their reservations.

housing bureau—Provided by a city's convention bureau, housing bureaus help place delegates into the city's hotels when large conventions are booked.

major arrival/major departure—The expected dates and times of arrivals and departures of large numbers of event attendees. Usually obtained from the group's resume, this information aids in staffing adequate front desk and bell staff.

no-shows—Customers who made reservations but do not show up at the hotel and did not cancel their reservations before the hotel's cancellation deadline.

overbooking—The hotel has committed more rooms that what are actually available for use (usually due to anticipated no-shows).

pre-registration—Often used for group business; with pre-registration, the hotel assigns the attendee a room that will be available upon the attendee's arrival.

rack rate—The standard rate established by a property for a particular category of room. May vary depending on the season.

reply card—A pre-printed, self-addressed card used for reservations for large conventions. Information on the card includes the name of the group, dates of meeting, and room rates.

reservation confirmation—Written agreement by a facility to accept a request for accommodations. To be binding, the agreement must state the intent of the parties—the particular date, the type of accommodations, and the number to be accommodated. Normally requires a credit card number.

room block—An agreed-upon number of rooms set aside for members of a group planning to stay at a hotel.

rooming list—A list of the names of attendees who will occupy the previously reserved accommodations, submitted by the meeting planner. It is also called a housing list.

run-of-the-house rate—An agreed-upon rate for all available rooms except suites. Generally priced at an average figure for group accommodations. Also called a flat rate.

self check-in, check-out terminal—A computerized kiosk system, usually located in the hotel lobby, that allows guests to review their registration information and receive their room keys at check-in. At check-out, they can review their folios and settle their accounts with the credit card used at check-in.

slippage—The number of guestrooms not used from the original room block. Also known as wash.

space available basis—Reservations that have no claim against the block of convention rooms because the request arrived after the official cut-off date.

split rate—The pricing of group guestrooms based on different room types, such as regular guestrooms versus tower rooms.

third-party housing provider—A private company that is contracted to manage the housing of convention delegates.

underdeparture—Occurs when a guest scheduled to leave decides to stay longer. Also called an overstay.

walk-in—A guest who does not have a reservation but requests accommodations at a hotel. Also called transient business.

walked customers—Guests holding confirmed reservations who are sent to another facility because of overbooking. If a hotel accepts a reservation but can't provide a room, the hotel has breached the contract and the injured guest is owed damages. The usual practice is for the guest to be compensated for the first night to stay at the second hotel (reimbursement for transportation between the two hotels is usually also included).

Review Questions

1. Describe in detail the types of reservations systems used to handle group bookings.

2. Trace the procedures used to service a citywide convention. Describe the forms used.

3. Distinguish between rack rates, run-of-the-house rates, spread rates, and split rates.

4. What three procedures are used by the Westin chain to assess the accuracy of a group's commitment?

5. What is the relationship between no-shows, underdepartures, and overbooking?

6. What factors are taken into consideration to ensure the smooth check-in and check-out of a convention group?

7. Assess the present-day application of the computer in servicing convention business and project technology's likely role in the future.

Additional References

Managing Front Office Operations, Eighth Edition, Michael L. Kasavana and Richard M. Brooks, AH&LA Educational Institute, 2009.

Internet Sites

For more information, visit the following Internet sites. Internet addresses can change without notice. If a site is no longer available at the address listed below, a search engine can be used to find the new address or additional, related sites.

Convention Industry Council, Hotel Best Practices for Managing Room Blocks
www.conventionindustry.org/projects/hotel_BP.htm.

Four Seasons Hotels and Resorts
www.fourseasons.com

Greenbrier Hotel
www.greenbrier.com

The Hospitality Sales and Marketing Association International (HSMAI)
www.hsmai.org

Hyatt Hotels and Resorts
www.hyatt.com

Destination Marketing Association International (DMAI)
www.destinationmarketing.org

Passkey
www.passkey.com

Project Attrition Final Report
www.conventionindustry.org/resources/project_attrition_report11204.pdf.

Sheraton Hotels
www.sheraton.com

Starwood Hotels & Resorts
www.starwood.com

Chapter 12 Outline

Competencies

1. Explain the purpose of a pre-convention meeting and the function of a key personnel roster. (pp. 389–394)

2. Describe the format and uses of the resume (specification sheet) prepared by the convention service manager. (pp. 394–398)

3. Describe the format and uses of the banquet event order (function sheet) in servicing conventions and group meetings. (pp. 398–402)

4. Describe the importance of communication and follow-up in servicing meetings. (pp. 402–407)

The Pre-Con: The Most Critical Meeting on the Program's Agenda

Marilyn McIver
Director of Convention Services
Marriott Desert Springs Resort, Palm Desert

"The pre-con meeting is possibly the most critical meeting on the program's agenda! Executive support is of paramount importance for any event, and general manager attendance at pre-cons is a real plus! After introducing the planner and allowing him/her an opportunity to give a brief of the program, our staff introduces themselves and their departments' roles during the convention. Don't make the mistake of confusing 'pre-con' with 'pre-planning.' By the time you've gathered the 'players' together, the majority of the work has been done via function sheets. I cannot stress enough the importance of detailed function sheets sent by the group, well in advance of the actual event. These sheets are usually transferred to a property format, so both parties should review function sheets to ensure accurate translation. Detailed function sheets, an accurate group resume with a timely distribution, and, finally, a well-run pre-con are all tools we can use to make our joint venture a success."

12   Preparing for the Event

FTER A LETTER OF AGREEMENT has been signed by both parties and the reservation cards sent, the event must be planned in great detail. Some conventions are planned a number of years in advance; others, a year or two. Some member of the organization's staff will be the primary coordinator for the group. It may be the executive director for a small or medium-sized association or a convention coordinator for a large organization. It could be a professional convention coordinator who is paid a fee by the association to run the event.

For the hotel, logistics are controlled by the convention service manager. As we discussed, the convention service manager is a most vital person on the hotel staff. He or she is the liaison person with the client and the control person within the hotel. It is not an exaggeration to consider the convention service manager as the key to the success or failure of an event. He or she is responsible for seeing that the event is properly planned and for taking quick, positive action should things go wrong during the event.

In many small hotels, the catering manager may serve as the convention service manager. It is not unusual in such a case for the catering manager also to be active in soliciting banquet business. If this is the case, communication with the sales department and use of the function book must be diligently controlled. This is doubly true when many promises are verbal, and not documented in correspondence or letters of agreement.

Preconvention Meeting

A **preconvention meeting (pre-con)** is essential and goes a long way toward eliminating problems that may surface during conventions. A smart hotel sales executive will arrange for a pre-conference meeting to introduce the hotel's convention service personnel, the organization's people, and all outside contractors involved in serving the group (see box titled "Pre-Con Meeting Agenda"). Hotels should make it a firm practice to bring the entire convention staff together for an unhurried preconvention session with the meeting planner and contractors for goods and services. This get-together gives all parties an opportunity to review the convention agenda item by item to ensure that everyone fully understands what is to take place and to finalize any last-minute details.

Westin's Larry Stephan, former director of sales at the Detroit Plaza, says that his chain services meetings with "Operation Excell." This program begins with a preconvention meeting held a day or two before the arrival of the group's main delegation (many convention service personnel feel that the ideal time to hold a pre-con is two days prior to the group's meeting or event). The hotel's CSM should determine the best time to schedule the meeting; morning meetings are commonly held, but an afternoon pre-con may enable the hotel's staff from two different shifts to attend. At this time, the meeting planner and his or her staff meet with the convention service manager and all the hotel's department heads who are involved in the direct servicing of the group. The upcoming program is thoroughly reviewed.

Attendees at the meeting vary. For simple or one-day meetings, the pre-con may include only the meeting planner and the convention service manager. For a large convention with a number of banquets, meetings, and complex setups, the following individuals are likely to be in attendance:

Pre-Con Meeting Agenda

The pre-con is held to reconfirm all written and verbal details of the event, discuss arrangements, and answer any questions relating to the program, but it should also serve as a relationship-building tool. Relationship-building begins with the hotel's staff. Staff members should dress professionally and wear name tags to help meeting planners identify and remember key personnel. Hotel staff also should stand and greet clients as they enter, and the meeting should focus on the client (this means that pagers, beepers, or walkie-talkies should not be allowed).

The pre-con meeting room should be set up to facilitate conversation between participants (a U-shape set up is typically used, with the client seated at the head of the "U").

To ensure that the meeting flows smoothly and all details are covered, a pre-con agenda should be established. Most pre-con briefings include a chronological review of the group's events, but the agenda may be modified as necessary. An agenda typically includes:

- Introduction of the planner (by the CSM).
- Brief review of the purpose of the meeting and agenda items.
- Introduction of attendees (by the meeting planner).
- Introduction of hotel staff, including a brief description of the job functions of each (by the CSM).

Meeting details to be discussed can include (but are not limited to):

- Review of meeting resume.
- Updated room pick-up report.
- Review of banquet event orders for each event.
- Review of master account, including authorized signers and billing instructions.
- Other pertinent group details, such as VIP and special considerations, business center requirements, recreational activities, and so on.
- Review of any items specific to the event (if the program includes a trade show, for example, union procedures should be covered).
- Review of the facility's fire, safety, and emergency procedures.
- Distribution of lists of contact names and contact numbers.

Remember that the pre-con is a confirmation of details, not the time for the planner to make drastic changes in the program. A continuing dialogue with the meeting planner as plans progressed prevents last-minute problems.

Source: Photograph of the Fairmont Banff Springs courtesy of the Fairmont Hotels & Resorts Image Library.

- Meeting planner and his or her staff.
- Director of convention services and the convention service manager responsible for servicing the group.
- Salesperson who secured the group and perhaps the director of sales.
- Food and beverage manager, catering/banquet manager, and the chef.
- Hotel's general manager and perhaps the comptroller or credit manager.
- Director of exhibit service, floor manager, and a convention service secretary.
- Representatives from the following departments:

- front office   - reservations   - publicity/public relations
- security   - uniform services   - housekeeping
- telephone   - recreational facilities   - concierge
- room service   - audiovisual
- garage/valet   - spa director

- Outside vendors who will play a significant role, such as third-party housing companies, destination management companies, or audiovisual firms.
- For large programs, a representative of the convention and visitors bureau may be invited.

Some astute hotel convention service managers suggest to the meeting planner that they invite a higher-up, such as the company president or association executive, to at least drop in at the introductions portion of the pre-con meeting. This helps the hotel's staff to recognize them as VIPs, gives the executives a clearer understanding of the complexities of managing meetings, and helps to strengthen the relationship between the hotel and the meeting group.

A small ceremony usually takes place at the end of the preconvention meeting. The meeting planner and his or her key personnel may be given VIP pins, which serve two functions. First, they give distinction to the meeting planner and staff, recognizing that the hotel is aware of their positions and the importance of the meeting. Second, they help the hotel staff single out members who are in charge, should there be any last-minute changes or requests.

This concept works well for Stephan, who offers a step-by-step review of his chain's "Operation Excell" program used to facilitate the servicing of convention groups in the "Best Practices" case at the end of this chapter. The procedure is not put into operation at every convention, nor

Marriott's VIP pin for meeting planners.

is it always necessary for all department heads to be present; the convention program determines which department heads will attend. Major conventions and smaller ones with complicated requirements, however, are preceded by such a meeting.

Regardless of who attends the pre-con, from that meeting on, it should be the service manager, not the salesperson, who deals with both the client and the hotel staff. If a hotel wants to suceed with convention business, it must develop good salespeople to bring in the right kind of business, and good convention service people, functioning in-house, to guide that business through to successful completion. In larger convention facilities, a convention service manager would have an assistant and possibly other specialists.

Key Personnel Roster

Meeting planners often request a **key personnel roster** from the convention service manager so they have someone to contact should trouble arise (see Exhibit 1). This roster would list the names and telephone numbers of hotel department heads and other specialists (such as the in-house audiovisual contact). Many convention service managers, however, are hesitant to provide such a list, preferring to have all requests channeled through them. We feel that the wisest course lies between these two positions.

If the convention service manager will *always* be on the scene and available to the meeting planner, it is possible for him or her to receive every request. But if this is not feasible, an assistant should be designated to act in such instances. If this is not practical,

Exhibit 1   Hotel Key Personnel Roster

HOTEL PERSONNEL

Hotel staff personnel contact for over-all service during the convention of _____

Period	Hours	Name	Title	Phone Extension
Early morning	___a.m. to ___p.m.			
Daytime	___a.m. to ___p.m.			
Evening	___a.m. to ___p.m.			
Saturdays	___a.m. to ___p.m.			
Sundays	___a.m. to ___p.m.			
Holidays	___a.m. to ___p.m.			

Hotel key staff by departments
Check marks on the hotel staff list given below indicate the departmental key personnel with whom the organization will come in contact during the servicing of the convention.

Check	Department	Name	Title	Phone Extension

The meeting planner should have a principal contact on the hotel staff at all times during the day. In addition to key personnel rosters, some planners insist on being supplied with a two-way radio, beeper, pager, or cellular phone to ensure immediate contact with the hotel staff.

The key personnel roster is given to the meeting planner at the pre-con, at which time it is also customary for hotel and meeting staff to exchange business cards. Laura Himelson, CSM for the Montage Resort in Laguna Beach, California, provides a plastic sleeve to enable meeting planners to conveniently store business cards in one place.

Sources: Form reprinted with permission from the *Convention Liaison Manual*, published by the Convention Industry Council. Business cards and plastic sleeve courtesy of the Montage Resort, Laguna Beach, California; used with permission.

Exhibit 2   Marriott Red Coat Service

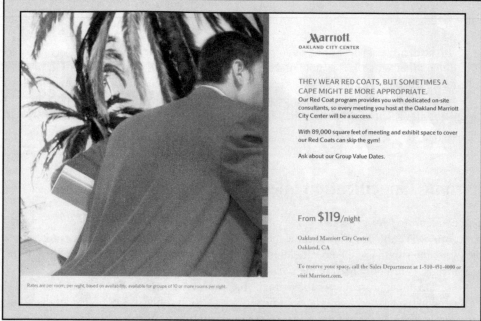

Marriott's Red Coat service, which provides dedicated service staff for meetings and conventions, is promoted by individual properties within the chain, including the Oakland Marriott City Center.
Source: Courtesy of Marriott Hotels. Used with permission.

department heads should be trained to inform the convention service manager of all requests.

During a convention, a meeting planner will often refuse to wait until the manager can be located before taking action in what he or she deems a crisis. In any case, prompt action on the part of the hotel staff is crucial; communication between key personnel and the convention service manager is obviously essential.

Minita Wescott, past president of both the Chicago Trade Association Executives Forum and the American Trade Association Executives, suggests:

> One person on the hotel staff should be assigned to the convention for the duration of the meeting. This person should be readily available to handle all on-the-spot needs. It makes for a smoother meeting if the executive of the association can meet and get acquainted with all top members of the hotel staff with whom this executive and his staff will have to work.[1]

The Marriott chain has responded to such meeting planners' requests for hotel contact people to act on last-minute needs and further expanded on it with the introduction of its Red Coat service (see Exhibit 2). A number of property convention staff personnel, easily identified by their red jackets, are both trained and empowered to handle last-minute details and crises. This program helps free up the property's convention service manager while still ensuring that immediate help is available to meeting planners who need it. The visibility and accessibility of these trained professionals helps to boost the confidence of even the least-experienced meeting planner and demonstrates the chain's commitment to service.

Crowne Plaza Hotels & Resorts offers the innovative HotPhone Service[SM] program, which provides a "hot phone" to meeting planners to enable them to keep in constant contact with the property's Crowne Plaza Conference Concierge[®] assigned to the group. The service, which is complimentary, features a digital two-line cell phone that not only lets the planner call for assistance with the touch of a button, but also provides communication with the "outside world" (the planner is free to make local and long-distance calls while on property).

In the pressure cooker of an ongoing convention, meeting planners are most appreciative of reassurance that last-minute problems will be dealt with, and promptly. Gestures of such reassurance go a long way toward making a property a favorite of convention planners.

In summary, we feel it a positive action to furnish a roster of key hotel personnel to the client, along with the request that all action be taken through the convention service manager, *whenever possible.*

Resume (Specification Sheet)

The convention service manager is responsible for writing a detailed schedule for each convention. The title for this schedule may vary. It may be known as the master prospectus, the bible, the summary, the specification sheet, or the resume. We will use the latter term, as it is most commonly used in the industry today.

Do not confuse the *resume* with the *banquet event order (function sheet)*, which is explained in the next section. The **resume** provides a comprehensive overview of the entire program in a chronological narrative, from preconvention to post-convention, to the hotel staff. The banquet event order details only a single event.

All convention hotels use similarly constructed resumes when servicing groups that meet for more than one day. Resumes set forth activities day by day and hour by hour, covering meetings, meals, refreshment breaks, cocktails, reservation procedures, billing, exhibit instructions, special events, guest programs, recreational activities, and anything else that needs the hotel staff's attention. It is undoubtedly the single most important element of the convention servicing process, providing a tool for planning and communication between hotel departments.

The resume is prepared by the convention service manager in conjunction with the meeting planner. Much of the information is extracted from correspondence and discussion with the convention group and from **event specification guides (ESGs)** prepared by the meeting planner (see box titled "Industry-Wide Event Specification Guides"). For larger groups (such as associations that meet annually), the convention service manager may request a copy of the group's previous year's resume. The group's information is then put in the hotel's format and the resume is distributed to everyone involved with servicing the convention. This must be done far enough in advance to ensure that departments will have time to staff and prepare appropriately (in most cases, at least a week before the group arrives).

The length of the resume varies, of course, with the convention's size and number of days, and the amount of detailed planning required for each convention. We have seen some group resumes that were more than 40 pages long. Most, however, run eight to 12 pages for a three-day session. Simply put, a resume should be long enough to include all the details.

The importance of putting every detail in writing cannot be overstated. And the more detailed, the better. "Nobody told me" is heard too often in hotels. Putting everything in writing lessens the chance of this occuring.

Exhibit 3 illustrates an abbreviated resume written for a ficticious convention, the Architectural Draftsmen International. Note that the resume opens with a preconvention setup and closes with a post-convention meeting. The resume begins with a general description of the group and a brief statement informing the hotel staff of the basic purpose

Industry-Wide Event Specification Guides

Event Specification Guides (ESGs), prepared by meeting planners, differ from the resumes prepared for events by hotel personnel. To ensure that the details compiled by the meeting planner could be effectively incorporated into hotel resumes, APEX (the Accepted Practices Exchange), an initiation of the Convention Industry Council, developed a template that could be readily used for this important function.

The term Event Specifications Guide or ESG (acronym) should be the industry's official term for the document used by an event organizer to convey information clearly and accurately to appropriate venue(s) and/or suppliers regarding all requirements for an event. This is a four-part document which includes:

- Part I   The Narrative – general overview of the event.
- Part II   Function Schedule – timetable outlining all functions that compose the overall event.
- Part IIIa Function Set-up Order – specifications for each function that is part of the overall event (each function of the event will have its own Function Set-up Order).
- Part IIIb Function Set-up Order (Exhibitor Version) – specifications for each booth/ stand that is part of an exhibition.

The 22-page template is essentially a staging guide (such as the one depicted in Exhibit 6). It can be accessed online at www.conventionindustry.org/apex/acceptedpractice/eventspecifications.htm.

The new ESGs have been praised by planners and hotel personnel alike. Vicky Betzig, CMP, president/owner of Meetings Industry Consulting, says:

The amount of time a planner spends putting together event specifications is enormous. The template includes all of the specs most often required by hoteliers. I will be one of the first to use it.

ESGs are also extremely helpful to a CSM preparing the group's resume. The CSM can take required information from the ESG, prepare a resume and banquet event orders in the hotel's format, and return them to the planner for approval. Richard Green, vice president of industry relations and association sales for Marriott International, states:

Standardized events specifications will help planners to focus their requirements around the information that hotels and convention centers need to deliver a zero-defect meeting.

Sources: *The APEX Event Specifications Guide Template,* ©2004, Convention Industry Council; quotes from an APEX audio conference (Betzig and Green were among the speakers), published in *PCMA Convene,* December 2004.

and objectives of the meeting. A list of the individuals and departments that receive this information is listed on the left-hand side of the first page. To facilitate hotel staff recognition of key meeting personnel, such as the meeting planner and other VIPs, the Montage Resort in Laguna Beach, California, also includes their photos within the resume. The first page also includes such information as complimentary accommodations, arrival and departure schedules, the reservation procedure, and billing to both master and individual accounts.

The next two pages provide an indication of the detail required in a resume. Every scheduled event is documented and thorough instructions provided regarding room setup and food and beverage arrangements. While reading through the sheet, keep in mind the importance of the meticulous recording required in the preparation of this form. As you can see, a large volume of information must be entered—and often changed—which is not only time-consuming, but may also result in costly errors.

Exhibit 3   Sample Group Resume

```
* * * * * * * * * * * * * * *
      GROUP SPECIFICATION SHEET
* * * * * * * * * * * * * * *
```

Left-column list (people and departments receiving the sheet):

General Manager
Food/Bev. Dir.
Front Office
Showroom
Exec. Chef
Beverage Mgr. (2)
Coffee Shop
Room Service
Group Billing
Hotel Manager
Asst. Hotel Mgrs. (2)
Food Checker
Reservations
Publicity
Security
Housekeeping
Head Houseman
Head Banquet Waiter
Sales (2)
Food & Bev. Control
Linen Control
Doorman
Benihana Manager
Stage & Sound (2)
Public Porters
Steward
Catering Director
Group Services (4)
Uniform Room
Purchasing

SUBJECT: Architectural Draftsmen International Attendees are the world's leading architects. The focus of the meeting is on customer service. The theme of the meeting is, "Building Better Relationships with Clients."

DATES: February 16-20, 20__

CONTACT: Jay Bryan
Master Draftsman
206 Clark - Suite 307
Lakeview, Michigan 48850

HOTEL SALESPERSON: Larry Kingsbury, National Sales Manager

ARRIVAL/DEPARTURE PATTERN:
ROOM RES. MANAGER
ASSISTANT MANAGERS
FRONT DESK
HOTEL CASHIER

300 rooms have been committed to this group. Most are arriving late Sunday, February 16 and departing Thursday, February 20, 20__. Arriving individually - Preregister

RATES - European Plan
$95.00 Single or Double occupancy, plus 6% County room tax, net, non-commissionable.

SUITE RATES - One Bedroom
$100.00 - Petite Suite
$120.00 - Deluxe Suite
$180.00 - Royal Suite

LOCATION: DESERT VIEW, FOUNTAIN VIEW, POOLSIDE HEXAGON, CENTRAL TOWER

COMPLIMENTARY ACCOMMODATIONS: A King Bedroom (North Tower) for Marney Vartanian, Associate Convention Manager
ARR: February 15, 20__
DEP: February 20, 20__

Additional complimentary units to be assigned based upon 1 complimentary unit for every 50 rooms actually occupied. (Names forthcoming)

HOSPITALITY REQUEST FOR: Ms. Marney Vartanian
Dewars Scotch w/setups
ARR: February 15, 20__

RESERVATION ACCEPTANCE PROCEDURE: This group utilized our return reservation cards.

MASTER ACCOUNT: All Group functions should be billed to the master account. Ms. Marney Vartanian will be the authorized signer.

INDIVIDUAL ACCOUNT: Room, tax, and incidentals to be paid by individuals.

(continued)

This form for a fictitious convention is similar to those used by hotels to provide an overview of a group's event. At the left is a list of the people and departments that will receive this sheet. In addition, the convention service manager usually sends the resume to the meeting planner well in advance of the pre-convention meeting to ensure that details are correct and that nothing has been overlooked. This saves time during the pre-convention meeting, as the major points have already been negotiated and accepted by both parties.

Exhibit 3   *(continued)*

```
*  *  *  *  *  *  *  *  *  *  *
       SCHEDULED FUNCTIONS
*  *  *  *  *  *  *  *  *  *  *
```

Saturday, February 15, 20__

3:00 P.M.   ADI/HOTEL STAFF PRECONVENTION MEETING   Board Room

                                   15 persons

Attn: Set-up Crew   "U" shape

Attn: Banquet Wtr.   Complimentary coffee, soft drinks, sweet rolls

Sunday, February 16, 20__

6:00 - 8:00 P.M.   ARCHITECTURAL DRAFTSMEN INTERNATIONAL   Sec. F
                                   COCKTAIL RECEPTION
                                   Approximately 30 persons. All are convention officials
                                   and board members

Attn: Set-up Crew   Cabaret style

Attn: Banquet Wtr.,
      Bar Manager   Call brand liquor to include: Beefeater, Johnny Walker Black,
                                   Dewars, Smirnoff, Jack Daniels Black, Old Grand Dad, CC,
                                   Bristol Cream Sherry @ $26.00 ++ and $30.00 ++. Two bottles
                                   Chablis and Pinot Noir @ $7.00 per bottle ++. Beer @ $1.00 ++.

Attn: Banquet Wtr.,   Following hors d'oeuvres: 5 orders Polynesian Pu-Pus @ $7.50++,
      Exec. Chef   5 orders Selection #3 @ $6.75 ++, 10 orders Selection #4 @ $6.75 ++
                                   10 orders hot seafood @ $8.00 ++, 10 orders cold seafood @ $8.50 ++,
                                   and one shrimp bowl @ $100.00 ++. Hors d'oeuvre table to be
                                   decorated with two gold candelabra and 6 silver chafing dishes, white tapers.
                                   Cold hors d'oeuvres to be passed by waiters.

Attn: Accounting   Bill to Texas Instruments - Exhibits Master Account.

Sunday, February 16, 20__

3:00 - 6:00 P.M.   REGISTRATION   Foyer

Attn: Set-up Crew   6' draped table rear of registration desk.
                                   2 house phones. 1 directory board. Ice water
                                   stand. Bb/c/e. (blackboard/chalk/eraser)

Monday, February 17, 20__

9:00 A.M. - NOON   GENERAL BUSINESS SESSION   Sec. F

                                   500 Persons

Attn: Set-up Crew   Theatre style with stage 12' x 40' x 24'
                                   twenty feet out from kitchen wall. Projection platform
                                   will be required against kitchen wall for rear screen projection.
                                   Size to be determined. Head table for 8 on stage. American
                                   Flag stage right. 1 35mm Carousel slide projector. 1 Lantern slide
                                   projector. 1 electric pointer. 2 center aisle mikes. Central dimmer
                                   to be located at projection platform. 1 projectionist.

9:30 A.M. - NOON   EXHIBIT HALL SETUP   Exhibit Hall

Attn: Hall Supervisor   20 - 8' x 10' exhibit booth to be set up by
                                   Scott Stubbs Service Company.

                                                                          (continued)
```
```

Exhibit 3 *(continued)*

<u>12:15 P.M.</u>	<u>LUNCHEON</u>	<u>Sec. B</u>
	500 Persons	
Attn: Set-up Crew	Rounds of 10 with raised head tables on 32" dais for 12 centered in south wall.	
	Lighted table podium mike center of head table.	
Attn: Banquet Wtr. Exec. Chef	Tickets to be collected except at head table. Linen will probably be alternated on this function. This is to be advised.	
Attn: Banquet Wtr.	Serve our Group Luncheon Menu #7 with tomato juice appetizer @ $6.10 ++.	
Attn: Accounting	Bill to ADI Master Account.	

<u>Thursday, February 20, 19   </u>

<u>3:00 - 5:00 P.M.</u>	<u>ADI/HOTEL STAFF POST-CONVENTION MEETING</u>	<u>Board Room</u>
	Same setup as on Saturday	

Banquet Event Order (Function Sheet)

When the program is finalized, each function should receive individual attention. Such attention to detail translates into service efficiency. This is done by means of a **banquet event order (BEO)**, such as the one illustrated in Exhibit 4. This banquet event order for a cocktail party shows the relationship between a resume and a banquet event order – the resume provides an overview of the event, while the banquet event order breaks the event down into minute details.

The banquet event order, like the resume, has been tagged with a variety of names: event form, worksheet, function sheet, and so on (we will use the term banquet event order, as that is the term most commonly used today). Banquet event orders can also vary from hotel to hotel in the amount of detail required. Individual banquet event orders, however, are generally prepared from the resume and are the working form for hourly employees (in Exhibit 4, for example, details are given regarding the staffing of a bartender, set-up crew, and cooks).

Ideally, the resume and any banquet event orders should be completed and two copies sent to the meeting planner two to three weeks in advance of the meeting and prior to distribution to the hotel staff. These materials should be accompanied by a letter asking the planner to review the copies, note any changes, and sign and return one copy to the hotel at least a week prior to the meeting (an example letter is shown in Exhibit 5).

Whether the function is a general session or a small committee meeting, document it. The basic seating layout, decorations, visual aids, and any other special services required should be detailed on the function sheet. Most hotels assign a specific number to each banquet event order for easy reference. Copies of each function sheet, as with the resume, should be distributed to hotel department heads at least a week prior to the event. There may be times when changes need to be made to banquet event orders. The most efficient way to communicate these changes is with a BEO addendum, commonly referred to as a banquet change order or banquet change sheet. These change orders contain the identification number and any other pertinent identifying information from the original banquet event order, and includes, very specifically, the changes to be made. In many cases, hotels use a color-coded system to immediately identify banquet event order status—the original BEO

Exhibit 4　Banquet Event Order (Function Sheet)

FUNCTION ORDER - FOOD AND BEVERAGE

EVENT DATE February 16, 19-	DAY Sunday	ORDER NO 126
ORGANIZATION Architectural Draftsman International		FILE NO N-614

POST AS
Architectural Draftsman International Cocktail Reception

BILLING ADDRESS
Bill to Master Account Texas Instruments, 120AK, Lakeview, MI 48851

CONTACT Deanne Pritchard	ON SITE CONTACT Robert Olson	BUS PHONE NO 363-1906	RES PHONE NO

EXPECTED 30	GUARANTEED 30	SET UP 33		BOOKED BY Amber S.	DATE TYPED 2/1

TIME	SETUP REQUIREMENTS	LOCATION	TIME	MENU	LOCATION

SETUP REQUIREMENTS

6:00 PM - 8:00 PM Cocktail   Sec. F

Cabaret Style Set-Up
Draped Cocktail Rounds with ashtrays,
no chairs

MENU

5 orders Polynesion Pu-Pus @ $22.50++,
5 orders selection #3 @ $20.25++,
10 orders selection #4 @ $20.25++,
10 orders hot seafood @ $25.50++,
10 orders cold seafood @ $25.50++,
1 shrimp bowl @ $300.00 ++

Hors d'oeuvre table to be decorated
with two gold candlabra and 6 silver
chafing dishes. White tapers.
Cold hors d'oeuvres to be passed by
waiters

Food @ $ 20.25+T+T
Seafood @ $ 25.50+T+T
Shrimp bowl @ $ 300.00 +T+T

HOTEL TO ORDER

_X_ Decorations
3 Tropical Florals
Charge to Master
___ Entertainment

REFRESHMENT BREAK

AUDIO VISUAL

Time   Location

SPECIAL NOTES

BEVERAGE REQUIREMENTS

RECEPTION

Call Brand Liquor to include: Beefeater,
Johnny Walker Black, Dewars, Smirnoff,
Jack Daniels Black, Old Grand Dad, CC,
Bristol Cream Sherry @ $78.00 ++, $ 84.00 ++
and $ 90.00 ++. Two bottles Chablis &
WINE SELECTION   Pinot Noir @ $21.00 ++ per
bottle. Beer @ $3.00 ++.

SUMMARY OF CHARGES

FOOD   See Menu
BEVERAGE   See Beverage Requirements
RENT
LABOR
PARKING
DEPOSIT RECEIVED
METHOD OF PAYMENT
BALANCE DUE DATE

TIME	LOCATION

WE NEED YOUR ASSISTANCE IN MAKING YOUR BANQUET A SUCCESS. PLEASE CONFIRM YOUR ATTENDANCE AT LEAST 3 BUSINESS DAYS IN ADVANCE. IF WE ARE NOT CONTACTED WITHIN THE SPECIFIED TIME. YOUR EXPECTED ATTENDANCE WILL SERVE AS YOUR GUARANTEE. THIS WILL BE CONSIDERED YOUR MINIMUM GUARANTEE. WE WILL ADD THE CUSTOMARY 17% SERVICE CHARGE AND SALES TAX. FOR GROUPS SERVED UNDER 25 THERE WILL BE A $50 LABOR CHARGE.
I HAVE READ AND I UNDERSTAND THE REVERSE SIDE OF THIS DOCUMENT.
IF IN AGREEMENT, PLEASE SIGN ONE COPY AND RETURN X _____

This form is used to detail each convention function listed on the specification sheet.

is printed on a white sheet, revisions can be printed on canary paper, and pink paper can be used for guarantees, for example. Other hotels reduce paper flow and instantly communicate changes via their computer systems.

Exhibit 5   Transfer of Resume and Banquet Event Orders to Client

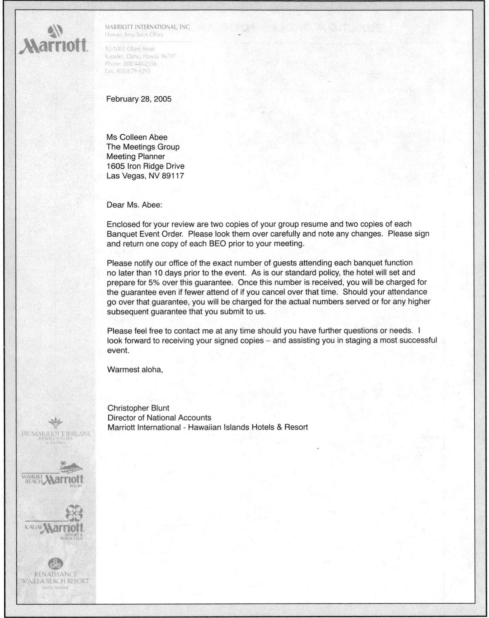

Hotels generally send copies of the group's resume to the meeting planner two to three weeks prior to the event for approval before distributing the resume and any accompanying banquet event orders to departments involved in servicing the event. This sample letter not only provides the meeting planner with these materials, but also requests attendance figures and reiterates the hotel's guarantee policy.

It is essential that *each program segment* have its own banquet event order (function sheet) to ensure that all details will be handled. Document the head table, platform, basic seating layout, and all other arrangements. But also have a checklist for small but needed items, such as water glasses, pads and pencils, audiovisual equipment, sound systems, floral arrangements, and so on.

You may find that many well-organized association and corporate meeting planners make their own checklists of what is needed. As we mentioned earlier in this chapter, some

Exhibit 6   Event Specifications Guides (Staging Guides)

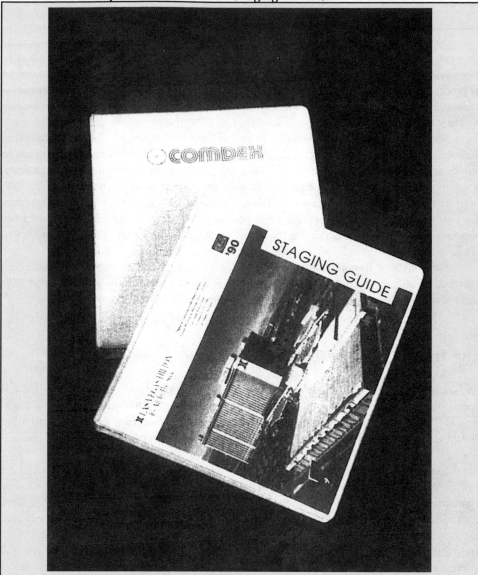

The overriding factor in the success of a meeting is communication. Meeting managers who provide event specification guides (ESGs) — detailed instructions for each event or setup in a loose-leaf notebook — facilitate the convention service manager's task of preparing the resume.

meeting planners will even provide you with a complete event specifications guide (ESG), also known as a staging guide or specifications guidebook, which is a concise document detailing how the meeting will proceed (see Exhibit 6). ESGs include activities (by day, time, room, setup, and requirements), complimentary room assignments, signature authority, and other details authorized by the meeting planner. You can use these guides to prepare your own group resumes, incorporating the itemized requests contained in the ESGs. One convention service manager shared the following with us:

> Most people think that all the convention service manager does is handle
> the group while it's in-house, but 90 percent of our work is the extraction

of details one to two years prior to arrival. My job is to direct, produce, and extract information from the meeting planner and in turn pass this information on to various department heads through specification and function sheets.

A master schedule should be made. This will assist you in determining the number of pieces of anything needed anywhere at any particular time. You may have specified on a number of function sheets that a digital slide projector is needed, but the master schedule would indicate how many such projectors are needed at the same time.

Many hotel people feel that such details are truly the responsibility of the meeting planner. However, it is the hotel staff that will be called upon under crisis conditions to rectify any oversights. You could avoid those last-minute panics by being well organized; develop your own checklists and suggest that the meeting planner do the same.

If planners are inexperienced and fail to anticipate their needs correctly, they may say you gave them insufficient notice and you may end up as the victim. Given a choice between blaming you and accepting the blame themselves, they may find it all too easy to blame you.

Not only is it important to plan defensively, but your suggestions and organization also will establish your reputation. Clients will retain the memory that meetings at your hotel always run smoothly. That memory is the one you want to leave with clients.

The Importance of Communication

Problems during meetings can be largely eliminated if a "pipeline" of communication has been established from the very beginning. It has been said that "the job of servicing meetings is 95 percent communication and 5 percent service." Securing detailed information and expectations from the meeting planner is one of the most important tasks of the convention service manager.

Letters, telephone calls, e-mails, and personal on-site visits are normally used to get initial information. Another excellent tool to initiate the communication process is to send a **resume questionnaire** (see the chapter appendix) to the meeting planner. This form consolidates a list of important questions and reduces the frequent telephone calls and exchanges of correspondence on individual items. Other ways to improve communication are for the convention service manager to provide the meeting planner with a formal and mutually agreed-upon timetable for communication of meeting details. Some convention service managers ask to be put on the meeting planner's mailing list, while others will send the meeting planners a sample specification sheet to inform the planner of the format used by the hotel.

Communicating Details Electronically

Computer technology has altered the way resume and banquet event order information is created. Exhibit 7 illustrates a computer-generated banquet event order (function sheet). Automated sales systems can build a function sheet as information is gathered and input by the salesperson into the client's file. Also, a computerized system allows the creation of a number of forms that can be tailored to specific servicing needs. For example, you can create a form that contains just menu information for your chef, or a form containing just setup information for your service staff.

Exhibit 7   Computerized Banquet Event Order (Function Sheet)

The Durham Resort
44 Newmarket Road
Durham, New Hampshire 038244
(603) 868-1500

GROUP NAME: Automobile Travelers Association
POST AS: Annual Meeting
IN CHARGE: Mr. Harry McArthur   **FUNCTION ORDER NO: 104**

DAY	DATE	TIME	FUNCTION	ROOM	PEOPLE	RENT
Tue	10/12	8:00 AM - 5:00 PM	Lunch Meeting	Cherry Room	75	$250

BEVERAGES	FOOD
Service: 17.5% Tax: 9.5% Bartender Fee: $65.00 each **ARRANGEMENTS** In charge of service: Banquet Service Chairs (18") 16mm Movie Projector 6' Round Dinner Table for Rounds of 10 Slide Projector with remote control capabilities Rear Screen Projection (10' x 10')	*Stuffed Pork Chop from 8:00 AM to 5:00 PM* *Room: Cherry Room Attendance: 75* Tender Pork Chop Filled with a Special Sausage Stuffing in a Mushroom Sauce Whipped Potatoes Vegetable du Jour Tossed Garden Salad, Choice of Dressing Assorted Rolls Coffee, Tea & Decaf *Charge: $18.00 Per Person* Billing: Master Account Address: 1234 Albany Drive Atlanta, GA 01234 Phone: (404) 555-2141

Client Signature:_____ Date:_____

Prepared By: Kathy McDonald_____ Date: June 14, 20_

> The contents of the above meet with my approval. I consider our agreement definite and confirmed.
> Guarantees must be sumbitted 48 hours in advance of all functions (Monday functions, 72 hours).
> Prices are subject to 17.5% gratuity and 9.5% sales tax (where applicable).

This function sheet, generated in an automated sales office, merges important account information and relative booking information on one display screen. This report retrieves the information from the hotel's meetings database.

In order to standardize resume data and to minimize error, Newmarket® International developed its Daylight® "ultimate electronic resume" software. This electronically-generated resume combines room block information, BEO information, and department information in one document (Exhibit 8 illustrates the initial page of a resume generated by the software).

Magnolia Hotels was one of the initial users of the ultimate electronic resume, and a representative of the chain states:

Exhibit 8   Newmarket® International's Daylight® Ultimate Resume

Daylight

Stratford Portsmouth Hotel
Welcomes
LRB and Associates

Main Contact:	Jared Goldman	**Arrival Date:**	Sunday, July 13, 2008
Address:	100 Main Street	**Departure Date:**	Wednesday, July 16, 2008
	Big Town, NY 10123	**Booking No:**	AA234567
Phone:	212-555-4567	**Catering Mgr:**	Susan O'Hara
Fax:	212-555-2345	**Service Mgr:**	Windy Hernandez
Email:	212-555-5678	**Sales Mgr:**	Jim Bento

Group Profile: *Group is here to discuss next year's plans and goals. Spouses are attending and have separate functions. This meeting is the high point for the staff; they look forward to it every year.*

Room Block:

Room Type		Sunday July 13	Monday July 14	Tuesday July 15	Wednesday July 16
King	Agreed	125	125	125	125
	Pickup	100	126	126	112
	Rate	$250.00	$250.00	$250.00	$250.00
Double/Double	Agreed	50	50	50	50
	Pickup	52	52	52	49
	Rate	$350.00	$350.00	$350.00	$350.00

Total Rooms:
Agreed: 700
Pickup: 669

Billing: **Master Account Number:** A123456

	Billing Method	Payment Method	Notes
Room & Tax	Combined	Direct Bill	Vendors as noted – pay their own Room & tax
Catering F & B	Master	Direct Bill	
On Own Dining	Individual	Credit Card	
On Own Beverage	Individual	Credit Card	
Incidentals	Combined	Direct Bill	Mr. and Mrs. Change have all incidentals posted
Transportation	Master	Direct Bill	
Golf	Combined	Direct Bill	Mr. and Mrs. Change have all incidentals posted
Spa	Combined	Direct Bill	Mr. and Mrs. Change have all incidentals posted
Tennis	Individual	Credit Card	
Internet	Combined	Direct Bill	Mr. and Mrs. Change have all incidentals posted

Program Details
Sunday, July 13, 2008

Times	Rooms	Event Type	Post As	EXP/GTD/SET	BEO #	Rental
3:00 PM - 1:00 AM	Little Room 1	Office	Office	1/1/1	10	$75.00
SETUP	2 - 6' Draped and Skirted Tables					
	4 - Chairs					
	1 - Large Trash Can					
	Clean Daily at prior to 8 am.					
SHIPPING	Please deliver all boxes marked for AASE to this room by 3:00 PM					

Times	Rooms	Event Type	Post As	EXP/GTD/SET	BEO #	Rental
3:00 PM – 4:00 PM	ROOMS	DEPARTMENT	DEPARTMENT	80/90/92		$0.00
FRONT OFFICE	Guests will arrive by bus					
	Please have key packets ready for distribution					
GUEST SERVICES	3 Buses to arrive					
	Have Bell Staff to assist with Luggage					

Page 1 of 9

This is the first page of a nine-page electronic resume created by Newmarket® International's Daylight® software. The form combines all time-sensitive resume and BEO information for all departments in chronological order.
Source: Courtesy of Newmarket® International. Used with permission.

As in many hotels, the catering staff at Magnolia was known to print out nine copies of a BEO. Now the team runs only one report. All the information and knowledge resides in one place, supporting seamless execution.

Database management programs also allow meeting information stored in the computer to be isolated, manipulated, or sorted to answer specific requests. With just a few keystrokes, the meetings can be sorted by location, time, date, size, and so on. For example, you may wish to ask the computer to list all meetings scheduled in the convention area that require overhead projectors on Monday between 7:00 a.m. and 7:00 p.m., or which rooms

Best Practices

Westin's "Operation Excell"

It is important for meeting planners and a property to get off to a proper start. A well-organized preconvention procedure such as Westin's "Operation Excell" eliminates many of the unforseen crises inherent to group meetings and could well mean the difference between a successful convention and one that is plagued by disorganization. The following, a step-by-step review of the "Operation Excell" checklist, is a concept for servicing meetings that can be used by any size property, whether resort, commercial hotel, or motel.

Source: Courtesy Westin New York at Times Square

1.   A preconvention date and time is agreed upon by the hotel and the meeting planner. A reminder is sent to all departments involved, with a notation that all department heads are to be there ten minutes before the meeting begins. This is to give the convention service manager a chance to prepare the staff for any unusual characteristics or demands of the convention group. All the normal procedures used in setting up meeting rooms should be applied in planning an Operation Excell meeting. Taking care of details such as proper seating setup, the right-size meeting room, and comfortable chairs gives the client the impression that the hotel will service his or her meeting as well as it runs its own. Coffee, soft drinks, and sweet rolls should be provided so there is an atmosphere of informality. To instill confidence that the hotel knows how to service meetings, the convention service manager should check the room an hour ahead of time for those little things — such as lighting, pads and pencils, and comfortable temperature — that make for a pleasant, attractive meeting setup.

2.   An inventory of nameplates of all department heads should be maintained so that the client may relate in the meeting to the key people on the hotel's staff. VIP identification pins are presented to the meeting planner and his or her staff.

3.   The meeting format gives department heads a chance to ask questions about matters that relate directly to their roles in servicing the group. The convention service manager then goes over the program event by event. A sample agenda might include:

- Review of the specification sheet and function sheets
- Review of the master account
- An updated room pick-up report

If there are areas of misunderstanding, or changes are needed, the client has an opportunity to inject input. A secretary should be on hand to take note of these changes. These last-minute changes are typed up after the meeting and distributed to all involved.

4.   A specification sheet (resume), which covers the entire convention program and is the hotel's in-house communication medium, should be distributed not only to those at the Operation Excell meeting but to every department in the hotel. Each department needs to be kept informed so it can forecast staffing needs. For example, if no luncheons or dinners are scheduled on a particular day, the people in charge of staffing the hotel's coffee shop and restaurants should be alerted to the possibility of extra volume. Likewise, if a late-evening activity is scheduled outside the hotel, security personnel should be informed to take extra precautions.

A postconvention meeting. When the event is over, convention service managers often meet with the meeting planner and key hotel personnel to review the convention. This is the opportunity to note what went well and to determine if there are areas for improvement.
Photo courtesy of InterContinental Hotels Group.

require classroom setup this week. This information is available instantly on a computerized data management program and would not require searching through numerous typed resumes. Additionally, changes and deletions are made simply by calling up the meeting in question and revising the individual fields or deleting the record.

In addition, new technology processes driven by the Internet and e-commerce will alter the way in which specification and function sheet information is communicated. Increasingly, this information will be transmitted electronically via a direct Internet link between the meeting planner and the hotel's convention service manager. Each will have all the details on-screen and will be able to make corrections online, eliminating the mailing of large amounts of paperwork.

Once approved by the meeting planner, the resume and banquet event orders will be distributed electronically to departments within the hotel rather than having sheets (even computer-generated ones) copied and distributed. With the click of a mouse, the exacting details of the meeting will be distributed to all involved with servicing the group.

The Importance of Follow-Up

Follow-up is an important part of showing your commitment to servicing a group's meeting. Follow-up, of course, should begin after initial contact with the client, as discussed in the communications section in this chapter. Checking details increases the likelihood that there will be fewer problems during the event.

During the meeting, frequent contact with the meeting planner and/or his or her staff is also important. Checking to ensure that all is going well reassures the meeting planner of your commitment to his or her group.

After an event, a **postconvention meeting** should be held. The same people who met for the preconvention meeting should meet for an after-the-fact review of the convention. This meeting is an opportunity for both the planner and the hotel staff to assess the success of the event and to address any problems (and determine ways to solve them in the future).

Summary

In this chapter, we have seen the necessity of working closely with the planner in the days leading up to a meeting or convention and the necessity of informing all hotel departments of their roles in the event. Preconvention meetings, detailed resumes and banquet event orders, and communication with both the planner and hotel staff will ensure the success of a meeting and will leave a good impression of the property's commitment to service. The banquet event orders discussed in this chapter cover the requirements discussed by the planner and the property to set the tone for and properly execute the planner's event.

Endnote

1. HSMAI Sales Manual.

Key Terms

banquet event order (BEO)—A form that provides a detailed breakdown of a single event. The banquet event order generally serves as a contract for the client and as a work order for the hotel's departments. Also called a function sheet.

event specifications guide (ESG)—A concise document, prepared and authorized by the meeting planner, detailing the specifics of a meeting or other event. ESGs include activities (by day, time, room, setup, and special requirements), complimentary room assignments, signature authority, and other important details. The ESG, which encompasses the full operation of the event, is shared with all key individuals. Also called a staging guide or a specifications guidebook.

key personnel roster—A list of hotel personnel who are available to the meeting planner to help service the event.

postconvention meeting (post-con)—A meeting held after the completion of a meeting or convention to evaluate the forecasting and planning that preceded the convention and the hotel's performance during the event.

preconvention meeting (pre-con)—A meeting held before the convention or event to review the entire program to ensure that the planner and hotel understand each other's requirements and expectations. This meeting is attended by the planner and key hotel personnel who will be involved in servicing the event to eliminate any misunderstandings and ensure a smooth event.

resume—A form providing a comprehensive overview of the entire convention program. Sent to the various hotel departments involved in the event, a resume provides specific instructions to the staff for servicing the event. Resumes include a summary of all group activities, billing instructions, key attendees, arrival and departure patterns, and other relevant information. Also called a specification sheet.

resume questionnaire—A form on which meeting planners answer questions relating to the upcoming event. Having detailed information readily available reduces the need for frequent contact with the meeting planner and assists hotels in preparing for both the pre-convention meeting and the event itself.

Review Questions

1. What is the purpose of the preconvention meeting? Who should attend?

2. What are the positions of the meeting planner and the convention service manager regarding a key personnel roster? What have some hotels done to compromise?

3. What key information is provided on a resume?

4. How does the the banquet event order differ from the resume?

5. How is the computer used to facilitate the communication of meeting details?

6. Why is follow-up so important? Describe three key times when hotel personnel commonly follow-up on a meeting.

7. Describe Westin's "Operation Excell." Outline the four stages of this program and discuss why each is important.

Additional References

Convention Industry Council International Manual, First Edition, Tony Carey, CMP, CMM, ed., Convention Industry Council, 2005.

Meetings and Conventions: A Planning Guide, Don MacLaurin and Ted Wykes, Meetings Professionals International, www.mpiweb.org.

Professional Meeting Management, Fifth Edition, Glen C. Ramsborg, Ph.D., ed., Professional Convention Management Association, 2006.

Internet Sites

For more information, visit the following Internet sites. Internet addresses can change without notice. If a site is no longer available at the address listed below, a search engine can be used to find the new address or additional, related sites.

Convene
www.pcma.org

Convention Industry Council (CIC)
  Accepted Practices: Event Specifications
www.conventionindustry.org/apex/accept-edpractices/eventspecifications.htm.

Delphi-Newmarket Software
www.newsoft.com

Marriott International
www.marriott.com

Meeting News
www.meetingnews.com

Meetings & Conventions
www.meetings-conventions.com

Westin Hotels
www.westin.com

CHAPTER APPENDIX

RESUME (SPECIFICATION SHEET) QUESTIONNAIRE
Resume questionnaire to be completed by the meeting planner.
(By permission, Penta Hotels)

Penta Hotel

RESUME GUIDELINES

1. EVENT TO BE POSTED AS FOLLOWS:

_____

_____

2. OFFICIAL OFFICERS:

    <u>NAME</u>   <u>TITLE</u>

_____

_____

_____

3. AUTHORIZED SIGNATURES:

    <u>NAME</u>   <u>SIGNATURES</u>   <u>TITLE</u>

_____

_____

_____

4. MASTER BILLING ADDRESS, TELEPHONE NUMBER AND TO WHOM'S ATTENTION IT SHOULD BE LISTED.
   (Upon approval of credit manager)

_____

_____

_____

5. NEW YORK STATE TAX EXEMPT: _____ YES _____ NO

       (If your organization is tax exempt, please forward a copy of the certificate to the Convention Service Department.)

6. CONVENTION HEADQUARTERS HOTEL : _____

   OTHER HOTELS USED: _____

_____   _____

7. EXPECTED CONVENTION REGISTRATION: _____ ADVANCE _____ ON-SITE

8. WILL THERE BE A NECESSITY FOR HOTEL SAFETY BOXES FOR THE CONVENTION OFFICERS? ____ YES ____ NO
   (If yes): HOW MANY? _____ AND WHAT NAMES SHOULD THEY BE LISTED UNDER:

_____

_____

_____

-2-

9. MONEY EXCHANGE: Will there be a necessity for the officers to exchange large bills during the conference? _____YES _____NO
    (If yes, in what denominations?)

    PENNIES _____   NICKELS _____   DIMES _____   QUARTERS _____

    $1 BILLS _____ $5 BILLS _____ $10 BILLS _____ $20 BILLS _____

10. RESERVATIONS: _____ HOTEL FORM   _____ OWN FORM   _____ HOUSING BUREAU

    _____ ROOMING LIST   _____ PHONE IN

11. ARRIVALS: Will most of your arrivals be arriving by:

    _____AUTOMOBILE   _____TRAIN   _____COMMERCIAL AIRLINE   _____CHARTERED BUS
    Note: For bus arrivals, please have the person(s) and/or organization contact our Reservation Manager directly.

12. HOSPITALITY SUITES: Please have the companies who will be sponsoring Hospitality Suites contact our Room Service Manager
    directly for their food and beverage needs. Also, our Reservation Manager and Credit Manager should be
    contacted to expedite their reservation and billing needs.

13. BUS DEPARTURES: Have you contracted for buses for tours, trips, etc. _____YES _____NO
    If yes, please advise us of your schedule in the program and setup instructions.

14. CELEBRITIES: Will any of your speakers attract media attention? _____YES _____NO
    If yes, please list their names and speaking date/time below:

    _____

    _____

    _____

15. SECURITY SPEECH: Do you require our Security Department to give a short speech on security tips on this city and the hotel?

    _____ YES   _____NO   If yes, it will be conducted at your first General Session.

16. OFFICERS, SPEAKERS AND VIP RESERVATIONS:

    NAME: _____   Double - 1 bed

    ADDRESS: _____   Twin - 2 single beds

    _____

    TELEPHONE #: _____

    ARRIVAL DATE:_____   ESTIMATED TIME: _____

    DEPARTURE DATE:_____   ESTIMATED TIME: _____

    ROOM TYPE: _____ SINGLE   _____DOUBLE   _____TWIN

    _____ 1 BEDROOM SUITE   _____2 BEDROOM SUITE

    (Sharing with: _____)

    Arrival: _____   Departure_____

    BILLING INSTRUCTIONS: _____ Pays own room, tax and incidental charges

    _____ Room and tax to the Master Account

    _____ Room, tax and incidentals to the Master Account

    SPECIAL REQUIREMENTS: _____

-3-

17. REGISTRATION: (Speakers - Exhibitors - Registrants)

<u>DAY</u>   <u>DATE</u>   <u>TIME</u>   <u>LOCATIONS</u>

_____

_____

18. ADMISSION: _____

19. EXHIBITS: <u>DAY/DATE</u>   <u>TIME</u>   <u>LOCATION(S)</u>

    Drayage setup: _____

                                 _____

    Exhibitors Setup: _____

                                 _____

    Show Opens: _____

                                 _____

    Exhibitors Dismantle: _____

                                 _____

    Drayage Dismantle: _____

                                 _____

20. NUMBER OF EXHIBITORS: _____   TYPE OF BOOTHS:_____
          Forward the exhibitors contract to the Convention Service department.

21. HOTEL HOLD HARMLESS CLAUSE: Please sign and return.

22. CONTRACTORS: (Contact, address and telephone number)

    DRAYAGE CONTRACTOR   SECURITY CONTRACTOR

    _____   _____

    _____   _____

    _____   _____

    AUDIOVISUAL CONTRACTOR   TYPEWRITER CONTRACTOR

    _____   _____

    _____   _____

    _____   _____

    SIGN CONTRACTOR   COPY MACHINE/OFFICE EQUIP CONTRACTOR

    _____   _____

    _____   _____

    _____   _____

-4-

SOUND/LIGHTING CONTRACTOR   OTHER CONTRACTORS

_____   _____

_____   _____

_____   _____

23. CONVENTION BUREAU PERSONNEL USED: _____ YES   _____NO

_____

_____

24. ROOM SERVICE/RESTAURANTS/BARS: L=Light, M=Moderate, H=Heavy

	BREAKFAST	LUNCH	DINNER	COCKTAILS
Room Service	_L _M _H	_L _M _H	_L _M _H	_L _M _H
Restaurants	_L _M _H	_L _M _H	_L _M _H	_L _M _H
Bars	_L _M _H	_L _M _H	_L _M _H	_L _M _H

25. TELEPHONE INSTRUCTIONS:

Will there be a need for outgoing calls?   _____YES   _____NO

If yes: _____LOCAL   _____LONG DISTANCE   _____BOTH

The special code word for all outgoing calls will be: _____

26. CHECKROOM FACILITIES:

The hotel does have a Main Checkroom located in the lobby. Will you require a second checkroom?   _____YES   _____NO

(If yes, our checkroom manager will contact you directly for charges incurred.)

27. PACKAGE ROOM:

Will you be shipping boxes to the hotel Package Room?   _____YES   _____NO

If yes, approximately how many?   _____Basic Size   _____Basic Weight

28. PROGRAM AND SET-UP INSTRUCTIONS:

On the following page, please find an example of the format followed for the Convention Service resume. We suggest this format for simpler communications and easy understanding. For more detailed set-ups, we suggest attaching a diagram.

This information will be included in the hotel's convention resume, which is distributed to all departments in the hotel.

Chapter 13 Outline

Competencies

1. Describe function rooms and how they are managed. (pp. 415–432)

2. Identify various meeting room setups and describe when each is commonly used, summarize how function rooms are broken down, describe meeting rooms of the future, and explain why it is important to monitor function room usage. (pp. 432–451)

How to Assign Meeting Rooms and Determine Meeting Room Setups

David Scherbarth, CMP
Director of Banquets and Convention Service
Sheraton Bal Harbour Beach Resort

"The convention service department is an extension of the sales department and must work closely with the sales manager to maximize function space while providing the group with a comfortable environment to achieve the goals of the meeting. Working closely with the meeting planner on the agenda will allow you to select proper function space so that the space is not too large or small for their meeting. The type of setup and the number expected to attend has a direct impact on how much space you need. You must know the various setups and what the capacity seating of each setup is for every function room in your facility. Other items that need to be considered when assigning function space are: noise conflicts with other meetings or banquets; traffic patterns of associated public space; lighting needs; ceiling heights; decor; electrical needs; and competitive groups."

Function Rooms and Meeting Setups

A NY HOTEL can supply guestrooms. A convention hotel is one that has a sufficient number of function rooms and the trained staff needed to handle the many different kinds of meetings and conventions.

Function Rooms

When the hotel sales representative originally solicited the convention, he or she presented the client with information about the hotel's meeting rooms. Most larger convention hotels have a number of suitable meeting rooms and often more than are needed for an event.

Often a convention planner will request that all the convention facilities be held for his or her event, at least until the program is roughed out and it is obvious what facilities are needed. This is rarely possible. Unless the convention is large and virtually sells out the house, the hotel management cannot lock up a precious commodity like meeting rooms for any longer than absolutely necessary.

It is urgent, therefore, for you to get together with the meeting planner to place a hold on the rooms thought to be needed and to urge that planning be done to determine realistically the needs of the event. There is no pressure if you have no other meetings scheduled for those dates, but most sizable hotels handle a number of smaller meetings simultaneously.

Types of Function Rooms

Before assigning rooms, the convention service manager must be aware of what the hotel has to offer. A common mistake is to assume you have only those rooms specifically designed as function rooms. Actually, all public space may be considered function areas, depending on the group and its needs.

Some of the most common **function rooms** depicted in the hotel's convention brochure are exhibit halls, ballrooms for banquets, and conference rooms for meetings. Unless meeting planners are advised otherwise, these are the rooms with which they will work as they lay out their schedules. Foyers and hallways outside the meeting rooms, however, can be used as **pre-function space**. These areas are often ideal for morning and afternoon refreshment breaks and as cocktail areas prior to evening banquets. Other possiblilities include use of the foyer, the parking lot, and swimming pool areas for cocktail parties; upper-floor suites equipped with conference tables for small, intimate meetings; and the garden area behind the hotel for an evening party. The possibilities are limited only by the imagination of the convention service manager. The unusual is often what makes a hotel unique, so it is important to keep in mind that all public areas may be used as function space.

Breakout rooms are used when a session divides into small groups for discussion and feedback. The trend toward breakout configurations as a method of training has become increasingly popular, so many hotels are making suites available near the main conference

CERTIFIED MEETING SPACE

Responding to the need to provide meeting planners with the actual dimensions of meeting rooms and their capacities under a wide variety of setups, the Professional Convention Management Association (PCMA) began a program to certify the dimensions of meeting rooms at hospitality properties.

Properties that take advantage of this program are given detailed computer printouts of their meeting space and permission to use the PCMA certification seal on promotional literature.

room. Others have provided rooms that can be subdivided with movable **air walls** to accommodate these setups.

Function Room Size and Layout

Many factors come into play when discussing meeting room size. First and foremost, of course, is the number expected to attend. Then you must consider the room setup desired and the number and type of audiovisual equipment needed. Additional space may be required for clothes racks, props, or tables to distribute literature. And you must allow more space if refreshment breaks are scheduled.

The basic layout indicates the style of seating. It is wasteful of labor to set each room to utmost capacity, but you obviously must provide enough seating. This is the time to examine the kind of sessions that will go on just before and just after this specific program to make sure the setup is the same or enough time is allotted to make the change. Hotels are frequently able to put similar meetings back to back and thus keep manpower and equipment change-over time to a minimum.

The meeting planner will also have to confer with you about the style and size of the head table. Pads, pencils, folders, and printed material may all be placed on chairs and tables. And water glasses and pitchers may be put at a number of tables (or stations if tables are not used). Each session has its own requirements; some, for example, call for name cards. Attention to details is the key to service.

Meeting Room Plans

It is important to include meeting room plans on resources used by meeting planners, including the hotel's convention brochure, websites, and directory advertising. For years, convention brochures gave general — often approximate — dimensions of meeting rooms, and meeting planners were often dismayed to find that there was not enough room to stage their functions. To eliminate this problem, the Professional Convention Management Association (PCMA) developed a program to help both properties and meeting planners by actually measuring the dimensions and capacities of meeting rooms. After the rooms are measured with sophisticated laser-powered equipment, computer software is used to accurately map out the room and determine room setup capacities. The detailed computer printouts generated are given to the property to be used in presentations. Properties that have had their space certified are provided with gummed seals that can be affixed to current promotional materials, and are given permission to use the PCMA seal in advertising to assure planners that they are getting the space promised (see box titled "Certified Meeting Space"). The PCMA partnered with Meeting Maker software to offer a diskette containing three-dimensional floor plans of their meeting rooms to properties that have been space-verified. Meeting planners can download, at no charge, a companion version of the software from the PCMA website. The PCMA and Meeting Matrix now advertise that "the combination of these software packages enables properties and meeting managers to send meeting room sets back and forth via the Internet, a whole new way of doing business."

In addition to the dimensions of rooms, meeting planners need to know the capacity of each under a variety of setups. Exhibit 1 illustrates a **capacity chart**, a diagram that shows the capacity of a room when various setups are used. While planners are made aware of the kinds of rooms available to them during a sales presentation, the convention service manager should be available to help planners decide which function would work best in

Exhibit 1   Meeting Room Capacities and Dimensions

INTERCONTINENTAL · TORONTO CENTRE

Name of Room	Banquet	Theatre	Classroom	Reception	Conference	U-Shape	Hollow Square	Dimensions	Area sq. ft.	Height
Ballroom 'A'	200	275	135	275	—	50	65	60x39	2340	9' 11"
Ballroom 'B'	270	400	198	400	—	65	80	60x57	3420	9' 11"
A&B Combined	510	700	342	700	—	—	—	60x96	5760	9' 11"
Simcoe	20	20	16	20	20	—	—	21x17	357	9' 6"
Ontario	150	200	84	200	—	42	52	53x38	2014	9' 6"
Niagara	70	100	45	100	28	32	38	29x38	1102	9' 6"
Ontario & Niagara Combined	240	280	120	320	—	—	—	82x38	3116	9' 6"

Dimensions are approximate and in feet

Most hotels, conference centers, and city convention facilities offer charts such as this one to meeting planners. This is a particularly good example, as it includes seating capacities for a variety of seating arrangements as well as detailed information on room dimensions, square footage, and ceiling heights. These statistics, coupled with the computerized scaled drawings now available, help meeting planners to assess the ability of properties to meet their requirements for various types of meetings and functions.

Source: Courtesy of InterContinental—Toronto Centre.

each room. We will discuss the setups commonly used and how capacity is affected by various setups later in this chapter.

Convention service managers should also be aware of the impact of the **Americans with Disabilities Act (ADA)** in regard to their property's function space. While there are still a number of "gray areas" in terms of responsibilities of the property, certain physical requirements must be met by properties offering convention space. These include (but are not limited to) adequate handicapped parking, easy accessibility (ramps, wide doorways, etc.), adapted restroom facilities, and assistive devices for the hearing and visually impaired. It is important to note that after the U.S. ADA was passed in 1990, other countries, including Australia (1992), the United Kingdom (1995), and Canada (2002) passed similar laws.

Not only must hotels be **barrier-free** (free of obstacles that prevent disabled persons from moving freely to all public areas), but meeting planners may also have special requirements for accommodating their attendees with disabilities. Wider aisles and increased space for seating arrangements may be needed to allow wheelchair access, or a signer may be required for hearing-impaired attendees. In some cases, it is not difficult for a property to make the necessary adjustments; in others, it will be up to the property and the meeting planner to determine who is responsible for providing the additional services needed.

Scaled Drawings. If a hotel does not present its meeting rooms in complete detail, it will be necessary to prepare other material. Most properties prepare scaled drawings of each room (see Exhibit 2). These should indicate doors, windows, pillars, elevators, electrical outlets, and any obstructions that might affect the setup of the meeting. Meeting planners will probably ask for scaled drawings of each room, so you should have accurately scaled drawings of each function room for your own use and for distribution to customers.

These drawings should be accurate enough to be used to designate meeting or exhibit layouts. If you indicate capacity on the drawings, keep in mind that different setups accommodate widely differing numbers of people.

Exhibit 2   Detailed Meeting Room Plans

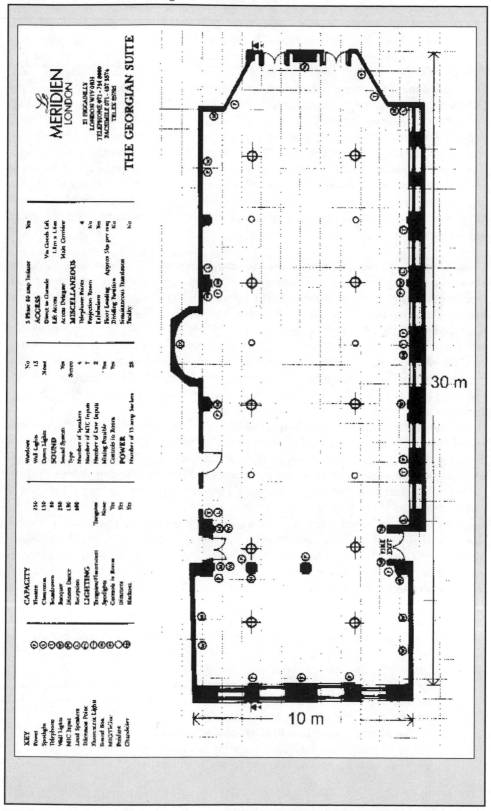

In addition, meeting planners also like to visualize the overall daily flow of their attendees as they participate in convention activities. Exhibit 3 shows an overall schematic of a facility. While this plan does not provide the detail inherent to scaled drawings of the meeting rooms itself, it may prove helpful to the planner in planning his or her program.

Scaled drawings of function rooms and overall schematics are important to meeting planners, and they are also used to ensure a safe event. For large events, detailed scaled drawings of the function are required by local fire marshals. These scaled drawings, unlike the scaled drawings provided to the meeting planner by the hotel, must include both the room's schematics and the proposed room setup. In most cases, this finalized scaled drawing is the responsibility of the meeting planner and should be a part of a hotel's contractual terms with the meeting planner. The Las Vegas Hilton, for example, advises: *"Your Company or Association is responsible for scaled diagrams for events with attendance of 300 guests or more. These must be approved by the Clark County Fire Marshal. The Las Vegas Hilton cannot guarantee these diagrams will be approved if submitted less than 30 days prior to your function. The Las Vegas Hilton can assist in providing a scaled diagram of your event."*

Using Computer Technology to Assist Meeting Planners. Many properties are taking advantage of today's computer technology to assist meeting planners in determining optimum room setups. Using **computer-assisted design (CAD)** programs is far quicker than manually drawing floorplans (often to find that the space does not accommodate the function), and offers the advantage of flexibility (features of a room — pillars, curved spaces, etc. can be considered when determining the best layouts — and a number of room setups can be compared). Additionally, they can show a number of options that the meeting planner (and the convention services staff) may not have previously considered, they enable meeting planners to see at a glance how various setups will work in terms of traffic flow as well as capacity, and they can be stored to enable them to be used for future functions.

Many hotel chains, such as Marriott (which utilizes its own software to offer computerized room drawings to meeting planners as part of its Network Plan), are finding this technology to be an invaluable tool for the varied needs of meeting planners. This technology is expected to be increasingly used by both properties and meeting planners themselves, and should be considered as part of your property's program to assist meeting planners with staging a successful function.

We have already mentioned the PCMA computer printouts that provide room capacities for varied setups, but still other software is available, such as MeetingMatrix, Room Viewer, and Delphi Diagrams for Meeting Managers, which also "draw" room setups, as well as Cast Software's innovative three-dimensional product, Vivien (see box titled "Using Computer Technology to Assist Meeting Planners"). Vivien, which is billed as a Virtual Event Design Suite, allows planners to view table-seating patterns or the stage from different angles, enabling them to "see" what attendees would actually see.

Jim Barr, catering/convention service manager at the Sheraton Chicago Hotel and Towers, states:

> MeetingMatrix diagrams are complete and easy to modify and read, and that helps us both with sales and operations. From a sales perspective, clients are more confident about their buying decision when we use MeetingMatrix to show how their function will work in our space. On the operations side, using the diagrams during final event preparations keep questions, miscommunications, and re-sets to a minimum.[1]

Monica Cheeks, director of convention services at the Hyatt Newporter in Newport Beach, California, is equally enthusiastic about the Room Viewer technology:

Exhibit 3   An Overall Facility Schematic as a Sales Tool

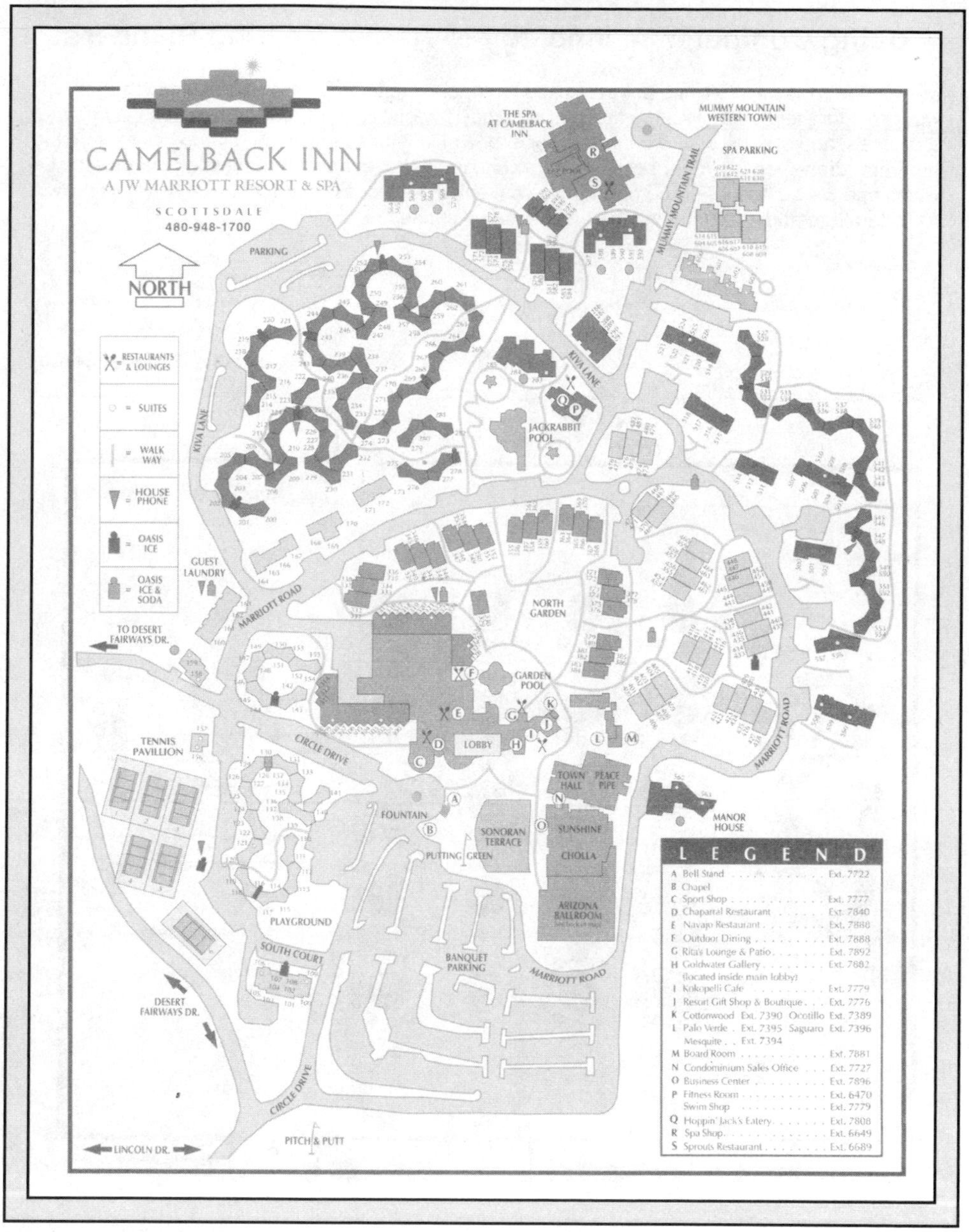

Using a plan as illustrated here, a salesperson can help the meeting planner visualize the attendees'
flow from guestrooms to function rooms.
Source: Courtesy of Camelback Inn, Scottsdale, Arizona.

We use it every day. Previously, we were sketching out meeting set-ups by hand, which is obviously neither precise nor very fast. Now with Room Viewer, I can plot out a planner's request very quickly and accurately, print it out and give copies back to the planner, as well as to our catering manager. Our sales team uses it in proposals, and it's helped to close deals. It even has six different aisle sizes, so it can conform to our complicated fire codes.[2]

Using Computer Technology to Assist Meeting Planners

MeetingMatrix is one software program used to enable meeting planners to see which setups will work best for their functions. After entering such basic information as room dimensions, number of attendees, and special requirements (size or shape of tables, space needed for exhibits, etc.), the program "draws" one or more possible room configurations, enabling the meeting planner to see which one will be best — and providing the convention services department with a list of function room furniture and equipment needed for the setup chosen.

Sample Banquet Setup

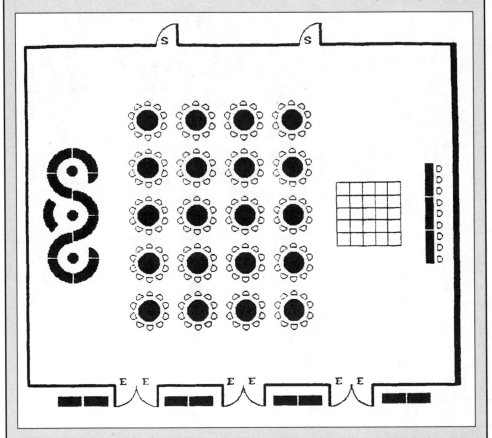

FUNCTION SPECIFICATION: Meeting name: Sample meeting   Facility name: Sample facility

Function name:	Banquet	Setup items used:	QTY	ITEM	
Room name:	Ballroom		209	18" x 18"	Chairs
Number of people:	209		8	6' x 30"	Rectangular tables
Setup:	Banquet —		3	8' x 30"	Rectangular tables
	10 per 5 foot diameter table		20	5' dia	Round tables
Distance between rows:	75 inches		2	5' dia	Quarter-round tables
Center aisle width:	5.0 feet		9	6' x 30"	Crescent tables
Side aisle width:	5.0 feet		25	3' x 3'	Dance floor squares
Cross aisle width:	5.0 feet				

MEETINGMATRIX is a trademark of SCLM, Inc. Used with permission.

FACTORS TO BE CONSIDERED WHEN ASSIGNING FUNCTION SPACE

David Scherbath, CMP, director of banquets and convention service at the Sheraton Bal Harbour Beach Resort, says that details are important when deciding how to effectively manage function rooms and meeting setups. Factors that should be considered include:

- Day(s) of meeting. If more than one day, try to keep the meeting in the same room. This minimizes labor and gives the group consistency.
- Beginning and ending times. Accurate times allow the room to be utilized more than once a day — sometimes for as many as three or four times for different functions.
- Setup style and attendance. The type of setup and number expected to attend has a direct impact on how much space is needed.
- Audiovisual and staging requirements. These two items can dramatically alter the size of space needed. A 24-hour hold may be necessary for extensive audiovisual and/or staging requirements.

Working closely with the meeting planner on the agenda will allow you to select proper function space so that the space is not too large or too small for their meeting. This is important, because the comfort of a meeting room can have an affect on the environment and on the focus of the meeting. This also allows the sales team every opportunity to maximize function space and guestrooms with additional bookings. Releasing space unneeded by one group may allow your sales team to book another group in the hotel, increasing your occupancy and revenues.

MeetingMatrix is available from SCLM Software Inc., 6 South Main, Stewartstown, Pennsylvania 17363. Room Viewer information can be obtained from TimeSaver Software, 10884 Kimball, Tustin, California 92680. Delphi Diagrams are available from Newmarket International, 135 Commerce Way, Portsmouth, New Hampshire. Free room layout software demos can also be downloaded from both MeetingMatrix (www.meetingmatrix.com) and Room Viewer (www.timesaversoftware.com).

Timetable for Setup and Breakdown

Most hotel brochures do an adequate job of presenting the basic contours of each meeting room, and many are designed to show how a room is used in a variety of ways. Few, however, tell the convention organizer how much time is required for room setup and breakdown. But there is a great need to communicate that information.

It is very important to know exactly how long it takes a crew to set up each room under the many seating arrangements. Many a meeting program has failed because those planning it did not take into account the time it takes to set up and break down, and the program was designed much too tightly to permit good service. The planner would have developed the program more realistically if he or she had some idea of the time needed to perform these services.

Too often, the hotel bears the stigma of failing to perform well, give good service, or show much expertise, so the hotel staff should make the meeting planner aware of its **function room turnover time** — the amount of time needed to tear down and reset a function room. Most meeting planners would gladly loosen up their timetables if they knew what was involved to assure that their shows ran smoothly and on time.

We strongly recommend that convention service managers have charts made up indicating such requirements. These charts should list the time it takes to set up each room for maximum capacity under each seating arrangement. They should give the time it takes to break them down, plus union regulations regarding workday, hours, overtime charges, and any unusual characteristics that may affect costs and time. Specify the number of people needed. Time may be saved by using a larger crew but this will cost more; at times a meeting planner might choose such an option.

Managing Function Rooms

Your hotel function space is a precious asset, and your goal as a convention service manager is to maximize its utilization (see box titled "Factors to Be Considered When Assigning Function Space"). Empty rooms, whether guestrooms or function rooms, are a perishable product.

The convention service manager is the person most qualified to assign rooms for specific events. This should be done in communication with the meeting planner. The service manager knows the hotel's facilities; the planner knows the event's characteristics.

In assigning a room, its size, its capacity under a specific layout, the type of event, and the presentation style should all be considered. The room size should "match" the expected attendance. Too much space or too many empty seats can create the wrong psychological setting. These fundamental requirements probably were hashed out during the sales presentations, but other factors must be considered, too.

Consider the room's location within the hotel in regard to traffic in corridors, elevators, escalators, parking arrangements, and coat check rooms. All program segments must be definitely allocated to specific locations about sixty days before the event, at the latest. This is especially important if a group wishes to reserve their space on a 24-hour basis. According to Maria Dempsey, director of sales and marketing North America for Pan Pacific Hotels and Resorts, this can pose a problem for the hotel:

> The request for access to public meeting space on a 24-hour basis means no other groups may use those rooms, even if the room is not occupied overnight.[3]

A number of groups, however, wish to reserve their rooms for the duration of their meeting, especially if functions involve exhibits or extensive staging or if there is the possibility that a meeting will not end on schedule. David Kilman, CMP, past president of MPI, offers this perspective:

> There is a tug-of-war between planners and suppliers regarding 24-hour space holds. It all comes down to the total value of the meeting. If a planner expects, or demands, the luxury of a round-the-clock hold on space, there must be an appropriate financial return to the supplier.... Once the economic impact of a meeting is resolved, it should be easy to determine if a 24-hour hold is a reasonable request.[4]

When considering a 24-hour hold, therefore, it is vital to analyze the economic impact of the meeting, including the value of the meeting itself and subsequent business from the group, and the time of year. If, for example, the group wishes to book during the Christmas holidays when you can expect to generate a large volume of lucrative catering business, it may not be a sound business decision to reserve function rooms on a 24-hour basis (see Sales Restrictions section in this chapter). If you decide to reserve the rooms around the clock, a clause should be included in the group's contract guaranteeing the 24-hour hold and any restrictions put upon it by the hotel.

You should get a list from the client of all the people on his or her staff who are authorized to move an event to a different location, should the need arise. Just before the event, and especially during it, it is absolutely essential to know the channels of authority within the convention staff. Time may be too short and the need for action too great to let you double-check any instructions. Cancellations of sessions, changes in timetables and the like may be made at the last minute.

Such a list should be in writing, of course. And the degree of authority should be specified. What can these staff members order? Changes in layout or location can be costly in terms of time and labor.

The list you get from the convention organizer should be similar to the list of your department heads that you give to the organizer. The key people of both the hotel and convention group staffs should attend the preconvention meetings. Let them get acquainted before the pressure begins. Discuss possible changes. This is the time to indicate what the hotel staff will need in the way of time and labor to bring about such program alterations.

Because association conventions must cope with optional attendance at both the convention and individual programs, it is often necessary to move workshops and meetings from one room to another to accommodate smaller or larger groups. Airing such possibilities in advance allows your staff and the client's staff to understand such conditions and to react more quickly and constructively in crisis situations.

Sales Restrictions on Function Space

Both the hotel sales staff and the catering department are involved in selling function space. The sales department is responsible for selling space that is used by convention groups requiring sleeping rooms. The catering department is responsible for selling function space to local groups. Since hotels are primarily interested in filling sleeping accommodations because of the high profit margin, the hotel sales department should have preference in booking the available function space.

Therefore, most hotels have local catering sales restrictions. For example, during its peak convention season, a hotel may limit local catering to a short booking cycle. That is, the catering department may only sell function space to local groups after the hotel is assured that the needs of groups needing sleeping rooms have been met. Once the hotel sales staff sells their group room allotment on a given day, any function space still available may be sold by catering.

In some cases, special **day packages** are created for groups that do not require overnight accommodations. Day packages typically include a single price per attendee for the entire day. This price is inclusive of all food and beverage, instead of having meals and breaks priced separately, so these packages can be an economical option for local groups or other groups that do not require sleeping rooms.

The further out a commitment is made by convention groups, the greater the opportunity for catering to sell the unused space. This period of time is frequently referred to as the **open sale period**. Holidays are often designated as open sales periods, as group guestroom business is traditionally slow around Christmas, Thanksgiving, and the Fourth of July. Any hotel business booked by catering during those times is not likely to displace conventions needing meeting space.

Function Room Charges

How do you determine what to charge for meeting space? Brochures list rates for guestrooms but rarely for meeting rooms. The latter situation is most flexible; it depends on the meeting group, the time, and the space required. If a group uses enough guestrooms, there is often no charge for meeting rooms. In the case of food functions, the cost per person often covers the use of the room.

Properties with unique function space may be able to charge more for their room rental. Function space characteristics that might command a premium include:

- Large ballrooms that are free of pillars or other obstructions
- High ceilings with retractable chandeliers
- Tiered theater-style auditoriums
- Advanced audiovisual-equipped rooms
- Meeting rooms that are convenient to guestrooms

It is important that the meeting planner understands your property's policy regarding function room charges. Many hotels include a clause similar to the one below to eliminate potential misunderstandings:

> *Meeting and function space is assigned based on the type of setup and the number of people in attendance. Should advance setup and late teardown or an abnormal amount of meeting space be required, a charge may be incurred. Specified meeting rooms cannot be guaranteed and are subject to change. If the final attendance figures are less than the original estimate, an adjustment to the meeting and function space will become necessary. Any changes requested in your agenda after receipt of this contract are based upon space availability at the time of your request. Any cancellation of food and beverage functions after acceptance of this agreement will result in the organization being charged the full dollar value of that function based on either the actual menu price or an average menu price. Should the hotel be able to resell a function of similar value in the originally scheduled room, there will be no charge assessed.*

There may well be circumstances in which the hotel management prefers to charge for a function room. A hotel that hosts a catering event where no guestroom nights are used, for example, may specify a *minimum sales amount* on the room. That is, the hotel could require that a group not using sleeping rooms spend a specific amount, such as $20,000, to secure a large ballroom rent-free for their event. You should consider having a listed price for each room; after all, it looks great when you waive the fee. When you do charge for a function room, a list of charges should be available. Function room rental rates should be determined for each meeting room by time of day. Some properties will list specific rates for morning, afternoon, evening, full-day, and 24-hour weekday hold, and weekend rates.

You might outline a sliding scale arrangement, tying the meeting room fees to the number of guestrooms used for the convention (see Exhibit 4). For example, if the group picks up 200 room nights or more, the $1,000 fee for the ballroom could be waived; if 100–199 room nights are used, the cost would be $500; and if the group uses fewer than 100 room nights, the cost would be $750.

There is a trend today to charge for space. A hotel that handles a number of small meetings would be wise to consider a fee, particularly if the group plans to meet in one

Exhibit 4   Guide to Function Space Charges

SHERATON FUNCTION SPACE CHARGES

The Sheraton Waikiki charges for function space under the following circumstances:

1.   All exhibits.
2.   All function rooms that are held on a 24-hour block.
3.   All function space for groups that have meetings only and are holding no sleeping rooms at the Sheraton Waikiki Hotel.
4.   All function space when unusual or costly setups are required.
5.   All function space when the sleeping rooms decrease proportionately from the original commitment.

FUNCTION SPACE VS. SLEEPING ROOM CONSUMPTION (PROPORTIONATE SLIDING SCALE)

Percent of Decrease From Original Block	Amount of Meeting Room Charges
Up to 40% decrease	No charge.
41%–60% decrease	50% charge for meeting rooms as listed on "meeting room charge sheet."
61%–80% decrease	75% charge for meeting rooms as listed on "meeting room charge sheet."
81%–100% decrease	100% charge for meeting rooms as listed on "meeting room charge sheet."

In addition to the above "sliding scale," the hotel will also take into consideration your definite food and beverage events when determining your meeting room charges.

The Sheraton Waikiki provides meeting planners with the following space pricing policy. Note the charges increase if sleeping rooms slip from the original room block commitment. In determining meeting room charges, many hotels consider "slippage" — when guestroom pickup decreases significantly, the charge for the group's function space increases. Meeting room rental at this 1,900-room property totals over $250,000 annually.
Source: Courtesy of the Sheraton Waikiki.

room, hold a food function in another, and conduct breakout meetings in another three to five rooms.

In such situations, room charges should be stipulated if the guestroom commitment is not enough to cover the labor costs of setting up, servicing, cleaning, and tearing down. After all, a hotel is in business to make a profit.

You might also want to charge for meeting rooms when companies participating in a trade show take the opportunity to hold dealer or sales meetings. The people attending may already be registered for the trade show, and the requirements of the trade show would place great strain on the allocation of meeting rooms. Of course, if the food functions of such additional meetings mount up, it may justify not charging for the use of the room. But a room charge may be justified if the food function is only a refreshment break. In the final analysis, there is no hard and fast rule on charging for meeting space. A hotel needs to look at the food, the rooms, and all other profit areas to determine its rate structure.

Function and Meeting Room Revenue Management

Increasingly, hotels are applying traditional guestroom yield management methods to meeting and function rooms. Yield management sets prices based on the forecasted demand for function space. Rental rates are increased or decreased from the established rates depending on the time and date of the meeting and on the total revenue the event brings to the property. Several Hilton hotels, for example, have begun to determine intricate yield management formulas for pricing their function space. Steve Armitage, senior vice president of sales at Hilton Hotels Corporation, states:

> The meeting buyer can expect to see meeting room yield management become more widespread as technology advances.[5]

The use of yield management techniques can be beneficial to both hotels and meeting planners. Setting prices according to predicted demand levels not only helps hotels to manage their revenues but also provides the opportunity for price-sensitive customers who are willing to purchase at off-peak times to do so at favorable rates. It is necessary, however, to identify and communicate high and low demand periods and to be able to justify the different rates available to different clients at different times of the year. And any fee increases should be made incrementally, to avoid alienating corporate buyers.

Fred Shea, vice president of sales operations for Hyatt Hotels Corp., says:

> We do not want to have huge swings where we charge $3,000 one day and nothing the next. We want to slowly move the margins up or down. We don't want there to be a big culture shock. It's a matter of degrees.[6]

When establishing your yield management strategy, you will want to consider a number of factors, including the performance of each of your function rooms (a large ballroom, for example, may actually yield a lower occupancy rate than a smaller meeting room that is used several times a day), physical "rate fences" (such as amenities offered, location, and so on, that can justify a higher charge), and non-physical "rate fences," such as customer characteristics (a property can justify lower rates to a potential customer likely to use other hotel facilities, such as sleeping rooms, restaurants, and so on).

Once these factors have been determined, you will want to develop a strategy that can be easily implemented. One simple approach is to color-code demand periods on a calendar or table. High-demand periods, for example, can be coded in red for instant recognition as a "hot" period, moderately high-demand periods can be coded in yellow to signify "warm" periods, and low-demand periods can be coded in blue. Each of the demand levels (colors) should have a different set of prices associated with it, and those prices should be communicated to all staff members involved in selling meeting space or catering functions. It is also important to communicate when qualified discounts can be offered to meeting planners or groups (usually in low-demand periods).[7]

Release Dates

When a convention buys out the house, a request to **hold all function space** seems reasonable. Such requests are typical from large groups that are booking two to three years out. But a request to "hold all function space" is difficult for a hotel, especially in periods of high demand. Groups requesting an all-space block on your function space should be closely monitored, and all-space blocks should be negotiated with reasonable **release date** increments, such as one year, nine months, or six months, to allow your property to sell the space with some lead time should the large group not materialize as anticipated.

Release dates should be set in every letter of agreement. At some early date when a rough program is available, the room assignments can be tentatively made. At this point, *some* function rooms can be released if there seems to be more than enough. The convention in the house should have a priority for meeting rooms, but you may get other calls. Here again, it is obvious why there is a need to have just one function book, under one person's control.

At a somewhat later date, when a detailed program is worked out, try to get unneeded rooms released. Planners often to try to hold onto every room indefinitely, to have a reserve for some occasion that may come up. But this practice can inhibit your other sales efforts.

Many properties specify their release date policies in meeting contracts. The following clause spells out one property's policy:

> *In order to ensure that adequate space is available for your meeting, please provide the Convention Service Department with a tentative function schedule six months prior to your meeting/convention, or as soon as possible. A final program is required no later than 90 days prior to the start of your convention. Space not assigned at 90 days will be released to the hotel for scheduling of other functions, as required.*

Several Meetings Simultaneously

Most meetings are small. More than 75 percent of all corporate meetings have fewer than 100 in attendance. To do much business in meetings, you must be able to house more than one simultaneously. Naturally, this is not the case when you virtually sell out the house, but most often the function book fills up with a number of more modest events.

Handling several smaller meetings calls for careful planning. You cannot negotiate with all groups at the same time, so you must take care not to commit all your public space to one group, leaving you with no facilities for the other. Most hotels want the option of moving groups around to maximize usage, especially when groups are not using guestrooms, and often include a function room assignment clause in their contracts. A typical clause might read:

> *The function room assignments listed in this contract are tentative. Final function and meeting rooms will be assigned by the Hotel three months prior to the meeting dates. The Hotel reserves the right to reassign function rooms to accommodate both Group and all other groups or parties using the Hotel's facilities during Group's meeting.*

Some meeting planners, who feel that they have negotiated for a specific room or rooms that will meet the objective(s) of their function, object to such a clause and try to negotiate it out of the contract. A hotel can address the concerns of the meeting planner by pointing out the reasonable time frame (most groups do not publish a program with specific room names more than three months before the function) and assuring him or her that the hotel will meet specific requirements if another room is substituted. The hotel should then follow through on its promises, ensuring that basic requirements (such as square footage and other needs, such as hard walls to minimize noise) are met.

Traffic patterns must be carefully planned to avoid confusion and congestion. Give thought, too, to the proximity of different kinds of groups. Don't forget to find out what will be going on in the room next door. Holding a training session next door to a college reunion is asking for trouble; a rock band next door to a speech could be disastrous. And even a seemingly ordinary meeting can become quite noisy merely by adding a sound film.

You may find it extremely profitable to go after smaller meetings. To begin with, there are more of them. And smaller meeting organizers are generally not as demanding of price and concessions, often can offer much repeat business, and tax your staff less in serving them. It is tempting to hit that home run by bagging a full-house convention. But a steady stream of good base hits in the form of modest-size meetings often wins the ball game by providing what every hotel wants — profitable business.

Use of Meeting Rooms by Others

Some organizations ask, or demand, that all requests by other groups for meeting facilities in the hotel at the time of their event be cleared with them. They are trying to control the entire environment of their event and they don't want rival organizations meeting at the same time under the same roof. Apprehensions of industrial security cannot be dismissed lightly.

The hotel must be careful about this. Imagine an IBM research seminar in the house at the same time as Toshiba or Honeywell meetings! When a competitive organization appears on the scene, the usually easygoing meeting planner gets quite uptight. And you may find yourself needing strict security systems for a relatively easy, small seminar.

And should you be concerned about only the exact date of the meeting, or must you worry, too, about the days immediately before and after the event?

Small properties that can handle only one average-sized group at a time can use such situations to sell themselves. In the off season the small resort can claim that walk-in business from competitive personnel is highly unlikely. The meeting organizer is assured of receiving all your facility and attention and need not worry about traffic pattern and unwanted guests.

The convention organizer may want to veto a meeting held in the hotel during his or her dates. Many companies hold dealer meetings at trade shows. Most association executives have no objections, and many feel that it adds importance to their event. But many worry that the timing of such meetings may pull delegates away from the main sessions or events.

It is safe to say that you can expect meeting planners to be interested in who and what is scheduled in the hotel during *their* time.

Employee Procedure Manuals

Convention service managers, as we have said, are the in-house coordinators of the convention. They work with virtually every department in the hotel. Their authority in dealing with these departments is to a great extent determined by their character and the respect they have earned from those with whom they work. In many hotels, convention service managers do not have direct line authority over rooms or food and beverage departments. This often necessitates that they use tact and discretion in getting the job done.

However, they do have line authority within their own department and must function as managers there. Serving under them are three to ten housepersons who set up the function rooms. Each of these people should be trained in the various types of meeting setups. Our experience shows this is best accomplished with the use of an **employee procedures manual** (see Exhibit 5).

A procedure manual is not a job description. A procedure manual tells the employee how to do the job, whereas the job description is prepared primarily for management and states the job's responsibility and authority. Ideally, the procedure manual should include illustrations or drawings. For example, setup illustrations similar to those used in this

Exhibit 5   Employee Procedures Manual

Setup Support Services for Functions		
STEPS:	**HOW-TO'S:**	**TIPS:**
To complete all steps, you will need tables, a banquet event order (BEO), change orders (if any), tablecloths, table skirts, standard amenities, trash cans, an easel, a message corkboard, and tacks or stick pins.		
1. **Set up registration tables.**	Check the banquet event order (BEO) for the number and type of tables to set up. Place tables in the lobby or near the entrance to the function room as stated in the BEO.	
2. **Cover, skirt, and flounce registration tables according to the BEO.**	Place tablecloths on function room tables, and skirt and flounce function room tables.	
3. **Place amenities on registration tables.**	Place the following items on registration tables: - Pens or pencils - Message pads - Pitcher with water and water glasses Arrange other items supplied by guests as indicated on the BEO.	Guests may have items sent ahead for the function.
4. **Place a trash can near the tables.**		
5. **Set up a message board.**	Put a message corkboard on an easel near the registration table to hold messages for guests who are at the function. Provide tacks or stick pins.	The message board prevents the interruption of meetings. Participants can check the message board during breaks.

Employee procedure manuals, such as this one, provide specific instructions for setting up the various components of a meeting or convention (this example provides instructions for setting up a registration area). Having detailed guidelines ensures that all aspects of the job are handled consistently.
Source: Adapted from Hospitality Skills Training Series, *Banquet Setup Employee Guide,* **American Hotel & Lodging Educational Institute.**

chapter should be included. The manual also should include a step-by-step outline of the houseperson's job.

The procedure manual will have the same importance for employees in the convention service department as the master recipe card does for a cook. Successful restaurants are largely successful because of consistency; the same should be true for convention servicing. A procedure manual will help ensure that setups will not be done in a slightly different way each day.

It is often difficult for employees to recall each procedure in a setup and all the required supplies. The manual eliminates the exclusion of certain setups, as well as serving as a valuable training tool for new employees. Manuals might also include rules and regulations that apply to the setup houseperson.

Efforts should be made to personalize the manual. It should be published in a small booklet form that can easily fit into a shirt pocket for quick reference.

No such manual is permanent. On the contrary, new tables, chairs, and operating techniques will necessitate updating. Hopefully, the employees themselves may suggest ways to perform certain aspects of the job better.

Meeting Setups

The physical arrangement of chairs and tables plays an important role in meetings. Convention planners know that the atmosphere of a meeting can be enhanced or destroyed by the size of the room and the manner in which it is arranged. Thus it is essential that you have an orderly presentation for each of your facility's meeting rooms, giving its dimensions and its capacities under a variety of layout designs.

Function Room Furniture

Hotel function rooms get heavy use. Often a number of functions are scheduled on one day for a single room, with only an hour or two between events. These events are usually quite different, and housepersons must work quickly to set up a variety of functions — business meetings, lectures, training sessions, fashion shows, banquets, and others. The only flexibility the room can provide is through the use of air walls or folding division doors. The major change must be provided by the equipment and setup.

Function room furniture is the term coined for equipment used in meeting and banquet rooms. Jacob Felsenstein of King Arthur Incorporated, a leading supplier of such furniture to the hotel industry, has suggested four general features to look for in function room furniture:

- *Strength and durability.* Watch for the weakest link, such as mechanical folding devices which are easily broken, or strong components which may depend on a weak hinge or spring. Safety of guests is a foremost consideration. There are simple and effective folding devices that minimize the possibility of failure. Keep in mind, frequency of use means frequency of cleaning. Parts in contact with the floor must be made to withstand and facilitate frequent scrubbing, waxings, and vacuuming.
- *Ease of handling.* All folding or knock-down equipment should be simple to set up. Equipment that is light in weight may not be the most durable. There are a wide variety of carriers, such as dollies and trucks, which are designed to aid in handling.

- *Ease of storage.* Equipment should be able to be stacked so that one piece does not mar the next, and in a manner that prevents vulnerable parts from protruding. In choosing dollies or trucks, check to see that they are designed to handle the particular piece of equipment in your particular setting.
- *Flexibility.* It may be advisable to buy function room furniture that serves two or more purposes in order to avoid extra handling or storage. For example, a Knock-Down Cabaret Table allows for different-sized tops to be used interchangeably with one column and base, enabling it to fill many different needs; one Dual-Height Folding Platform serves two different levels, many different purposes, can save up to 50 percent on initial outlay, and an additional 50 percent on handling costs and storage space.[8]

Chairs and Tables. Meeting room chairs and tables vary a great deal, but there are certain types and sizes that are used most frequently. We will use these basic types when we present layouts and schematics for setups. Your capacity figures should be based on such equipment, and will vary when you use equipment other than the standard. Most variations are used in small meeting setups, such as board room facsimiles; we have relaxed during many such meetings in posh swivel chairs. Conference centers frequently boast **ergonomic** chairs, which are bigger than a regular chair, upholstered in leather, come with a cushion seat and swivel, and are said to be comfortable for 18 hours at a stretch (see box titled "Crowne Plaza® Rolls Out Ergonomic Chairs").

Most chairs used for meetings are 18 inches wide by 18 inches deep by 17 inches high. Stacking armchairs (not the deluxe type mentioned in the previous paragraph) are slightly larger, such as 20 by 20 by 17. Most folding chairs are smaller and not as comfortable, and are generally used for last-minute overflow accommodations. Planners want their attendees comfortable so they can concentrate on the program.

CROWNE PLAZA ROLLS OUT ERGONOMIC CHAIRS

Just as the Westin chain revolutionized the guestroom with its Heavenly Bed, the Crowne Plaza® Hotels & Resorts brought comfort to the meeting room with ergonomic seating. After a survey commissioned by the chain revealed that over 60 percent of the respondents felt that a more comfortable chair would help them focus during meetings, the chain refitted meeting rooms in its properties in the United States and Canada with Herman Miller Caper® chairs. The chairs, which offer greater comfort with their ergonomic backs, flexible mesh net seat, and casters for mobility, are just the chain's first step in meeting the demand for more comfortable seating. Crowne Plaza® is also outfitting larger rooms with flex-back banquet-style chairs that feature contoured seats and flexible backs.

Source: Courtesy of Crowne Plaza Hotels & Resorts.

Kevin Shanley, director of sales and marketing at The Kalahari Waterpark Resort & Convention Center in Wisconsin Dells, Wisconsin, says:

> You don't want people thinking about how uncomfortable they are or how much they want to get up and stretch [instead of paying attention to the presentation].[9]

Rigid chairs are recommended for food functions. They are more comfortable than folding chairs, which are smaller and lower. Folding chairs should only be used for emergency backup or for outdoor events.

The standard height for tables is 30 inches; the standard depth, either 30 or 18 inches. When people are to be seated opposite each other, the 30-inch table is required. When people sit on only one side of the table, as we shall discuss in *schoolroom* setups, the 18-inch depth is sufficient and saves much space. The 30-inch-deep rectangular table, however, is used most frequently for head tables, even when people are seated on only one side. This deeper table is also used as display tables, exhibit stands, and for other purposes. It is most versatile and comes in lengths of four, six, and eight feet so that a variety of total lengths may be achieved easily.

Round tables (also called **rounds**) are used for many food functions and also for some kinds of meeting sessions. They most often are five, five-and-one-half, or six feet in diameter. Comfortable seating calls for a five-foot round table for six to eight people; a five-and-one-half foot table for eight to ten guests; and a six-foot table for ten to 12. A **cocktail round** (also called a cabaret table) of about three feet in diameter is used for **reception style** setups. In this type of setup, the tables, which vary in height from 30 to 50 inches, are placed throughout the room to allow for the mixing and mingling of guests. There is usually limited or no seating — if seats are provided, they are usually set against the perimeter of the room.

An almost infinite number of variations can be created by using half-rounds and quarter-rounds. The more imaginative curved **serpentine** tables (also called crescent tables) are commonly used for buffets. You are restricted only by your imagination in developing unique buffet arrangements.

Tablecloths, mitered on the corners, are used on tables because most banquet and meeting room tables are damaged and unsightly from continual breakdown and storage. When ordering tablecloths, you will have to specify the exact measurements needed (see box titled "Tablecloth Sizes for Round Tables"). Tablecloths for round tables should be approximately 18 inches wider than the table diameter to allow for a nine-inch drape over the sides (a 90-inch round tablecloth should be used for a 72-inch diameter table, for example). Since the standard table measures 30 inches from the floor and the average chair seat is 17 inches from the floor, the nine-inch drape will not touch the chair seats or interfere with the guests' comfort. Floor-length tablecloths are sometimes used at formal functions, however.

Several companies have begun to market folding tables that are attractive and not easily damaged, and they can be used without tablecloths, saving on laundry and labor costs. Such tables, however, are expensive and fail to provide the warmth and color of tablecloths.

Head tables, as well as display and buffet tables, stages, and platforms, require special drapery. Traditionally, T-pins and tacks have been used to attach floor-length linens for such setups, but **velcro** is now being used by many hotels.

Snap-drape skirting is also available. Plastic clips are fitted along the top edge of platforms and tables, and grippers sewn into the upper pleat of the skirting are snapped into place quickly. Snap-drape skirting is made of permanent-crease polyester and fiberglass, making it easy to clean and wrinkle-free.

Platforms and Staging. Folding platforms are used in many ways; they elevate head tables for banquets and speakers. They come in different sizes, with different names: platform, riser, stage, **dais**, podium, or rostrum. You must construct them to size. Check local safety regulations carefully. The usual heights are six, eight, 12, 16, and 24 inches, plus a 32-inch high *riser*. Lengths may be four, six, or eight feet, or any combination of these. Widths vary from four to six feet. If you maintain adequate stocks, a variety of combinations can be created. If the platforms are old and unsightly, put pleated skirting around the bottom and perhaps carpeting on top.

Staging height is determined by the room length. In general, divide the room length by 50 to determine the stage height. For example, a room that is 100 feet in length would require a 24-inch (two-foot high) stage or platform. A room that is 75 feet in length divided by 50 equals 1.5 feet or 18 inches needed for stage height.

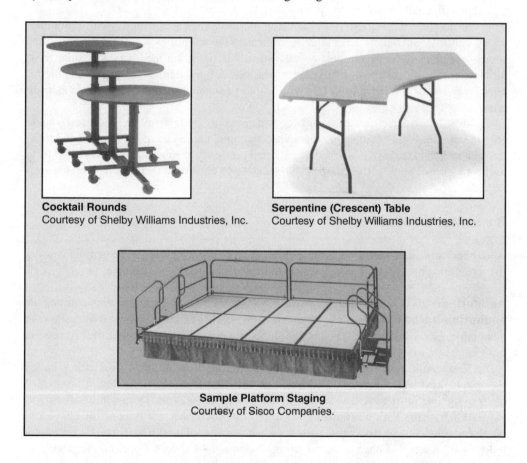

Cocktail Rounds
Courtesy of Shelby Williams Industries, Inc.

Serpentine (Crescent) Table
Courtesy of Shelby Williams Industries, Inc.

Sample Platform Staging
Courtesy of Sisco Companies.

Lecterns. Lecterns are reading desks used to hold the speaker's papers and come in two basic types. The smaller *table lecterns* are placed on tables, while full-size *floor lecterns* are set on the floor. Both sizes should feature built-in light fixtures to enable the speaker to manipulate lighting and audiovisual equipment directly, and enough connecting wire to reach wall outlets.

Many a room becomes difficult to set up because the wall outlets are on the same circuits as the overhead lights and are controlled by a common switch. Make sure the lectern's light unit is connected to a wall outlet that will not be cut off with the overhead lights. Cables must be taped, like those for microphones or light units — tripping the guest speaker is not a recommended way to start a session.

House lights are often dimmed for effect or for greater visibility of audiovisual presentations. Check each setup carefully; smart meeting planners will double-check such items themselves.

Lecterns (and head tables) should be easily accessible. They often must be approached in a relatively darkened room, so the access path must have some illumination. They should not be located near an entrance or other high-traffic area to ensure that speakers and their audiences are not distracted by people moving about. If a video or PowerPoint presentation is planned, the room should be set up so that any doors are off to the side so latecomers will not have to walk in front of the projector.

You should have a good inventory of table lecterns, floor models, and some lecterns with contained sound systems. It is helpful if the lectern has a flat area that securely holds at least a water glass. This area should be large enough so that writing implements, such as a pen, pencil, chalk, or an electric pointer, can be stored.

Permanent stages allow you to develop more sophisticated lecterns with full audiovisual controls. Such units don't lend themselves to the temporary setups of most meeting rooms, but they are received most enthusiastically by program members. Consider these units whenever a permanent installation is possible. A must item that is most versatile for temporary setups is a portable lectern with a built-in sound system that plugs into an ordinary outlet.

Most hotels have their names or logos painted on the lectern faces. Because speakers are commonly televised or photographed, the hotel name can result in much publicity through local and national news media. It is often necessary to show some goodwill gestures to the TV people so they will compose the scene large enough to include the hotel logo.

Basic Meeting Setups

A number of basic seating arrangements have evolved. Be sure that your customer is using the terminology correctly. Layout or schematic sheets will help in this area.

Auditorium or Theater Style. One of the most common seating arrangements, termed the **auditorium/theater style**, calls for chairs to be set up in rows facing the speaker, stage, or head table. Good for lecture sessions with limited note taking (see Exhibit 6), it is used in both large and small meetings.

To set auditorium style, place two chairs first to position the aisle. Two inches, called the *space*, must be left between chairs side by side. The *distance* is the dimension from a chair to the one in front of it. Minimum distance is 36 inches from chair center to center.

When chairs have been positioned to indicate the aisles, the bulk of the chairs can be placed. One-square-foot carpet patterns is the most popular with hotel people because it helps to align setups. If there is no carpeting, the lines in hardwood floors might guide you.

Aisle sizes and numbers are regulated by local fire departments. If you have any doubts, get the specifications from the fire department. Most regulations call for aisles to be six feet wide if 400 or more people are involved; aisles of four or five feet are sufficient for smaller groups. Double aisles are preferred if the meeting format calls for questions from the floor or anything that will result in back-and-forth movement of people or passing of objects such as microphones.

The first row of chairs should be about six feet from the front edge of the head table or platform. The most popular auditorium style uses a center aisle, but many experienced

Exhibit 6   Variations of the Auditorium Style Seating Arrangement

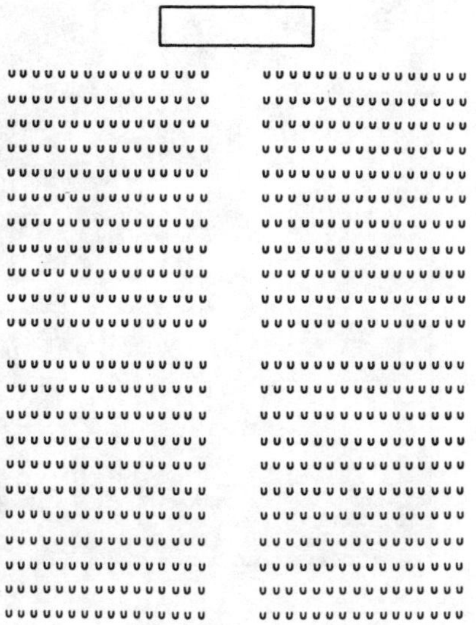

Straight

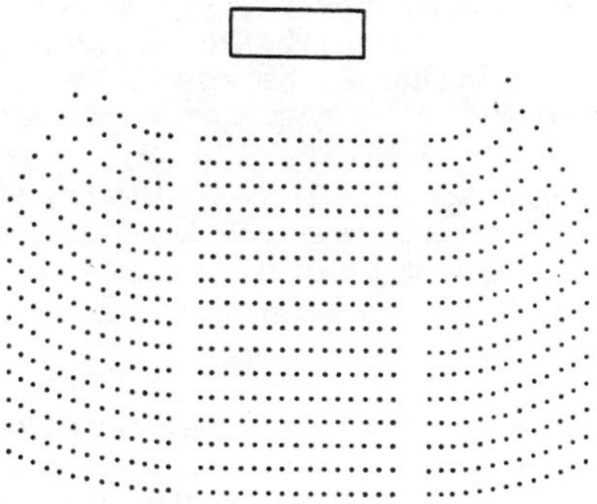

Senate

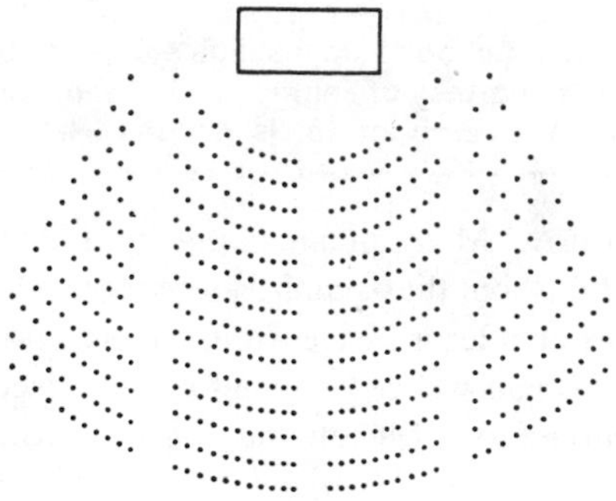

Semi-circular

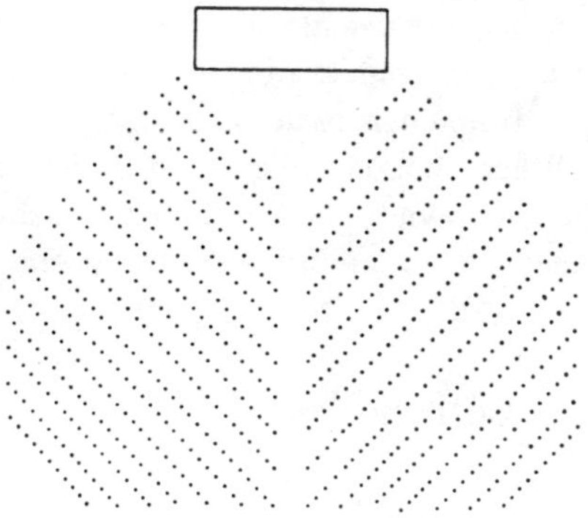

Many planners prefer the V-shape or semi-circular rather than the straight setup because attendees will have a more direct line of sight to the speaker. Aisles are generally four to six feet wide and when possible should align with exit doors. Aisles are required across the front and rear of the room as well as along the sides. When attendance is large, requiring several rows of chairs, cross aisles should be placed for every 15 rows.

Source: Reprinted with permission from *Function Room Set-Up Manual* by Gerhard M. Peter; published by the Hospitality Sales and Marketing Association International.

planners avoid a middle aisle because the presenter is facing an empty space. Many planners prefer to divide the seating area into three sections with two aisles of four feet. In larger halls, fire departments may require aisles across the front and back of the room and an additional horizontal aisle halfway down. It pays to check and to keep a record of local fire regulations.

Keep in mind the number of chairs in a row. It is extremely uncomfortable for an attendee to have to make his or her way across fifteen people to find a seat in the middle

Seating Principles

1. *Avoid center aisles whenever possible.* The center area should be used for seating meeting attendees because it offers the best viewing.

2. *V-shaped and semicircular seating is preferred over straight-line seating.* Angled seating improves sight lines and brings attendees at the outside ends of the rows closer to the speaker.

3. *The speaker should be positioned on the long side of rectangular meeting rooms.* While not as space efficient, placing the presenter on one of the long sides of the room allows the audience to be closer to the speaker.

Source: Schoolroom V-shape setup photograph courtesy of Fairmont Hotel Vancouver. From the Fairmont Hotels' Image Gallery.

of the row. Many planners opt for a "mini row" of no more than seven seats. There are variations, but they require more room. One is *auditorium style, semicircular, center aisle.* You need at least 12 feet from the head table or platform to the front row of chairs. Set the outside chair where you want it. Use a piece of string tied loosely between the two ends of the curved row. Line up the rest of the rows measured from the first one.

Auditorium, V-shape (sometimes referred to as a **chevron setup**) sets up similarly; the side sections form an angle to the center aisle. This is an ideal setup if space isn't an issue, as, by offsetting each row, attendees are not sitting directly behind one another.

Space and distance vary from the norm when armchairs with writing arms are used. Because of the bigger dimensions of these chairs, use three-inch spacing and a 40-inch distance from chair center to center.

When on a dais, regardless of the floor arrangement, make sure that the head tables are draped down to the floor. Place water and glasses at the lectern and on the head table. Use one water carafe for every two people seated on the stage.

Setups with Tables

A great many meetings and most food functions require tables as well as chairs. In this section, we will take a look at some of the most commonly used setups and their variations.

Schoolroom Style. One of the most popular setups among both large and small groups is the **schoolroom/classroom style** (see Exhibit 7). This is the best setup for meetings in which most of the talking will be done by a presenter and attendees will take notes, refer to information in binders, or work on computer equipment such as laptops. It is also the most comfortable design for very long sessions. This setup, however, is not the preferred setup for encouraging conversation among attendees, although it can be used for small group interaction — participants at every other table can turn to face those behind them. In the most common arrangement, people sit on just one side of the table. In such cases, use the 18-inch-deep rectangular tables and, most of the time, allow for a center aisle. Allow about 24 inches

Exhibit 7   The Schoolroom Style Arrangement and Variations

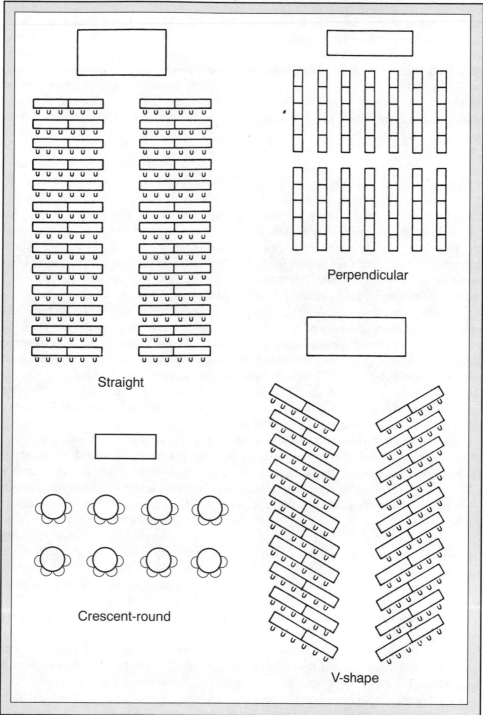

Straight

Perpendicular

Crescent-round

V-shape

The V-shape schoolroom allows the best sight-lines between attendees and the speaker. If attendees are expected to use laptops, 30-inch-wide tables are preferred rather than the standard 18-inch-wide tables. The crescent-round setup is often used when a planner wishes to follow a meal function with a presentation and desires to keep participants in the same room. Once the meal is finished and tables are cleared, attendees are seated on one side of the round, facing the speaker.
Source: Reprinted with permission from *Function Room Set-Up Manual*.

of space for each person. However, if attendees will be using binders or laptop computers, allow 2.5–3 feet per person. While this means that a six-foot table will seat only two people, it is better than seating three people uncomfortably (both physically and psychologically).

Schoolroom tables are either six or eight feet in length. Six-foot tables can seat two or three persons per table; eight foot tables seat three or four. For groups requiring space to spread out, the smaller number should be set for each table.

The 30-inch-deep tables are usually too wasteful to use in schoolroom setups because people are seated on only one side. But there are instances when you do have to use them, especially if a great deal of paperwork is to be done. In such cases, allow 60 inches from center of table to center of table. The length of each row depends on the room size and attendance.

The tables should be draped. Place pads and pencils at each setting, plus water pitchers for every 16 persons. You can put a glass at each setting or provide a tray with ten or 12 glasses for every 16 persons. A variation is *schoolroom perpendicular style.* In this arrangement, the rows of tables are perpendicular to the speaker's table. The 30-inch-deep tables are used because people will be seated on both sides. It is necessary to allow additional room for each person because the seats must be turned somewhat to face the speaker. Allow 30 inches of table space per person instead of 24 for the wide table and 60 inches from center of table to center of table. Tables should be six feet from the head table, with six-foot aisles on both sides of the room and a four-foot horizontal aisle in the center.

Schoolroom setups may also be *V-shape*, off a center aisle. Angled seating improves sight lines and gives attendees a sense of being closer together. Angling the rows to form a herringbone or chevron pattern brings attendees at the outside ends of the rows closer to the speaker. Schoolrom styles may also be set up using round tables. The **crescent-round** setup uses either 60-, 66-, or 72-inch diameter rounds. Seating is used on only one side, so all attendees can face the speaker. This setup works well when the same room will be used for meals and an educational session, and for general sessions in which in attendees break into small discussion groups in the same room.

Many groups schedule a break if a meeting is longer than two hours. The break should be programmed so that your staff can take the opportunity to **refresh the meeting room**. When the meeting breaks, housepersons should refill ice water pitchers, replace dirty glasses with clean ones, replace soiled or wet linen, straighten all chairs, and pick up all obvious trash on the tables and floor. Such procedures help project a positive image of the hotel.

U-Shape. Some smaller meetings require a more face-to-face arrangement, making the **U-shape setup** popular (see Exhibit 8). This setup is often used for board of directors meetings, committee meetings, and breakout sessions with audiovisual presentations, as all attendees can see the presentation when it is placed at the open end of the U (for optimal learning, group size should be limited to 20–24 people). The U-shape can also be used for banquets, with seating on all sides of the U.

Use 30-inch rectangular tables if people will be seated on both sides. Eighteen-inch-deep tables can be used if only the outsides will be used, but most planners prefer 30-inch-deep tables. The usual per-person allowance is 24 inches, but training and technical groups may need more space (2.5–3 feet per person) if attendees will be using training materials or computer equipment.

Drape the front part of the U all the way to the floor. When the tables are draped, make sure that the crease is straight; it should run continuously along the center of the table.

Exhibit 8   The U-Shape Seating Arrangement

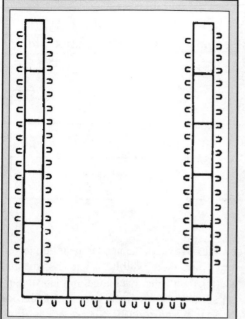

Exhibit 9   The Horseshoe Arrangement

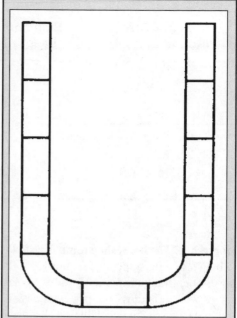

Source: Reprinted with permission from *Function Room Set-Up Manual*.

Quick Calculation—Theater Style

Allow 12 square feet per person for groups of less than 60 people
11 square feet per person for groups of 60–300 people
(the most common size for a breakout session)
10 square feet per person for groups of more than 300 people

Quick Calculation—Schoolroom Style

Allow 22 square feet per person for groups of less than 60 people
20 square feet per person for groups of 60–300 people
(the most common size breakout session)
17 square feet per person for groups of more than 300 people

Quick Calculation—U-Shape and Horseshoe

Allow 35 square feet per person

Quick Calculation—Hollow Square and Conference

Allow 30 square feet per person

TABLECLOTH SIZES FOR ROUND TABLES

Table Size (Round Diameter)	Standard: Banquet-Length Tablecloth	Formal: Floor-Length Tablecloth
72"	90"	132"
66"	84"	126"
60"	78"	120"
36" (cocktail)	54"	96"

Horseshoe. The **horseshoe setup** is just like the U-shape except the head table is connected to both legs with serpentine sections to soften the corners (see Exhibit 9). The U-shape and horseshoe arrangements are good for board meetings and idea exchange and lend themselves well to audiovisual presentations. The horseshoe and U-shape setups are ideal for training meetings in which the speaker needs access to the participants. These setups allow all participants to see and hear each other, but the size of the group is limited to approximately 24 persons.

Hollow Square and Hollow Circular. The **hollow square setup** and the **hollow circular setup** are preferred by meeting planners who want to do away with the head table concept (see Exhibit 10). This setup, which makes efficient use of space in a room, works best for small groups (up to 30 people) for which there is a facilitator leading the discussion or decision-making or problem-solving sessions, as there are good sight lines and the setup is conducive to eye contact between participants. There is also no sense of preferential seating, so there is a sense of equality among participants. This type of setup, however, does not work well for sessions requiring audiovisuals.

These setups are formed like the U-shape (using 30-inch-wide tables) except that the open end is filled in. Naturally, chairs are placed only on the outside. The hollow square and the hollow circular are popular for small meetings. Both arrangements should be skirted on the inside and are usually constructed to accommodate up to 30 persons.

Variations. The **E-shape setup style** is a variation of the U-shape (see Exhibit 11). You need about four feet between the backs of the chairs to facilitate traffic. The *T-shape setup* has a head table 30 inches deep. A single leg extends from the center of the head table for as long as is needed. The leg is often set with double tables to make a 60-inch solid rectangular unit.

Board of Directors. The **board of directors/conference setup** is a popular arrangement for small meetings. It calls for a single column of double tables making a draped table of 60 inches by as long as necessary (see Exhibit 12). Allow 24 inches of table space per person. The board of directors arrangement is so popular with meeting planners that many convention hotels have permanent setups with fine wooden tables and deluxe executive-type chairs. Suites equipped with such permanent fixtures are versatile small meeting rooms.

The *board of directors oval setup* is simply the board setup with a 60-inch half-round table at each end of the long table. Chairs may be set at the curved end.

Exhibit 10   The Hollow Square and Hollow Circular Arrangements

Exhibit 11   The E-Shape and T-Shape Arrangements

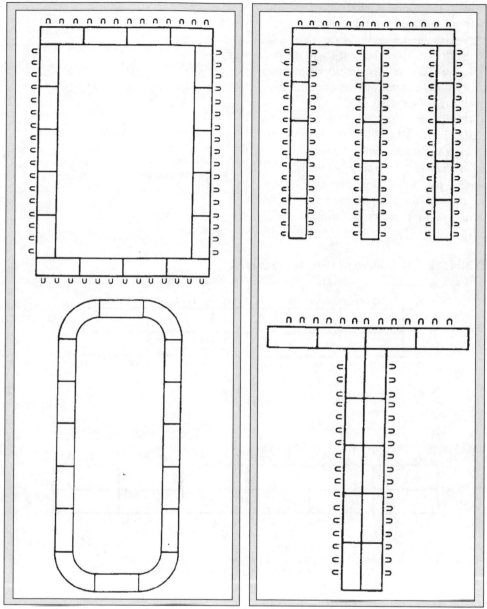

These setups are used for groups that do not want a head table concept. The T-shape arrangement shown here uses a row of two tables for the base of the "T"; the T-shape is also commonly seen with a row of single tables forming the base.

Source: Reprinted with permission from *Function Room Set-Up Manual*.

Round Tables. *Round tables* (see Exhibit 13) can be used when meetings break up into smaller discussion groups without leaving the room. Round tables are also used most often for food functions.

Use the design in the carpet or lines in the floor to align the tables in neat rows. Allow at least 54 inches between round tables for chair and service space for banquet setups (see diagram).

Waiters need 36 inches between chairs and walls. Place chairs near the tables and position after the waiters have set the tables. The front edge of the chair should just touch the tablecloth. Afterward, stack the chairs immediately to facilitate cleanup and breakdown.

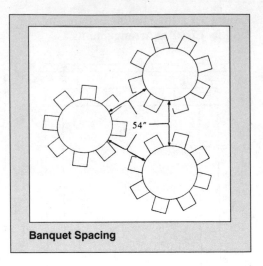

Banquet Spacing

Exhibit 12   The Board of Directors Setup

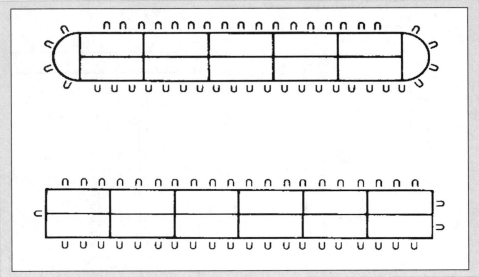

Popular seating arrangement for small meetings shown with its oval variation.
Source: Reprinted with permission from *Function Room Set-Up Manual*.

Circular Buffet Table. The *circular buffet table*, most useful at food functions, is made by using four serpentines and four 30-inch-deep four-foot tables (see Exhibit 14). This makes up a 20-by-20-foot buffet table. A round center table can be used for flowers or a display. Tier arrangements can be made with risers.

Many variations can be made by using tables of various shapes. You are limited only by imagination, time, and space.[10] If you design one you particularly like, draw a schematic of it. You can show this to a prospective client and use it for future reference.

Exhibit 13   Round Table Arrangements

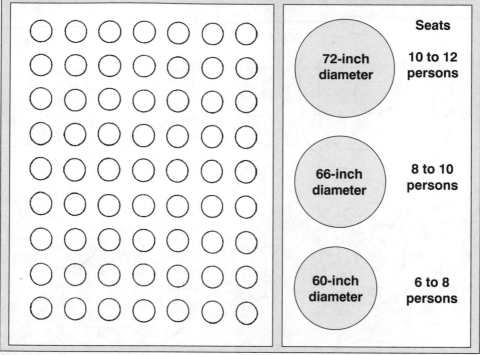

Rounds can be used for food functions and for meetings that break up into smaller discussion groups. Seventy-two-inch rounds seat ten to 12 people. Sixty-inch rounds seat six to eight persons. There are also 66-inch rounds, that seat eight to ten. For greatest comfort, the lesser number of seats is preferred.
Source: Reprinted with permission from *Function Room Set-Up Manual.*

Breakdown of Function Rooms

After a meeting or party is completed, housepersons should break down the room and clean it. The reason for this is obvious. Business could be lost, or a poor impression given, if a prospective customer saw an untidy meeting room while walking through the convention area.

Chairs and tables need to be stacked. Function chairs probably receive more damage than any other furnishings in a hotel. Housepersons who display more speed than caution in setup and dismantling should be instructed to avoid such carelessness.

If the meeting room isn't scheduled for immediate use, tables and chairs may need to be stored. Storage is a common headache to convention servicing. Hotels unfortunately often do not allot adequate and accessible storage space for function room equipment. Space that is too small or is too difficult to maneuver in shortens the life of the equipment. Furniture that is "forced" into storage is often damaged.

Some properties keep formal control over the location and storage of their equipment. In large convention hotels where the volume justifies it, a requisition system is used for issuing equipment and supplies. An inventory is taken periodically and all articles are locked up when not in use.

Exhibit 14   The Circular Buffet Table Arrangement and Variations

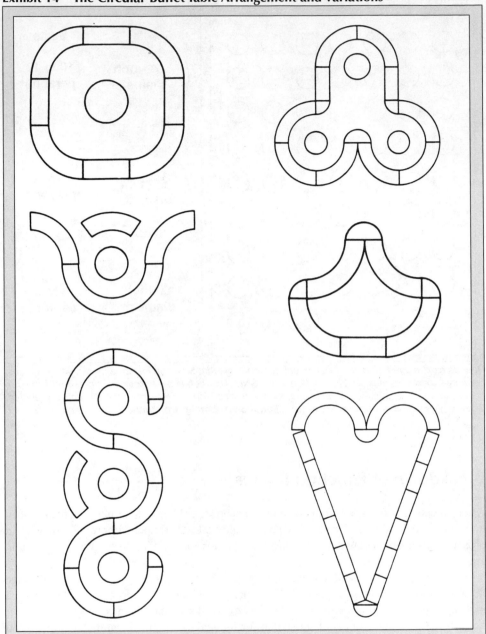

Source: Reprinted with permission from *Function Room Set-Up Manual.*

Meeting Rooms of the Future

As we entered the 21st century, dramatic changes were already taking place in how meeting rooms were designed and equipped. Hyatt Hotels, for example, replaced drywall construction with open-structured ceilings in their ballrooms, providing greater versatility as well as faster setup time. In its meeting rooms, the chain installed infrared lighting controls, giving the speaker the ability to make instant adjustments to the lighting system. Distracting noises were eliminated by adding light and sound vestibules between public areas and the actual meeting space, and by creating double walls between the subdivisions of the ballroom to eliminate noises from adjacent meetings. The chain also installed permanent state-of-the-art communications systems featuring fiber-optic cable, Category 5 data cable, and ample telephone wiring.[11]

A growing number of properties are also providing wireless, high-speed Internet access in their meeting rooms – and throughout the hotel (including lobbies, guestrooms, business centers, and even food and beverage areas). While Internet service has been offered for some time, the wireless technology has made accessing such information as exhibit directories, seminar schedules, and other data easier than ever before, and both meeting planners and attendees have come to expect the technology to make their meetings more productive.

Another development for meeting rooms of the future is the use of plasma screens. These three-inch-thick, self-contained units will not only change the way in which presentations are made, but will also change the shape of meeting rooms. As plasma screens become the dominant feature in meeting rooms, lighting requirements will change—and the sizes of the rooms themselves will have to be adjusted to accommodate the new wide screens. Acording to Martin Dempsey, director of the media and business center at the Scottsdale Conference Center in Arizona, "Ambient light is not an issue with the plasma screen."[12] There is no need to dim lights to see the image.

Other changes cited by architects in the field include changes in table shapes, room decor, and simplifying controls used for presentations. Tomorrow's tables, although they will have the look of heavy wooden tables, will be hollow, light, and easily moved. Rooms will be white or light-colored to provide for better contrast when video cameras are used, while rooms in which plasma screens are dominant can be painted in lively hues. While high technology will continue to play a major part in presentations, it is expected that

---

🖥 INTERNET EXERCISE

Radisson Blu Hotels and Resorts operates over 150 hotels in Europe, the Middle East, and Africa. The hotel company, which is based in Denmark, has sponsored several research studies, including one that focuses on "The Conference Room of the Future." Log on to the company's website, www. radissonblu.com, and click on the Meetings & Events tab. Next, click on "Tools and Resources" and then on "Meetings & Event Tips." Go to the "Red Book" section and click on "Download (PDF)" to find five topics related to meetings of today—and the future.

1. Why is flexibility important when planning a meeting or conference?

2. What roles do space and function furniture play in a successful meeting?

3. In what new ways are lighting, acoustics, and color being used in conference rooms of the future?

Note: Click on the Yellow Book section of the website to see nine learning techniques to help attendees get the most out of their meetings.

control panels will become less visible (concealed yet readily accessible). To see a virtual tour of some of these new innovations, visit the site of Next Gen Boardrooms (www.ng-boardroom.com).

Despite these exciting innovations, there is, conversely, a trend toward a traditional look for boardroom setups. Cindy Carney, an interior designer with Debra Myers Associates, says:

> Five years ago, everyone wanted laminates and a techy look.[13]

Now, clients want a more conservative, throwback style. Wood paneling, leather seating, and traditional light fixtures add to the trend toward a masculine, conservative, "clubby" atmosphere.

A SENSORY APPROACH TO MEETING ROOMS OF THE FUTURE

When Omni Hotels set about to craft the perfect meeting room, it wanted to go beyond the three essential elements — proper room temperature, the ability to hear well, and the ability to clearly see the presentation — and create an atmosphere that would provide the type of environment that would ensure that the  goals of a meeting were met. To do so, the chain started with a year of research, which included creating a Sensory Advisory Board, staffed by representatives from several high-profile companies (including the Elizabeth Arden Red Door Spa, the Julliard School, and Whole Foods Market). The panel focused on the five human senses to determine which colors, lighting, sounds, scents, and even tastes best contributed to the optimum experience for meeting attendees.

The result was the chain's Sensational Meetings program, which offers customized settings for three meeting approaches: energetic meetings, challenging meetings, and recognition meetings. For energetic meetings, brainstorming, planning, and training are enhanced by the use of vibrant, high-energy colors and stimulating flavors for meals and break fare. Challenging meeting settings provide a relaxed environment to mitigate stressful points of discussion through the use of subdued lighting and soothing music (and breaks featuring green tea). **Recognition meetings**, which focus on honoring past successes and building on them for the future, are highlighted by upbeat music, vibrant floral designs, decadent champagne truffles, and stimulating scents.

 Loews Hotels has also picked up on the trend, offering the Color Break option that allows meeting planners to theme their meeting rooms — and even food choices — by color. The program is currently available in three color themes: blue (representing peace, spirituality, and youth), which stimulates thought and communication; yellow, which represents wisdom and happiness — and sharpens memory and concentration skills; and green, which represents nature and well-being, to encourage ideas.

The elements of each theme color include wall coloring, color-inspired floral centerpieces, and onscreen color flashes. The color schemes also translate well to meals and break snacks. A yellow theme, for example, would feature a mix of sweet, healthy, and salty foods — personal dishes of pineapple, yellow M&Ms, and potato chips — in individual dishes.

Both the hotels and meeting planners are seeing positive results with the new programs. According to Ellen Burke Van Slyke, the corporate creative director of food and beverage at Loews Hotels, "The value of color as a stimulant is undeniable. All elements of a meeting room must be in place to create the right mindset."

Sources: "A Sensory Approach to Meetings," *Meetings & Conventions*, May 2007, p. 48; Francine Cohen, "Ending Meeting Madness," *Hotel Interactive*, March 25, 2008; and "Color-Coded Meetings Featured at Loews," *MeetingNews*, January 28, 2008, p. 10.

Another trend that has impacted both hotels and restaurants is the growing demand for environmentally friendly facilities and services. Hotel and convention meeting space is "going green" in a number of areas. In building and construction, for example, the use of such products as stone and recycled materials is growing in popularity, as is the use of natural sources of light and energy, including skylights and solar panels. It is also becoming more common for meeting facilities to eliminate the need for copious amounts of paper — many are providing individual computer terminals for data storage or, if that is not an option, establishing recycling programs for paper and other materials, such as ink and toner cartridges, commonly used at meetings.

Whatever trends finally emerge as dominant, it is important that hotels keep abreast of the latest innovations but make decisions concerning design and function with the actual needs of the meeting planners they are serving in mind. If a hotel caters primarily to SMERF segments, for example, a large investment in plasma screens and other high-tech gadgets would be a waste of money. Corporate groups, however, would demand the latest in technology.

The InterContinental Toronto Centre is regarded as the most technologically advanced hotel in Canada. The property's two Next Generation Boardrooms, named Conquest and Visionary, offer drop-down LCD projector screens, 60-inch plasma SMART boards, high-end sound equipment, and video web conferencing. Attendees sit in sleek, ergonomic black leather chairs around contemporary oval conference tables that feature recessed "Plug & Surf" high-speed dataports and electrical outlets for each participant. **Source: Photo courtesy of InterContinental Hotel Group.**

PUTTING IT ALL TOGETHER

This time, *you* will be using the information that you have learned in this chapter to demonstrate how a property's meeting space can be utilized to its maximum potential. You have been named convention service manager of a hotel with fairly limited meeting space (see diagram below). It is your job to fill this space as effectively as possible, so you have booked a number of functions. On Thursday of next week, your property will be hosting:

1. A morning (9:00 a.m.–noon) training seminar for 50 distributors of a multi-level marketing company. The distributors will need to check in and will receive packets of information before entering the training room. A refreshment break will be taken at 10:30 a.m.
2. An afternoon (1:00 p.m.) press conference for a local official announcing her candidacy for Congress. Attendance is projected to include approximately 20 news reporters, three television crews, and the candidate's key staff of nine people. In addition, the candidate has requested the provision of additional seating in the event the public wishes to attend. She has also requested the availability of floor microphones for a question and answer session.
3. A two-hour afternoon (2:00 p.m.–4:00 p.m.) meeting of twelve directors of the board of the community's hospital.
4. A local charity's evening fund-raising dinner. A cocktail reception will be held from 6:00 p.m. to 6:30 p.m., with dinner following at 7:00 p.m. Dancing will follow from 8:30 p.m. until midnight. Expected attendance is 300 people. Special requirements include a head table for 20 VIPs and the availability of an area for ticket collection and the viewing of prizes that will be raffled throughout the evening.

The following morning, another training session will be held from 9:00 a.m. to noon, and you will want the room set up before the staff goes on overtime at 1:00 p.m.

1. Which room(s) would be most suitable for each meeting? What factors did you take into consideration in making your decision?
2. What style of seating would you choose for each meeting? Draw up a sample floorplan for each function.
3. Develop sample function sheets that detail the special needs for each function and how these requirements will be met.

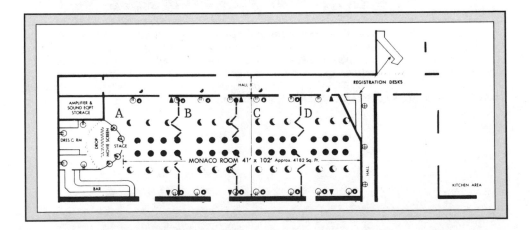

Monitoring Function Room Usage

It is important to understand the dollar value of function room space. One chain calculated that meeting space cost $.08 per square foot per day when it was not being utilized. In other words, a 10,000-square-foot ballroom costs $800 per day just sitting vacant. To get a handle on function space utilization, it is useful to track and monitor the following:

- Function room occupancy by meal period
- Types of functions
- Use of guestrooms by function groups
- Popularity of individual banquet menu items
- Sales revenue per square foot of function space
- Average banquet check by type of function
- Pattern of unused times and days
- Average number of persons by type of function

Reporting function room statistics can be revealing. While the hotel's function rooms may seem very busy, during certain times of the year only one function per day is often booked in each of the meeting rooms. The data gathered will help you to develop an effective strategy for yield management, which was discussed earlier in this chapter.

Summary

In this chapter, we have taken a look at the various types of function rooms and the setups that are commonly used when servicing convention groups. We have discussed the importance of assigning function rooms for maximum efficiency and revenue, and detailed the factors that should be considered when assigning function room space. We have also seen that the use of function rooms must be monitored to ensure maximum profitablilty for your hotel.

Endnotes

1. Jim Barr, Catering/Convention Service Manager, Sheraton Chicago Hotel and Towers, MeetingMatrix advertising brochure.

2. Bryant Rousseau, "Low-Cost Software for Room Layouts," *Meeting News*.

3. M. Jill Wien, "Holiday Holds," *The Meeting Manager*.

4. Ibid.

5. Chris Davis, *Business Travel News*, May 15, 2000, p. 39.

6. Chris Davis, "Room Rental Rising: Hotels Revisiting Meeting Room Yield Management," *Business Travel News*, April 26, 2004, p. 37.

7. Information in this section adapted from Sheryl L. Kimes and Kelly A. McGuire, "Function-space Revenue Management: A Case Study from Singapore," *Cornell Hotel and Restaurant Administration Quarterly*, December 2001, pp. 43–44.

8. *Guide to Function-Room Furniture*, Jacob Felsenstein; King Arthur Incorporated, Pennsauken, NJ.

9. Elaine Yetzer Simon, "Comfort, ease of use help determine seating selection," *Hotel & Motel Management*, April 7, 2003, p. 30.

10. "Quick Calculations" charts in this section were developed by David Lutz, managing director of Velvet Chainsaw Consulting (www.velvetchainsaw.com) from the *CONFERON Guide* published by *Convene* magazine. Used with permission.

11. Doug Fox, "Hyatt's Improvements Upgrade Presentations," *Convene*.

12. Justin Henderson, "21st Century Box," *Successful Meetings*, January 2000, p. 20.

13. Ibid, p. 21.

Additional References

The Americans with Disabilities Act: A Review Course for Meetings and Conventions Industry Professionals, by Ciritta Park, CAE, Professional Convention Management Association. Available online in the PCMA Publications Library at www.pcma.org/publications.

The Convention Industry Council Manual, Eighth Edition, Susan Krug, Executive Director, 2007 – www.conventionindustry.org.

Pocket Guide to ADA, Revised Edition, by Evan Terry Associates, P.C. www.mpiweb.org.

Internet Sites

For more information, visit the following Internet sites. Internet addresses can change without notice. If a site is no longer available at the address listed below, a search engine can be used to find the new address or additional, related sites.

Cast Software
www.castgroup.inc

Event Sketch
www.timesaver.com

Meeting Matrix International
www.meetingmatrix.com

Next Generation (Next Gen) Boardrooms
www.ngboardroom.com

Professional Convention Management Association
www.pcma.org

3D Event Designer
www.eventsoft.com

TimeSaver Software – Room Viewer
www.timesaversoftware.com

Review Questions

1. What is a function room? List the basic types of function rooms.

2. What is mean by the statement: "All public space may be function areas, depending on the group and its needs." What other areas can be used to host functions?

3. What factors must be considered in charging a group for meeting space? For assigning meeting rooms?

4 List the basic styles of meeting room setups and tell when each is used. What styles are commonly used for food functions?

5. What is "function room furniture"? What features should you look for when selecting function room furniture?

6. How will meeting rooms of the future differ from today's meeting space?

7. What methods are used to monitor function room space?

 **Key Terms**

air walls—Moveable barriers that partition large areas into smaller ones. Not necessarily soundproof.

Americans with Disabilities Act—U.S. legislation that requires public buildings (offices, hotels, restaurants, etc.) to make adjustments to meet minimum standards to make their facilities accessible to individuals with physical disabilities.

barrier-free—Absence of obstacles preventing handicapped persons from moving freely to all public areas within a building.

auditorium/theater style—Chairs set up in rows facing head table, stage, or speaker. Number of aisles may vary. Some variations are V-setup and semicircular.

board of directors/conference setup—One wide table or series of tables set up in a rectangular shape with chairs on both sides and at the end. Some hotels have permanent board setups featuring expensive furniture and executive chairs. Oval setup is also used.

breakout rooms—Smaller meeting rooms used when larger sessions divide into smaller groups for discussions and group work. Usually planners request that these rooms be located near the main meeting facilities.

capacity chart—A diagram that details the specifics of a meeting room, including the name of the space, the dimensions of the room, and the room's capacity in various room setups, including classroom, rounds, boardroom, and so on.

chevron setup—Seating arrangement in which chairs are arranged in rows slanted in a V shape facing the head table or speaker (rows are separated by a center aisle). Also called a herringbone set-up and a V-shape set-up.

cocktail round—Small round table, available in 18-, 24-, 30-, or 36-inch diameters, used for cocktail-type parties. Also called cabaret table. For sit-down service, use 30-inch height; use bar height for stand-up service.

computer-assisted design (CAD)—A computer program that allows meeting planners to graphically implement meeting room designs and layouts.

crescent-round—Seating arrangement in which 60-, 66-, or 72-inch diameter rounds have seats on two-thirds to three-quarters of the table and no seats with their backs to the speaker. It is often used for banquet-to-meeting or meeting-to-banquet quick setups.

dais—Raised platform on which the head table is placed.

day package—A special package created for groups that will be utilizing the hotel only during daylight hours. A day package is often the most economical option for meetings that do not require overnight accommodations, as they typically include a single price per attendee for the entire day — the price is inclusive of all food and beverage, rather than having meals and breaks broken down.

employee procedures manual—Instructions for employees to do specific jobs. Often includes illustrations or drawings. Helps ensure consistent setups.

E-shape setup style—Tables set in the shape of an E with chairs on the outside of the closed ends and on both sides of each leg.

ergonomic—Furnishings, especially tables and chairs, specifically designed to provide maximum comfort and alertness in a conference environment.

function room turnover time—The amount of time needed to tear down and reset a function room.

function rooms—Rooms specifically designed to house meetings or social gatherings.

head table—A table, often elevated on a dais or stage, used to seat VIPs, speakers, and other dignitaries.

hold all function space—Blanket hold on all available space in a facility without specific meeting or function rooms named.

hollow circular setup—Same as horseshoe setup except both ends are closed; chairs placed on the outside.

hollow square setup—Tables set in a square with a hollow middle; chairs placed only on the outside.

horseshoe setup—Similar to U-shape style; set in the shape of a horseshoe. Chairs can be placed around both the inside and outside.

lectern—A reading desk used to hold the speaker's papers. Either rests on the floor (full size) or on the table.

pre-function space—Area adjacent to the main event room; used to assemble attendees prior to a function. Often used for receptions prior to a meal or for refreshment breaks during an event.

open sale period—Period of time during which catering is free to sell function space due to projected slow convention business (catered events would not be likely to displace convention groups needing meeting space).

reception style—A room setup designed to encourage the flow of traffic to enable participants to mix and mingle. Usually consists of high-top tables placed throughout the room, and limited or no seating is provided (if chairs are used, they are usually placed along the perimeter of the room).

recognition meetings—Meetings held for the purpose of honoring past successes and building on them for the future. Typically festive events, featuring awards presentations, guest speakers, and possibly entertainment to motivate attendees.

refresh the meeting room—Clean a room after or between meetings (refilling water pitchers, changing glassware, and other general housekeeping).

release date—Date when the hotel or conference facility will require the meeting planner to designate final space needs and release any unneeded space back to the facility.

rounds—Circular banquet tables, usually 60 inches (152 centimeters) in diameter (also available in 66-inch and 72-inch — 168- and 183-centimeter — sizes). The 60-inch diameter table provides place settings for eight people; the 72-inch size for ten people.

schoolroom/classroom style—Tables six feet by 18 inches are lined up in rows on each side of a good-sized center aisle. Usually six chairs to two tables. All tables and chairs face the head table. Variations are the V-shape and perpendicular style.

serpentine—Curved, S-shaped tables that make a snake form when placed together.

U-shape setup—Tables set up in the shape of the block letter U; usually used for small meetings. Chairs are placed on the outside of the closed end and on both sides of each leg.

velcro—Brand-name special tape with loops and fabric that is used to adhere table drapery.

Chapter 14 Outline

Competencies

1. Identify different types of food service and service-related issues related to food functions. (pp. 457–478)

2. Identify control issues related to food functions. (pp. 479–481)

3. Describe service and control issues related to beverage functions. (pp. 481–490)

4. Describe post-function activities for both food and beverage functions, and compare large properties with small ones in terms of in-house coordination. (pp. 491–494)

Planning Food Functions

Gene Meoni
Director of Food and Beverage
Grand Traverse Resort and Spa, Michigan

"The catering or conventions services department is the most profitable division of any hotel food and beverage operation, provided the proper planning, controls, service, and creativity are utilized for an event, be it a refreshment break for 20 or a five-course gala dinner for 1,000. When planning meetings, conventions, or catered events, you must utilize the controls planned to guarantee service to your guests and the profitability of your operation. Function sheets for food and beverage products and services must be detailed and specific. When setting up for a convention, meeting, or catered event, organization and pre-planning are necessary for a successful execution. The plans, controls, and teamwork involved in food and beverage service are immense, but, if effective, will lead to operational success, which I define as exceeding guest expectations, motivated employees who take pride in their accomplishments, and exceeding budgeted bottom line profits."

14   Food and Beverage Service

FOOD AND BEVERAGE FUNCTIONS have always played an important part in meeting and convention programs, but the "traditional" food and beverage options of past years, such as the choice between one chicken and one beef entree at a banquet or simply providing an urn of coffee and hot water for tea for meeting delegates, have been replaced with new choices that add variety and excitement to meetings and conventions (see box titled "Latest Food and Beverage Trends").

These changes have resulted from the public becoming more knowledgeable about food and beverages and meal presentation, thanks in part to such food personalities as Emeril Lagasse and Rachel Ray.

Robert Briggs, associate director of continuing education at the Culinary Institute of America in Hyde Park, New York, says:

> People are reading culinary magazines, watching the Food Network, taking cooking classes, traveling, and becoming much more food savvy in recent years.[1]

The result is that attendees have higher expectations regarding the food and beverages served at their meetings or conventions, they are more willing to experiment with new foods, and they expect attractive presentations. Hotels are responding to their demands with creative menus, including incorporating local specialties into meals and staging themed functions, and offering alternate food and beverage options.

Hyatt Hotels, for example, has led the way in several service trends. George Vizer, vice president of food and beverage, says:

> We are trying to create a restaurant-quality dining experience in a banquet setting. Having a banquet doesn't have to mean that you have servers in a banquet setting with large service trays, distributing food in an institutional manner. Instead, servers come to the table and introduce themselves to the guests. They recite the menu. They announce what wine they're pouring. So that there's interaction with the guests, just as you find in a restaurant setting.[2]

Steve Enselein, assistant vice president of catering and convention services for the chain, adds:

> We're also offering guests a choice of entree selection at dinner, which creates more of a restaurant feel than a banquet feel ... [and] it's been well received by groups. Anytime you give people an opportunity to choose, you increase their satisfaction.[3]

This concept is part of the chain's Personal Preference Menus for banquets (see box titled "Hyatt's Personal Preference Banquet Menus"). This concept allows meeting planners to select one appetizer, a salad, and a dessert, and to choose three entrees from a selection of six. Banquet attendees are served the pre-selected appetizer and salad, but then opt for one of the three entree choices (a vegetarian entree is also available).

LATEST FOOD AND BEVERAGE TRENDS

Years ago, foods and setups available for meetings were generally unimaginative and predictable. Banquet attendees, for example, were all usually served the same dish (or possibly a choice of chicken or beef), buffet tables were typically square and skirted, while banquets were set at round, skirted tables, and refreshment breaks usually consisted of sugary pastries and the choice of coffee or tea.

Today's food and presentation methods are a far cry from that standard fare. As attendees have become more health-conscious and food savvy, the old "stand-bys" have become a thing of the past. New food and beverage trends, which we will be discussing in greater detail in this chapter, include:

Presentation — The skirted buffet or banquet table is fast becoming a relic, and yesterday's round banquet tables are being replaced with clean, exciting looks. At the Four Seasons Hotel Philadelphia, for example, elegant, unskirted tables are put together in a variety of ways, while Hyatt Hotels & Resorts opts for an assortment of benches, ladders, and stainless steel tables to add atmosphere to the function.

Even the presentation of the food has changed. At buffets, chafing dishes are rapidly being replaced by woks, paella pans, cast-iron skillets, heated bricks, and marble slabs, while other foods are presented on risers or as part of an elegant display or edible centerpiece. Today's banquets now rival fine-restaurant dining, with attendees being offered a menu of entrees from which to choose, and other options, such as mini-meals and tasting stations, are replacing traditional sit-down dinners. The Harbor Castle Westin in Toronto promotes tasting stations as an opportunity for attendees to mingle as well as try a variety of bite-sized foods.

Food and Beverage Options — Today's meeting attendees are both food savvy and health-conscious, and hotels have responded by offering **organic foods**, low-fat foods, low-carb choices, sugar-free options, and foods prepared with no trans-fats or corn syrup. And not only is fresh food preferred, attendees want smaller portions of healthy foods — and a wide choice — making such options as tapas, dim sum, and mini-desserts popular. Also popular are "trendy" foods, such as sushi, "spa cuisine," and "bad foods with good ingredients" (blueberry muffins, zucchini bread, carrot cake, pumpkin pie, and banana nut bread instead of sugary doughnuts and Danish).

Dolce Hotels and Resorts emphasizes nourishment with such break offerings as fresh fruit and vegetable juices, vitamin water, fruit, yogurt and granola bowls, small salads, and interactive juice bar stations, while the Hilton Suites Phoenix offers interactive F&B stations featuring made-to-order juice beverages blended for each guest, stations for custom-made salads, and "Fire and Ice" bars with cold stations (chefs preparing sashimi) and hot stations (chefs cooking up spicy Cajun-style fare).

Other Innovations — Other innovations in the F&B industry include online banquet menus and the "customization" of banquet events. Rarely do today's meeting planners order strictly off a pre-printed menu; they prefer to work with a hotel or convention bureau's catering staff to create "signature events" using local regional fare. At the Washington State Convention and Trade Center (WSCTC), for example, fresh Northwest seafood, shellfish, beef, fruits, berries, vegetables, microbrews, and wines are incorporated into events to provide a unique experience for attendees.

Sources: Jonathan Vatner, "Banquets Reborn: An Inside Look at the Latest F&B Trends," *Meetings & Conventions*, December 2006, pp. 41 & 43; Patti J. Shock, CPCE, "What's Hot in F&B," *Corporate Meetings & Incentives*, May 2007, p. 22; publications by Dolce Hotels and Resorts and Hilton; and Andrea Doyle, "Haute Cuisine on the Menu at Today's Convention Centers," *PCMA Convene*, October 2006, p. 60. Photograph courtesy of Mandarin Oriental Hotel Group.

Increased attendee satisfaction means more attendees at an organization's next function — and repeat and word-of-mouth business for a hotel that makes food and beverage functions memorable. In this chapter, we will discuss the various types of food functions typically staged for meetings and conventions, and detail how creativity and communication play important roles in successful functions ranging from simple refreshment breaks to elaborate, themed events.

Food Service

Banquets, parties, and other business or social functions involving food and beverage can produce additional, often high, revenues for your hotel. Bill Carlin, managing editor of *Nation's Restaurant News*, states:

> Banquets are the most profitable area of hotel food and beverage operations.[4]

Successful banquets can contribute greatly to overall profitability, because the profit margin on sales for banquets often runs 35–40 percent, as opposed to 10–15 percent for hotel restaurants. There are several reasons for this difference:

- In convention-oriented hotels, banquet sales volume often exceeds restaurant volume by as much as two to one.
- Banquets allow flexibility in pricing. A New York steak dinner priced at $45 on the restaurant menu may bring $60 on the banquet menu. The justification for this difference is the cost of setting up and tearing down the banquet area and also the short time allowed for serving a large number of people in one seating.
- Food costs are lower due to volume preparation and no large inventory is needed, since ordering can be done as needed and all attendees normally receive identical meals.
- Beverage profits are high because beverage costs are easily controlled and revenues are greater because of pricing flexibility.
- Labor costs are significantly lower because banquet servers and bartenders are often part-time employees used on an as-needed basis. The cost of restaurant employees, in contrast, is largely fixed, because a regular staff must be maintained even during slow periods.
- Employee productivity is high, since staffing levels can be set for a predetermined, guaranteed attendance.

Types of Food Functions

Meetings may call for breakfasts; luncheons; dinners; dinners with entertainment and/or dancing; refreshment breaks; bars; receptions; buffets; and continuous hospitality setups in suites, meeting rooms, or exhibit halls. Gene Meoni, Director of Food and Beverage at The Homestead, a resort in Hot Springs, Virginia, says that banquet menus should be varied in selection and price range to meet your market segments. Menus should include regional specialties, property specialties, and upgraded menus that have been executed during past events.

HYATT'S PERSONAL PREFERENCE BANQUET MENUS

In response to the increased emphasis on updating meetings cuisine, the Hyatt chain introduced its Personal Preference Menus for banquets, which allows attendees to choose their own dinner entrees, just as they would in a fine-dining restaurant.

Steve Enselein, VP of catering and convention services for Hyatt Hotels & Resorts, says:

> We wanted to get away from predictable food choices. Part of our thinking behind Personal Preference is that Americans are becoming more educated about food. It's a new sense of food entitlement: "I want what I want when I want it." We are trying to meet those higher food expectations with all of our new options.

Troy Wood, director of catering and convention services at the Hyatt Regency Tamaya Resort & Spa in Santa Ana Pueblo, New Mexico, adds:

> Often our client is planning grand closing dinners or special occasions as a part of the booking, and that's when Personal Preference Menus are a perfect fit. When we discuss Personal Preference Menus with our clients, the first response is, "Wow, can you do that?"

The concept works as follows:

- The meeting planner selects one appetizer and one salad that will be served to each attendee.
- The meeting planner chooses three entrees from a selection of six. At their table, attendees may pick from these three entrees or choose a vegetarian option.
- A dessert sampler is also included.

Helen S. Pollard, CMP, director of meetings and conference services for the Emergency Nurses Association, is enthusiastic about the program:

> At our big lunches or galas, you always have people who won't touch the food — people who are allergic to seafood, or won't touch meat, or just will eat chicken. Our population is so varied, something like the Personal Preference Menus is appealing.

Not only do Personal Preference Menus for banquets offer unique selections that appeal to food savvy attendees, the experience itself rivals that of a fine-dining restaurant. Eye-catching four-color menus are presented to each guest, and, once waiters explain the concept to attendees, the appetizer course is served. Bread is served between the appetizer and salad, giving the kitchen staff enough time to prepare the entrees. The final course, a trio of three elegantly presented desserts, caps off the "fine dining" experience.

Sources: "Multiple Choice: Banquet Dining Becomes a Matter of Personal Preference," *The Hyatt Edge*, **Fall/Winter 2005, p. 5; and "The Preference Is Clear: Hyatt's Flexible Banquet Menus Are a Hit Among Meeting Planners and Attendees Alike,"** *The Hyatt Edge*, **Summer 2007, p. 4.**

💻 INTERNET EXERCISE

Log on to the websites of the hotels listed below and review their banquet menus:

- Manchester Grand Hyatt, San Diego, California — http://manchestergrand.hyattemenus.com
- Marriott Harbor Beach, Ft. Lauderdale, Florida — www.marriottharborbeach.com (Click on "Plan Events," then "Banquet Menu" tabs)
- Hilton Anaheim — www.hotelfandb.com/features/images/eat_naturally_menu.pdf
- Fairmont Hotel Vancouver — www.fairmontmeetings.com/hotelvancouver/pdf/banquet_menus.pdf

1. How well do each of the menus reflect the menu guidelines presented in the chapter?

2. Which hotel's menus do you feel are most appealing to meeting planners? Why?

3. What is unique about the Hilton Anaheim's banquet menus?

4. What service charges does each hotel impose?

Group menus come in a variety of forms and sizes. For convenience, we recommend a small bound booklet, such as used by Radisson hotels (see Exhibit 1). The Radisson booklet gives both sit-down and buffet suggestions for breakfast, lunch, and dinner.

These Radisson menus are effective because of their descriptions of the various items offered and the use of graphics to showcase menu choices. Many hotel banquet menus, however, simply list the foods and beverages offered; there are no detailed descriptions or illustrations.

In designing your own group menus, your presentation is just as important as the choices you offer. Begin by collecting sample menus from other properties to glean ideas you may want to incorporate into your own design. If your budget is limited and you can't afford expensive graphics, you can still get your point across with mouth-watering word images (words such as "melt in your mouth," "piping hot," "savory," "flaky," and so on create a word picture — and a desire to purchase).

Be sure that your menu conveys your image — and generates sales — by following basic design elements, such as an attractive cover, an appealing design format, and an easy-to-read layout. Menus should always be printed on a good-quality paper stock. Dark ink on ivory or cream paper stock gives a more "cultured" look. Pages should not look cluttered — always allow plenty of white space between items and columns. Don't forget contact information — always include your property's logo, name, address, telephone numbers, and e-mail addresses. An original copy (not a photocopy) should always be presented to meeting planners (the only exception to this rule is sending menu information to a meeting planner via fax).

Two other types of food functions held in conjunction with beverage service are **refreshment breaks**, which are increasingly being called **energy breaks**, and cocktail **receptions**. Refreshment breaks, which take place between meeting sessions, are generally offered for 30 minutes at mid-morning and mid-afternoon. Ideally, breaks should be set up in a room adjacent to the meeting room. If this is not possible, beverages and/or food items can be setup in the hallway or lobby outside the meeting room (you will want to ensure that any setup required will not disturb the meeting program) or brought to the meeting room itself. Serving carts or portable tables can be used outside the meeting room, or the items can be carted outside the meeting room and wheeled in when the person in charge of the

Exhibit 1   Sample Menus from the Group Menu Booklet Used by the Radisson Hotel

Breakfasts

The aroma of freshly brewed coffee. Fresh juices, pastries, muffins and breads warm from the oven.

Launch a successful day at the Radisson Hotel St. Paul with breakfast full of homemade American goodness.

Chef's Breakfast Recommendations

The French Connection
Grapefruit Juice or Orange Juice, Egg Dipped French Toast Topped with Apples, Bananas, Pecans and Maple Whipped Butter. Canadian Bacon or Sausage. Freshly Ground and Brewed Guatemalan Antigua Coffee or Colombian Supremo Decaffeinated Coffee. Granola Bars and Assortment of Whole Fresh Fruit Basket.

Midwestern Sunrise
Vegetable Juice or Cherry Cider. Scrambled Eggs with Wisconsin Cojack Cheese, Fresh Chives, Canadian Bacon or Smoked Ham Steak and Sautéed Red Potatoes. Blueberry Muffin Basket. Freshly Ground and Brewed Guatemalan Antigua Coffee or Colombian Supremo Decaffeinated Coffee.

The All American
Grapefruit Juice or Orange Juice, Scrambled Eggs, Bacon, Hash Brown Potatoes, Assorted Breakfast-Bakeries, Butter, Jams and Marmalades, Freshly Ground and Brewed Guatemalan Antigua Coffee or Colombian Supremo Decaffeinated Coffee, Assorted Herbal and Premium Teas

Breakfast Buffets (minimum 50 people)

Sunrise Buffet
Orange Juice, Grapefruit Juice, Fresh Fruit Medley, Scrambled Eggs, Home Fried Potatoes, Bacon and Sausage, Assorted Muffins and Pastries, Beverage

Northwoods Buffet
Apple Cider, Orange and Vegetable Juice. Country Style Eggs Scrambled. Display of Seasonal Fruits and Berries. Homemade Granola. Smoked Fish and Cheese Platters, Hickory Smoked Ham. Flapjacks with Blueberry Compote, Grilled Homefried Potatoes. Assorted Muffins and Pastries, Beverage.

Omelette Bar (maximum 75 people)
Orange Juice, Apple Juice, Fresh Fruit Medley, Omelettes or Eggs cooked to order, Home Fried Potatoes, Hickory Smoked Ham, Yogurts, Granolas and Muffins.

*Low Cholesterol Eggs Available

A la Carte Breakfasts

FRUITS AND JUICES   (Choice of One)
Half Grapefruit, Grapefruit Juice or Orange Juice, Fresh Fruit Medley, Chilled Melon

COMBINATIONS
Served with Basket of Muffins and Breads, Butter, Jams, Marmalades and Beverage

Scrambled Eggs, Sausage or Bacon Strips
Home Fried Potatoes

Scrambled Eggs, Ham or Canadian Bacon
Home Fried Potatoes

Ham and Cheese Egg Croissant
Home Fried Potatoes

Roast Beef Hash with Poached Eggs
Home Fried Potatoes

Grilled Tenderloin Steak with Scrambled Eggs
Home Fried Potatoes

(Continued)

group gives a signal for the food service staff to enter (see box titled "Refreshment Break Guidelines").

Refreshment breaks generally include such beverages as coffee, tea, soft drinks, and bottled water, and usually feature various light food items. A break between morning sessions, for example, may include muffins, low-fat yogurt, and fruit in addition to beverages. Serving heavy, sugar-laden foods may lead to attendee sluggishness, especially between afternoon sessions.

Receptions are usually stand-up social functions that bring attendees together to socialize, and they may be held at various times during a meeting program. Sometimes, there are welcoming receptions for attendees; other receptions precede a meal function (this

Exhibit 1 *(continued)*

Lunch

Take a memorable mid-day break. Introduce the occasion with our Chef's creative soups of the day or a picture-perfect salad. Select one of our savory main courses. Then top off the meal with a dessert guaranteed to set your guests to talking.

Chef's Luncheon Recommendations

Chicken Salad Plate with Fresh Fruit
Soup of the Day, Breadsticks, Beverage

Roasted Top Sirloin of Beef
Mushroom Sauce, Tossed Green Salad, Fresh Vegetable, Potato, Rolls and Butter, Beverage

Grilled Breast of Chicken
Basil Cream Sauce, Fresh Fruit Salad, Fresh Vegetable, Three Rice Blend, Rolls and Butter, Beverage

Deli Platter
Soup of the Day, Roast Beef, Turkey, Ham and Salami, Assorted Cheeses, Relishes, Potato Salad, Assorted Breads in a Basket, Beverage

Tuna Salad, Canteloupe
Soup of the Day, Hard Boiled Egg, Cottage Cheese, Relishes, Rolls and Butter, Beverage

Roast Breast of Turkey
Gravy and Dressing, Apple, Orange Waldorf Salad, Fresh Vegetable, Whipped Potatoes, Rolls and Butter, Beverage

Baked Chicken Breast
Mustard Sauce, Filled with Spinach Wild Rice and Jarlsburg Cheese, Fresh Vegetables, Rolls and Butter. Tossed Green Salad, Beverage.

Grilled Chicken & Shrimp Stirfry
Florentine Rice, Peapods and Carrots, Luncheon Salad, Rolls and Butter, Beverage

Broiled Orange Roughy
Fresh Dill Sauce, Danish Cucumber Tomato Salad, Three Blend Rice, Fresh Vegetables, Rolls and Butter, Beverage

Grilled Salmon Filet
Dilled Salsa Verde, Butter Lettuce Salad, Three Rice Blend, Steamed Broccoli, Rolls and Butter, Beverage

Desserts A La Carte
Chocolate Fudge Cake, Vanilla Ice Cream with Berries in Season, Chocolate Rum Mousse, Carrot Cake, Apple Pie, Cheesecake, Pound Cake Compote

Hearty Deli Box Lunches
Choice of One in Each Category:
Mustard Glazed Ham, Roasted Turkey Breast, or Lean Roast Beef
Cheddar, Smoked Gouda or Swiss
Onion Bun, Whole Wheat Bun or Pumpernickel Bread
Marinated Vegetable Salad, Pasta Salad or Dill Potato Salad
Granola Bar, Chocolate Chip Cookie, Peanut Butter Brownie, Banana or Apple
Soda or Spring Water

LUNCHEON BUFFETS

New York Deli
Soup of the Day, Roast Beef, Turkey, Ham and Salami, Assorted Cheeses, A Variety of Breads, Condiments, Salads, Relish Platter, Cheesecake, Beverage

Picnic Time (minimum 25 people)
Sliced Tomatoes, Sliced Cucumbers, Potato Salad, Southern Style Fried Chicken, Rolls and Butter, Apple Pie, Beverage

Boulevard Buffet   (minimum 75 people)

Tossed Green Salad, Fresh Fruit Medley, Soup of the Day, Sliced Tomatoes, Sliced Cucumbers, Relish Platter, Potato Salad, Salad Dressings, Breads and Butter, Assorted Cold Cuts, Assorted Cheeses

Select Any Two:
Fish and Chips, Grilled Chopped Sirloin, Roast Top Sirloin, Fried Chicken, Baked Ham, Roast Half Chicken
Chef's Select Fresh Vegetable, Potato,
Carrot Cake, Apple Pie, Chocolate Rum Mousse, Beverage

(Continued)

ensures that all guests are in the same place before a sit-down dinner), or receptions may be held to enable attendees to socialize with outside participants, such as vendors, outside sales representatives, and so on.

At most receptions, beverages, usually including alcoholic beverages, and light foods, often **hors d'oeuvres** (hot or cold finger foods) and **canapes** (hot or cold appetizers with a bread or cracker base), are served. Foods may be presented on small buffet tables or passed by servers.

When presenting foods in a buffet style, keep in mind that easy access to food results in greater consumption. Exhibit 2 details how different types of buffet setups affect the amount of food that would be required for a reception. If a planner has a limited budget

Exhibit 1 *(continued)*

Dinner

Select menus to round out the day's events . . . or a beginning to your evening's production. A leisurely ambiance of taste and imagination.

Chef's Dinner Recommendations

Roast Prime Rib of Beef
Caesar Salad, Potato, Fresh Vegetable, Rolls and Butter, Chocolate Cheese Cake, Beverage

Char-broiled Pacific Salmon
Mustard Dill Sauce, Tossed Garden Greens, Fresh Vegetables, Wild Rice Blend, Rolls and Butter, Chocolate Chip Cheesecake, Beverage

New York Cut Strip Sirloin
Peppercorn Sauce, Caesar Salad, Potato, Fresh Vegetable, Rolls and Butter, Four Layer Chocolate Cake, Beverage

Char-broiled Center Cut Pork Chop
Apple, Orange Waldorf Salad, Potato, Fresh Vegetable, Rolls and Butter, Carrot Cake, Beverage

Roasted Top Sirloin of Beef
Mushroom Sauce, Caesar Salad, Potato, Fresh Vegetable, Rolls and Butter, Chocolate Chip Cheesecake, Beverage

Grilled Breast of Chicken
Spicy Tomato Sauce, Tossed Garden Greens, Fresh Vegetables, Fettucini, Rolls and Butter, Pound Cake Compote, Beverage

Hardwood Grilled Chicken Breast and Beef Tenderloin Filet
Peach Chutney, Tossed Garden Greens, Brown Rice and Lentils, Fresh Vegetables, Rolls and Butter, Irish Cream Mousse Cake, Beverage

Grilled Swordfish
Minted Tomato Sauce, Caesar Salad, Potato Gnocchi, Fresh Vegetables, Rolls and Butter, Bread Pudding with Caramel Sauce, Beverage

Chicken Breast Porcini
Mushroom Cream Sauce, Tossed Garden Greens, Wild Mushroom Chicken Mousse, Fresh Spinach, Wild Rice, Fresh Vegetables, Rolls and Butter, Cheesecake with Amaretto Cream Sauce, Beverage

Stuffed Pork Loin
Pistachio Apple Brandy Sauce, Caesar Salad, Sweet Potato Tart, Fresh Vegetables, Rolls and Butter, Dutch Apple Pie, Beverage

Grilled Chicken Breast and Shrimp Marinara
Caesar Salad, Fettucini, Fresh Vegetables, Rolls and Butter, Four Layer Chocolate Cake, Beverage

Midwestern Grill
Four Season Salad, Beef, Veal and Lamb Chop Grilled to Perfection, Potato Au Gratin, Fresh Vegetables, Rolls and Butter, Irish Cream Torte, Beverage

Hardwood Grilled Tenderloin and Baked Salmon Filet
Peppercorn Sauce, Caesar Salad, Lentil Brown Rice, Fresh Vegetables, Rolls and Butter, Amaretto Cheesecake, Beverage

Sliced Tenderloin and Grilled Shrimp
Port Wine Cherry Sauce, Marinated Tomato and Spinach Salad, Wild Rice, Fresh Vegetables, Rolls and Butter, Walnut Layer Cake, Beverage

Dinner Buffet   (minimum 75 people)

Tossed Green Salad, Fresh Fruit Medley, Sliced Tomatoes, Sliced Cucumbers, Relish Platter, Potato Salad, Salad Dressing, Breads and Butter

Select Any Two:
Roast Loin of Pork, Natural Gravy; Breast of Chicken, Cordon Bleu; Roast Half Chicken; Rainbow Trout Almondine; Grilled Pacific Salmon, Orange Butter; Roasted Top Sirloin of Beef, Mushroom Sauce; Baked Ham; Roast Breast of Turkey, Gravy and Dressing

Vegetables and Starches to Complement Buffet

Assortment of Pies, Cakes and Mousse, Beverages

Dinner Grand Buffet   (minimum 75 people)

Tossed Garden Greens, Fresh Fruit Medley, Marinated Mushroom Tomato Salad, Danish Cucumber Salad, Antipasta Salad, Relishes, Bread Display

Carver Attended: Select One
Roast Prime Rib of Beef or Baked Ham

Select Any Three:
Roast Loin of Pork, Breast of Chicken Cordon Bleu, Roasted Chicken, Sole Roulades, Seafood Creole, Roasted Breast of Turkey.

Vegetables and Starches to Complement Buffet
Grand Dessert Display, Beverages

or simply wants to ensure that the food he or she has ordered lasts through the event, you should suggest the round buffet or 180-degree buffet arrangements.

A cocktail reception with hors d'oeuvres should create a festive atmosphere, so many receptions include music, dancing, and entertainment. There should also be plenty of room to allow attendees to socialize (as a rule of thumb, allow seven to 10 square feet per attendee and provide seating for 25 percent of attendees). Not only do these activities put attendees in a good frame of mind, they also serve as distractions that will cut down on reception food consumption (this not only ensures that attendees will have room for dinner if the reception precedes a meal, but also helps the meeting planner's budget).

Refreshment Break Guidelines

1. Prices for breaks may be quoted per person or on a consumption basis.
2. Space stations so bottlenecks are kept to a minimum.
3. Open stations farthest from the main entrance first to draw people into the room.
4. Separate coffee and soda stations.
5. Identify each hot beverage with a sign.
6. Lay out stations for quick service: coffee cups, followed by regular coffee, decaf, tea bags, and hot water. Accessories, cream, sugar, sweetener, and spoons should be available on a separate table a short distance from the beverage station.
7. Set one beverage station per 75 to 100 attendees.
8. Staff one server per 100 people for refreshment breaks; one server per 50 people at receptions and buffets.
9. Figure 20 six-ounce cups of coffee in a gallon.
10. "Marry" (combine) coffee stations toward the end of the break.

REFRESHMENT BREAK ESTIMATES FOR 200 PEOPLE

	A.M.		P.M.
Coffee	65% x 200 = 130 cups = 6.5 gals	Coffee	35% x 200 = 70 cups = 3.5 gals
Decaf	30% x 200 = 60 cups = 3 gals	Decaf	20% x 200 = 40 cups = 2 gals
Tea	10% x 200 = 20 cups = 1 gal	Tea	10% x 200 = 20 cups = 1 gal
Soda/		Soda/	
Water	25% x 200 = 50 drinks = 50 sodas	Water	70% x 200 = 140 drinks = 140 sodas

Exhibit 2   Sample Reception Buffet Setups

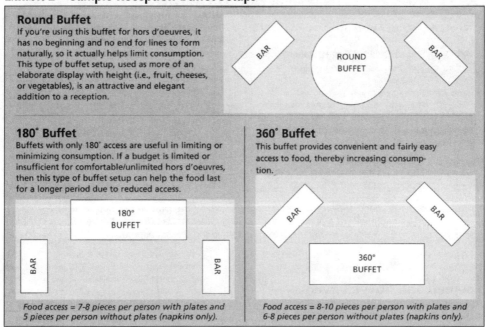

The physical layout of a reception buffet controls access to food, therefore limiting or expanding the amount of time that food lasts. This chart details how much food can be expected to be consumed per person using the three most common reception buffet setups, enabling you to assist a meeting planner in deciding which setup to use and how much food to order for the event.
Source: From the *Experient Guide to the Food and Beverage Experience*, sponsored by Hilton Hospitality, Inc., and published by Hammock Publishing. Used with permission.

To assist meeting planners in ordering food for receptions, the following guidelines have been developed:

Dry snacks	1 ounce per person
Anchor foods (cheese, vegetables, fruits)	enough for 1/3 of attendees
Action stations (carving station, pasta station)	enough for 1/2 to 2/3 of attendees
Passed hors d'oeuvres	1 of each for all attendees
Dessert and coffee	enough for 1/3 to 1/2 of attendees

Source: From the *Experient Guide to the Food and Beverage Experience*, sponsored by Hilton Hospitality, Inc., and published by Hammock Publishing. Used with permission.

Keep in mind that many guests at receptions enjoy sampling every item. Therefore, encourage meeting planners to order at least one piece of every item for each attendee. For a reception for 500, for example, it is wiser to order 500 pieces of three types of hors d'oeuvres rather than 250 pieces of six different types. If the planner wants more variety, the menu can be supplemented with less expensive items, such as cheese and crackers, chips and dip, and vegetable and fruit trays.

Two basic methods are used in charging for hors d'oeuvres and **finger food**: by the person per hour, and by the bowl or tray. Exhibit 3 shows these two methods.

Each function should be dealt with separately to make sure of details. A banquet event order should be filled out for each event, listing all the information needed for smooth execution.

Exhibit 3   Pricing Catered Items

Canapés and Hors D'Oeuvres	
No.1: $6.50 per person	**No. 2:**
Hot Grilled Cocktail Franks, Mustard Sauce Swedish Savory Meatballs Knishes Chinese Egg Rolls Butterfly Shrimp, Cocktail Sauce	**Cold Canapes** Large Tray...**$68.50** (Serves approximately 25 persons) Medium Tray...**$46.00** (Serves approximately 15 persons)
Cold Canapes Savory Cheese Spread, Pimento Cornets of Imported Genoa Salami Smoked Nova Scotia Salmon Deviled Eggs with Anchovies	Selection: A variety of Assorted Cold Canapes, including Stuffed Eggs Moscovite

This hors d'oeuvres menu shows two methods of pricing: by the person per hour and by the tray or bowl. While the eating habits of groups may vary, the industry standard for a two-hour reception is eight pieces per person for the first hour and four per person during the second hour.

Themed and Special Events

Every meeting planner tries to do something different at each event. Most conventions have a high percentage of people who repeatedly attend, so the planners want to "add a new twist" to the program, from adding flair to the cocktail party to staging a themed banquet.

Experienced meeting planners disguise the same old cocktail party by introducing a different theme each year. **Themed events**, both large and small, are very popular and are remembered by the attendees. In addition, themed events do much to enhance the reputation of the hotel. The focal point of any such function is the menu, and hotels that offer several different types of themed menus are a step ahead of the competition. There are many themes that can be effectively executed, even if the meeting planner has a limited budget. An "Old Mexico" theme, for example, can offer taco bars, a chili bar, an interactive fajita bar, and chips with salsa and guacamole. Not only are most of these menu items inexpensive, but it also takes time for guests to assemble a taco, which greatly cuts down on the amount of food consumed. Other low-cost themes include a State Fair or Fourth of July theme (featuring traditional, low-cost foods such as hot dogs, hamburgers, and so on) and a Western theme (beef stew served from a "chuck wagon," or typical barbecued foods).

If you are in a locale that offers unique cuisine, consider featuring a locally grown themed menu. In Calgary, for example, themed "local" menus might include Alberta beef, caribou, lamb, salmon, halibut, or goat cheese. Amy Johnson, director of catering and convention services at the Hyatt Regency Calgary, says:

> One of our biggest sellers right now for banquets is venison.[5]

At a recent event, Johnson served Alberta venison and wild mushroom soup in an acorn squash, veal wrapped in an Alberta potato, and a Canadian cheese platter. These menu items were an excellent way to introduce delegates to the "flavor" of the destination.

The menu should be served in creative ways that will enhance the theme. **Action stations** featuring costumed chefs, for example, are more memorable than having a guest simply choose from pre-prepared dishes on a buffet table. A chef wearing colorful garb as he or she makes fajitas at an Old Mexico event, or dressed as a cowboy while preparing cooked-to-order steaks for a Western-themed party, are just two examples. Costumes for servers can also add to the atmosphere, as can creative decorations and entertainment. Incorporate the theme into your table and serving ware; use clay dishes and colorfully decorated serving platters and bowls for a Mexican theme tin plates and cups at a barbecue, and so on. The theme should also be reflected in table and wall decorations and lighting (paper lanterns for an Oriental theme or torches for a Hawaiian luau, for example).

Many decorations and other enhancements, such as bubble machines, fog machines, and other "effects," are inexpensive and can be easily stored for future functions. Themed props may also be obtained at low (or even no) cost from such sources as vendors (most beverage vendors can supply "game-themed" props, such as Super Bowl decorations or NASCAR posters), travel agencies, and airlines (good sources for travel posters). If you have requests for unusually themed events, it can be cost-effective to work with outside sources and rent props needed for special functions.

Action stations featuring chefs serving or carving food are more memorable than having a guest simply choose from a buffet table.
Source: Photograph courtesy of Loews Hotels and Resorts.

When you have developed functions that work well, these can easily be promoted to other groups. Some properties and chains, such as Fairmont Hotels & Resorts, offer brochures promoting their popular themed events. Brochure pages detail the setting and decorations for the event, the food and beverages that will be served, entertainment provided as part of the function, and "extras," such as a fireworks show to end the evening. Themes range from a Mexican party (complete with a performance of the Mexican Folkloric ballet) to a Bohemia Party to a Las Vegas Night.

This type of promotional material (as well as photographs taken during past events) is a great help in selling other business. If you have successfully staged themed events, clients will likely respond to your suggestions. This is especially true if you can offer not only the expertise but also the other elements needed to stage such an event. While planners usually love themed events, many have budget constraints or need help with stimulating their thinking. When you help meeting planners stage events that guests remember long after the meeting or convention, everyone benefits. The guests have a memorable experience and meeting planners have the confidence to book more, bigger, and better events with the hotel, which can look forward to both future repeat business and word-of-mouth bookings resulting from satisfied planners and guests.

In addition to themed events, meeting planners may also want to include other **special events** in their programs. These functions, which are primarily social in nature and are generally celebratory, can range from receptions for attendees, VIPs, and speakers to elegant, black-tie **gala dinners** that include gourmet food, music, dancing, other entertainment, and awards presentations.

No matter what type of event is planned, the property's food and beverage department will play a major role in making it a success. That means offering special foods and beverages, perhaps serving the food more elegantly (passed by waiters in tuxedos, for example), and creating a setting that gives the event the "flavor" desired by the meeting planner.

A property's food and beverage department is critical for the execution of special events. While some hotels have an in-house special events manager and can provide a vast inventory of linens, serving ware, and so on, many hotels work closely with destination management companies (DMCs) or special event companies that are hired by the meeting planner. These companies may be better able to work with specific vendors or arrange for off-site locations, such as private homes, clubs, and golf courses for the function.

Off-Premises Catering

In addition to servicing functions in-house (known as **on-premises catering**), a great many hotels and restaurants are turning to **off-premises catering** — preparing food and/or beverages for events away from the hotel — to boost food and beverage revenues. While some events are held on the grounds of a property or restaurant, these are still serviced directly by the hotel's on-premises kitchen(s). With off-premises catering, food must be either partially or fully prepared in the hotel's kitchen and then transported to the site of the function or fully prepared at the event site.

Off-premises events can be held at a local attraction (in Dallas, some events are held at the Southfork Ranch, where the *Dallas* TV show was filmed, for example), or at other venues, such as a fund-raising dinner at a museum or an opening reception at an art gallery, or at outdoor locations. The location of the event will be an important factor in determining both the menu and the method of food preparation.

Before a hotel or restaurant gets into the off-premises catering business, it is important to determine the feasibility of such an operation. Off-premises catering can be an

Best Practices

Off-Premises Catering:
Fairmont The Queen Elizabeth, Montreal, Quebec, Canada

The 1,039-room Fairmont The Queen Elizabeth in Montreal generates $1.6 to $1.9 million annually with its off-site catering department, which brings in almost 18 percent of the hotel's total food and beverage revenues. The service, which began when the hotel began catering meals to one nearby office building in 1976, now handles some 300 events a year, which translates into 130,000 to 140,000 covers.

Headed by Armando Arruda, director of outside catering for the hotel, the department prepares a variety of cuisine, including Canadian, continental, and French dishes. Most of the food for the off-site events, which range from continental breakfasts to high-end gala dinners, is prepared in the hotel's kitchen, which is manned by 80 chefs. For some events, the food is finished in off-site kitchens. Although outside help, including wait staff, is sometimes hired for large events, the hotel maintains quality control by employing its own chefs.

Head Chef Pignard

In addition to providing food for corporate events, the Fairmont also caters a number of off-premises functions, such as fund-raising or award dinners, for hospitals, art organizations, and other groups.

Other Fairmont hotels, such as the Fairmont Pallister in Calgary, Alberta, and the Fairmont San Jose in California, also offer off-premises catering at venues that range from large barbecues at Calgary's rodeo grounds to intimate dinners on private jets.

expensive proposition. Mobile kitchen equipment and other equipment, such as portable furniture and decorations, may have to be purchased. Since off-premises catering may be seasonal in some locales, storage would have to be arranged for equipment not being used on a regular basis.

Some hotels opt to partner with local venues or work with destination management companies to get the maximum value from off-premises catering. In some cities, hotels can partner with unique local venues, such as the Liberace Mansion in Las Vegas, for example, or a reception facility (such a facility usually stocks its own furniture and props; all the hotel or restaurant would have to do is provide the food and/or beverages). Destination management companies can help with such off-site arrangements as equipment, decorations, entertainment, and other services.

Revenue potential can also be maximized by preparing menus that are both cost-effective and easily prepared and transportable. A barbecue menu can easily be executed at local parks or other facilities, for example, or a property may opt for catering only one or two types of events, such as receptions or buffet breakfasts, off-site.

Changing Tastes

Banquet menus should reflect meeting attendees' desire for a more healthful diet. People are increasingly conscious that the food they eat and the way it is prepared has an impact on

The "Greening" of Banquets

Healthy, natural food is becoming more important to both meeting planners and attendees, and many hotels are responding to this trend by offering organic foods, including locally-grown produce that is free from pesticides and chemical fertilizers; and beef, chicken, and other meats that have not been injected with anabolic steroids, antibiotics, and growth hormones.

The Fairmont Hotels & Resorts chain was the first hotel company to commit to using sustainable, locally sourced and organically grown products as part of everyday food service operations whenever possible. Serge Simard, Fairmont's vice president of food and beverage, says:

> Our guest are very savvy, experienced diners, and they also are becoming more conscious of how their consumer choices affect the planet. We want our guests to know that when they dine at Fairmont, not only can they count on the very best, freshest ingredients and a true experience of the destination through their culinary choices, there will always be a range of sustainable options for them to consider.

Other hotels and chains offering organic choices include the InterContinental Chicago, which promotes "Green Menus" that are anchored by local vendors who supply products that are organic and cruelty-free in addition to being locally grown. The chain reports that their green menus now account for approximately 50 percent of their event business, and other properties, including the Walt Disney World Swan and Dolphin Resort, have also introduced organic banquet menus.

Buying local produce isn't always an option for some properties, especially those in arid climates. Some hotels, such as The Boulders Resort & Golden Door Spa in Carefree, Arizona, have responded by creating their own gardens. The 5,280-square-foot garden at The Boulders not only supplies the property's restaurants and spa café, but has also become a refreshing event space for small groups. Some hotels have to resort to having organic produce shipped in, and some of their choices may be limited — it may be impossible to serve range-free chicken to a large group, for example.

Keeping costs reasonable is another concern. Organic produce, for example, may be ten to 50 percent higher (although the average is 25 percent) than traditional fruits and vegetables, and the cost of free-range chicken and grass-feed beef may be prohibitive. The key is to offer as many

Rooftop herb garden.
Source: Photograph courtesy of Fairmont Royal York Hotel, Toronto, Ontario, Canada.

organic, locally-grown products as possible to appeal to health- and environmentally-conscious meeting planners and attendees.

Sources: "From the Farm to the Fork: Fairmont Offers a Fresh New Take on Menus," *ehotelier.com,* **August 27, 2007; "Fresh, Local & Gorgeous,"** *Meetings & Conventions,* **December 2007, pp. 61 & 62; and "Thinking Green," excerpted by InterContinental Chicago from** *Hotel F&B Magazine,* **September/October 2008.**

their overall health. Hotels have responded by offering lighter, low-cholesterol items and providing alternative menus for attendees with dietary or religious restrictions. These menus may offer vegetarian, gluten-free, and lactose-intolerant substitutes, and offer choices that reflect the latest dietary trends (see box titled "The 'Greening' of Banquets").

Ruth Butler, CMP, CMM, manager of event operations at Experient's northeast regional office in Norwood, Massachusetts, says:

> The low-carb craze has really hit. All the meeting and event managers in our office are dealing with it.[6]

The Sheraton chain has responded to the low-carb trend by introducing Lo-Carb Lifestyle, the most extensive line of low-carb food offerings in the hotel industry. Recently, four senior chefs from Hilton Hotels Corporation attended an extensive three-day nutrition course at Johnson and Wales University. Upon their return, they created a roster of recipes geared toward low-carb dieters and people with diabetes.[7] New York–based Loews Hotels responded to the trend with its "No Carb-tails" drink menu, which includes such libations as diet-friendly daiquiris and vodka-infused green tea,[8] while Marriott has a program called Fit for You, and Renaissance offers Eat, Drink, and Balance.

The biggest change in eating habits has occurred at breakfast. Meagan Kiessling, the association conference manager for Alcoholism and Substance Abuse Providers of New York State in Albany, New York, says:

> Low-carb and protein are definitely playing a larger role in menu planning, particularly with breakfast. There is almost no point to adding a continental breakfast for your group without at least two low-carb options.[9]

Eggs, potatoes, bacon, and sausage have given way to a variety of lighter, health-conscious offerings such as whole grain muffins and rolls, low calorie yogurt, fresh fruits, and low-fat dairy products. Hot oatmeal, cooked wheat cereal, and shredded wheat are very popular alternatives to traditional breakfast fare. Lunches and dinners have also become less formal. Diet-conscious attendees appreciate extensive salad bars featuring fresh vegetables and low-calorie dressings. Poultry, fish, veal, and lean pork entrees, grilled rather than fried, are popular with fitness-conscious attendees. Heavy meals promote sleepiness, so offer moderate portions and food groups that are high in protein.

Today, new technology is being used to assist planners in making their decisions — and to improve the quality and variety of food and beverages offered to meeting and function guests. Sheraton's "Sheraton Cuisine," the umbrella name for the chain's hotel kitchen software, provides colored pictures of the 365 dishes offered in its "Cuisine of the Americas" menu, along with the recipes and a breakdown of the nutritional content of each entrée. Scott Geraghty, director of culinary services for the Sheraton New York Hotel Complex, is enthusiastic about this program and its next phase, which calculates nutritional content after substitutions have been made. He states:

> A catering manager will be able to sit down with a meeting planner, call up a color picture of what a plated dish would look like, and make substitutions like: "What would this dish look like with carrots instead of zucchini?"[10]

Refreshment breaks no longer require doughnuts, Danish, and other surgary bakery items. Health-conscious participants know that simple sugars provide few nutrients and

play havoc with the waistline. Fruit juices; flavored mineral waters; yogurt; muffins; fresh
fruits such as pineapple, melon, and strawberries; plus decaffeinated coffee and hot tea are
popular items. One conference service manager tells us that today's meeting breaks also
feature such healthy options as fresh vegetables, nuts, power bars, and other foods "that
can help to keep the brain power going during the day." Because of this growing health-
conscious trend, many hotels now market energy breaks instead of refreshment breaks.

Types of Service

An important planning decision is the type of service to be used at food functions. The
kind of banquet service selected influences pricing, staffing, and the overall effect of the
function.

  American/plated service is the most common form of banquet service. The food is
assembled in the kitchen and waiters deliver plates to the tables. Cold food may be plated
ahead of time and stored in refrigerators. Hot food is plated just prior to delivery and is
sometimes served from a number of stations set up in the kitchen. Guests are served food
from the left and beverages from the right. All items are picked up from the right at the
end of the course. Plate service requires the least skill on the part of the service personnel.

  With **Russian service**, all food is fully prepared in the kitchen and courses are served
to the guests directly from soup tureens, platters, or an escoffier dish by waiters working
in teams. While Russian service, also called *platter service*, requires more space between
tables to enable waiters to move freely, and a larger, skilled labor force, it is an efficient
way to control portions, as waiters place a pre-determined amount of food in the bowls or
on the plates of guests.

  French service, also called *cart* or *tableside service,* is generally used only for small
groups, but also requires sufficient space between tables for waiters to move about freely.
More experienced waiters are required for this type of service, as much of the food is prepared tableside on a gueridon (rolling cart).

  Pre-set service is frequently used for luncheons where fast service is needed. The
first course of soup, salad, or appetizer is set on the table prior to the guests' arrival; occasionally the dessert may also be pre-set. While pre-set service works well when the schedule is tight, pre-set food is rarely as attractive as food delivered in courses during the meal.

English/family-style service is similar to Russian service, as food is brought to the table on a platter or tray. In most cases, the food is presented to the host, who either cuts the main course himself or herself or chooses to have it done by the server away from the table. Vegetables and other accompaniments are placed in bowls or other serving dishes on the table, allowing the guests to serve themselves.

Buffet service is a presentation of several food items from which the attendee makes a selection. Buffet service is efficient because a large number of people can be served in a short period of time with a small serving staff. Since buffets can be more expensive to serve than plated meals, because there is no portion control and surplus food must be ordered to ensure adequate amounts of offerings, hotels may suggest several alternatives to the "traditional" unlimited buffet. These choices can include *attended buffets*, at which guests are served by chefs or attendants (this not only offers better portion control, but is also more elegant), *combination buffets*, in which inexpensive items, such as salads, are presented buffet style and expensive items, such as meats, are served by an attendant for portion control, and *plated buffets*, at which a selection of pre-plated foods is set on the buffet table.

Butler service is sometimes used at receptions or upscale dinners. At receptions, servers circulate with trays, from which guests help themselves. At formal dinners, food is presented on silver trays, and serving utensils are offered to allow guests to help themselves from the tray.

Another trend in food functions is **a la carte catering**, which offers more options to both planners and diners. Under the a la carte system, catering departments develop menus offering two or three items from which guests can choose, or unique combinations of entrees to suit more palates (a combination of meat and seafood or creative vegetarian entrees, for example).

Just as Hyatt introduced its Personal Preference Menus for banquets, mentioned earlier in this chapter, the Marriott chain has made extensive use of a la carte catering, even offering seated guests a menu to give more of a sense of fine dining. The Peabody Orlando,

Butler-style service, such as this example of hors d'oeuvres being passed on silver trays by waiters wearing white gloves, conveys an upscale atmosphere.
Source: Photograph courtesy of Jumeriah Hotels and Resorts.

which has offered a choice between beef and chicken for some time, has extended its a la carte service to include duo and trio entrée choices in its regionally-oriented banquet dishes (such as jerk chicken and Caribbean-style pork). Karl Edlbauer, executive chef of the hotel, explains:

> The clientele is looking for more upscale menus that are daring, but with a classical presentation.[11]

Chef's Tastings

In order to enable planners to sample banquet dishes so they'll know in advance how the food will look and taste, many hotels offer a "tasting dinner," also called a **chef's tasting**. A chef's tasting is especially important to meeting planners who are staging larger, unusual events or one that is extremely important, such as a board dinner.

Chef Gordon Marr of the Hilton Washington in Washington, D.C., recommends that the tasting meal be an exact replica of the banquet meal and that it should approximate meal service. Exhibit 4 shows a sample tasting given by the Grand Hyatt New York.

Chef's tastings can take place at two crucial times during the meeting planning process. Some planners opt for a tasting shortly after they have selected the menu. This gives them the opportunity to talk with the chef to let him or her know what they hope to achieve with the banquet. Chefs can then come up with other inventive ideas to enhance the experience for attendees. Planners may also schedule tastings one or two weeks before the function to enable them to experience seasonal foods that may be on the menu.

Exhibit 4   Chef's Tastings

The elements of a tasting firsthand at the Grand Hyatt New York by Convene *staff members Jamie Roberts and Michelle Russell. They were joined by Grand Hyatt staff James Dale, senior director of catering; Chef Arbeeny; Jerry Perez, executive sous chef; Ricardo Morales, banquet captain; and Chris Reed, sous chef. Terry Dale, formerly of NYC & Co., sits next to PCMA's Peter Shure.*
Source: Reprinted with permission of Convene**, the magazine of the Professional Convention Management Association, www.pcma.org ©2005. Photo courtesy of Grand Hyatt, New York.**

Hotels do not charge for chef's tastings, but properties sometimes limit the number of attendees. To be fair to the venue, attendees should be directly involved in the function. Therefore, attendees would include the meeting planner and such executives as the executive director of an association or the program chairman of a group event. Some hotels also allow one or two guests to attend, but it is more cost-effective if these guests will have direct input into the meeting (a board member who will be attending a function, an actual attendee, and so on).

Pricing Food Functions

Many convention planners prefer to complete all negotiations in detail before signing the letter of agreement. Some even want to go so far as to select menus and agree on prices. A planner would prefer this because it makes budget projections so much easier. But with conventions planned years in advance, it is not possible for a hotel to make exact quotations.

Most hotels will gladly say what they charge for menus currently in use, feeling that this is a sufficient guide for meeting planners. There is obvious danger in pricing a menu so far in advance. Most meeting planners with any experience at all realize that any such agreements may have to be modified because of rising costs. If you examine the currency values of the past fifty years, you see constant inflation. When the spiral goes up sharply, everyone recognizes the inflation, but in reality there has been a steady curve upwards over the years.

You must be very careful when you have to make price guarantees for dates several years ahead. Most hotels have adopted a policy of quoting room rates not more than one year in advance and firm menu prices not more than six months before the event. Some hotels even quote a more restricted policy. For example, the Orlando Marriott contract reads:

> *Menu prices cannot be confirmed more than 60 days prior to the function due to the daily fluctuation of market prices. The organization grants the hotel the right to make reasonable substitutions on the menu to meet increased market prices or commodity shortages.*

You cannot avoid such a policy unless you have no need to be competitive and can build in a fat reserve in your quotations. But few of us have such prerogatives. To be competitive, you figure prices closely and cannot absorb inflationary additions to cost.

You will find some exceptions, but most meeting planners understand such limitations and are concerned about unduly squeezing a hotel. After all, each event is a custom production and the planners are concerned with the quality of what they will receive. If they *are* obliged to set an early price on tickets, they understand that a flexible attitude on the menu can enable them to carry out the meal function while allowing the hotel a fair profit. Some astute meeting planners attach a copy of the hotel's current menu to the contract and specify that prices cannot be raised "more than X percent per year" over current prices.

All agreements on menus, prices, and terms must be made in writing and signed by both parties. This eliminates misunderstandings.

Attendance

The planner initially will estimate attendance at a food function. This is vital, as it indicates the scope of the event. The figure is only for preliminary preparations, and must be reviewed.

The convention planner owes it to the facility to keep it informed of the closest possible estimates of attendance at each food event. The planner may not know for sure, but a time will be set by which a firm guarantee must be given in order to prepare for the event.

Properties doing banquet business face the problem of determining a fair and workable **guarantee** policy. A typical guarantee clause might read:

> *In order to best serve your guests, a final confirmation of attendance or "guarantee" is required by NOON, three (3) business days prior to your meal event. The guarantee is not subject to reduction after the 72-hour deadline. If no guarantee is received, the hotel will charge for the expected number of guests indicated on the Banquet Event Order (BEO) or the original contract, whichever amount is greater. The hotel will set 5% over the guarantee for all food functions with less than 500 attendees and 3% for all groups exceeding 500 guests. Guests arriving over and above the guaranteed number may be served an alternate menu.*

The convention service manager can assist the planner in determining banquet attendance figures by suggesting that there be a **ticket exchange** and reserved seating for the *final* banquet, which is usually the most cost- and labor-intensive function. A ticket exchange is a control procedure that requires attendees to exchange a coupon from their registration packet for an actual event ticket and a reserved seating arrangement for the final gala banquet. The attendee typically turns in the ticket shortly after registering. Using this method, the planner can set a reservation deadline that falls during the meeting but still within the hotel's deadline for a head count.

No one policy is applicable to all hotels or all situations. However, the Hospitality Sales and Marketing Association International surveyed a number of hotels and found that most adhere strictly to their guarantee policies. Those surveyed stressed the importance of explaining the guarantee and working with the planner to set a realistic attendance figure.

Most hotels require a guarantee either 48 or 72 hours before a food function. The meeting planner then agrees to pay for the guaranteed number of people whether or not that many appear. If 200 people are guaranteed for luncheon at a per-head charge and only 185 show up, the organization will pay for all 200. It is a touchy situation, but the obligation is clear-cut.

What happens when more show up? The experienced planner will ask that places be set for more than the guaranteed number; an **overset safety margin** of three to five percent is common. It is to the advantage of both the hotel and the convening group to avoid last-minute scrambling with chairs, tables, and place settings.

Often the guarantee is included in the function sheet and is signed by both the hotel and a convention representative. Any agreement between the hotel and client is binding. If the guarantee calls for 200 and the hotel agrees to set for 5 percent over, the hotel sets tables and chairs for 210. If 210 show up, all is in readiness and the bill indicates 210. If 230 show up, the hotel is allowed to substitute 20 meals of a quickly prepared item.

Another guarantee method suggested by meeting planners, but seldom used, is to guarantee only labor. If only 185 of the guaranteed 200 showed up, the association would pay for only the cost of one waiter and not the extra fifteen meals prepared. Obviously, a hotel should never consent to this unless the extra meals can be used somewhere else.

The organization must designate, in writing, who is authorized to make changes in attendance estimates, menus, and prices. A guarantee sheet (see Exhibit 5) summarizing the functions and the guarantees for each day is printed daily and distributed to appropriate staff.

Exhibit 5   Guarantee Sheet

The Durham Resort
Guarantee Sheet
For February 8, 20_

Time	BEO #	Room	Func.	GTD	Set	Sources	Post As
4:00A-4:00A	121	Madison	EXHB	25	28	DJ/AO/JH/CH	Kopykat Sales
7:00A-9:00A	378	Monroe	BMTG	150	165	AO/AO/JH/JH	Auto Travelers Assn
7:00A-9:00A	127	Grant	BMTG	100	110	DJ/DJ/AO/AO	Auto Travelers Assn
7:00-11:00A	382	Ballroom J	RECP	200	220	KZ/KZ/JH/JH	Kopykat Sales
7:30A-8:00A	352	Ballroom J	CONT	50	55	AO/AO/JH/JH	Kopykat Sales
8:00A-4:00P	482	Ballroom A	EXHB	20	22	ML/ML/MW/MW	Auto Travelers Assn
8:00A-6:00P	482	Ballroom A	EXHB	20	22	DJ/DJ/AO/AO	Auto Travelers Assn
8:00A-6:00P	371	Webster	EXHB	20	22	AO/AO/JH/JH	Auto Travelers Assn
8:00A-12:00P	487	Coolidge	REG	20	22	AO/AO/JH/JH	Auto Travelers Assn
8:00A-5:00P	877	Washington	GS	80	88	DJ/DJ/AO/AO	Kopykat Sales
10:30A-4:30P	472	Jackson	MTG	75	85	JH/JH/DJ/DJ	Kopykat Sales

This computer printout lists all food functions on a particular day. Copies of the form are generally distributed to the executive chef, banquet chef, executive steward, food and beverage controller, function book coordinator, banquet manager, and convention service manager.

Attrition

Hotels must be certain that the food and beverage revenue generated by a group can support the amount of space required for the event. Increasingly, hotels are using clauses that deal with attrition and/or cancellations to protect themselves. Attrition is the difference between the actual number of food and beverage covers consumed and the number agreed to in the contract between the meeting planner and the hotel. When hotels book a piece of business, they often base the room rate quoted to the group on the amount of food and beverage and the meeting room rental anticipated. Typically, hotels look at the type and size of functions planned for the convention, put a dollar value on each one, add up the numbers, and then allow about 20 percent of that number for attrition (slippage). The resulting number is the minimum amount the group is expected to spend on food and beverage and meeting room rental. If the group fails to spend this amount because of poor attendance or the need to cancel banquets, the attrition clause in the contract allows the hotel to collect damages for lost profits.

A typical clause might read:

> *The Hotel is relying on, and the Group agrees to provide, a guaranteed minimum of 80 percent of the total anticipated food and beverage revenue ($_____). If Group's total actual food and beverage revenue slips below this amount, Group agrees to pay as liquidated damages (agreed not to constitute a penalty) the lost profit on the food and beverage revenue; 30 percent of the difference between the agreed minimum and the actual total food and beverage revenue. Group also agrees that, with respect to guaranteed functions, Group will pay the greater of (1) actual attendance or (2) the guaranteed attendance, with the revenue from such payments counting toward the satisfaction of Group's minimum total food and beverage revenue commitment.*

Function Rooms

The type of function room to be used for a food event depends on the nature of the session, its location in relation to other functions and the hotel traffic flow, and the kind of seating arrangement desired. Pay attention, too, to the decor, lighting, and other decoration requested. And, thought must be given to heating and cooling controls.

All these factors must be considered when the convention service manager sits down with his or her counterpart in the convention organization to select a room for the function. Priorities may dictate that the most suitable room go to another event, but any room used for a food function must be able to provide satisfactory results. Exhibit 6 shows how one hotel promotes its commitment to serving food "hot and fast" to meeting attendees by offering fully equipped, fully staffed kitchens adjacent to every ballroom.

A reminder is in order here to note the time it takes to set up the food function room and clean it up afterward. It is important to know whether the cleanup noises will disturb the meeting session going on next door. It may not be possible to avoid such proximity, but it shouldn't come about because no one thought about it. The clash of silver and china can be most distracting at a serious meeting and can reflect on the hotel's image.

On one occasion, the Salvation Army had a meeting scheduled next door to a luncheon for the governor of Hawaii. As the governor was presenting his opening remarks, the Salvation Army opened its meeting in the traditional way with a song to the resounding beat of the bass drum. Needless to say, the hotel's convention service manager gave greater consideration to a group's program after this incident.

Exhibit 6   Ad Promoting the Proximity of the Kitchen to Meeting Space

Control Procedures

Most food functions are charged on a per-head basis. Every hotel should devise a **head count** procedure to determine the actual number of **covers** (meals) served. Guesswork has no place in banquet billing. The charges should be agreed to in writing, and the menu selection should be indicated.

Many meeting planners prefer to use coupons or tickets. The delegate at registration is issued a coupon book with tear-out tickets for each function. There is need for caution if this system is suggested. Here are the two most common methods of ticket collection:

At the door — A table should be set up with a representative from the association and one from the hotel there to collect tickets.

At the banquet table — In this case, the waiter collects the tickets. This can be a touchy area if delegates do not have their tickets. A common delegate response is, "I left my ticket in my room." This is a difficult situation to police; if the hotel is paid for only the tickets collected, the waiter is forced to refuse service. Hotel personnel should be instructed what to do if a conferee shows up without the proper ticket.

Counting the dishes expected to be used in advance is another method of determining the number of covers served. The chef or convention service manager then counts the number of dishes that were not used and subtracts this from the first figure. Perhaps the best system is to simply count the people seated. The convention service manager and the meeting planner should both take counts. This should be done immediately after the entree has been served.

Some food functions, such as refreshment breaks and hospitality suites, obviously cannot be charged in this way. Spell out clearly the formula used. You may charge for coffee by the cup or by the gallon, fruit juice by the gallon, Danish pastry by the piece or by the tray, and so on.

Some canny sales managers will give away hors d'oeuvres or favors. In such cases, it enables them to close the deal at higher rates for rooms or meals. Psychologically, the practice may make for a better presentation; economically it may represent less than the price advantage. In addition, the higher rate will bring in a further dividend should more people attend. The buffet and hors d'oeuvres are fixed costs on your part, while the higher rate for additional guests adds to your profit.

Small food functions are often tagged with additional charges. If the function is not large enough to cover labor and setup costs, hotels frequently add on to the bill. Exhibit 7 provides an example of banquet labor and miscellaneous charges.

Staffing

Hotels generally provide more waiters per guest as the price per cover increases. The minimum wait service for standard plated dinners is one waiter per 20 guests (at rounds of ten, one waiter per two tables; at rounds of eight, two waiters per five tables). French and Russian service generally require one server for every ten guests. For buffet meals, the standard is one wait staff to 40 persons for breakfast and one wait staff for 30 persons at lunch and dinner. The minimum bus staff is one for every three waiters. If the menu calls for wine service poured by wait staff, the minimum is one waiter per 16 guests.

Pre-meal briefings should be conducted before all large banquets by the **banquet captains** (one banquet captain should be staffed for every ten to 12 servers). Menus, special service requirements, station assignments, and other pertinent items should be reviewed. The setup and service of the head table should be assigned to the captains. Special attention is paid to silverware, glasses, and proper arrangement of place settings.

Finally, the times for serving must be carefully controlled. The salad course typically takes about 20 to 30 minutes, the entree about 30 to 50 minutes (from serving to the removal of plates), and desserts can usually be handled in 20 to 30 minutes. Normally, complete service takes about 1½-hours for a lunch and about two hours for a dinner event. Keep in mind, however, that a more elaborate function will take additional time, so staff accordingly.

Exhibit 7   Miscellaneous Function Charges

Banquet Labor and Miscellaneous Charges

A. Waiter Labor Charge...........$30.00
   All functions with less than 20 guests

B. Overtime Charge, Waiter...$9.00/hr
   Breakfast over 2 hours
   Lunch over 3 hours
   Dinner over 4 hours

C. Service Charge $10.00/extra table
   For setting less than 10 covers per table

D. Carver (Chef).............. $30.00/hour
   After 2 hours

E. Housepersons.............$12.00/hour
   4 hours minimum

F. Early Setup of Banquet
   Rooms........$12.00/hour per waiter
   Prior to meal functions

G. Porter....................$80.00/8 hours
   If no food functions and meeting room
   complimentary

Hotels frequently add on to the bill if the food function is not large enough to cover labor and setup costs. In addition to the charges listed above, it is common for properties to apply a flat service charge to food and beverage functions under a certain size (typically 25 people or less). In some cases, labor and charges are waived entirely or based on the total dollar amount spent on the function. Any specifics negotiated should be clearly spelled out in the contract.

It is necessary to adhere closely to scheduled meal times, so extension of cocktail parties should be kept to a minimum. Meal functions should also run on schedule. Not only are some attendees reluctant to attend a catered event that will run over two hours, but an overly long event may also give the impression that there is something wrong with the catering department.

Uniserve or Duoserve

The food and beverage service is generally handled in one of two ways by hotels. In a **uniserve** system, the meeting planner makes all arrangements for both function space and food and beverage through one service contact, the convention service manager. In this system the banquet/catering department reports to convention services.

With a **duoserve** system, the food and beverage responsibilities are separated from the scheduling of function space. In this case, meeting planners must work with the banquet/catering department for their food and beverage requests and with the convention services department for their function room needs. When the duoserve approach is used, the banquet/catering personnel generally report to the food and beverage director. As we indicated earlier, most meeting planners want to deal with only one contact person at a hotel. The assistant director of convention services at the Sheraton Tucson El Conquistador makes a strong case for the uniserve system (see box titled "Should Hotel Catering and Convention Services Departments Be Combined?").

Beverage Service

More discontent has been voiced over beverage service and charges than over most factors of a convention. Of all the price policies at a convention, the liquor arrangement brings the loudest and most frequent outcry.

Should Hotel Catering and Convention Services Departments Be Combined?

by Nora May, Assistant Director Convention Services, Sheraton Tucson El Conquistador

"UNISERVE" — the word used by the Sheraton Tucson El Conquistador to define a manager who specializes in catering AND convention services. When it was announced that our hotel would be switching to the Uniserve concept, there was a definite concern that arose in my mind on how a person could "do it all!" After all, in my experience as assistant catering director, catering alone took all of my time, including my personal family time, and now they want to add to my responsibilities? It seemed almost impossible.

Several years have passed since the Uniserve concept was put into action, and there is no doubt in my mind that this is THE BEST way to run the business. The positive aspects of this concept outweigh the negative aspects. As a matter of fact, I can't think of a negative aspect. These are the positives:

1. **Efficiency!** The meeting planner benefits from working with just one person. It simplifies the job. Plus it saves on communication time for the meeting planner and the Uniserve convention service manager. When working the split method, oftentimes I would get little notes on my desk from convention services that said something like, "Spoke with ABC Company on the phone. They want to add a continental breakfast to the meeting on Monday." It is incredible how much time it takes to find out exactly what this message means. Which meeting? There are three breakouts and a board meeting scheduled. How many people? First you go to the convention services person to obtain more details, and usually you have to call the client to confirm. Uniserve eliminates this type of time waste.
2. **Control!** As a sole person handling all of the group's conference requirements, one has a grasp of the whole picture. The Uniserve CSM is responsible for every detail of the conference.
3. **Rewarding!** Opportunities and challenges continuously arise prior to a group's conference and during the conference. There is no getting around the problem-solving issues that tend to keep our blood flowing in the hospitality industry. That is what makes our jobs so interesting, exciting, and sometimes exhausting. In Uniserve, when the group departs and the guests are grinning from ear-to-ear, sending compliments in every direction, and the meeting planner re-books for the following year on the condition that YOU are assigned to work their file... rewarding? You bet!
4. **Free Time!** It's the best part of Uniserve! Prior to Uniserve, I literally spent 90% of my time at work. Family life barely existed. And although this type of job can be addicting, everyone has a right to a personal life. Uniserve permits a personal life. I say this with caution, as this is dependent on a number of things:

A. Adequate staffing is necessary in the Uniserve department. The Sheraton El Conquistador convention services department consists of four Uniserve people who handle the convention groups, one local catering manager, and a one-stop-shop manager who blocks, contracts, and caters to groups of 20 sleeping rooms and under. Of course, staffing varies from hotel to hotel and is dependent on the type of market the hotel pulls.
B. The convention files must be assigned strategically between managers to allow adequate days for paperwork between groups and allowing for *days off.*
C. The banquet manager, banquet captains, and conference floor manager *must* be trained to handle problem-solving situations effectively and with confidence. The same captain should handle as many of the group's meal functions as possible so that the meeting planner can feel comfortable with familiar faces.
D. A daily meeting with the hotel staff to include the chef, banquet manager, conference floor manager, and Uniserve CSMs is a MUST! The purpose of the daily meeting is to cover all functions in the hotel for the upcoming three days.

I cannot claim that the Uniserve system will work for all hotels. However, I believe there are many hotels that could use this system and it would relieve many of those catering and convention service managers who are "burned out."

Unfortunately, meeting planners or the hosts at hospitality suites usually specify their favorite brands of liquor, and they are familiar with package store prices. Many planners and hosts resent what they consider to be unfair markups on name-brand liquor by the hotel. Some hotels have taken to charging the same prices as local liquor stores, but most have a much higher rate — two, three, or even four times the cost. This is a management decision. The additional revenue gained by marking up must be weighed against the frequent ill will engendered.

Types of Setups

A number of beverage arrangements are used in catering to private parties. We will discuss the four most common procedures specified by meeting planners:

The **host bar**, also called an *open bar* or *sponsored bar*, is used most frequently by corporate meeting planners. At a host bar, guests drink freely of the beverages offered and the host pays the bill at the end of the function (average consumption at a hosted bar is two to three drinks per person for a one-hour open bar). This type of bar is stocked to prepare for all types of drinks and is staffed by a bartender. A purchase amount is almost always guaranteed. If, for example, at least $300 worth of beverage is not consumed, the host will pay for what was consumed, plus an additional amount to cover labor. Exhibit 8 shows typical labor costs for beverage service.

The **cash bar**, also called a *C.O.D. bar* or *no-host bar*, is the second most common arrangement. At a cash bar, each person pays for his or her own drinks. A minimum guarantee is also specified by the hotel in this case. Beverage consumption at a cash bar is usually lower than when the bar is hosted; during a one-hour cash bar, the consumption is about 1½ to two drinks per person.

Coupon sales are used at many private parties. Delegates buy tickets or coupons ahead of time and give them to the bartender when the drinks are served. The coupons may be sold by the hotel management or the host organization. Coupon sales eliminate the use of cash and the need for a cashier at the function.

Exhibit 8   Typical Labor Costs for Beverage Service

Beverage Labor and Miscellaneous Charges

A. Bartender Charge —
If less than $300 sales, labor charge
....$125.00

B. Bar Supplies — If group supplies liquor
Cocktail Napkins
Stir Sticks $1.00/person
Assorted Bar Fruit
Mix—Sodas $2.50/quart
Bloody Mary Mix, Orange Juice,
and Sweet and Sour........$8.00/quart
Blenders.......................$10.00/each

C. Extra Bartender Charge $20.00/hour
4-hour minimum

D. Extra Barback Charge $96.00/8 hrs
8-hour minimum

In addition to the charges listed above, it is common for properties to apply a flat service charge to functions under a certain size (typically 25 people or less). In some cases, labor and charges are waived entirely or based on the total dollar amount spent on the function. Sometimes, bartender fees are waived altogether (many meeting planners insist that they not pay bartender fees for the staffing of large hosted bars). Any specifics negotiated should be clearly spelled out in the contract.

Stanley Stearman, executive vice-president of the National Society of Public Accountants, said of the use of coupons for beverage functions:

> We give everyone two drink tickets along with their banquet ticket. They are actually perforated stubs which are turned in to the bartender in return for drinks. Not only does this method limit consumption to two drinks per person, but it gives me control over my liquor costs. I pay a certain amount for each stub that has been turned in. The only disadvantage to me is that I have to pay full price even if someone redeems his stub for a soft drink.[12]

The South Coast Plaza in Costa Mesa, California, uses still a different method in servicing private parties. The **captain's bar** is a self-service or make-your-own-drink bar that has been stocked with full bottles of liquor and mixes needed to make all the basic bar drinks. This bar is always hosted. The meeting planner and the convention service manager inventory the bar before and after the party, and the group is charged for how much is consumed. There is no guarantee on this type of setup because there is no bartender labor cost.

Hospitality Suites

Hospitality suites are beverage or food and beverage functions held by the sponsoring organization or by other groups (such as exhibitors at an organization's trade show). They are usually held in a suite on a sleeping room floor, which means that hospitality suites are typically sold by the catering department but serviced by room service. Larger functions, such as those offering entertainment, are held in public function rooms (in this case, they would be both sold and serviced by the catering department).

While hospitality suites have traditionally been evening hospitality functions, there has been a trend for hosting breakfast or luncheon events as well. These hospitality suites are **auxiliary business**, commonly referred to as in-conjunction-with (ICW) business, for hotels. This means that even if the ICW business is not necessarily booked directly by the meeting sponsor, it should be considered part of the group's meeting history, as it increases the value of the meeting to the hotel.

Some meeting planners and exhibitors wish to avoid what they consider to be excessive prices charged by the hotel by bringing in liquor purchased outside the hotel. They then order mixers, ice, and glasses from room service. Hotels have varying policies regarding such action. Some hotels have a **corkage** charge to cover the use of liquor that is purchased elsewhere.

Katie Kannapell, the banquet manager of Cipiriani 42nd Street in New York City, tells of a recent corporate event in which the champagne provided by the sponsor was $20 pricier than Cipriani's in-house stock due to the corkage charge. She says:

> Corkage is complicated. People often think corkage is cheaper, but you [the meeting planner] have to ask what is included and then compare it to what the venue serves. Very often you are not saving anything.[13]

Union regulations often dictate the circumstances under which a bartender must be employed. Tell your client in advance about such regulations. Explain the hours involved, overtime charges, and other pertinent details. Spell out the circumstances under which no such help is required. Include information about gratuities and taxes.

Brands

Most hotels offer a varied selection of liquor brands to the meeting planner. Brands are commonly offered in three categories: house (well) brands, call brands, and premium brands. **House brands** are the least-expensive liquors and wines, and will be used for the function unless the meeting planner requests otherwise. Actual brands of liquor offered may vary from venue to venue, so be sure to inform meeting planners of the brands your hotel uses to avoid any confusion.

Call brands are brands specifically asked for by name, such as when a meeting planner requests Jim Beam Bourbon or Beefeater's Gin. These brands are generally priced in the mid-range and must be requested as replacements for house brands.

Premium brands are quality, expensive liquors, such as Crown Royal, Chivas Regal, or Tanqueray Gin. When a planner selects a top-of-the-line drink menu, a guest at the function will not have to settle for the one brand offered on the standard drink menu. He or she will likely be able to choose from two or three brands of quality liquor.

Be sure that the meeting planner understands these categories, his or her options (using house wines but call brands, for example), and associated charges so that he or she can make an informed decision. This will avoid complaints over liquor charges.

Pricing Methods

Meeting planners often ask for advice on how much liquor will be needed. The consumption of liquor varies, of course, with the makeup of the attendees. A chart such as the one shown in Exhibit 9 should prove helpful to you and your customers in making such decisions.

Liquor charges can be figured *by the person, by the bottle,* or *by the individual drink.* Whichever is used, make sure that someone on the convention staff has been designated to tally up after the affair with a designated member of the hotel staff. This will help avoid misunderstandings after the event and avoid last-minute searching for someone of authority on the convention management staff to corroborate the tally.

By the Person. When liquor is priced **by the person**, a flat rate is charged for each person present during a specified period of time. This type of pricing is also referred to as the *per person/unlimited consumption plan.* Sometimes a flat rate is charged for a cocktail party of a specified time period and additional time is charged on an hourly basis. At other times, the rate is given only as an hourly charge. If food is to be served, what kind and how much must be discussed and listed in the agreement.

From the meeting planner's perspective, this flat rate per person can be the simplest, but not necessarily the cheapest, pricing method. Unless the group has a lot of drinkers, this is usually an expensive plan.

You will need a way to determine the number in attendance. Collecting tickets or invitations at the door is one way to do this.

Extension of the time period and the admission of people who do not have tickets require approval by an authorized person. The head count and the time period should be acknowledged immediately after the event by having the authorized person initial the tally.

Exhibit 9   Guide to Help Estimate the Amount of Liquor Needed for a Beverage Function

Reception Drink Estimator

Based on an all-male attendance and easy access to bars. With 50% female attendance, average is 2 1/2 to 3 per hour, with 100% female attendance, average is 2 to 2 1/2 per hour.

Number of Guests	1/2 hr	3/4 hr	One hr	1 1/4 hrs	1 1/2 hrs	1 3/4 hrs	Two hrs
25-55	2	3	3 3/4	4	4 1/4	4 1/2	4 3/4
60-104	2	3	3 3/4	4	4	4 1/2	4 3/4
105-225	1 3/4	2 1/2	3	3 1/2	4	4	4 1/2
230-300	1 1/2	2	2 1/2	2 3/4	3	3 1/4	3 1/2
315 & up	1 1/2	2	2 1/2	2 3/4	3	3 1/4	3 1/2

Drink Estimator

Bottle size	Drink size	Number of drinks
Liquor		
4/5 quart	1 oz.	25
4/5 quart	1 1/4 oz.	20
4/5 quart	1 1/2 oz.	17
Quart	1 oz.	31
Quart	1 1/4 oz.	25
Quart	1 1/2 oz.	21
Wine		
750 ml	5 oz.	5
Liter	5 oz.	6.7
Magnum	5 oz.	10.2

While guides such as the one above can be helpful in determining how much liquor will be needed for an event, several other variables should also be considered. Alcohol consumption is usually less if the event is on the evening of a major arrival day, the event is before 5:00 p.m. or after 8:00 p.m., hors d'oeuvres are served, or if there are other activities available in the function area. Consumption typically increases if the event is on the final night of the meeting, is held between 6:00–7:30 p.m., only dry (salted) snacks are served, or if the event is held during a major sporting event and a large video screen is in use.
Source: Reprinted with permission from *The Schenley Guide to Professional Hosting*. Published by Schenley Affiliated Brands Corp.

By the Bottle. The convention organizer may prefer to pay **by the bottle** consumed. Liquor by the bottle can be cost-effective for large groups. If you are charging $6 per drink and serving one-ounce drinks from a fifth, the meeting group pays $150 for the bottle (25 drinks per fifth). A by-the-bottle charge would reduce this cost to $80 to $100 per bottle.

The by-the-bottle system is very popular for hospitality suites, both with and without bartenders. This system calls for charges on all bottles opened regardless of how much of the contents is consumed. Some hotels permit the host to keep the opened bottles; others do not. Some hotels agree to store opened bottles of liquor from one reception and use them for the group's next reception. Obviously, the bartender must be made aware of the arrangement, and it must be made part of the work order for the beverage event.

Sometimes the charges for the bartender are part of the per-bottle price. If so, this should be indicated in the work order or agreement; if not, list the rates and hours.

Make sure that the liquor supply given is stored securely. Good hotel people assist their guests in arranging storage. It is imperative that both the hotel and the convention organization have people designated to tally and record the number of bottles used and returned for credit. Meeting planners will want to ensure that they have a good inventory system in place to ensure proper billing. This means taking an inventory of the bars both before and after a function (this should always be done in the company of a hotel banquet person, who verifies the planner's totals). The inventory should not only include bottles of liquor, but also mixers, soft drinks, and bottled water (as well as any other items for which the group is being charged). Soft drinks are usually charged at about $3 each, so it is becoming more prevalent for these items to be inventoried.

When buying liquor by the bottle, meeting planners often request the banquet bars be closed in staggered order, moving the partials from one to the other (this is termed *marrying* the bars). Their instructions also frequently call for the bartenders to pour measured drinks, as bartenders could pad the bill by overpouring.

Food may be served, but is charged separately. And, under certain conditions, there may be a room charge. Much depends on the anticipated volume and the basic agreement under which the event takes place.

By the Drink. Charges can also be made **by the drink**, based on the number of individual drinks served. This type of function always includes the mandatory use of bartender service (no less than one bartender for every 75 guests is the rule of thumb). There should be an agreement on the size of the drink to be poured, and the bartenders so instructed. Meeting planners often specify that portion control measuring pourers (called Posi-Pours) be used.

This arrangement is used by many meeting planners, especially those planning for small groups. Most meeting planners feel the most economical bar for receptions of under 100 persons is by the drink; for over 100 persons, by the bottle.

The guests may pay for drinks in cash or prepaid coupons, or the host may pay for it all. Food charges are a separate item, and there may be a room charge. Give the meeting planner advance notice of gratuities, taxes, and a schedule of bartenders' work regulations.

Beverage Control

Rigid procedures for issuing liquor and the use of it should be maintained. The banquet department is generally responsible for issuing the liquor. Since it is impossible to judge how much or what kind of liquor will be preferred, it is customary to stock 25 percent over what the group is estimated to consume. This policy eliminates shortages, but it must be controlled.

The excess must be returned to the storeroom at the end of the function. Special banquet requisition forms are used for private parties, showing all the bottles issued, consumed, and returned. Immediately after each function, all bottles — full, empty and partially used — should be accounted for.

The Renaissance Hotel uses the requisition form shown in Exhibit 10. The banquet manager uses this form for each function, showing the number of bottles originally issued, any additional issues, and all returns. Each bottle issued is marked with a distinctive means of identification. At the end of the party, the banquet manager totals the requisition by determining the amount of each item consumed and its price, and then making the appropriate extensions. The total is transferred to the banquet guest check, which is verified and signed by the meeting planner. A percentage of the check total is usually added to the bill as a gratuity for the staff.

Exhibit 10　Bar Requisition Form

RENAISSANCE HOTEL

BANQUET WINE/LIQUOR REQUISITION

NO. 001399

DATE: 8-25-
DAY OF WEEK: MONDAY
TIME: 6:00 PM

FUNCTION: RECEPTION
ROOM: Foyer / Renaissance Ballroom

ORGANIZATION NAME: SINGER
BANQUET CHECK #: 06272

BANQUET EVENT ORDER #: 02135
TENDERS IN CHARGE: Bill / Cheryle

CLIENT'S ACCOUNT #: 12948

NUMBER OF GUESTS: 275

MANNER OF SALE:　☒ BY DRINK　☐ BY BOTTLE　☐ BY HOUR

TYPE OF BEVERAGE:　☐ PREMIUM　☒ HOUSE　☐ SPECIAL LIST

TYPE OF SALE:　☒ HOSTED　☐ CASH BAR

CODE	DESCRIPTION	ISSUED QUANT.	ISSUED SIZE	RETD. BOTT.	USED BOTT.	NO. DRINKS	DRINK PRICE	TOTAL	LIQUOR	WINE	MISC.	% POT.
	HOUSE BOURBON	3		1.7	1.3	43	3.00	$129.00	8.35			65%
	HOUSE SCOTCH	3		1.9	11							
	HOUSE GIN	4		2.4	1.6							
	HOUSE VODKA	4		1.1	29							
	HOUSE BRANDY	2		1.8	2							
	HOUSE RUM	2		1.6	.4							
	HOUSE TEQUILA	2		1.3	.7							
	HOUSE WHISKEY	2		1.8	.2							
	HOUSE WHITE WINE	18		2	16							
	HOUSE RED WINE	6		3	3							
	MILLER LITE BEER	24		5	19							
	HEINEKEN BEER											
	PREMIUM BOURBON											
	PREMIUM SCOTCH											
	PREMIUM GIN											
	PREMIUM VODKA											
	PREMIUM BRANDY											
	PREMIUM WHISKEY											
	PREMIUM TEQUILA											
	PREMIUM RUM											
TOTALS												

(COST: LIQUOR / WINE / MISC.)

ISSUED BY: _____　RETURNED BY: _____　APPROVED BY: _____

RECEIVED BY: _____　RECEIVED BY: _____

WHITE - FOOD AND BEVERAGE CONTROL　　CANARY - BANQUET MAITRE D'　　GOLDEN ROD - BEVERAGE MGR.

This form details the number of bottles issued, consumed, and returned. The form also specifies the pricing method to be used (by drink, by bottle, by hour), the type of brand (premium, house, special list), and the type of setup (hosted, cash bar).

Automated Bars. Several hotels are making use of automated bar systems. A long-standing complaint of meeting planners is the tendency of bartenders to over-pour in host bar setups (pouring drinks without the use of shot glasses or other measuring devices is called **free pour**). They feel the staff members are encouraged to pour on the heavy side because their tips are figured as a percentage of sales. Another problem area is the counting and storing of open bottles. Both of these problems are eliminated with automated bar setups.

Automated bars operate much like soft drink bars, with individual push buttons for each liquor item — vodka, gin, bourbon, scotch, rye, etc. Quart bottles are placed upside down in the wells and dispensed by a vacuum system. Each bottle has its own dispensing unit and meter. The size of the drink is determined by the meeting planner, and the dispensing unit is set accordingly (this method of dispensing exact amounts of liquor per drink is known as **electronic pour**). The meters are checked and recorded before and after the party, with the difference being the amount consumed.

The control feature offered by the metered bars is what makes them attractive to both the meeting planner and the hotel. They provide a consistent drink and eliminate overpouring, but they are not without their limitations. The machine dispenses only the alcohol; mixed and blended drinks still must be prepared by a bartender. And only eight bottles can be filled on most units, limiting the choice of drinks. Some observers also say that metered bars are impersonal, lending a mechanical atmosphere to cocktail parties.

The Peabody Hotel in Memphis uses a RFID tracker system to monitor its bar and banquet operations. RFID, which is short for "radio frequency identification," is a technology similar in theory to bar code identification. RFID-enabled liquor pour spouts provide a clear picture of how each drink is prepared, identifying over-pouring, missing drinks, and unaccounted pours — all of which translate into reduced liquor costs.

Liquor Liability. Can a hotel be held liable to an innocent third party for wrongful acts of an intoxicated attendee? The answer depends on the individual state, but due to alcohol-related automobile accidents, many states have passed **dram shop laws** imposing liability on the dispenser of alcohol sold illegally, terming a sale is illegal if to a minor, intoxicated person, or known alcoholic. Management must take reasonable care in serving alcoholic beverages at functions. Managers should be trained to be alert to potential problems with intoxicated patrons and how to deal with unruly meeting attendees. A typical contract clause might read:

> *If alcoholic beverages are to be served on the Hotel premises (or elsewhere under the Hotel's alcoholic beverage license) the Hotel will require that beverages be dispensed only by Hotel servers and bartenders. The Hotel's license requires the Hotel to (1) request identification (Photo ID) of any person of questionable age and refuse service if the person is either under age or proper identification cannot be produced, and (2) refuse alcoholic beverage service to any person who, in the Hotel's judgment, appears intoxicated.*

Some provisions are stricter, prohibiting attendees from bringing alcoholic beverages into the hotel from outside:

> *Alcoholic beverages may not be brought into the hotel from outside sources. The sales, service, and consumption of alcoholic beverages are regulated by the State Alcoholic Beverage Commission. The Hotel, as a licensee, is subject to the regulations promulgated by the Commission, violations of which may jeopardize the Hotel's license. Consequently, it*

is the Hotel's policy that alcoholic beverages may not be brought into the hotel from outside sources.

Staffing and Logistics. A typical rule of thumb is to staff one bartender per 75 to 100 people. You will also need to staff one bar back for every three bartenders (bar backs are responsible for replenishing stocks of liquor, ice, glassware, and garnishes used during the function). When food is served at receptions, staff one server per 50 people, and one waiter per 100 people for receptions without food service.

Bar locations will vary according to the room's dimensions and the placement of other provisions such as staging, dance floors, and buffet tables. Generally, one bar station is required for every 75–100 guests. Avoid grouping bars too close together. With large receptions requiring several beverage stations, open those bars farthest from the entrance first in order to bring people into the room. This helps to spread the crowds. The chart below summarizes staffing requirements for receptions based on attendance.

Reception Service Estimator

Number of Guests	Number of bartenders	Number of waiters with food	Number of waiters without food
25-100	1	2	1
105-205	2	3	2
215-325	3	3	2
350-475	4	4	3

Beverage Labor Charges. In addition to charges for the liquor and other drinks served at beverage functions, hotels also assess labor and miscellaneous fees for events. Generally, clients must hire a minimum number of bartenders for a minimum number of hours (typically for shifts of four hours). Some bartender fees, for example, are based on a sliding scale, such as $125 for the first hour, $75 for the second hour, and $50 for each hour thereafter. If bartenders are hired for a four-hour shift and the function extends beyond four hours, additional overtime charges may be assessed. In addition to bartenders, beverage functions require bar backs. Some hotels include the salaries for these employees in the bartender charge, except in cases where additional bar backs are required.

Some beverage functions may also require cashiers. Many hotels do not allow clients to schedule cash bars unless at least one cashier is employed. Having a cashier eliminates the need for the bartender to handle cash, which slows down beverage production and service and can create security problems. Cashiers can be eliminated if the client sells drink tickets that guests can redeem for beverages.

Planners may also wish to employ cocktail servers, although servers can cost almost as much as bartenders. Therefore, most meeting planners eliminate the need for servers by having two or three portable bars set up in the room and having guests give their orders directly to the bartenders. If the client wishes to have cocktail servers, however, they can be used to best advantage by circulating the room with trays of poured wine or champagne. This eliminates the need for wine drinkers to slow down the flow at bar stations.

Other charges incurred at beverage functions are the costs for supplies and mixers, which are not considered part of a liquor order. It is important that all charges, whether they be for labor or supplies, be clearly spelled out in the contract in order to avoid any misunderstandings.

Post-Function Actions

Prompt action must be taken at the end of each food function to eliminate possible billing difficulties and to bring each function segment to a satisfactory close.

If billing is based on attendance, the captain in charge should tally the number of persons served or the number of tickets collected and have the authorized convention person sign an acknowledgment of the total. Make sure the person signing is designated in writing.

If beverages were served, tally the unopened bottles of liquor and/or soft drinks and have the amount acknowledged by signature. Bottles to be returned for credit must be signed for.

Most convention groups use a master billing account for the food functions. If the terms are cash, the money or check should be presented when the tally is certified as correct. If cash is collected by the organization, the hotel should provide a safe place for it or accept it in payment and give a suitable receipt. Place a summary of the food functions in the file folder for the analysis of the convention.

In-House Coordination: Large vs. Small Properties

We have referred to the convention service manager as the person who coordinates the convention. This person, however, does not do it all; many departments are involved. The competence of the department heads determines the extent to which the convention service manager becomes involved. If the reservations, front-desk, and catering managers are on top of their jobs, the convention service manager's headaches are minimized. If not, the convention service manager must spend more time overseeing the operation.

Role of the Catering Manager

The in-house coordination at small properties is generally not handled the same way as at larger properties; the major difference is the role played by the *catering manager*. At larger properties, catering managers are only in charge of food and beverage; seldom do they become involved in sales and seldom are they required to account for more than the food and beverage service. But at small properties, their areas of responsibility branch out.

A property with insufficient sales volume to justify carrying a convention coordinator must nevertheless give one person that responsibility. Usually, it is the banquet or catering manager who wears two hats: head of his or her department and head of group business.

What distinguishes a large property from a small one? There is no definition, but hotels with fewer than 250 guestrooms might well handle servicing differently than larger ones.

Exhibit 11 gives a catering manager's job description adapted from the operating manual of Doubletree Hotels, whose hotels range from 140 to 300 guestrooms and are typical of such properties whose catering managers double as convention service managers.

Servicing and Selling

The division between servicing and selling is less pronounced at small hotels than at large ones. There is wide variation among hotels in the extent to which the sales department participates in servicing.

Exhibit 11   Job Description of a Catering Manager

Catering Manager's Job Description

1. **Basic Function**
   To service all phases of group meeting/banquet functions; coordinate these activities on a daily basis; assist clients in program planning and menu selection; solicit local group catering business.

2. **General Responsibility**
   To maintain the services and reputation of Doubletree and act as management representative to group clients.

3. **Specific Responsibilities**

   a. To maintain function book. Coordinate the booking of all meeting space with the Sales Department.
   b. To solicit local food and beverage functions.
   c. To coordinate with all group meeting/banquet planners their specific group requirements with the services and facilities offered.
   d. To confirm all details relative to group functions with meeting/banquet planners.
   e. To distribute to the necessary inter-hotel departments detailed information relative to group activities.
   f. To supervise and coordinate all phases of catering, hiring, and training programs.
   g. To supervise and coordinate daily operation of meeting/banquet setups and service.
   h. To assist in menu planning, preparation, and pricing.
   i. To assist in referrals to the Sales Department and in booking group activities.
   j. To set up and maintain catering files.
   k. To be responsive to group requests/needs while in the hotel.
   l. To work toward achieving Annual Plan figures relating to the Catering Department (revenues, labor percentages, average checks, covers, etc.).
   m. To handle all scheduling and coverage for the servicing of catering functions.

4. **Organizational Relationship and Authority**
   Is directly responsible and accountable to the Food and Beverage Manager. Responsible for coordination with kitchen, catering service personnel and accounting.

As seen by these duties detailed by Doubletree Hotels, the catering manager often serves as the convention service manager at small properties.
Source: Courtesy of Doubletree Hotels.

At small hotels, servicing and sales, particularly of food and beverage functions, are more likely to be handled by the same person. Part of the catering manager's job might be to actively solicit and schedule group banquet business. Often, the catering manager is given charge of the function book. This is fine as long as the lines of authority, responsibility, and communication are clearly understood.

Problems arise when the left hand does not know what the right hand is doing; for example, when the sales department books a convention that conflicts with the catering department's efforts. The problem is likely to be acute when the two departments are located in different areas of the hotel. In this case, the sales department rarely sees the function book and must rely on the phone or memos to communicate with the catering department. There may even be inter-departmental rivalry for function space, with each trying to show greater sales and profit. This communication problem is eliminated at properties using computerized function books.

Communication and Cooperation

Servicing requires clear communication channels at all properties. When the property has a convention service manager (which is typical at large properties), there is generally good cooperation, with one independent person coordinating the efforts of other departments. But when the catering manager serves as the coordinator (which is typical at small properties), there seems to be more autonomy of departments. The catering manager may be unfamiliar with the problems in the front of the house; reservation and front office departments lack understanding of the handling of food and beverage.

Such a situation is not necessarily detrimental, as long as each department does its job and there is good inter-departmental communication. The difficulty may arise when the association executive questions the hotel's handling of his or her membership's registration.

 PUTTING IT ALL TOGETHER

Your property has been approached by the corporate office of a large multi-level marketing company that wishes to hold a convention for approximately 600 distributors and spouses. While funds are unlimited, the meeting planner is totally inexperienced and will need your help to plan a successful function.

At this time, plans are sketchy. The meeting planner does want to incorporate the company's "Pot of Gold" promotion into an Awards Banquet and stage a luau to celebrate the vacations won by the company's top five distributors. The meeting planner is open to your suggestions regarding creative menus for these two functions, but wants to serve traditional American fare for the buffets and other meal functions.

The convention will run from Wednesday afternoon through Sunday afternoon. Events currently being considered are:

Wednesday	(Afternoon)	**Registration**
	(Evening)	Registration and **Hospitality Suite**
		Dinner on own
Thursday	(Morning)	**Three seminars** (Approx. 100 people each room)
		Refreshment Break
	(Afternoon)	**Three seminars** (Approx.100 people each room)
		Refreshment Break
	(Evening)	**Buffet Dinner** (Approx. 500 attendees)
Friday	(Morning)	Same as Thursday
	(Afternoon)	**Buffet lunch** (Approx. 500 attendees)
	(Afternoon)	Same as Thursday
	(Evening)	**Directors Dinner** (24 in attendance)
		Other attendees: optional dinner show (on own)
Saturday	(Morning)	**President's Breakfast** (approx. 300 attendees)
		General Session (600 attendees)
		Lunch on own
	(Afternoon)	**Continuation of General Session**
	(Evening)	**Awards Banquet**, **Entertainment** (music and dancing)
		(600 attendees)
Sunday	(Morning)	Breakfast on own
	(Afternoon)	**Farewell Luau** (Approx. 350 attendees)

Develop a presentation that you will use in your pre-convention planning session with the meeting planner. Cover the following areas:

1. A proposal detailing what food and beverages could be offered at the food functions (hospitality suite, refreshment breaks, buffet lunch and dinner, the directors dinner, president's breakfast, the awards banquet and luau). Include how the client could be charged for each function.
2. An outline of what your property can offer in the way of decorations, staffing, and meeting requirements (musicians, additional entertainment, staging, lighting, etc.) for the awards banquet and the luau. Provide room set-up plans detailing suggested seating, food service, and entertainment area options.
3. A sample room set-up for the seminars and the general session. Include the style of seating, a list of available audiovisual equipment, and staffing (set-up, registration personnel, etc.) that your property can provide.

If the catering manager is the planner's contact in the hotel, the planner may find little relief for the problem. Perhaps the catering manager is too busy with the upcoming dinner or has not been schooled in the procedures for registering guests. Or perhaps — and this is a more common problem — the catering manager doesn't have the authority to go to the rooms department to straighten out the situation. The meeting planner's nightmare is a contact without the muscle to get the job done.

The autonomy of departments also leads to the lack of resumes (specification sheets), which are the backbone of control and communication in servicing. Substituting for the resumes (specification sheets) are memos from the sales department to the rooms department and individual function sheets prepared by the catering manager for all meeting room and food and beverage setups. Memos and function sheets are fine ways of communicating, but a comprehensive schedule of the overall convention program is still needed.

Beverage stations should be set up toward the rear of the function room to draw people into the room. The most popular beverage pricing plans are by the person, by the bottle, and by the drink.
Source: Photograph courtesy of Dolce Hotels and Resorts.

Summary

Food and beverage functions are an integral part of most meetings. Both association and corporate meeting planners rate the quality of food and beverage service as "very important" in their selection of meeting facilities. Food and beverage functions are second only to guestrooms in generating revenue at most convention hotels. So, while hotel sales and service people are generally primarily concerned with filling guestrooms, it is imperative that convention sales and service managers also be knowledgeable in the food and beverage area.

Endnotes

1. Carol Bialkowski, "Emerging Trends: A Conversation with Top Hyatt F&B Executives," *Unconventional Cuisine*, © 2002, Hyatt Hotels Corporation, p. 6.

2. Ibid, p. 2.

3. Ibid.

4. *Meetings & Conventions.*

5. Carol Bialkowski, "Infusing Your Meeting With Local Flavor," *Unconventional Cuisine*, © 2002, Hyatt Hotels Corporation, p. 24.

6. Carol Bialkowski, "What's on the Menu? Staying Ahead of Attendees' Food Issues," *pcma convene*, April 2004, p. 30.

7. Ibid, p. 32.

8. Bruce Myint, "Hotels Scramble to Cut Carbs," *Meetings & Conventions*, May 2004, p. 42.

9. Ruth Hill, "Association Meetings," *Meetings West*, August 2004, p. 1.

10. Jeanne O'Brien, "Sheraton Reveals New Food & Beverage Program," *Meeting News*.

11. Toni Giovanetti, "A La Carte Catering Emerges as the Favored Choice of Meeting Planners," *Hotel Business*, August 7–20, pp. 25–27.

12. Bob Skalnik, "Liquor Control," *Association and Society Manager*, ©Barrington Publications.

13. Cheryl-Anne Sturken, "Bar Codes: Understanding How Liquor Tabs Are Tallied," *Meetings & Conventions*, February 2004, p. 19.

 ## Key Terms

a la carte catering—Catered events at which guests may choose from a number of different menu items.

action station—At action stations, chefs prepare foods to order and serve them to guests. Popular items for action stations include omelets, crepes, pasta, grilled meat or shrimp, carved meats, sushi, Caesar salad, and flaming desserts. Also called performance stations or exhibition cooking.

American/plated service—Food is arranged on plates in the kitchen and brought to the guests.

auxiliary business—Affiliate and sub-group business that is brought to the hotel because of the meeting or event. Also called in-conjunction-with (ICW) business.

banquet captain—Person in charge of banquet service at food functions; supervisor of the servers. For small functions, the banquet captain also serves as maitre d'; for larger functions, he or she may be responsible for a specific area of the dining room.

buffet service—A presentation of several food items from which the guests choose and serve themselves. Variations include attended buffets, at which chefs serve attendees, and plated buffets, at which a selection of pre-plated foods is set on a table from which attendees choose.

butler service—At receptions, servers offer a variety of hors d'oeuvres on platters to guests. At dinners, food is presented by butlers on silver trays.

by the bottle—A charge for liquor based on full bottles served.

by the drink—A charge for liquor based on the number of drinks served.

by the person—A fixed price for liquor per attendee. This charge may cover all consumption of food and beverage (this is sometimes referred to as the per person/unlimited consumption plan). In some cases, beverages are charged per the person and food is ordered separately by the piece.

call brand—Brand name liquor, distinguished from "house brand," selected by customer according to personal preference. Usually of higher quality than house brands.

canape—Hot or cold appetizer with a bread or cracker base.

captain's bar—Self-service bar at which guests make their own drinks. This type of bar is always hosted.

cash bar—Guests pay for their own drinks. Also called a no-host bar or C.O.D. bar.

chef's tasting—The opportunity to sample a menu in advance of the event, usually in the company of the chef.

corkage—Charge that is placed on beer, wine, and liquor purchased elsewhere and brought into the facility.

coupon sales—Attendees at a function purchase tickets for drinks from the hotel or from the host organization.

covers—The number of meals served at a meal function.

dram shop laws—Laws covering the liability of people serving alcoholic beverages. Under dram shop laws, a party injured by an intoxicated person can sue the establishment that contributed to that person's intoxication.

duoserve—A meeting service system in which food and beverage responsibilities are handled by catering while other aspects of servicing the group are handled by the convention service manager. Because responsibilities are separated, meeting planners have two hotel contacts.

electronic pour—System of dispensing pre-determined exact amounts of liquor or non-alcoholic beverages per drink.

energy break—Refreshment break at which nutritious food and beverages are served. These breaks also may include some form of exercise.

English/family style service—Food is brought to the table and guests serve themselves. In some cases, the host cuts the meat and passes the tray to guests; the host may also have the meat cut by a server away from the table before it is placed before guests.

finger food—Food, typically served at a reception, that does not require the use of a knife, fork, or spoon.

free pour—Alcoholic drinks poured without the use of shot glasses or other measuring devices.

French service—Food service in which items are prepared tableside from a cart or gueridon. This type of service is best suited to small groups.

gala dinner—An evening event at which a multi-course, seated dinner is accompanied by entertainment, such as dancing, speeches, or the presentation of awards. Standard dress is black-tie.

guarantee—The minimum number of meals to be paid for by the client, even if some are not consumed. Usually, the hotel requires the planner to set this number no less than 48 hours prior to the event.

head count—The actual number of people attending a food function.

hors d'oeuvres—Small appetizers; hot and/or cold finger foods served at a reception.

hospitality suite—Guestroom or suite used for receptions and entertainment. Usually stocked with beverages and light food. Often used by exhibitors at trade shows to entertain and sell delegates on their firms' products.

host bar—Beverage plan for banquets or other functions in which the guests do not pay for drinks; the host is charged either by the drink or by the bottle. Also called an open bar or a sponsored bar.

house brand—Brand of wine or distilled spirits selected by a hotel or restaurant as their standard when no specific brand is specified. Also called a well brand.

off-premises catering—The transportation of food, either fully prepared or in various stages of preparation, from a hotel's kitchen to a site away from the hotel.

on-premises catering—Servicing food and/or beverage functions in meeting rooms, function rooms, and sleeping rooms within the hotel. Some on-premises events may extend to the hotel or restaurant grounds, but food and/or beverage is still served within the confines of the establishment.

organic foods—Food products that are free of pesticides, commercial fertilizers, or other chemicals.

overset safety margin—Number of covers set over the guarantee. Billed to the client only if actually consumed.

premium brand—High-quality, high-priced hard liquor (spirits). The best and most expensive brands.

pre-set service—Placement of some foods on banquet tables prior to the seating of the guests.

reception—Stand-up social function, sometimes preceding a meal, at which beverages and light foods are served. Foods may be presented on small buffet tables or passed by servers.

refreshment break—Short breaks between meeting sessions. Usually offering beverages and/or light food items, some are planned around a theme. See also **energy break.**

Russian service—Food is fully prepared in the kitchen and all courses are served on platters (or from tureens) to guests at their tables. A plate is placed in front of each diner and a server places food from the tray or platter on each plate.

special events—Unique activities or functions staged one time, usually for the purpose of entertaining event attendees. See also themed event.

themed event—A function with a creative theme to make it more memorable. Themed events utilize elements that appeal to all five senses, incorporating sights (decorations and costumes), sounds, tastes (special food and beverages), touch, and smells to create a unique experience for attendees.

ticket exchange—Banquet control procedure whereby guests exchange an event coupon from their registration packet for an actual event ticket and seat assignment. This procedure increases control and tends to reduce the number of "no shows" to provide more accurate guarantees.

uniserve—A meeting service system in which the meeting planner makes arrangements for both function space and food and beverage events through one service contact, the convention service manager.

 Review Questions

1. Explain why the profit margin for banquets is considerably higher than that of hotel restaurants.

2. Name several types of food and beverage functions commonly requested by meeting planners. Why is it necessary to have a separate function sheet for each?

3. What trends have affected the types of food served at functions? How have hotels responded to these trends?

4. What types of service are used for food functions? What factors determine the most effective type of service for a function?

5. Discuss the procedures used in establishing a guarantee for food functions. In what ways is attendance monitored to ensure the guarantee has been met?

6. What three different pricing methods are used to bill for liquor? How is control maintained for billing purposes?

7. Discuss the staffing and logistics common to beverage functions.

8. How does control of the food and beverage function differ between large and small properties? Distinguish between the role of catering manager and convention service manager.

Additional References

Alcohol and Meeting Planning, Meeting Professionals International www.mpiweb.org

Controlling Alcohol Risks Effectively (CARE). www.ei-alha-org/care.index.htm

Dining Room & Banquet Management, Third Edition, Anthony J. Strianese and Pamela P. Strianese, Thomson Delmar Learning, 2002.

The Meeting Planner's Legal Handbook, James M. Goldberg, MPI www.mpiweb.org

Meetings & Liability, John S. Foster, CHSE www.mpiweb.org

On-Premise Catering, Patti Shock and John Stefanelli, John Wiley & Sons, 2001.

Special Events Magazine, Penton Media, P.O. Box 2100, Skokie, Illinois 60076

Special Events: Event Leadership for a New World, Fourth Edition, Dr. Joe Goldblatt, John Wiley & Sons, 2005.

Internet Sites

For more information, visit the following Internet sites. Internet addresses can change without notice. If a site is no longer available at the address listed below, a search engine can be used to find the new address or additional, related sites.

The Catering Connection
www.caterconnect.com

Chef's Store
www.chefstore.com

Controlling Alcohol Risks Effectively
  (CARE)
www.ei-ahma.org/care.index.htm

Cuisine
www.cuisinenet.com

Food Net
www.foodnet.com

Internet Food Channel
www.foodchannel.com

National Association of Catering Executives (NACE)
www.nace.net

Training for Intervention Procedures by Servers of Alcohol (TIPS)
www.gettips.com

Virtual Vineyards
www.virtualvin.com

Chapter 15 Outline

Competencies

1. Summarize factors in the decision about which audiovisual requirements to service in-house and which to outsource. (pp. 501–504)

2. Describe types of audiovisual equipment and their uses. (pp. 505–525)

3. Identify issues related to providing audiovisual equipment and services, and explain the hotel's responsibilities in terms of signs and notices. (pp. 525–530)

Understanding Audiovisual Requirements

Lee Sterbens
Director of Sales, Creative Services Division
Greyhound Exposition Services

"In the field of communications and information exchange, equipment and the technology used to operate it are changing rapidly. More and more people are using computers interfaced with monitors and video projectors to exchange information, compared to a few years ago when slides and transparencies were the norm. While convention service managers are rarely expected to be expert audiovisual technicians, they should be able to assist meeting planners with the selection of appropriate space and proper audiovisual equipment. Having a basic understanding of what equipment is required to achieve the desired goal will allow you to better serve your meeting groups and yourself."

Audiovisual Requirements

I T IS A RARE MEETING TODAY that doesn't incorporate an audiovisual presentation somewhere in its program. The more sophisticated users of AV systems require little help from the hotel staff. They know precisely what equipment they need and what is required in the facility. They may bring their own equipment or contact an AV service company for support.

In the past, most meeting needs were fairly simple. Meeting planners typically requested a few microphones, a slide projector and screen, a few flip charts, and an occasional movie projector. Over the past two decades, however, technological developments in communication have led to audiovisual equipment and techniques that have greatly enhanced the meetings market. And today's sophisticated meeting planners want to take full advantage of these advanced capabilities (see Exhibit 1). It is not unusual for a meeting planner to request teleconferencing equipment, DVD players, personal computers, and even multivisual synthesizers, quadraphonic sound, and total immersion environments.

The meeting planner who is less knowledgeable about audiovisual systems will need support. Someone on the hotel staff should at least be familiar with, if not expert at, AV systems to provide such service or to help the planner get it locally. It is not realistic to expect convention sales and service personnel to be expert in every facet of the convention business, but all, especially the convention service manager, should keep abreast of new developments as well as be conversant in the terminology and requirements of today's AV technology.

Outside or Inside?

Since audiovisual equipment plays such a vital part in today's meetings business, properties are faced with the dilemma of how to make AV equipment available. Is it feasible to maintain a large in-house inventory, and, if so, what should be stocked? Or, would it be more cost-effective to have an outside AV firm provide the requested equipment? Or, as yet a third alternative, should the most commonly used items be stocked and outside AV firms be called upon to supply any special equipment requested by the meeting planner? In this section, we will take a look at the advantages and disadvantages of supplying AV equipment from outside sources or in-house (see box titled "Outside or Inside?") and look at what factors figure into a property's decision on meeting AV requirements.

Audiovisual Specialists

Many hotel managers prefer to use a local AV service organization rather than cope with this area in-house. Outside rental firms are used when:

- The hotel lacks adequate storage space
- Equipment is used so infrequently that investment in a piece cannot be justified
- The call for certain equipment, such as video projectors, is so heavy that it is not feasible for a hotel to inventory so many pieces

Exhibit 1   Today's "Wired" Meeting Rooms

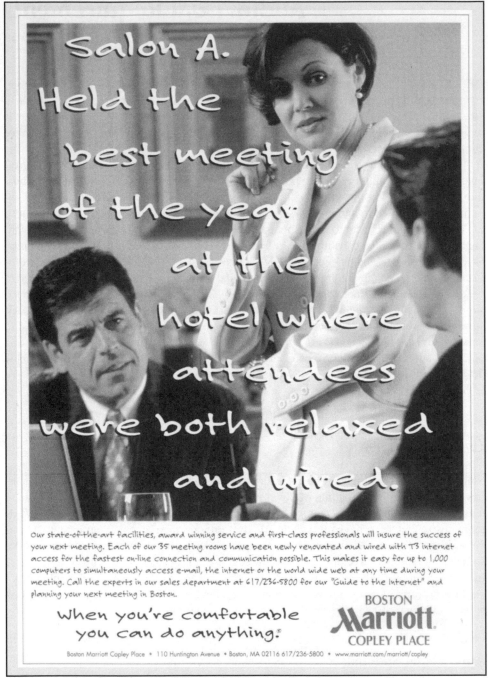

Today's hotels are advertising their ability to meet the needs of meeting planners with meeting rooms and equipment designed for the high-tech meetings common today. Note that this ad promotes T3 Internet access to enable attendees to access e-mail and the web during the meeting.

When an outside firm is used, many convention service managers prefer to order the equipment themselves rather than have the corporation or association do it. There are three reasons for this. First, they are assured that the equipment will arrive in plenty of time to set it up. Second, they can determine how large to set the stage, since the screen is often placed on a raised platform. A third, not so admirable, reason is that AV companies often pay a commission to hotels that book them instead of the competition.

An outside company offers the hotel's client a specialist with a full staff and inventory of equipment. An expert staff can be relied upon to maintain the equipment and to handle any on-the-scene malfunctions. Many hotel managers have said that they would install an inventory of such equipment only when the volume of such rental would enable them to hire at least one full-time specialist to manage a small department. That person would assist in planning, setup, operation, and service.

This is sound thinking when the hotel is in an area with good service companies. But in the more remote resort areas, the nearest AV dealer may be some distance away. If that is the case, last-minute malfunctions or additional needs can constitute a severe problem. A convention services manager in Lake Tahoe, Nevada, for example, gave this explanation for opting to stock equipment in-house:

> We are in a very isolated area, so each time I need to order a single piece
> of equipment due to a group change, the service charge is outrageous.
> The AV company's office is in Reno, 35 miles away, and the weather can
> be a factor on equipment delivery nine months out of the year.[1]

Large conventions often contract with AV service companies that will go anywhere to handle the convention. The fees they charge are usually a small price for the convention organization to pay for a smooth AV presentation.

It is not practical to call in such organizations for a small meeting. Yet some small meetings, particularly training ones, use a great deal of such equipment and need some assistance.

Outside or Inside?

Hotels are faced with the decision of either owning AV equipment and leasing it to the meeting group or entrusting the AV needs of a group to an outside firm. The final decision will vary depending on individual property needs, and the following factors should be taken into consideration when making that decision.

Advantages of Using an AV Company Outside the Hotel

1. Audiovisual equipment is expensive. In the event of theft or lost items, the outside firm, rather than the hotel, would incur the loss.
2. Many audiovisual pieces are used so infrequently that the cost of maintaining an inventory would be prohibitive.
3. The cost of maintaining and repairing equipment is expensive and may not justify the hiring of a staff specialist to service audiovisual items.
4. With advances in audiovisual equipment, some items may become obsolete, which would require additional expenditure by the hotel.

Advantages of Owning AV Equipment and Leasing It to the Meeting Group

1. There may be a lack of suppliers in the area, or it may be difficult to rent a particular piece.
2. The property can purchase pieces that best meet its needs rather than have to rely on an outside contractor whose equipment may not be adequate.
3. The property has greater control over the quality of equipment if it owns it. Rental equipment may have been misused and may not function properly.
4. The property directly benefits from renting its own equipment to meeting groups, rather than turning the profits over to an outside firm.

In-House Equipment

If an arrangement with a local AV service company cannot be made, a hotel may decide to stock at least the basic AV requirements. Rick Stanfield, senior vice president of Opryland Lodging Group, cautions:

> It is essential to track usage before investing in equipment. Do you have enough demand? Who will coordinate the AV service? These are important questions to answer. Go through a year's worth of records to see how often certain equipment is rented and calculate how many rentals will be necessary to break even. Look carefully, plot it on a graph, because it's hard to get payback if your equipment is sitting on a shelf.[2]

The question might well be asked, "If a hotel is going to have its own equipment, what types and how much of each must be stocked?" Naturally, the type and quantity vary from hotel to hotel. No one list or rate schedule can be applied to every hotel; a hotel must consider the needs of its clients in offering the proper assortment of AV equipment.

Some hotels are reluctant to bring in local companies on a one-time rental basis for fear that the service may not be up to their own staff's standards. But if you call on a local company frequently, you have the muscle to demand *excellent service*, rather than the business-as-usual kind. After all, the malfunctions generally happen on the weekend or at night. If you can achieve a good working relationship with an alert and eager AV company, your problems are solved. If not, you had better set up some sort of department of your own.

Several hotels now contract with an AV company to set up an office at the hotel and store equipment there. Referred to as **in-house contractors**, these AV firms are often provided space rent-free but are required to pay a commission to the hotel when meeting planners contract for AV equipment (commissions vary, but 30 percent is common). Bauer Audio Visual Inc. provides in-house services at 80 hotels. Other companies, such as AVW Audio Visual and Presentation Services/Audiovisual Headquarters, have signed corporation-wide contracts with hotel chains. Exhibit 2 shows an example of an audiovisual rate schedule for equipment provided to the Yarrow Hotel by an in-house contractor, Wasatch Audio Visual. These AV firms know the facility and what will and won't work in each meeting room. Last-minute needs can be met quickly from the on-site storage of AV equipment. And, in-house companies provide convenient, consolidated billing for the planner.

Equipment used at a convention, then, can come from any of three sources—the *convening organization*, the *hotel,* or an *outside AV specialist* hired by either the convention organization or the hotel. And equipment can come from any combination of the three.

The first need is to coordinate service. Another is to identify hotel equipment permanently to facilitate sorting equipment afterward. Use decals or permanent stencil imprints in paint. Many properties with in-house audiovisual departments are utilizing *bar coding* to both inventory equipment and to facilitate billing. Each type of equipment is labeled with its own bar code that can be scanned to generate reports as to where and how much is used, and charges can be instantly calculated and posted to the client's account.

Your own equipment will fare better from security and maintenance standpoints if responsibility for it is assigned to specific individuals. These people should receive special training in the care and operation of such equipment. Everyone in convention sales and service should be at home with the kind of equipment needed for most meetings. The dealer from whom the merchandise is purchased should agree to train your personnel; it requires merely some demonstration, not a lengthy course. And technical representatives of AV equipment manufacturers can be reached through the dealer to provide advice and training assistance.

Exhibit 2   Sample Audiovisual Equipment Rates

AUDIO VISUAL

PROJECTORS
• Overhead Projector $30.00
• 35mm Slide Projector $30.00
• 35mm 50% Brighter $75.00

SCREENS
• 6' Tripod Screen $30.00
• 8' Tripod Screen $40.00
• 12' Cradle Screen $65.00

MICROPHONES
• Handheld Podium Mic. ... $15.00
• Wireless Lavalier $60.00
• Wireless Handheld $60.00

SPEAKER PHONES
• Speaker Phone
  (6 people) $30.00
• Polycom System
  (20 people) $75.00
• Gentner System
  (large groups) $250.00

TAPE RECORDERS
• Portable Cassette $15.00
• Stereo Cassette $40.00
• CD Player $40.00

VIDEO CAMERAS
• Camcorder $100.00
• Digital Video Camera $550.00

VIDEO MONITORS & TV's
• 25" Monitor $80.00
• 31" Monitor $150.00
• 51" Monitor $275.00

VIDEO PLAYERS/RECORDERS
• 1/2" VHS $50.00
• Beta SP $400.00

DATA & VIDEO PROJECTION
• LCD for Computer $350.00
• LCD for Video $400.00
• LCD 2000 Lumens $550.00

PRESENTATION AIDS
• Easel Only $10.00
• Flipchart (pad & easel) $25.00
• Whiteboard $20.00
• Corkboard $15.00

CARTS & STANDS
• Projection Carts $15.00
• TV/VCR Cart $20.00
• Safe Lock Stand
  (adjustable) $10.00

Additional Information:

Please call (435) 655-9898

Fax (435) 655-9899

**WASATCH
AUDIO VISUAL
BUSINESS CENTER**

Equipment is supplied and serviced by our on-site audio visual specialists, Wasatch A/V Business Center.

An experienced event consultant will preview your needs and arrange for hardware and technical support. This could range from the latest in giant screen projection from video or computer sources to an overhead projector and screen or a simple flipchart with colored markers.

Prices subject to change.   Equipment subject to availability.   This is a partial list only.

The Yarrow Hotel contracts with Wasach Audio Visual to supply AV equipment to meeting planners. An in-house contractor, the company maintains an office within the hotel.
Source: Courtesy of Yarrow Hotel, Park City, Utah.

Types of Audiovisual Equipment

The audiovisual equipment used for today's meetings can range from a simple flip chart to a sophisticated computer-generated multi-media presentation. In this section, we will take a look at the various types of AV equipment commonly used by meeting planners and see how each can be used to help stage a successful meeting.

Sound Systems

A sound system is the kind of AV system that most hotels own. A supply of microphones, microphone stands, amplifiers, and speakers is typically the first AV equipment purchased by a hotel staff.

Top-quality sound **amplifier** systems are a must. Speakers should be distributed so that there are no "dead spots" in sound. When sound systems are used with projection equipment, they should be located in the same area as the screen. Studies have shown that people tend to comprehend better when the sound and the visuals come from the same direction.

You need a variety of microphones, stands, and long extension cables to handle meeting situations. It may be necessary to supply a mike for every one or two panelists at the head table or speakers at lecterns, and/or to have several microphones on the floor for questions from the audience. Ideally, the moderator and each speaker on a panel should have a microphone; if this is too costly, only then should microphones be limited to one for every two or three panelists (who should be reminded beforehand to speak into the nearest microphone).

If you join any but a brand-new facility, take inventory and have a list ready of what is available for use, in good working order. Call in a consultant on sound systems and find out what constitutes a basic inventory. Discuss this with experienced convention coordinators too.

Any basic inventory should include a variety of microphones. A **lavaliere microphone** is popular with speakers because it hooks around the neck with a ribbon or cord, leaving the hands free. This type of mike, which is also called a *lapel*, *neck*, or *pendant microphone*, has a variety of optional positions. For best results, however, the head should be as close to the speaker's mouth as possible—men should be encouraged to place them on their neckties or coat lapels, and women should wear their mikes high on their blouses or on the upper part of a jacket lapel.

It is important that all microphones used with public address systems (lectern, table, and floor mikes) be unidirectional. A **unidirectional microphone** picks up sound from only one direction (the speaker) and background noise (sounds coming from the sides and back of the microphone) is rejected. Windscreens (porous covers) also reduce the possibility of distracting sounds, such as blowing or popping.

A **standing microphone** is attached to a free-standing floor stand that is adjustable for height and angle. The stand has a sleeve or collar into which the mike can easily be placed. This type of mike, which is omni-directional (which means it picks up sounds from all directions), is typically used for questions or comments from the audience (in which case it is usually positioned in one of the aisles) or it can be used by a speaker or entertainer from the floor or stage.

A **roving microphone**, which is used to reach different parts of the audience, can also be equipped with a floor stand. Some models require a long cable to reach audience members, but some meeting planners prefer a **cordless/wireless microphone** when roving mikes are required. Cordless/wireless mikes come in two types: UHF (ultra high frequency) and VHF (very high frequency). UHF is usually preferred, but both types work well and offer freedom of movement. Wireless mikes offer the convenience of being able to move around the room without worrying about a cord (although you will want to make sure that these mikes have fresh batteries), but they are more expensive than microphones with cords and, in some cases, an audio mixer is required to control the sound if the cordless mike doesn't feature a volume adjustment. To avoid any problems, it is always best to suggest that the meeting planner have a hard-wired back-up mike in place.

A **table microphone** has a short stand that rests on a table, desk, or lectern (the microphones, therefore, are sometimes called *lectern* or *podium mikes*). The mikes are usually attached to a gooseneck mike holder, enabling more than one speaker to use a mike in close proximity to his or her position on the stage.

Mikes should be tested in each room to make sure the signal doesn't come through neighboring amplifiers. Cordless microphones should only be used in situations where freedom of movement is important, as they can cause problems. Signal interference is possible from a number of sources: metal structures in the room, wire mesh in the walls, and even suspended ceiling framework can cause disruptions or distortion in the sound. Even the more expensive models can face such problems as weak signals and quality as batteries wear down. If wireless microphones are used, then, it is wise to have a back-up system (such as a wired lavaliere microphone) immediately available.

All cables should be taped to the floor or carpet to avoid accidents in a darkened room. Avoid at all costs cables that run across the dais. Run such connectors along the front of the stage, hiding them in the draped skirting.

Have an attendant available during conventions. It helps to have the person on hand for large events and available for troubleshooting at smaller events, such as workshops.

All systems should be set up and *tested* before the meeting. And spare microphones should be available; equipment is not indestructible. Find out if the meeting group plans to have someone in charge of volume control and distribution of microphones. The amplification system is crucial to the success of the meeting, and is an important part of the testing process. In cases where multiple microphones will be used, or when proceedings will be recorded, a sound technician will be needed to run a **mixer board**; the mixer board (sound board) raises and lowers the volume from each input source, and will be located in the audience to enable the technician to hear exactly what the audience is hearing. In general, one mixer is required for two to four microphones, and two mixers should be used for five to eight mikes.

If your hotel uses Muzak or similar background music or a paging system, make sure you can control or eliminate such distractions in each meeting room. This is essential. And many times larger rooms are subdivided by temporary walls and the controls are in only one segment. The meeting planner may not know which subdivision has the controls. Orient the convening organization's staff to control locations.

Lighting

Lighting requirements should be handled by a specialist. If the hotel has a permanent stage, a professional service company should equip it for versatile lighting. But most often, platforms are temporary and lights must be furnished on stands. If platforms are always placed in the same position in certain rooms, a permanent lighting booth may be constructed and equipped. Even smaller rooms need skillful light placement to improve visibility of screened presentations.

While the technical details should be left to a lighting professional, the convention service manager should have a working knowledge of the basic types and uses of lighting equipment.

Lighting requirements for small rooms are simple; for large rooms and auditoriums they are more complex. Union regulations recognize this. Attendants are required for spotlight use when large rooms use stage lighting, and so on. They are usually not required for simple setups in small rooms. Don't forget to tell the client about union regulations and rates.

Some of the basic types of lighting include profile spots, follow spots, floodlights, and special effects lighting. **Profile spots** are also known as *ellipsoidal spots* or *lekos*, and are ceiling mounted with a range from 500 to 1,000 watts. Employing a halogen lamp, they are used to light lecterns, signs, and the area of the stage nearest the audience to project background light patterns (colored filters are often used for this effect). Profile spots can also project **gobo patterns**, pre-cut designs that fit over the projected light to form light shapes, such as a company logo.

Follow-spots are cannon-shaped, movable lighting devices that are usually located to the rear of the auditorium. They are used to highlight and follow the speaker or performer, and require the services of a technician to ensure this added visibility is maintained. These lights are extremely brilliant, and may also be used with colored filters for a variety of effects.

Floodlights are usually used to light objects rather than people, and are often used to light backdrops (known as cycloramas) that serve as neutral backgrounds for the speakers. Floodlights are used to project a diffused, even light, and feature frames that can accommodate color filters for different effects. The par cam is the most commonly used floodlight. This type of floodlight can be used for a variety of lighting options, from filling large areas with light to creating mood and atmosphere by lighting only the front of the stage or providing "mood" lighting as a backdrop. In addition, gels can be inserted to provide color, creating a dramatic effect.

Special effects lighting is used both for illumination and to "create the mood." Ballroom globes, strobe lights, ultraviolet lighting, and laser lighting can be used to create a number of effects that enhance special functions—and can serve as visual centerpieces.

Computer-controlled lighting instruments, which are commonly called **intelligent lighting**, are capable of performing a wide variety of functions with the touch of a button. Although intelligent lighting equipment is significantly more costly than traditional lighting, its flexibility makes it a popular option with hotels that frequently host theme parties and large-scale productions that require complex lighting effects.

Dimmer switches on house lights are a must for meeting rooms. Delegates need partial illumination to take notes, while still being able to see the projection on the screen clearly. A control board is used to balance lighting to achieve the desired effect, and, depending on the complexity of the board, it may require lighting personnel or a lighting technician.

Screens

Projection screens are often purchased by hotels. Larger ones must be tailor-made for the larger rooms, especially those hampered by a low ceiling. The charts in Exhibit 3 offer a guide to screen size selection under a variety of conditions and can help you decide where to place the projection stands when setting up.

There are several formulas used for determining seating capacity and screen placement. The two most commonly used are the *five feet rule* and the *two by eight rule*.

The five feet rule states that the minimum distance from the bottom of the screen to the floor is five feet, while the average height of a seated person is four feet, six inches. Therefore, to view the screen clearly, the bottom of the screen must be a minimum of five feet off the floor.

The two by eight rule states that no one should be seated closer to the screen than two times the screen's height or farther from the screen than eight times the screen's height. For example, if the meeting room's ceiling height is 15 feet, the maximum height for the projection screen is 10 feet, and if a 7½-foot-high by 10-foot-wide screen is used, the farthest seat from the screen should be no more than 60 feet and the closest seat no closer than 15 feet. Screen sizes are always listed height first, so a 7' x 10' screen is 7 feet high and 10 feet wide.

Several other guidelines also apply to ensure maximum visibility. First, the distance from the projector to the screen should be at least 1.5 times the width of the screen. Second, the projection platform must elevate the projector to at least the bottom of the screen. Third, the projection platform should be placed at a 90-degree angle to the screen.

Exhibit 3   Guide to Screen Size Selection and Seating Distance from Screen

Choosing a screen size that takes full advantage of the specific type of projector and room size is as important as choosing the proper screen surface. Today's shorter projection lenses and larger rooms permit bigger, more lifelike projecting than ever. Now, for example, a 4" lens projects a 35mm slide to 60" height and width from a distance of only fifteen feet. And the zoom projectors need big screens to make the most of their capabilities. These charts are accurate guides to screen-size selection. Make sure the screen selected is on the basis of the largest-size slides or movies intended for projection.

16mm Movies

Lens Focal Length	P r o j	Screen Width			
		40"	50"	60"	70"
1"	D	9'	11'	13'	16'
1 1/2"	i	13'	17'	20'	23'
2"	s	18'	22'	26'	31'
2 1/2"	t	22'	27'	33'	38'
3"	a	26'	33'	40'	46'
3 1/2"	n	31'	38'	46'	54'
4"	c e	35'	44'	53'	61'

35mm Slides

Lens Focal Length	P r o j	Screen Width			
		40"	50"	60"	70"
3"	D	7'	9'	11'	13'
4"	i	10'	12'	15'	17'
5"	s	12'	16'	19'	22'
6"	t	15'	19'	22'	26'
7"	a	17'	22'	26'	30'
8"	n c e	20'	25'	30'	35'

Audience Capacity

Farthest Seat—Eight times the screen height. First consideration when picking ideal
screen for any room. (Assuming choice of lenses).
Closest Seat—Two times the screen height.
Audience capacity—Ten square feet per person after aisle space is deducted.
(Assumes ideal seating arrangement.)

Screen Size	Farthest Seat from Screen	Closest Seat to Screen	Audience Capacity	Square Feet Seating Space
6' x 8'	48'	12'	150	1,500
7½' x 10'	60'	15'	200	2,000
9' x 12'	72'	18'	300	3,000
10½' x 14'	84'	21'	500	5,000
12' x 16'	96'	24'	750	7,500
15' x 20'	120'	30'	1,500	15,000

There are three options for placement of a screen: the center of the stage, to one side of center stage, or in a corner. In deciding where to place the screen, it is important to determine which is more important in the presentation—the speaker or the information on the screen. If the speaker is conducting training, for example, the screen should be centered and the speaker should stand or sit off to the side. If the presenter is a motivational speaker or other special guest, he or she should be the focal point and the screen should be placed off to the side. Placing the screen in a corner is usually reserved as a space-saving measure when rear-screen projection is used.

You will also want to have a seating arrangement that offers an optimum relationship of the audience to the screen. The most desirable angle is between 45 and 90 degrees, although an angle of 22–45 degrees is acceptable, especially if the on-screen presentation is secondary to the speaker. Angles of less than 22 degrees are undesirable, as these angles would make it difficult to read the projected material.

When placing screens, you will also want to be sure that you do not block fire exits and that lighted exit signs or other lighting do not shine through the rear of the screen. The darker the area above the screen, the brighter the projected image will be. And, since most people are right-handed, place the screen to the speaker's right to enable the presenter to refer to projected material with his or her right hand.

There are many types of screens available. Exhibit 4 compares the advantages and disadvantages of the three most common screen types:

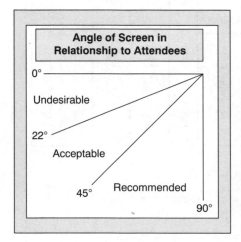

· Fastfold screens
· Wall and ceiling screens
· Tripod screens

The most popular of the larger screens is the **fast-fold**, available in sizes up to 30 feet high. The screen comes with adjustable legs to vary the height of placement off the floor (or it may be hung from the ceiling). They last a long time when taken care of and the smaller fast-folds represent a relatively minor investment. Local AV dealers may have a hard time supplying the huge screens, but no trouble supplying any number of small units.

You can give your fast-fold screens a "movie theater" look by purchasing full dress kits made especially for these screens. Dress kits are curtains designed to be placed at the top and around the sides of the screen. The curtains add weight to the top of the screen, but additional support brackets will eliminate any potential problems. While using dress kits increases costs somewhat, meeting planners appreciate the "finished" look that dress kits provide for general or plenary sessions or other types of meetings for which a professional-looking backdrop is important.

Wall or *ceiling screens* come in a variety of sizes and are designed to be hung from hooks or lines or mounted on the wall or ceiling. They are inexpensive, and the metal tube casings make for easy storage. They are activated like the old-fashioned window shades.

Tripod screens, which come in a metal tube like the wall screen, are mounted permanently on folding tripod stands so that they can be placed anywhere. Light, portable, versatile, and inexpensive, they are extremely useful in smaller meetings. Tripod screens should be tilted forward or back at the top to avoid **keystoning**, an effect in which an image appears noticeably wider at the top than at the bottom and appears unfocused. And, for a more professional image, the bottom of the screen should be skirted.

There is a variety of screen fabric in use today. A favorite is **glass-beaded** (white), which offers great brilliance. As their name implies, these screens have surfaces covered with tiny glass beads that reflect a bright image back toward the audience. A disadvantage of this type of screen is that they have a narrow viewing angle. Smooth white **matte-surface screens** offer consistent brilliance from a wider angle, which is important in small rooms where some seats may be at a sharp angle to the screen, and are the most commonly used types of screens. Silver metallic and **lenticular screen** surfaces combine the best features of both types, offering maximum brilliance and wide-angle light consistency. They are somewhat

Exhibit 4   Advantages/Disadvantages of Types of Screens

SCREEN TYPE	ADVANTAGES	DISADVANTAGES	AUDIENCE SIZE
Fast-Fold	Excellent appearance Available in large sizes Good for rear projection Dress kits available to improve appearance	More expensive No anti-keystoning device available More labor intensive	6'x8' - up to 150 people 7.5'x10' - up to 200 people 9'x12' - up to 300 people 10.5'x14' - up to 500 people 12'x16' - up to 750 people 15'x20' - up to 1500 people
Wall/Ceiling Screens	Usually complimentary Can be large in size	Screen can't be moved Meeting room must be set around screen	Audience size will vary depending on size of screen
Tripod	Less expensive Anti-keystoning device available in sizes less than 8 ft. Fast installation	Largest size is 8-ft. Less attractive Full dress kit not available Cannot be used for rear-projection	60"x60" - up to 25 people 70"x70" - up to 50 people 84"x84" - up to 100 people 96"x96" - up to 150 people

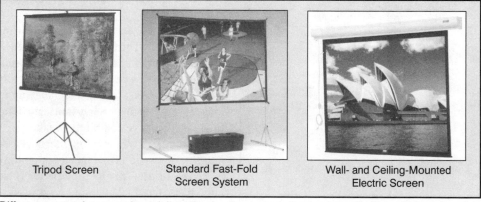

Tripod Screen	Standard Fast-Fold Screen System	Wall- and Ceiling-Mounted Electric Screen

Different types of screens have inherent advantages and disadvantages that should be taken into consideration when determining the best screen(s) to be used for presentations. This chart provides an "at-a-glance" comparison for easy reference.
Source. Courtesy of Da-Lite Screen Company, Inc. Used with permission.

more costly than the others. Any local AV dealer can assist you in selecting the proper screens for your facility.

Slide Projectors

Slide projectors were once the mainstay of the meetings industry, but today they are increasingly being replaced by high-tech computer projection systems. In cases in which slide projectors are used, the most popular option is the 35mm, 80-slide **carousel projector**.

A remote control device is often used for slide projectors. Both wired remotes and cordless remotes are available, with the wireless device giving the speaker additional mobility. When a remote device is used, it is advisable to have an assistant near the machine in case of a malfunction.

A **dissolve unit** is required when two or more projectors are used in combination. A dissolve unit activates fade-in and fade-out of slides when two or more slide projectors are focused on the same screen. Dissolve units are widely used by meeting planners to avoid the light flash between slides when only one projector is used. When multiple slide projectors are used, a prerecorded tape may be synchronized with the slide sequence. The signal from the tape will activate the slide projector at the right moment.

To ensure proper functioning of equipment, the convention service manager should also have a working knowledge of the components of slide projector systems. Lenses, for example, are commonly a 4-to-6 zoom lens, but larger lenses are available if there is a need to project over longer distances. Specialized lenses are often quite expensive, but may be available from an AV company if there is a need for a non-standard lens.

Most slide projectors use a quartz-halogen bulb, but **xenon bulbs** are also available in cases where increased brilliance is required (when projecting over long distances, for example). The xenon bulb can be dangerous, however; it is filled with a high pressure gas, and its use and care is best left in the hands of an experienced operator. The availability of bulbs can be crucial to a presentation; it is wise to ensure that replacement bulbs are readily available in the event of a blowout during a presentation.

Overhead Projectors

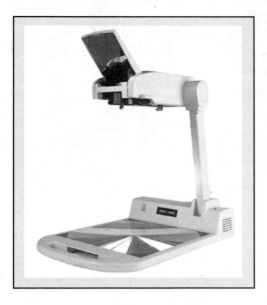

An **overhead projector** is popular for instructional use. The projector is positioned near the speaker and projects behind him or her onto a screen. Overhead projectors handle any brands of transparencies up to nine by nine inches. Such units are relatively inexpensive and rarely break.

One of the most versatile developments in the field of overhead technology is the **computer projection panel** (also known as the LCD—liquid crystal display). The LCD projector has largely replaced traditional overhead transparencies and the 35mm slide projector, and it is the instrument of choice for PowerPoint slides and web presentations. The special attachment is attached to a personal computer, projecting whatever is on the computer monitor to the projection screen. Not only does this device make the image large enough for easy audience viewing, but it can also store and select data at the operator's command (see Exhibit 5).

Although most meeting planners are well versed in the layout of meeting rooms, occasionally the convention service manager will be called upon to advise in the placement of audiovisual equipment. Few things can destroy the effectiveness of a meeting more than the improper positioning of projectors and screens. No one wants to look down the back of

Exhibit 5   Liquid Crystal Display (LCD) Technology

An image may be projected from a computer monitor to a larger screen with the use of Liquid Crystal Display (LCD) technology. The LCD panel is used with an overhead projector; the LCD projector has a built-in light source.

someone's neck while the speaker explains the visuals. Obscured views can be prevented with a simple understanding of AV layout.

Exhibit 6 illustrates the proper positioning of an overhead projector so that the speaker does not block the audience's view. Exhibit 7 shows the best positioning of an overhead projector, a slide or filmstrip projector, and a movie projector. Review these illustrations thoroughly. Good visibility is foremost in communicating with visual techniques.

Rearview Projection

A visual presentation that is receiving wide use is **rearview projection**. The term "rearview" is somewhat of a misnomer, because the audience still views the picture (slides, film, or video visuals can be projected) from the front (see Exhibit 8). The projector, however, is set up behind the screen. By using a curtain or similar room divider, hotels can cut off one part of a room from the other. The audience sits on one side of the partition, the projector on the other. A **translucent rear-projection screen** is framed by the curtain, and the projection equipment is hidden on the darkened rear side.

Three of the most commonly used self-contained rear-projection units are Telex's Caramate, Kodak's Audioviewer, and Bell & Howell's Ringmaster. These units resemble small television sets with a slide tray on top; slides can be advanced manually or through the use of an audio tape programmed with silent "cues" (pulses).

The primary advantage of this technique is that all projection equipment is hidden from the audience, eliminating the need for an aisle. Additionally, the projection area can be blacked out, allowing for higher **ambient light** in the audience area without washing out the image. The disadvantage is that the room cannot be fully used for seating (rearview projection reduces the available square footage for seating up to one-third). Another disadvantage is that rear projection requires an almost completely dark projection area behind the screen, requiring complete draping of the screen—sides, bottom, and top (the area of the room where the audience is seated does not need to be darkened). In addition, if space behind the screen is limited, a more expensive wide-angle lens may be required. On the

Exhibit 6   Seating Arrangements When Using Overhead Projectors

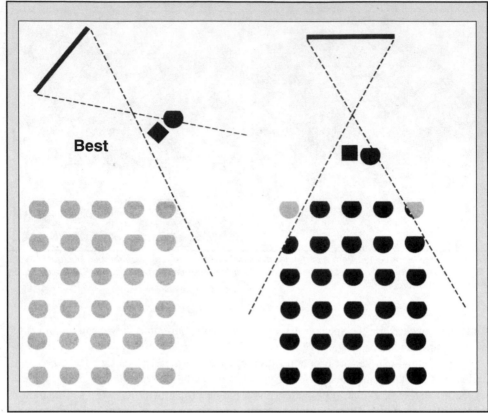

When using an overhead projector, the room should be arranged so that the audience's view of the screen is not blocked by the speaker and the projector. The seating arrangement on the left is best for viewing.
Source: Courtesy of the 3M Company.

positive side, however, rearview projection can be effective, as it allows the speaker more freedom of movement and the presentation can appear more dramatic because the image seems to appear out of nowhere.

Motion Picture Film Projectors

When movies are shown at meetings, they are most frequently the 16mm size. Fortunately, any 16mm film can be shown on any 16mm projector.

The sound system built into motion picture projectors is often poor; in larger meeting rooms, an independent subsidiary sound hookup should be used. The sound from a 16mm projector can be "patched" into the property's built-in sound system for greater clarity.

Motion picture film projectors require an operator to thread the film into the projector, although some have an automatic feeding system (preferred by most convention service departments). To be on the safe side, however, a trained projectionist should be available in the event of a malfunction in the automatic system.

Another consideration when dealing with motion picture projectors is the lamp system. As with slide projectors, a higher intensity bulb is required when images must be projected over longer distances. A MARC (mazda closed arc) projector can be used when

Exhibit 7   Multimedia Arrangements in U-Shaped Setup

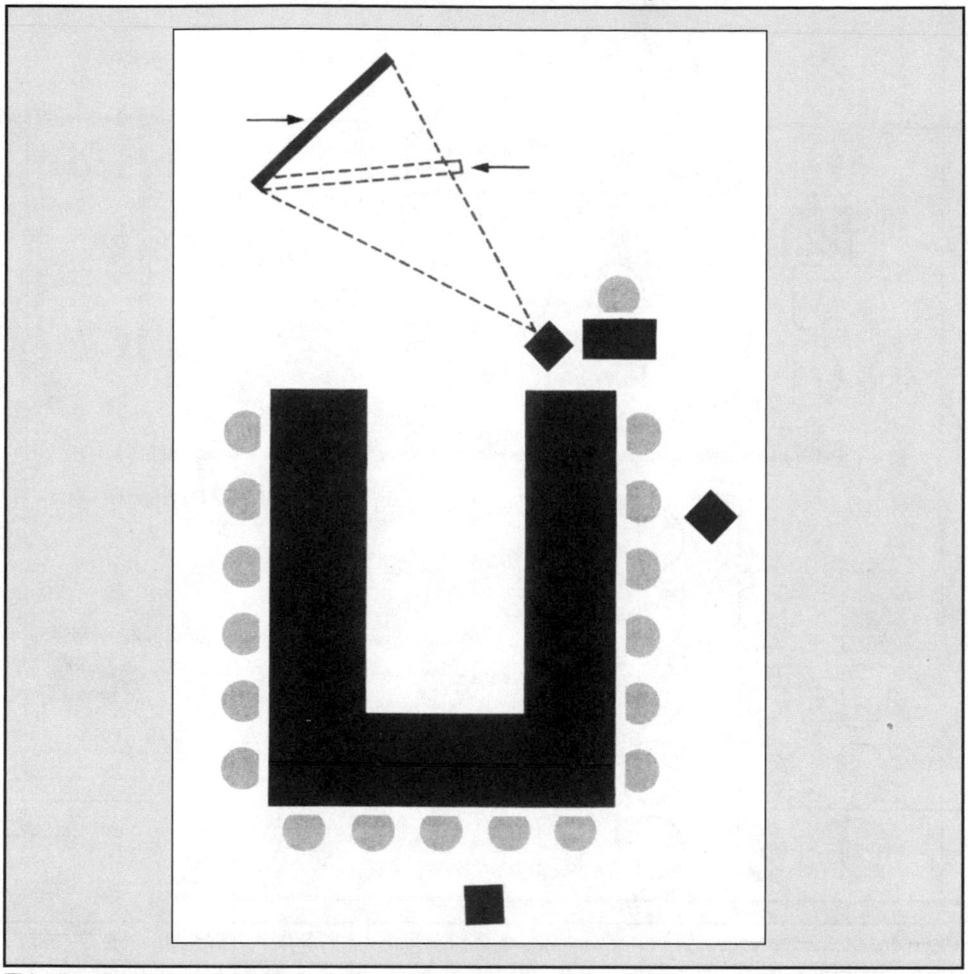

This diagram illustrates the best position for an overhead, slide, or filmstrip projector in a U-shape table arrangement.

greater clarity is required, while a Xenon 16mm projector is the most powerful projector for long-distance projection (a professional projectionist is required for this equipment).

It is wise for the convention service manager to check out the room setup and the audiovisual equipment supplied before the meeting starts. He or she should check:

- The *screen,* to see if it is above the audience's heads so that all will be able to see clearly from where they sit
- The *projector,* to see that it is secure on the stand and that an extra lamp is available
- The *speaker,* to see that he or she is near the screen
- The *electrical cords,* to be sure they are out of the aisle and hidden

Videotape and DVD Projectors

With the growing use of videotape and DVD (digital video disks) for meeting presentations, many properties are finding it imperative to provide video playback equipment and support.

Exhibit 8   Comparison of Common Projection Systems

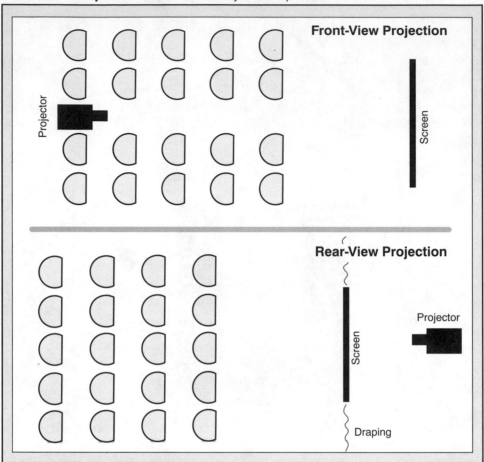

There are both advantages and disadvantages to the two common projection systems detailed in this figure. Front-view projection systems do not take up a lot of space. Disadvantages include possible interference (as when attendees walk across the projected beam of light) and the danger of speakers or attendees tripping over cords or other equipment. With rear-view projection systems, there is no need to dim lights, allowing attendees to take notes. The primary disadvantage of these systems is their size; not only do they take up a lot of space (typically 15 to 30 feet behind the screen), but the area behind the screen must also be completely dark, reducing the square footage available for seating. Another disadvantage is that special projector lenses are required, which also adds to the expense.

Video projectors and DVD projectors are essential for viewing videotapes or digital video disks in all but small groups. A self-contained video projector has a curved six-foot screen that can easily be seen by audiences of up to 100 people.

While several of these units can be used for larger groups, it is usually more effective to use a detached video or DVD projector and a fast-fold projector screen in larger rooms. This equipment offers a quality image 12 feet wide, and can be used for both front or rear projection.

For arenas and other larger areas, light-valve video projectors must be used. This type of projector projects up to 400 feet and creates an image roughly 40 feet wide. It may not be feasible to purchase this type of projector. It is more practical to rent them when the need arises.

On the other end of the meetings spectrum, television sets can be used to service small meetings. Television falls into two categories: monitors and receivers.

A **monitor** has no tuner, and interprets signals directly from a videotape player, DVD player, or video camera. Monitors are more costly than television receivers, but are often requested by meeting planners due to the crisper image they produce. The next level of video monitors is high-definition television (HDTV) and plasma screens. These monitors are only three inches thick and up to 80 inches in size. Although these monitors are costly, they are being increasingly used by meeting planners.

Receivers are used to interpret and reproduce television signals, but cannot play videotapes without the use of a videotape player. While television receivers have built-in audio systems, these are usually of a mediocre quality; it is advisable to patch sound into the property's sound system rather than rely on the units' audio systems.

Signals from videotapes can be split to feed a number of monitors and television receivers, and the number of units needed will depend on the size of the audience. A general rule of thumb is 25 viewers per 25-inch set and 50 viewers per 25- to 52-inch set.

Since video is widely used, it is important that the property have compatible tape equipment readily available. The basic formats available in the United States are:

- DVD (Digital Video Disk)—is popular for the consumer market, readily available, and is easy to read on home computers and DVD players.
- VHS (Video Home System)—uses 1/2-inch tape and, before the introduction of DVD, was the most popular variety of tape with meeting planners.
- Betacam, Beta SP—is the common video format for presentation graphics.
- U-Matic or Industrial—uses 3/4-inch tape and generates a better image than VHS. These formats are generally used for educational tapes.
- Broadcast video—1- or 2-inch tape, used primarily by television stations and production houses; will rarely be requested by meeting planners.
- Video 8—another Sony product that uses small cassettes (only slightly larger than standard audio cassettes). This format is rarely used, but may be found in exhibits, where space is at a premium.

It is important to note that none of these tape formats is compatible with any of the others. And, problems may also arise if speakers or presenters are from foreign countries. A NTSC standard is used for VHS and DVD in the United States, while Europe, Africa, Australia, and Southeast Asia use a PAL standard, and the SECAM standard is used in Russia, France, and the Middle East. It is usually impractical to stock equipment to accommodate foreign standard tapes, but the convention services department would be wise to locate audiovisual suppliers that can provide this equipment when needed.

Projection Systems for Computer Presentations

Throughout the meetings industry there has been a very rapid movement to computer-driven presentations. Slide, film, and overhead transparency projection is being replaced by computer projection at many gatherings.

There are two primary types of projection systems available for personal computer-based presentations: liquid crystal display (LCD) computer panels and computer projectors.

Liquid crystal display computer panels, discussed in the previous sections, are units that sit atop an overhead projector. The LCD panels are connected to a computer, and images on the computer screen are then displayed on the overhead projector.

A more recent innovation, and one that is preferred by many meeting planners, is the **computer data projector**. These stand-alone projectors are equipped with their own built-in light source into which the computer plugs directly. There is no need for an overhead projector when using this device.

Computer programs, such as Microsoft PowerPoint, are commonly used with this type of projector. These programs allow color, animation, and graphics to be projected from computers onto a screen.

An even higher-end projector used in large function rooms where a large screen is required is the **DLP projector (digital light projection)**. DLPs are lighter (three to seven pounds is common), more portable, brighter (with extremely high light output of up to 15,000 lumens), and have a better image quality. While more expensive, they provide better resolution at greater distances.

Projector Stands

Projectors have to be placed on something. It may be a table or desk, but it is more versatile and convenient to have special projection tables or stands. These come in folding and rigid types. Some have casters for easy movement; with these stands, projectors may be placed anywhere in a room.

There are two basic types of projector stands: the **Safelock stand** and the rolling cart. The Safelock is ideal for large projectors, and has four telescoping legs that adjust to heights up to 56 inches. Rolling carts come in several fixed heights, with the 32-inch and the 54-inch the most commonly used. The 32-inch rolling cart is ideal for overhead projectors, while the 54-inch cart is usually used for television monitors. When using rolling carts, regardless of height, **skirting** (pleated or ruffled draping) should be used to wrap the lower portion of the cart. (Skirting, which gives a professional, finished look, should also be used at the bottom of projection screens.)

Permanent projection booths can be constructed for larger rooms. The screen chart in Exhibit 3 will help you choose the proper lens to fill the screen from such a fixed position. Lenses of extra-long focal lengths for long projection distance may not always be in stock but can be ordered from local AV dealers. Check local fire and union regulations regarding projection booth operations.

Multimedia Presentation Equipment

This concept uses several types of audio and visual equipment to create total sight/sound environments. **Multimedia** can range from the very simple to highly sophisticated systems, and convention service managers should have a working knowledge of the basic types of equipment commonly requested by meeting planners.

The simplest form of multimedia is the sound/slide synchronizer. It uses a sound tape that automatically advances the slides and provides music or narration during the slide presentation.

Slide projectors can also be teamed with dissolve units. Dissolve units alternate two or three slide projectors focused on the same screen. These units fade and overlap images to create a smooth multimedia presentation.

Programmers are the ultimate in multimedia equipment. The computerized control can be used to synchronize sound tracks and multiple slide projectors on multiple screens (and can even turn the lights off in the room) for a stunning audiovisual performance. And, as video continues to become a popular alternative to slides, multimedia is becoming even more exciting as a motivational and communications tool.

Simultaneous Interpretation Facilities

As meetings become more international in scope, many properties have found it necessary to provide **simultaneous interpretation** facilities. This involves having a speaker's words translated into the language(s) of the meeting participants, and requires specialized equipment and personnel.

In most cases, the speaker addresses the group and interpreters in soundproof booths relay what the speaker has said to the attendees via wireless headsets. The number of booths and headsets needed will depend on the number of languages required for the meeting.

Today's technology has enhanced this process. Loop antennas can be used within certain areas to enable attendees to hear their language within that area. Infrared signals are also used to beam a language to attendees. Another development is multiple channel selection, which enables attendees to channel back and forth between different languages.

While simultaneous interpretation can be costly, both in terms of equipment (sound booths, headsets, and antennas or infrared radiators) and personnel (interpreters and technicians), more meeting planners will require this service in today's increasingly international business world, and the properties that offer this capability can capture a share of this growing—and lucrative—market.

Virtual Conferencing Equipment

In an increasing number of cases, meeting planners have found that it is virtually impossible—or too costly—to bring all persons that should be involved in a meeting together in person. Conflicting schedules and the high cost of travel are the prime factors for the use of **virtual conferencing**. The most recent Meetings Market Report conducted by *Meetings & Conventions* found that approximately 25% of corporate meeting planners use virtual conferencing.

Virtual conferencing can be broadly defined as the electronic linking of more than two people at different sites, and falls into four basic categories: audio, audiographic, video, and web conferencing.

Audio conferencing, the most basic form, is generally used when budget is a major consideration. Audio conferencing simply utilizes the telephone lines and speaker phones to connect several parties. A speaker can give a presentation to meeting "attendees" at several locations via speaker phones or special microphones and amplifier systems tied directly to the telephone lines of the participating properties or alternate remote sites.

Audiographic conferencing is generally used for planning sessions, project reviews, and briefings because it combines both audio interaction and visual capabilities. Specially designed conference rooms offer the ability to "show" documents, slides, and objects via television monitors at the remote sites.

Video satellite conferencing provides full-motion, "face-to-face" networking, and is the most expensive and sophisticated form of virtual conferencing. Remote sites are "linked" through the use of satellite technology; many properties now offer this type of conferencing network.

Video conferencing involves considerable expense. First, it is necessary to provide full video production, which involves multiple video cameras, technicians, and special effects equipment. Second, it is necessary to provide a playback system at each location. This equipment includes multiple video monitors or video projectors. Third, uplink/downlink and satellite facilities are required. Special equipment (telephone lines, cable, or a microwave system) sends the signal from the origination point to a satellite dish ("uplink" or "earth station") which beams the image to the satellite (22,000 miles or more above the earth). The signal is received by a transponder (an access point on the satellite), the frequency is changed, and the signal is beamed down to satellite dishes ("downlink") at each remote location before it travels, again via telephone line, cable, or microwave system, to the remote receivers.

While this process requires a large initial investment, many properties have found it worthwhile to purchase or lease uplink systems or find other ways to offer video-conferencing services. Sheraton Hotels & Resorts, for example, went into partnership with VueCom, which provides videoconferencing services transmitted over high-speed, fiber-optic lines. The system, which is easily adapted to various meeting sizes, is installed at approximately 140 properties.

Other chains, including Marriott, Westin, and Hyatt, currently offer videoconferencing or are in the process of reintroducing this service. Their investments in this technology may pay future dividends, as adverse circumstances—a fuel crisis, worsening economic trends, or other negative shifts in the business world—make video conferencing a viable alternative to costly meeting travel and accommodations.

The newest alternative to face-to-face meetings is **web conferencing**. Web conferencing refers to conducting meetings, events, and seminars over the Internet. Web-based presentations utilize an Internet connection rather than satellites. The sponsoring organizations have the advantage of saving time and travel expenses as "attendees" can participate without leaving their offices, plus the Internet is less costly than satellite uplink/downlink services.

There are a number of different ways that speakers can connect to the Internet. The easiest, least expensive, but slowest connection is through a telephone line. Many planners find this access too slow and prefer the high-speed connections possible with ISDN (Integrated Services Digital Network), T1, or T3 lines (T1 lines operate at a higher capacity than an ISDN line and can be "split" to accommodate several users at once; T3 lines are even faster than T1 lines, allowing more tasks to be performed simultaneously at the higher speed). Since these lines ensure that web information will appear very quickly on computer and projection screens, many hotels, conference facilities, and convention centers are installing these types of lines throughout their meeting rooms. Exhibit 9 shows how the Chaparral Suites Resort in Scottsdale, Arizona, promotes its meeting technology, including ISDN, voice, and modem lines at T1 speed.

Spare Parts

If you have your own projectors—slide, movie, video, computer-based, or overhead—you should maintain a stock of spare lamps. Keep fuses at hand if the hotel is not wired with

Exhibit 9   High-Speed Internet Services

*Today's meeting planners often require high-speed access for presentations generated from remote
locations for viewing on computers and projection screens. Hotels, conference facilities, and convention
centers are meeting this requirement by installing—and promoting—their state-of-the-art, high-speed
Internet services.*
Courtesy of Chaparral Suites Resort, Scottsdale. Used with permission.

circuit breakers. Someone on the convention service staff should know how to select the
proper lamps, replace burnt-out ones, and instruct others in the operation of the projectors.
This attention to detail can be very important to meeting planners (see Exhibit 10).

Other Presentation Devices

Not all presentation is done by film, of course. Many speakers use *chalkboards*. Some
call them *blackboards*, but most of them are green these days. These may be permanently

Exhibit 10 Solving Problems for Meeting Planners

A "No Excuses"® guarantee for your next meeting.

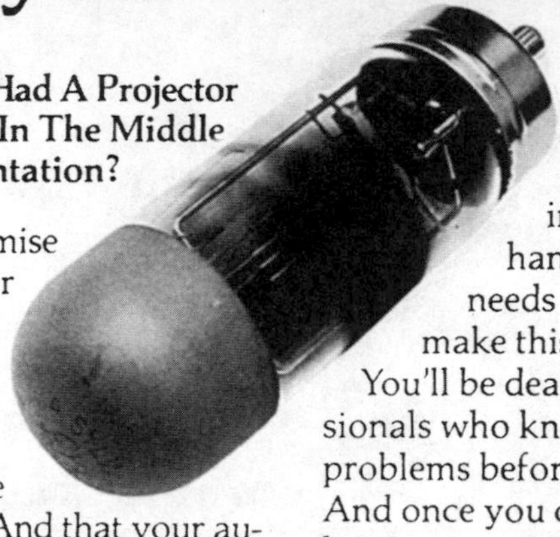

Have You Ever Had A Projector Bulb Burn Out In The Middle Of A Big Presentation?

We can't promise that you'll never have another bulb burn out.

But we can promise that we'll have spare bulbs on hand. And that your audio-visual and sound equipment will be set up per your specifications and in good working order.

The same is true for the way we set-up your meeting space and the timing and manner in which we serve your coffee breaks. If any of these individual requirements are not the way we agreed in our meeting contract, we'll either make it right or charges for that item will be deleted from your bill.

That's the whole point of our "NO EXCUSES"® Meeting Guarantee. We have to have a lot of confidence in our ability to handle your meeting needs or we wouldn't make this promise.

You'll be dealing with professionals who know how to solve problems before they happen. And once you check-in, you'll have someone to handle your needs 24 hours a day.

They'll also be on hand to review the charges with you before you check-out. And you will be billed per the agreed format and with appropriate back-up documentation.

For more information about our "NO EXCUSES" Meeting Guarantee contact the Director of Sales at any of the participating hotels, or fill out and return our coupon, or call 1-800-MEETING.

Holiday Inn

Many meeting planners worry about small details. This ad featuring Holiday Inn's "No Excuses" meeting guarantee assures meeting planners that each property is ready to handle any problem that might arise—including having spare lamps on hand to ensure that presentations can go on as planned.

installed, hung on a wall, or used on a tripod **easel**. Make sure the chalkboard is washed clean and that chalk and *clean* erasers are supplied. To enliven the presentation, an assortment of colored chalk is preferable to white or yellow chalk only. It is the hotel's responsibility to provide the meeting planner with first-class chalkboards, blackboards, and easel charts. Such equipment that is in need of repair is unsightly and difficult to work with.

A *whiteboard* is cleaner and more convenient than a chalkboard, and can be used as an impromptu projector screen as well as for easy-to-read, readily correctable presentations.

Advantages and Disadvantages of Popular AV Equipment

Advantages	Disadvantages
Slide Projectors 1. Can be operated with wireless remote control device. 2. Can be connected with audio-sync tape. 3. Excellent color reproduction on slides. 4. Can be computer programmed for multi-image productions. 5. Can project a larger image.	1. Limited motion capabilities compared to video. 2. Fan noise can be distracting.
Motion Picture Projectors 1. Full motion capabilities. 2. Excellent color rendition. 3. Can project large, quality images.	1. Difficult to feed unless equipment has automatic threading mechanism. 2. Built-in speakers are often of poor quality; sound may have to be "patched" to the facility's sound system.
Flip Charts and Chalkboards 1. Very inexpensive. 2. Take up very little seating space. 3. Ideal for "brainstorming" and training meetings.	1. Limited to small audiences (50 persons or less). 2. Messy and often difficult to erase.
Computer-Based Projectors 1. Most are compatible with laptop computers. 2. PowerPoint and electronic graphics make for powerful presentations. 3. Possible to provide Internet connection.	1. Resolution (sharpness of image) doesn't match slides or film. 2. Technology changes about every 18 months, so equipment can become obsolete. 3. Not as bright as overhead projectors, so glass-beaded screens may be needed to provide a brisker image.
Overhead Projectors 1. Can be used in a lighted room. 2. Simple to operate, and transparencies can be produced quickly on a copy machine. 3. Speaker can control presentation by highlighting or marking on transparency during presentation. 4. Speakers can face audience and do not have to turn their backs (as is the case with chalkboards or flip charts).	1. Noise from built-in fans can be a distraction. 2. Limited color reproduction.
Video Projectors 1. Instant playback capabilities. 2. Full motion and color capabilities. 3. Simple to operate. 4. Video display of computer-generated information is possible.	1. Various formats of playback equipment are incompatible. 2. Difficult to project to large audiences.

Instead of chalk, dry-erase markers are used, and many whiteboards are marked like graph paper, making it easy for a speaker to write or draw in a straight line.

Whiteboards are also available in electronic versions. One model, Panasonic's Panofax, reproduces everything written on it or taped to it. When desired, a photocopy of everything on the board can be made with the push of a button. This eliminates extensive note-taking, which often distracts attendees from what the speaker is saying.

The Gemini Blackboard is another technological improvement of the whiteboard. This device has capabilities to send materials written on it to another board (sometimes thousands of miles away) via a telephone line. This application has become increasingly popular as more meeting planners are turning to teleconferences.

The SoftBoard, shown in Exhibit 11, is another example of this technology. Soft-Boards are connected to a computer and store everything written on them into the computer using two infrared lasers mounted at the upper corners of the boards. Information is generated through the use of bar-coded dry erase markers, allowing the lasers to track their position and color. Information is captured stroke by stroke and can be "played back" at various speeds or stored on disks, e-mailed, or cut and pasted into other files.

Exhibit 11   High-Tech Computer Applications for Presentations

The SoftBoard shown above connects to a computer, which stores information written on the board with bar-coded dry erase markers. The device's playback mode works like a VCR, and information generated can also be stored on a disk, e-mailed, or cut and pasted into other files.

Paper easel pads or **flip charts** are commonly used with broad soft-point pens, markers, or crayons. These are always portable, using handy tripod easels. There are special cabinets to house them. If you have rooms used extensively for training classrooms, you may find it convenient to mount such flip charts. The Oravisual Company has a selection of these, which are readily available from audiovisual and art supply dealers.

Flip charts are generally 27x34 inches in size, and should be limited to use in small meeting rooms. When ordering flip charts, the convention services department needs to specify "flip chart easel with pad"; this will differentiate from the order for "tripod easels," which support signs but not the heavy flip chart pads. Some properties charge extra for pads and markers and supply the easels only; others include all materials needed for the presentation (easel, pad, and specified colors of markers) in the basic charge.

Pointers have become more sophisticated since the days of long wooden ones. Many speakers use metal pointers that telescope down to ball-point pen size. There are also electric hand-held **laser pointers** that can project an arrowhead onto the screen from 100 feet away, allowing a greater freedom of movement for the speaker.

Another device, which is used for presentations, communication, and training, is the personal computer. Most meeting planners realize that computers can easily become damaged in transit, and look for properties that can supply personal computers for workshops and training sessions (as well as for on-site convention registration).

While the cost of stocking computers may be prohibitive, many properties make arrangements with a local computer rental center when needed. Other properties have found that the establishment of computer systems has generated sufficient bookings to prove profitable. Yet a third alternative is for the property to "link up" with a nearby computer facility.

Hotels are not expected to supply the gear for sophisticated AV presentations such as multi-screen extravaganzas. These are usually handled by specialists. Local AV dealers or service organizations can handle such needs if you get requests for such sources.

It is usually enough for hotels to be able to supply on short notice such basics as slide projectors, overhead projectors, 16mm sound projectors, screens, chalkboards, and easel pads. Beyond this, advance notice should be given and a specialist dealer called in. A meeting planner should supply a list of all AV needs in advance.

To sum up, a hotel should have a good working relationship with a local audiovisual dealer/service organization. If such a company is not available, the hotel may decide to stock a department of its own. In either case, a hotel may choose to stock a minimum number of basic items and train staff people to maintain and operate them.

🖥️ INTERNET EXERCISE

Visit the websites for Audio Visual Solutions (www.avwtelav.com) and Presentation Services (www. psav.com). Both of these companies provide extensive audiovisual services to hotels and resorts. Navigate through these sites and answer the following questions:

1. Which of these sites offers a glossary of audiovisual terms?

2. Which site is the audiovisual firm for Freeman, a leading exposition service company?

3. What additional information have you learned about audiovisual equipment?

Charging for Audiovisual Equipment

No single rule can be established for how much a hotel should charge for AV equipment. Competition and the availability of outside firms, the number of guestrooms occupied, the extent of food and beverage functions, and the amount invested in equipment are some of the variables that must be considered in establishing a policy.

In some cases, the client deals directly with the AV supplier if an outside supplier is used. In other cases, you may contract with the outside service and pass the charges along to the client. Whether you use outside services or provide in-house equipment, you should supply a list of your prices to the client. A form detailing the specific equipment to be used and the cost for each piece is commonly used to provide an at-a-glance overview of AV charges (see box titled "Sample AV Equipment List/Price Sheet").

Remember when figuring your prices to include any additional charges, such as delivery costs, set-up charges, labor requirements (technician, sound mixer, etc.), and other miscellaneous fees (the cost of bringing extra electricity to a room, for example). These costs

Sample AV Equipment List/Price Sheet

A listing such as this one can be used to give the meeting planner an at-a-glance look at exactly what audiovisual equipment will be used for a meeting or function and its overall costs. This list can also be helpful to the property's convention service department, as it provides an overview of the equipment that will be in use on specific days.

Source: Bill Masheter, "AV Bids," *Association Meetings*. **Used with permission.**

AV Flowsheet

Meeting: **American Association of Widget Waxers**
Property: **Hotel Unique**
City: **Heartland**

Room: **All**
Session:

EQUIPMENT	BASE COST	Thu 14 (QTY)	Fri 15 (QTY)	Sat 16 (QTY)	Sun 17 (QTY)	Mon 18 (QTY)	Tues 19 (QTY)	Wed 20 (QTY)	TOTAL
Tripod screen 70" x 70"	$18.00		5 — $90.00	8 — $144.00	6 — $108.00	6 — $108.00	7 — $126.00		$576.00
Tripod screen 84" x 84"	$24.00		1 — $24.00	1 — $24.00	1 — $24.00	1 — $24.00	2 — $48.00	1 — $24.00	$168.00
Tripod screen 96" x 96"	$30.00							2 — $60.00	$60.00
CPE fastfold screen 10' x 10' front	$55.00		2 — $110.00	1 — $55.00	1 — $55.00	1 — $55.00	2 — $110.00		$385.00
CPE fastfold screen 12' x 12' front	$85.00		1 — $85.00	2 — $170.00	2 — $170.00	2 — $170.00	2 — $170.00	1 — $85.00	$850.00
2 x 2–35mm slide projector Kodak EKIII	$27.50		4 — $110.00	7 — $192.50	6 — $165.00	5 — $137.50	8 — $220.00		$825.00
2 x 2–35mm slide projector Kodak EKIII Britelite projector	$48.00		4 — $192.00	3 — $144.00	2 — $96.00	3 — $144.00	2 — $96.00	4 — $192.00	$864.00
2 x 2–35mm slide projector 500w xenon	$200.00			1 — $200.00	2 — $400.00	1 — $200.00	2 — $400.00		$1200.00
2 x 2 long lens	$15.00		7 — $105.00	7 — $105.00	7 — $105.00	7 — $105.00	8 — $120.00	4 — $60.00	$600.00
Safelock stand	$10.00		5 — $50.00	9 — $90.00	7 — $70.00	6 — $60.00	8 — $80.00	1 — $10.00	$360.00
Overhead projector	$27.50		5 — $137.50	10 — $275.00	6 — $165.00	5 — $137.50	8 — $220.00		$935.00
32" cart w/drape	$15.00		5 — $75.00	10 — $150.00	4 — $60.00	8 — $120.00	11 — $165.00	3 — $45.00	$615.00
16mm projector	$35.00		1 — $35.00				1 — $35.00		$70.00

may be figured into the price of the equipment, in which case you may wish to add a notation to that effect on your form. Or, additional costs may be listed separately on your form.

In any case, it is bad business to surprise the meeting planner with hidden costs; he or she must often work within an AV budget and should know exactly what will be charged for the entire meeting beforehand.

A logbook should be used to control the rental of audiovisual equipment. The log should contain the date ordered, the item, the delivery date, the guest billed, and the banquet check number. If an outside agency is billing the hotel, each invoice should be approved by the convention service manager and recorded in the logbook before sending it to accounting.

🖥️ INTERNET EXERCISE

Log on to the websites of Janus Displays (www.janusdisplays.com) and Four Winds Interactive (www.fourwindsinteractive.com) and answer the following questions:

1. What types of displays does each company offer?

2. List at least three hotels that have used each company's digital displays.

3. Which site did you find to be the most user-friendly? Why?

Union Regulations

One of the biggest complaints of meeting planners is the influence that unions have on the operation of audiovisual equipment. When AV equipment is ordered from outside firms, technicians are often part of the package. Projectionists, sound recording engineers, spotlight operators, and other specialists with expertise in complicated equipment are required. The problem arises when the services of a projectionist really aren't needed, but the union contract calls for such a person whenever the equipment is used. One convention manager told us:

> One of the biggest complaints by convention groups coming to our city is the requirement to pay the high union scale for some person to sit idly by and run a machine that anyone can operate. In some cities the meeting planner or his people can't even plug the equipment in, but must wait for a union projectionist.

While this may seem a little farfetched, the situation is actually becoming more common. And it is unlikely that union restrictions will be eased. Hotels should inform meeting planners of such rigid union regulations; a violation can lead to work stoppage and a crisis in the convention.

Signs and Notices

While signs are not considered audiovisual equipment, proper signage can add a great deal of visual impact to a convention or meeting as well as provide needed information. Only the simplest meeting can make do without *signs* and *notices*. They are most obvious when absent. The convention organization has a great stake in making sure that all goes smoothly, and signs are a great help within the convention area. Many convention planners are inexperienced, so the hotel must stand ready to advise and supply. Unless you want to scramble at the last moment, you should remind the client of the need for such signs and notices and expedite the creation of them.

Hotel Rules

Hotel and convention facilities need rules about the use of signs to avoid damage to walls and doors by indiscriminate use of tapes and tacks. It is a wise hotel that builds sign holders in crucial areas of its convention space. The best kind are permanent frames on or near doors of meeting rooms that hold standard-sized card stock for signs. Bulletin boards and other movable signboards are handled easily on short notice. Those reliable tripod easels make great sign holders and are most versatile.

A printed form outlining the hotel rules on signs should be submitted to the convention organizers to be included in their convention manuals. Exhibit 12 shows a typical sign policy regarding signs and their placement.

Hotel rules regarding distribution of notices also should be outlined clearly. Companies at trade conventions frequently request to distribute printed material at strategic points within the hotel or even to place them at the door of each delegate's room. Daily convention newspapers, newsletters, and advertising material are distributed in this manner.

The hotel should inform the organization if it is willing and able to undertake such distribution and if it charges for the service. The convention organizer should be directed to inform the participants about the recommended procedure to follow for such service.

It is important to learn if the convening organization has any policy about signs and distribution of newspapers, magazines, newsletters, advertising materials, or any other printed matter. The policy should be aided by the hotel staff's compliance, and all such requests should be referred to the convention staff. Hotel personnel should either handle or supervise the hanging of posters or signs.

Exhibit 12 Hotel Sign Policies

- All signs must be professionally printed or painted. Handwritten signs are not permitted.
- All signs must be displayed from easels.
- Placement of signs is restricted to meeting room area.
- No signs allowed in main lobby or guestroom corridors. The hotel has an electronic event board in the lobby for daily meeting room and registration information, as well as electronic signs outside of each function room.
- No pins, tacks, or adhesives of any sort are permitted on any hotel wall or door.
- No tape or glue permitted on painted walls. We realize that visual aids have to be displayed occasionally on the vinyl walls of our meeting rooms, but please check with your convention service manager on the type of tape to use on vinyl walls.
- The hotel's staff will be happy to assist in hanging any banners or large signs. Please check with your convention service manager for any restrictions.
- Please be advised that you will be held liable for damages if the above-mentioned policies are not adhered to.

This is a typical hotel policy regarding the placement of signs.

Sign Responsibility

It is the convening organization's responsibility to create signs. The convention service manager should be alert and advise when he or she notices that they are not being planned. A discussion of signs is helpful. The inexperienced meeting planner will appreciate it; the old pro won't mind the reminder.

The program indicates the need for signs. If the organization supplies them, the hotel is freed from the responsibility. We would suggest documenting that decision with a memo or letter. Most often, however, it is easier for the organization to have the signs made through the hotel to save the bother of transporting them.

Regardless of who accepts the responsibility of supplying signs, invariably a few more are needed at the last minute. Some arrangement must be made for such service. If the hotel cannot do the job in-house, a local supplier must be on call. In view of the fact that setup usually is on weekends and evenings, it is a wise convention hotel that sets up some sort of sign-making capability in-house.

Price Schedule

Establish a price schedule for all sign work, whether the hotel has an in-house shop or farms the work out. A work order should be made out for each sign; its location, if predetermined, should be noted. No verbal orders should be taken. State whether the hotel will bill the organization or the group will deal directly with a local sign company.

Locations

The purpose of signs is to give information, direct pedestrian traffic and activity, and assure a smoothly flowing meeting. Thus signs are needed in logical locations. Trace the progress of attendees step by step to determine what signs are needed and where.

To facilitate this process, which is especially important for large conventions, a convention service manager should provide a facility floor plan to meeting planners. This will enable the hotel and the meeting planner to develop a *way-finding plan*, which will not only show the convention attendees how to get around the hotel, but will also help the meeting planner to determine exactly where signs will be placed, what each sign should convey, and the size of the sign, among other details. A way-finding plan is especially useful if the convention service manager indicates the most common sign locations within the hotel and suggests sign sizes and recommended materials (in today's eco-friendly environment, natural materials are often suggested or requested). It is important to note that all signs should serve a distinctive purpose. A giant at-a-glance agenda sign may be obsolete before the meeting starts, so the wise convention service manager should suggest alternate choices, such as a video display board, to convey such information.

Large banners may be placed outside the hotel entrance or over the marquee. Or, **reader boards** listing the day's events, times, and locations can either be printed or displayed on video screens. The goals are to prevent delegates from milling around and to direct traffic.

Notices on the bulletin board in the lobby, in elevators, and at crucial places in the corridors will help facilitate movement of people. The hotel staff also must be informed about events so it can answer questions intelligently. Such informed staff people should include the assistant manager, the bell captains, the door attendants, and front desk personnel.

At some properties, the creation and placement of signs and notices may come under union contract. In this case, the client should be notified about any union jurisdiction to avoid difficulties.

Today's technology is also being used to convey convention information. Many hotels have an in-house television channel that is programmed to display meeting information (in most cases, there is no charge for scheduling information, and the convention organizer or vendors have the option to purchase time for additional messages or advertisements approved by the hotel). When guests awaken, they merely turn on the TV to access the schedule of events for the day. This method of communication is especially useful when last-minute changes have been made in the convention program.

An increasing number of properties are using **digital signs** to convey information outside meeting rooms and in high-traffic areas. While the initial cost of installing digital signs is higher due to installation or rental of the flat panel screens, programming costs, and electrical work needed for the units, the use of digital signs is appealing to meeting planners, as there are reduced costs (there is no need to change out placards daily, saving on labor and material) and less environmental impact. Janus Displays (www.janusdisplays. com) offers motion video, live RSS feeds, and flash animation to enable hotels to promote both convention events and advertise hotel amenities. Other applications of the software include way-finding displays and floor plans, and the broadcast of emergency warnings.

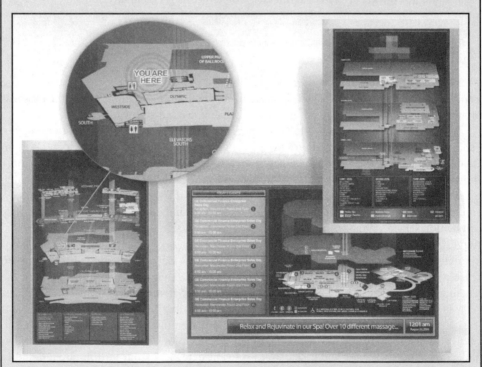

Sample Way-Finding Digital Displays

Two examples of how digital signs are used to assist convention attendees in finding their way around the convention facility. The hotel has advertised its amenities at the lower portion of the display on the right.

Summary

Convention programs are becoming more sophisticated and often involve the services of both the hotel and a number of outside suppliers to carry them out. Today's hotels must have—or be able to obtain—the latest in presentation devices in addition to the traditional flip charts and slide projectors used in the past. Today's meeting and convention attendees expect a professional presentation and come to the meeting with high expectations.

Endnotes

1. Hotel Convention Sales, Services, and Operations, Pat Golden-Romero, Elsevier.
2. Vicki Meade, "Picture This," Lodging, September 2000, p. 94.

Key Terms

ambient light—Level of illumination from natural lighting sources already existing in an environment.

amplifier—A device that enables sound signals to be intensified.

audio conferencing—A conference between two or more sites using only voice transmissions.

audiographic conferencing—Conference that combines visual capabilities with voice transmissions.

carousel projector—Most popular 2" by 2" (35mm) slide projector. Projects images from slides in mounts measuring 2 by 2 inches, presorted in round trays.

computer projection panel (LCD)—A device that projects the image on a computer monitor onto a screen. The self-contained unit, which contains a liquid crystal display panel, light source, and lens, works with both PC and Mac computers and DVD, VCR, and digital HDTV signals.

computer data projector—Similar to LCD panels used with an overhead projector, except it is a self-contained unit and uses its own light source to project the computer image onto the screen.

cordless/wireless microphone—Small, portable microphone that operates without any direct electrical connection. Often used when taking questions or comments from the audience.

DLP projector (digital light projection)—High-end projector with extremely high light (up to 15,000 lumens) and scan output. Most commonly used for very large screen and room applications.

digital signs—Signage that features electronic displays rather than printed copy.

dissolve unit—Device that activates fade-in and fade-out of slides; can be used with several projectors. Used to create a "seamless" slide presentation.

easel—Portable three-legged stand with a rack that is used to hold signs, boards, posters, charts, cork boards, magnetic boards, or other objects.

fast-fold screen—A large screen with a frame. The legs of this screen are attached at the sides to allow the screen to be folded down into a small case for storage (some fast-fold screens are also suspended above the viewing area). Most popular of large viewing screens. Available in sizes up to 30 feet high.

flip charts—Large pads on a tripod stand. Used by speakers for illustrations and drawings.

floodlights—Lights designed to provide general illumination.

follow-spots—Movable lights used to highlight the speaker or performance.

glass-beaded screen—Screen on which the surface is covered with tiny glass beads that reflect a bright image back at the audience but have a narrow viewing angle.

gobo patterns—Possibly derived from "go between," gobos are metal plates perforated with a pattern of holes to produce a projected image or outline, such as a corporate logo, when placed in front of a light (more sophisticated gobos rotate to create moving patterns). Gobos can also be made of glass that contains colored patterns.

in-house contractor—Contractor retained by a facility to provide on-site services as needed. In some cases, planners are not required to use their services, but may be charged a surcharge or facility fee for using outside contractors to provide the same service.

intelligent lighting—Lighting instruments that can be computer-controlled to move light around the room and project color and patterns on screens, scenery, walls, or the floor.

keystoning—Distortion of a projected image; the image is wider on the top and narrower on the bottom. Tilting the top of the screen can correct the problem, and many data projectors allow the operator to tilt the lens to correct keystoning.

laser pointers—Compact instruments consisting of a visible light laser. Used for pointing out features on a projected visual display.

lavaliere microphone—A microphone that hangs around the neck, leaving the hands free. Also called a lapel, neck, or pendant microphone.

lenticular screen—Screen with a silver-colored finish that has brighter reflective characteristics than a matte screen and a wider viewing angle than a beaded screen.

matte-surface screen—Screen having a flat or matte white finish that does not reflect as effectively as a glass-bead screen but can be viewed from virtually all front angles.

mixer board—Regulates the sound from multiple microphones. Also called a sound board.

monitor—Device used to view a video or computer image.

multimedia—Refers to the use of two or more audiovisual devices for a presentation.

overhead projector—Projects a transparency onto a screen. Speakers can write on transparencies as they are projected.

profile spots—Adjustable spotlights used to light lecterns, signs, and areas that need a tightly focused pool of light.

reader board—A sign, either printed or displayed on a video screen, that lists the times and locations of a group's events.

rearview projection—Movie, slide, or computer image projected from a projector positioned behind the screen onto the back of a screen placed between the viewer and the projector. Also called back projection.

receivers—Devices that convert electric currents or waves into visible or audible signals. Similar to a monitor, but with poorer picture quality.

roving microphone—Hand microphone, with or without a cord, that can be moved easily through an audience to take questions.

Safelock stand—Audiovisual equipment stand with four adjustable telescoping legs.

skirting—Pleated or ruffled draping used on audiovisual stands and stagings. Also used to drape buffet, reception, and head tables for food and beverage functions.

simultaneous interpretation—The interpretation of the presentation into another language while the speech is in progress.

standing microphone—Microphone attached to a metal stand placed on the floor. Can be adjusted for angle and height. Also called a floor microphone.

table microphone—Microphone attached to a small stand placed on a table, desk, or lectern.

translucent rear-projection screen—Plastic screen with a special gray coating that allows images to be projected from behind the screen and viewed by the audience in front.

tripod screen—Portable projection screen with three folding legs and a pull-up surface supported by a rod on the back. Usually not larger than 10–12 feet.

unidirectional microphone—A microphone that picks up sound from only one direction. Used for speeches, it is different from omni-directional devices, which pick up sound from all directions.

video satellite conferencing—Two-way, full motion, full-color, interactive electronic form of communication. Various transmission technologies can be used to link groups of people at two or more communications for face-to-face meetings, seminars, or conferences.

virtual conferencing—Any meeting at which people at two or more distant locations are linked using video, audio, and data for two-way communication via satellite communications or the Internet. Parties see and hear each other via TV screens or computer monitors and audio speakers.

web conferencing—Multiple participants take part in an online, real-time meeting.

xenon bulbs—Extremely high-intensity lamps that are replacing carbon arc light sources in follow spots and long-distance projectors.

 # Review Questions

1. In what cases would a hotel prefer an outside AV specialist rather than coping with in-house service? What have some hotels done to offer on-site service without the expense of purchasing AV equipment?

2. Discuss the types of sound systems, lighting, lecterns, and projection screens usually offered by hotels.

3. What types of projectors are commonly used in meeting presentations? When is each type typically used?

4. How has technology changed the presentation of information? What high-tech AV equipment is used today?

5. How do union regulations affect meeting presentations?

6. What factors are considered when hotels determine charges for AV equipment?

7. How do signs and notices improve convention traffic flow? Where is signage commonly posted to enhance the convention experience? What other methods are used to provide information to convention delegates?

 # Additional References

The Boston Handbook on Meeting Technology, Doug Fox, City of Boston and PCMA. Contact PCMA at (877) 827-7262.

Meeting Professionals' Guide to Technology. Contact EventCom Technologies by Marriott, 9550 West Higgins Rd., Suite 400, Rosemont, IL, phone 1-888-833-3572. www.marriott.com/eventcom

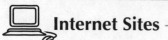

Internet Sites

For more information, visit the following Internet sites. Internet addresses can change without notice. If a site is no longer available at the address listed below, a search engine can be used to find the new address or additional, related sites.

AVW Audio Visual
www.avw.com

American Society of Training and
 Development
www.astd.org

Aspen Productions, Inc.
www.aspenproductions.com

Bauer Audio Visual, Inc.
www.bauerav.com

CP Communications
www.cpcom.com

In Concert Productions, Inc.
www.in-concert.com

International Webcasting Association
www.webcasters.org

Janus Displays
www.janusdisplays.com

Kodak—Meeting in a Box
www.kodak.com/90/mpi

Presentation Services
www.psav.com

Projection Presentation Technology, Inc.
www.projection.com

Chapter 16 Outline

Competencies

1. Describe registration and types of admission systems used for meetings, and summarize exhibit security issues. (pp. 537–546)

2. Identify special services properties sometimes offer meeting groups. (pp. 546–554)

3. Describe programs that hospitality properties offer for guests and children of meeting attendees, and explain the importance of checklists in planning meetings and conventions. (pp. 555–561)

Building Attendance: Mixing Business with Pleasure

Alan T. Brenner, CMP
Manager, Monterey Conference Center
Monterey, California

"Mixing pleasure into business is an attendance-builder. If the program includes pleasure along with the work, with leisure time activities and entertainment arranged and scheduled just for the fun of it—well now, there's a meeting with some of the drudgery taken out of it. Getting together just for the fun of it does more than just entertain. It refreshes the mind and uplifts the spirit. The fun times promote a different level of exchange: unstructured, open, less risky, easier to be heard, more attentive, even confidential. Managers and planners should arrange good times ahead of time. As the working sessions march along, it's good business to mix in some pleasure!"

16

Admission Systems and Other Services

O NCE THE PLANNER has made arrangements with the hotel for his or her event, the next step is to get the word out to the organization's members and provide a way for them to register for the convention. While registration is a function of the convening organization (it is not the same as room reservations, which are handled by the hotel), it is up to the property to ensure that everything runs smoothly on-site and to assist the planner with other aspects of the event, including security and activities for attendees and their guests. If problems arise, attendees may unfairly blame the hotel, so it is important to take whatever steps are necessary to ensure that convention guests have a positive impression of the hotel. In this chapter, we will take a step-by-step look at the registration process and detail ways that hotels can help with registration and other aspects of the organization's program, both before and during the event.

Convention Registration

The first step in the **convention registration** process is getting the word out to potential **attendees**, who may be called delegates at some conventions. This may be done by mail, e-mail, fax, via the organization's newsletter, or over the Internet (many organizations today set up a link to their convention information and registration on their home pages or create a dedicated convention site, such as the one illustrated in Exhibit 1). No matter which method is used, the planner should include complete program details, including dates and times of the event and specific functions, housing options (some are handled by the organization; others require that reservations be made directly through the hotel or an outside party designated to handle room reservations), and other services available, such as details on transportation, free shuttles, guest and children's programs, and so on.

Registration information is of special importance, so the **registration form** should clearly spell out fees, cut-off dates, and methods of payment accepted. Some registration fees are all-inclusive (the registration fee covers both the program and housing), while others include only the convention program or portions of it. If the registration fee is not all-inclusive, it is important to detail any extra charges, such as special events, tours, spouse and children's programs, and so on. Some organizations keep the registration fee as low as possible by offering attendees the option of choosing which functions they wish to attend (a budget-conscious attendee, for example, may opt for a less-expensive luncheon rather than the more expensive closing banquet, or forego smaller functions in favor of the banquet).

Most planners prefer **advance registration** over **on-site registration**. When attendees are given the opportunity to register in advance of the event, attendance is usually better, there are less on-site traffic problems, planners are able to create customized convention packets containing badges and tickets to selected functions ahead of time, and, last but not least, advance registration generates cash flow before the event. In order to encourage advance registration, some organizations offer a discount to attendees and/or promote the advantage of having a guaranteed place at functions that may be sold out by the time of the event.

Typically, a majority of attendees pre-register by mail, fax, and the Internet (the number of **registrants** opting for **online registration** is growing year by year), while a small percentage register on-site (this can vary, of course, depending on the organization). No matter which method is used for advance registration, it is important to follow up immediately with a confirmation that includes specific details, including the fee paid (and any balance due) and functions, courses, or activities selected; this eliminates the possibility of errors when the delegate arrives on-site. In addition to a confirmation, some organizations send out a registration packet that contains program information for registrants.

Exhibit 1   Online Convention Information and Registration

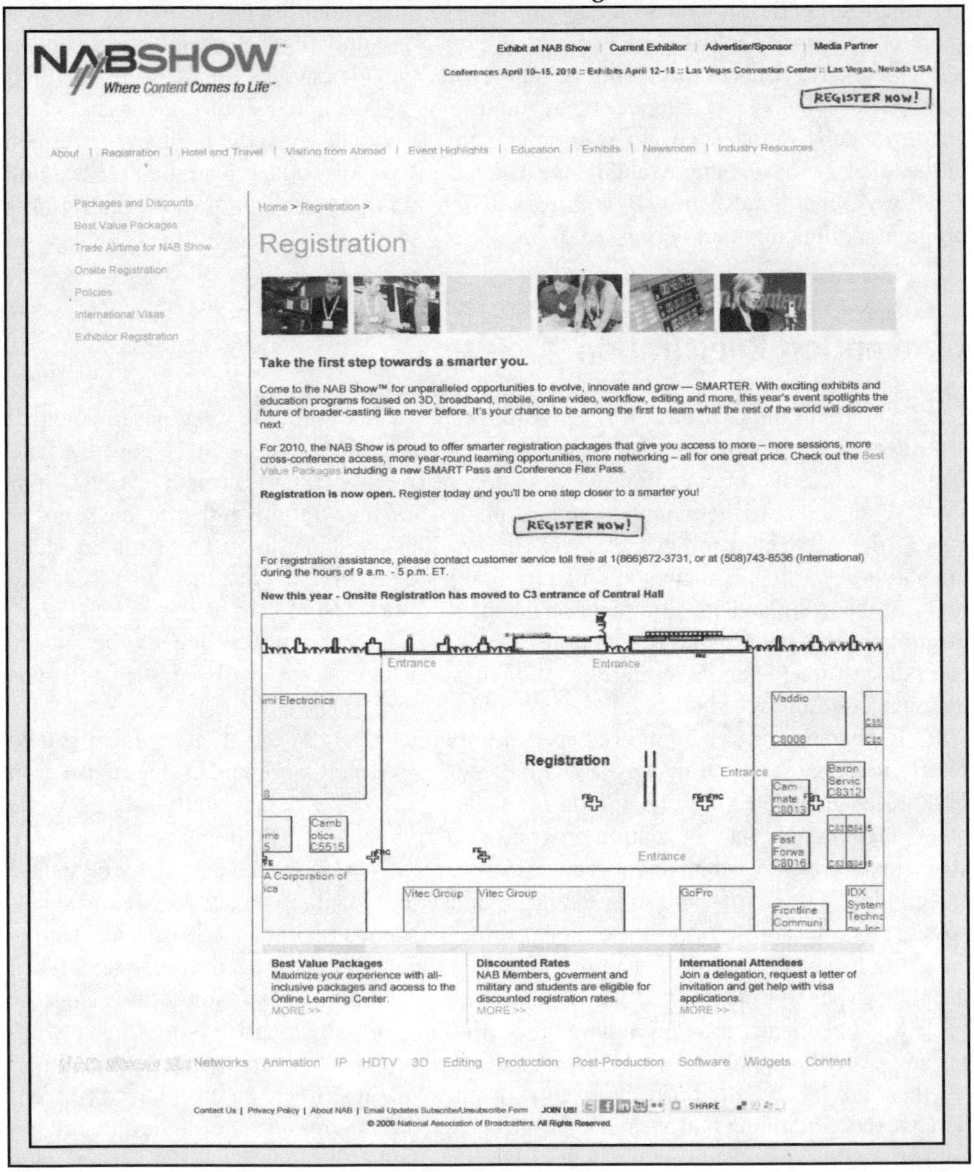

This website, created by the National Association of Broadcasters to promote their 2010 convention in Las Vegas, is one of many examples of how organizations create an online presence to provide information to potential attendees — and to allow them to register securely online for the event. Online information can also be offered on the convening organization's main site as well as on a separate site, such as the one that the NAB created, or the host hotel may offer a dedicated web space for the convenience of the planner and his or her organization.
Source: Courtesy of the National Association of Broadcasters.

Sending pre-convention information is an excellent way to market products and services. The organization, for example, may offer CDs of the meeting program or provide details on baby-sitting and other services. Hotels can also take advantage of this opportunity to reach future guests early by providing brochures or other printed advertising to be sent to attendees with the pre-convention information.

Once attendance is confirmed, the planner can begin to put together a **convention packet/kit** to be distributed to each attendee on site. Items provided by the convening organization in convention packets typically include:

* An introductory letter stating the purposes and aims of the meeting
* A list of scheduled events
* Information about speakers and entertainers
* Coupons or tickets to all pre-paid functions
* A badge or name tag

Hotels often provide meeting planners with information to be included in convention packets. Items commonly included are:

* Hotel facilities available to guests
* Times of operation for hotel restaurants and hospitality suites
* Details on check-in and check-out procedures and the handling of hotel bills
* Special favors, such as notepads and pens imprinted with the hotel's logo

Convention packets can be distributed in several ways. If rooms have been pre-assigned, packets can be left in guestrooms. Or, a pre-registered guest may pick up his or her packet upon registering at the front desk. Most planners prefer to hand out packets at the group's **registration area,** even though the first two methods help to eliminate traffic congestion (in most cases, the group has a separate area for pre-registered guests). Handing out packets gives event staff the opportunity to welcome attendees, answer questions, and immediately attend to any problems.

The location of the registration area is important, and may vary depending on the size of a group. An area may be set aside off the lobby or in front of the meeting rooms for a small group; a larger group will require a separate room (many convention hotels have separate lobbies near their meeting rooms) or, in the case of large conventions, may even be placed in a tent in the facility's parking lot. No matter which type of location is required, the registration area is usually broken down into three stations: a *packet pick-up area*, where pre-registered attendees sign in and receive their packets; an *area for on-site registration*, where delegates register and payment exchanges hands; and an *information* or *tour desk*, where delegates may register for special tours and other optional services.

Robert Paluzzi of Caesars Palace in Las Vegas, speaking to a class of ours, defined the convention registration area as the "headquarters place for the meeting." Since it will be visited by all the attendees at one time or another, careful attention must be given to the traffic flow and other aspects of the registration process. It is a wise convention service manager who works with the planner to ensure smooth traffic flow. In the case of smaller conventions, a straight line queue can be used to register attendees. With larger conventions, however, a **serpentine queue** is often used to minimize space needed for lines (to see examples of both types of lines, see sidebar titled "Registration System with Queue"). Serpentine queues offer the advantage of being positioned to direct people to various stations, and portions of the barricades can be removed as traffic lessens. This type of line also provides an opportunity for face-to-face communications between attendees.

It is important to remember that no one likes to stand in line. Therefore, offering diversions can make the time pass more quickly. Some registration areas are set up near video screens that provide information on the convention and the property, including directions to meeting rooms, information about property amenities and services, and information about area attractions. An electronic **message board** may also be set up in the registration area to provide up-to-date program information (nearly every convention registration area includes a "traditional" message board that enables attendees to post notes to each other, but an electronic board makes it easier for convention staff to provide last-minute updates).

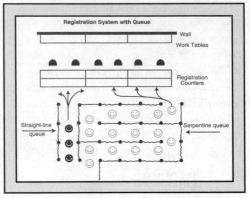

Source: *Professional Meeting Management, Fifth Edition, Kenneth G. Carlisle, "Taming the Registration Beast," Chapter 24, p. 369. Published by the Professional Convention Management Association, 2010.*

The second station in the registration area, which is for on-site registration, is generally handled exclusively by the meeting planner. The hotel, however, can make a positive impression and ensure that things run smoothly by having an adequate supply of back-up computers and printers (and other supplies) available for use in an emergency. The hotel may also offer assistance to the meeting planner regarding staffing needs.

Since convention registration has gone "high-tech," it is important that registration staff be fully trained to understand the computer programs used in the registration process (one such program is Experient's EventXL™). They should also be trained in payment procedures and be able to answer any questions that may arise (or know whom to contact if the problem is beyond their expertise). For these reasons, registration is sometimes handled by the convening organization's staff; in other cases, outside help is contracted through the city's convention and visitors bureau. In some cities, convention bureaus have their temporary help, which they offer at no charge or for a nominal fee. Temporary workers can be contracted through outside staffing agencies (these temporary workers are usually referred to as **temps**). If the convening organization wishes to use temps, the hotel or convention bureau should be able to provide a list of reputable staffing agencies.

Exhibit 2 shows a typical example of the third stop in the registration process, the tour and special service desk. City tours, trips to local attractions, exhibit setup instructions, and similar services are provided at this point.

Convention Security

Another important area of concern to meeting planners is staging a worry-free event. Meeting planners want to ensure that their attendees and exhibitors don't have to worry about their personal safety or their property. Hotels have responded to this requirement for greater security by installing electronic door locks, providing well-lighted parking and public areas, and offering high-tech alarm and surveillance systems in their exhibit halls.

In the wake of the terrorism threat following the attacks of September 11, 2001, hotels are also taking other measures to ensure the safety of their guests and their facilities. This begins with having all employees wear hotel-issued photo identification badges and putting plans in place to ensure heightened security at both front-of-the-house and back-of-the- house areas.

Exhibit 2   Tour and Travel Desk

The tour and travel desk is one of the stopping points in the delegate registration process.

Some hotels require checks of car trunks and baggage during heightened security alerts, while other properties, such as the Wynn Las Vegas, have beefed up security by putting specially trained dogs on patrol (see box titled "Security Goes to the Dogs").

Depending on the risk level, spot checks of delegates and their luggage may be made at the front desk and in the registration area; if the risk level is elevated, inspection may be mandated for all delegates and their belongings.

There should also be plans in place for back-of-the-house areas such as loading docks and entry points for exhibitors. In some cases, exhibitors may be required to be accompanied from the loading docks to the exhibit area; if the security risk level is high, exhibitors may be barred from the loading docks.

To assist hotels in planning for safety and security at their convention centers and exhibit halls, the International Association of Assembly Managers (IAAM) has released such publications as *Security Planning Guide* (for arenas, stadiums, and amphitheaters) and a *Best Practices Planning Guide* (for convention centers and exhibit halls).[1] Guides such as these help hotel people assess security risks and take the steps necessary to ensure a safe event.

The meeting planner can also contribute to a hassle-free meeting by controlling access to the group's functions. There are a number of ways in which this can be accomplished. The following pages will offer some insight into methods of controlling access to the event.

Controlled Admission

Most conventions insist upon registering all attendees, even when there are no charges for admission. At the very least, good mailing lists are derived from the data collected at the registration desk.

Security Goes to the Dogs

Security officers are a common sight in the hotels and casinos of Las Vegas, but eight "officers" stand out — the two Labrador retrievers and six German shepherds that patrol the Wynn Las Vegas. Wearing harnesses that say "Security" and displaying official hotel employee identification badges, the dogs, who have such Vegas-themed names as "Ace," "Blackjack," "Casino," "Jackpot," and "Keno," patrol all areas of the property — the two main entrances, the public promenade, the luggage distribution center, and back-of-the-house facilities. Wynn Las Vegas Vice President of Security Jerry Keller, a former two-term Metropolitan Police Department Sheriff, says of his canine "officers":

> The dogs are a deterrent. We want them visible for both our employees and guests. Visibility is a key element.The dogs are part of the overall security measures we've developed.

The dogs, who were specially trained in explosives detection techniques in Europe, accompany a select group of eight officers who have more than 35 years of combined canine-handling experience. If a suspicious scent is detected while on patrol, the dogs give a subtle reaction to their handlers, and a security team and the Las Vegas Metropolitan Police are notified to deal with the situation.

Although the dogs, like those in other canine units, go through extensive training with their handlers to build bonds, the Wynn security dogs do not go home with their handlers, as is typical in canine units. Instead, the dogs are housed in a $500,000 climate-control kennel complete with a bathing area and two large outdoor exercise pens.

Source: Howard Stutz, "Two Labrador Retrievers and Six German Shepherds Key Components of Wynn Las Vegas Security Operations," *Las Vegas Review-Journal*, May 7, 2005. Photograph courtesy of Wynn Las Vegas.

Admission often is limited to people with particular jobs or professions. People are screened at a central registration desk, fees are collected, and some sort of credential, usually a **badge**, is presented (Exhibit 3 shows two different types of badges). The registrant's name and affiliation are typed, printed, or written on the badge. Since adhesives, pins, and even clips can damage garments, putting plastic-encased badges on a **lanyard** that can be worn around the neck is a popular choice (if using this type of badge, names and other pertinent information should be visible on both sides in case the badge flips over). To avoid tangled lanyard cords, some planners include this type of badge in the attendees' individual registration packets. Another planner tells us that he places lanyard badges on jewelry stanchions purchased for this purpose; this practice not only eliminates tangled cords, but also makes the registration area look more organized and professional.

A more sophisticated type of badge is a plastic card embossed with the registrant's name and address, similar to a charge card. Exhibitors are supplied with "lead retrieval" devices that scan the badges of the attendees. At the end of the show, the exhibitor returns the machine to the lead retrieval company and receives a printout of all the attendees who visited the booth. (Exhibitors use trade shows to develop new trade contacts, and follow-up of these new contacts may result in additional business. That's the system that feeds the exhibits, which certainly support the entire convention.)

More sophisticated systems include barcoded badges, which can be used not only for on-site registration to identify guests, but also for billing purposes. Some registrants, for example, are coded to authorize the rental of audiovisual equipment or meals and special services. The bar codes will permit instant access to these charges, making cost-accounting far more accurate and up-to-date.

Another type of sophisticated badge that is being increasingly used by meeting organizers is the **radio frequency identification tag** (RFID). Each RFID SmartBadge has a small (often one-quarter-inch or smaller) chip — which is part computer chip, part transmitter — that is encoded with a unique identification number. The identification number, which corresponds to information in individual attendees' registration files, can be accessed by other badges via infrared sensors over a wireless network with a central server. One such badge, the nTAG by nTAG Interactive, allows badges to exchange data and find mutual areas of interest to facilitate networking.

RFID devices, which can also be accessed by special readers located at such strategic points as the registration desk, outside meeting and banquet rooms, and at exhibitors' displays, have proven invaluable in a number of areas besides networking. Meeting planners can use the ID codes to analyze registration information, track attendance at various events (the technology is often used to track attendance at educational sessions to verify completion of Continuing Education Units — CEUs), and even to help attendees find colleagues and friends at large sessions or banquets. Exhibitors can use ID codes to determine traffic flow to their booths and to qualify prospects and then follow up with them.

The convention service manager should be able to supply the names of local companies that stock different kinds of badges. However, it is generally not the hotel's responsibility to supply badges. This is the job of the convening organization. One innovative hotel stepped over this rule and designed a combination convention badge-service directory as a giveaway item. The badge-directory could be put into a suit coat pocket. The top of the badge provided space for the delegate's name and organization, and the bottom had the directory of the hotel's services.

Exhibit 3   Sample Convention Badges

Badges for attendees and exhibitors at conventions can range from an adhesive name tag (not pictured); to a badge placed into a plastic holder and worn around the neck; to today's sophisticated, interactive badges, such as the nTAG by nTAG Interactive. This badge not only displays the name of each meeting and convention attendee, but can also communicate with other badges to facilitate the tracking of attendees and provide networking opportunities.
Sources: Name badge courtesy of *Corporate Meetings & Incentives*; nTAG photograph courtesy of nTAG Interactive.

Badges are often color-coded to sort out the different categories of registrants. In some cases, all but exhibitors are barred from the exhibit hall area except during certain show hours, and the color-coding helps the security guards police this policy. Color-coding also helps the exhibitors recognize prospective customers.

Ticket Arrangements

Tickets provide a simple way of presenting evidence on which to base charges. If the agreement is to charge twenty dollars for each person served at a luncheon, each of those lunch tickets represents a twenty-dollar bill. The tickets must be counted immediately after the affair, and the number verified by an authorized person from the convention staff.

Systems for collecting tickets are simple enough, but nothing should be left for the staff to improvise. Suggest one system.

If the admission is to be by ticket, a small table or two, with chairs, is set up to handle the transactions. The table is especially needed if tickets may be purchased at the door and not merely presented. Sometimes tickets or badges are to be claimed at such a table. If you expect a crowd, you'll need several table stations. It is easier to bring up the subject and discuss it in advance than to scramble for tables and chairs at the last minute.

The tables and chairs may be placed just outside or just inside the door of the function room. Space is a consideration in deciding where to put the tables.

Waiters can collect tickets at a sit-down meal, while a hotel employee can collect tickets at the door for a buffet. It is worth repeating that a person on the convention staff should be at the door, too, to troubleshoot and to identify and greet VIPs. The tables also serve as a focal point for those who have questions, for notices to be placed, and for material to be picked up.

Tickets are often sold in advance by convention organizers. The associations make money from such functions in many ways. The price they charge might be more than they pay the hotel. In addition, not every ticket is used and no refunds are made. This happens especially when the convention sells a package of tickets for all the meals of the event at a flat fee.

Lots of ruffled feathers can be avoided if the hotel staff meets with the convention staff to decide what to do when delegates lose or forget their tickets. Don't expect a security guard or a waiter to improvise in such cases. If a convention executive is authorized to approve a number of admissions at each function, make some provision for recording that number. The simplest way to handle the problem of lost or forgotten tickets is for the convention executive to have extra tickets to supply when he or she sees fit to do so.

Sometimes, the count must be verified and the bill submitted to someone other than the convention organization. Many companies sponsor food functions as a way of helping an organization and to promote their image within that industry. The procedures are all the same except that you deal with another person. Arrangements should be made to ascertain who should be billed — the convention organization or the sponsor. And an authorized person should be designated to verify counts. Payment arrangements should be spelled out.

Uncontrolled Admission

There are times when the doors are open to all who care to enter. However, this is relatively rare. But it is common to permit all who have badges to enter, allowing a free flow of people into and out of the meeting and function areas. This is where color-coding helps a great deal.

When admission requires only a badge, and the badge is readily available, a security guard or other hotel person, such as a captain, stationed at the door may be all that is needed.

In such uncontrolled arrangements, it is most common for all liquor and food to be paid for with cash or coupons.

Exhibit Security

Conventions accompanied by exhibitions pose a number of potential problems that can be both embarrassing and costly to a hotel. Communication is needed between the convention service manager and the person responsible for security. Coordination and cooperation are necessary to provide the protection required.

When exhibitors are involved, the hotel's security force may have to be beefed up with outside help. The extra cost should be figured into the selling price and absorbed by the organizing group. There are a number of national **security contractors** that might be called in. However, many hotels maintain an on-call list of reliable off-duty police and fire officers. They have been trained in basic security procedures and are an excellent source of help.

All security personnel, whether part-time or full-time, experienced or inexperienced, should go through a training session and orientation of the hotel's facilities. A job description such as that shown in Exhibit 4 might be given to each guard. It outlines the guard's duties and responsibilities as an employee of the hotel.

Security in the modern hotel is becoming a more complex problem. There are four critical periods involved in security: move-in, open show hours, closed show hours, and move-out. Each is different.

Move-in and move-out periods are the most critical times because of the many transitory, poorly identified persons who have access to exhibits and displays. People have been known to take anything from calculators to operating tables. Security personnel must be wary of anyone who looks suspicious. For example, it is strange to see someone wearing an overcoat when it is quite hot outside. The security guard should make tactful inquiries of such people immediately. Security guards must be alert and observant to spot the unusual.

Tight security is essential at the loading docks and truck entries during move-in. Any materials or displays that go in and out of the door should have a pass-check from show management. Security personnel often encourage exhibitors during move-in to put their

Exhibit 4   A Typical Job Description for Hotel Security Guards

Hotel Security Personnel Job Duties and Responsibilities

1. *Help take care of an antagonist calmly.* Security must know how to take care of troublemakers through the use of logic or force without attracting too much attention from the guests.
2. *Watch for fire.* Security must know what to do about extinguishing small fires when fire trucks are still in transit.
3. *Report accidents.* A report must be presented to the hotel office for insurance purposes.
4. *Know how to take care of bomb threats.* Security must learn how to warn guests of bomb threats without making them panic.
5. *Emergency evacuation plan.* Security must know the hotel's exits so that in an emergency they can direct people.
6. *Crowd control.* Security guards must know how to handle crowds during a mass panic.
7. *Policing loading areas.* Loading areas must be checked for stolen hotel property or stolen exhibits.

And in addition to these duties, a security officer must have a law enforcement background and be familiar with local and state laws.

display goods in a "safe room," if one is available. If it is not available, they are encouraged to put their displays under their booths, away from the view of passing persons. This will help to eliminate theft.

It is advisable to have a roving officer rather than one who merely stands at the door; this more often is a psychological deterrent to would-be thieves.

During the show or exhibit, much of the responsibility for guarding the booths falls on the exhibitors themselves rather than the security guards; this is especially true of large conventions, where it is just not feasible to have a security guard at each exhibit. Exhibitors who decide to leave their booths for any period of time should have replacement personnel so the booths are never left unattended.

Burns Security Institute once surveyed exhibitors and show personnel around the nation about exhibit hall security problems. The 200 exhibitors who responded to that survey felt that one of the primary problems in exhibit areas was internal pilferage, with both exhibit hall and exhibit workers taking advantage of managements' trust by stealing items.

Likely times for employees to steal is during dismantling. Security needs are crucial at this time because so much is going on in the hall. The employee knows the hotel, its hiding places, and the exits that are unguarded. Because of this, employee thefts are often successful.

Exhibits are also very vulnerable to theft during the evening when exhibitors are gone. Exhibitors often leave in a hurry to join the merriment without putting expensive exhibits in the security rooms, if they are available.

Electronic surveillance is a new feature of hotel security systems. Burglar alarms and closed-circuit television are used now, but not to the extent that people might believe. Certainly there is going to be better control with such equipment, but there will be a greater expense, which the organizing group will have to bear. Thus many conventions will decide not to use such surveillance because of their tight budgets. If, however, the exhibition is a large one with highly valued items, this electronic equipment will be used.

Other Services

There are a number of other services that may have to be arranged by the convening organization or that will require your input and assistance to execute. Press facilities may have to be designated (most **press rooms** include a place for the press to do interviews, as well as telephones and computer access to enable reporters and photographers to submit coverage). Sources for computer and printer rentals and other needed equipment must also be found. Local modeling agencies, public stenographers, and similar services may have to be called in. Most of these services do not require special handling, just advance notice and some thought.

Convention Headquarters Room

The administration of a large convention often requires a staff of five to ten people, so the association needs a room to work out of as an office. Hotels recognize this need and usually provide such a room free as part of the package. Ideally, this room should be adjacent to the meeting rooms and equipped with tables, computers and printers, duplicating machines, and perhaps a stenographer. Naturally, the hotel will charge for any such equipment supplied.

The Sonesta Hotel chain has gone a step further. A secretary is assigned to large groups free of charge to work in the headquarters room. The secretary's functions might include typing, handling messages, and arranging show tickets, among other functions.

Convention Hospitality Suites

Planning something for the evening hours is sometimes a real problem for meeting sponsors. One solution a convention manager might suggest to a client is a company **hospitality suite**. This calls for coffee, a bartender, card tables, a television — in general, a lounging atmosphere where the members may congregate informally. The advantage to the hotel is that the delegates stay in the hotel and spend their money there rather than being out on the town.

Another service provided by the hotel is what might be called "controlled hospitality suites." There is a tremendous demand for hospitality suites when a large convention and exhibition move into a hotel. Exhibitors rush for these rooms as places to entertain and transact sales. But the association executive also needs these suites for board and convention officials. When the demand for hospitality suites is greater than the number available, *the hotel's first obligation is to the meeting planner.*

Meeting planners are specific about the assigning of suites. Ground rules often state that:

- Exhibitors are not to have their hospitality suites open while meetings are scheduled.
- Non-exhibitors will not be allowed to have hospitality suites.

Guest Packages

Convention exhibitors and convention delegates frequently bring samples and promotional material that they would like to distribute at the meeting. Procedures for accepting these guest packages must be determined and communicated to the employees involved. If adequate storage space is available, packages are generally stored free. But it should not be a hotel's practice to store large packages, or any packages for an extended period of time.

To avoid any misunderstandings, the hotel's policy can be stated in a clause, such as the following, in the organization's contract:

> ### Storage of Exhibit Materials
> *The Hotel cannot accept and store shipments of exhibit materials in advance of a show. Due to County fire department regulations, crates, boxes, and other items to be used for the storage of exhibit materials cannot be stored on the Hotel premises during a show. It will be necessary for you to make arrangements with your exhibitor service to receive and store exhibits for delivery to the Hotel on the move-in date. These arrangements must also include the removal of empty crates, their storage during the show, and their subsequent return to the Hotel on the move-out date. Should any property not be removed by the designated move-out date, the Hotel management may store, or cause to be stored, any such property and your organization or the exhibitor will be charged a reasonable fee for all expenses incurred.*

A package log book should be maintained, showing the date of receipt, where a package is stored, and both the addressee and addresser.

Exhibitors occasionally misdirect packages to the hotel. Such packages should be referred to the decorator's warehouse for later delivery. If exhibitors ask the hotel at the end of the convention to wrap and send out packages, the service should be provided at a charge.

Telephones

Telephone service should be discussed with the convention staff before the event; it may be necessary to bring in telephone company representatives. Many conventions want provisions made for incoming calls to meeting rooms and exhibit areas. Outgoing telephone service from meeting rooms can be abused if it is not controlled. If outgoing service is requested, it must be planned. You should discuss who is to pay and when. Exhibit 5 details the fees of the Ritz-Carlton Lake Las Vegas for telephones and other communications.

Exhibit 5   Sample Telephone and Communication Charges

THE RITZ-CARLTON®
LAKE LAS VEGAS

Event Technology
CONNECTIVITY
PRICING GUIDE:

Meeting Space Connectivity:

❋ **House Phone: <u>No Charge</u> for first house phone.**
   ($25.00 per phone/per day for each additional phone.)

❋ **D.I.D. Phone Line: $50.00 per day + calls**
   (All calls billed through PBX.)

❋ **Conference Phone: $125.00**

❋ **Speaker Phone: $75.00**

❋ **T1 Connection: $700.00 Per room or location**
   Up to 5 terminals per location. (One time connection charge.)

Client Communications:

❋ **Client Walkie Talkies: $35.00 Per day.**
        (Each includes spare battery and charger.)

❋ **Nextel Communicators: $125.00 Per Week.**
      Phone capabilities $1.00 per minute
        (Includes incoming/outgoing and Long Distance.)

Most hotels prepare a detailed listing of charges for telephones and other communications equipment available for meetings and conventions. This form details the fees that the Ritz-Carlton Lake Las Vegas charges for telephones, high-speed Internet connections, and other communication devices.
Source: Courtesy of the Ritz-Carlton Lake Las Vegas. Used with permission.

Printing and Duplication

Most printing is done by the organization before the event, but last-minute work is often needed. You should be able to supply the names of cooperative printers nearby who have proved their reliability. Some hotels have in-house print shops.

You should inform the convention staff of what types of duplication you can handle, what the lead time is, the costs, and the kinds of material you can handle. Have a fee schedule printed and presented beforehand or on display. You may have an in-house shop with offset printing capability, a stencil or spirit duplicator, or one of the more sophisticated models of office copiers. All of these can handle notices and the like. The convening organization is not the only one to seek such services. Many of the exhibitors look for last-minute

---

Executive Business Center Services

Facsimile

Local Fax:	$1.00/page
Domestic Fax:	
First Page	$4.00
Additional Pages	$2.50/page
International Fax:	
First Page	$10.00
Additional Pages	$3.00/page

Computer

Workstation:

Word Processing	$25.00/hour
Printing	$0.25/page
Includes Complimentary Internet	

Clerical:

Typing	$10.00/page
Statistical Typing	$15.00/page

Rental Equipment

Fax Machine	$400/3-7 days
Copier	$400/3-7 days
Printer	$190/2 days
Color Printer	$440/2 days

Additional equipment available upon request

Comb Binding

Small Comb	$4.50/each
Medium Comb	$5.00/each
Large Comb	$6.00/each

Office Supplies

Legal Copy Paper	$12.00/ream
Formatted Diskette	$1.00/each
Legal Note Pad	$2.00/each
Name Badges	$2.00/badge
(plastic sleeve, clip, printing)	

Additional supplies available upon request

Photocopying

Black & White Copies:

Letter Size	
1-200	$0.25/page
200-500	$0.20/page
500-1000	$0.15/page
1000+	$0.10/page
Legal Size	
1-200	$0.30/page
200-500	$0.25/page
500-1000	$0.20/page
1000+	$0.15/page
Ledger Size	
1-200	$0.50/page
200-500	$0.45/page
500+	$0.40/page

Double sided copies, add $0.10/page

Color Copies:

Letter Size	
1-100	$2.50/page
100-200	$2.00/page
200-300	$1.50/page
300+	$1.00page
Legal Size	
1-100	$3.00/page
100-200	$2.50/page
200-300	$2.00/page
300+	$1.50/page

Double sided copies, add $0.50/page
Colored and Three-hole Paper, add $0.10/page

Transparencies

Black & White	$2.50/page
Color	$5.00/page

Taxes not included in copy and facsimile prices

The Ritz-Carlton, Lake Las Vegas
1610 Lake Las Vegas Parkway
Henderson, NV 89011
Phone: (702) 567-4700
Fax: (702) 567-4777

A Sampling of Specialized DMC Services

(Including but not limited to)

- Creative proposals for on- or off-site themed special events—including decor, conception, audiovisual, sound and lighting professionals, entertainment, centerpieces, and more.

- Entertainment procurement—DJs, musicians, impersonators, comedians, games

- Customized off-site tours—historic, industry related, spouse, or fun

- Off-site venue and entertainment logistics and suggestions

- Airport transfers—sedans to coaches—including VIP Meet and Greet

- Shuttle services—hotel to venue

- Company picnics: catering, entertainment, and permits

- On-site registration and hospitality services

- Teambuilding design: ropes Courses, scavengers hunts

- VIP amenities—themed gift baskets and promotional items

Source: Vivian K. Elba and Renee T. Mulvey, "The Destination Management Company: A Hotel's Partner in Sales," *HSMAI Marketing Review*, Spring 2005, p. 72.

printing to fill needs of their exhibits and/or the sales meetings that are frequently held in conjunction with the convention.

Hotels that handle a large number of meetings and conventions often have business centers to meet printing and duplicating needs and other secretarial or business services. The box titled "Executive Business Center Services" details some of the services (and their costs) offered to meeting planners at the Ritz-Carlton Lake Las Vegas.

Decorations

From time to time you will get calls for special draperies, flowers and plants, and special flags and banners. Exhibit decorators usually handle such items; they have the expertise and the trained personnel to take care of these requests.

Hospitality suites may need floral decorations. You should have an arrangement with a florist to facilitate service and billing. Make clear to your clients whether they are to pay you or deal directly with the florist. Unless you have an arrangement with a florist for exclusive business, you really shouldn't care if the florist and your clients make their own arrangements. Often, clients are happy to be steered to firms in the house or recommended by the hotel so that they can feel sure of prompt service, especially when they are not obliged to use that particular vendor.

Entertainment

There are union regulations and tax liabilities to be considered when live entertainment is used. This varies from area to area and should be part of the general information included in the letter of agreement and discussed at the pre-event meetings.

Live entertainment will also affect your table and chair setups. Bands may call for raised platforms. Entertainers have different requirements, too. The entire stage area should be discussed to make sure you have enough space and meet all specifications.

Hotels are often called upon to supply dressing rooms for entertainers. A problem is that entertainers prefer to rehearse on the scene, which may not be possible because the room may be in use for other convention events. This should be taken into consideration when the program is arranged and rooms selected. It may not be possible to honor such requests.

Preferred Suppliers/Exclusives

Because meetings and conventions have gotten so sophisticated and complex, it is not always possible for the planner to make the necessary arrangements for each of the services described in this section. In this case, the help of an outside party is often sought. Convention decorators, drayage companies, florists, printers and duplicators, photographers, **ground operators,** and audiovisual specialists are a few of the outside organizations that can be used.

Yet another outside source is the *special event planner*. The services of special event planners vary a great deal; some catering and production companies, for example, advertise "event planning services" to give the impression that they provide complete planning services, when, in fact, they do not. A true special event planner brings together a combination of the best vendors (florists, caterers , entertainers, staging companies, and so on) to meet a client's needs and budget. In an effort to identify qualified special event planners, the International Special Events Society (www.ises.com) offers a certification program. Meeting planners who hire a planner with the CSEP designation are ensured of getting a highly trained professional who can, indeed, provide all needed services.[2]

Today, many meeting planners turn to **destination management companies** to manage such details of their meetings as transportation, group tours, and elaborate functions. The advantages to using a DMC are that they are experts on their particular area and that they have built relationships with local vendors who can provide reliable services, often at a discounted rate due to the volume of business that DMCs generate from them. As with special event planners, however, the expertise and services offered by DMCs can vary. The sidebar titled "A Sampling of Specialized DMC Services" provides a list of services most commonly offered.

🖳 *INTERNET EXERCISE*

Destination Management Companies Join Forces to Form a Global Presence

In 2008, the DMC Network, an Orlando, Florida–based company representing more than 50 North American destinations, formed an alliance with Ovation Global DMC, a Dublin, Ireland–based consortium of European and Middle Eastern DMCs. Log on to the companies' websites, listed below, to answer the following questions:

- dmcnetwork.com
- ovationdmc.com

1. What are the key points in the mission statements of each group?

2. What standards must be met for consideration in the DMC Network?

3. Briefly describe the Ovation Strategic Partner Programme.

4. What advantages has teaming up provided to each company?

BEST PRACTICES

The San Francisco Marriott: In-House Destination Management

Marriott has led the way in offering in-house destination management services. Destinations by Marriott, a new division of Marriott Lodging, has been established at several properties. Resort properties were the first to offer in-house event planning, but now a growing number of city hotels are adding it as well.

The trend toward more elaborate meetings and conventions has been on a collision course with company downsizing, forcing more meeting planners to rely on outside help for planning the myriad details associated with group functions. More and more, planners have been turning for help at the scene of their functions—destination management companies (DMCs) that can arrange for everything from ground transportation to decorations to elaborate theme parties.

Many properties, who see this type of service as a logical extension of the sales effort, are getting into the act as well; either offering hotel office space to outside DMCs or setting up their own in-house DMCs. This enables the hotel to offer everything required by the meeting planner—from planning through execution of the function—with the added benefits of consolidating deposits and posting all charges to the group's master account.

Barbara Morris, director of Destinations by Marriott at the San Francisco Marriott, says her hotel's in-house destination management program is "awesome." She says:

> Customers are so pleased to have the ability to work with one supplier. They like the Marriott name and the service level behind it.... It's wonderful for the meeting planner who comes to us. They have a master account with everything on it. And they generally get a better deal if everything is done in-house.

Naturally, the entry of hotels into this area has sparked some resentment from private DMCs. They claim that the DMC staff at the hotel may not have the experience—or contacts—of established DMCs. But the entry of hotels into this arena can only make things better for meeting planners—there will be increased competition for business, resulting in even more creative options—and better service.

Meeting planners are not required to use the services of an in-house DMC; a property's service bids for the business just as outside services do. Many meeting planners, however, appreciate this "one-stop shopping" option, making it likely that the number of in-house DMCs will continue to grow—and offer more and better service to stay competitive.

Source: Ruth A. Hill, "The Entertainers: Hotels Assume the Role of Destination Managers," *Lodging.*

DMCs can range from one-person shops to franchise operations to large companies, and they may handle diverse business; some, for example, handle specific groups, such as corporate or incentive groups, others may service only associations, while the larger DMCs typically handle a mix of all three categories of clients. Location can also play a part in the focus of a DMC; for example, The Meeting Manager Company, which has offices in Southern California, specializes in association programs in San Diego and incentive business in Palm Springs.

Costs and methods of payment for DMC services will also vary. Some DMCs bill by the hour, while others have a set commission. When a commission is charged, most DMCs charge 15 to 20 percent above their costs, which may actually be a bargain, as DMCs can often negotiate lower rates with vendors.

In addition to planners, hotels that have their own convention services departments can benefit from joining forces with local DMCs. Partnering with a DMC that can handle outside details allows the property's staff to concentrate on meeting needs and food functions.

Rather than tie up staff to research special requests, a DMC that is familiar with what is available in the area can provide an immediate solution to a meeting planner.

DMCs that regularly work for hotels are familiar with the specific needs of planners and the importance of providing reliable service to them. And a hotel's willingness to leave important details to a trusted outside firm demonstrates that the property is committed to ensuring the best experience possible. Payment for the use of DMC services can be billed separately, or, as is often the case, added to the master billing.

The increasing use and success of outside DMC services has prompted some hotels and chains to establish their own DMCs (see Marriott "Best Practices" box). Nashville's Opryland Hotel and the Pointe Hilton Resorts, for example, own and operate their own DMC services outright rather than deal with outside suppliers. At the Boulders Resort and Golden Door Spa, the Destination Service Department and the Catering/Conference Services department work together to provide complete in-house destination management services, including off-property theme events, recreational activities, tours and sightseeing, transportation services, and room amenities and gifts in addition to meetings support and team-building programs. By providing in-house, "one-stop shopping" to meeting planners, the hotel generates additional revenue that would otherwise have gone to an outside vendor.

Receptive agents, who perform such services for delegates as guided tours and local transportation, are also extremely important to the success of a convention, as are local talent and modeling agencies, speakers bureaus, and temporary personnel services. Most hotels maintain a list of *preferred suppliers* who can provide specific services to meeting planners. In many cases, the hotel receives a commission for recommending these suppliers.

Many times, hotels allow their preferred suppliers to maintain an **on-site office**. In this case, the supplier has a greater chance of getting most of the convention business, and pays the hotel rent and a percentage of sales. While some meeting planners appreciate the convenience of such on-site service, many are expressing concern over the growing number of properties that insist that the convening organizations use the property's preferred supplier (see box titled "Preferred Suppliers: What Meeting Planners Have to Say").

Sometimes, hotels and convention centers not only have a list of preferred suppliers or their own DMCs, but also have **exclusives** with some vendors. This means that only a specified vendor is allowed to provide a service or product (catered food and beverage, Internet/telecommunications equipment, decorating and/or floral service, security, cleaning services, and so on) within the facility. When a hotel has an exclusive, meeting planners do not have a choice of suppliers—and cannot bring in products or services from off-property sources.

Exclusives, which benefit hotels by generating more revenue, are becoming more common, but they are not popular with all meeting planners. Hotels can "sell" these exclusives to meeting planners by promising a better service level (hotels must select vendors that deliver, of course, and can point out vendors' familiarity with the facility and locale and his or her accessibility). Sometimes, hotels can also demonstrate that their exclusive vendors can offer services or products (such as audiovisual equipment, for example) cheaper than the organization can purchase or rent them and have them delivered to the function.

Meeting planners are more likely to accept the idea of exclusive suppliers if they understand the rationale behind using them. John Houghton, vice president of sales and marketing for the Metro Toronto Convention Centre, says:

> When you talk about the benefits of using an exclusive supplier, you need to keep in mind the service they provide. Electrical services are exclusive because we don't want just any company having access to critical systems like electrical. You want someone who is intimately familiar with

---

Preferred Suppliers: What Meeting Planners Have To Say

"The value of a preferred supplier list depends on where my meeting is located. In my home area — Greater Chicago — I have my own resources and preferred suppliers. I have had experience with most suppliers or know someone else who has used the vendors and service providers.

"Away from my home base, I'd welcome a preferred supplier list to tell me who does a good job in the area, but I still would do my own calling to compare prices. I wouldn't be bound to using that list, but I would appreciate that the hotel offered it."
Roseanne M. Hoban, account executive, Association Management Systems, Naperville, IL

"I like to find my own suppliers and negotiate with them directly. I think you get a better price. If you go through the hotel to book your photographer, for example, there's going to be an added cost. The hotel is going to make some money. But it takes a lot of time to find suppliers on your own. The advantages of using a hotel's preferred suppliers are that they are familiar with the property's quirks and are likely to do a good job because their position with the hotel is at stake. And even if a planner is working with an in-house supplier, he or she can still negotiate with them directly and pay them directly."
Pat Fagan, conference service manager, Sun Life of Canada, Wellesley Hills, MA

"The issue of preferred suppliers is a hot one right now. More and more hotels are doing it, and I have even heard of hotels that are telling meeting planners that there will be a 15-percent surcharge if they do not use a preferred supplier. That's because the hotels are getting a commission from suppliers they recommend.

"I don't like it. I want to be able to choose the decorating firm, the florist, and the audiovisual company I use for my meetings. Now, if I am in a city where I have no contacts, a list of preferred suppliers might be helpful. But I don't want to be bound by it.

"Hotels that tell planners which suppliers they should use — or penalize them with a surcharge — should realize that the practice is going to cut into their business. For example, our association has a decorator we've used for the past seven or eight years. He knows our show and travels with us on site visits to cities we'll be using. While I am negotiating with the hotel, he meets with local decorators to explain exactly what we need and to find someone to contract for the job. I want his advice, not that of the hotel.

"Other groups have two- or three-year contracts with audiovisual people who will go to their meeting sites and run locally rented equipment to make sure the show goes the way it's supposed to. Now, if the hotel insists the planner employ a preferred supplier, the association is still bound to a contract with its own audiovisual firm and duplicate services could get very expensive."
Janet Balletto, national meetings coordinator, American Mathematical Society

---

our infrastructure and knows what can and cannot be done. We never want the lights to go out during an event due to someone who "thinks it should have worked without any problems," but didn't understand the electrical load of everything else that is going on in the building.

Our exclusive suppliers maintain offices within our facility and are linked into our communication systems. They have a warehouse full of gear on-site to be able to deal with last-minute requests or last-minute changes. These are also "event savvy" people who are used to *working with the idiosyncrasies of the business and people who have immovable deadlines.*[3]

In some cases, hotels may compromise to secure the group's business; they may allow the convening organization to bring in its own decorator if it agrees to use the property's photographer, for example. Meeting planners should always be advised beforehand of existing exclusives, and all arrangements made—whether agreeing to the sole use of exclusive vendors or otherwise—should be clearly understood during the negotiating process and spelled out in the group's contract to avoid any misunderstandings.

Guest/Companion Programs

Many hotels have neglected a potentially profitable market in not promoting guest attendance at conventions. The average convention delegate spends approximately $200 per day in the hotel. If the delegate brought a guest, the expenditures for both might well exceed $250 per day. It is a general conclusion that members stay longer and spend more money when a spouse or guest is along; both result in more money for the hotel.

This additional revenue, which is known as **auxiliary business**, typically comes from money spent in the property's restaurants, lounges, and gift shops and for the use of its recreational facilities; it also includes extra revenue for guestrooms and other services rendered to exhibitors at conventions and trade shows. The hotel can also generate extra income by offering **ancillary services or activities**, such as baby-sitting services or local tours and other programs to complement the meeting. This is added revenue for the hotel and doesn't require the selling of another guestroom. For a 500-delegate convention, this could mean an *additional* $25,000 a day in sales—no small sum for any hotel.

More often than not, attendance at today's conventions includes the spouse or a guest. According to the most recent *Meetings & Conventions* Meetings Market Report, over 11 million spouses or guests attend conventions and association meetings each year. And for some groups the annual convention has become a family affair. Convention service people should make provisions for entertaining these additional guests.

The first step, after recognizing the significance of attendance by spouses, is to sell the idea of a **guest/companion program** to the meeting planner, who after all must increase the convention budget if these programs are part of the plan. Point out that the presence of spouses and guests may be healthy for the meeting. The attendees are less likely to come to

Cooking classes are popular activities for guests/companions at conventions.
Source: Photograph courtesy of The Ritz Hotel, Paris, France.

the morning session bleary-eyed after a late night on the town if their spouses or guests are accompanying them. Sessions will probably be more businesslike and delegates more alert, attentive, and receptive. In addition, ticket sales for food and social functions will increase markedly, with positive effects on the meeting planner's anticipated revenue.

Suggest to meeting planners that they often determine the attendance figure. If delegates anticipate they'll have a good time, they encourage their mates or guests to attend the convention. Spouse and guest attendance at conventions fosters a close-knit family feeling, which improves the company's image. If a poll were taken, it would probably show that the most successful meetings were those attended by both the husband and wife. This is a strong factor in corporate decisions to invite the spouse or a guest to attend.

Discussing options to cover the costs of these activities may also increase their appeal. In some cases, the organization subsidizes all or part of the costs of additional activities, but attendees may pay themselves, which does not add to the meeting planner's budget. Activities such as tours may be added as options to the group's program and included in the convention fees, or the attendee may purchase tickets for a tour directly from the tour operator. A third — and often attractive — option is to arrange for sponsorships for outside programs. A local attraction, such as an outlet mall or theme park, for example, may cover part of the costs, offer discounts, or provide transportation to and from the hotel because the attraction can expect to generate additional revenue from the participants.

Building Guest/Companion Attendance

Once a meeting planner is convinced of the value of inviting guests, much can be done by hotels to promote their attendance. Working in conjunction with the meeting group, the convention service manager should suggest ways to create interest and thus increase attendance. The following methods might be used:

- Supply the meeting planner with the hotel's brochures and internal marketing pieces and suggest that he or she include them with group mailings. Include such items as menus, pictures of the hotel, and highlights of the city.
- In addition, you might secure a complete and up-to-date membership mailing list from the meeting planner and send personalized letters describing the planned activities. Also tell potential guests about the climate and offer suggestions on appropriate attire.
- Suggest that the convening group designate a chairperson for a guest/companion program. Offer to work with this person in arranging shows, sightseeing, and other interesting programs.
- Advertise in the popular trade journals of the conferring group. Your ad should extol the virtues of having the delegates' guests come along.

Activities for the Attendees' Guests

Hotels have recently taken positive steps to increase spouse and guest attendance; a few properties have even created guest/companion service departments with directors to meet the needs of these attendees. Working alongside the convention service manager, the program's director helps convention committees plan and coordinate interesting programs.

Most hotels cannot afford to staff a special director for spouses and guests, but every hotel dealing in group business should at least prepare a directory of possible activities for

Developing Attendance With Guest/Companion Programs

Janet H. Wright, CEM
President, The Wright Organization, Inc.

"One of the most challenging aspects of meeting and exposition management is developing memorable recreational and social programs for both attendees and spouses and guests. In order to do so, you must know what the local area has to offer, and, equally important, know your audience. In some recreational areas, such as Orlando, Anaheim, etc., it is foolish to plan tours that compete with existing recreation. In those cases, we try to negotiate discounted tickets, line passes, etc. Yet in many locales where there is an abundance of activities we have found our more successful activities are those which we have created with the help of a convention service manager or a destination management company. Since we know our audience, the broad strokes of an idea are normally generated by us, with the convention service manager supplying the details and implementation. For example, one of our corporate meetings featured a 'Beach Olympics.' Since it was obvious we would lose attendees to the beach in the afternoon anyway, we made the beach part of the corporate program. The event consisted of surfing, volleyball, sand castle building, hula dancing contests, and, during rest periods, participants heard a brief — and usually humorous, always instructive — message from the sponsor. With the tightening of tax laws, it is imperative that these supplementary activities fall within IRS guidelines as education rather than recreation to be considered tax-deductible."

these attendees. This directory should be freely distributed to meeting planners. Exhibit 6 provides examples of unique guest programs created by several properties.

Shopping Trips. A very popular event that promotes goodwill is the shopping trip. Proper planning is very important. Normally, chartered buses take care of the transportation. A store guide should be scheduled to greet the attendees and, if possible, the group should be shown behind the scenes.

Timing is important. Often the attendees will break into smaller groups to go through different stores, so a rendezvous time should be clearly communicated. Be sure that the attendees are back at the hotel in time to get ready for the evening's festivities.

Sightseeing and City Tours. Sightseeing and tours are also popular. A competent guide is paramount. The convention service manager should have a list of sightseeing and tour agencies contacted in advance.

All cities have points of interest: colleges, historic spots, gardens, and so on. One of the best-received tours is the home and garden type. Local residents open their homes for conventioneers' guests, often in an effort to raise money for charity. Generally five homes for viewing is ample. As in the case of shopping trips, timing is important. Discourage the use of cars; go by bus to keep the group together.

Guest Lecturers. Many guest/companion programs present speeches by professional people, such as doctors, lawyers, chefs, company executives, and psychiatrists; questions

Exhibit 6   Creative Guest Programs

When creating memorable guest programs, it is important to take both the location of the property and the guests' preferences into consideration. The properties in the examples below have each put a twist on typical guest program activities by offering an experience unique to their locales.

Las Ventanas al Paraiso, Los Cabos, Mexico. The 71-suite Rosewood Resort offers tequila lessons taught by "trained tequileros." Groups learn about the history, classification, and distillation of tequila — and get practical advice on how to drink it. Guests can earn a "Tequila Aficionado" certificate after tasting three different kinds of the liquor and passing a quiz.

Ojai Valley Inn & Spa, Ojai, California. Located in California's wine country, the 312-room property on an 800-acre ranch offers several "Short Courses in Living Better." Local artisans conduct group workshops in drawing, painting to music, and making sarongs using the batik dyeing technique. Other courses include horsemanship, aromatherapy, and golf etiquette.

Sheraton Wild Horse Pass Resort & Spa, Chandler, Arizona. The 500-room resort serves as a cultural liaison to guests, working with groups to incorporate Pima and Maricopa tribe culture into meetings and activities. Pottery, basket weaving, and other artistic workshops are available, and tribal elders are available to speak at functions. Team-building activities include building bicycles for children who live on the nearby reservations.

The Equinox Resort & Spa, Manchester Village, Vermont. The 183-room property offers such unique programs as falconry sessions, as well as an archery school and the opportunity to drive its fleet of Land Rovers and Hummers over 80 acres of off-road vehicle trails.

Mohonk Mountain House, New Paltz, New York. The 261-room property in New York's Catskill Mountains has developed wacky group activities that include game shows, remote-control car races, tricycle polo, and "human foosball." Other activities include gnome hunts, a "musical chairs" painting workshop, during which participants contribute to a group canvas, and cardboard boat regattas.

Hotels often offer guest/companion programs to boost attendance at conventions and meetings. The properties featured above have developed creative programs that provide unique activities and appeal to a wide range of interests.
Source: Tom Isler, "Property Rites: Inspiring On-Site Activities for Groups," *Meetings & Conventions***, March 2006. Photographs courtesy of The Equinox Resort & Spa.**

and answers follow. Perhaps there are local speakers you might suggest to the organization. The range of these lectures is great, from flower arranging and dancing lessons to how to prepare a will.

Other Activities. Certainly the list of possibilities is nearly inexhaustible. Other suggestions gleaned from our readings and discussions with convention service managers include theaters and concerts, special business meetings for spouses and guests only, and finale parties. Local cultural activities, such as visits to museums, galleries, and historical districts; "behind-the-scenes" tours of the property and nearby attractions; and tours of local businesses (such as wineries, chocolate factories, and manufacturers of popular products) are also well-received. Or, you may wish to offer self-improvement courses, such as cooking classes and classes on time management, stress reduction, dress for success, family life, parenting, child development, and so on, based on the interests of members of the group and their guests.

When planning guest activities, it is important to know your audience and gear your program to their specific interests and tastes. For example, the Hudson Valley Resort and Spa in Kerhonkson, New York, has developed a "menu" of ideas to customize activities to match the interests and personalities of the meeting group. Planners can choose from indoor and/or outdoor activities. A sampling of offers includes paintball battles, rock climbing excursions, and wine or antiquing tours. If possible, find out what was done in previous years (you won't want to duplicate last year's program) and gauge which activities were most favorably received.

You will also want to schedule activities carefully. Keep in mind that many spouses and guests consider conventions as vacations and like to sleep in; suggest that guest/companion programs be scheduled in the afternoons. Spouses and guests may also dislike being rushed from one activity to the next; ample free time should be allotted.

Activities for Children

Over the past several years, a growing number of attendees have been combining the annual convention with their family vacation. Smart meeting planners are aware that working parents want to spend more time with their children, so many organizations are inviting the entire family to conventions as a way to boost attendance (see Exhibit 7). Hotels also benefit from family attendance, but some properties have found it a challenge to balance family-friendly services with the needs of business travelers, who may also be an important market segment for the property. Anne Hamilton, vice president of resort sales and services for Walt Disney World Hotels, says:

> We identified that we would have two types of guests before the actual construction of our resorts, so because of the layout, there's no reason for, say, a leisure guest to walk through the convention center. We pre-block the groups' sleeping rooms in an area where they're together. Groups normally like that anyway, and it limits the concerns of being disturbed by, or disturbing, other guests.[4]

Another challenge for hotels and meeting planners wishing to build attendance is having to plan activities and supervision for children of various ages. Some hotels have established in-house programs for junior attendees. The Hyatt chain, for example, offers Camp Hyatt, a program that offers structured recreation and learning activities for several age groups. The Walt Disney World Swan offers Camp Swan, with activities (featuring Disney characters) available until midnight. The box titled "A Rundown of Kid-Friendly Programs at the Major Hotel Chains" lists programs and activities for children and teens that are offered by major hotel chains.

Other properties may offer licensed child-care facilities on-site or, at the very least, provide a list of registered baby-sitters for the youngest children. Some hotels contract with an outside service, such as Kids Quest, which provides hourly child-care and entertainment at the property. Or the hotel or sponsoring organization can look to such companies as KiddieCorp and KidsAlong to create programs that are customized for the children of attendees. One of KiddieCorp's clients is the Rancho Bernardo Inn near San Diego, where the children of attendees enjoy "Camp RBI" during the summer and on various holidays.

Exhibit 7   Guest and Children's Programs

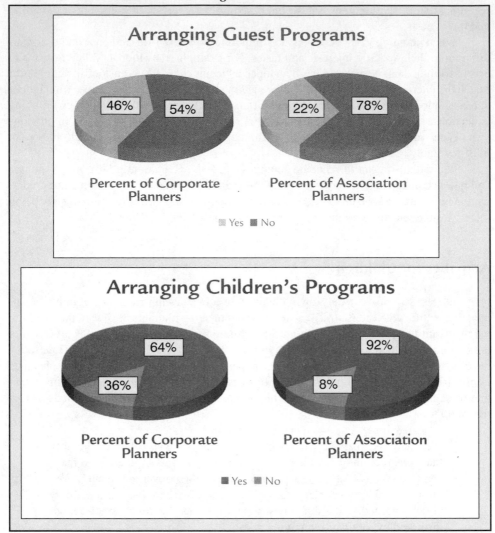

The most recent "Meetings Market Report" conducted by Meetings & Conventions *magazine shows the extent to which corporation and association planners accommodate guests and children at meetings.*

There are a wide variety of choices available, from on-site supervised recreational activities to field trips to local attractions. The wise meeting planner will schedule children's activities to entertain young guests while their parents are tied up in meetings as well as activities for the entire family to enjoy together after the meetings (one organization, for example, stages a variety show for the entire family, while others may arrange for discounted family passes to nearby attractions).

No matter which avenue is chosen, there are a number of factors to consider when hosting family-oriented groups. First and foremost is liability. The hotel must protect itself (and its guests) in regard to the safety of facilities used and the personnel supervising children. All child-care facilities should carry a minimum of $1 million in liability coverage, and most require that parents sign a waiver when dropping off children; this should also be done for any in-house programs, and especially for any field trips off-site. Background checks should be performed on all personnel having direct contact with children, and the hotel should ensure that there is a small ratio of children to staffers to ensure adequate

A rundown of kid-friendly programs at the major hotel chains			
HOTEL CHAIN	**PROGRAM**	**AGES**	**NOTABLE FEATURES**
Doubletree	kidsCAREpak	3-12	Gift bags for children during the summer
Holiday Inn	KidSuites	All ages	Special guest rooms to give kids their own "fun" space
Hyatt	Camp Hyatt	3-12	Activities that incorporate local culture
Four Seasons	Kids for All Seasons	5-12 (may vary)	Children's bathrobes; supervised activities
Hilton	Hilton Vacation Station	2-12	Free toy rental; supervised activities at some resorts
Le Méridien	Penguin Club	4-12	Supervised activities available at offshore properties
Loews	Loews Loves Kids	10 and under	Family concierge trained to cater to children's needs
Omni	Omni Kids	13 and under	Pre-trip planning at www.omnikidsrule.com
Ritz-Carlton	Ritz Kids	4-13	Healthful kids' menu; etiquette classes for ages 8-12
Sonesta	Just Us Kids	5-12	Free activities and excursions
Westin	Westin Kids Club	12 and under	"Heavenly" cribs; free beverages and teddy bears
Wyndham	Wyndham Family Retreat	All ages	Program for families to cook and play games together

supervision (the accepted **adult-staff-to-child ratio** is one adult for every three infants, one adult for every four toddlers, and one adult for every six children up to eight years of age).

When the details have been worked out, it should be up to the meeting planner to communicate to the attendees exactly what will be offered—and who is responsible for paying for various activities and programs. This will eliminate any misunderstanding by participants, ensure a happier time for all involved, and establish the hotel as a family-friendly property that will likely be considered for future group activities and family vacations.

Checklists

There are numerous details that must be worked out to ensure a successful meeting or convention. The use of checklists can help to avoid overlooking important items, and can assist in contracting for the special services that will be needed.

There should be an overall checklist giving an overview of the entire meeting as well as for each function. Many companies, such as Sheraton and InterContinental, offer meeting planners guides that include these types of checklists (see Exhibit 8). Save good checklists that you run across in your travels and adapt them to meet the needs of your convention clients.

Exhibit 8   Convention Checklists

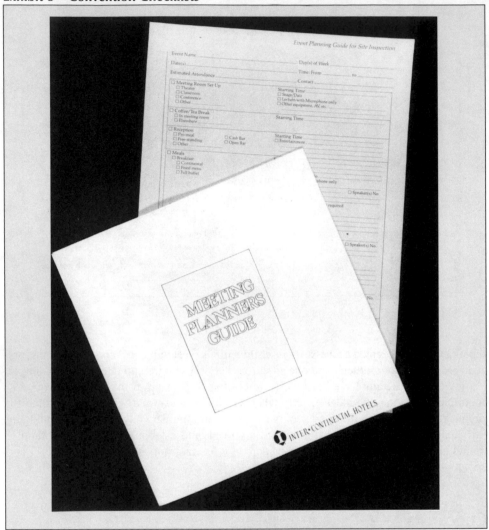

Many chains offer planning kits that include checklists that the meeting planner can use to ensure that all the details of his or her meeting or event have been covered.
Source: Courtesy of InterContinental Hotels.

Summary

Hotel personnel are often involved in a number of activities to ensure that convention programs run smoothly. When servicing a large convention, the convention service department may be involved in everything from suggesting effective admissions systems to providing security to delegates and exhibits to arranging for in-house or outsourced decorations, entertainment, and printing services. To be effective, your property must be willing to "go the extra mile" in assisting the meeting planner with these details—as well as helping to build attendance through guest/companion and/or children's programs. Building your skills in these areas will enable you to handle any type of meeting—including the largest of conventions and trade shows.

Endnotes

1. Michelle Russell, "Planning Convention Center Security," *Convene*, April 2003, p. 46.

2. Barbara Scofidio, "Up Front: Special Events Intelligence," *Corporate Meetings & Incentives*, February 2007, p. 6.

3. "Leave Your Vendors Behind: Exclusive and Preferred Providers," *Meeting Budget*, June 2006, p. 11.

4. Susie Amer, "The Family Business," *Successful Meetings*, March 2007, p. 59.

 # Key Terms

adult staff-to-child ratio—The ratio of adults to children required during a child-care/ youth program. Accepted ratios are 3:1 for infants, 4:1 for toddlers, and 6:1 for children up to eight years old.

advance registration—Attendees register for an event before it takes place, either by mail, fax, phone, or over the Internet. Also called **pre-registration**.

ancillary services or activities—All event-related support services, including stewards, technicians, interpreters, and tour guides. Many activities, such as local tours, are arranged or promoted by the meeting manager to complement the meeting, and these non-essential meeting components may result in extra revenue to the hotel if facility services are used (see auxiliary business).

attendees—People present at the convention; may be determined in terms of registered members of the convening organization or also include spouses, children, guests, and vendors.

auxiliary business—Business that is brought into the facility because of or in conjunction with an event.

badge—Identification card with registrant's name and affiliation printed on it for control and security reasons. Usually given out during convention registration, a badge can be an adhesive, pin, clip-on, or necklace style, or a digital interactive badge.

convention packet/kit—A comprehensive collection of conference documentation and/ or event materials presented in a bag, binder, envelope, or folder. Materials can include a program book, tickets, maps, and so on, and hotels often provide information about the property for inclusion in the packet. Sometimes called a registration packet.

convention registration—Process during which attendees pay convention registration fees and receive packets outlining the convention program.

destination management companies (DMCs)—Professional management companies that specialize in the creation and/or delivery of events, activities, tours, staffing, and transportation, utilizing their local knowledge, expertise, and resources.

exclusives—Agreements that limit who may provide specific products or services. A florist or a photographer, for example, may have an exclusive contract in a particular facility, meaning that no other contractor is allowed to provide the same services or products in that facility.

ground operators—Company or person in a city that handles local transportation and/or other local travel needs.

guest/companion program—Entertainment or activities, such as sightseeing, shopping, and lectures, planned for guests and companions of those attending conventions.

hospitality suite—Suite or room for the convenience, comfort, and socialization of attendees and/or guests. Drinks and snacks are usually available.

lanyard—A cord or string worn around the neck, as in corded badges.

message board—A board, also sometimes called a *bulletin board*, on which convention attendees can review messages left by others and leave their own messages if they desire. May also be electronic or online message centers for attendees.

online registration—Attendees register for an event on the sponsoring organization's website.

on-site office—A convening organization's temporary headquarters, which is set up at the site to handle business during the event.

on-site registration—Attendees register at the site of the event, usually on the day the event starts (or sometimes the day before or while the event is in progress).

press room—A separate area in which members of the press may obtain exhibitor kits, conduct interviews, and file their stories by telephone, fax, or the Internet.

radio frequency identification tag (RFID)— An interactive badge that shares information between a receiver and a small transponder.

receptive agents—Tour operators or travel agents who specialize in services for incoming visitors.

registrant—Individual who has submitted a registration form and attends an event; also called an attendee or a delegate.

registration area—Designated area where event registration takes place.

registration form—A form, either printed or online, that is filled in by an attendee to sign up for the event and specific functions during the program. May also include housing options.

security contractors—Companies hired by exhibit or event management to keep the entire event floor and individual exhibits safe during the function. Guards, closed circuit TV, and other methods may be used.

serpentine queue—Unlike a straight-line queue, a serpentine queue makes use of barriers, such as ropes, to either save space or direct attendees to different service stations. As the crowd thins, barriers may be removed, resulting in a straight-line queue.

temps—Temporary workers hired for convention registration and other duties, such as clerical support, traffic control, and security.

 Review Questions

1. What is the difference between hotel registration and convention registration? What three methods are used to distribute delegates' convention packets?

2. There are four critical periods for convention exhibit security. Identify them and detail the methods for control of each.

3. Why is it important for hotels to work with or to be able to recommend reliable outside suppliers? How do these arrangements benefit the hotel? the meeting planner? the outside supplier?

4. Discuss the importance of guest/companion attendance at conventions. List possible programs for encouraging adult attendance.

5. Many conventions are planned at vacation resorts or other family-friendly locations so delegates can bring their children along. What activities are typically planned to entertain children while their parents are occupied with convention business?

Additional References

The Convention Industry Council Manual, Eighth Edition, Susan Krug, Executive Editor, 2007.

Event Management, by Lynn Van Der Wagen and Brenda R. Carolos, Prentice-Hall, 2005.

Special Events: The Best Practices in Modern Event Management, Third Edition, by Joe Jeff Goldblatt, John Wiley & Sons, 1997. www.hospitality@wiley.com

Internet Sites

For more information, visit the following Internet sites. Internet addresses can change without notice. If a site is no longer available at the address listed below, a search engine can be used to find the new address or additional, related sites.

Association of Destination Management Executives
www.adme.org

The DMC Network
www.dmcnetwork.com

Global Event Partners—Destination Management Companies
www.globaleventspartners.com

International Special Events Society (ISES)
www.ises.com

Kiddie Corp
www.kiddiecorp.com

Marriott Hotels, Resorts and Suites
www.marriott.com

National Speakers Association
www.nsaspeaker.org

nTAG Interactive
www.ntag.com)

PC/NAMETAG
www.pcnametag.com

USA Hosts Destination Services
www.usahosts.com

Chapter 17 Outline

Competencies

Exhibitions Require a Team Effort

Sam Lippman
President
Integrated Show Management and Marketing

"Producing trade shows is an exciting, demanding, complex challenge that requires teamwork and communications. The trade show industry is completely interdependent. Associations depend on the income generated by trade shows to keep their membership fees low and still offer their members many benefits and services. Show managers depend on their trade show team for the success of their trade's show. Trade show contractors depend on healthy trade shows for their livelihood. Facility managers depend on accurate floor plans to deliver their services to the correct booths. Exhibitors depend on qualified labor to set up and dismantle their displays. Because of this interdependency, successful trade shows have a commitment to communications. Trade show managers communicate early and constantly with their exposition contractors, facilities, labor and exhibitors. This constant, interactive communication among all members of the trade show team helps to create shows that provide a cost-efficient marketing and education forum for exhibitors and attendees."

17   Exhibits and Trade Shows

T HE EXHIBIT is a very important part of the convention business. It is a key element in most trade conventions, with over 80 percent including an **exhibition** in their annual meeting, and a very important part of technical, scientific, and professional conferences as well. Associations see exhibits both as a way to attract attendance and as a very essential revenue producer. Additionally, **trade shows** are viewed by organizers as educational opportunities for attendees—an extra component of the event's educational program, supplementing seminars and workshops.

Exhibitors, in turn, consider exhibitions as unique opportunities to market their products. There is no other way they could reach so many buyers so quickly, and face to face. Most of the attendees present at the shows are decision-makers, so much effort is put into exhibits as marketing tools.

The Scope of Exhibits and Trade Shows

Exhibits and trade shows are a lucrative and fast-growing segment of today's convention and meetings market. Growing at an annual rate of over four percent, an increasing number of companies are taking advantage of this excellent marketing opportunity, and some trade shows are becoming major international events (see Exhibit 1).

The association makes a profit from exhibits by charging exhibitors for booth space. Exhibits also offer the association a cash flow, which helps finance the convention planning. The exhibitor's reservation for booth space is usually accompanied by a check for half the cost of the space. The rest is sent in later, but still in advance of the convention.

The association's only costs at this stage have been for promotion of the event and payroll, a year-round burden. This advance money from exhibitors amounts to a great deal, and it literally finances the convention. The only additional revenue of any consequence comes from admission and registration fees. It, too, is solicited in advance for the same reason.

The importance of the trade show is reflected in the development of hotels with considerable convention space. These hotels have had great success in going after conventions with exhibits.

It is a rare convention organizer who does not prefer to house the entire convention under one roof. When this is not possible, separate exhibit centers are often used in conjunction with neighboring hotels. The largest exhibitions use huge convention centers such as McCormick Place in Chicago, which has 2.6 million square feet, and the Las Vegas Convention Center, which boasts over 3.2 million square feet of space.

Convention hotels with built-in exhibit areas are successful even in a city with a giant convention center. In Las Vegas, for example, the attraction of a one-house event brings lots of business to individual properties, even with the convention center available. While the very largest conventions would use the convention center and several hotels near it, a somewhat smaller event might be held at the MGM Grand Hotel (5,700 rooms and suites and over 600,000 square feet of exhibit space), Wynn Las Vegas and its sister property, Encore (4,750 rooms and 223,000 square feet of exhibit space), or Mandalay Bay (3,754

Exhibit 1   Top Trade Shows

		Net Square Feet of Exhibit Space	Attendance
1.	International CES Consumer Electronics Show	1,804,070	143,695
2.	International Construction and Utility Equipment Expo	1,155,000	17,950
3.	MAGIC (Men's Apparel Guild in California)	1,100,885	120,000
4.	WSA (World Shoes and Accessories)	1,100,250	37,500
5.	SEMA (Specialty Equipment Market Association) Show	1,063,970	125,000
6.	NBAA (National Business Aviation Association) Show	1,038,600	32,052
7.	International Builders' Show	1,037,000	103,921
8.	National Association of Broadcasters	906,000	93,159

Source: 2009 Trade Show Directory.

rooms and suites and an exhibit area of nearly 1.7 million square feet). All of these hotels, as well as other hotels in the city, have the necessary supporting rooms that can accommodate conventions with exhibits.

Las Vegas enjoys as much event business as it does because of its excellent convention facilities and tourist attractions. However, trade show business is not limited to large properties only. Smaller hotels around the country use in-house exhibit areas as an asset in selling convention business and as a lucrative source of revenue. Research by the Center for Exhibition Industry Research (CEIR) reveals that approximately one-third of the conventions involving trade shows have fewer than 50 exhibits per convention. A common rule of thumb is that twice the amount of space is needed for each square foot of booth space. For example, 50 eight-by-ten-foot booths need 4,000 square feet of space for the actual booths plus an additional 4,000 square feet of space for aisles, entrance and exit areas, and registration desks (see box titled "Formula For Determining Exhibit Space Needs).[1]

Types of Exhibits

Exhibits are used to showcase or demonstrate products or services at trade shows. There are three basic types of exhibits: a **table top exhibit**, that is often used when there are few exhibitors or space is limited; an **area exhibit**, in which the exhibitor is assigned a specific floor space for displaying large, tall equipment or two-tier displays or **multi-level exhibits**; and a **booth exhibit**, which is usually constructed with either **pipe and drape** or **hardwall**.

The most common arrangement is the booth plan. Exhibit booths are ten feet wide by eight feet deep or ten feet wide by ten feet deep and limited in height to eight feet or 12 feet along the back wall with four-foot high side dividers. There are four basic types of booths:

(1) **standard booths** (also known as in-line booths) are placed back-to-back with adjacent booths on the sides and have maximum heights of eight feet; (2) **perimeter booths** are located on outside walls and maximum heights of 12 feet are allowed; (3) **peninsula booths** consist of four or more spaces and are bordered on three sides with aisles; and (4) **island booths** are bordered on all four sides by aisles and include four or more spaces.

Exhibit Planning

Normally the trade show is held in conjunction with the trade association's annual meeting, but other groups or corporations may also sponsor a trade show as a profit-making venture. The association or corporation may manage the trade show from in-house, using its own personnel, or may hire an outside show manager to plan, organize, market, and operate the show.

Trade show managers who work directly for a particular association or corporation are represented by the International Association of Exhibitions and Events (IAEE), formerly the International Association for Event Management (IAEM), a professional association of approximately 7,000 trade show managers. The Society of Independent Show Organizers (SISO) also provides information on the value and role of exhibitions, and offers practical tips and how-to information on exhibition management.

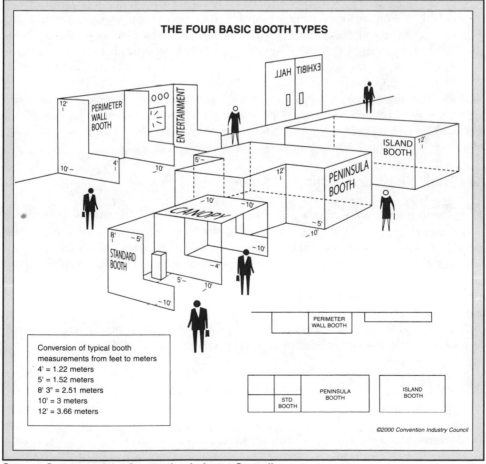

Source: Courtesy of the Convention Industry Council.

Formula for Determining Exhibit Space Needs

Factors that need to be considered when determining the space needed for an exhibition include:

- The number and size of regular and nonstandard booths (island booths, peninsula booths, and so on).

- Space needed for additional features, including special feature exhibits, display areas, lounge areas, concessions, and so on.

- Placement of the show's registration area and management office— additional space will be needed if these are located inside the exhibit hall.

Square footage needed for an exhibit is determined by doubling the net square footage required for the booths and adding any space required for ancillary needs. The basic formula is to multiply the number of booths x booth length x booth width x two. This formula also works in reverse. If you have 12,000 square feet of exhibit space available and want to determine how many 8'x10' booths would fit in the space, for example, you would divide 12,000 by two, then by eight (length of booths), then by 10 (width of booths)—or simply divide the square footage once by 160. Using this formula, you would see that 75 booths would fit into the 12,000 square-foot space.

Some hotels with substantial dedicated exhibit space may staff a director of exhibit service. This person functions as the principal liaison between the hotel's convention service manager and the meeting group's show manager. There is a wide range of professionalism in show management. Local committees generally have little background in exposition management, while association and corporate meeting planners responsible for annual shows have developed considerable expertise in conducting a show. Hotels committed to the trade show market are well advised to employ a knowledgeable director of exhibit service with a good understanding of exhibit and trade show jargon to assist committees and meeting planners in producing a successful event.

Key Trade Show and Exhibit Personnel

Trade shows provide a forum at which companies can exhibit their products and services to convention attendees. They are, essentially, a "live" marketing event, with about sixty percent of today's trade shows held in conjunction with an association convention and forty percent sponsored by independent corporations. Both associations and independent corporations have also taken advantage of today's technology to offer **virtual trade shows**—exhibits, displays, and programs are made accessible to remote "attendees" through Internet and data feeds.

No matter how an exhibit is managed, if your property plays host to such an event, you will be working with a number of different people, including:

- Trade show managers
- Exhibition service contractors/decorators
- Exhibitors

Trade Show Manager. The **trade show manager** (also called the show producer, exhibition manager, or show organizer) produces and manages the exhibition. He or she is responsible for developing a list of potential exhibitors, marketing the show to both exhibitors and attendees, contracting with an exhibition service contractor, and overseeing all logistical planning.[2] The trade show managers you work with will be employed in one of two ways:

- Directly for the organizing group, serving as an in-house staff member assigned to organize, market, and manage the show for the association (the National Restaurant Association operates in this manner). Or, the trade show manager may be an outside individual or firm contracting with the association to oversee the trade show aspect of the convention.
- As a private entrepreneur or corporate entity, organizing an independent trade show for profit. A recent trend is for associations to either sell their trade show and use the invested funds to benefit the association or partner with a multi-management trade show firm and get a percentage of the profits. Examples of such trade shows include the sale of the American Booksellers Association's trade show to Reed Exhibition Companies and the sale of the National Sporting Goods show to Miller Freeman, Inc.

The show manager's first priority is to sell floor space to exhibitors. To attract exhibitors, the trade show manager prepares an **exhibitor prospectus** that includes the location and dates of the show, a profile of prospective and past attendees, floor rental prices, and other pertinent information to assist potential exhibitors in making a decision as to whether to participate (see box titled "The Exhibitor Prospectus"). High attendance figures from past shows are particularly important in recruiting exhibitors.

Exhibition Service Contractors/Decorators. It is customary for the hotel to furnish the basic exhibit area, perhaps with a floor covering, but perhaps with nothing. The trade show manager usually selects an exhibition service company to work as an "official" **exhibition**

The Exhibitor Prospectus

The exhibitor prospectus is the most important marketing piece that will be produced for the event, as it will help to influence an exhibitor's decision to participate. The exhibitor prospectus should include:

- A cover letter, on official letterhead from the show's sponsor (which should prominently feature contact information), inviting the exhibitor to the show. It is particularly effective if the invitation comes from an industry leader who has had past experience with the show.
- The show's unique rationale (and, if applicable, brief highlights of the show's educational content).
- The show's important statistics and successes (exhibitor and attendee testimonials should be included).
- The features of the show and benefits for exhibitors (photographs of crowded aisles are a good selling point).
- A listing of attendee categories and demographics (location, buying power, influence).
- A listing of other exhibiting companies.
- A listing of the products and services that will be displayed at the show.
- The exhibit floor plan.
- General information (hours, days, booth furnishings).
- Pricing, payment schedule, and deposit information.
- The exhibitor contract with rules and regulations.

service contractor (decorator, general service contractor) for the event. While the trade show manager will contract with an exhibition service firm, this does not generally preclude exhibitors from using an outside contractor for the installation and dismantling of their booths. Some companies have contractual agreements with firms that travel around the country setting up the corporation's exhibits. These firms, called **exhibitor appointed contractors**, participate in several shows throughout the year (see box titled "Changes in the Role of an Exhibition Services Contractor"). Show management and the "official" service contractor require a letter of intent to use an outside contractor.

Sam Lippman, who is quoted at the start of this chapter, considers the exhibition service contractor the most important member of the trade show team. He says:

> The exhibition service contractor's account executive is the show manager's "eyes and ears" on the exhibit floor, allowing the show managers to focus on their many other responsibilities. From the unloading of

---

Changes in the Role of an Exhibition Services Contractor

Don Freeman is chairman of Freeman, which has grown into a family of full-service contractor services that includes AVW-TELAV Audio Visual Solutions, Party Time Rentals, and Stage Rigging. Many of his clients are shows that move around the country, and Freeman has seen a dramatic shift in how his firm meets the needs of these exhibitors:

> Since I started in the 1960s, the biggest change I've seen is the increasing sophistication of shows. It used to be a trade show was either hard-wall booths or pipe and drape. We were essentially a furniture rental company, and we didn't even do a lot of materials handling. Then we progressed to a full-service contractor and now things are moving even beyond that. We do so much more than take orders for signs and carpet. We consult with clients about how they want to convey their brand's image.

Today, exhibitors want more than themed show graphics and signage—they are focusing more on reflecting their show brands, and Freeman says:

> We have to better understand the objectives of the organizations we're working for and the objectives they have for each event. Then we've got to find ways to support those objectives and bring value to the table.

To do so, Freeman, which had focused primarily on the service they provided for show organizers, stepped up efforts to better meet the needs of exhibitors. The company constantly looks for ways to improve the exhibitor experience, including redesigning their Exhibitor Service Centers to be easier to use and more consistent from show to show. One thing, however, remains the same—the company's commitment to customer service. Freeman says:

> Now every one of our 3,000 employees receives customer service training, even if they don't deal with outside clients…. There's no secret to creating great customer service. It's just something you've got to build into your culture in everything you do and remind people of it often.

Source: "5-minute interview: Don Freeman, Chairman of Freeman," *Expo*, February 2007, p. 14.

the first truck to the dismantling of the last exhibit, a happy exhibitor is the goal of both the show manager and the exhibition service contractor. Exhibitors that have a successful show will increase their budget for the next show, for more exhibit space and more complex displays, which means more revenues for both show management and their exhibition service contractor.[3]

The contract with the show manager generally calls for general decorating of the exhibit hall (includes entrance signage, aisle carpeting, and basic construction of pipe and drape booths), the design of the **exhibition floor plan**, and on-site coordination for the show. The floor plan is a scaled, schematic drawing of the exhibit area, including dimensions, design, shape, entrances, aisles, numbered exhibit booths, lounges, concession areas, restrooms, and electrical/plumbing accessibility.

It is the exhibition service contractor's job to organize, coordinate, and execute all the services required to set up the exhibit area. The old-time decorator was basically a window trimmer, carpenter, and sign painter whose function was to construct eight-by-ten foot booths. Decorators' work today is much more encompassing. They are in charge of labor, plumbing, electrical work, signs, cleaning, telephones, florists, booth hostesses, audiovisual information, and drayage (shipping and warehouse storage of exhibits).

In fact, exhibition service contractors are key persons in the convention process. They work with meeting planners from the pre-show planning until the exhibit hall is cleaned and all the exhibitors' equipment is returned to the home offices. They prepare floor plans for approval by local fire marshals. They contract with a number of suppliers, such as audiovisual dealers and florists, removing this task from the meeting planners. They provide **floor managers** to supervise and control the setup and dismantling of exhibit booths.

Equally important, they consult with hotel convention sales and service staffs in an effort to bring about understanding and acceptance of each other's procedures and responsibilities (see box titled "Do's and Don'ts of Exhibit Planning"). This mutual understanding is best facilitated through a pre-event meeting or a series of meetings between the decorator and the convention service manager.

The exhibition service company's contract with the exhibitors is initiated through the **exhibitor service kit** (see Exhibit 2). This kit or manual provides information, pricing, and order forms for booth items including floor coverings, signage, janitorial services, electrical services, furniture rental, shipping of materials, and so on (see box titled "The Exhibitor Service Kit"). The service contractor of today frequently uses the power of technology to carry on business with exhibitors. Using the Internet, the exhibition service contractor can display the floor plan, allowing exhibitors to determine space availability. Additional linking allows the exhibitor to browse the exhibitor's service kit and complete forms for drayage, carpet, phone lines, and other needs online.

Often, the exhibition service contractor will subcontract special services, such as floral, catering, and audiovisual, to specialty contractors. But, regardless, the exhibitor normally contracts directly with the exhibition service contractor for all services.

The exhibition service manager oversees the move-in, setup and tear down of the trade show and is present throughout the event to service any last-minute needs of either of its two main clients—the exhibitors or the trade show manager.

Because of the tremendous coordination required in staging an annual show, many associations and independent trade show sponsors seek multi-year contracts with an exhibition service company. A good working relationship between the sponsoring organization and the exhibition service contractor is of obvious importance and should receive the very highest priority by all parties.

Exhibit 2   Sample Exhibitor's Service Kit

A typical exhibitor's service kit includes a number of forms, such as the ones above, that provide information and enable the planner to order specific products and services for various aspects of the function. The forms above can be accessed online to allow planners to quickly and easily enter required information and forward it to the convention facility. While it was previously necessary to either mail or fax requests to hotels or other convention facilities, many venues now make their forms available online to facilitate the ordering process.

Courtesy of Sands Expo, Las Vegas, Nevada.

Exhibitors. The **exhibitor,** who can be an individual or a firm, sees the trade show as an opportunity to demonstrate products or services to prime decision-makers and is therefore diligent in selecting and participating in what he or she considers to be the most important events.

Exhibitors are first contacted by the trade show manager through the prospectus. After deciding to participate, they rent floor space from the trade show manager. The exhibitors are then introduced to the exhibition service contractor via the exhibitors service kit and buy (or rent) other services and materials, such as booth signage and decorating from the exhibition service contractor.

Do's and Don'ts of Exhibit Planning

Exhibition service contractors do find fault with hotels. GES Exposition Services, a leading decorator with offices nationwide, has outlined the following hotel problem areas from actual convention situations:

1.   Poor Planning for Exhibit Layout

How many times has an exhibitor walked into his assigned booth space to find a beautiful gigantic and low-hanging chandelier right smack in the middle of the booth—or a column or similar obstruction? Reason? The convention sales personnel just pulled out a basic stock floor plan and submitted it to the client—without consulting the exhibition service contractor—and nowhere did the plan indicate the column or chandelier.

2.   Plumbing

Neither the plumbing contractor nor the exhibitors will ever be the same after this session—140 booths in 30,000 square feet of exhibit space, and two water and drain outlets from which to supply all the plumbing lines and connections required by the exhibitors.

3.   Electrical

This was an electronics show; power load was so great that existing equipment in the hotel was inadequate to provide half the required current. Additional lines had to be brought in by the utility company at the time of the show move-in. An electronics show obviously involves a heavy power load, and the hotel could have saved everybody a lot of headaches if this had been taken into consideration while booking the show—balancing requirements against electrical facilities available—and increasing the power in advance.

4.   Labor

How many times have we set up a one hundred or two hundred booth show, all custom constructed displays, and found we would be allowed six hours for dismantle, pack-up, and move out from the area? This unreasonable rush causes breakage and damage to property, misdirected shipments, and, worst of all, an unhappy client who will not do business with you again.

5.   Heavy Equipment

Heavy equipment shows do not belong on ballroom floors, nor should this heavyweight material have to be moved over marble or plush carpet. Further, the live load limit of a floor is not equal to the static load limit. One of the machines exhibited in a ballroom weighed 12,800 pounds, in a single unit 12' long and 8' wide. Not only that, but there was another part meant to be attached to the machine, weighing an additional 6,000 pounds all by itself, which was to be hoisted and attached to the top of the machine, to complete the unit, to a total height of 20'. We regret to say the hotel took a dim view of the whole operation, and refused to allow use of the hoisting rig necessary to raise the 6,000 pound attachment, so the show went on without it. A perfect show for a concrete floor, but never a ballroom.

6.   Control of Dock

Here, we meet the drayage contractor's most serious problem. The most important single function of the drayage contractor is to get the exhibit freight in and out on schedule, a schedule not determined by him, for his convenience, but predetermined by the meeting group and the hotel. No hotel has unlimited facilities for receiving, storing, and handling tons of exhibit freight. Most have limited dock space. Some much tighter than others, but none so extensive that they can accommodate miscellaneous common carriers, display house vans, and independent exhibitors' vehicles, out of control of the official drayage contractor. The official drayage contractor assumes the responsibility for prompt, orderly move-in and move-out of all freight for the show, and the only way he can fulfill this obligation is by being allowed absolute control of the loading dock, and with all freight movement through his hands.

As we said, a meeting of the convention service manager and the decorator before showtime is a must. Most of the difficulties outlined above could be resolved through communication and joint cooperation.

The Exhibitor Service Kit

The exhibitor service kit, which is sent to exhibitors who have contracted for and been assigned booth space, should be sent to exhibitors at least 90 days prior to move-in and should include such information as:

- List of official service contractors
- Checklist of forms and deadlines for their return
- Days/dates and hours for move-in and move-out
- Pertinent rules and regulations (fire/safety regulations, labor union rules, and so on)
- Rates and pricing and order forms for such items as:

Booth furniture, carpeting and signage	Labor and equipment
Utilities	Telephone/Internet connections
Booth security	Booth cleaning
Audiovisual equipment	Computer rental
Catering	Photographers
Floral needs	Greeters, demonstrators, models, and
Exhibitor insurance	other personnel
	Lead retrieval

- Contractor's payment policies, liability, labor, and material-handling authorizations
- Information and order forms for promotional opportunities (list rentals, invitations, sponsorships)
- Exhibitor registration, housing information, and other pertinent forms

---

Many participating companies appoint an **exhibit manager** to coordinate the exhibit. Large companies that participate in several shows throughout the year may assign a corporate exhibit manager to coordinate their company's exhibit. Smaller companies give sales managers or sales staff managers the additional part-time responsibility of organizing the exhibit and selling at trade shows.

While many properties do not deal directly with exhibitors, it can be very beneficial to work with an **exhibitor advisory committee**, which consists of representatives of an event's exhibiting companies. Committee members update properties and inform management on industry trends and issues, and act as a liaison between show management and exhibitors in regard to show rules and procedures.

Exhibitors can have an enormous impact on the property. They require guestrooms, patronize food and beverage outlets, and often host hospitality suites. It is a wise convention service manager who works with a show organizer to ensure that the organization's overall plan includes analyzing how exhibitors will affect the overall strategy for the function.

In some cases, for example, a limited amount of guestrooms may be available at the host property, and an overabundance of exhibitors may result in convention attendees being forced to find lodging elsewhere. The convention service manager may suggest that exhibitor registration be limited to ensure that enough guestrooms are available for convention delegates. Or, the convention service manager may work with the trade show manager to find alternate accommodations for exhibitors.

In cities that host a number of conventions, such as New York, Chicago, Orlando, and Las Vegas, for example, hotels have addressed this problem by building larger convention facilities so they can both provide accommodations for large groups and hold all exhibits in-house. These **hotel shows**—exhibitions held entirely within the hotel rather than at a convention facility—have become increasingly common as a result of both meeting space expansion and the downsizing of some exhibits that previously required extensive floor space.

Hotel shows offer a number of advantages. Meeting planners like the idea that their attendees are somewhat of a "captive" audience in the hotel. They also like hotel shows for the financial advantages they can offer. While convention centers rely on exhibition hall and meeting room charges and other fees, the planner can often get free function space by booking blocks of rooms and other business, such as food and beverage functions. Hotels, of course, benefit from the extra business, but careful thought should be given regarding how many rooms are set aside for hotel shows—and when. Booking shows during peak times, for example, can result in the loss of large blocks of rooms that could have been sold at higher rates. Conversely, booking exhibits during valley or shoulder times can greatly contribute to the hotel's bottom line.

Scaled Drawings

We have discussed the need for the hotel to have scaled drawings of its meeting rooms. Obviously, the same need exists for the exhibit area (see Exhibit 3). Large, accurate drawings to scale should note the presence of columns, doors, windows, obstructions of any kind, the **floor load** capacity, and ceiling heights. The latter two factors are essential, because some displays rise high in the air and some merchandise is heavy.

Supply the drawings to association clients in sizes that make good work sheets. It is important to keep drawings to scale. Many office copiers reduce the image to save paper or to increase sharpness. Some do it slightly; some, a great deal. But reduction destroys the key to the scale. If the scale is given as one-quarter inch equaling one foot, a *reduced* drawing carries such a notice, but a rule laid across the drawing would give a false reading. Imagine setup day with a layout that was planned on the basis of such a false print!

If you have your scaled drawings printed, perhaps in a fair quantity by the offset printing process in a convention booklet, be sure to inform your printer of the need to maintain the strict scale. Usually, printers reproduce your copy exactly as it is presented, but it doesn't hurt to make sure. Sometimes, a slight reduction in overall size helps the job get done on a specific-size sheet of paper, and it usually does not affect the overall quality of a

Exhibit 3   Scaled Drawings

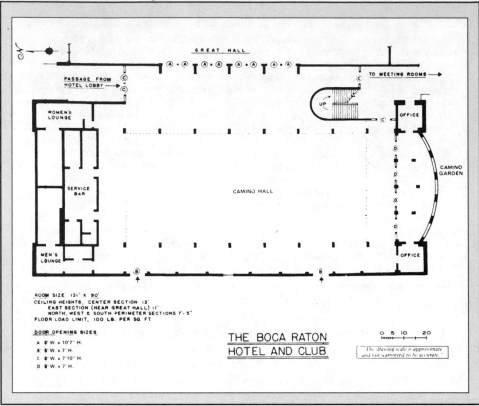

This scaled drawing for the Boca Raton Hotel and Club provides information on ceiling heights, sizes of door openings, and floor load limits. Note that although a scale is provided, it is approximate.
Source: Courtesy of the Boca Raton Hotel and Club, Boca Raton, Florida.

job. But not in your case. If the printer knows the importance of maintaining your scale, you might eliminate costly and aggravating problems later on.

Layouts

You should also offer a convention planner a variety of layout schemes for a specific hall (see Exhibit 4). An exhibit in a hall seemingly too large for it looks awful—it carries the stigma of failure on the part of the convening group to attract enough exhibitors. A different layout might provide wider aisles, or conference or rest areas; or perhaps the exhibitors could be spaced out to make for a better looking, more efficient exhibit. Screens (run-off drapes) or temporary walls could be used to block off unoccupied areas. The appearance of the exhibit is important to the hotel as well as to the convention planner. It is in your interest to make the exhibit look great.

The schematics should be presented to the convention executive early enough to help him or her prepare convention solicitation brochures. After all, the executive sells specific areas designated by numbers, not general space. It is difficult to change the layout after positions have been assigned. Exhibition service contractors might be helpful in supplying these exhibit layouts for your hall.

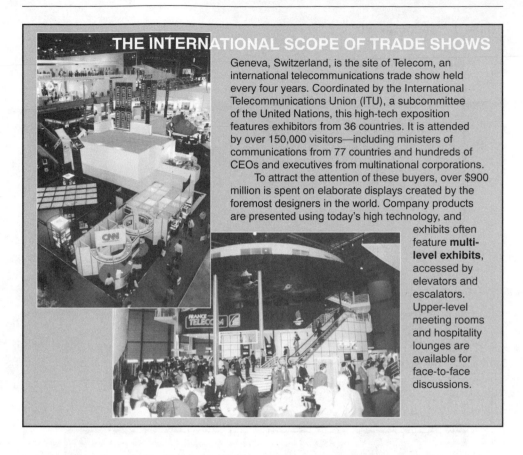

THE INTERNATIONAL SCOPE OF TRADE SHOWS

Geneva, Switzerland, is the site of Telecom, an international telecommunications trade show held every four years. Coordinated by the International Telecommunications Union (ITU), a subcommittee of the United Nations, this high-tech exposition features exhibitors from 36 countries. It is attended by over 150,000 visitors—including ministers of communications from 77 countries and hundreds of CEOs and executives from multinational corporations.

To attract the attention of these buyers, over $900 million is spent on elaborate displays created by the foremost designers in the world. Company products are presented using today's high technology, and exhibits often feature **multi-level exhibits**, accessed by elevators and escalators. Upper-level meeting rooms and hospitality lounges are available for face-to-face discussions.

The service contractor will know the local fire regulations in regard to aisle width, room capacity, access to exits, and anything peculiar to that locality. In many places, the local fire inspector must approve exhibit layout and setup. It is so much easier to conform to local fire regulations from the very onset of the planning of the exhibit. It avoids those headache-provoking late changes and explanations that can plague a planner.

Photo File

It is also helpful to maintain a file of photographs of conventions held previously in your establishment. The convention executive can check out aisle width, exhibit heights, and overall appearance from the photos. All too often, printed material shows only open rooms. Besides guiding the planner for his or her layout, the photos carry the endorsement of past patronage by convention organizations.

Guide the photographer by listing the characteristics you want shown clearly in the photographs. Build a file of floor setups with and without people in the scene.

Timetable

When planning for the exhibit, it is necessary to block out the time that each exhibit area will be in use. This includes the time needed to bring in the exhibit material, remove it from the crates, set it up, remove the packing cases, and clean up before the exhibit opens (this process is known as **move-in**).

Exhibit 4 Booth Layouts

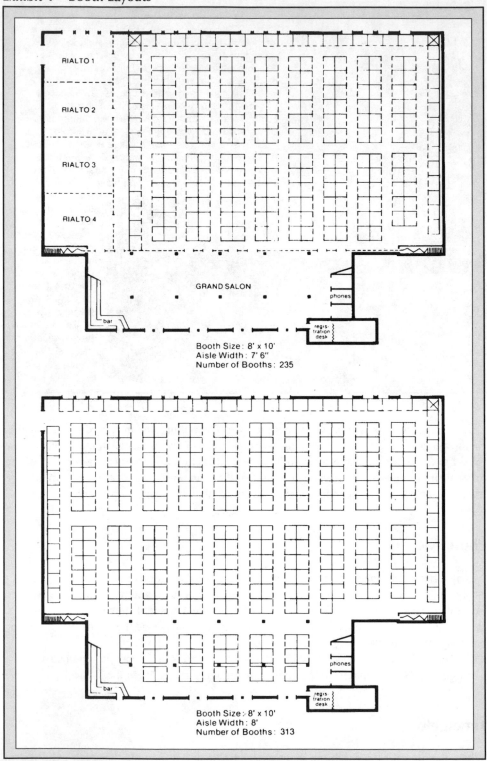

RIALTO 1

RIALTO 2

RIALTO 3

RIALTO 4

GRAND SALON

phones

bar

regis-
tration
desk

Booth Size: 8' x 10'
Aisle Width: 7' 6"
Number of Booths: 235

phones

bar

regis-
tration
desk

Booth Size: 8' x 10'
Aisle Width: 8'
Number of Booths: 313

These graphics from the Bally Grand Hotel's convention brochure show two examples of booth layouts
for the same room. Note that the layouts shown are based on both 8'x10' booths and 10'x10' booths.
Aisle widths are also noted.
Source: Courtesy of the Bally Grand Hotel, Las Vegas.

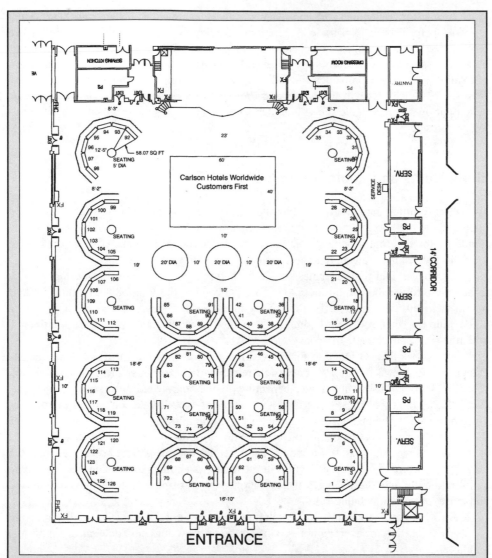

Carlson Hotels Worldwide used a unique booth configuration for its Annual Business Conference Customers First Partner Trade Show at the Bellagio in Las Vegas. Instead of the traditional 10'x10' booth, each booth is pie-shaped and set within a pod (each pod of booths showcases exhibitors selling similar products). The back of each booth is 10' wide—large enough for a standard portable display—and each space contains 58 square feet. The distance from the outer edge of the seating area in the center of each pod to each exhibition table is approximately 12.5 feet. The unique floor plan is a major tool for selling exhibit space. Freeman, the exhibition service contractor for Carlson Hotels Worldwide, prepared this floor plan (drawn to scale) on a template of Bellaglo's Grand Ballroom.
Source: Courtesy of Carlson Hotels Worldwide and Freeman.

After the event, the exhibition contractor must plan the logistics of bringing in the packing cases, delivering them to the individual booth areas, dismantling the booths, arranging for shipping or storage of the units, and cleaning up in time for the next exhibit to move in (this is commonly referred to as **move-out**).

A day or two is needed for **installation and dismantle** at most exhibitions (see Chapter Appendix). Labor charges are important in this process. The most common complaint of exhibitors is the need to use high-priced labor at overtime rates.

In an effort to negotiate the improvements they feel are needed, exhibitors have joined together to form their own trade associations. Exhibitors in the health care industry are represented by the Healthcare Convention and Exhibitors Association (HCEA). The International Association of Exhibitions and Events (IAEE) is another professional association of exhibit managers. Companies and individuals who design and produce the exhibits are represented by the Exhibit Designers and Producers Association (EDPA). These groups have their own annual trade shows at which the newest ideas and designs in exhibit building are presented.

Show Hours and Room Assignments

Two other common complaints of exhibitors are the hours the exhibit hall is scheduled to be open and the method in which guestrooms are assigned. Actually, both of these are determined by the meeting group, not the hotel, but it is important for the convention service manager at least to be aware that there are complaints.

Exhibitors feel that delegates should have free time from meetings during the day to browse through the exhibit area. Many are annoyed at the long days of sitting in their booths with little delegate traffic flow. They maintain that they are too tired after sitting all day and that there is too little time left to make their important business appointments, which is why they came to the convention.

How does this all relate to the convention service manager? Bill Tobin of Caesars Palace said to a class of ours: "If I notice there is a particularly busy meeting and function schedule, I will tactfully encourage the meeting planner to give exhibitors more exposure."

The assigning of guestrooms is another source of exhibitor discontent. One of the services provided to the planners by the hotel is "controlled hospitality suites," which means the meeting group gets first choice on all of the hotel rooms and suites it needs. After all, it is the group's meeting. Exhibitors would like to see less of this policy, however, because it leaves many of them in hotels other than the headquarters hotel. And when forced to stay in a different hotel than the delegates, the exhibitors naturally find it more difficult to transact, and close, important evening sales.

So what can the hotel do? One solution is for the hotel to rent its smaller meeting rooms to exhibitors for evening hours. This arrangement would help delegates, exhibitors, and hotels.

Labor Regulations

The trend of trade shows beginning on Sunday has made it difficult to avoid night and weekend labor charges. This overtime, added to what many exhibitors consider already exorbitant labor rates, has caused some to reconsider their commitment to exhibitions. Whenever possible, a hotel should allow exhibitors to set up early to avoid such charges.

Some cities, such as Chicago, New York, and San Francisco, are referred to as "union cities," as there are formal working arrangements between the city, labor unions, and primary convention facilities. While surrounding hotels are not always bound by such agreements, some are **union houses**—properties that have agreed to abide by negotiated labor agreements. Typically, these labor agreements cover *teamsters*, who are licensed to handle and unload freight and oversee drayage; *decorators, riggers,* and *show installers*, who install booths and carpeting and decorate the finished booths and exhibition area; *electricians*, who handle all electrical needs; *stage hands*, who facilitate the installation of stages,

lighting, and audiovisual equipment; and *food and beverage workers* (this category sometimes includes janitorial functions as well).

While it is understandable that some functions, such as the installation of complicated electrical connections and lighting, are best left in the hands of an expert, labor regulations in some cities prohibit exhibitors from even plugging in a projector or pounding a
nail. The labor contractor does all the work, even the simple jobs that the exhibitor could
easily do. Ed Johnson, past Trade Show Exhibitors Association (TSEA) president, says of
this situation:

> Every show contract specifies an official contractor and spells out certain
> functions the official contractor will perform exclusively. Usually these
> services are limited to plumbing, electrical work, and drayage, but some
> contracts include carpenters, model agencies, and photographers. We be-
> lieve the exhibitor should be able to select his own florist, photographer,
> and models rather than have to be forced to use someone who may not
> suit his needs. (Often these subcontracted services lead to a kickback
> situation.) We want to make it clear, however, that if we use someone
> besides the official contractor, he will be a bonafide contractor located in
> the show or convention city. Associations are afraid the exhibitor wants
> to bring in non-union help, and that just isn't true.[4]

Labor regulations vary a great deal throughout the country. In San Francisco, for
example, stage hands and riggers often perform similar functions; in Chicago, teamsters
can carry power strips to the floor, but only electricians can plug them into sockets. Convention service managers should not close their eyes to the varying restrictions and trust
to luck. Remind the association to alert its exhibitors to the labor regulations that apply to
your hall. The convention service manager must also keep abreast of labor developments
and advise the show organizer and exhibitors of any potential problems, such as impending
labor disputes. The membership of some organizations will honor union picket lines, so
it is important to have a contingency plan. One option is the purchase of strike insurance,
which should include coverage for such losses as shipping and transportation costs and the
reimbursement of sponsorship fees as well as covering the refund of fees paid by the show
organizer and exhibitors.

You must live with the labor contracts in your city. Most experienced convention
executives are aware of the labor situations and have learned to live with them, but be wary
of the inexperienced client.

Insurance

Accidents do happen, and claims do come up, so insurance coverage is absolutely essential.
It should be provided by the convening organization, and smart exhibitors will carry their
own as well.

The convention organization should be encouraged to contact its own insurance
agents to provide full coverage for liability, fire, theft, and breakage. In turn, if notified
early, the convention staff should pass along such advice to exhibitors.

Too often the subject is not discussed until the need for coverage is at hand. Then
someone says that he thought the hotel was covered. This is another area in which the hotel
must be wary of inexperienced convention personnel.

For the protection of the hotel, each exhibitor should be presented with a contract
containing a **hold harmless clause** such as the one shown in Exhibit 5. A hold harmless

Exhibit 5   Insurance and Hold Harmless Clause

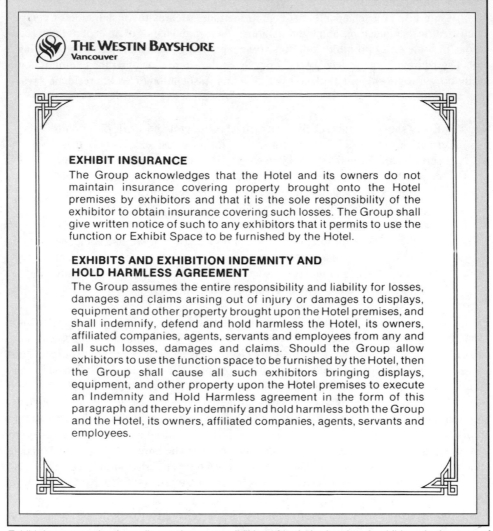

THE WESTIN BAYSHORE
Vancouver

EXHIBIT INSURANCE

The Group acknowledges that the Hotel and its owners do not maintain insurance covering property brought onto the Hotel premises by exhibitors and that it is the sole responsibility of the exhibitor to obtain insurance covering such losses. The Group shall give written notice of such to any exhibitors that it permits to use the function or Exhibit Space to be furnished by the Hotel.

EXHIBITS AND EXHIBITION INDEMNITY AND HOLD HARMLESS AGREEMENT

The Group assumes the entire responsibility and liability for losses, damages and claims arising out of injury or damages to displays, equipment and other property brought upon the Hotel premises, and shall indemnify, defend and hold harmless the Hotel, its owners, affiliated companies, agents, servants and employees from any and all such losses, damages and claims. Should the Group allow exhibitors to use the function space to be furnished by the Hotel, then the Group shall cause all such exhibitors bringing displays, equipment, and other property upon the Hotel premises to execute an Indemnity and Hold Harmless agreement in the form of this paragraph and thereby indemnify and hold harmless both the Group and the Hotel, its owners, affiliated companies, agents, servants and employees.

Exhibit insurance clearly spells out the responsibilities of both the hotel and exhibitors in the case of loss or damage. In the example above, exhibitors are required to carry their own insurance, and they assume the responsibility for loss or damages to their property as well as damages incurred by the hotel.
Source: Used with permission of the Westin Bayshore, Vancouver, B.C.

clause releases the hotel from liability should there be an injury, loss, or breakage. These clauses also spell out exhibitor liability; if exhibitors damage hotel property, they should be held liable for repair charges.

Exhibit Billing Procedures

What does the hotel charge for? There is no reason why a hotel cannot set its own policy regarding any aspect of the exhibit, providing, of course, that the client agrees to it (see Exhibit 6).

Exhibit 6   Exhibit and Decorator's Charges

Exhibit and Decorator's Charges

There are *two charges* that you should be aware of for your budget purposes:
- A)   *Hotel Exhibit Charge*
- B)   *Decorator Charge*

A. Hotel Exhibit Charge

Sheraton-Waikiki exhibit charge is on a *Sliding Scale Per Room basis. Sliding Scale* is based on a *Per Booth Basis Per Room Per Day*, as follows (When we use the terminology "Booth", we are speaking of an 8' x 10' area):

Sliding Scale

Number of Booths in a Room Respectively	Per Room Respectively Kauai/Maui/Molokai/Lanai
35 - 44	$30.00 per 8' x 10' booth per day.
26 - 34	$35.00 per 8' x 10' booth per day.
18 - 25	$40.00 per 8' x 10' booth per day.
10 - 17	$60.00 per 8' x 10' booth per day.
05 - 09	$180.00 per 8' x 10' booth per day.

All Foyer booths $30.00 per 8' x 10' booth per day. Entrance and exit days are full price on Fridays and Saturdays. One-half (1/2) price on Sunday through Thursday.

Exhibit Pavilion:	$2000.00 each day, plus 4.16% tax Daily charges include set-up days and exit days.

All above subject to 4.16% sales tax.

There are two *money-saving opportunities* contained in the above:
- a)   By careful planning of your entrance and exit dates and time, you can save money.
- b)   By containing your exhibits to the capacities that the respective rooms will hold offers money savings.

Kauai Room	(44) 8' x 10' exhibits	Maui Room	(44) 8' x 10' exhibits
Molokai Room	(44) 8' x 10' exhibits	Lanai Room	(37) 8' x 10' exhibits
2nd Floor Foyer	(28) 8' x 10' exhibits		

B.   Decorator Charge

The decorator, when selected, also has a booth charge which includes rod and drape, electrical outlets and other specific equipment as negotiated between the decorator and the association.

The hotel agreement with the decorator is as follows:

- a)   The decorator will provide all chairs and tables negotiated with the association. The hotel cannot provide the tables and chairs for exhibits.
- b)   The respective booth electrical specifications, including spotlights, are negotiated between the decorator and the association. The hotel is not involved.
- c)   Storage equipment responsibility rests with the decorator. Equipment is stored in the decorator's warehouse prior to and after each convention.
- d)   Drayage—The decorator is responsible for the following:
    1. Receipt of exhibits from the mainland.
    2. Storing of goods.
    3. Transfer to hotel.
    4. Transfer to second floor exhibit area.
    5. Removal of exhibits back to warehouse.
    6. Shipping to mainland.

Source: Courtesy of the Sheraton Waikiki.

Common trade practice calls for the hotel to make a basic charge for the room. This charge may be (1) a flat fee, or (2) it may be based on the number of booths sold.

This latter method of pricing is popular with meeting planners because it protects them from a poor showing by exhibitors. Of course, it means that the hotel is locked into the convention's success, or lack of it, in selling exhibit space. And the hotel's role in such sales efforts is necessarily a passive one.

Hotel's Rental Charge

Hotels historically have been paid for guestrooms and food and beverage, but only recently have they capitalized on the sale of exhibit space. Exhibitions more and more frequently are held concurrently with conventions, and hotels with adequate exhibit areas are in the best

Exhibit 7   Exhibition Service Contractor's Fees

FREEMAN

INVOICE

HOWARD JOHNSON/TRAVELODGE/KNIGHTS INN

BALLYS CASINO & RESORT - LAS VEGAS, NV

BOOTH #:	522					INVOICE #:	124444-54
BILL TO:	AAA					INVOICE DATE:	
						BRANCH #:	111
						PO #:	

EXHIBITOR: AAA

DESCRIPTION	MEN	HOURS	QTY	UOM	RATE	EXT	TAX
6'L X 42"H DRAPED COUNTER			1	EA	123.60	123.60	
8'L X 42"H DRAPED COUNTER			1	EA	138.40	138.40	
CASEY PADDED STOOL			4	EA	65.75	263.00	
9' X 10' CARPET			1	EA	113.00	113.00	
CARPET PADDING - (SQFT)			90	SQFT	.50	45.00	
					BOOTH FURNISHINGS TOTAL	**$683.00**	
WAREHOUSE-CRATED-OT ONE WAY Received DT: 05/20/05 02:23 pm Target DT: Shipper: AAA Receiver #: 1000087 Carrier: FREEMAN DECORATING COMPANY Pc Cnt: 4 Pro #: 67884-71			2	CWT	65.40	130.80	
WAREHOUSE-CRATED-OT ONE WAY Received DT: 05/16/05 02:46 pm Target DT: Shipper: AAA Receiver #: 1000015 Carrier: AIRBORNE EXPRESS Pc Cnt: 5 Pro #: W38589624371			2	CWT	65.40	130.80	
SHOWSITE-CRATED-OT ONE WAY Received DT: 05/24/05 10:00 am Target DT: Shipper: AAA Receiver #: 2000025 Carrier: DHL WORLDWIDE EXPRESS Pc Cnt: 2 Pro #: 38589689073			1	CWT	62.20	62.20	
					MATERIAL HANDLING CHARGES	**$323.80**	

Most exhibitor service contractors charge a flat fee for setting up simple booths and charge additional fees for additional items, including furnishings and booth decorations. This excerpt from an exhibitor service contractor's invoice details the charges for booth furnishings and carpet and padding, as well as shipping costs for the listed items.
Source: Freeman.

position to book these groups. Some hotels have not only been able to show profits from the rental of their exhibit areas, but they have also taken on the role of decorator, providing booths, furniture, drapery, etc., for which there is an additional rental fee. This is not the rule, however; most meeting groups use independent decorating firms.

There are two common types of exhibit arrangements for shows held within a hotel—the exhibit held concurrently with a convention, and the exhibit held as part of a trade show. The first is sometimes termed a private trade show, with preregistration required and attendance restricted to individuals within the association. The latter, often called a **consumer show** or *gate show*, is targeted directly to consumers and open to the public, although attendees are usually charged an entrance fee at most shows. These categories require different considerations in determining rental charges.

The exhibit held concurrently with a convention is the more common type of arrangement, and rental charges vary to a greater extent. As we mentioned, it is a common hotel practice to make a basic charge for the exhibit area. Associations, which make a sizable profit reselling the space to exhibitors, are willing to pay a reasonable fee. While there are no hard numbers and fees vary from city to city, time of year, and demand, it is common for the facility to charge the association or trade show company from $2.00 to $5.00 per square foot. The association or trade show company then resells the space for considerably more—in the $15–$30 per square foot range or even more.

Hotels frequently establish a figure from which they are willing to negotiate. Each group must be analyzed individually. Various factors must be considered in arriving at an agreed rate, just as in determining the charges for meeting rooms. Here are some of the considerations:

- What is the extent of the group's guestroom commitment? Its meeting room commitment?
- How much can the members be expected to spend for food and beverage?
- Is there the possibility of repeat business with this group?
- Are there any unusual problems in catering to this group (e.g., a large electronics show)?
- How great is the demand from other groups for these particular days?
- How much of an exhibit area will the group need?

The exhibit held as part of a trade show is often open to the public, as in the cases of boat, gem, and antique shows. In other cases, such as the Snowsports Industry of America, the exhibit is restricted to dealers. Trade show organizers are primarily in the business for a profit and fully intend to make their profit from subleasing the hotel exhibit space. In this case, the markup for exhibit space is considerable.

Hotels can generally command a bigger rental charge for trade show exhibitions than those used in conjunction with conventions. Meeting rooms are seldom used by trade shows, and there is no assurance that attendees will stay in the hotel guestrooms. A case we know of is when antique dealers were booked into the Las Vegas Hilton. Most of the dealers were not financially able to pay the Hilton's high room rates, so they stayed in nearby budget motels.

Another consideration justifying a higher rental charge is the likelihood of damage to the hotel with the increased traffic flow. Such business, however, might well provide the hotel with increased food and beverage revenue in its restaurants and lounges.

Exhibition Service Contractor's Fee

The exhibition service contractor usually receives a flat fee of $100 to $150 for setting up each booth, using pipe frame dividers and drapery for separation on the back and sides (see Exhibit 7). The service contractor charges the exhibitor extra for such furnishings as tables, chairs, and wastepaper baskets. Sometimes, the exhibition service contractor will offer a **booth package** to exhibitors. In this case, the exhibitor pays a single price for the booth and such additions as a table, chair, carpet, electrical outlets, and so on instead of having to pay for the added items separately.

The fees the hotel charges for the room usually include the overall lighting (but not that for individual exhibits), heating and air conditioning, and cleaning services. The individual exhibitor orders from the decorator and pays directly for extra lighting, booth decorations, the furnishings described above, electrical connections, water and gas connections, telephone service and installation, extra signs, graphics, floral decoration, and photography.

Convention Shipping and Receiving

The convention service manager can avoid many frayed tempers and difficulties by advising the convention organization about shipping procedures. Such advice should be given early enough for the convention executive to include it in mailings to exhibitors. This is accomplished by working backwards from the meeting date to create a schedule to ensure that materials are ready for shipment and arrive when they are needed on site. Specific instructions should also be provided for the routing and storage of exhibit materials (see Exhibit 8). In some cases, small packages (such as attendee handouts) may be addressed directly to a hotel contact person; in most cases, however, exhibit materials are handled by outside companies. It is important, then, to provide detailed information on the procedures and costs for handling exhibition materials.

Exhibit Shipping

Many hotels do not have adequate storage space to receive and store exhibit material prior to the event. A **drayage company** thus plays an essential role in the flow of exhibit material. **Drayage** refers to material handling, and is the work and cost of transferring an exhibitor's materials to and from the booth.

The drayage company receives all the exhibit material. It has adequate storage facilities in another part of town, probably where real estate is less expensive and zoning allows large warehousing operations. It also has adequate trucking equipment to move the material from its storage area to the convention site within a day or two of setup time. It is the aim of every exhibition hall manager to reduce to an absolute minimum the time the hall is not used for an active exhibit. When setup day comes, the manager wants the material moved in quickly.

Exhibit handling and storage are paid for by the exhibitors. When the exhibitor doesn't understand that the drayage company is to store all material, cases start coming to the hotel. But if the drayage company is selected early enough, such shipments are rerouted to the drayage company facility, and the drayage company can have the convention organizer include its facility as the proper shipping address for the exhibit crates. The exhibitor then ships directly to the drayage company, which accepts the material, stores it, and starts

Pictured are exhibits using only a portion of the more than 218,000 square feet of the exhibit space available at the John B. Hynes Veterans Memorial Convention Center in Boston, Massachusetts.
Source: Courtesy of the Massachusetts Convention Center Authority.

to deliver all the crates to the convention site on setup day. When the time comes to break down, the entire process works in reverse.

Frequently, the decorator will handle all the drayage. He or she will send the exhibitor labels for any freight that will be sent to the convention. The labels are pre-stamped with the name of the convention to ensure that the service company gets the freight to the right show. The service company sometimes gives exhibitors thirty days of free storage prior to the convention; this is to make sure all freight arrives in time.

Drayage material will be delivered to the booths prior to the show. After the convention, the service company delivers the freight to a common carrier or other means of transportation, such as air or padded van.

It is important that the decorator know the truck line and invoice number of the shipment in order to trace freight if it is not received in time. Reforwarding instructions are also required by the service company.

Recommended Address Terminology

Proper address terminology facilitates handling and delivery of crates and parcels. If a drayage company is used, have all shipments addressed and consigned directly to its facility.

The *event* the shipment is intended for and the *dates* of the event should be marked clearly. This is essential, even if in-house storage is provided. It is also important for small parcels sent through the mail, so there can be a logical grouping and storage within your hotel package room.

Exhibit 8   Hotel Shipping Guideline

THE BOULDERS
RESORT AND GOLDEN DOOR SPA

Incoming Shipping Guidelines

> Please make sure that the following information is on the outside of the packages when shipping materials for your event

- Address the packages to the individual (with your company) who will be receiving them once on property (i.e. Joe Smith, guest with _____ group).
- Send To:

> The Boulders Resort
> 34505 N. Scottsdale Road, Suite K1
> Scottsdale, Arizona 85262

- The name of the Catering/Conference Service Manager
- Number of Pieces (i.e. 1 of 10, etc.)
- Conference Name and Dates

Send your packages to arrive approximately 3 days before your function begins. Packages cannot arrive any earlier than 5 days prior to the conference due to limited storage facilities. Any shipments that do arrive earlier will be charged a storage fee of $5.00 per box per day. Crates and/or large boxes will be charged $25.00 per box per day.

Incoming packages will be charged the following handling charges:

1 – 5 boxes	$15.00
6 – 10 boxes	$25.00
11 – 20 boxes	$50.00
21 – 30 boxes	$70.00
31 – 50 boxes	$100.00
51 – 99 boxes	$150.00
100+ boxes	$200.00
Crates/Pallets	$125.00 each

All shipments must be prepaid. The Boulders Resort cannot be responsible for collecting shipments.

Please Note:
The preferred carriers for The Boulders Resort are UPS and Federal Express. They arrive once daily, usually between 10am and 2pm, regardless of the package service used. Both couriers will deliver on Saturday, but only when specifically requested.

34505 North Scottsdale Rd. Suite K1 Scottsdale, Arizona 85262 Phone 480-488-6720 Fax 480-488-7462

In order to ensure prompt delivery of materials needed for exhibitions and trade shows, hotels prepare guidelines for organizers and exhibitors and mail the required information out well in advance of the show date to avoid any problems with the receipt of materials. In some cases, materials are handled by drayage companies or shipped to an outside facility; in this example, The Boulders Resort and Golden Door Spa in Scottsdale, Arizona, provides guidelines for materials to be sent directly to the property. Note that arrival date and storage information/fees are provided, and the property also lists its preferred carriers.
Source: Courtesy of The Boulders Resort and Golden Door Spa.

A convention service manager often will prefer to have the association address its material marked to his or her attention. Lost or misplaced crates create havoc; the first inquiries made by exhibitors are often in regard to their crates and parcels.

It is important to set up a procedure on handling material addressed to the hotel. Even if the exhibitors' manual instructed that shipments were to be sent directly to the drayage company, you'll always get some sent to the hotel. How you handle such shipments depends on how much room you have at the hotel and how much time is left before the event.

Lost shipments are always a problem. It is difficult for convention service managers to help when cases are lost en route, but they should do what they can to calm concerned and aggravated exhibitors. They, of course, should help exhibitors trace their shipments and expedite installation at the earliest moment after arrival.

Shipping Methods

You help your client and you help yourself if you indicate a preferred shipping method. There are several options:

- Air freight/parcel delivery (overnight or two-day service) gets packages to the facility quickly and facilitates tracking, but this option is expensive and there are often weight/size limitations for packages.

- Common carriers are trucking companies that combine shipments (from several clients) that are going to the same destination. This is an economical way to ship, but delivery dates are not always guaranteed and tracking can be difficult.

- Trucks can be hired exclusively from van lines or trucking companies —or exhibitors, especially those who participate in numerous shows, may own or rent their own delivery vehicles.

- Using an exhibit contractor as a shipping agent.

From your vantage point, a preferred carrier or trucking company may mean smooth delivery of many shipments. The client is assured of delivery with little trouble.

Local companies don't all offer the same degree of service. Some truckers may have a larger installation in your city, or more trucks, or perhaps just a better, more concerned traffic manager. One desirable characteristic is delivery on weekends. Whatever the reason, recommended firms with consistently good performances ease the bottlenecks that appear on setup day. Good local trucking arrangements help a great deal.

Even using the best trucking company available does not always eliminate problems. To reduce risk, some planners opt to insure their materials. This decision is made based on the value of their items, how critical the materials are to the meeting, and the risk of their loss or damage due to the shipping method. If, for example, a package of speaker handouts is lost in transit, insurance would cover the cost of replacement printing and copying.

On the hotel's part, you will also want to ensure that there are no scheduling conflicts at your **loading docks**, the area where goods are received. This is especially important if you are using your loading docks for more than one function—or if exhibitors are bringing in goods or merchandise (such as a fleet of cars, for example) that may tie up the docks for some time. The hotel's convention service manager should be aware of the number and type of deliveries expected and the amount of time required to unload incoming trucks to avoid conflicts with additional deliveries or the receipt of incoming shipments.

Incoming Shipping Costs

Some arrangements must be made to handle shipments that come in with postage or freight charges due. Drivers are not empowered to leave shipments when money is due. Without a clear arrangement, a truck might remain at the loading platform, keeping others from unloading and generally causing havoc.

Exhibitors should be advised to prepay all shipping charges, but inevitably a number of cases and cartons arrive with some money due. A procedure should be set up to pay such charges and arrange for reimbursement. This responsibility clearly belongs to the convention organization, but the hotel should make sure that some sort of system is set up. When it isn't, the hotel is generally blamed as being unable to handle incoming shipments without trouble.

Outgoing shipments should be handled properly, too. One reason so many shipments come in with charges due is the ease of shipping that way, eliminating the need to weigh and evaluate shipping costs on the scene. If exhibitors prefer to ship that way from your hotel, keep in mind that those shipments may not be going back home. Many go to other events. Similarly, the exhibit cases you receive may be coming from another event freight-collect.

Working with good shipping companies can ease your outgoing shipment problem. Alert them to the breakdown schedule of the show, and they can arrange for the trucks and drivers to be there. Those companies that work well with you to clear the cases out of your hotel are very likely the companies you'll be recommending for incoming shipments. Good local service companies are a comfort to a convention service manager, and they should be cultivated carefully.

Inform the convention staff of the time needed to set up the exhibit and to break it down. Reminding exhibitors about overtime charges works well. Some exhibitors rush to get ready for the exhibit but have to be prodded to get out quickly.

Summary

Trade shows can be a lucrative business for hotels that are willing to make the effort to organize for them. This involves developing a capable sales and service staff that understands the needs of both the trade show organizer and the exhibitor. While a hotel's role in the trade show may vary, it is important that its staff be able to assist meeting groups or trade show companies as needed. This may involve contracting exhibition service contractors or other outside services (such as florists, security staff, personnel to set up and dismantle booths, and drayage companies), or directly assisting with specific requirements. No matter what the hotel's involvement, the property has a stake in the success of a trade show. Trade shows bring in guestroom and food and beverage business, and satisfied exhibitors and trade show organizers often result in repeat business—not only for future trade shows but also for other meetings and leisure stays.

Endnotes

1. Total number of booths = 50 booths
   Size of each booth (8'x10') = 80 square feet
   Total number of booths multiplied by the size of booths
   80 square feet x 50 booths = 4,000 net square feet
   Net square feet multiplied by 2 = 8,000 gross square feet

2. To view the most recent salary surveys for both association and independent show managers, go to www.expoweb.com.

3. From correspondence with Sam Lippman. Used with permission.

4. Jane Chase, "Exhibitors Have Their Say," *Association & Society Manager*, ©Barrington Publications.

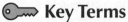 ## Key Terms

area exhibit—Exhibitors are assigned specific floor space for displaying equipment and other displays.

booth exhibit—A standard unit of exhibit space (usually 10 ft. by 10 ft.) occupied by an exhibitor. Usually constructed of pipe and draping.

booth package—An exhibitor receives a variety of services for a single price. Carpet, a six-foot draped table, a 500-watt outlet, and 500 pounds of drayage may be included in the price of each booth, for example.

consumer show—Show open to the general public. Also called a gate show or public show, these shows may include travel destination shows, recreation shows, home and garden shows, and so on. These shows are not generally connected to any convention or meeting and usually charge an entrance fee.

drayage—Delivery of exhibit materials from the dock to the assigned exhibit space, removal of emptied crates, return of the crates to be repacked at the end of the event, and delivery of the crated exhibit materials back to the dock.

drayage company—Company that handles drayage for a show and returns exhibit materials to the exhibitor.

exhibition—An event at which products and services are displayed. In addition to stimulating sales and enhancing public relations efforts, exhibitions provide face-to-face contact with prospective buyers and the opportunity to build business-to-business (B2B) relationships.

exhibit manager—Person in charge of individual exhibit booth/stand.

exhibition floor plan—To-scale plan showing spacing of booths, aisles, and the design of the exhibition. Prepared by the exhibition service contractor for the show manager and approved by the fire marshal.

exhibition service contractor—Independent firm or individual responsible for setting up and dismantling an exhibit, including supplying booth and display equipment, rental furnishings, floor coverings, labor, drayage, and signage. Sometimes referred to as a general service contractor or a decorator. Usually contracted by the planner's organization. If the sole agent, said to be the exclusive contractor.

exhibitor—Person or firm that displays products or services at the show. Also refers to the staff of a booth or display.

exhibitor advisory committee—Representatives from an event's exhibiting companies who act as advisers to show managers regarding rules and procedures; they also advise managers of industry trends and issues.

exhibitor appointed contractor (EAC)—Any person or firm other than the designated "official" contractor providing a service to an exhibitor. Can refer to an install and dismantle company (I&D house), florist, or any other type of contractor. Rather than working in one city, exhibitor appointed contractors often travel throughout the country to set up and dismantle the booths for companies that exhibit at a number of shows throughout the year.

exhibitor prospectus—Promotional materials that promote the benefits of exhibiting in a show, sent to current and prospective exhibitors to encourage their participation. Information includes a floor plan of the exhibition, cost of exhibition space, special requirements, and an application for participation.

exhibitor service kit—Contains information about the services needed by the exhibitor for a successful convention. Usually developed by the exhibition service contractor. Contains general event information, labor/service order forms, and rules and regulations pertinent to an exhibitor's participation in an exhibition. Also called an exhibitor's manual.

floor load—Weight per square foot/meter that the exhibit can safely accommodate.

floor manager—Person retained by event management to supervise the installation, operation, and dismantling of the exhibit area.

hardwall—A type of exhibit construction in which the walls are made of a solid material, such as plywood, plastic, or similar materials, rather than the fabric used in pipe and drape.

hold harmless clause—A type of indemnity clause that requires one party to fully protect the other from a claim (this would include the payment of costs for attorney fees). States that neither party will hold the other responsible for any damages to or theft of materials or equipment.

hotel shows—Exhibitions held in hotels as opposed to a city's convention center.

installation and dismantle—The set up and tear down of exhibits. Also, the firm that does this work.

island booth—Booth or display with aisles on all four sides.

loading dock—The area on premises where goods are received. Loading docks are usually raised areas that facilitate the unloading and loading of trucks.

move-in—Date or dates set for the installation of exhibits.

move-out—Date or dates designated for the dismantling of exhibits.

multi-level exhibit—An exhibit with two or more levels or stories. Often used by large companies to expand their exhibit space without taking up more floor space.

peninsula booth—A booth or exhibit with aisles on three sides.

perimeter booth—A booth or exhibit located on an outside wall. Also called a perimeter wall booth.

pipe and drape—Lightweight aluminum tubing draped with fabric to create separate exhibit booths.

standard booth—A basic 8'x10' or 10'x10' booth configured in rows of adjacent and back-to-back booths of the same size.

table top exhibit—Used where space is limited or where there is a limited number of exhibitors.

trade show—An exhibition of products and services held for members of a common or related industry. Not open to the general public.

trade show manager—Individual who plans, organizes, and operates the trade show. Responsible for renting the site and soliciting exhibitors. May work directly for the association or corporation or as an independent. Also called the show organizer or show producer.

union house—Facility at which workers are governed and regulated by an organized union.

virtual trade show—Exhibition of products or services that can be viewed over the Internet.

Review Questions ───────────────────────

1. Why are trade shows important to both meeting planners and hotels?

2. What are the three types of exhibits used at trade shows? Describe the four basic booth configurations.

3. Who are the key personnel responsible for executing trade shows? What is the role of each?

4. Explain the difference between the exhibitor's service kit and the exhibit prospectus.

5. List the types of information and some of the forms provided in the exhibitor's service kit.

6. Identify the two types of clients served by exhibition service contractors and detail the services provided to each.

7. Discuss how such factors as labor regulations and insurance coverage affect exhibitors.

8. What are the billing procedures typically used by hotels to bill trade show participants? What factors play a part in determining hotel charges?

9. Discuss the shipping of exhibits, including address terminology, shipping methods, and shipping costs.

 Additional References ───────────────────────

The Art of the Show, by Sandra Morrow, Association for Exhibition Management Foundation. www.iaee.org

Exhibit Marketing: A Success Guide for Managers, by Edward Chapman, McGraw-Hill.

Expositions and Trade Shows, by Deborah Robbe, John Wiley & Sons: 2000. www.hospitality@wiley.com

Meeting Manager Standards and Meeting Coordinator Standards, by MPI Canadian Council and the Government of Canada, the Department of Human Resources Development, Meeting Professionals International. www.mpiweb.org

 Internet Sites ───────────────────────

For more information, visit the following Internet sites. Internet addresses can change without notice. If a site is no longer available at the address listed below, a search engine can be used to find the new address or additional, related sites.

Canadian Association of Exposition Management
www.caem.ca

Center for Exhibition Industry Research
www.ceir.org

EventWeb
www.eventweb.com

Exhibit Designers and Producers Association
www.edpa.com

Exhibition Service Contractors Association
www.esca.org

Exhibitor Appointed Contractors Association
www.eaca.com

Exhibitor Magazine
www.exhibitornet.com

ExhibitorNet
www.exhibitornet.com

Expo Magazine
www.expoweb.com

Expo Net: Tradeshow Marketing Resource
   Network
www.exponet.com

The Freeman Companies
www.freemanco.com

GES Exposition Services
www.gesexpo.com

Healthcare Convention and Exhibitors
   Association
www.hcea.org

International Association of Exhibitions
   and Events
www.iaee.com

National Association of Consumer Shows
www.publicshows.com

Society of Independent Show Organizers
www.siso.org

Trade Show Central
www.tscentral.com

Trade Show Exhibitors Association
www.tsea.org

Trade Show News Network
www.tsnn.com

Tradeshow Week
www.tradeshowweek.com

CHAPTER APPENDIX

A BEHIND-THE-SCENES LOOK AT A TRADE SHOW

The Consumer Electronics Show (CES), held in January in Las Vegas, is the premier trade show for the consumer electronics industry. Sponsored by the Electronics Industries Association/Consumer Electronics Group, this trade show features audio- and video-based products, multimedia, home computing, interactive, electronic gaming, and cellular products. The large number of displays require the use of several facilities, including the exhibit halls of the Las Vegas Convention Center, the Convention Center parking lot, and several hotels that offer exhibit space.

Naturally, a show of this magnitude requires extensive planning and pre-show preparation. In the following photographs, we will take a behind-the-scenes look at the steps taken to prepare just one hall for this trade show.

Exhibit Hall S2 has been cleaned after a prior event and spaces for the CES exhibitors' booths have been marked and numbered. The Winter CES show will utilize over 1 million square feet of exhibit space and will host more than 1800 exhibitors.

On December 28 and 29, trucks begin moving in cargos of freight, including construction material that may be used to build exhibitor booths and displays. These crates will be stacked prior to booth construction and removed as booth construction progresses.

On December 30, additional freight, including the exhibitors' merchandise and components for the display, continues to arrive, the first overhead directional and exhibitor signs are hung, and booth decorating—including the laying of individual booth carpet—begins.

On January 3, booths are beginning to take shape.

By January 4, booth construction is well underway, as is booth and hall decorating, including the draping of booth and exhibit hall walls.

On January 5, the last of the freight, including rental furniture and last-minute decorating items (such as plants and flowers), is moved in. Later that evening, the aisle carpet will be laid in preparation for the next day's opening.

On January 6, the four-day show opens. Over 100,000 people, including buyers, international, and editorial press will attend.

On January 10, the day after the show, dismantling is already in progress. Aisle carpet was rolled up immediately after the show's close to facilitate the removal of freight, crates are returned for the packing of show merchandise, and booth dismantling begins.

By January 11, most of the show has been crated and is in the process of being removed from the exhibit hall.

Photographs courtesy of Stephen A. Stoney. Special thanks to the Las Vegas Convention and Visitors Bureau and the Electronic Industries Association/ Consumer Electronics Shows for their help in the preparation of this appendix.

Chapter 18 Outline

Competencies

1. Explain how hospitality properties handle billing for conventions and meetings. (pp. 601–616)

2. Describe typical procedures for conducting a postconvention review. (pp. 616–624)

Establishing Convention Billing Procedures

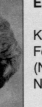

Karen Hudson
Former Sales Manager, Four Seasons Hotel
(Now the Island Hotel Newport Beach)
Newport Beach, California

"At our hotel, convention billing procedures are set up prior to the meeting. Once a contract is signed and the group requests direct billing of charges, a credit application is forwarded to the client. If the credit manager approves the credit application, a master account is established for the group. In the event credit is not approved, a deposit is then required either immediately or at some point prior to group arrival. When a master account is established in the computer system, any and all charges that the company or association is responsible for are posted to that account. These charges are processed through the front desk, which posts these charges daily. Once the group checks out, charges are collected by the credit department and compiled into one bill. If the group uses outside vendors such as entertainment or special flowers or plants, it is the responsibility of the conference service manager to post the supplier or vendor charges to the group's master account."

18 Convention Billing and Postconvention Review

AFTER A BOOKING has "gone definite," the convention service manager begins to collect information from the meeting planner about various aspects of the convention so that he or she can prepare the meeting **resume**. The resume, or specification sheet, is the major internal means of communication for hotel personnel involved with the convention. There are three basic areas that every convention service manager looks at as he or she puts together the resume: reservations, program, and billing. Open and honest communication is paramount in all three of these areas. In this chapter, we will address questions about function *billings*.

Convention Billing

Convention billing is much too important to be handled haphazardly. Ranking near the top of the list of meeting planners' pet peeves are surprise billing charges. Open communications can help tremendously to have the event end on a happy note. When it is clear who pays for what, everything seems to go more smoothly.

As with most aspects of convention planning, the time to avoid billing problems is at the beginning and not at the end. Billing policy is usually established months before the group gets into the hotel, not at the end of the convention, and should address:

- What areas does the master account cover?
- How are the delegates' charges to be handled?
- Will there be more than one master account?
- Who is authorized to sign?
- What about tips and gratuities?
- How should early arrivals and late departures be handled?
- Should the hotel or the group be billed by outside service companies such as florists and audiovisual suppliers?
- What are the charges for the various types of guestrooms? Meeting rooms? Exhibit area?
- What are the arrangements for food and beverage?
- How are transportation charges to be handled? How are special events, such as golf tournaments and tours, to be priced?
- What are the arrangements for audiovisual, electrical, and phone charges?
- Will there be a charge for security and other labor provided by the hotel?
- How does the meeting planner want the bill broken down?
- Are deposits required?
- Who will prepare and collect chits? Tickets? Banquet checks?

All of these aspects need to be prearranged, and each detail should be clearly spelled out. **Billing instructions** for each function should be clearly outlined in the resume, as shown in Exhibit 1. The accounting department, as well as the other service departments in the hotel, wants explicit instructions on the billing procedure. You definitely want to avoid the problems that arise at the check-out desk when the specification sheet doesn't deal in detail with billing arrangements.

Exhibit 1   Corporation and Association Billing Examples

Example I — Arizona Biltmore Hotel, Phoenix

_____**Corporation**

Controller: Corporation will guarantee all personal checks up to $250 for all members.
Reserve suites 67-66-63-62-61-59-58 from 4/28. Charge 5 to Master Account—other 2 to be complimentary.

Billing: MASTER ACCOUNT to cover American plan room rate, tax and service charge of all guests.
Master Account also to cover: receptions, surcharges, recreational activities on tournament day, breakfast trail ride, cowboy hats, bandanas, refreshment breaks, entertainment, hostesses, etc. PREPARE INCIDENTAL FOLIO for each guest. Post all incidental charges to their respective accounts. To be paid prior to departure. (LIST IN ACCOUNTING OFFICE OF ENTIRE ACCOUNTS TO BE TRANSFERRED TO M/A).

Night Auditor: NOTE: Extend $4.50 inclusive credit per person for those taking shopping tour on 4/4 or leaving prior to luncheon on 4/5. MUST NOTIFY CASHIER 24 HOURS IN ADVANCE IN ORDER TO RECEIVE THIS CREDIT. THIS CREDIT GOES TO MASTER ACCOUNT—NOT INCIDENTAL ACCOUNT.

Example II — Caesars Palace, Las Vegas

_____**Association**

Master Account I: All group functions should be added to the master account.
Mr. _____ and Ms. _____ will be the authorized signers.
NOTE: Please post a charge in the total amount of $250 to this group's master account. This charge is for the purchase of 250 Caesars Palace medallions at a cost of $1.00 per medallion.

Master Account II: A second master account is to be set up. To this master, charge the entire accounts of all _____ Association Directors and Staff.
Mr. John M._____ will be the authorized signer.

Individual Account: Rooms, tax, and incidentals to be paid by the individuals.

Billing instructions from actual resumes for a corporate meeting and an association convention.
Source: Courtesy of the Arizona Biltmore Hotel and Caesars Palace.

The Master Account

The biggest problem when working with convention billing is usually unclear communication. Therefore, an understanding of billing procedures begins with terminology.

A *folio* is a collection of charges incurred by an individual or an organization. There are three types of folios to which charges are posted:

- **Master Account Folio**—charges are paid entirely by the sponsoring organization.
- **Individual Guest Folio**—charges are paid entirely by the individual guest.
- **Split Folio**—charges are paid partially by the sponsoring organization and partially by the individual guest. Most meetings in hotels are accounted for as split folios.

A **master account** is generally set up to facilitate billing to the convention organization. The hotel executive and the convention executive should discuss the charges that should be billed to this account. All other charges are billed to the guests on their individual accounts.

Increasingly, meeting planners are looking for hotels that are willing to divide the overall bill into sub-master accounts to enable planners to quickly and accurately review actual charges against their budgets. For example, many groups will specify a separate master account for group food and beverage functions, another for audiovisual, and still another for miscellaneous items such as telephone and business center use. Sometimes a participating company will sponsor a program event, such as a luncheon or cocktail party, and a separate master account is set up for this affair.

Deirdre Bourke, CMP, a senior account executive at Experient, advises meeting planners to:

- Provide clear instructions to the hotel about specific charges that should be posted to the master account, such as room and tax, food and beverage, audiovisual, electrical, telecommunications, and business center.
- Advise the hotel in advance if separate master accounts are required. Establishing multiple master accounts is a simple way for meeting planners to segregate bills in advance so they don't have to be sorted out after the event.
- Confirm with the hotel that all charges posted to the master account must have backup, including invoices, signed checks, and banquet event orders (BEOs).[1]

It is imperative that the convention organization put down in writing all people authorized to charge to the master account, and they sometimes provide samples of **authorized signatures**. Signers are usually the convention staff personnel. If *all* their charges are to be allowed on the master account, say so. The understanding is that these people are also authorized to sign charges. If this area of authority is to be limited in any way, those limitations should be spelled out.

Failure to detail the extent of charges to the master account can lead to difficulties in the case of convention guests, speakers, and program presenters. The hotel doesn't care who pays what or how, so long as it is made clear who is to pay. It is the convention staff's responsibility to inform its guests about the extent of the hospitality, but it is your desk clerk or cashier who must face these people when they check out.

Ask the convention staff to inform you, as well as the guests, who will pay for rooms, food, beverage, telephone, valet charges, and other incidentals. It helps to inform the guest when he or she checks in that the room charges will be paid for by the association, but many hotels feel that this is the convention staff's task. Unfortunately, it is surprising how infrequently the convention staff follows through to tell its guests the extent to which they are responsible for charges. Bringing the matter to the attention of convention executives will at least alert them to potential embarrassing problems and maybe move them to set policy.

Such arrangements apply to corporate meetings as well those of associations, since corporate meetings may be attended by persons other than company employees. The arrangements should be spelled out completely. This applies to corporate personnel, too. Some companies pay *all* charges through the master account, while some pay only room and food charges, with the rest paid through individual expense accounts. All variations will be encountered.

The hotel should have no policy of its own, but should merely follow the *clear* instructions of the company meeting planner. These instructions should be in writing. Generally speaking, if you get the meeting planner to spell it out to you in writing, the corporate personnel stand a much better chance of receiving detailed instructional memos telling them how to check out.

In some cases, group deposits are required. The need for group deposits is based upon such factors as credit worthiness and group history. The Financial & Insurance Conference Planners association has prepared a guide providing possible solutions to problems usually associated with master account billing to be used by meeting planners and hoteliers alike. Two forms from this guide are illustrated in this chapter. Exhibit 2 illustrates a **master account billing authorization form**, which provides a comprehensive set of instructions on:

- How hotel charges are to be posted (master account or individual guest's room folio).
- The limit of financial responsibility the meeting group will accept.
- The names and specimen signatures of those who are authorized to sign for any master account expenses (only those with an authorized signature are permitted to sign for group charges).

Exhibit 3 illustrates a **rates and charges bulletin**, which communicates to the convention attendees the specific rates for rooms, meals, **incidental charges,** and billing procedures, as agreed to by the convening group and the hotel. The bulletin is sent to the convention attendees one month prior to the convention date. Use of this communication bulletin reduces disputes and speeds guest check-out.

Time of Payment

Methods and time of payment vary a great deal, depending on the policy of the hotel, the credit and reputation of the convening organization, past history, the frequency of group business, and other factors.

Master accounts can add up to a considerable amount of money, and it is hard to blame hotel managers if they try to get as much of it as possible up front. This is not only because of concern about being paid, but also because of a desire to accelerate time of payment and to ease the hotel's cash flow.

The usual practice in the trade is a payment when the contract is signed, a pre-convention payment at an agreed date, on-the-scene payments, and a final payment. The final payment can be broken into two parts—one at the end of the event, and a final settlement later. In most cases, payment is due in full approximately 30 days after the event. To ensure prompt payment, some hotels offer discounts to groups that pay their master account

Exhibit 2   Master Account Billing Authorization Form

MASTER ACCOUNT BILLING AUTHORIZATION

Convention
Name_____
Dates_____
Food Plan_____

NOTE: Please post charges as indicated below. Master Account charges noted here apply only on meeting dates. See separate letter for exceptions and additional Master Account information.

	MA	IND		MA	IND		MA	IND
ROOM & FOOD PLAN			**HOTEL SERVICES**			**SPORTS**		
Room & Tax			Telephone • Local			Golf Greens Fees		
MAP (FAP)* Guest			• Long Distance			Golf Lessons		
MAP(FAP)* Spouse			Parking			Golf Driving Range		
Other			Valet & Laundry			Golf • Caddie Fee		
			Bellmen			Golf • Cart Rental		
FOOD & BEVERAGE			Maids			Tennis • Court Fees		
			Pool/Beach Attendants			Tennis • Lessons		
Restaurant • Food			TV Movies			Tennis • Racquet Rentals		
Restaurant • Bar			Beauty Salon			Sports Merchandise		
Room Service • Food			Barber Shop			Spa/Health Club		
Room Service • Bar			Merchandise Shops			Stables		
Bar Charges			Other			Other		
Cover Charge								
Other			**MISCELLANEOUS**			**TOURNAMENTS**		
BANQUET CHARGES			Airport Transfers			Refreshments		
_____			Other			Club/Racquet Rental		
_____						Golf/Tennis Balls		
_____						Greens Fees		
_____						Cart Rental		
_____						Caddie Fees		
_____						Court Fees		
_____						Other		

*Including tax & Service Charge, if any.

The _____Company
    (Sponsor Organization)

1. (Is/Is not) responsible for payment of delinquent charges to individual accounts.
2. (Will/Will not) guarantee payment of its attendees' hotel bill whether paid by check or charge card.
3. (Will/Will not) guarantee personal checks cashed by its attendees up to $_____.
4. Some persons (list attached) will have entire room and incidental accounts posted to Master. These persons should be preregistered and will not check themselves out. Their room bills will be reviewed and signed by the sponsor organization's planner.
5. Authorizes these signatures (Type) _____ _____ _____
   for its MA charges   (Sign)_____ _____ _____
The hotel should consider these billing instructions definite and authorized by_____
                                              (Planner/ Date/Telephone Number)

The meeting planner uses this form to provide the hotel with a comprehensive set of instructions on how specific charges are to be billed.
Source: Courtesy of the Financial & Insurance Conference Planners.

charges in full within ten days after departure. In other cases, hotels offer discounts to groups who pay with certain credit cards. The American Express® program, for example, offers discounts and other amenities at several hotel chains and properties when the card is used for payment.

Hotels have been known to be flexible about payments, depending on what they know about the client. Political organizations certainly should not be allowed to run up large bills, because the payment may be uncertain or delayed. But a prestigious local corporation that has dealt with you many times may cause your controller little concern about the bill.

Exhibit 3   Specimen Rates and Charges Bulletin

SPECIMEN RATES AND CHARGES BULLETIN

To: Convention Attendees

The following rates and charges, which have been agreed to by ABC Company and the XYZ Hotel, will be in effect during your stay at the XYZ Hotel. The rates listed in this bulletin represent the maximum you should be charged for the listed services during the length of your stay at this convention.

DAILY ROOM RATE: Modified American Plan (2 meals)

$ 140.00 Per Person, per day plus
     11.00 Per Person,
             daily service charge* plus
       4.53 Daily state tax (3%)
	$ 230.00 Per Person, per day plus
	     11.00 Per Person,
	             daily service charge* plus
	       7.23 Daily state tax (3%)

$ 155.53 Daily Total	$ 248.23 Daily Total

These Rates: Include lodging, breakfast and dinner daily, and gratuities for maids and MAP dining room personnel.

Don't include bellman, doorman, or limo driver gratuities, parlor charges, or incidental charges.

MAP CREDITS

Tavern Room   A credit of $8.00 per person will apply and the balance would be charged at a la carte prices.

Golf Club   Dinner in Golf Club carries a surcharge depending on items selected.

Main Dining Room   A few items are a la carte, depending on items selected.

All Extra Meals   (A la carte) charges will be billed to your individual hotel account.

Room Service   A room service charge of $2.00 per person ($2.50 in cottages) will apply to all room service orders.

NOTE: MAP includes dinner on check-in day, and breakfast on check-out day. Should you dine in a group, be certain that all room numbers are listed or only that person who signs will get the total charges for the group.

TRANSPORTATION

Airport to Hotel $6.50 per person
                     $3.25 per person (small children)

*Applicable if the hotel imposes a Service Charge

One month prior to the convention, a listing of specific rates and charges is sent to the convention attendee by the meeting planner. This type of communication clearly spells out exactly what is covered by the convening group and what charges the individual attendee will be responsible for, greatly reducing the chances of any misunderstandings at the time of the meeting or convention.
Source: Courtesy of the Financial & Insurance Conference Planners.

Many meeting planners insist on talking with someone from the hotel's accounting department before the convention begins. The standard policy for the Hyatt Hotel chain is to take the meeting planner to the accounting office at the first mutually convenient time to go over billing procedure. The understanding agreed upon earlier is reinforced and problems are solved before the service is performed.

Convention organizers frequently complain that hotels cannot present the final accounting at the end of the event, while the convention staff is still on the premises and memories are fresh. If complete billing is not ready, they can still review the charges and initial approval. Some charges lag, but at least the bulk of the account can be settled. The Hilton chain requires that if bills are not available at the postconvention billing, they be

Exhibit 4   Daily Meeting Debriefings

Daily Meeting Debrief

Daily Meeting Debrief – With a limited budget and lots of attendees, it's common for even a well-planned budget to run over. Now, at the end of every day of your meeting, you'll get a Daily Meeting Debrief. This itemized accounting of your bill will be presented by your Crowne Meetings Director so that you may discuss, in detail, all of that day's expenditures. This will provide the perfect opportunity for you to track and manage your budget before it becomes a problem. During the Daily Meeting Debrief, you'll also be able to raise any issues, special requests or needs for the following day so your meeting will continue to run smoothly and as you planned.

The Daily Meeting Debrief: another way we set the standard.

FOR MORE INFORMATION ON HOLDING A SUCCESSFUL MEETING WITH
CROWNE PLAZA HOTELS, CONTACT US AT 1-800-MEETING,
VISIT MEETINGS.CROWNEPLAZA.COM OR CALL A HOTEL DIRECTLY.

CROWNE PLAZA

HOTELS & RESORTS

The Crowne Plaza Hotels & Resorts has developed a "Meeting Success" program to assist meeting planners to plan and host successful meetings and events within their budgets. Part of this service is their Daily Meeting Debrief, which provides planners with an itemized accounting of each day's expenditures to enable them to track and manage the function budget.
Source: Courtesy of Crowne Plaza Hotels & Resorts.

Best Practices:

Daily Meeting Debriefings
The Crowne Plaza Hotels & Resorts Chain

To successfully attract meetings and functions business, hotels must keep abreast of the needs of meeting planners. The Crowne Plaza Hotels & Resorts chain relies on market research to ensure that they are meeting those needs. In a recent survey, the chain found that, in regard to billing, the most critical issue for the majority of the respondents was accuracy, especially in relation to correct line items and consistent formatting. Many of the planners responding suggested a pre-departure bill review meeting, an estimated pre-bill prior to the meeting, and/or a daily bill review.

Kevin Kowalski, vice president of brand management for the chain, says:

> We are currently monitoring the needs of meeting planners. These survey results reveal that services like the Crowne Meetings Director and our daily expenses debrief are directly addressing planners' needs.

As part of its "Meeting Success" program, the chain offers a daily meeting debrief between the Crowne meetings director and the planner. At the meeting, an itemized accounting of charges posted to the account is presented to the planner. This enables him or her to track and manage his or her budget and also offers an opportunity to raise questions about specific items.

This daily tracking of expenditures allows the meeting planner to make any necessary changes or special requests for the next day's activities, and ensures that charges on the master account are accurate and up-to-date, facilitating the presentation of the final bill (in most cases, an accurate billing can be presented before the group leaves the hotel).

Source: "News Briefs," *Meetings West*.

sent out within five days after the meeting (and, to further facilitate the billing process for the planner, bill formats are consistent at all properties within the chain).

A good practice, endorsed by many convention service managers, is to arrange for the meeting planner to meet with the property controller daily to go over the previous day's charges on the master account. Some hotel chains, such as the Crowne Plaza Hotels & Resorts, offer a *daily meeting debriefing* to allow meeting planners to review an itemized accounting of that day's expenditures (Exhibit 4 shows how the chain promotes this service). Daily meeting debriefings allow meeting planners to track and manage the function budget on a frequent basis, and any discrepancies and questions can be addressed during these meetings. The daily reviews eliminate surprises for the meeting planner and, since issues are clarified before the group leaves the hotel, they facilitate the correct posting of master account charges (ideally, the master account can be presented before the event organizers leave the hotel). All banquet checks, audiovisual charges, and other service invoices should be reviewed and signed daily by the meeting planner. Days or weeks after the event, it is extremely difficult to dispute the number of dinners served at a banquet or soft drinks consumed during a break.

The hotel doesn't want the entire account held up while a relatively minor matter is adjudicated, of course. One suggestion is to set this amount aside pending further investigation and/or discussion while the rest of the bill is settled. Some meeting planners ask that a certain amount be held back after the event to handle any adjustments. The amount of money held back and the time allowed should be part of the letter of agreement or other correspondence. Otherwise, the entire bill might be held up and perhaps used unfairly for leverage.

At some conventions, a considerable amount of cash is generated through registration and ticket sales. Some arrangements should be made to count this money and keep it safe. If such cash is applied against the master account, receipts should be issued for all payments. If agreed-upon payments have been made on schedule, organizations may request checks from the hotel in return for such cash. Clear such arrangements with the hotel controller.

The increasing use of the computer for accounting functions has greatly enhanced the billing process. But in addition to more efficient billing (some charges can be added instantaneously if the property uses point-of-sale terminals), computers increase the speed with which hotels can analyze convention groups for future billing.

One hotel sales executive sees technology helping both the hotel and the meeting planner:

> Among the things that are different these days is that you can see the arrival/departure pattern of a group. You can see what food and beverage sales are per occupied room because they play a role in what's charged for meeting and sleeping rooms. Now the planner can get a report that will show the exact value of his or her group to the hotel. We still need to offer good meeting space, but now a lot of the competition is going to revolve around who can make the planner's job easier. And technology is helping us to accomplish that.[2]

With computer systems, the bill can be broken down for each function and quickly tallied to provide the total charge within an hour of the last meeting. Confusion and long hours of labor are minimized, and the bill can be reviewed and finalized while details are still fresh in the minds of the hotel staff and the meeting planner.

Guest Credit

Another matter to be discussed by the hotel staff and the meeting planner is **guest credit**. With national credit cards, it is simply a matter of saying which cards the hotel will accept. If the hotel limits the cards it will take, this information should be given in time for inclusion in the convention brochure so the guests will be forewarned. But most national and international cards are accepted in most hotels, so this seldom constitutes much of a problem.

The extension of credit directly to the guest is more of a risk. The convention executive should be told if this is contrary to hotel policy. Then the recommended procedure by which a guest could establish credit with the hotel might be outlined.

The hotel should also state its policy about cashing checks for guests. Maximum amounts should be made clear. Cashing checks for people with no established credit is a courtesy, not an obligation. Many associations, and certainly corporations, guarantee the checks cashed for members or employees. A maximum limit, if any, should be indicated.

Gratuities and Service Charges

Gratuities and service charges are a generally accepted part of convention costs. These items are always covered in all sales proposals and later in the contract (letter of agreement), yet few areas of convention management seem to cause as much controversy. While the common industry practice is to use the terms tips, gratuities, and service charges interchangeably, the CIC glossary makes clear distinctions between the terms. **Gratuities** or tips are monetary gifts given *voluntarily* in appreciation of excellent service. A **service charge**, generally a set percentage of the total bill, is a *mandatory* fee added to the group's bill (the fee is then distributed among service personnel).

Meeting planners are often confused about how much to tip, who should be tipped, and when the tip should be given. One hotelier states:

> The end of tipping is a long way off in America. I feel the planner should settle the gratuities subject in advance. If he or she feels uncomfortable with the amount specified, he or she should go to another hotel. Likewise, if he or she feels there is dissatisfaction with the amount of the gratuities, he or she should think twice about returning to that hotel. Most of the problems with gratuities are the result of not discussing the matter with the hotel convention staff—in the beginning, when everything else is being settled. Nobody should ever feel strange about asking the hotel for advice on this matter.[3]

When hotels are approached for advice on tipping, they should be prepared to explain the types of gratuities typically given and the usual amounts given to specific personnel. Although tipping procedures and amounts may vary by location and type of facility, gratuities and service charges can be categorized into four distinct groups:

- Gratuities for hotel hourly personnel, such as bellpersons, food servers, housekeepers, and door attendants.
- Service charges for group functions and banquets. These are automatic and mandatory, and are generally figured as a percentage of the bill and added to the check.
- Blanket service charges. These charges are added to the room charge and delegates are not encumbered with further tipping.
- Special gratuities given to management personnel, such as the convention service manager, banquet manager, and head houseperson.

Our first classification, tips for hourly service personnel, primarily covers the following:

Door Attendants	Restaurant Servers
Bell Staff	Cocktail Waitresses and Bartenders
Concierge	Wine Stewards
Valet Parking Attendants	Room Service Staff (unless tip is included
Housekeeping Staff	in room charge)

Other hourly service personnel may include shuttle drivers, recreational personnel (golf and tennis pros, pool attendants), childcare workers, and so on. Hourly service personnel may be tipped by individual delegates or by the event staff, depending on meeting arrangements. If a meeting organizer is handling tips, he or she should take into consideration such factors as the size of the group, the complexity of an event, and the destination, since expected gratuity amounts can vary from location to location—and from venue to venue.

Generally, gratuities for hourly service personnel are given when the service is rendered—a valet parking attendant is tipped when he or she returns a car, housekeepers appreciate a daily tip, and banquet staff should be tipped at the end of the meal. But, especially if gratuities are handed out by the convening organization, tips can be given to department managers to be distributed at the end of the event—or even after the postconvention meeting takes place.

In those cases where a meeting organizer handles gratuities, a hotel convention service manager may be asked to issue **paid-out slips** to employees. These in-house forms authorize the hotel to charge the group's master account for the tips, eliminating the need for the planner to handle large amounts of cash. Employees present their slips to the facility's cashier or payroll or accounting departments to receive their cash. Amounts needed can be gauged from past events or calculating three to five percent of the event's spending and integrating gratuity money into the event budget. Whether tips are handled through paid-out slips or distributed through department management, it is totally acceptable for the planner to ask for proof that the money was distributed—and to whom.

Our second classification, service charges, seems to present the most problems. The flat service charge rate is 15 to 20 percent or more in most cities, and many meeting planners justifiably decry being assessed a 15-plus–percent service charge regardless of the service. In many cases, however, the hotel is following the terms of a union contract, and this should be explained in the initial negotiations to avoid misunderstandings.

It is important to note that in some states the amount will be subject to sales tax if it is listed as a service charge rather than a gratuity. If a planner hosts a lunch for 100 people at $25 per person, for example, and a service charge of 18 percent ($450) was added, the resulting total of $2,950 would be subject to the state's sales tax—not just the original cost of $2,500.

To combat this problem, some hotels eliminate the term *service charge* and replace it with *gratuity*. A gratuity can legally be added to the bill after the state sales tax has been levied on the cost of meals only. This results in major savings for meeting planners, and most of them prefer to be charged in this way.

No matter which approach is used, it is important that your hotel clearly spell out its policy to eliminate unpleasant surprises for the meeting planner. If mandatory service charges on food and beverage functions or sleeping rooms can legally be replaced with agreed-upon gratuities not subject to state taxes, this arrangement should be spelled out in the convention contract.

When there is a flat percentage on food and beverage setups, the hotel normally distributes the service charge among the service personnel. While the bulk of any mandated service charge will go to the workers servicing the function, it is not uncommon for a portion to be distributed to other hotel staff members. The Royal Palms, an upscale resort in Phoenix, Arizona, for example, charges a 22-percent service charge on food and beverage service. This money is distributed beyond the service staff—both the catering director and the convention service manager receive a portion of the service charge, although no portion is given to the hotel executives, sales-staff, or owners.[4]

Many planners will ask the convention service manager for a breakdown of who shares in the distribution. There is a greater willingness to pay a mandatory service charge if the planner knows it will go to employees and not be used as an additional source of revenue by the property. In fact, a recent survey conducted by *Meetings News* showed that knowing how the service charge was distributed was "Very Important" to over half of the planners interviewed and "Somewhat Important" to over another third (see box titled "Show Me The Money").

Meeting planners should be advised, however, that it is not uncommon for a portion of a service charge to be used by management to offset labor costs. The director of convention services at a well-known San Francisco hotel says:

The union contract specifies the apportionment of the 19 percent gratuity. No part goes to convention service staff, banquet managers, or room setup; but just 75 percent is equally distributed among the waiters—the people who worked the function. The other 25 percent is allocated to a category called "salaries recovered," reducing labor costs on the profit and loss statement.[5]

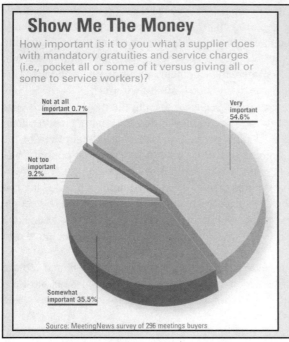

Show Me The Money

How important is it to you what a supplier does with mandatory gratuities and service charges (i.e., pocket all or some of it versus giving all or some to service workers)?

Not at all important 0.7%

Very important 54.6%

Not too important 9.2%

Somewhat important 35.5%

Source: MeetingNews survey of 296 meetings buyers

A recent survey by Meeting News *showed that knowing how mandatory gratuities and service charges were distributed was considered important to 90.1 percent of the 296 meeting planners surveyed.*
Source: Rayna Katz, "Planners Nix No-Choice Tips," MeetingNews.

Blanket service charges, our third classification, are becoming common. Planners and delegates often favor this form of tipping; it means they tip only once—when they register—and are not faced with it again. Some resorts have used this method for years, and now commercial convention hotels are trying the system, which is called the **American plan**—a single charge for rooms, meals, and gratuities (the more common **European plan** prices rooms, meals, and tips separately).

If a blanket tipping policy is to be used, this must be communicated to the delegates to avoid double tipping. Often the meeting planner will point out the policy in the registration packet. Notices declaring "Your gratuities are completely covered in the room charge; do not tip hotel personnel" are common. Similarly, the hotel must communicate this procedure to its employees and discourage them from accepting tips. Again, the resume is the medium whereby the tipping policy is communicated internally.

To help clarify blanket tipping charges, we have outlined below the policies of two well-known resorts:

- The Greenbrier
  White Sulphur Springs, West Virginia

  In lieu of gratuities for housekeeping and Modified American Plan food service personnel, a service charge of $12.00 per person is added daily to guests' accounts. Bellmen, doormen, and others who render personal services are not included in the service charge.

- Boca Raton Hotel and Club
  Boca Raton, Florida

For the convenience of the convention group, the hotel adds $14.00 per day per person to cover the following hotel personnel:

- *Front door and parking attendants*
- *Handling of luggage on arrival and departure*
- *Chamber maids*
- *Dining room personnel for meals served under the meal plan*

For a la carte food and beverages an automatic service charge of 15 percent is added to the check. Other personnel are tipped at the convention group's discretion.

Even if gratuities for hourly employees are included in service charges, there may be occasions when either the meeting planner or the event's attendees wish to recognize exceptional service with an additional gratuity. A meeting planner may give a tip to a banquet captain whose expert handling of a function has made the event especially memorable, for example. Or, a delegate may wish to show appreciation to a staff member who has provided an additional or unexpected service.

The final type of gratuity is that used in rewarding special personnel. Meeting planners may ask the hotel about the accepted practice and internal policies for giving such tips. Hotels that do recommend tipping for special services will offer a suggested minimum scale. Exhibit 5 shows the results of a survey of meeting planners regarding how they tipped special service personnel.

Surcharges and Resort Fees. While surcharges and resort fees may seem similar to blanket service charges, they are far more encompassing. **Surcharges**, which have been

Exhibit 5   Gratuity Structure for Special Tips

Gratuities Vary Based On Hotel Staff Positions

Q. Assume that the following hotel personnel have been equally attentive. Indicate whether you would give them a gratuity, and if so, how much:

PERSONNEL	YES	NO	HIGH	LOW	AVERAGE
Convention Service Director (main contact)	75%	25%	$500	$25	$125
Food and Beverage Manager	68%	32%	$500	$15	$ 88
Assistant Convention Services Director	65%	35%	$150	$15	$ 58
Setup Crew Supervisor	62%	13%	$200	$10	$ 44
Hotel General Manager	0%	100%	—	—	—
Convention Sales Manager	10%	90%	$200	$35	$ 69
Account Executive on your convention	17%	83%	$400	$15	$ 80
Catering Manager	63%	37%	$400	$20	$ 78
Front Desk Supervisor*	69%	31%	$100	$10	$ 36
Head Banquet Waiter**	82%	18%	$125	$10	$ 42
Audio Visual Operator	41%	59%	$200	$ 5	$ 44
Switchboard Operator***	39%	61%	$ 50	$10	22

* Other gratuity: candy (1)
** Other gratuity: $10 per event (1); $20 per function (1)
***Other gratuity: $10 for each operator (1); $250 to PBX Fund (1); $150 to include operators (1); candy (4); and gift (1)

In a recent survey, Meeting News *asked meeting planners which hotel personnel they tipped for special service and the average amount of such tips.*
Source: Courtesy of *Meeting News.*

implemented to bring additional revenue to hotels, are often added to guestroom bills for energy usage and Internet access, telephone calls and faxes, mini-bar restocking, and baggage handling. Meeting charges may include such surcharges as fees for electricity for audiovisual equipment and lighting, fees to cover the cost of banquet staff, and even charges for using credit cards to pay the master account.

Like service charges, surcharges are mandatory, and many meeting planners and delegates feel that they are paying for services they don't need. One SMERF meeting planner's take on surcharges and resort fees, which we will discuss next, is:

> The whole concept of surcharges goes against our grain. The so-called daily resort fee is another way hotels try to squeeze extra dollars from their customers. For $10 a day, for example, they will cover a number of things "for your convenience!" Well, all my luggage is on wheels and I don't need the bellman to carry my luggage. I'm smart enough to open the hotel room door, and even smart enough to turn on the light. Free telephone access for local calls doesn't help, because I don't know anybody local to call. For long distance, I've long since learned that it's a lot cheaper and easier to use my cell phone. So paying $10 a day for a newspaper I don't normally read is simply not for my convenience. That's why, if I sign a contract, I make sure that the rate specified is "all-inclusive" except for taxes, an element beyond the control of the hotel.[6]

It should be noted that a surcharge does not always include fees for other services and facilities that planners and attendees may use. Some hotels charge daily fees for valet and self-parking, the use of its fitness center, spa access, tennis court access and racquet rental, sports equipment storage, and Internet access, if that is not included in the surcharge. The difference between these fees and the surcharge is that they are only paid if meeting attendees make use of them, and planners should make attendees aware of these additional charges—especially if guestrooms and gratuities are covered by an all-inclusive plan.

The **resort fee**, which is similar to blanket service charges and surcharges, was originally added by resorts, especially those in out-of-the-way locations, to help raise revenue as they did not enjoy the benefits of walk-in traffic. These fees, which are now common in most resorts, are automatically added by resorts for services ranging from in-room amenities to local telephone services to resort facilities such as business centers, fitness centers, and tennis courts. The Boulders Resort in Arizona, for example, lists a number of amenities that are included in its resort fee:

> *A Resort Service Charge currently of $29.00 per Casita per day and $33.00 per Villa per day will apply to all guestrooms utilized. This fee includes daily newspaper, nightly turndown service, valet parking, all cash gratuities for bellstaff, housekeepers, on-property drivers, pool attendants, concierge, and all other service personnel (**excluding food and beverage gratuities**). This nightly service charge also includes a daily membership to the Golden Door Spa. This membership allows access to the locker room and all the amenities, full use of the weight room and cardio room, access to the sauna, steam room and O'Furo, Golden Door Spa pool area, Niwa, Labyrinth and Access to the Golden Door Spa Café (**excludes treatments and classes**).*

Other resorts may include such amenities as in-room coffee and movies, shuttle service, access to sports facilities, Internet access, newspapers, and valet parking. When 395 meeting planners were questioned in a recent survey, they detailed 15 services typically included in resort fees (see box titled "Which Amenities and Services Are Included in the Resort Fee?").

Meeting planners frequently balk at resort fees, which average $12 per day, and most feel that these fees should be eliminated. They often try to negotiate them out of the contract, or, if that is not possible, ask for a reduction in resort fees or have them rolled over into the overall room rate.

To combat the fees, which are becoming more prevalent—and more costly—some planners insist on clauses in their contracts that protect them against unexpected fees. John

WHICH AMENITIES AND SERVICES ARE INCLUDED IN THE RESORT FEE?	
Fitness center use	88%
Newspaper delivery	83%
Local phone service	78%
In-room coffee/tea	77%
Use of recreation facilities (tennis, pools)	73%
Turndown service	57%
Internet access	55%
Spa access	34%
Shuttle service	33%
Parking	32%
Housekeeping tips	26%
Bottled water	23%
Bellman tips	22%
Fax service	21%
Fitness classes	9%

Source: Art Pfenning, "Who's Paying Resort Fees?", *Meetings & Conventions*.

Foster, CHME, an attorney with the Atlanta law firm of Foster, Jensen & Gully LLC, adds the following clause to all his contracts:

> *1) No additional charges not specified in this contract, or any addendum, will be incurred by XYZ Group for work performed or for service items provided by HOTEL unless HOTEL has first obtained prior written permission from XYZ Group to have the work completed or the service or item provided.*

> *2) Neither XYZ group nor attendees will be responsible for additional surcharges, gratuities, or service fees not included in this contract without XYZ Group's or an attendee's written consent, respectively.*[7]

Hotels are responding to the concerns of meeting planners in several ways. Marriott, for example, does not charge resort fees, and it bundles telephone and Internet charges to save money for their customers. While Hilton continues to use add-on fees, including resort fees, these charges are now optional for meeting planners—and a full disclosure is always made before the customer is charged; a group cannot be charged an additional fee unless it "opts in."

In conclusion, the handling of gratuities and service charges, as with all elements of convention management, should be carefully reviewed and understood by both the meeting planner and the convention service manager. Even though tipping is a touchy area, no difficulties should arise if guidelines are clearly established at the outset.

HSMAI's Suggested Payment Schedule

The Hospitality Sales and Marketing Association International offers a list of standardized procedures that help reduce problems in convention accounting. Here are the guidelines:

- Establish a formal procedure for the hotel and the meeting planner to review periodically the room block arrangements before the meeting. The recommended schedule: up to one year before the meeting; six months before; then every month; and, with one month to go, weekly. The use of rooming lists is encouraged.
- Meeting room usage and charges should be thoroughly reviewed before the meeting.
- The hotel should clearly specify what credit cards are accepted and the maximum that can be charged.
- A master statement of all functions should be organized daily.
- Night auditors and cashiers should be instructed about the details of posting convention charges.
- It is desirable to have corporate meeting planners guarantee all attendees' bills.
- The hotel should inform the company of any delinquent accounts after thirty days.
- A representative from accounting, the head cashier, and perhaps the accounts receivable department head should also attend the pre-convention meeting.
- The resume and individual function forms are to be supplied to the meeting planner before the convention; charges to be clearly specified in advance.
- At the conclusion of each function, a copy of the master statement and supporting vouchers should be furnished to the meeting planner for his or her signature.
- It is recommended that the master account be submitted in full no more than five days after the event. Prepayment of a portion of the master account is encouraged.

The emphasis of this checklist is *communication*. Every aspect of billing must be clearly and concisely communicated to the accounting department and the meeting planner.

Postconvention Review

It is wise to review a job when it is completed. Much can be learned. Such a review should be done with an eye toward constructive improvement. The purpose of a review is to evaluate performance during the event and the forecasting and planning that preceded the convention. The goal is to improve technique so that the next event will go even smoother.

A convention service manager we interviewed about postconvention meetings said:

> A good, thorough pre-convention meeting can lead to a very short and satisfying postconvention wrap-up.

We recommend two review sessions. The first, an intra-staff meeting, should involve the hotel staff only. The second, termed a **postconvention meeting (post-con)** should be attended by both the hotel staff and the meeting planning staff.

The hotel meeting should include the hotel sales manager, convention service manager, and all departments involved in servicing the group. The purposes of this meeting are to review the meeting's rough spots, to discuss how the event could have been expedited, and to recognize any efforts that went well as examples for the future. Often in such a meeting an internal report, called a **performance report**, is prepared. Kirby Smith, vice president of sales skills training for Marriott, says his company takes post-meeting performance reports seriously:

Postconvention Reporting

Mike Gamble
Sr. Vice President, Sales and Marketing
Philadelphia Convention & Visitors Bureau

"Postconvention reporting has become one of the over-looked, underrated, and irritating duties that convention professionals face every day. Cities and hotels are still faced with inaccurate reporting of history and typically do not have the adequate information available to make a good business decision on whether or not to book a group or convention. With the fast pace of the hospitality industry, it is easy to move on to the next meeting or convention and forget about the one that has just finished. A thorough postconvention report will give a much better picture of the overall value of the meeting that most times is not conveyed. During the qualifying and pre-sales activities, the hotels and convention bureaus often ask for an extraordinary amount of information about the group's history, buying habits, and ancillary spending. The irony is that typically hotels and cities are unable to provide the same amount of information back to the planner once the meeting is completed."

> We use one form that's designed to hold people accountable in every facet of a hotel's operation, channeling to them with our bonus system. The form is broken down into the sales process—pre-event, event, and post-event phases—and addresses transitions from sales to service.[8]

The second meeting should involve both the meeting planner and his or her staff and the hotel staff. If the convention is city-wide, the convention bureau, exposition service contractor, destination management company, and audiovisual supplier may be invited. This meeting is also held to go over the many things that happened at the convention while they are fresh in everyone's mind. A good time to hold this meeting is when the master account gets its final review and approval. Everyone is in the hotel and relaxed after the great effort.

Don't duck discussions about the rough spots. Talk them out and try to agree on how they can be handled in the future. Both teams learn much from these inter-staff meetings.

This is also a time to begin the pitch for more business. Many hotel staff people are reluctant to start selling at this time, but if all went well, it may very well be the best time to make the pitch. If not for the convention itself, for other types of meetings. Corporations hold meetings all the time, and you should make your bid for more of their business.

Every aspect of the meeting should be reviewed and discussed candidly. Association executives should feel free to express their views on the staff's service and performance. Meeting planners appreciate having the opportunity to share their comments. If they sense the hotel is honestly concerned about improvement, they will more readily book future business.

Comparison with Projections

Compare what happened with what was expected to happen. Prepare a **pick-up report**, comparing the number of guestrooms originally blocked out with the number actually used.

Review the flow into and out of the hotel. Were there early check-outs or late departures? Did you have adequate help on hand to receive the guests? Were no-shows a problem? Did you overbook? If so, how did you handle it? Compare attendance with that of other years.

Early departures wreak havoc with hotel income. Yet they generally reflect at least as much on the convention programing as on the hotel attractions. If early departures were greater than in previous years, the program could be at fault; but the hotel still might give some thought to what it can do to make its facilities or area more inviting.

If this convention continually has a problem with early departures, the executive should make some effort to get members to estimate their stays more accurately and honestly. Most convention executives realize that healthy hotels are their concern, too.

Late departures create a different problem when they interfere with other group commitments that are beginning. There is enough evidence of intentional overbooking by hotels that late departures add fuel to the fire. Late departures are a problem, of course, only when the house is overfilled. Otherwise, it's a pleasant bonus.

The entire projection of arrival and departure patterns should be reviewed. The mix of rooms used—single, doubles, twins, and suites—should be compared with what was blocked out in order to polish the technique for the next time. Compare the pattern with the work schedule of your front desk people and other personnel needed for heavy arrival traffic.

Function Attendance

Both the hotel staff and the convention executive are most interested in how actual attendance at special functions compared with expectations. Guarantees at food functions don't tell the whole story. If actual attendance fell below the guarantee, the convention executive still has to pay for the full number guaranteed or try to persuade the hotel to accept payment for only those served. On the other hand, if more than an extra five percent showed up, the hotel is hard-pressed to seat and serve them. The convention organization is chagrined not to serve its members; the hotel is undeservedly shown in a bad light.

Review function room allocations. It is difficult to conduct a meeting in a room only 30-percent filled. A smaller room would have helped, if one were available. If not, dividers and screens could have helped. Perhaps the larger room could have been used for something else.

Special Services

Feedback on the hotel's services also is of interest. Each convention is different, but the hotel can learn from each one about room service, the restaurants, the play at the athletic facilities, the elevator service, and so on. Keep an eye on these services, because hotel reputations depend on them. It is an interesting phenomenon that the people who shape the image in the hotel business are the ones who get the least pay. The telephone operator and the front desk people probably have more contact with hotel guests than anyone else on the staff. If they have been congenial throughout the convention, the customer probably will carry away a good image of the hotel.

Individual Comments

A very different picture may emerge if you take the trouble to invite comments from your own staff, too. Staff members have a different vantage point than the convention service manager. Ask the bell staff, housekeepers, and front desk people how they think the convention went.

Stand near the cashier at check-out time to hear candid comments from guests. Some hotels make post-event mailings to guests. The benefits are twofold: the hotel projects a sincere desire to render good service, and it is often able to detect unspotted problem areas.

The Grand Sierra Resort, for example, uses a service evaluation form (see Exhibit 6) to quiz the respondent on all service aspects of the meeting. An analysis of the results has proven to be very advantageous when it comes to booking repeat business.

Exhibit 6   Service Evaluation Questionnaire

GRAND SIERRA
RESORT AND CASINO · RENO

Name:
Group:
Dates:

M & C Manager:
Catering Manager:

Performance Survey

PLEASE RATE YOUR SATISFACTION WITH OUR PERFORMANCE:

MEETINGS & CONVENTIONS   1: NOT SATISFIED - 5: EXTREMELY SATISFIED

1.	The review and confirmation of your meeting arrangements?	N/A	1	2	3	4	5
2.	Requests were responded to in a timely manner?	N/A	1	2	3	4	5
3.	The Service Manager Team's visibility and accessibility during your meeting?	N/A	1	2	3	4	5
4.	The meeting rooms were set-up on time and according to your specifications?	N/A	1	2	3	4	5

CATERING & BANQUETS

1.	The review & confirmation of your Banquet Event Orders (BEO's)?	N/A	1	2	3	4	5
2.	Requests were responded to in a timely manner?	N/A	1	2	3	4	5
3.	The Catering Team's visibility and accessibility during your meeting?	N/A	1	2	3	4	5
4.	The banquet rooms were setup on time and according to your specifications?	N/A	1	2	3	4	5
5.	The quality of banquet food & beverage selections?	N/A	1	2	3	4	5
6.	The banquet service level during meals?	N/A	1	2	3	4	5

AUDIO VISUAL PRODUCTIONS PLUS!

1.	The AV equipment set-up according to your specifications?	N/A	1	2	3	4	5
2.	The AV equipment working properly?	N/A	1	2	3	4	5

PRIORITY NETWORKS HIGH SPEED INTERNET SERVICE

1.	Quality of service & equipment provided by Priority Networks?	N/A	1	2	3	4	5

OVERALL EXPERIENCE AND SUGGESTIONS

What did we do well?

Where can we improve?

Were there members of our staff that went above and beyond your expectations?

Prepared by:

NAME: _____
              Please print

DATE: _____

Forms such as this one, used by the Grand Sierra in Reno, Nevada, ask delegates to give their rating of the hotel's performance during a meeting or convention. Used with permission.

Hyatt Hotels recently employed third-party telemarketing assistance to receive feedback from planners about service delivery. Fred Shea, vice president of sales operations, says:

> Nobody can tell you what to do better than your customers. Hyatt commissioned the Gallup polling organization to survey meeting planners by telephone. With results of the canvassing, the company is making changes in its culture that are tied to service accountability.[9]

Whatever your approach, some effort should be made to determine the staff's and guests' feelings about how the event went and how the hotel fared.

Postconvention Reporting

Postconvention reports have become one of the most discussed topics in today's meetings market, as accurate and thorough reports are important to both planners and hoteliers. Meeting planners know that information is power, and when it comes to negotiating, a thorough meetings history provides leverage in ensuring better rates. Catherine Roper, director of meetings for the Health Industry Distributors Association, says:

> As a planner, I need help from the hotel in knowing the value of my business. This is so I have a history to bring to negotiations. For instance, my people are in the gift shops, the restaurants, playing golf and tennis, and using the spa. I want to know the total picture of my meeting's value.[10]

Another meeting planner says:

> Writing a clear and compelling postconvention report is as important as the flawless execution of the event itself. A postconvention report is a summary of our meeting experiences that creates history, and showcases our talents and professionalism. Postconvention reports assist us in managing and controlling event management systems, and they summarize information and facts (not emotions), persuade change, and move others into action.[11]

Hotels, likewise, recognize that postconvention reports allow them to more accurately evaluate and qualify business. The Hilton chain, for example, offers a guaranteed Post-Event Report (PER) that will be delivered electronically within 14 days after the end of the event (see Exhibit 7). Convention bureaus need accurate histories when trying to establish room blocks for citywide conventions, and hotels need them to determine their level of participation.

Accurate postconvention reports also lead to better service. For example, the convention service manager can staff to handle peak arrivals based on past experience.

To ensure they receive postconvention reports, some planners are stipulating in the contract that they won't pay until they get an accurate report. Planners are also asking hotels to provide postconvention information on **auxiliary business**—affiliates and subgroups as well as exhibitors. Planners recognize that the auxiliary revenue to hotels from associations with exhibits can be huge. Not only do exhibitors utilize guestrooms, but many also hold events ranging from meals to hospitality suites to meetings.

Exhibit 7   Hilton's Post-Event Report Commitment

One of the most important tools that the Hilton chain offers to meeting planners is the Post-Event Report (PER), which is guaranteed to be delivered electronically within 14 days after the end of an event. The chain also promises to provide the group's master account billing five days after the event's conclusion.
Source: Courtesy of Hilton Hospitality, Inc.

Responding to the need for postconvention reports, most major hotel chains now have a company-wide standardized system for postconvention reporting. Hyatt, Hilton, and Marriott automatically provide postconvention reports for all groups using 100 rooms or more on peak nights.

Industry-Wide Post-Event Report

Since compiling accurate meeting histories is essential in evaluating business, standardized information is becoming increasingly necessary. To ensure that complete, standardized data could be collected for analysis, APEX (the Accepted Practices Exchange), an initiation of the Convention Industry Council, developed a template that could be readily used for this important function.

After extensive research, the History/Post-Event Reports Panel of APEX spent a year compiling a History/Post-Event Report (PER), that meets an established set of guidelines, including:

- The necessity of a Post Event Report (PER) citing details and activities of an event—its history
- A face-to-face meeting between the primary event organizer and each venue or facility involved in an event that should occur immediately following the end of the event, to focus on completion of the PER
- Once the PER is complete, the organizer should file report copies with each venue or facility used for the event (i.e., CVB, hotel, conference center, etc.)
- The most recent PER for an event should accompany any request for proposals sent to solicit proposals for future occurrences of same
- The APEX PER should be completed for events of all sizes, especially those of 25 peak room nights or more

Approved as an "Accepted Practice" by the CIC, the 14-page template, which is available on line at www.conventionindustry.org/APEX/acceptedpractices/posteventreporting.htm and is also available on computer disks and in a paper version, includes instructions for use; forms for entering information on group event(s), contacts, hotel rooms, room blocks, food and beverage, function space, exhibit space, and future event dates; a section on report distribution; and tracking and Post-Event Report FAQs.

The report has proven invaluable to both hotels and meeting planners. Dave Scypinski, senior vice president of industry relations for Starwood Hotels and Resorts, says:

> All the information we want to report on is contained in the APEX post-event report. If this is to become our industry standard, we said let's get a jump on it for internal purposes.

One meeting planner who praises the PER is Barbara Zamora, program director for the Association of Hispanic Advertising Agencies. She says:

> It is very thorough; there is no room for error. The PER can be customized for small or large groups; I use it for both my larger meetings, and even for board meetings. Suppliers and planners can communicate much more effectively.

Sources: The APEX Post-Event Report Template, Convention Industry Council; Christie Hicks and Christine Shimisaki, CMP, "APEX in Action: Bridging the Gap," *PCMA Convene.*

When the event concludes, the hotel's convention service manager and the meeting planner should schedule a time for convention analysis and review. We recommend an on-site review of the master account prior to departure, while the meeting is still fresh in the minds of both parties.
Source: Photo courtesy of InterContinental Hotels Group.

Many in the meetings industry would like to see an industry-wide, single database of postconvention information. One possibility proposed by industry groups is to have post-convention information submitted by hotels to their convention bureaus.

It is important to note that databases and other exchanges of information regarding a group's history should never include dollar amounts. It is a violation of antitrust law to exchange pricing information, such as room rates or banquet charges. Exchanging the number of rooms blocked, rooms picked up, number and size of food functions, and describing room service and restaurant volume as light, moderate, or heavy is an acceptable practice.

Since it is so important to get accurate meeting statistics, there has been a growing consensus within the industry that standardized forms would facilitate the process. In response, the Convention Industry Council (CIC), which has been active in trying to standardize many areas of the hospitality industry, developed a post-event report template. This fourteen-page template is not only available on paper, but on computer disks and online as well, making it easy to enter data and get an almost immediate picture of the convention success (the online version can be viewed at www.conventionindustry.org/APEX/acceptedpractices/posteventreporting.htm). The box titled "Industry-Wide Post-Event Report" further explains the Post-Event Report (PER) and its importance to meeting planners and hotels alike.

Final Appraisal

Before breaking down the working file and returning appropriate correspondence to the account file, ask if you could do a better job if the clock could be turned back to give you another chance. That question should be considered with complete frankness in the cold light of postconvention experience. If the answer discloses areas of difficulty, you should take steps to eliminate the problems in the future. The problems could deal with personnel or facilities. Solving them could help the sales manager set priorities on the kind of business you want and can handle. If the answers please you, don't forget to send a thank-you letter to the meeting planner, and to put that name in your follow-up file for some time in the very near future.

Summary

As we have seen throughout this chapter, selling to and servicing the conventions and meetings market requires careful planning and attention to details. The convention billing process and postconvention follow-up are important factors in building a group's goodwill and generating future business. A property must clearly spell out billing procedures and make it easy and convenient for the meeting planner to keep abreast of meeting charges. And, after the convention or meeting, follow-up is necessary to determine areas of strengths and weaknesses and to build a group history that can be used in the future to negotiate additional events.

Endnotes

1. Deirdre Bourke, "Bill Review Made Easy," Experient special to PCMA.
2. Don Nichols, "High-Tech Comes to Hotels," *Association Meetings*.
3. Roger Sonnabend, "The Hotelier Looks at the Business of Meetings," *3M Business Press*.
4. *Meeting News*, March 5, 2007.
5. Julie Barker, "The Ultimate Guide to Tipping and Gratuities," *Successful Meetings*.
6. "A Good Contract," *TRNews*, July 2005, p. 26.
7. Nicole Brudos Ferrara, "Stop Those Surcharges!" *Meetingsnet.com*, June 2005, p. 36.
8. Ruth Hill, "Planner's Lament," *Lodging*.
9. Ibid.
10. Ruth Hill, "Confronting the Bull in Today's Market," *HSMAI Marketing Review*,
11. Michele Wierzgae, "Writing a Post-Con Report," *Meetings South*, January 2006, p. 6.

 ## Key Terms

American plan—Charge includes room, food and beverage, and gratuities. Includes three meals per day.

authorized signature—Signature of person(s) with the authority to charge to a group master account.

auxiliary business—Affiliates and subgroups, such as exhibitors, who contribute to the overall value of the meeting. Often, this type of business that is brought to a facility because of an event is called "in conjunction with" business.

billing instructions—Notice as to how charges for an event should be handled and to whom invoices should be addressed.

blanket service charges—Service charges added into the room charge so that attendees do not have to tip during their stay. Primarily used with the American Plan (AP) system.

European plan—Guestrooms, food and beverage, and tips are priced separately.

gratuity—A voluntary payment added to a bill to signify good service. Also called a tip.

guest credit—Credit extended to a guest based on information collected by the hotel's credit department. This is a courtesy of the hotel, not an obligation.

incidental charges—Expenses (telephone, room service, and so on) other than guestroom charges and taxes billed to a guest's folio.

individual guest folio—An account on which all individual guest charges not covered by the master account will be posted for payment by the individual guest.

master account—The group's primary record of transactions to be paid for by the event's sponsoring organization. Charges may include guestrooms, taxes, food and beverage, audiovisual equipment, decorations, incidentals, and so on. Since delegates may be responsible for some charges at some events, all items to be charged to this account should be agreed-upon in advance. Also called a master account folio or a master bill.

master account billing authorization form—A form that provides instructions on the types of folios to be established, limits of financial responsibility, and the names and signatures of personnel authorized to sign for group charges.

paid-out slips—In-house forms that allow cash withdrawals to be charged to the event's master account for employee tips. Using paid-out slips eliminates the need for the event organizer to have to carry large amounts of cash for tips distribution.

performance report—An internal report used by hotels to evaluate a convention. The hotel can use this research to determine how the convention facilities matched the client's needs.

pick-up report—A post-meeting document detailing the number of hotel rooms used each day of an event. This report includes the total number of guestrooms originally blocked for each night and how many were actually used.

postconvention meeting (post-con)—A meeting at the primary facility at which an event occurred just after the event has ended. Attendees usually include the primary event organizer, representatives of the host organization, department heads of the facility, other facility staff as required, and event contractors. Its purpose is to evaluate the implementation of the event and to complete the postconvention report. A final review of the master account with a representative from the hotel's accounts payable department is usually part of the post-con meeting.

postconvention report—A report of the details and activities of an event. A collection of post-convention reports over time provides a complete history for an event. Also called a post-event report.

rates and charges bulletin—Communicates specific rates for rooms, meals, gratuities, and billing procedures agreed upon by the various parties involved.

resort fees—Charges automatically added by a hotel for services ranging from in-room amenities to local telephone services to resort facilities, such as business centers, fitness centers, and tennis courts.

resume—A form that provides a comprehensive overview of an entire event, from preconvention to postconvention, for the hotel staff. These sheets detail activities from day to day (and hour by hour), and cover complete details of functions, reservations procedures, billing, recreational activities, and anything else that may require the attention of the hotel's staff. Also called a specification sheet.

service charge—An automatic and mandatory amount added to standard food and beverage charges or other hotel services.

split folio—Convention charges are paid partially by the sponsoring organization and partially by the guest. Communication is needed to ensure that all parties involved understand who is responsible for specific charges.

surcharge—A mandatory charge added to guestrooms for such items as energy, Internet access, and telephone usage; and to meeting rooms for products and services (electricity, additional charges for service personnel, and so on).

 Review Questions

1. Discuss the statement: "As with most aspects of convention planning, the time to avoid billing problems is in the beginning and not at the end." What procedures are recommended for avoiding billing problems?

2. What are the three different folios that can be used for a meeting or convention? Who pays the charges for each?

3. What factors should be considered when determining a time of payment for a meeting group? When are charges typically billed?

4. List the four groupings for service gratuities and distinguish between blanket service charges and special tipping.

5. Outline the HSMAI's suggested payment schedule.

6. Why is a postconvention review important? Who should attend post-convention review meetings?

7. What should be included in the postconvention report? What are the benefits of post-convention reports? Design a sample report that would help your hotel to gauge the success of a convention.

 Additional References

The Convention Industry Council Manual, Eighth Edition.
www.conventionindustry.org

Professional Meeting Management, Flfth Edition, Kendall Hunt Publishing, 2006.

 Internet Sites

For more information, visit the following Internet sites. Internet addresses can change without notice. If a site is no longer available at the address listed below, a search engine can be used to find the new address or additional, related sites.

Caesars Palace
www.caesars.com

Convention Industry Council
www.conventionindustry.org

Convention Industry Council Accepted
 Practices: Post-Event Reporting
www.conventionindustry.org/apex/
acceptedpractices/posteventreporting.htm.

Delphi-Newmarket Software
www.newsoft.com

Event Web
www.eventweb.com

Experient
www.experient-inc.com

Hospitality Sales and Marketing
 Association International (HSMAI)
www.hsmai.org

Financial & Insurance Conference Planners
www.ficpnet.com

The Original Tipping Page
www.tipping.org

Philadelphia Convention and Visitors
 Bureau
www.libertynet.org/phila-visitor

Appendix

Convention Management and Service Case Studies

The following cases have been developed through the involvement of industry leaders. The issues and problems presented in these cases illustrate the types of situations you can expect to encounter when working in convention sales and services. The discussion questions at the end of each case direct your attention to important issues, but you needn't limit your analysis to finding the answers to these questions. Examining the cases from different perspectives can help you get more out of each case.

Here are some guidelines that might be helpful in analyzing the cases:

- Read each case study carefully, noting important information and facts.

- Construct a time line of events leading to the situation being considered.

- Identify all of the significant characters in the case.

- Identify the problem presented by the case and define it. Is there more than one problem?

- Analyze the problem. What are its causes? Whom does it affect?

- List important factors in the case that affect your analysis (for example: type of property, location of property, time of year).

- List items you think should be addressed in developing a solution to the problem.

- Identify a solution (or solutions) to the problem. Remember that often times the first solution that comes to mind is not the best.

- Evaluate your solution. If your solution was implemented, would it solve the problem? What would be the possible consequences? Might it cause new problems?

- Look at the case again, taking the perspective of a different character in the case. Explore the problem and your solution(s) from that character's perspective.

Studying these cases will help you learn important lessons and develop critical thinking skills that will be valuable to you in your hospitality career.

SUMMARY OF CASE STUDIES

Chapter 2—**Leadership at the Hamilton: Impasse Between the General Manager and Director of Sales**

The general manager of a 500-room first-class downtown hotels calls in a marketing consultant to shake up the sales staff. Year-to-date occupancy is down 4 percent with a year-end projected shortfall of $700,000 in revenue, but marketing expenses are already $55,000 over budget. The consultant's recommendations must temper the unrealistic expectations of the GM and refocus the efforts of the director of sales.

Chapter 3—**Departmental Conflict at The Ultra Hotel**

This case pits marketing and sales against the rooms division in a battle over a sensitive hotel issue: how many rooms can marketing and sales have for group sales? To land an important piece of group business, the marketing and sales director wants more rooms than are usually allocated to group sales; the rooms director thinks the group's business is not worth inconveniencing the hotel's regular transient guests.

Chapter 5—**Overcoming Rate Resistance—Among the Sales Staff**

The 263-room Park View Hotel has too much contracted business at a low rate. The director of sales works with the sales staff to replace a third of this business—about 5,000 room nights—with higher-rated transient and group business. They look at what business to keep, new sources of business to replace the contract business, and scripts for the sales staff to use with current clients of the preferred group rate.

Chapter 6—**Reviving Revenue Management**

After surviving the opening of a competing hotel, the GM and sales staff at the Hearthstone Suites Hotel are challenged to revive the property's revenue management program. While occupancy is at budget year-to-date, average daily rate (ADR) is down by $6.00. Also, the mix of commercial business is lower than planned (40 percent of guest mix instead of 50 percent) and the SMERF segment is higher than it should be (15 percent of guest mix instead of 5 percent).

Chapter 7—**Don't Just Tell It—Sell It! or Needs Satisfaction Selling: Booking Business by Turning Features into Benefits**

In this case, veteran salesperson Sandra Savvy shares techniques for combining courtesy and customers' needs satisfaction to build business, a common sense approach often overlooked in sales. New salesperson Drew Newbie also gets some tips from Sandra on how to turn property features into benefits.

Chapter 9—**No Vacancy**

The negotiation process is one of the most challenging aspects of hospitality sales—particularly if both sides at the negotiation table are to be satisfied. In this case, the sales manager of the Monte Sereno Hotel negotiates with Jon Stonewall, the unyielding manager of a national computer software company, who wants to hold a regional meeting at the hotel. The challenge is to arrive at a win-win situation for the hotel and the client.

Chapter 11—**Sales Underperforms Even While Meeting Budget**

The new general manager at a 180-room economy/business property in a booming suburb of a major city is challenged by the regional director of operations to increase the hotel's market penetration rate. The case focuses on increasing the volume of group business as well as raising the ADR for groups.

Chapter 14—**Distributing Sales Functions Between a Hotel's Sales and Catering Departments**

Year-end projections for a 400-room first-class suburban hotel show banquet food sales will be off by $60,000 to budget and audiovisual revenues and room rental revenues will miss budget by $30,000. The director of catering learns to rely less on the hotel sales department and takes ownership of the problems.

Case Study: Chapter 2

Leadership at the Hamilton: Impasse Between the General Manager and Director of Sales

It was hard for Susan Fontenot to keep her mind on her driving as she made her way through the city's early morning rush-hour traffic. She was on her way to a potentially difficult meeting with Thad Johnson, the director of sales for The Hamilton, a 500-room first-class hotel right in the heart of downtown. Susan was a marketing consultant that the general manager of The Hamilton, Rick Martin, had called last week, all in a dither. "I can't believe it," Rick had said. "I just got this month's profit and loss statement, and occupancy year-to-date is down four percent, while marketing expenses are over budget by $55,000. How can that happen? Months ago I raised the sales-call quotas for our salespeople, started sending them to every trade show in sight, and re-did all of our collateral materials so they are really first class. And still we get these numbers! I don't know what else to do to help Thad—my background is in F&B, not sales. Will you come in and help us with a plan to turn things around?"

Susan knew from experience that there were two sides to every sales-are-down story, and this was no exception. When she arrived in Thad's office and sat down across the desk from him, it didn't take him long to get to the point. "Rick doesn't know what he's doing," he said bluntly. "Three months ago, when the occupancy numbers first began to go down, he started bugging me about sales calls. I told him to be patient, things would turn around. But they didn't turn around fast enough for him, and a month ago he raised our sales-call quotas. The only thing raising our call quotas did was raise everybody's stress levels in the department."

"Yes, Rick mentioned raising the quotas," Susan said, taking a yellow pad and pen from her briefcase. "Just how high did he raise them?"

"He wanted each of us to make 50 in-person client calls a week! Two breakfast site inspections, two lunch site inspections, two dinner site inspections, and four other on-site visits in between, every day. He just pulled those numbers out of the air. It's ridiculous."

"How many calls were your salespeople supposed to make before?"

Thad frowned. "I don't believe in quotas," he said. "I came up through the ranks, and I know how much I resented the director of sales I used to work for. She insisted on a certain number of calls every week, with all sorts of end-of-week and end-of-month sales call reports to fill out, and I told myself I wasn't going to operate that way. I trust my people and I don't look over their shoulders all the time. Besides, they're always busy. Because we're a first-class hotel, I emphasize personal service. I make sure the salespeople baby-sit their groups when they're in the hotel. 'Make sure the client sees you all the time and knows you care'—that's my motto. If the client has a problem, the salesperson is right there to take care of it personally."

Susan smiled. "It must make it hard for your salespeople to find time to make outside calls."

"Well, as a matter of fact, it was pretty rare for us to make an outside call before Rick handed down his quotas," Thad replied. "I never had quotas before; our hotel sells itself. Everybody know what we stand for and what we offer. If someone wants to go first-class in this city, this is the place to stay."

"How close are your salespeople coming to actually making 50 calls a week?"

"To be honest, I don't know," Thad said. "I just told them to do the best they could. Like I said, I don't believe in quotas and paperwork and I'm hoping Rick won't push it."

Susan made some notes on her yellow pad.

"Besides," Thad went on, "we're too busy going to trade shows! That's another thing Rick insisted on. Just between you and me, I think it's because he enjoyed going to the National Restaurant Association show in Chicago every year back when he was a food and beverage director. Now we're constantly packing and unpacking our trade show booth and making travel arrangements to travel hither and yon. Most of the time these trade shows don't generate any business. People just pick our booth clean of brochures—that's another thing!" Thad grabbed a brochure sitting on his desk. "Look at this thing! Ten pages, full color! Back at the beginning of the year Rick insisted that all of our collateral materials be in color, so he scrapped everything except for this brochure and a 30-page banquet menu collateral piece we send out to prospective banquet clients. That used to be a two-color piece, but now it's full color too. He said a first-class hotel should have first-class collateral. That sounds nice, but I don't have to tell you how expensive full-color stuff is."

"Full-color costs money, no question about it," Susan agreed.

"And while we're on the subject of expenses, how fair is it that every manager in the hotel signs for meals and drinks and it gets charged to my department as 'advertising and promotion'? If they are legitimately with a client, that's one thing. But they eat at the hotel because they don't want to eat in the employee break room, or it's raining outside, or they're short on cash this month—they even treat their spouses to dinner, and they sign the bills like it's a management perk or something. And it all gets charged to marketing. If Rick is so concerned about marketing expenses, why doesn't he do something about that? I've complained and complained about it."

"I've seen that privilege get abused at other hotels, too," Susan nodded. "How do you keep track of other department expenses, like office supplies, sales trip expenses, and so on?"

"Oh, I just wait for the profit and loss statement to come out at the end of the month and see where we are. If we're over one month, I try to cut back the next."

Susan made a note, then tapped her pen on her chin. "Let's backtrack for a moment. I'd like to know more about your staff—Rick didn't go into details with me. How many people do you have and what's their experience level?"

"I'm lucky—when I came on board two years ago, I inherited a staff of four veteran salespeople. Two had been with the hotel for five years, the other two had just come on board but had worked for other hotels for a number of years." Thad smiled. "I didn't have to do any training or coaching, I was able to just do my job and let them do theirs."

Susan smiled. "Sounds like you're pretty confident in their abilities. Have you ever gone out on a call with them?"

"No, why should I?"

"Well, because you're so confident in them, I was wondering if you had actually seem them in action, selling to a client."

"No. Up until this year, we've always made our number, and like I said earlier, we didn't make many outside sales calls anyway. People know our hotel's reputation. Most of our clients call us."

"So you don't provide your salespeople with sales targets to meet or action plans to follow?"

"Not really. Like I said, they're busy fielding all the incoming calls and taking care of clients. They're good people and they know what they're doing."

"I see." Susan made some more notes on her pad. "Well, as you know, Rick has asked me to make some recommendations to help the hotel raise its occupancy numbers. Four percent doesn't sound like much, but I'm sure you are as aware as anyone that, with your hotel's average daily rate and budgeted occupancy levels, a four-percent shortfall comes out to about $700,000 below budget for the year. I have some preliminary notions about what might be helpful, but do you have any ideas for turning things around?"

Thad leaned back in his chair and thought for a moment. "To tell you the truth, I think Rick overreacted to the situation," he said finally. "Of course I'm willing to take a look at any ideas you come up with, but I think the numbers would eventually have come up on their own if we had just stayed our course. To my mind, personal service is the key to this market. A continued emphasis on really serving our clients once they get to the property will keep them coming back, and word-of-mouth from happy clients will keep our phones ringing." Thad paused. "I think Rick's directives are doing more harm than good, so my suggestion would be to call off the call quotas and cut way back on the trade shows."

Susan nodded and returned her pad and pen to her briefcase. "You have a point about the trade shows," she said. "Rick wants to bring marketing costs down and increase occupancy. I think I'm going to concentrate on three marketing expense areas: the trade show issue, the hotel's collateral materials, and the advertising and promotion expense account. On the occupancy side, I'm going to look at ways to determine whether your salespeople have the sales skills they need to meet the booking objectives, and I'm probably going to recommend that you give your salespeople more direction as to where you want them to focus their efforts."

Susan rose and shook hands with Thad. "I know it can be difficult to have an outsider come in to look at what you're doing, but my job really is to just try to be helpful and look for ways to make sales targets easier to make. I'm going to schedule a meeting with both you and Rick sometime next week, and I hope you'll be happy with the recommendations I come up with for you."

Discussion Questions

1. What are some recommendations Susan can make for decreasing the hotel's marketing expenses?

2. What are some recommendations Susan can make to Thad to help him evaluate his staff's sales skills?

3. What are some recommendations Susan can make to Thad to help him give his staff more direction to ensure that their efforts are focused and targeted?

Case Number: 370CI
This case was developed in cooperation with Lisa Richards of Hospitality Softnet, Inc., a marketing resources and support company.

This case also appears in *Contemporary Hospitality Marketing: A Service Management Approach* (Lansing, Mich.: Educational Institute of the American Hotel & Lodging Association), ISBN 0-86612-158-7.

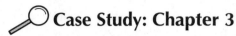 Case Study: Chapter 3

Departmental Conflict at the Ultra Hotel

A quick glance out the lobby window revealed wind-blown gray clouds bunching up over the city. "Storm's brewing out there," thought Rick Roland, the Ultra Hotel's marketing and sales director. In here, too, he thought as he walked past the lounges and restaurants on the ground floor of the 500-room, three-star convention property.

Unconsciously, Rick's pace slowed as he got closer to the meeting room where the end-of-the-month executive committee meeting was due to start. How ironic, he thought, to feel so apprehensive even though I'm almost ready to close on one of the biggest pieces of business I've landed in quite some time.

Taking a deep breath, Rick paused before entering the room. Images of the people waiting inside flashed through his mind: Fred Franklin, the general manager, a tough but fair boss who liked to give his staff members a chance to present their side of an argument; Norma Lopez, the no-nonsense controller with the laser-like focus on the bottom line; Claude van Fleet, the temperamental food and beverage director piloting a department through a terrible month; Camille Petrocelli, self-described "people person" and human resources director; and last, Jeanelle Causwell, rooms director, a fast-track performer, a favorite of Mr. Franklin's, and possibly my mortal enemy by the end of this meeting, Rick thought wryly.

Exhaling, Rick entered the meeting room. The meeting raced by for Rick until the moment he was waiting for. Mr. Franklin turned to him and said, "What have you got for us, Rick?"

"Well, gosh," Rick began, trying to inject some folksiness into a speech he had rehearsed a dozen times, "I'm about to land a nice piece of business for us. As all of you know, we've been after the ConveyorMatic meeting planner for months. The good news is, I think the guy's ready to commit in a big way. We're talking 250 rooms the second week of September, Sunday through Thursday, and—get this—it's a mandatory sales meeting for their big-spending sales staff, so filling up at least 240 of those 250 rooms is a cinch."

Seeing some nods and looks of interest, Rick went on. "Claude, you'll love this. We're getting three dinners, three lunches, three upgraded breakfasts, and two cocktail receptions with heavy hors d'oeuvres, which is big-time food and beverage sales—and that doesn't include spending in the outlets. It projects out to $130,000 in business for the hotel Last year, we had only about $80,000 the same week."

"Excuse me, Rick, but isn't it hotel policy that you're only allotted 200 rooms for group sales?" Jeanelle said, launching her first salvo.

"Good point, Jeanelle, but if I book this group this year, they could be repeat customers every year. Plus, this guy is active in Meeting Professionals International, so he could give us some great referrals."

"I love it. Let's book 'em," Claude interjected, looking relieved and grateful.

"I do have to book it today, by five o'clock. That's why I want to get us all together on this," Rick explained.

"Excuse me, again, Rick," Jeanelle said, "I'm sure you didn't make any promises to this group that would affect our room assignments, right?"

"Not really." Rick turned quickly to the controller. "What do you think, Norma?"

"I think we need to take a look at the numbers and make sure they're as good as you say," Norma said.

"Camille?" Rick continued eagerly.

"What?" Camille smiled, looking up from an issue of *HR Weekly*. "Oh, it sounds good; we could keep ten or fifteen people a day working for four days. Might slow down the turnover of our part-time kitchen staff."

"Rick, let's back up a minute." It was Jeanelle again, refusing to be sidetracked. "When I asked whether you'd made any promises to this group that would affect room assignments, you said 'Not really.' Could you define 'Not really' for me?"

"Well, I, uh," Rick looked down and mumbled rapidly, "I told them they could have fifty percent of their block in our new wing."

"What!" Jeanelle yelled, "You gave away my new wing! What do I tell my transient, repeat guests? My regulars stay three or four days, six times a year. You want me to tell them I'm kicking them out of the new wing? Why don't we just save time and tell them to go stay across the street from now on, because that's just what they'll do."

"But we're talking about 250 rooms!" Rick protested.

"At what rate?" Jeanelle shot back.

"Well, because of the F&B business, I gave them a discount—$79 a night."

"Wow! That's twenty percent off our regular $99 rate. Give those rooms back to me, Mr. Franklin. If we open up the corporate reservations center for discounts, I'll sell every one at $89. And I won't have to dump my best guests out of the new wing for these conveyor salesmen."

"Now, Jeanelle ..." Rick pleaded.

"Now, nothing!" she snapped.

"But Jeanelle, the F&B revenue!" Claude said, dreaming of making up last month's budget shortfall. "You know as well as I do that transient guests don't eat at the hotel. This group will mean big bucks in F&B."

"Mr. Franklin, you're the general manager; it's your call," Rick said resignedly. Jeanelle and Claude nodded in agreement. The staff leaned back, waiting for the GM's decision.

Discussion Questions

1. What reasons might the GM have for deciding to turn down the business? What conflicts on the executive committee would have to be resolved if the GM decides to turn down the business?

2. What reasons might the GM have for deciding to take the business? What conflicts on the executive committee would have to be resolved if the GM decides to take the business?

Case Number 370CA

This case was developed in cooperation with Bill Flor and Randy Kinder, authors of *No Vacancy: A Tried & True Guide to Get More Rooms Business!*

This case also appears in *Contemporary Hospitality Marketing: A Service Management Approach* (Lansing, Mich.: Educational Institute of the American Hotel & Lodging Association), ISBN 0-86612-158-7.

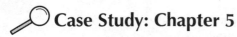

Case Study: Chapter 5

Overcoming Rate Resistance—Among the Sales Staff

Conversations stopped as Fran walked into the meeting room where the sales staff of the 263-room Park View Hotel had gathered. The director of sales surveyed the anxious faces that turned toward her as she approached.

"Lighten up, folks," Fran said reassuringly. "This is a strategy session, not a wake. I know you're all aware I had a meeting with the general manager last week, and he'd like us to make a few changes to our marketing plan. I'd like us to sit down together and brainstorm ways to solve some problems we identified in our meeting."

Fran passed around a handout as the salespeople took their seats. The objections started as soon as they began reading the agenda.

"Get rid of 5,000 room nights of our corporate contract business? That's crazy!" said Angela. "Most of my best accounts are corporate preferred. I worked hard to get those accounts and I'm not dropping them now."

"Where are we going to find the customers to replace these 5,000 room nights?" Michael asked. "You can't just expect that kind of new business to come strolling through the door right away."

Murmurs of agreement filled the room. "And how am I supposed to break it to my accounts that they're not going to get their preferred rate any more?" asked Tanisha. "I wouldn't know what to say, and I don't think I could sound real convincing."

Fran raised her hands. "Let's take this one step at a time. Here's the situation. The hotel has too much contracted business at a low rate. We need to replace about a third of this business—about 5,000 room nights—with higher rated transient and group business. I just want to evaluate which accounts we should keep, which ones might accept a higher—but still discounted—rate, and which ones don't make good business sense to keep."

Fran stood up next to a flip chart and uncapped a marker. "Let's set up some criteria for reviewing our contract accounts. What kinds of things should we look at? I'll start." She wrote, "Keep accounts with attractive arrival/departure patterns."

She continued to write as the staff began calling out ideas.

After a refreshment break, Fran called the group together again. "Great work, folks. Now, let's think about how we're going to replace that contract business with some new business that will bring in more revenue. I'd like to make a list of market segments and sources we could solicit more strongly. Then we can evaluate which areas we should concentrate our sales efforts on. Any ideas?" Fran worked the flip chart again.

That job done, Fran turned to the issue that Tanisha brought up earlier: how to tell clients about the change in the hotel's corporate preferred rate policy. Together, the staff decided they would be more comfortable and effective if they had scripts to work from.

Fran assigned two of the sales staff to write some scripts that everyone could use when talking with their accounts, whether they were increasing their rate or eliminating their preferred rate. As the meeting adjourned, Fran still heard grumbles from some of the salespeople. "My work's not done yet," she thought, and began planning her next steps for helping her staff accept these new rate changes.

Discussion Questions

1. What are some of the criteria the sales staff should use to evaluate whether a corporate contract account should be retained or dropped?

2. What factors should the staff consider when determining new sources of business to replace the displaced contract business?

3. What would the scripts look like that the sales staff could use when talking to clients about the rate change?

4. How can Fran help her staff become comfortable with the changes in the hotel's rate structure?

Case Number: 370CJ

This case was developed in cooperation with Lisa Richards of Hospitality Softnet, Inc., a marketing resources and support company.

This case also appears in *Contemporary Hospitality Marketing: A Service Management Approach* (Lansing, Mich.: Educational Institute of the American Hotel & Lodging Association), ISBN 0-86612-158-7.

⌕ Case Study: Chapter 6

Reviving Revenue Management

The Hearthstone Suites Hotel is an all-suite property with 250 rooms. A new property, the Fairmont Hotel, opened near Hearthstone Suites three months ago. Several months before the opening of the Fairmont, Laurie, the GM at the Hearthstone Suites, pushed all her front office and reservations staff to sell as many rooms as possible. As she put it, "Whatever it takes, to stay competitive." The director of sales, Pat, supported the plan from day one, but Jodie, the front office manager, had misgivings from the start. Jodie was concerned that the revenue management program that managers implemented a year and a half earlier would be totally useless because of the push for occupancy.

The most recent profit and loss statement indicates that Jodie's fears were realized. Though the occupancy is at a budget year-to-date, the average daily rate (ADR) is down by $6.00. Also, the mix of commercial business is lower than planned—40 percent of guest mix instead of 50 percent. Also, the SMERF segment is higher than it should be—15 percent of guest mix instead of 5 percent. SMERF is a catch-all term for group business at substantially lower rates—Social, Military, Educational, Religious, and Fraternal groups.

Jodie, Pat, and Laurie are in a meeting to discuss these latest figures.

Laurie, the general manager, opens the meeting by saying, "Well, we've weathered the storm caused by the opening of the Fairmont. We managed to hold on to our occupancy level. But it looks like we have some regrouping to do. I trust you've each received the profit and loss statement I sent you. I'm concerned about the fact that we've lost so much of our share of the commercial business. And, our ADR is much too low."

"I agree," says Jodie, "but I was just following orders when I had my staff focus on selling rooms. Our good occupancy rate has come at the cost of both yield management and revenue. It will take quite a while to regain our former position."

"We all sat down and agreed months before the Fairmont opened that we should do our best to keep our occupancy numbers, and that's what we've done," says Pat. "You and your staff have worked hard and are to be commended, Jodie."

"Hear, hear," says Laurie. "And now we have some time to re-evaluate our position and start targeting that corporate segment again."

"I just hope it's not too late to win it back from Fairmont," sighs Jodie.

Later that day, Jodie gathers her front desk and reservations team to brief them about re-implementing the revenue management program. "I know you've all been putting a lot of extra effort into filling rooms over the past several months. I'm proud of you; the whole management team is. We've met our occupancy goals. The down side is that our guest mix is off. We've lost some of our commercial segment and gained too much of the SMERF segment. And, our ADR is down a full $6. It's time we reviewed the revenue management program we use...."

"The revenue what?" blurts Jack, a fairly new front desk agent. "You never told us about that."

"Now hold on a minute," counters Jodie, "some of you are so new that you haven't been fully trained in this program, but I know I've talked about it to some extent with all of you."

"Sure, you told me a little about it," offers Tracey, a reservationist. "I never have been comfortable with it, to tell the truth. One day I quoted a guest $85 and he books a suite. A month later he calls back to book another and I quote $105. Then the guest asks why the rates went up—what am I supposed to say?"

"Well, there are things you can tell guests who ask that, but we're not going to get into that right now," says Jodie.

Bill, the most experienced front desk agent, speaks up. "I've been using the yield management program all along, just like you showed me." He turns to his co-workers. "It's really not unreasonable when you look at the big picture of the hotel's revenue. I just tell inquisitive callers that our rates depend on their arrival dates. Some periods are busier for us than others, and that affects rates."

"Bill, it's good to hear that you continued using the yield management program," Jodie says. "We can get into more detail on applying it in formal training. We've had a lot of changes since the push for volume began—changes in personnel and even changes in the yield management program itself. It's clearly time I evaluated training needs in our department in the area of yield management program execution. You can be confident, Tracey—and all of you—when you quote rates that they are competitive for what we offer. That reminds me," and here Jodie pauses a moment, "how many of you have actually been inside some of our suites?"

Three of the six employees raise their hands. "How many have seen rooms at the Fairmont or any of our other competitors?" continues Jodie. Only Bill raises his hand. "So almost none of you have seen the difference between our suites and the single rooms other properties are offering?"

"There hasn't been much time to look at what we're selling," protests Jack.

"… much less to look at what anyone else is selling," adds Linda, another reservationist.

"That's what I was afraid of," says Jodie. "In the next two weeks or so, as I'm re-evaluating training needs, I'm going to have each of you spend time gaining an appreciation of the value we offer—especially in comparison with the value of Fairmont's offerings and those of our other competition."

"Are we still going to be offering the $84 supersaver rate?" asks Tracey. "We've had a lot of repeat business because of that rate."

"I've had callers tell me we're the best deal in town," adds Linda.

But Bill cautions, "We won't need to use it next week. The Home Builders' convention is in and every room in town will be booked. We can afford to charge more next week."

"That's good thinking, Bill," says Jodie. "I know it's nice to be popular with guests and it's easy to use that discount whenever a potential guest shies away from a quoted rate; but the supersaver rate is intended to be used only as a last resort or in other special cases. We shouldn't be offering it too frequently. We also need to adjust our selling strategies when special events, like this convention, come along."

"Speaking of selling strategies, when are we going to get to go through that training module on selling skills you were talking about?" inquires Linda. "I've heard about it but I haven't gone through it yet."

Discussion Questions

1. How can the management team address the problem of low ADR?

2. What are some ways Jodie could make employees such as Jack and Tracey more familiar and comfortable with a yield management program?

3. What selling skills should training focus on for the Hearthstone Suites Hotel staff?

4. How can the Hearthstone Suites Hotel regain some of the commercial business it has lost?

Case Number: 370CF
This case was developed in cooperation with Lisa Richards of Hospitality Softnet, Inc., a marketing resources and support company.

This case also appears in *Contemporary Hospitality Marketing: A Service Management Approach* (Lansing, Mich.: Educational Institute of the American Hotel & Lodging Association), ISBN 0-86612-158-7.

Case Study: Chapter 7

Don't Just Tell It—Sell It! or Needs Satisfaction Selling: Booking Business by Turning Features into Benefits

Sales at the 112-room Goodsleep Inn have been down lately. The number of room nights sold has dropped and, due to turnover, the sales staff is inexperienced. Today, the hotshot sales director, Sandra Savvy, begins training Drew Newbie, one of the new salespeople.

At their first meeting in Sandra's office, Sandra explains, "Drew, to sell our hotel you have to understand what it is you're selling and how it appeals to your potential clients."

"That's easy—we're selling rooms," Drew said.

"That's true," Sandra replied. "But it's not that simple. To be a successful salesperson, you must be able to identify the hotel features that can benefit your potential clients and satisfy their *specific* needs."

"What do you mean?"

"How would you describe the Goodsleep Inn to someone who's never been here before?" Sandra asked.

"Well," Drew said, "it has 112 rooms and is three stories high, with external corridors. Is that the kind of information you mean?"

"That's a start. What else?"

"Hmm, let's see," Drew continued. "We have a swimming pool, and our rates are pretty reasonable. We have a great, free continental breakfast, too."

"Right," Sandra said. "What about the property's location?"

"I think I see what you're getting at," Drew said enthusiastically. "We have a coin-operated laundry for guests. We're in the suburbs near the business district. The area is safe. It's also close to the interstate. And even though we don't have any food and beverage outlets at our property, there are a lot of family restaurants and convenience stores within walking distance."

"Excellent! You're getting the hang of it," Sandra said. "Some other things you may want to mention a potential client are: recent updates to the hotel, like the $150,000 guest-room renovations we just did; the free movies we offer; and our non-smoking rooms. These may seem like little things, but to some guests they mean a lot. The key is to find out what your potential guests need, then match the property's features to your guests' needs and show them how the property can benefit them."

"So, it's not just telling someone you've got rooms available, is it?" Drew asked.

"No, that's called *tell* selling," Sandra said, shaking her head. "That's what the stereotypical salesperson does—you know, the pushy person trying to sell you a used car you don't want. To really be successful in sales, you have to look for a win-win situation with clients. Find out what they really want, then describe the features of the hotel that match what they want. Keep in mind, though, that it's not just selling them a line. You don't make up stuff about the hotel that isn't true. You merely make the effort to match what you've got to what they want and describe what you have in terms of how it benefits the client. That's the way you can build long-term relationships with clients, which will increase the number of room nights sold in the long run."

Drew thought for a minute. "It sounds like common sense."

"It is. You'd be amazed at how successful you can be by simply listening to what your prospects need, describing how your hotel can meet those needs, and using a little common courtesy," Sandra said.

"Common courtesy," Drew said. "I've got that. I always say please and thank you."

"It's more than that," Sandra said. "There are simple things you can do that will really impress your potential clients and win you business for life. For example, greet potential clients at the front door, or even meet them in the parking lot and walk them to the front door; don't make them ask for you at the front desk. During the hotel tour, introduce them to the property manager and hotel employees. You'd be amazed at how little details like these can set the right tone."

"So, how do you find out what the potential clients' needs are?" Drew asked.

"That's simple—ask them! Also, take the time to get to know your markets. I do a little research before I meet with a potential client so I have some ideas about what he or she might want. Not only does it help me prepare, but it shows that I care about meeting the person's needs, not just making a sale. Then, when you give property tours, simply ask potential clients what's important to them in a hotel and give it right back to them by describing the hotel features and benefits that fit those needs."

"I guess I have my work cut out for me," Drew responded.

"Yes, Drew, but you're up for the job." Sandra picked up her planner and flipped it open. "I've got an idea. I'm giving three property tours next week. Let me tell you what I've found out about each potential client and you tell me how you would sell the property to each."

"The first tour is for the local terminal manager who handles accommodations for long-distance drivers. These guests often use a room for only eight or nine hours, just enough time to get some sleep before getting back on the road. They want time to unwind, but they don't socialize. They stay in their rooms and watch TV or sleep. They want king-size beds, clean rooms, and respect. They want to be reassured that you don't look down on them because they drive trucks or buses."

"The next tour is for a youth soccer league organizer from the parks and recreation department. She's responsible for recommending properties to out-of-town soccer teams that come here for games. Team members are usually 12- to 16-year-old boys and girls. Parents, coaches, and chaperons look for safe properties close to affordable restaurants and the soccer fields where the kids play. Luckily, we're really close to the soccer fields and we have a lot of affordable restaurants nearby. These guests want rooms with two double beds and an on-site laundry. Also, the property they choose has to be tolerant of the athletes. Everyone wants to have a good time, and the kids can get pretty rowdy."

"The third tour is for the pastor of a local church that offers a weekend couples conference twice a year. The couples attending this conference are very rate-conscious, but they want safe, clean, well-appointed rooms with king-size beds and some amenities for their weekend stay. They often do some socializing at breakfast and after the conference, although most of their time is spent away from the property."

Sandra closed her planner and looked up. "OK, Drew, it's your turn. We'll generate about 4,000 extra room nights a year if we can win the business of these potential clients. That means $125,000 in revenue. How would you present our hotel to each of these potential clients to win their business?"

Discussion Questions

1. How can Drew show common courtesy to each of these three potential clients?

2. How should Drew present the Goodsleep Inn's features and benefits to the local terminal manager?

3. How should Drew present the Goodsleep Inn's features and benefits to the soccer league organizer?

4. How should Drew present the Goodsleep Inn's features and benefits to the church pastor?

Case Number: 370CC
This case was developed in cooperation with Bill Flor and Randy Kinder, authors of *No Vacancy: A Tried & True Guide to Get More Rooms Business!*

This case also appeared in *Contemporary Hospitality Marketing: A Service Management Approach* (Lansing, Mich.: Educational Institute of the American Hotel & Lodging Association), ISBN 0-86612-158-7.

Case Study: Chapter 9

No Vacancy

Jon Stonewall is a regional manager for IntelTech, a Seattle-based company that produces computer software. He is responsible for planning the annual meeting of his account representatives in District 12, which encompasses the entire Pacific Northwest. The meeting, normally just an opportunity for education and socializing, will be especially important this year because the company is introducing several new products. After reviewing several locations, Jon decided to have the meeting in Sacramento and asked his secretary, Chris, to gather information and solicit bids from at least five Sacramento hotels. Jon is a hard-nosed businessperson who likes to get what he wants. To waste as little time as possible, he systematically examined his choices and narrowed the selection down to two. Now it was time to make a deal.

Jon was in his office when he received a call from Julia Chavez, the sales manager of the Monte Sereno Hotel in Sacramento. She began the conversation by introducing herself and her property, a mid-range hotel with 248 rooms, 8,000 square feet of meeting space, and a 5,200-square-foot ballroom that could be divided into four equal sections.

"We're so pleased you've selected the Monte Sereno as a possible site for your next meeting," Julia continued. "I've spoken at length with your secretary and wanted to speak with you personally to be sure we understand your needs. Do you have a moment to talk?"

Jon was at the start of a busy day and was a little annoyed at the interruption, but brusquely told her to go on. Concerned by his tone, Julia thanked him for his time and proceeded cautiously.

"I understand your group will arrive Sunday afternoon and leave Thursday. You'd like 48 rooms, single occupancy, and an opening night reception with heavy hors d'oeuvres. Is that correct?"

"Yes," Jon grunted.

"Chris told me that you'll begin each morning with a continental breakfast at 8:00 a.m., followed by a general session at 8:30. The general session meeting room is to be arranged classroom-style, with a luncheon in a separate room beginning at noon. From 1:00 to 5:00 p.m., your account reps will break into groups of 10 to 15 and require separate meeting spaces."

"That's right," Jon replied, "except that everyone will be on their own at lunch time."

Julia had carefully considered this sales opportunity, weighed the options, and decided on an appropriate rate before making the call to Jon. She had taken into account the property's sales history, which showed a 92 percent occupancy rate on the particular days IntelTech had in mind. She was concerned because this meeting would use only 20 percent of the hotel's rooms while using 65 percent of the hotel's meeting space. From her standpoint, it wasn't a great piece of business. Julia wanted the business, but she wanted it on her own terms. She took a deep breath and continued.

"Well, we do have those dates available for your meeting. We can offer the guest-rooms at $99, a reduction from our standard $110 rate, and offer the meeting space you need at $1,000 per day. However, I know that getting high value for your dollar is a consideration for everyone these days, so, if you can be flexible and change your dates to a Wednesday arrival and a Sunday departure, I can offer the rooms to you at $85 and waive the $1,000 charge for the meeting space—if you will hold your farewell banquet with us."

"I can't believe this!" Jon said, his voice rising. "The Salton Hotel down the street has the dates I want *and* they can give them to me at the rate you quoted! Granted, I prefer your hotel overall, but I have to consider my company. This meeting has been set for a long time;

some of my people have already made travel plans. We've even scheduled the speakers. I can't go back and change things now! Why are the rates so different later in the week?"

Julia was prepared for this response and answered him as tactfully and honestly as she could. "I'm aware of your concerns and know it would be difficult to move the meeting, but I wanted to give you the option. Since we're both businesspeople, I know you'll understand that I have to consider my property's financial position in all of this. Our sales history shows that we have our highest occupancy during the first part of the week—between 90 and 100 percent—but later in the week that number declines to around 60 percent; that's why I can give you a lower rate at that time. Because we're sold out or almost sold out from Sunday through Thursday, it doesn't make sense financially for us to offer you the lower rate early in the week."

"Look," Jon said, "I can appreciate where you're coming from, but I don't see how I can change this meeting—even if I can save a lot of money."

"I understand your situation and want to work with you in the future," Julia replied, "but I'm not sure we can meet your needs this time. Down the road, if you bring me your next meeting, I'll throw in a free cocktail party. I think you'd be very pleased with our hotel. We have outstanding food and a very friendly, courteous staff. I hope you'll come and visit us when you're in town."

Jon hesitated. Since he really wanted to stay at the Monte Sereno rather than the other hotel, he didn't want to let the matter drop. "What about this, Julia: if I agree to the higher rates and choose you over a competitor, will you do a few things for me? I'll pay the $99 room rate if you'll throw in the meeting space for nothing. I also want the free cocktail party you just mentioned. In addition, I'd like you to give us turndown service throughout our stay, a free *USA Today* in every room, and waiting for my account reps when they arrive on Sunday, a mint and a welcome note from me in every guestroom."

Discussion Questions

1. Do you think Julia should agree to host the meeting on Jon's terms? Why or why not?

2. How could Julia further negotiate each of Jon's demands and end with a win-win conclusion?

Case Number: 370CB
This case was developed in cooperation with Bill Flor and Randy Kinder, authors of *No Vacancy: A Tried & True Guide to Get More Rooms Business!*

This case also appears in *Contemporary Hospitality Marketing: A Service Management Approach* (Lansing, Mich.: Educational Institute of the American Hotel & Lodging Association), ISBN 0-86612-158-7.

Case Study: Chapter 11

Sales Underperforms Even While Meeting Budget

The Christopher Hotel is a 180-room economy/business property of a national chain located in a booming suburb of a major city. Tony, the regional director of operations, is orienting the property's new general manager, Janice.

Generally, the hotel is close to meeting most of its budgeted targets. However, when Tony compares the hotel's activity with competing hotels in the area, the picture changes dramatically. Other hotels are enjoying much higher occupancy levels than the Christopher and they are selling rooms at higher rates. The Christopher's market penetration is only 84 percent, when its baseline goal should be to achieve at least 100 percent of its fair share of the market. Tony calculates penetration rate by dividing the hotel's actual market share by its fair share (based on the proportion of rooms available in the local market).

Tony and Janice also review the Christopher's group business. Year-to-date, the hotel sold 4,796 group room nights—short of the budgeted target of 6,500 group room nights. The average room rate (ADR) for group business is down $4 from the budget.

Tony tells Janice, "While I'm here I want to investigate these problems with you and help come up with an action plan to address them. How can we increase the Christopher's penetration rate, Janice?"

"I'd start by examining what kind of new business—group and otherwise—is being generated," says Janice. "What is the mix of corporate, leisure, government, or educational groups that is looking for rooms? I bet that new college is putting together a sports program; visiting teams will need someplace to stay."

"You could be right," says Tony. "The school is so new that you might be too early on that idea, but it couldn't hurt to get a start with the sports program developer. Let's see what the hotel has historically done with groups." He pulls out some reports. "They've got corporate groups contributing 3,000 room nights and other groups contributing the rest of their total 4,796."

"Other groups? Is that how it's listed—'other groups'? Aren't there classifications within that 'other' category?" asks Janice.

Tony responds, "That's how it's listed."

Janice shakes her head and asks, "Do we have a group room control log to look at so we can see how individual group segments are performing? How about a pace report so we can see how group bookings kept up with budgeted amounts?"

Tony shuffles some of the papers and replies, "The previous GM did keep a GRC log and a pace report. He may not have used them to fullest advantage. He also could have kept better track of what the property's competitors were doing. That information is crucial to success, especially in this local area. In the next few months, I would like you to keep up to date on what our competitors are doing and how they're doing it."

"How good a networker was the previous director of sales?" asks Janice. "Did he have relationships with area churches, mosques, and synagogues for wedding and other special ceremony business? Was he in touch with the manager of the local convention center? How about city officials?"

"He focused more on officials of agencies serving the whole metropolitan area than on officials of this suburb." Tony replies. "Maybe he was hoping to land some of the business for conventions held downtown. He was using the right technique but on the wrong people. Our competitors here keep in touch with the city Department of Parks and Recreation. As far as wedding and ceremony groups, there's been no sales effort specifically targeting them, though some large bookings have come from that segment. I'd encourage you to pursue that option with the staff. And don't be shy about using the yellow pages of the phone book. So many salespeople use that as a last resort. Just think about all the kinds of business represented there...."

"It does sound like this is a very competitive area." Janice offers. "I wonder if our sales contacts with those buyers for groups are everything they should be. How experienced are our sales staff?"

"I'm not sure, but that's another good area to look at. Now how about this problem of the group ADR?" asks Tony.

Janice picks up a management binder labeled Rate Guidelines from the GM office bookshelf. "It's great that they had some of these, though having guidelines and making sure staff know and use them are two different things. Hmm, it doesn't have a date listed; do you know when it was last updated?"

"No, I don't," replies Tony.

"That could be important; I'll check on it. Maybe we also need to change our rooms inventory management guidelines to make sure we sell out on every night when there's potential to do so," Janice responds.

Tony closes with, "I think you've got a good handle on the most pressing issues facing the Christopher Hotel, Janice. Why don't you draft an action plan in the next couple of days and we'll refine it together."

Discussion Questions

1. What factors should Janice consider when planning to increase the hotel's market penetration rate?

2. What factors should Janice consider in relation to increasing group business?

3. What initial steps should Janice take to evaluate the low average room rate for groups?

4. How can Janice find out what the competition is doing and how they're doing it?

Case Number: 370CH
This case was developed in cooperation with Lisa Richards of Hospitality Softnet, Inc., a marketing resources and support company.

This case also appears in *Contemporary Hospitality Marketing: A Service Management Approach* (Lansing, Mich.: Educational Institute of the American Hotel & Lodging Association), ISBN 0-86612-158-7.

Case Study: Chapter 14

Distributing Sales Functions Between a Hotel's Sales and Catering Departments

Carla Mills is the general manager of the Woodfield Plaza, a 400-room first-class suburban hotel. It's early July, and Carla has just reviewed the forecasted year-end profit and loss statement. A couple areas concern her. First, assuming the hotel will hit budget the rest of the year, banquet food sales will be down $60,000 to budget. Also, the audiovisual revenues and room rental revenues will miss budget by $30,000. Carla calls a meeting with her director of catering, Alan Jenkins, to discuss ways to remedy the situation.

Carla opens the meeting by contrasting the forecasted statement with the budget and asks Alan what he plans to do about the decrease in banquet food sales.

"You've been here sixty days now, Alan. You should have a good feel for the property and the community. Tell me, why are sales down in your area?"

Alan shifts in his seat. He thinks about the question for a moment, then responds. "Well, I think ultimately it comes down to a problem with selling," he says. "The sales staff knows how to sell guestrooms, but they don't seem to sell function rooms. They don't seem to be aware of opportunities to sell catering, or how to take advantage of those opportunities. I can't remember one event since I've been here that was generated by sales. And from what I've seen in past reports, this has been an ongoing problem."

"OK. That's a legitimate point," Carla replies. "Salespeople certainly could take advantage of those kinds of opportunities. Sales and catering aren't often as united as they could be when it comes to selling our services—"

"It's just that no one in sales will take ownership for selling catering," Alan interrupts.

"Then you take ownership of it," replies Carla. "Look, in fairness to sales, it's not their job to sell function rooms and banquet events, primarily. Their job *is* to sell guestrooms. In some situations they could probably work a little harder on selling function rooms. But the responsibility for selling catering events ultimately belongs to catering, not sales … and since you're so concerned about *sales* selling *functions*...how many *guestrooms* has *catering* sold? The street goes both ways."

Alan sits back in his chair, thinking about what Carla has said. "Not many, actually," he finally says. "As far as catering taking responsibility for its own sales … you're right. We need to. But we're so busy taking the calls coming in, and we're trying to process them as fast as we can. We haven't had time to focus on increasing our sales skills."

"You can't continue to be just order-takers and expect your sales to do fine," Carla says. "You need to take responsibility for your sales. You need to take an active role in this. In your own words, you need to take ownership of it. Let me ask you: Do you know where you're losing business, and why?"

"Not offhand, no."

"Do you know how you're going to solve the problem?"

"Well, I think I can come up with a solution," Alan replies.

"I know you can. And I know your staff is capable. What'd I'd like you to do is come up with a plan as to how you'll sell catering, and how you'll work with the sales staff to sell catering. Could you get that to me...let's see," Carla looks at her calendar. "Two weeks from today?"

"I think I can do that."

"Great. Now on to my next concern." Carla holds up the forecasted statement. "As you can see from this forecast, by the end of the year audiovisual revenues and room rental revenues will miss budget by $30,000—that's if all goes well the next six months. Now, what do you suggest we do about *that*?"

Alan thinks about the problem. "With the room rentals, I think the problem is that we're giving function space away to book more room nights. I understand we have to do this, to some degree, but we're losing money doing it."

"But don't you think that's a worthy trade-off, to get more room nights?"

"I would be if it were necessary. But I don't think it is."

"What do you mean?" Carla asks.

"I think we can keep the room nights without losing the room rental completely, if we institute a sliding-scale function fee."

"Yes," Carla nods.

"For example, if the customer picks up 80 to 100 percent of a room block, there's no rental. If they pick up 50 percent of the room block, they'll get 50 percent off the rate, and so on."

"Excellent idea. That should increase room rental revenues. You may want to consider putting a similar scale in place for catering revenues."

"Hmmm … come to think of it, my staff does seem a little too eager to lower rentals. Maybe scales will help them deal more effectively with that issue."

"Good. Now, what about audiovisual rentals?"

Alan pauses. "I need to look into that. I know there are several ways to increase the AV revenues, as well as additional ways to increase room rental revenues. How about if I think about the problem in the next couple of weeks, and include my proposals in my plan?"

"I trust your judgment. Let's get together again in two weeks and see what you've come up with."

"Great. I'll see you then."

Alan leaves the room. Both he and Carla feel that they made some progress in solving their budget problems. And they're confident that in two weeks they'll have a plan in place to help prevent similar problems in the future.

Discussion Questions

1. In an ideal situation, what should the distribution of sales functions between a hotel's catering and sales departments look like?

2. Given the responsibilities of a hotel's catering department, what challenges will the director of catering face as the department shifts from simply being production-focused to being sales focused?

3. How could the catering department at the Woodfield Plaza recover more audiovisual and room rental revenues?

4. What steps should the director of catering at the Woodfield Plaza take to identify the specific causes of his budget problem? Once the specifics of the budget problem have been identified, how should he address the problem?

Case Number: 370CG

This case was developed in cooperation with Lisa Richards of Hospitality Softnet, Inc., a marketing resources and support company.

This case also appears in *Contemporary Hospitality Marketing: A Service Management Approach* (Lansing, Mich.: Educational Institute of the American Hotel & Lodging Association), ISBN 0-86612-158-7.

Index